ISBN 978-1-331-48611-4
PIBN 10196630

Similar Books Are Available from
www.forgottenbooks.com

HISTORY OF
SEATTLE

From the Earliest Settlement to the
Present Time

BY

CLARENCE B. BAGLEY

ILLUSTRATED

VOLUME I

CHICAGO
THE S. J. CLARKE PUBLISHING COMPANY
1916

Copyright, 1916, by

C. B. BAGLEY

PREFACE

The reader, who may give these pages more than a passing glance, will discover that the writer has presented an account of events and not a history of the men who were the actors in them.

The reasons for this are twofold. First, lack of fitness for biographical writing; and second, of far more importance, the belief that the time is not yet ripe for a truthful and impartial work of that kind. The city is young; of its founders and of those who helped to erect the present structure, in all its magnificence, many are yet here. When these shall have gone to their final account will be time enough to deal with the personal element of its pioneers and builders.

The preparation of a History of Seattle has, in effect, been the exploration of a new field and the amount of patient research and careful investigation involved has been a task of colossal proportions.

The printed and written records of the first twenty years of Seattle's existence are scanty almost beyond belief. Not until 1863 was a newspaper established here and, for many years, more space in it was devoted to eastern and foreign politics than to the record of local passing events. Few, if any, pioneers kept diaries and none of these, except that of the writer, has been accessible.

His own local recollections cover nearly all the years since Seattle's founding and he has not deemed it necessary, excepting upon rare occasions, to quote authorities regarding matters within the range of his personal knowledge.

When this work was begun it was contemplated that his connection with it should be that of editor only; to give aid and counsel in its preparation and to read and approve it in advance of its publication. Not until late in the year 1915 was the constructive work placed in his hands and, the publishers being desirous of its delivery to the subscribers as soon as possible, he and his co-workers have since given to it long hours of unremitting toil. The utmost condensation has been observed consistent with a proper presentation of the topics under discussion.

Messrs. Welford Beaton, Floyd C. Kaylor and Victor J. Farrar have done much work in its preparation and the writer's thanks are also here extended to Judge Roger S. Greene, Dr. H. Eugene Allen and Messrs. Harry W. Bringhurst and A. A. Braymer for notable aid and kindly counsel during the progress of the work.

Seattle, Washington, May 1, 1916.   CLARENCE B. BAGLEY.

ILLUSTRATIONS

CONTENTS

CONTENTS

CONTENTS

HISTORY OF SEATTLE

CHAPTER I

IN THE BEGINNING

It is the intention of the writer of this work to bring into it only facts and accounts that belong to a history of Seattle. However, the history of the City of Seattle and of the Sound country are so closely interwoven that it will be necessary to go far anterior to the arrival of the pioneers in Elliott Bay to present a clear understanding of the later years. It is believed the readers of its pages will be more pleased with this plan than to consume much space in describing remote incidents about which they are, perhaps, better informed than the writer.

For more than a century preceding the settlement at Alki Point maritime expeditions into the North Pacific had been made by the Spanish, British, Russian and American navigators, and a brief account of these is proper as a prelude to the later events which made the rise of the City of Seattle possible.

In April, 1596, Michael Lok, an Englishman, met an old Greek navigator called Juan de Fuca, at Venice, and in the course of their conversation, de Euca opened up to him certain of his voyages. On one of these, in 1592, while in the service of the Viceroy of Mexico, he sailed up the coast of North America until he came to latitude forty-seven degrees where he found a broad inlet between the forty-seventh and forty-eighth, and entering it sailed for more than twenty days, passing many islands. The viceroy promised him a great reward for his discovery, but the reward never came, and de Fuca said that he then left the service of the viceroy, and intimated to Lok that he would like to enter the service of the English if for no other reason than to get revenge on the Spanish for their vile treatment of him. Lok tried to get the old man employment, but never succeeded, and the old man died. It has since been proved that Juan de Fuca or Apostolos Valerianos, as he was known in the Greek language, is a myth and that Lok had been imposed upon by a clever seaman. However, the story became widely known and was published in the leading geographies of the day. It is a remarkable coincidence that his story should be so nearly in keeping with the facts.

The Spanish had been pushing northward from Mexico and, witnessing the efforts of all the other civilized nations in the Pacific Northwest, began to send explorers into these waters. On May 21, 1775, the Spanish sent out from San Blas, Mexico, the Santiago, in command of Bruno Heceta, accompanied by the schooner Sonora, in command of Bodega y Quadra. This expedition

sailed northward as far as Alaska, and on its return narrowly missed the discovery of the Columbia River. But they failed to sight the entrance to the
Strait of Juan de Fuca.

On Sunday, March 22, 1778, Capt. James Cook, of the British navy, sailing on his third voyage, made his way along the northwest coast of North
America and sighted a prominent cape which he called Cape Flattery. He had
in mind the supposed strait or inlet advertised by Juan de Fuca and Lok, but
after considerable search was unable to find it. It appears that a heavy wind
arose during the night and when morning came he had passed the entrance.
Cook remained at Nootka Sound, on what is now Vancouver Island, for over
a month, engaged in scientific work.

To Capt. John Meares belongs the honor of sighting the Strait of Juan de
Fuca. In May, 1788, while sailing under the British flag, but in reality under
double colors, having a Portuguese partner, Meares in the Felice arrived at
Nootka, and purchased for two pistols some land from the Indian chief,
Maquinna. He erected a fort here and built a little vessel called the North West
America. In the latter part of June Meares set out to explore the surrounding
country, and on Sunday, June 29, 1788, he sighted the great inlet which he
called after its real discoverer John de Fuca. Of course Meares believed
implicitly in the story of Juan de Fuca. He made for the southern coast and
landed upon the shores of what is now the State of Washington, probably at
Neah Bay, and there was received by a chief called Tatoosh. He saw the
large mountain to the southward and called it Mount Olympus. He then went
southward and entered Willapa Harbor which he called Shoalwater Bay, but
was unable to find a river where the Columbia empties into the Pacific and so
dubbed the site where he had labored in vain Cape Disappointment and Deception Bay. Returning to Nootka, Meares dispatched one of his officers and
thirteen men in a boat to examine the shores of the Strait of Juan de Fuca.
Meares then left with a cargo of lumber for the Chinese markets and made
arrangements for his aids to winter in the Sandwich Islands. Later he organized a joint stock company for trading purposes under a license from the East
India Company and proceeded to build up a colony at Nootka of Chinese men
and Hawaiian wives. In April, 1789, two captains of Meares', Douglas and
Funter, arrived at Nootka.

In the meantime, the Spanish, alarmed at the fact that the Russians were
extending their colonies and forts north of California, sent Estevan Jose Martinez northward to examine the Russian settlements. He secured information
that the Russians intended to send four frigates from Siberia to Nootka, whereupon he was directed to repair to Nootka and take possession of the place in
the name of the Spanish king and build a fortress there. By so doing he would
out-general the Russians. When he arrived at Nootka, however, he found the
English ships instead of the Russian, and proceeded to take possession of the
place and to seize the ships and men, taking them to Mexico. The Spanish
then occupied the fort erected by Meares and established a garrison, first under
Martinez and later under Francisco Eliza. This was almost an act of war and
for a while it looked as if Spain and England would leap at each other's throats.
The Spanish began to compromise by releasing the ships and men and promising
indemnities to the owners of the vessels for delays, etc. But Meares had now

arrived in England and 1e set t1e matter before t1e Englis1 government on April 30, 1790. England demanded not only a payment of damages for t1e individual losses of s1ips and stores, but demanded also t1at t1e lands be restored to t1e sovereignty of t1e Englis1 crown. England was able to secure t1e prom- ise of aid from Holland and Prussia, but as Spain's c1ief ally, France, was now in t1e midst of a revolution, Spain was forced to meet t1e Britis1 demands, and signed a treaty dated October 28, 1790, w1ic1 provided for an indemnity ultimately amounting to $210,000 to be paid by Spain, and t1e transfer of t1e lands at Nootka to England. Subjects of bot1 powers were left free to visit t1e port. T1e entire matter was patc1ed up at Nootka in Marc1, 1795.

It was during t1ese years t1at t1e Spanis1 became quite intimately acquainted wit1 t1e Strait of Juan de Fuca, and made fairly accurate surveys of t1e coasts as far east as Belling1am and as far sout1 as Admiralty Inlet. In 1790, Francisco Eliza, who was in command at Nootka, sent Manuel Quimper to explore t1e Strait of Juan de Fuca. He placed Spanis1 names on most of t1e bays, points, and islands, few of w1ic1 1ave survived. In 1792, two scientific men, Dionisio Galliano and Cayetano Valdes, were added to t1e expedition, and t1ey made furt1er surveys. T1e principal names added to t1e nomenclature of t1e Sound were San Juan Arc1ipelago, Sucia Islands, Matia Islands, Canal de Haro, Port Angeles, Guemes Island, and Fidalgo Bay. Most of t1e ot1ers 1ave long since disappeared, alt1oug1 subsequent explorers 1ave 1onored t1e Span- is1 commanders by naming several places for t1em.

On t1e two principal maps left as a 1eritage by t1e Spaniards, t1at portion of t1e Sound now known as Admiralty Inlet, w1ic1 connects Puget Sound proper wit1 t1e Strait of Juan de Fuca, is called Boca de Caamano. Quimper says in 1is journal, t1at from 1is station (now called Port Discovery) 1e saw ot1er inlets and openings to t1e east, w1ic1 1e called Boca de Fidalgo and Boca de Flon. He 1ad, 1owever, no time to explore t1em. Don Francisco Eliza, who advanced in 1791 to t1e eastern end of de Fuca Strait, recognized for t1e first time t1is inlet, and called it Bocas de Caamano, probably in 1onor of t1e Spanis1 navigator, Caamano. Eliza, 1owever, did not furt1er explore t1e interior of t1is inlet, because 1e understood from t1e Indians t1at, t1oug1 it was very long, still, from t1e end of it, one could not advance furt1er unless wit1 canoes. Eliza's object was not to explore s1ut-up inlets, but to find a passage to ot1er waters.

Following closely upon t1e voyages of Cook and Meares was the expedi- tion of George Vancouver who was t1e first recorded w1ite man to enter Puget Sound above t1e entrance to Admiralty Inlet. Vancouver's expedition was partly scientific, partly commercial, and partly diplomatic, for 1e was detailed to meet t1e Spanis1 at Nootka Sound and arrange terms of settlement. He sailed from England April 1, 1791, wit1 the sloop-of-war Discovery and t1e armed tender C1at1am, and after rounding t1e Cape of Good Hope visited t1e Sout1 Seas and t1e Hawaiian Islands, and t1en made his way to w1at was t1en known as New Albion, but w1ic1 is today called Oregon and Was1ington.

He examined t1e region about Cape Disappointment, but came to the con- clusion t1at t1ere was only an inlet t1ere, and t1en proceeded nort1ward nam- ing Point Grenville and passing Cape Flattery and entering t1e Strait of Juan de Fuca. Here 1e met Capt. Robert Gray of t1e s1ip Columbia who told 1im that he had discovered a large river at Cape Disappointment, but Vancouver would not believe him, and only later did he come to the same conclusion. Vancouver named the mountain which appeared to the eastward Mount Baker after his third lieutenant, Joseph Baker; New Dungeness after its resemblance to old Dungeness in England; Port Discovery after his vessel, the Discovery, and the little island at the entrance to the harbor, Protection Island, because it served as a protection to the harbor both from contrary winds and armed attacks from an enemy if the island were fortified. He now came in sight of a large mountain to the south-eastward which he called Mount Rainier in honor of Rear Admiral Peter Rainier, his friend. Port Townsend he named after the Marquis of Townshend. [About 1850 the "h" was dropped as the word, so spelled, proved difficult for the Americans.] He sailed into Hood's Canal which he so called after the Right Honorable Lord Hood, and Marrowstone Point because it was here that he found deposits of marrowstone.

He then quickly sailed southward into the main port of the Sound and established his party in headquarters on what is now Restoration Point on Bainbridge Island. This point he first called Village Point, probably because it was here that he found an Indian village, but he changed the name to Restoration Point in honor of the fact that the day was the anniversary of the restoration of the Stuart monarch, Charles II, to the throne, after the long rule of Oliver Cromwell. From his headquarters at Restoration Point Vancouver sent out small boat parties to make surveys. His lieutenant, Peter Puget, went up the Sound, through the narrows and made a fairly good survey of the waterways and inlets. This portion of the Sound was called by Vancouver Puget Sound, and the name is probably as euphonious a one as has ever been given to any portion of the earth's surface. It must be remembered that Vancouver intended that only that portion of all these northwest waters should be called Puget Sound, but it is interesting to note the development of this word Puget Sound as a generic term for all these Northwest waters. Vancouver designated these waters by five names, viz.: Strait of Juan de Fuca, Canal de Arro, Gulf of Georgia, Admiralty Inlet, and Puget Sound, but at the present time all save two, Puget Sound and Strait of Juan de Fuca, have ceased to be terms of popular parlance. Only the United States Coast and Geodetic Survey Charts officially recognize them. Nor is the term Strait of Juan de Fuca safe from ultimate extinction. In 1859 no less a person than Governor Douglas of British Columbia spoke of Vancouver Island as being in Puget Sound, and in a recent decision of the Superior Court of Clallam County, Judge Ralston held that for the purposes of the fishing laws, the Strait of Juan de Fuca was a part of Puget Sound.

Vancouver, himself, surveyed the land to the southward of Restoration Point, and found and named the large island Vashon Island, in honor of a friend, James Vashon. This brings up an interesting relationship of names. Rainier's sister, Sarah, married Admiral James Vashon, and Joseph Baker married Vashon's niece, so that in a way Mount Baker, and Mount Rainier are related.

The survey of the waterways to the westward of Restoration Point Vancouver intrusted to his clerk, H. M. Orchard, and that is how we get the name Port Orchard. Not wishing to be forgetful of the honors which the board of admiralty in England had bestowed upon him in selecting him as leader of the expedition, Vancouver named the watercourse which extends from the narrows to the Strait of Juan de Fuca, Admiralty Inlet, which name is still officially used upon all Government charts, but which is not very generally used by the public at large. On Vancouver's chart a fairly good representation of the harbor which is now known as Elliott Bay is set down, but there is no evidence to show that Vancouver's surveyors did any more than sketch it in the rough from small boats perhaps a half a mile from mainland.

His expedition now repaired to the inlet or watercourse to the eastward of Whidby Island and landed somewhere on the mainland within the present limits of the City of Everett. Here he prepared to celebrate the king's [George III] birthday, it being June 4, 1792. As this region is so near to the present limits of the City of Seattle I take leave to quote a few words from Vancouver's Journal.

"Sunday, the 3d, all hands were employed in fishing with tolerably good success, or in taking a little recreation on shore; and on Monday, the 4th, they were served as good a dinner as we were able to provide for them, with double allowance of grog to drink the king's health, it being the anniversary of his majesty's birth; on which auspicious day, I had long since designed to take formal possession of all the countries we had lately been employed in exploring, in the name of, and for his Britannic majesty, his heirs and successors.

"To execute this purpose, accompanied by Mr. Broughton and some of the officers, I went on shore about one o'clock, pursuing the usual formalities which are generally observed on such occasions, and under the discharge of a royal salute from the vessels, took possession accordingly of the coast, from that part of New Albion, in the latitude of 39° 20' north, and longitude 236° 26' east, to the entrance of this inlet of the sea, said to be the supposed Straits of Juan de Fuca; as likewise all the coasts, islands, etc., within the said straits, as well on the northern as on the southern shores; together with those situated in the interior sea we had discovered, extending from the said straits, in various directions, between the northwest, north, east and southern quarters; which interior sea I have honored with the name of The Gulf of Georgia, and the continent binding the said gulf, and extending southward to the forty-fifth degree of north latitude, with that of New Georgia; in honor of his present majesty. This branch of Admiralty Inlet obtained the name of Possession Sound; its western arm, after Vice Admiral Sir Alan Gardner, I distinguished by the name of Port Gardner, and its smaller eastern one by that of Port Susan."

Recently the Daughters of the American Revolution erected a monument, in commemoration of this event, within the present limits of the City of Everett. A bronze tablet upon the monument reads: "On The Beach Near This Spot Vancouver Landed June 4, 1792. Erected by the Marcus Whitman Chapter Daughters of the American Revolution. June 4, 1915."

Port Susan has almost disappeared as a name; Possession Sound is still used for Everett Harbor; Port Gardner has been replaced by Saratoga Passage; while Alan Point is still the southern cape of Camano Island; and the term Possession is further used as the name of the south cape of Whidby Island. It is a matter of regret that his celebration could not have taken place nearer the City of Seattle. It is, however, interesting to note that all the land once taken possession of by the English and later transferred to the United States

of America, is connected in some way with the name of George III. It was
this king who was reigning when the American Revolutionary war was fought;
while this country, called by Vancouver, New Georgia, later known as Oregon
and Washington, was definitely ceded to the United States in 1846.

Other names which Vancouver gave were: Whidbey Island, in honor of
the master of his ship Discovery, Joseph Whidbey, who had made extensive
surveys in this region, and who proved this to be an island. Vancouver never
determined that Camano Island was an island but has it set down on his chart
as a part of the mainland. Point Partridge was named in honor of the family
into which Vancouver's brother John had married. Other names are: Cypress
Island, Strawberry Bay, Deception Pass, Bellingham Bay, Point Hudson,
Birch Bay and Point Roberts. This latter name is of some interest. Vancouver was not the first choice of the admiralty as leader of the expedition.
Another person, Capt. Henry Roberts, had been selected, and Vancouver was
to go along in the capacity of lieutenant, but just as the expedition was on
the point of sailing, a war with Spain was imminent, and Roberts was sent in
command of a ship of war to fight the Spanish, if war were declared, in the
West Indies. But Vancouver and Roberts were on good terms and in recognition of their friendship as well as a recognition of former intentions, Vancouver
perpetuated his name in the region which he was once selected to survey.

Vancouver had other work to do in this Northwest region besides make
surveys, namely, to carry out certain provisions of an agreement between Spain
and England, which is known as the Nootka Convention, with the Spanish
officer stationed at Nootka Sound, Don Juan Francisco de la Bodega y Quadra,
by name. The two met at Nootka but were unable to come to any agreement,
although each had a high regard for the other personally, and Vancouver was
treated with great respect. Quadra suggested that some place be named after
them both not only to commemorate their meeting but the friendship that
existed between them as well, so Vancouver named the island upon which
they met, Quadra and Vancouver Island. Then the two separated. Spain
gave up her claim to this region, and the fortunes of the country, generally
known as Old Oregon, fell to the United States and Great Britain which nations
possessed them under a joint occupancy agreement until 1846, when the present boundary was drawn. The name of the island, Quadra and Vancouver,
persisted upon some maps until in the '50s' but the Quadra was dropped, and
the Vancouver remains. Vancouver gave many names to British Columbia and
Alaska as well as to the State of Washington.

After his return to England he devoted himself entirely to the preparation
of his journal for publication; but died while the work was on the press, May
10, 1798. His brother John, with the assistance of Captain Puget, completed
the work which was dedicated to King George III, the first edition being published in 1798.

In 1670 Charles II of England granted to Prince Rupert and associates a
charter giving them the exclusive right to trade with the Indians of the region
about Hudson Bay, and a company was then formed to take advantage of
this charter. It was called the Hudson's Bay Company, and like most of
the early English companies did the threefold work of fur-trading, governing
the region, and defending the country from a possible foreign enemy. For

over two centuries this company maintained a monopoly; but after that time a rival company which disputed its monopoly, the Northwest Company, was organized, and these two organizations expanded, moving across the Canadian wilds. About the beginning of the nineteenth century they moved from northwestern Canada into the unowned country known as Oregon, and proceeded to organize it.

The Americans had been keenly alive to the opportunities of the fur-trading business in the West, but they never succeeded as well as their English rivals. Chief among the American companies was the one promoted by John Jacob Astor, but just as he was getting started the War of 1812 with England came on, and the English compelled the surrender of his post at the mouth of the Columbia. His associates on the ground lost no opportunity in accepting the offer of the Northwest Company to buy them out, and the fort, known in history as Astoria, became the property of the English, and its name changed to Fort George, in honor of the ruling monarch, George III.

About 1821 the two English companies grew tired of the rivalries of each other and merged into one company retaining the name of the older company, the Hudson's Bay Company. With a view to organizing the Oregon country, Governor Simpson came down from Northwest Canada and arrived at Astoria or Fort George, in the fall of 1824. He organized this region as the District of the Columbia and placed Dr. John McLoughlin in charge as chief factor; he made arrangements for the removal of headquarters from Astoria to a newly selected site further up the Columbia River to be called Fort Vancouver because it was near to the site generally known as "Vancouver's fartiest." This was in 1824. A second post, a trading post, was planned and built on the Fraser River and known as Fort Langley. The expedition which located Fort Langley is interesting to us, as one of the clerks, John Work, recorded it in his journal, also some of his descendants live in Seattle. The proposed expedition left Fort George or Astoria in November, 1824, and was under the command of James McMillan. It made its way by canoe and portage from the Columbia River to Gray's Harbor via Baker's Bay and Willapa Harbor; thence up the Chehalis River to the Black River, up that stream to its source, Black Lake, then by portage to Eld Inlet, and finally by Puget Sound to the Fraser River. After a brief examination of the river the party returned, but when reaching the Chehalis River divided into two groups, one going by the route whence it had come, the other making overland to the Cowlitz River and down that stream to the Columbia. This is one of the first recorded uses made of the Cowlitz trail, so well-known to the early pioneers. In June, 1827, the same commander, James McMillan, headed the expedition which was to build Fort Langley. The Cadboro, a vessel famous in the history of the Sound was to assist, and she went by way of the Pacific. The overland expedition, however, came up from Vancouver by the Cowlitz trail, which shows that the trail was just coming into use. Fort Langley was built in the fall of 1827 and James McMillan was placed in command. At this place a few of the entries in the journal of John Work are quoted as they throw much original light and color on the early nomenclature about Seattle:

"Tuesday, 7th. Wind Easterly. Overcast cold weather, foggy in the morning. Embarked at ½ past 7 o'clock and proceeded 3 miles N. E., 6 E. and

26 North, in all 35 miles. Encamped at 4 o'clock in the evening. Our course lay through narrow channels about ½ mile wide and some wide openings formed by traversing bays and channels formed by islands and points. 'Passed a channel on the E. side, the last of the bays receives the Qualax River. [Puyallup] Stopped at another little river where there was a village [Steilacoom] of the Nisqually Nation consisting of six houses, these are miserable habitations constructed of poles covered with mats, we were detained 1½ hours at this village, getting two men and a woman, wife to one of them, to act as interpreters and guides for us. The men are both of the Sanahomis tribe [Snohomish] and are not intelligible to any of our party, neither do they well understand us but they, at least one of them, understands the language of the Coweechins which is the name of the tribe at the entrance of what is supposed to be Fraser's River. The woman speaks and understands the Chenook language pretty well and is to interpret to the men. Two canoes with 8 Indians passed our encampment in the evening, and when it was dark the Indians visited our camp, these people are from the Interior and belong to the . . . The Nisqualy Indians speak a language different from any we have seen yet. Where we are encamped is an island [Vashon] where we see the marks of some horses which the Indians have on it. The appearance of the shores is much the same as yesterday, still bold and high, composed of clay and generally wooded to the water's edge. Where we encamped last night we found abundance of mussels at low water.

"Wednesday, 8th, some rain in the afternoon, wind Easterly. We were on the water at 7 o'clock and made according to estimation a distance of 36 miles, N. 5 miles, W. 3, northeast 5 and north 23. We were 7¾ hours on the water, 3¾ of which we both sailed and paddled with mild breeze, we concluded that we made at least 5 miles per hour. We, this day, proceeded through a fine channel formed, as the other, by the mainland and an island. Passed an opening on the E. side in the morning and on the same side a bay [Elliott Bay] into which the Sinananimis River [Duwamish River] flows. On the West side we came through the Soquamis Bay from which there is a small opening to the Westward. Where we are now encamped opposite to a wider channel or opening [Admiralty Inlet] which runs to the Westward, it is very deep with a number of islands in its north side and through its entrance. The channels through which we passed may be 3 or 4 miles wide, the shores appear the same as yesterday. We stopped at the Soquamis village situated in the bay, Port Madison of the same name. It consists of 4 houses, we saw only 8 or ten men, but understand several of the inhabitants were off fishing. Our object in stopping here was to get the chief to accompany us as an interpreter, but he was not at home. The houses are built of boards covered with mats."

The line of communication between Forts Vancouver on the Columbia and Langley on the Fraser River was too great and difficult of passage, and before a half dozen years had elapsed the company decided to locate a post midway between the two. It is not known why the choice fell to a little prairie at Sequalichew Creek, but it is probable that the locators desired a port on Puget Sound where sea going vessels could land, and also a place not far removed from the Cowlitz trail.

Here, in the spring of 1833, Archibald C. McDonald built the trading post known as Nisqually House or Fort Nisqually. It was more of a post than a fort, consisting of a main hall for business, a hall for the assembled Indians to congregate in, quarters for the men, who seldom numbered more than a dozen, shops, barns and other buildings. The buildings were crudely constructed of hewn timbers and whip-sawed boards, plastered within and covered with cedar bark without. The business of the post was three-fold: Trading in furs with the Indians, raising grain for export to Russia and the Hawaiian Islands, and salmon packing for the export trade. In time the beef, salmon and grain trade became the chief form of enterprise of the posts of Langley, Nisqually and Vancouver, for the Sound country was never very rich in furs. As time went on several extensive farms were added to Nisqually post. While the plowing and more skilled work was done by the employes of the Hudson's Bay Company, among whom were natives of the Sandwich Islands, a large amount of work was also done by the Indians who were fairly quick to learn some of the more menial tasks.

Nisqually secured the Indian trade of most of the Sound region. The Makah, Clallam, Skagit, Snohomish, Twana, Duwamish, Nisqually, Chehalis and Cowlitz tribes were frequent visitors to the post. At times Indians from east of the mountains brought their furs to Nisqually, coming either by way of Naches Pass or a more northern route. The chief furs secured were from the beaver, sea otter, black bear, lynx, musquash and deer, and these the Indians bartered for blankets, guns, and various other articles, chiefly those of dress. A blanket brought two first-class beaver skins. The employes of the company were very closely allied with the Indians with whom most were intermarried, and the halfbreed children usually remained in close contact with the post. While the Indians disliked the Nisqually officials because of the high tariffs imposed, nevertheless, they soon regarded the trading post as an indispensable adjunct to their civilization. The Indian never had much use for the settler, but he had a common interest in the trading post.

Here at Nisqually, in the early '30s, the Indians received their first instruction in the white man's religion, and seemed to make some progress, although the example set by the employes was hardly inspiring.

In the spring of 1834 the company decided that the posts Langley and Nisqually could be supplanted to advantage by a post established midway between the two, and several surveys were taken of the country on Whidby Island in the vicinity of Ebey's Landing and Fort Casey. It was decided that a post should be erected there and the men and materials were on their way from Nisqually when the expedition was recalled owing to disorders at Nisqually which needed the immediate attention of the commander. It seems hardly possible that the fate of a post on Whidby Island should hang on so slight an accidental factor, but although the company continued to speak of Whidby Island as a future site, the post was never built, and Langley and Nisqually served as they had in the past. It is interesting to note the possible effect such a post might have had on the subsequent history of the State of Washington. Had the British been in possession of a post on Whidby Island in 1846 when the Oregon question was settled and a boundary line permanently established it might have been so drawn as to include as British Territory the entire San Juan archipelago as well as Whidby Island.

While looking for the proposed site for the new post, one of the employes of the company, Ouvrie, by name, suggested the site later known as Seattle. Under date of July 8, 1833, the following entry is recorded in Dr. William Fraser Tolmie's diary at Nisqually House:

"Ouvrie having frequently talked about a spot favorable for an establishment, it has been agreed that I am to start this evening accompanied by Ouvrie and five or six Indians in canoe to examine the place and return tomorrow night." The diary for the succeeding day mentions passing "Payillipa Bay" and other points along the east side of the Sound, and in the forenoon "landed on the prairion so much admired by Mr. A. and Ouvrie. It was about one mile in length and from one hundred to one hundred and fifty yards in extent, raised about thirty feet above the sea level, towards which it presented a steep, clayey bank. Surface flat and dotted with small pines, but soil composed almost entirely of sand. Its breadth was measured from the base of the steep wooded bank which lines the coast throughout to the margin of the same. At its northern extremity the coast is indented with a bay five or six miles wide, and perhaps three long, into which Ouvrie's River flows, described by him as equal in size to the Cowlitz. On the opposite shore of this bay was pointed out to me the countries of Sannahomish, Keatchet and Shalatchet tribes lying in the above order from the mouth of Ouvrie's River, to the point marking the extremity of the bay. The south side of bay and river is inhabited by the Tuamish [Duwamish] Indians, of whom we saw several parties along the coast, miserably poor and destitute of fire arms. The opposite coast of Sound is possessed by the warlike Soquamish with whose chief all were on friendly terms. A fort well garrisoned would answer well as a trading post on the prairie where we stood. It would have an advantage of a fine prospect down the Sound and of proximity to the Indians but these would not compensate for an unproductive soil and the inconvenience of going at least one-half mile for a supply of water.". The next morning they breakfasted on parboiled peas eaten with a shell out of a potlid. This place later became known as Alki Point. No future attempt to establish a post there was made by the Hudson's Bay Company.

With the completion of Fort Nisqually the old route to the Columbia River via Eld Inlet, Black River, Chehalis River, Gray's Harbor, Willapa Harbor and Baker Bay, was abandoned, and henceforth the portage route to the Cowlitz River was used instead. Every old pioneer is familiar with Cowlitz Landing and the old road to the northward. This route was the heritage of the Hudson's Bay Company, and in its day did good service. When the pioneer settler came to Washington Territory he complained of the trials he had to endure in the way of poor roads; had it not been for the work done by the company he might have been in a worse plight.

In the spring of 1846 the British frigate, Fisgard, forty-two guns, and a crew of 352 men, under the command of Capt. J. A. Duntz, anchored at Nisqually. This was just before the settlement of the Oregon question, and President Polk's aggressive policy of "Fifty-four Forty or Fight" had made war a possibility even if not a probability. Another British vessel of similar mission, the Modeste, anchored in the Columbia River. The Fisgard was accompanied by the paddle-sloop Cormorant, six guns, commanded by G. T. Gordon.

SEATTLE WATER FRONT ABOUT 1878, LOOKING UP MARION STREET

On board the Fisgard was Robert M. Inskip, naval instructor, who proceeded to erect at Nisqually a naval training station wherein to instruct the young midshipmen. Most detailed surveys of the upper portion of the Sound were made by this instructor and a few new names added to the nomenclature of that region. The hall wherein the school exercises were held was standing when the first settlers came to the Sound, and was for a long time known to them as the "castle of indolence."

British vessels came up and down the Sound and Fort Nisqually became a place of some consequence. However, the war talk subsided; Polk did not secure all he wanted, and the Oregon question was peacefully settled by the Treaty of 1846 by which the Forty-ninth Parallel of north latitude was continued westward to Puget Sound and the boundary line then drawn through the lower Sound waters through the Strait of Juan de Fuca to the Pacific Ocean. By the terms of the treaty the region north of the Columbia River became United States Territory, and Nisqually and Vancouver lost their sovereign power. They ceased to be forts, and were subject to the laws of the United States. The Hudson's Bay Company, and its subsidiary company, the Puget Sound Agricultural Company, continued to operate these establishments as private individuals, until the property was purchased by the United States Government.

Thus passed a great enterprise. It had rendered a great service on the Sound. It had educated and pacified the Indians for thirty years. The early pioneers were well treated by the trading posts, which helped many of them by loans of cattle and advances in foodstuffs to carry them over the unproductive periods when they were getting started in the world.

Many persons were in charge of Fort Nisqually during its existence. Perhaps the best known of these was Dr. William Fraser Tolmie. He was born in Inverness, Scotland, and educated as a naturalist which included medicine and surgery. Botany was his special study. Under the patronage of Sir William Hooker, the famous naturalist, he secured, in 1832, an appointment with the Hudson's Bay Company and in company with another appointee, a Mr. Gairdner, also a naturalist, set sail from London, aboard the Ganymede, and arrived off Cape Disappointment April 30, 1833. Here he received orders from Doctor McLoughlin to repair to Milbank Sound to assist in founding of Fort McLoughlin. While enroute he arrived at Nisqually, and because of an accident to a valuable employe, Doctor Tolmie was forced to remain there and treat him. While here, he made the first attempted ascent of Mount Rainier. In November he reported for his destination. In 1834 he was surgeon with an expedition under Ogden on the Stikene River, then served at Fort Simpson; finally going to Milbank Sound where he remained until February, 1836, when he took up his abode as surgeon and trader at Fort Vancouver, remaining until 1840, when he was granted a year's leave of absence. The year 1841 he seems to have spent in organizing agricultural establishments in the Willamette Valley. In 1841 he returned to England where he remained until 1843, attending to the agricultural interests of the company. During these years he had acquired a knowledge of Spanish, having in mind an appointment to the post at Yerba Buena, but upon his return was given the superintendency of the Puget Sound Agricultural Company at Nisqually, where he remained until 1859, moving to Victoria, but still managing affairs for both the Hudson's Bay Company, and the Puget Sound Agricultural Company at Nisqually.

The cause of the purchase of Nisqually and other posts of the Hudson's Bay Company in United States Territory was the antagonism of incoming settlers who coveted the lands occupied by the company. When Doctor Tolmie left, Edward Huggins, a clerk, remained as custodian at Nisqually. There were many attempts at settlement in the '50s. The American Civil war delayed a settlement, although Secretary of State Seward and Lord Lyons completed an arbitration treaty in 1863. Under the terms of that treaty a decision was reached in 1869. Under its terms the company was paid for its property. Mr. Huggins became an American citizen, and took over the site of Nisqually as his homestead which he continued to occupy until about ten years ago when he sold out to the Du Pont Powder Company.

By far the most interesting, although the least known of the expeditions to the Sound was that of Lieut. Charles Wilkes in 1841. It was this explorer who, on November 8, 1861, intercepted at sea the English mail steamer Trent and took off the confederate commissioners James Mason and John Slidell assigned to France and England. Wilkes was born in New York, April 3, 1798, and entered the navy as a midshipman in 1818, and after successive promotions was given command of the expedition which was to be known as the United States Exploring Expedition. The object of this expedition was scientific, but if the secrets of the war office were known it is quite probable that it was also political. Wilkes received his instruction August 11, 1838, and sailed from Norfolk, on the 18th of the same month and year, with a squadron of vessels consisting of the sloops of war Vincennes and Peacock; the brig Porpoise; the ship Relief; and the tenders Sea Gull and Flying Fish. His instructions required him to visit Rio Janeiro, Tierra del Fuego, Valparaiso, the Navigator Group, Figi Islands, Hawaiian Islands, the Northwest Coast of North America, San Francisco, Japan, China, and other places.

Only that portion of the expedition which has to do with the immediate vicinity of the City of Seattle is considered. After a cruise of over two years the expedition arrived off the mouth of the Columbia River on April 5, 1841; but finding it almost impossible to effect an immediate entry, made its way to Puget Sound and anchored in Port Discovery May 2, 1841. Here he dispatched some Indians to make known his arrival to the Hudson's Bay Company's officials Anderson and McNeil at Nisqually House, and to secure a pilot to lead his vessels through the narrow maze of the Sound waters; but failing to hear anything from them in due course of time, made his own way cautiously southward, when he met the officials and named the place Pilot Cove because it was here that he secured his pilot. After a short sojourn at Nisqually House, where he received a cordial welcome, he set his men to work making surveys of the Sound; he sent out an expedition under Lieutenant Johnson across the Cascades Mountains and into various parts of what is now the eastern part of the State of Washington. This party, so far as is known, was the first to ever pass through the Nachess Pass, although it is reasonably certain that the Hudson's Bay Company's servants were acquainted with the pass, as two of their men accompanied Lieutenant Johnson in the capacity of guides. Wilkes, himself, made an excursion down the Cowlitz River to the Columbia and thence into Oregon; while another of his lieutenants, Eld, by name, made a trip to Gray's Harbor and made a survey of the region. Many volumes were the fruits of this expedition and much new information was gathered by his eminent scientists, and on almost every subject. Historically the expedition is of most interest to the people of Seattle because of the surveys which it made. Prof. Edmond S. Meany of the University of Washington, in the Sunday editions of the Seattle Post-Intelligencer for May 23, May 30, and June 6, 1915, gave a thorough account of the work done in these surveys. His articles are entitled Origin of Point Defiance and Other Names of Puget Sound; Origin of Geographical Names in the Vicinity of Seattle; and Origin of Geographical Names in the San Juan Archipelago. A few of the most important will be given. Commencement Bay on which the City of Tacoma is now situated he so called because it was here that he commenced his work. Point Defiance received its name from the fact that it commands the narrows "which, if strongly fortified, would bid defiance to any attack and guard its entrance against any force." Maury Island was in honor of William L. Maury of the expedition. Colvo's Passage to the west of Vashon Island was secured from the name of Lieut. George W. Colvocoressis, but Wilkes wisely dropped the Greek sounding appendix. Hale's Passage was in honor of Horatio Hale, his philologist. Fox Island was in honor of J. J. Fox, assistant surgeon of the expedition. Anderson's Island and McNeil Island were named in token of the services received by Wilkes from them both in providing him with a pilot and in other ways at Nisqually House. Alexander Anderson was a chief factor for the Hudson's Bay Company, and Capt. William Henry McNeil was the second commander of the famous steamer Beaver. Carr's Inlet and Case's Inlet for two of his lieutenants. Hartstene Island for Lieut. H. J. Hartstene. Other important names he gave in the upper part of the Sound were: Henderson, Budd, Eld, Totten and Hammersley inlets, in honor of officers aboard his vessels. A half hundred or more of points and capes were likewise named by Wilkes, most of which persist to this day. Blake Island opposite Elliott Bay was named in honor of George Smith Blake, who had charge of the United States Coast Survey from 1837 to 1848, and who was always more or less in close touch with Wilkes. Alki Point is a recent name which will be treated on other pages; Wilkes named this point Point Roberts to honor Armourer Humphrey Roberts. Elliott Bay, on which our city is situated, is in honor of the chaplain of the Vincennes, Rev. J. L. Elliott.

Before Wilkes made these surveys it was thought that what is now Bainbridge Island was mainland, and it was Wilkes who first made this discovery. As Professor Meany pointed out, the naming of Bainbridge Island in honor of a hero of the War of 1812 brought together a group of names of famous personages. On this island is Port Blakeley, and what is now Yukon Harbor Wilkes called Barron's Bay. William Bainbridge acted as second for Commodore Stephen Decatur who fought a fatal duel with Barron. Not far from this group of names the sloop-of-war Decatur was stranded on a reef in 1856, hence the name of Decatur Reef.

Eagle Harbor was named because of some supposed resemblance to a bird, and the two capes to the harbor are called Bill Point and Wing Point. Port Madison and Points Monroe and Jefferson are all in honor of former presidents of the United States. Port Ludlow was in honor of Lieut. Augustus Ludlow who was with Captain Lawrence in the famous naval duel between the Chesapeake and Shannon, in 1813, and who lost his life. He named Appletree or Apple Cove because he saw supposed apple blossoms on shore. There are no apple trees but an abundance of dog-wood trees which produce blossoms which probably deceived him. West Point, which is the north cape of Elliott Bay, was named by Wilkes. The present passage between Whidby and Camano Islands is called Saratoga Passage, and many old pioneers can no doubt recall the time when Camano Island was called McDonough's Island. Wilkes called the passage Saratoga Passage and the island McDonough's Island. Now Captain McDonough commanded the expedition which defeated the British squadron on Lake Champlain, and his ship was the Saratoga. McDonough's Island has disappeared as a term and Camano has taken its place but the term Saratoga Passage is meaningless without the knowledge that the Island of Camano once honored McDonough, her commander.

It is a matter of regret that all the names given by Lieutenant Wilkes cannot be reproduced. A few names in the present San Juan Archipelago cannot be passed by. Wilkes was a young naval officer who had entered the service of the navy in 1818—too late to take part in the War of 1812. He had read of all the war heroes and knew their deeds by heart. So he decided to honor them by placing their names on the various islands, bays, points and mountains in this archipelago. The largest of the islands, San Juan of the present time, he called Rogers' Island, in honor of Commodore John Rogers, who as commander of the President captured the British sloop of war Little Belt. Lopez Island he called Chauncy's Island for Chauncey was in command of the entire naval forces operating on the Great Lakes. The most interesting bit of nomenclature history relates to the naming of places about the present Orcas Island. This island he called Hull's Island; West Sound he called Guerriere Bay; East Sound he called Ironsides Inlet; and the large mountain upon the island he termed Mount Constitution. Only one of these four names has persisted to the present day— Mount Constitution. The story is simple and known to all readers. Capt. Isaac Hull commanded the United States frigate Constitution, nicknamed the Old Ironsides, which captured the British frigate Guerriere. Likewise Wilkes named Fidalgo Island Perry's Island in honor of Commodore Perry who won the victory over the British on Lake Erie, and to the beautiful mountain he gave the name Mount Erie. Like Mount Constitution Mount Erie is the only surviving piece of nomenclature. One can almost make a history out of the nomenclature given by Lieutenant Wilkes among what is today the San Juan Islands.

Lieutenant Wilkes was interrupted in his work upon the surveys of the San Juan Islands by a messenger who brought word that his ship Peacock had been wrecked at the entrance to the Columbia River, and he was forced to make a hurried departure, never to return to the Sound. His account of the expedition was published in several small editions in the early '40s' but his complete works took many years before completion and several of the proposed volumes were abandoned. There were only 100 sets of the complete works published and these were distributed to all the friendly powers and one set to each state and territory then in the Union. Portions of the works are now in the state library at Olympia. Unfortunately, the historical part of the expedition is brief; and the scientist part more voluminous. The Atlas of Charts, however, is remarkable, considering the time which was spent and the instruments at hand. Wilkes made the first calculation of the height of Mount Rainier. From Puget Sound he departed to the Columbia River where he was regarded with suspicion and even hatred by the sturdy pioneers who wanted to see an American Government in Oregon, and to whom Wilkes was not very sympathetic. From Oregon the party went to California and then left to cross the Pacific Ocean

In the light of later events it appears that Wilkes never regarded Elliott Bay as remarkable. Of the harbor he made a detailed map, but he did this of many harbors about the Sound both good and bad. In his narrative he has no word of description about the harbor. He seems to have regarded the upper portion of the Sound most favorably, at least from the military standpoint. But this is going to be the case with most of our early discoverers, pioneers, explorers and others. Seattle was not located or planned. It arose because of inherent commercial advantages which had to be learned by later promoters through experience.

Wilkes' was the last of the exploring expeditions, and the Hudson's Bay Company, despite the fact that it made a pretense as an agent of civilization, was in reality nothing more than a frontier post. With them we pass from the history of the wilderness to the history of civilization, of the farmer, settler and manufacturer.

The early '40s witnessed the coming of that class of persons whose activities formed the basis for our great cities on the Sound. In the fall of 1849 Samuel Hancock, started from Olympia in a canoe with a crew of Indians, in search of coal, which he had been informed had been noted at several points along the Sound. He says: "The first night we camped at the mouth of the Puyallup River. We left here and proceeded slowly northward, for the prevailing winds are so violent at this season that at times it is unsafe to travel in canoes. My Indians were anxious to stop, but I insisted on continuing, though the wind was now blowing a half gale, and they seemed a good deal alarmed for our safety. However, we reached Alki Point, an excellent harbor against the prevailing winds in winter, without accident. [This journal was prepared for publication in 1860, but never published. The notes were taken from day to day by Mr. Hancock. This will explain why he mentions "Alki Point" years before its naming.] A great many Indians came from their houses to the beach here to ascertain where we came from. All the Indians I have met with in this region have a great deal of curiosity, and they are certain to know very soon after your arrival amongst them all that the Indians who are with you are in possession of in relation to you. So they were soon pretty well posted in regard to me; indeed, such was the nature of my business that I desired they should know, as I expected to derive considerable information from them about the coal. As they seemed well disposed, I opened my valise and gave them all presents, to the men pipes and tobacco, to the women small looking-glasses and brass rings."

From Alki Point he went down the Sound and during his explorations he went up the Snohomish River and visited and described the falls of the Snoqualmie, the first recorded account, though the visit of Capt. Robert Fay was made about the same time, probably.

In the fall of 1850 Col. I. N. Ebey wrote from Olympia to M. T. Simmons an account of an exploration he had recently made of the valleys of the Puyallup and Duwamish rivers.

He gave a vivid and truthful description of the rich Puyallup Valley as far as where the Muckleshute Indian Reservation was afterward established. Coming on down the Sound he entered this bay which he called the Duwams. His party ascended the crooked river that he also called the Duwams to the forks. What is now called Black River he spoke of as a continuation of the main stream. He says:

"The river meanders along through rich bottom land, not heavily timbered, with here and there a beautiful plain of unrivaled fertility, peeping out through a fringe of vine maple, alder or ash, or boldly presenting a view of their native richness and undying verdure. Other plains of more extensive character are represented as being near at hand, and of sufficient fertility to satisfy the most fastidious taste.

"At a distance of about twenty miles from the bay the river forks—the right fork bears the name of Duwams. It has its source about ten miles to the north in a large clear lake [Lake Washington]. This stream has an average width of about twenty yards. The country along its banks partakes of the same character as that lower down the river. A few miles of this stream will be found quite rapid, offering many fine opportunities for mill privileges. Sandstones of a good quality for building materials make their appearance along this stream. The lake from which this stream has its source is of considerable extent, surrounded principally with woodland, consisting of cedar, fir, ash, oak, etc. It varies in width from one to six miles. I traveled on it to the north a distance of more than twenty miles without finding its terminus. The water is clear and very deep; from the beauty of the lake and the scenery surrounding it we christened it by the name of Geneva. Another lake of less extent lies about six miles east of Geneva, and connected with it by a small stream.

"Between Geneva Lake and Admiralty Inlet there appears an extensive country of low land that has never been examined by white men, and when examined I have no doubt will be found very valuable. The distance from the Inlet to Geneva Lake in many places cannot exceed a few miles, as the Indians make portages across with their canoes."

Colonel Ebey also went up the valley of what is now called White River, but did not give it a name. He intersected his former trail up the Puyallup.

CHAPTER II

THE PIONEER PERIOD

The history of Seattle began September 28, 1851, when the vanguard of the first settlement at Alki Point arrived there. The settlement on the Duwamish River two weeks earlier was only a farming enterprise, and their claims were beyond Seattle's boundaries for thirty years or more.

When they left their homes in the East the majority of the settlers at Alki and Seattle intended to locate in the Willamette Valley, but on reaching the country west of the mountains they heard so much about the Sound country that they determined to investigate it sooner or later.

While the members of the pioneer party were at Portland, John N. Low and David T. Denny, who were on the lookout for homes, set out for Puget Sound after they had driven Low's cattle to the Chehalis Valley for winter range. Arthur A. Denny, the elder brother, and the leading spirit in the expedition which had crossed the plains from Illinois, had heard so much of the Sound country that he decided to become better acquainted with it before deciding to settle elsewhere, but an attack of ague made it necessary for him to remain at Portland while his brother and Low went on ahead.

At Olympia the two were joined by Lee Terry and Capt. Robert C. Fay, and the four came on to the Duwamish River on a prospecting tour. They spent their first night under the trees on the promontory of what is now West Seattle, called Sgwudux by the Indians. The next morning Low, Denny and Terry hired two young Indians of Chief Seattle's band to take them to the Duwamish River in a canoe.

After ascending the Duwamish several miles Low and Terry landed and set out over an Indian trail to look at the country, leaving Denny to follow in the canoe with the Indians. As they did not appear when night set in Denny landed and camped for the night at a place afterward known as Maple Prairie. His companions arrived the next morning in a canoe which they had obtained from the Indians at the mouth of Black River. The party returned to Sgwudux, where they remained during the night of the 27th. In the evening a scow passed them on the way to a settlement which had been made a few days earlier by Luther M. Collins, Henry Van Asselt and the father and son, Jacob and Samuel Maple, on the banks of the Duwamish River. Two women, the wife and daughter of Collins, conversed in Chinook with Captain Fay. On September 28th the party moved their camp to Alki Point, where a permanent settlement was begun.

They made up their minds that they had reached the end of their journey. Terry and Low had visions, and in their enthusiasm they determined that some day a city would build itself back of the point. It is not strange that this place that later was called Alki should have been selected by these earliest settlers for a townsite. It was either a natural prairie or the timber had mostly been burned off. This made it easy to put up the first buildings. The beach was sandy and gravelly and the upland easily accessible. It had an unobstructed view of the Sound northward and southward and of the Olympic Mountains. The few sailing craft then visiting the upper Sound passed near it, and the smaller boats and canoes made of it a convenient port of call. Elliott Bay was guiltless of settlers and there was then nothing that attracted visitors. The point was well protected from southerly storms but the small craft that harbored there soon found it dangerous when the winds and waves swept in from the north.

They erected a rude shelter to protect them while they put up a more pretentious cabin. Their townsite was called by them New York but visitors smiled and said, "Yes, by-and-by." This was translated into its Chinook equivalent, "Alki," and ere long that was its only name.

Captain Fay had been on the Sound for some time and was the owner of the boat on which they had come from Olympia. While they had made their prospecting trip up the river he had gone on down the Sound looking for a good place at which to put up salmon to ship to San Francisco. He returned on the 28th and spent the night with Low, Denny and Terry. It was in compliance with his advice that the first houses were put up with logs instead of split cedar boards because they would offer greater protection from bullets in case of troubles with the Indians.

Low immediately hired Denny to remain on the claim with Terry while he returned to Portland for his family. He carried with him a letter from David Denny to his brother urging him "to come at once."

The first structure erected at Alki Point was a brush shelter made with boughs laid over a pole supported by crotched sticks. Here Terry and Denny slept while they began the erection of the first log cabin, the foundations of which were laid September 28, 1851. In the construction of Seattle's first building they enlisted the services of the Indians who had already begun to congregate there, giving them in payment bread and trinkets. While they were thus engaged Luther M. Collins and an Indian passed along the beach driving oxen to Collins' claim. These are believed to be the first draught animals brought into King County. Early in November Collins again passed on his way to Olympia with his scow, and Terry joined him, leaving young David alone on the claim among the Indians to continue work on the cabin and complete it if possible before the arrival of the main party from Portland.

At this time the schooner Exact, Captain Folger, was fitting at Portland for a voyage to Queen Charlotte Island with gold prospectors, intending to touch at the Sound with emigrants. The party determined to take passage on her. She sailed on November 5, 1851, and cleared at Astoria on the 7th. On November 13th the schooner dropped anchor off the point and there disembarked from her the party that founded Seattle. David Denny was glad to see them. Just previous to their arrival some skunks had invaded his quarters and partaken so generously of his rations that there was little left for him to eat. Mr. Denny says, "Our first work was to provide shelter for the winter and we finished the work begun by my brother and Lee Terry for J. N. Low." Thus the first house was built for Mr. Low. D. T. Denny was hired to assist in the construction, had no ownership rights either in the claim, the house, or the town-site, all up to this time being owned by Low alone or by Low and Lee Terry jointly. In the party were twelve adults and twelve children, A. A. Denny and family, John N. Low and family, C. D. Boren and family, W. N. Bell and family, and Charles C. Terry, who with Lee Terry and David T. Denny brought the number of adults up to twelve.

After the Low house was finished it was occupied by the others in order to avoid the rain which was falling every day. The second house was a log struc-ture for A. A. Denny which increased the house-room so that all were com-fortable. With the construction of this house the timber adjacent suitable for log houses was exhausted, whereupon the settlers split cedar puncheons and built houses for Bell and Boren. These were considered quite fancy but not as substantial as the log houses. The winter quarters were no sooner completed than commerce found the little colony and there commenced the trading that has since made Seattle one of the well known seaports of the world.

In December, 1851, the brig Leonesa, Capt. Daniel S. Howard, dropped anchor off the little settlement seeking a cargo of piles. The settlers took the contract to load his vessel and while the rest of the men and boys devoted themselves to taking out piles and hauling them out by hand, Lee Terry went to Puyallup and secured a yoke of oxen, which he drove to Alki Point along the beach. After the arrival of the cattle the contract was speedily completed.

During their first winter on the Sound Denny, Boren and Bell explored the surrounding country and early in 1852 seriously took up the task of selecting claims for themselves, for their cabins had been erected on the land of Lee Terry and Low. Accordingly they examined the coast toward Puyallup, but not lik-ing the prospect in that direction began to examine the country around Elliott Bay. They realized that the life of the settlement would depend upon its abil-ity to sell piles and timber, for there were several other thriving settlements on Puget Sound and a market had already been established; in fact it was the important consideration, for the land was pretty much alike in all directions.

They used a canoe as their craft, and Bell and Boren handled the paddles. With a bunch of horseshoes attached to a heavy line, Arthur Denny "heaved the lead," and noted the soundings which convinced them that Elliott Bay offered the greatest promise. They began their work about daylight, passing over to the north shore and taking soundings from Smith's Cove southward. The water proved very deep in the bay and they were forced to keep close to the shore for quite a distance for the line to reach bottom. Stopping at a spring near the beach, they rested for a time. As he looked over the bluff Mr. Denny observed a break in the forest. Thinking this indicated a break in the continuous woods, he climbed up the bank to discover a gently sloping hillside over which a fire had passed, deadening the trees. Some of these, particularly the alders, of which there were many at that particular place, had fallen over, leaving an opening. It was this place, which by his right of dis-covery, he afterwards chose for his home. During the afternoon the party paddled south, up the bay. As they passed slowly along the shore from their noon resting place, they saw the bluff diminish in height, lowering from thirty or forty feet down to fifteen, and, in less than half a mile, to only five feet or less. Then it disappeared, and they came upon a little crooked tide stream, with muddy banks and salt grass on the margin along the tiny meadow. Near this point was a curious circular knoll thirty or forty feet high, with steep sides. Beyond was observed an Indian house, no longer inhabited, partly overgrown with wild rose bushes, which flourished along the shore. It stood near the present corner of First Avenue South and Yesler Way. South of the little tide stream they coasted past a low wooded flat but a few feet above tide water. They continued their voyage around the head of the bay, reaching home by nightfall, not only well pleased with the excursion, but thoroughly satisfied as to the fitness of the bay as a harbor and the promise of its eastern shore for a home. Thus they explored for timber, harbor and feed for live stock, and finally on February 15, 1852, marked three claims in one body at the present heart of Seattle. The southern boundary was fixed at what is now King Street and First Avenue South. This was the southern boundary of the claim of C. D. Boren. Next north was the claim of A. A. Denny, and north of this claim was that of W. N. Bell, all fronting on the Sound. A little later D. T. Denny located his claim north of Bell's, fronting on the Sound and on Lake Union as well. Each claim embraced about three hundred and twenty acres. All were in township 25 north, range 4 east, Willamette Meridian, though the land, of course, had not been surveyed, nor obtained by treaty from the Indians.

Meanwhile there were neighbors to the south along the banks of the Duwamish, who were to have a vital interest in the making of the city, and we must go back for a minute to pick up the incidents which brought them in touch with the first settlers here. On September 14, 1851, Luther M. Collins, Henry Van Asselt, Jacob Maple and his son Samuel, whose names have already been mentioned, arrived at the mouth of the Duwamish River, having come overland from the Columbia River to the Sound. At Olympia they hired two Indians and a canoe, and after two days of travel reached their destination. They made the first settlement in King County.

The four men took claims; Luther M. Collins, who with his wife and two children, had first settled in the Puyallup Valley, the nearest the mouth of the river; Jacob Maple next; above him, Samuel Maple; and adjoining him on the south, Henry Van Asselt. On the claim of the latter the city plant of the Denny-Renton Clay and Coal Company is now located. They experienced much difficulty in bringing their live stock to their new location. A scow used at first proved unequal to the task and was abandoned. The animals were then driven along the tide flats with great difficulty and not a little danger. They finally arrived at Alki Point and soon reached the place afterward called Milton and still later named West Seattle. But it was found that the mud flats could not be traversed, neither could the woods, so the scow was again brought into use, and the animals were finally landed in safety at Collins' claim. They then returned to Nisqually and moved the Collins family down and built cabins on their claims. Mr. Denny said their permanent location was made September 14, 1851; but E. B. Maple claimed that it was made June 22, 1851, on the day of their first arrival. Other settlers on the river later were G. Holt, G. Hograve and William Ralston, whose claims were where South Park now is.

SEATTLE EARLY IN 1865
Looking North from Main Street

For a time Maynard had carried on a small merchandising in Olympia, where he had made friends of his customers but not of his competitors in a business way. The doctor had done a good deal of traveling about the Sound and made the acquaintance of large numbers of Indians. He had gained the friendship and confidence of Chief Seattle, after whom the village was named, and was persuaded by him that this region was a most favorable trading point. Maynard was not long in deciding to make the change. He put all his unsold stock on a scow, and with Indians as his only companions set sail down the Sound. On his arrival at Alki he found most of the settlers there arranging to remove to the eastern shore of Elliott Bay. These urged him to join them, which Maynard soon decided to do. By mutual agreement he selected the most southerly claim, its northerly line meeting Boreu's at Yesler Way.

At that time the "Point," as it was soon called, was an island at times of full tide, of about eight acres in extent. At Washington Street the inlet extended across First Avenue South from about Railroad Avenue. From First Avenue South eastward it covered a much wider space and then narrowed again near the present Union Depot. Thence westerly along the general course of King Street to Railroad Avenue; thence northerly to Washington Street. It was covered with a heavy growth of fir and cedar and the usual dense underbrush. The sawdust and waste from Yesler's mill were used to fill in the low ground at Washington Street and the flow of the tides was soon shut off, but it was more than thirty years later when it was shut out at the easterly inlet.

Maynard's official land entry named April 3, 1852, as his date of settlement. With his accustomed energy he at once set to work to provide himself with a store building, availing himself of white and Indian labor, and in a few days was selling goods in it. It was eighteen feet wide and twenty-six long, with an attic in the front half of it. The walls were of logs and the roof of shakes, the usual name for split boards about four feet long. It stood at the present northwest corner of First Avenue South and Main Street. The unbroken forest was a few feet away on the east and the steep bank above tidewater on the west. The stores of that period included under one roof the necessaries of pioneer life as far as attainable, clothing, hardware, groceries, tools, ship chandlery, and Maynard's was the first of its kind in Seattle, although Low and Terry had conducted a similar business at Alki.

Among his other activities he immediately set to work to put up salmon for shipment. That season he sent to San Francisco nearly one thousand barrels of salted salmon. The barrels were made on the ground where they were packed, though where he got the coopers is not recorded. Procuring the fish was a simpler matter, as the Indians supplied him with all he could use. On its arrival in San Francisco most of the shipment was found to be spoiled, and his venture proved almost a total loss.

During this time he had men skilled with the broadax squaring timbers, and others cutting piles and shaving shingles. A cargo of these was shipped to San Francisco on the brig Franklin Adams; 12,000 lineal feet of squared timbers, 8,000 lineal feet of piles, 10,000 shingles, and 30 cords of wood. All of this cargo found a ready market at good prices and from it he more than recouped his losses on the salmon.

In the Columbian Maynard's advertisement of the "Seattle Exchange" appears later as follows: "The subscriber is now receiving direct from London and New York, via San Francisco, a general assortment of dry goods, groceries, hardware, etc., suitable for the wants of immigrants just arriving. Remember, first come, first served. Seattle, October 30, 1852."

He also advertised for a blacksmith and promised him constant employment.

At the time of these pioneer settlements all the northern part of the Sound country was included within Thurston County. Col. Isaac N. Ebey was the only member from Thurston County of the Legislature which met in Salem, in the Willamette Valley, in December, 1852, his colleague having resigned. Colonel Ebey introduced bills to have Pierce, King, Jefferson and Island counties set off from Thurston, and these bills became laws during that session.

In July, 1852, the commissioners of Thurston erected a voting precinct and a school district here and named it Dewamps. All of the eastern shore of Puget Sound north of the Puyallup River was within its limits.

At an election that fall Arthur A. Denny received all of the votes in the precinct and was elected to a seat in the Legislature, but he never took his seat. The election was December 7th. The Legislature convened at the same time. The official returns were so slow in reaching the capital that the Legislature had adjourned before he could receive his certificate and reach Salem.

The Columbian was then the only newspaper published north of the Columbia River and in politics it was ardently democratic. It spoke about the election at the time, but as Mr. Denny was of the opposite party the paper did not publish the fact of his election.

On April 3, 1852, Bell, Boren's family and Doctor Maynard moved from Alki to their claims, leaving behind A. A. Denny, who was too ill from ague to come over until a house could be built. At first Bell camped on the north side and Boren on the south side of the claims, continuing thus until they could build cabins. This they soon did and then built one for A. A. Denny at what is now the intersection of Western Avenue and Battery Street. This location was undesirable, and a little later Denny built another residence at the northeast corner of First Avenue and Marion Street. The united claims were so divided that each could have access to the Sound and the claims were made as nearly equal as possible.

Had the first settlers on the east side of the bay been seeking farms they would not have chosen their claims where they did. The prospect of clearing off the heavy timber that extended from the banks overlooking the Sound everywhere to the lakes would have appalled them; but as this forest was to be the means of affording them a livelihood for years, it was calculated to attract rather than to repel them. The estimate that the clearing of the forest and underbrush from the present site of Seattle has cost more than all the filling in of the tide flats is a modest one. Not even the actual excavation of the earth during the progress of the city's numerous regrades has amounted in cost to the sum total involved in removing the trees and their enormous roots. No great city on the American continent has overcome so many natural obstacles encountered in its growth. The expense of clearing the land, leveling down the hills and filling up the waters of the bay and the lakes, together with the enormous added cost of sewer tunnels, intercepting and trunk sewers, to keep the sewage out of the lakes and carry it six or eight miles off to the Sound, make an aggregate that must have reached twenty, perhaps twenty-five, millions of dollars.

So quickly was it known after the hegira from Alki began that Seattle was soon to have a sawmill that only a few log cabins were put up, perhaps eight or ten, and only a couple of these, Maynard's store and Yesler's cookhouse, were of considerable size. All of these but the cookhouse disappeared during the later '50s.

The type of log cabin of the American pioneers has not greatly changed since the landing of the pilgrims. Usually it was about sixteen feet square. At each end of the logs the upper side was hewed into triangular shape; the next tier had notches cut in them on the lower side to fit closely over the lower logs. About eight feet from the ground, at each end of the structure, the logs were carried up from four to six feet farther and gradually shortened and sloped toward the ridge. On these were laid, three or four feet apart, substantial rafters, to hold the shake roof. The shakes were usually held in place by poles placed over each rafter and the two substantially fastened together with wooden pins. After the logs for the cabin had been brought on the ground and fitted for use it was the custom for the neighbors to aid in rolling them into place by means of "skids," or long poles.

With ax, adze or broadax, two or three augers, drawshave and a handsaw, wonders were accomplished in building and furnishing these cabins. Often not a piece of metal entered into their construction. Between the logs they were first "chinked" with moss, and this was held in place by strips of wood outside and inside, though often clay served the same purpose. Where straight-grained logs could be secured "puncheons" were split and hewed into a semblance of smoothness, and out of these the floor, tables, benches, stools and door were fashioned. Often the latter was made with an upper and lower section, and was a triumph of art and strength, with hinges and bars equally calculated to resist all ordinary methods of breaking it open. At one end the bar worked on a pivot and at the other end it dropped into a notch. At this end a strong leathern thong was fastened and its free end passed through a hole above in the door. By this simple expedient the door could easily be barred or unbarred. In peaceful times the thong was not drawn in at night, and from this custom the phrase originated, "The latch-string is always out," equivalent to open-handed hospitality. The door with its two sections served a double purpose. When the upper section was open the interior was well ventilated and also lighted, after a fashion. By keeping the lower section closed the dogs, pigs and chickens were kept out and the babies kept in. Some of the cabins boasted at least one small window with glass panes, though often instead of glass it had thin cotton cloth or even strong white paper oiled to make it semi-transparent. In the cabin where the writer was born in Illinois the oiled paper served this purpose.

Wherever most convenient an opening was left in the wall to a height of about six feet from the ground and the same width. Into this the face of the fireplace was fitted and the chimney built outside reaching above the peak of the roof. If stones suitable for the purpose could be obtained they were used, but more often sticks were laid neatly one above the other, forming a crib, and on the inner face of the fireplace and chimney a coating of clay was liberally plastered. After fires had been kept for a time the clay hardened and·not often required patching or to be removed.

At night many primitive methods of lighting were in use to supplement the firelight in the open hearth. Pitchwood, tallow dips and fish oil lamps were in frequent use. Even a shallow dish filled with oil in which one end of a wick or piece of cotton cloth was immersed and the other end lighted served at times to partially dispel the darkness.

Sixty years ago the kerosene lamp first made its appearance on the Pacific Coast, and was regarded by its fortunate possessor as the ultimate in convenience and dazzling brightness. The depravity of the gas meter was then unknown and electric lighting undreamed of, also the exactions of the plumber and the building regulations of later years vexed not the soul of the householder.

Pins driven into holes in the walls supported substantial shelves for the dishes and the few articles of clothing that might be in use. Longer pegs, held up at the inner ends by uprights driven into the earth or in holes in the floor, supported long strips of split boards, and on these were laid cedar boughs, moss from the trees or dried fern or grass. On such a mattress were spread the blankets, and no sweeter slumber now comes to the couch of down than visited the pioneer in his rude bunk in the olden time.

The crane in the fireplace, the bakeoven on the hearth for the bread, and the reflector for the biscuit, all were a part of the household economy. Soap was made out of grease and lye; ax handles and brooms were whittled from ash, oak or maple sticks; much of the cobbling, as well as carding of wool, spinning of yarn and knitting of socks and stockings, was done in each household. "Quilting bees" among the women and "log-rolling" among the men were about the only opportunities for relaxation and social enjoyment. On such occasions the neighbors gathered from near and far to take part in them.

A most vivid presentation of the conditions existing here in the early days is made in Inez Denny's "Blazing the Way," from which several paragraphs are extracted:

"These primitive habitations were necessarily scattered, as it was imperative that they should be placed so as to perfect the titles of the donation claims. Sometimes two settlers were able to live near each other when they held adjoining claims, others were obliged to live several miles away from the main settlement and far from a neighbor, in lonely, unprotected places.

"What thoughts of the homes and friends they had left many weary leagues behind visited these lonely cabin dwellers!

"The husband was engaged in clearing, slashing and burning log heaps, cutting timber, hunting for game to supply the larder, or away on some errand to the solitary neighbor's or distant settlement. Often during the livelong day the wife was alone, occupied with domestic toil, all of which had to be performed by one pair of hands, with only primitive and rude appliances; but there were no incompetent servants to annoy, social obligations were few, fashion was remote and its tyranny unknown; in short, many disagreeable things were lacking. The sense of isolation was intensified by frequently recurring incidents in which the dangers of pioneer life became manifest. The dark, mysterious forest might send forth from its depths at any moment the menace of savage beast or relentless man.

THE COOK HOUSE IN 1865. BUILT IN 1835.

"The big grey timber wolf still roamed the woods, although it soon disappeared before the oncoming wave of invading settlers. Generally quite shy, they required some unusual attraction to induce them to display their voices.

"On a dark winter night in 1853 the lonely cabin of D. T. and Louisa Denny was visited by a pair of these voracious beasts, met to discuss the remains of a cow, belonging to W. N. Bell, which had stuck fast among some tree roots and died in the edge of the clearing. How they did snarl and howl, making the woods and waters resound with their cries as they greedily devoured the carcass.

"The pioneer couple who occupied the cabin entered no objection and were very glad of the protection of the solid walls of their primitive domicile. The next day Mr. Denny, with dog and gun, went out to hunt them, but they had departed to some remote region.

"On another occasion the young wife lay sick and alone in the cabin above mentioned and a good neighbor, Mrs. Sarah Bell, came to visit her, bringing some wild pheasant eggs the men had found while cutting spars. While the women chatted, an Indian came and stood idly looking in over the half-door and his companion lurked near in the brush near by.

"John Kanem, a brother of the chief, Pat Kanem, afterward told the occupants of the cabin that these Indians had divulged their intention of murdering them in order to rob their dwelling, but abandoned the project, giving as a reason that a 'haluimi kloochman' (another or unknown woman) was there and the man was away.

"Surely a kind Providence watched over these unprotected ones that they might in after years fulfill their destiny."

In October, 1852, H. L. Yesler, of Portland, arrived at Seattle in search of a suitable location for a sawmill. The point on the bay where the claims of Boren and Maynard joined (now Pioneer Place) suited him, and as none of the claims had yet been filed at the land office in Oregon City, the two settlers, Maynard and Boren, agreed to surrender to him a strip of land where their locations joined in order to give him a water frontage for his claim and at the same time secure a sawmill, a very important industry for the contemplated village. All the settlers were willing to make concessions, sacrifices, in order to expand the settlement. The plat of the proposed village and the name were agreed upon before the arrival of Mr. Yesler, so that his name did not appear as one of the proprietors of the first town plat.

When Yesler's mill started, in 1853, the first logs were furnished by Doctor Maynard. Hillory Butler and William Gilliam had the contract to take these logs to the mill from a tract adjacent to First Avenue South and Main Street, which they did, rolling them down with handspikes. Doctor Maynard designed to lay out lots where these logs were cut. George F. Frye, Edward Hanford, John C. Holgate, T. D. Hinckley, David Phillips and Jack Harvey helped supply the mill with logs during the first few years. When white help was lacking Mr. Yesler employed the Indians. George Frye was Mr. Yesler's sawyer, and his engineers at the different times were T. D. Hinckley, L. V. Wyckoff, John J. Moss and William Douglas. A. A. and D. T. Denny also worked in this mill, as did nearly all of the early residents. Lumber from this mill was sent to China and other foreign ports, as well as to San Francisco.

On November 19, 1852, Dr. D. S. Maynard, justice of the peace, married,

at Seattle, John Bradley and Mary Relyea, both of Steilacoom. This was probably the first marriage ceremony performed in Seattle and in King County.

During the year 1852 the settlers spent their time building homes, planting
gardens, getting out piles and timber, and providing for the care of live stock.
Several vessels visited the Sound settlements that year, among them the brig
Franklin Adams, Captain Felker, and the brig John Davis, Captain Plummer.
Each vessel carried a stock of general merchandise from which the settlers
secured their earliest supplies. During the winter of 1852-53, which was very
severe, there were several months when vessels did not visit the Sound settlements and the settlers suffered greatly in consequence. Late in 1852 Mr. Denny
paid $90 for two barrels of pork and $20 for one barrel of flour. One of the
barrels of pork was lost on the beach. The settlers lived on potatoes, fish,
venison, sugar, syrup, tea, coffee. Flour sold at one time during the winter as
high as $40 a barrel. Flour came from Chili, sugar mostly in mats from China,
and pork and butter around The Horn from the Atlantic cities. On one occasion A. A. Denny and J. N. Low went to Fort Nisqually in a big canoe propelled
by four Indians and returned with fifty bushels of little red Indian potatoes,
which were heaped up on green hides in the bottom of the canoe.

It was not only difficult to travel in early days, but was difficult to live. The
high cost of living was then burdensome as now. In the winter of 1852-53
flour sold in Portland at from $20 to $24 a barrel, and butter at $1.50 a pound.
At Olympia flour was $25 a barrel; potatoes, $2.50 a bushel; and beef, 16 cents
a pound. But as a compensation, in San Francisco squared timbers sold at $45
and sawed lumber at $70 per 1,000 feet.

One of the arrivals of 1852 was Dr. Henry A. Smith, for whom Smith's
Cove was named, and who was the innocent creator of a joke that went down
in the annals of the city. In the course of his work of settlement he started
out one day to blaze a trail from the cove which still bears his name to the
Village of Seattle, became lost without knowing it and described a huge circle
which brought him to his own back fence. Here he sat for some time and
reflected on the similarity between this strange clearing and his own. The story
was too good to keep, and Seattle laughed at him for many a day.

Another important arrival of the same year was George N. McConaha, a
lawyer by profession. He had come from Missouri, first to Sacramento, where
he was esteemed as one of the brightest men at the bar. Hoping to win higher
honors here, he came to the territory in 1852, and was elected from King and
Pierce counties a member of the Council of the First Territorial Legislature,
and was chosen president of that body.

There seems to be no record of the exact time that the name Seattle was
chosen by the founders for the new town. However, it had become well
known by that name as early as the fall of 1852. The first few settlers realized
the importance of selecting a name that would reflect credit on the metropolis
they hoped some day to build and various suggestions were made. It was found
that some of the land upon which the city now stands already was known by
name, the Indian words Mukinkum and Tsehalalitch having been applied to
some of it. The Thurston County officials, being under the necessity of giving
the precinct some name by which it could have a place in the official records,
called it Dewamps, from which the modern name Duwamish was evolved.

There was at the head of a colony of Indians who lived in the neighborhood of the new settlement a dignified old chief by name Seattle. He was popular among all the whites, and as his name was short and euphonious the movement to name the town after him gained some headway. The sentiment was crystallized May 23, 1853, when the plats were filed under the name "Town of Seattle." The chief was not moved to emotional depths that made any ripple on his usual dignified bearing when he became acquainted with the fact that the honor had been conferred upon him, but throughout the remainder of his life he continued to manifest his friendship for the whites upon every occasion, and no one ever regretted that his name was adopted as that of the great city that subsequently replaced the forests in which he and his braves pursued game.

Thomas Mercer left his family in Salem during the winter of 1852-53 and came over to Puget Sound to investigate conditions here, and he was so well satisfied with the village that he went back and in the spring brought his family with him. Dexter Horton and wife were members of the same party. They arrived here in April, 1853. Even though they then gave no indication of the prominent part they were later to play in the development of the city, their arrival was one of the most exciting things that had occurred in the settlement, for Mercer brought a team of horses and a wagon. Mercer speedily became Seattle's entire transfer system, and by adding dairying to his teaming grew to be an important factor in the life of the town. He took up a donation claim, the eastern end of which was the meander line of Lake Union, and what is now known as Mercer Street was the dividing line between his claim and that of D. T. Denny.

There is no contemporaneous published record of early events in this region, save here and there an advertisement or a paragraph in the Olympia papers, excepting the official account of the Indian war. Seattle's first newspaper did not appear until the fall of 1863; the men were mostly all too busy to keep diaries. Arthur A. Denny's charming little book was published in 1888. Fred Grant's history of Seattle was written about 1890, and published the following year. Nearly all the pioneers were then living and its facts were obtained first hand, and are well and accurately presented. Inez Denny had her father's diary to consult and her own memory and that of other members of her family older than she to aid her in writing "Blazing the Way." Thomas W. Prosch had access to the diary of Doctor Maynard and the valuable personal aid of Mrs. Maynard while preparing his monograph of David S. Maynard. These four books are almost the only original sources extant, and under strict historical interpretation even they do not fall within the category, but their substantial accuracy is indubitable. Personal acquaintance with nearly all the first local pioneers and much knowledge of those early days, and of the actors amid them, has led to frequent and copious selections from their pages. It was a sad coincidence that the author of two of these four books should have been drowned, though Mr. Prosch did not meet with the fate that befell his one-time friend and companion, Fred J. Grant, until twenty years later.

Previous to the appearance of the white settlers the Alki site had not been a general camping ground for the Indians, but they soon began to come and build rude houses near those of the whites until it is claimed over one thousand were there. They were friendly and seemed to regard their location near the whites a protection against their Indian enemies, and the whites did not object for fear of offending them.

The first store in King County was opened at Alki Point in November, 1851, and Charles C. Terry was the pioneer merchant. From notes in a little memorandum book of his that has been preserved it appears he had the forethought to secure a small lot of merchandise in Portland and have it shipped around on the Exact at the time the families were brought to Alki. The list includes the following: 1 box tinware, 1 box axes, 1 box tobacco, 1 keg brandy, 1 keg whisky, 1 box raisins. Terry lost no time in putting up a little cabin in which to display his goods. In addition to his Portland shipment he had bought from a trading schooner 25 barrels pork, 3,500 pounds flour, 150 gallons molasses, 800 pounds hard bread, 1 case boots, 1 case brogan shoes, 1 bale domestic, 1 dozen pieces prints, 1 cask whisky, 6 dozen hickory shirts, 1 dozen window sash, 1 box glass 8x10, 1 dozen grindstones, ½ dozen crosscut saws, ½ dozen files, 1 case mustard, 1 case pepper sauce, 400 pounds sugar. With these goods opened up, young Terry put up a sign that he was ready for business. So far as the memorandum book discloses, Mr. L. M. Collins was the first customer at the new store; at least, he opened the first account, and is charged with 6 pans, 1 large and 2 small water pails, 6 pint basins, 1 coffee pot, 2 frying pans, 2 candlesticks and 1 dipper.

Alki had a number of business houses in addition to that of Charles C. Terry. In April, 1853, Samuel Lambert and W. M. Smith opened an establishment which they called the "New York Wholesale and Retail Store and Ship Chandlery," in which they kept a general assortment of merchandise. They advertised that they were "constantly receiving goods from San Francisco by the clipper brig Leonesa, which makes the quickest trip of any vessel coming into the Sound." They also kept a letter box for the reception of letters of strangers and residents, and a "register for travelers and others to register their names." In September the firm dissolved partnership and called for a settlement of accounts.

In the spring of 1853 Stilwell & McMillen announced that they had established a cooper shop at Alki, where they would keep a full line of barrels particularly for the salmon industry.

George & Co. advertised a full supply of groceries, flour and liquors received through the bark Harriet Thompson and the schooner Willimantic.

The enterprise of Seattle pioneers was beginning to attract widespread attention. The Columbian of August 20, 1853, said

"Seattle is thriving. All the accounts that we receive from thence tell us of new buildings and other improvements. Yesler's steam sawmill is working finely. Alki is full of vigor and goaheaditiveness; her commerce is increasing and her men of business are doing well. Renton's steam sawmill will be in operation in a few days. The enterprising inhabitants of these two places, near together as they are, seem determined that their full, high and important destiny shall be achieved as soon as possible. Success attend them, say we."

Immediately after the founding of Seattle new arrivals began to make their homes in the village or to take claims nearby.

Hillory Butler and wife, George N. McConaha and family, Thomas S. Russell, Robert Russell, George F. Frye, Franklin Matthias, David Phillips, L. V. Wyckoff, M. D. Woodin, Ira Wooden, John A. Chase, William G. Latimer,

Charles Plimmer, Joseph Williamson, David Maurer, Robert Gardner, Jacob Wibens and George Bowker soon identified themselves with the affairs of the village permanently. While William Hebner, S. M. Holderness, J. W. Margrave, John Margrave, N. H. Oglesbee, Gideon Hibbard and Thomas Stewart settled here, and were for a time active in affairs, they did not long remain in this community.

On the bay to the south claims were taken by John C. Holgate, Edward Hanford, John J. Moss and Seymour Hanford. The latter did not perfect his title to his claim. On Lake Washington were E. A. Clark, Walter Graham, John Harvey, Timothy D. Hinckley and Lemuel J. Holgate. About half way between bay and lake Seymore Wetmore and family took up their claim.

To the north was Dr. Henry A. Smith on Smith's Cove and about and near Salmon Bay were Edmund Carr, E. M. Smithers, David Stanley, Ira W. Utter, John Ross, Francis McNatt and William A. Strickler, besides Joseph Overholts, Henry R. and Burley Pearce, who remained but a short time.

At the mouth of the Duwamish River was Charles Walker, and a little farther up the river were D. Conklin and wife. Above these the Maple-Collins settlement has been mentioned elsewhere. Farther up the river were John Buckley and wife, J. C. Avery, G. T. Grow, Dr. S. L. Grow, George Holt and August Hograve. Of these only Buckley and wife long remained in the county.

On the Duwamish, not far below the confluence of Black River and nearby on Black and White rivers, were William H. Gilliam, Joseph Foster, Stephen Foster, John Carr, H. H. Tobin, A. F. Bryant, Dr. R. M. Bigelow, Charles E. Brownell, O. M. Eaton and Joseph Fanjoy. The latter two were murdered by the Indians east of the mountains while they were going further north on a prospecting tour.

William P. Smith and family were the first to settle on Cedar River near the present Town of Renton.

On White River below the present Town of Auburn were William H. Brannan and wife, George King and family, Harvey Jones and family, Enos Cooper, Moses Kirkland, Samuel W. Russell and family, Joseph and Arnold Lake, Henry Adams, John M. Thomas and wife, Robert H. Beatty and D. A. Neely and family.

On the upper reaches of the White River were A. L. Porter, Dominick Corcoran and James Riley.

In the summer of 1853 there were in King County 170 white settlers, of whom 111 were men and voters. In the whole territory there were 3,965 white inhabitants.

David S. Maynard and Catharine T. Broshears were united in marriage January 15, 1853, by the Rev. Benjamin Close at the bride's home near Olympia, and they came at once to Seattle to live.

Mr. Close had recently been assigned to the District of Northern Oregon and stationed at Olympia. He was at that time the only Protestant clergyman on the Sound.

On the 23d day of January, 1853, David T. Denny and Louisa Boren were united in marriage by Justice of the Peace Maynard, at the home of her brother Arthur. Their certificate of marriage was the first issued in King County. It is attested by D. S. Maynard, J. P., and H. L. Yesler, clerk. Not long afterward they bundled their few effects into a canoe and moved into a small cabin that recently had been erected near the water front on their donation claim. Their daughter Inez writes that the first meal partaken of in this cabin consisted of salt meat from a ship's stores and potatoes. At times this diet was varied by substituting fresh salmon for "salt horse."

In the Town of Seattle, December 29, 1853, by the Rev. David E. Blain, Mr. William H. Brannan, recently from Winnebago County, Illinois, was united in marriage with Miss Elizabeth Livingston, recently from Marion County, Indiana. They were among the victims of the massacre by the Indians near the present Town of Auburn in October, 1855, as noted elsewhere.

The story of Seattle's development is written in epochs. The first was the erection of the steam sawmill by Yesler. It gave the settlement a start and a guaranty of future existence. The stack that emitted the Yesler smoke was the pioneer of thousands of others; the city grew up around it, and Henry L. Yesler was the father of the city's industries.

The action of Boren and Maynard in moving their lines to accommodate Yesler is a significant episode in the life of Seattle, as it marked the first concerted attempt of the town to attract industries to itself. True, the motive was entirely selfish, for the presence of the sawmill could have but one effect on the adjacent land, which prior to the establishment of the mill could not rightfully claim to be of any more value than any other shore lands for miles in either direction. But all civic loyalty may be the offspring, in part at least, of enlightened selfishness; a campaign for more railroads or more factories is carried on with money cheerfully subscribed by people whose idea is to benefit the city in which they live and thereby enhance the value of all the property within that city. The enterprise of Boren and Maynard was on a par, therefore, with the later efforts greater bodies of her citizens have put forth to bring new industries to Seattle.

In the case of Yesler's mill the advantage to the small settlement became apparent as soon as work of construction was commenced. Work was given every adult in the settlement, and when the operation of the mill began logging became practically the only source of revenue of the settlers. By sheer strength of their bodies the men laid low the stately trees that made the site of the future city a forest, rolled them to tidewater and towed them with small boats to the mill. There was no other way to do the work and full advantage had to be taken of the accommodations which the gods had provided, as the steep hills back of the water front presented grades that eased somewhat the work of handling logs without the equipment that makes them the playthings of the machinery of today.

The Columbian of October 20, 1852, remarked: "We have heretofore neglected to notice the fact that there is a new steam mill in process of erection by Mr. H. L. Yesler at Seattle, north of the Duwamish River, and which, we are told, will be ready to go into operation early in November next and no mistake. Huzza for Seattle! It would be folly to suppose that the mill will not prove as good as a gold mine to Mr. Yesler, besides tending greatly to improve the fine town site of Seattle and the fertile country around it by attracting thither the farmer, the laborer and the capitalist. On with improvement. We hope to hear of scores of others ere long."

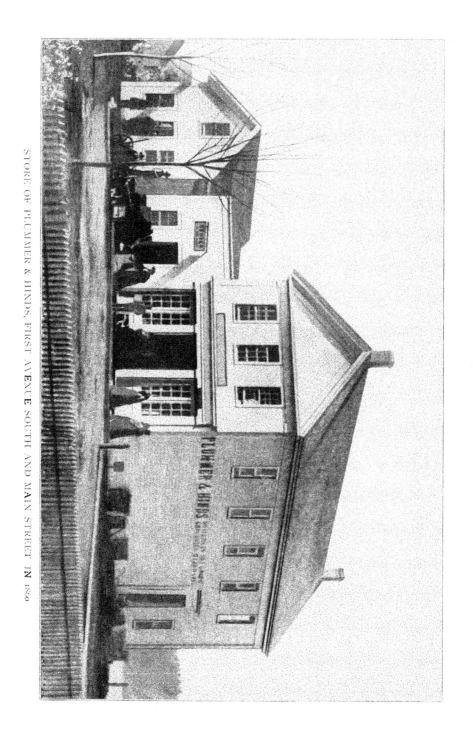

STORE OF PLUMMER & HINDS, FIRST AVENUE SOUTH AND MAIN STREET IN 1869

September 10, 1852, the Columbian, the first newspaper published north of the Columbia River, made its appearance in Olympia. In it appeared the advertisement of the "New York Cash Store," as follows·

"Chas. C. Terry & Co., thankful for past favors, take this opportunity to inform their numerous friends and customers that they still continue at their well-known stand in the Town of New York on Puget Sound, where they keep constantly on hand and for sale at the lowest prices all kinds of merchandise usually required in a new country. N. B.—Vessels furnished with cargoes of piles, square timber, shingles, etc."

Early in 1853, Low sold his interest at Alki Point to Charles C. Terry and moved to the neighborhood of Olympia. As Terry's brother Lee had previously returned to his old home in New York, he became the sole owner of the point. April 11, 1853, Terry advertised that the copartnership with Low had been dissolved by mutual consent and that the business of the firm would thereafter be conducted under the name of C. C. Terry. It was about this time that the name of the settlement was changed from New York to Alki, and the following announcement appeared in the Columbian

"Our enterprising friend, C. C. Terry, has made an excellent change of name for his flourishing town at the entrance of Duwamish Bay, hitherto called New York. It is henceforth to be known by the name of 'Alki.' We never fancied the name of New York on account of its inappropriateness; but Alki we subscribe to instanter. It is a pretty word, convenient, not borrowed or stolen from any other town or city, and is in its meaning expressive even unto prophecy. The interpretation of the word Alki being 'by-and-by,' 'in a little while,' or 'hereafter,' we must approve its application to a growing and hopeful place. Well done, friend Terry, success to thee and thy Alki. We are informed that a steam sawmill and several business houses are being erected at Alki. An extensive square timber and pile business is done there, and good assortments of merchandise are kept by the merchants. The brig Leonesa, Captain Howard, is now fully due at the port of Alki with merchandise for C. C. Terry and Lambert & Smith." In April, 1853, C. C. Terry advertised that he had just received a large and splendid assortment of goods of all kinds from San Francisco by the ship Sarah Parker and the brig Leonesa. He offered for sale 15,000 pounds of barley seed, and stated that he would receive timber and piles in exchange for his goods.

Additional mills soon began operations and the lumber trade increased steadily. In the winter of 1853-54, J. J. Felt arrived and built a mill at Appletree Cove, which early in 1854 was moved to Port Madison. It was owned later by George A. Meigs. In the spring of 1853 Capt. William Renton went to Alki and he and Terry erected a sawmill there, but it was soon found that strong northerly winds and a lack of abundance of fresh water made the place unsuitable, so the mill was moved to Port Orchard. The same year Talbot & Company built a mill at Port Gamble. The Port Ludlow mill and the one at Utsalady were also started in 1853.

The brig Kingsbury, Captain Cook, sailed for San Francisco in April with 250 piles, 20,000 feet of sawed lumber and 30 cords of wood on board. A little later the bark Sarah Warren, Captain Gove, took away a large cargo of piles, square timbers, shingles and cordwood. The brig Cyclops, Captain Perkins, sailed for San Francisco with 190,000 feet of sawed lumber, 14 cords of wood and 2 tons of coal. The Leonesa sailed with a cargo 8,000 lineal feet of piling and 4,000 lineal feet of squared timber and 20 cords of wood, all shipped by Terry.

Soon afterward he shipped by the Sarah Parker 10,000 feet of squared timber, 15,000 feet of piling and 100 cords of wood. The ship Mason brought him a large shipment of merchandise and provisions. In December, 1853, the brig John Davis sailed from Alki with a cargo of piles and timber, and about the same time the ship Brontes, similarly loaded, sailed from Seattle for the same destination.

The farms on the banks of the Duwamish River showed prospects of great development and furnished the people of Seattle and the lower sound with their products.

In 1853 the crop raised by L. M. Collins was valued at $5,000. The enormous size of the products of his farm excited surprise even here. He raised turnips weighing from twenty-three to thirty-five pounds each, potatoes weighing as much as four pounds each, and onions two pounds each. Already he was advertising 200,000 apple, peach, plum, cherry and other trees for sale at the low rate of $12.50 per hundred.

Rev. David E. Blaine and wife sailed from New York for Puget Sound October 5, 1853, by way of the Isthmus and San Francisco and reached Olympia November 20th. This was making good time for that period. They came down to Alki November 26th. The little hamlet then contained eight houses and a sawmill. The clergyman and his wife were entertained by Mr. Samuel Russell and wife, who were the only white family there at the time. The other houses were used as stores and homes for the bachelor residents.

Samuel Russell and wife not long afterward moved to their donation claim in the White River Valley and lived and died there. Their sons and daughters were active and prominent in the social and business life of this community for nearly a half century. The sons were Thomas, Robert and Alonzo. The elder daughter married John Thomas. They spent all their years afterward on their donation claim not far from where Kent now stands. Mary Russell married Charles C. Terry and was the mother of Ed and Charles Terry and Mesdames Scurry, Kittenger and Lewis. The youngest daughter, Emeline, married James J. Crow and the City of Kent was founded on their land claim.

Of his first ministrations in this new field of labor Mr. Blaine wrote a few days later as follows: "I preached in the afternoon and evening. In the evening after the sermon a young man (Charles C. Terry) took his hat of his own accord and passed around among the auditors, of whom I should think there were about thirty. When we counted the collection it amounted to $12.50.

"It rained hard most of the way from Alki to this place. We came to Mr. Denny's, a member of the M. E. Church, and were kindly received. Here we are yet. His home contains two rooms. I had purchased a stove in Olympia for $25, such as would cost me in Seneca Falls six or seven dollars, and we put this stove up in Brother Denny's room till we could make other and better arrangements. Last Sabbath I preached two sermons and organized a church of four members of whom Catharine (his wife) was one."

No clearer presentations of conditions 1ere in t1ose early days could be given t1an in t1e foregoing paragrap1.

Mr. Blaine's first letter from Seattle was dated December 6, 1853, and gave an acco1nt of t1e voyage from San Francisco to t1e Sound. It 1ad consumed only twelve days but at one time considerable uneasiness was occasioned because of faulty reckoning and consequent narrow escape from being driven on t1e rocks sout1 of Cape Flattery. T1e letter gave a description of t1e Sound from t1e cape to Olympia and many details of t1eir first experiences at Olympia, Steilacoom, Alki and Seattle. Several paragrap1s will be of more t1an ordinary interest to t1e reader of today. He wrote:

"I suppose Cat1erine will take t1e sc1ool 1ere for t1e next t1ree mont1s, at abo1t sixty-five dollars per mont1. A subscription was started yesterday. One man w1o 1as only two c1ildren to send 1as signed $100. We 1ave a few generous 1earted men 1ere. I am offered a lot anyw1ere in town to build our 1ouse upon, wit1out c1arge. I 1ave not yet selected it. One man 1ere has donated t1irty acres of land for a seminary just outside of t1e village survey. Anot1er is to give me a lot for a c1urc1 and parsonage. Our village contains about t1irty 1ouses and I t1ink twenty-six of t1ese 1ave been p1t up during t1e last six mont1s, but as yet it is mostly in t1e woods. T1ere are emigrants coming in, every now and t1en and augmenting our numbers.

"T1e people seem disposed to take very good care of us and give us enoug1 to do. Brot1er Denny offers me a lot for a first best garden, w1ere it will not require muc1 labor to clear it. We s1all not need to secure a claim. Village lots will be more val1able and t1ese we can 1ave given to us for t1e asking or on condition t1at we will make some improvements on t1em. T1e prices of lots vary from twenty-five to one 1undred dollars. As for fruit, we can very well live wit1out it as t1e superabundance of berries 1ere will serve as a substitute. T1ese abound during nine or ten mont1s in t1e twelve. We 1ave strawberries, raspberries, dewberries, salal berries, salmon berries, cranberries, w1ortleberries and wild grapes of a superior kind. T1ese ripen successively and are picked by t1e Indians and broug1t in by t1e barrel. Cranberries and w1ortleberries are still 1anging on t1e bus1es in abundance. T1ey are larger and more solid t1an our berries at 1ome in t1e states.

"T1ere is an abundance of game in t1e woods. consisting of deer, wild cattle (t1ese belong to t1e Hudson's Bay Company but 1ave run wild), bears, wolves, pant1ers, squirrels, skunks and rats. P1easants, grouse, gulls and ducks and crows are as tame 1ere as t1e 1ens at 1ome. T1ey are very numerous. T1ere are also a great many eagles, ravens and cranes. Our Sound, or inland sea, besides its many ot1er excellent qualities, abounds in fis1 of almost every variety. Salmon are very abundant, cod fis1, 1erring, sardines, oysters and clams. Whales come spouting along now and t1en. Halibut are caug1t at certain seasons of t1e year. T1e Indians do most of t1e fis1ing. T1e oysters here are of an inferior quality and small size."

Under date of January 11, 1854, 1e writes: "I 1ave just seen Governor Stevens. He came to Seattle last night; is expecting to go up our river tomorrow to visit our coal mines and make arrangements for t1e exploration of our country back to t1e pass in t1e Cascade range, wit1 a view to ascertaining t1e most feasible sit1ation for t1e terminus of t1e Pacific railroad. Many in t1is territory are very sanguine in the opinion that this terminus will be at some point on Puget Sound. This place, in view of the natural and easy route hither and of our excellent and commodious harbor, said to be the best on the Sound, will probably be the place."

January 17th Mrs. Blaine adds a postscript: "Our governor is now arrived, and we are to have a Territorial Legislature. The members are to be elected next month. The governor's home is at Olympia at present. He was down last Friday with Governor Lancaster, the nominee for congressman. They both addressed the people here. I did not hear them, being occupied in my school. They gave very good satisfaction. I did not see the governor, but the judge called on us twice. He appears well, has the reputation of being a fine man, a Christian. The governor is as rough in his appearance as any of our backswoodsmen. They say he wears his red flannel shirt, no white one, coarse clothes and unshaven beard. You probably know he came the overland route with a company to see what were the facts in regard to the practicability of a northern road, where would be the best passes, etc. He unhesitatingly declares the advantages of the northern route, and thinks, as we all here know, that if such a road is ever built, its western terminus will be somewhere on the Sound. He is a skillful, practical engineer, having served in that capacity in the Mexican war, and well qualified to judge in such matters. He pronounces himself pleased with the country, considers its resources abundant, and says he is astonished at the degree of intelligence he finds wherever he goes. He has quite encouraged the people, given them new life and vigor."

March 7, 1854, Mrs. Blaine writes: "We are now laboring under some excitement in consequence of some circumstances which have recently occurred. Just before we arrived here, the whites had hung an Indian that had killed some Indians and threatened to kill the whites. The Indians made no resistance and were apparently indifferent. Since that time there have been some white men missing and the Indians say they have killed them in revenge. One day last week a man started from Alki to go down the Sound in a canoe with three Indians. The Indians returned with his canoe, clothing, watch, money,.etc., and were quite badly wounded so that one of them died. Suspicions were raised that all was not right, and last Saturday three white men, and three Indians of another tribe, went to make inquiries. The Indians who were suspected of murder had left Alki and were found among their own tribe. The whites demanded them and they were given up without hesitation. They put them in a canoe, but it was aground which caused some delay in getting away, during which time the Indians from the land rushed upon the men with drawn knives, and one man fired upon them. This commenced hostilities and the whites killed from five to ten (they do not know the exact number) of the Indians. During the fracas one of the Indians they had arrested managed to escape. The other behaved so badly they shot him. The whites were all wounded, one of them mortally. He died last night. Mr. B. preached his funeral sermon this afternoon. Another was wounded in the thigh, a bullet going through it. The other received a bullet in his cheek, which flattened against his teeth and he spit it out. One of the Indians they took with them was wounded so they think he cannot live. Their return to this place yesterday excited the people very much. A company immediately volunteered to go this morning and attack them, but·upon more mature thought they decided to refer the case to the governor for his action upon it. The citizens convened last night, drew up a set of resolutions, informing him of affairs and requesting him to take immediate action. They sent it off in a sloop to Olympia, but unless the winds should be very fair, we cannot hope for aid from him before Saturday. Meantime we feel considerably alarmed for ourselves. The Indians are all well armed with guns, knives and more ammunition than the whites. They are very much alarmed, but if they knew their strength they might dispatch every white person on the Sound. There have been a great many of them about here this winter. At one time it was said there were 500 in this town and vicinity. They have left so that now we have no more than one hundred or two hundred. There are two things in our favor, the Indians are very cowardly, and the different tribes are at enmity with each other. Should their mutual fear of and hatred to the "Bostons" impel them to unite against us, the terrible scenes enacted in the settlement of the Atlantic states, the accounts of which used to chill my blood with horror, may be re-enacted here."

An engineer named William Young, employed in Renton & Terry's mill at Alki, had gone down the Sound in search of a claim and was murdered by the Indians he had employed to accompany him. The murderers fled to Whidby Island. Sheriff Thomas Russell organized a posse, consisting of Doctor Cherry and Mr. Tyson and three Indians of another tribe. One of the Indians of the sheriff's party died from the effect of his wounds soon afterward. The excitement and alarms incident to the murder and the bloody affray between the Indians and the officers of the law soon subsided and no further ill results followed in their train.

August 4, 1854, Mr. Blaine wrote a long letter to his mother on a great many topics, some connected with the old home and more with the affairs of the little village in which he and his wife had established a new home. The following is the writer's views regarding the local Indian as he then existed. The present day writers of Indian romances will hardly recognize the picture:

"You tell Kate she must love the coarse, filthy and debased natives in order to do them good. We can imagine, in some degree, your feelings on this subject, and you will need the help of imagination to appreciate our situation and relation to these pitiable objects of neglect and degradation. Once we could have hoped to do them good, but alas, they are most undoubtedly beyond our reach. They are but a remove above the digger Indians in California in intellect or humanity. Those who cannot talk the jargon or Chinook are beyond our reach because we cannot converse with them except through an interpreter. They have already learned enough of religion through the Catholics to make the sign of the cross and say (ikt papa ikt sockala Tiee) one pope and one God. Their ideas of a future state are very indefinite. They are taught that there is a lower region and an upper one and that the good and bad will be separated in the future state, but moral feelings seem to be blunted or quite blotted out, and they lie, gamble, steal, get drunk and all the other bad things almost as a matter of duty because it is so deeply innate and so fully acquired by habit. Those who can speak the Chinook are apparently more intelligent because from their intercourse with the whites they have acquired some cunning and artifice, but they are even lower in immorality than their less informed elders who speak not the jargon. They have also associated with the worst of white men and their example and influence have been most pernicious. Seeing the whites paying no regard to religious obligations nor even to moral principle they could scarcely do likewise. A prominent trait of Indian character east of the Rocky Mountains, we were taught, was gratitude, but these possess not a vestige of this noble feeling. You may feed them all they can eat and give them all they can put on today, and tomorrow they will come back and ask for more and not be satisfied unless you give them a more munificent present which they would take without the least show of thanks. And should you wish to get the use of their canoe, even for a few minutes, they would want pay for it. The principle which actuates almost all here is, 'Get all you can and keep all you get,' no matter how you get it. This is fairly illustrated by a case that occurred a day or two since. An Indian wore a very nice pair of pants when he came to call upon us, and when Kate, who was in the house alone, asked him if he got them by working in the saw-mill, he replied ('wake, nika iseum momook tolo') meaning, 'No, I got them by gambling' when she said 'Momook tolo hias mussachee' (gambling is very wicked) he replied 'wake mussachee—wake mussachee, iseum hiyou dolla' ('No bad, no wicked, gets plenty dollars'). This is the principle. Nothing is wicked which gets plenty of dollars. The first article is the creed of nearly all."

Mrs. Blaine added a postscript:

"Would you like to visit us? I do not know how long you would be contented here but I think for a time the novelty of everything would make you forget to be discontented. What would you think to go through a town which has but one street built on, and that but thinly, with nothing to mark the different lots, the sides and middle of the street all alike, stumpy, with miserable Indian shanties scattered all about and Indians meeting you at every step? We have now become so accustomed to these things they do not seem so strange to us, but I often think what would our folks say if they could see them. This warm weather they go almost naked, and it is no unusual sight to see quite a number of men around the tents entirely so. I can pass a long row of their tents on the beach within a few feet of the water and see children of all ages from a few months up to those twelve or fourteen years old running around without an article of clothing, sometimes chasing each other in the water and sometimes rolling on the sharp stones on the beach. Their skins seem as tough as horse hide, and they know as little of shame as the beasts of the field. Besides seeing the sights, we could amuse you by taking you out to pick berries. We went yesterday and picked a fine lot of raspberries. We went over and under logs, through brush and tangled weeds, up hill and down, but we had a very pleasant time."

At that time in Seattle trees had to be felled and stumps dug out to get sites for the little homes and the little gardens. Members of the cloth were too poor to hire this work done and all the other members of the community were engaged in the same tasks, so clerical ministrations were interspersed with long hours of severe manual labor. The following is illustrative of the pioneer experiences of all circuit preachers in those days. Writing of her husband she said:

"He does indeed need some new clothes as you would think if you could see how he goes dressed. He dirties and wears out a great many clothes as he has such dirty hard work to do. I have made him a hickory shirt that he puts on over his clothes when he is doing the worst. I do not know as you sisters would own him for a brother if you should see him as he looks nowadays. His hands are coarser and rougher than any farmer's I ever saw, and his clothes to match. I go out in the garden after school and help him. Making gardens here is a different thing from what it is with you where the ground is all cleared off nicely. Here are stumps, roots, bushes and plenty of such things to be cleared away. We have had fires burning for two weeks in the yard to burn up the stuff."

This yard and little garden was where the New York Block now stands. Probably few pioneers now living who often saw the residence of Dexter Horton when he lived on the east side of Second Avenue, just north of Cherry Street, knew that the Rev. David Blaine built that house long prior to the Indian war and that Mr. Horton bought it from him.

The early part of 1854 Charles C. Terry was planning a trip to the Atlantic states. Collection of accounts due him, securing men to operate the sawmill at Alki and supplying it with sawlogs, and keeping his store running were a part of his activities. In February he advertised that he had just received by the Leonesa a full and general assortment of provisions, groceries, drygoods, clothing, liquors, stoves, etc., and being anxious to close out the present stock he would sell cheaper than could be purchased elsewhere on the Sound.

However, a trip to the eastern states at that time was not a matter of a few days' travel and of slight consideration. It would probably consume five or six months, and the actual expenses for travel and subsistence amount to five or six hundred dollars. Mr. Terry appears to have sold out his store before starting east, as George & Co., in July of that year, advertised that they had bought his stock of goods.

Terry believed in the value of newspaper advertising, and during all the early years the Olympia newspapers seldom failed to have something in their columns about him and his different lines of business.

A stroll through the Village of Seattle in the summer of 1855 would lead one around stumps and over broken ground. The most noticeable building on First Avenue South was the branch store of Bettman Bros., who had begun business here the year previous. They had a very presentable establishment and kept on hand a full stock of goods. The Indian troubles impelled them to leave the city, and they disposed of their business to Charles C. Terry, who took possession after the war was over. They were engaged in the same business in Olympia, where the elder Bettman continued it during his lifetime, and it is still carried on by his son.

On the northwest corner of First Avenue South and Washington Street was the store of Denny, Horton & Phillips. The latter had come to Seattle from Olympia where he had at first settled.

Arthur A. Denny was among Seattle's first merchants. Commercial interests began at Seattle in the most natural manner, being but an outgrowth of the trading from the vessels that came to the harbor for piling and square timbers for the San Francisco market. While thus taking on cargo the captain carried on trade with the settlers and Indians on board the vessel. It was found to be profitable to leave the remaining stock behind at the village, to be sold off on commission. To Mr. Denny fell the lot of taking such goods and disposing of them. A store was built, one story high, 20x30 feet in size, on the northwest corner of First Avenue South and Washington streets, where Dexter Horton & Co.'s beautiful bank building afterward was erected, and in this unpretentious structure Mr. Denny sold all sorts of goods on commission. Trade increased rapidly, and 1e soon tiereafter associated with 1imself, Dexter Horton and David Piillips. Tiey carried provisions, 1ardware, cloties, cutlery and notions. It was not long before Mr. Denny and his partners were able to place themselves on an independent basis, tie founder of tie 1ouse visiting San Francisco to purciase 1is annual stock. Wien tie Indian war broke out, Mr. Denny disposed of 1is interest in tie business to enter tie volunteer service. Horton and Piillips continued business at tie old stand for a number of years, until tie institution of tie bank by Horton and tie deati about tie same time of Piillips. Atkins & Shoudy succeeded to tie mercantile department, and tiey in turn sold out in 1869 to Crawford & Harrington, afterwards transformed to Harrington & Smiti. Mr. Smiti died in San Francisco many years ago, and owing to complications tie affairs of tie partnersiip were wound up., Mr. Harrington is now living in Alaska.

Tie tiird and remaining store was tiat of Dr. Josepi Williamson, a widower, and a very successful merciant wio continued in tie same line of business until 1is deati many years later.

A sciooliouse was provided by William A. Strickler, a young man of fine attainments, and an engineer and surveyor by profession. He vacated a dwelling 1e 1ad erected and it was turned into a schooliouse.

The 1otel of tie place was the Felker House, tiat stood away out on the point near tie corner of Jackson Street and Railroad Avenue. It was tie best building in tie place; was a two-story, framed structure, finisied witi lath and plaster inside, tie first hard-finisied 1ouse in tie village.

Hillory Butler's 1ouse was on tie corner of James Street and Second Avenue on tie present site of tie Butler Hotel. It was riddled witi bullets during tie attack by tie Indians January 26, 1856, but it stood, a well-known landmark, until 1888, wien it was demolisied to make room for a business block.

Anotier 1ouse was occupied by Samuel Russell and family wio 1ad moved over from Alki and remained 1ere for a time before moving onto tieir farm in tie Wiite River Valley.

Boreu's was a notable structure, two stories in 1eigit, on tie corner of Second Avenue and Cierry Street. It was later known as tie Bell house.

Doctor Maynard's 1ouse was at tie corner of First Avenue Souti and Main Street; Edward Hanford's and Mrs. Holgate's on Cierry Street; Artiur Denny's was out quite a way on First Avenue near Madison Street, and Yesler's was at tie corner of James Street and First Avenue.

Bell's was at tiat time far out to tie north near Battery Street. It was burned by tie Indians tie day of tie battle.

At a general election in King County in July, 1855, about one hundred and forty votes were cast. Artiur A. Denny, A. B. Webster and David Piillips were elected to tie Legislature; Tiomas Mercer, county commissioner; T. S. Bordwell, auditor; E. M. Smitiers, assessor; A. F. Bryant, surveyor. For proiibitory liquor law eig1ty-one, against forty-four. Sixty years later King County reversed tiis verdict.

In October, 1855, just before the Indian war troubles broke out in King County, Luther M. Collins gathered a crop of 300 busiels of peaches. As this

CHARLES PLUMMER'S RESIDENCE. OCCIDENTAL AVENUE AND JACKSON STREET

THE FELKER HOUSE. JACKSON STREET AND WESTERN AVENUE

was only four years after the orchard was planted this was a good demonstration of fertile soil and favorable climate.

Under date of November 12, 1855, Col. M. T. Simmons, special Indian agent, published a notice directing all the friendly Indians within the limits of the Puget Sound District to rendezvous at North Bay, Nisqually, Steilacoom, Gig Harbor, Vashon's Island, Seattle, Port Orchard, Penn's Cove and Oak Harbor. Sub districts were formed with Dr. J. B. Webber, Dr. D. S. Maynard, Capt. R. C. Fay and Dr. N. D. Hill in charge.

The subject of one of the chapters of Grant's History of Seattle was "The Town and People," most of which is presented here.

"By the summer of 1855, preceding the siege, the number of houses of all descriptions in Seattle had reached about forty or forty-five. They were clustered on both sides of First Avenue South for three blocks. There were no houses north of Madison Street and none east of Second, except a building or two between James and Columbia, and a house near Jackson Street and Fourth Avenue South.

"The most important structure in the village was Yesler's sawmill. In more senses than one it was the life of the place. Here most of the men in town earned their money; here the ships came for cargoes and discharged their groceries. Its puffing, buzzing, and blowing of steam made the music of the bay, and the hum of its saws was the undertone of every household. By its whistle all the clocks were regulated and the whole business of the village was carried on. It was not a large mill, having only some fifteen thousand capacity, but as the price of lumber was very high, the value of its output was not inconsiderable. The next house in interest was Yesler's log cook and mess-house. As the name implies, this was the eating house of the mill hands. But in addition to this use it was town hall, court room, meeting house and hotel. All the legal business was transacted here and here nearly all social gatherings were held. It was the lounging place where the men collected and heard the news and told stories. A low, long, rambling affair without architectural pretentions, it possessed a certain homely attractiveness and was the last of the log buildings to be taken down. Soon after the mill began running the people built frame houses in a style that we should now call old fashioned, with clapboards and white paint, and one-story or story and a half in height. Such comparatively good houses, however, were quite few, the rest were shanties or cabins. The streets were unimproved, full of stumps and mud holes, and a single team did the carting. Bell's house, in what is now known as Belltown, was not in the town at all, and was burned by the Indians. Mercer's house was far in the country on Lake Union, and was the only dwelling out of town spared at the time of the attack. The forest closed down on the city and it was deep woods beyond Third Street.

"Thomas Mercer was one of the most useful members of the little community. By trade and education he was far from a pioneer, having worked until he was twenty-one in a woolen mill. He went, however, from his native Ohio to Illinois and learned some of the hooks and crooks of pioneer life on the prairie, finding that hands as soft as a girl's might soon be made strong and hard enough to swing the ax and maul, and guide the plough.

"But the excessive cold of the prairies led him to look at length for a milder climate, and for a number of years he made a study of Oregon. He became so thoroughly conversant with the subject that he was frequently called upon by the neighbors to come and tell them about Oregon as if he had been there. Indeed, he fell to dreaming of being here and in one of his dreams appeared to be in a forest where there was a sidehill swamp with a lake beyond and bay upon which one might come to his home all the way in a boat—his home in Illinois being some eight miles above river navigation. The particulars of this dream correspond curiously well with the surroundings of his present home on Lake Union, and the dream is a sort of life touch showing the somewhat mystical element which entered into early life on our coast; although Mr. Mercer is not in the least a superstitious man. When he started from Illinois he planned to come to Puget Sound, thus being an exception to the rule, as most of the settlers were directed hither after reaching Oregon. On the way, just as he was nearing the end of the tedious journey, being at the Cascades, he met with the greatest bereavement that can befall a man, the loss by death of his wife. With his four little motherless girls he came on to the end of his journey. At Portland he was invited by Lot Whitcomb and Thomas Carter to join a party to Gray's Harbor, but declined on the ground that he was too old, nearly forty, to wait for the development of that region. As for his children, there were kind people that offered to take them and bring them up, but his oldest daughter said she would keep house for him, she was thirteen, and they must all stay together. She kept her word nobly, denying herself that she might send her three little sisters off through the wood path to the log schoolhouse. It is a comfort to reflect that the endeavors of these brave children met before long the attainments of education and culture that they so much valued. For seven years Mr. Mercer had to be both father and mother to his girls.

"Among the effects that he brought to the Sound was a wagon, alluded to heretofore, and a span of horses. One of these animals was an old mare useful chiefly in bucking straw from the thresher. He was about to sell this animal upon his departure for Illinois. A neighbor, however, advised him that she would be his best animal on the plains, and after due deliberation he decided to take her. He found that she proved equal to the occasion, and for eleven years served her master most faithfully. She was the pioneer horse of Seattle; Tib was her name, and her grave near the old Mercer homestead is still carefully marked. With his horses and wagon, the only team in town, Mr. Mercer had a monopoly of the express business, and recalls with great enjoyment the fact that he was the first of all the teamsters. The roads were far from good, but he boasts that he surmounted all the difficulties of driving about the stumps and backing his loads of lumber even into the houses to which they were destined. He also did much in the line of delivering wood on the wharf for the steamers, among which he remembers the historic Massachusetts. Sometimes he did the wood-chopping himself, but he usually found it more profitable to hire Indians. Among the Indians he was able to move with perfect security, even going out for loads of wood during the time of the siege. Of all the houses in the county left to the depredations of the savages his alone was left unburnt and unharmed. The Indians were afterward asked the reason of this and answered that they thought he might want to use it again. It was said to him by a neighbor that if he stayed on his place with his little girls the Indians would not have hurt a hair of his head. He was always exceedingly kind to them.

"To him must be given the credit of naming the lakes. Up to 1854 they had gone without a name other than the Indian designation 'tenas chuck' and 'hias chuck' (little water and big water), barren of even proper Indian names. All agreed that distinctive names should be given to the lakes, but for some reason it was not easy to find satisfactory ones. A public meeting was called to settle the question, and Mercer's suggestion, that the larger one be named Washington for the father of his country, and the smaller Union, as sometime to become the connecting or uniting link between the larger lake and the Sound, met with hearty approval, and these names were adopted. Mr. Mercer lived a part of the time on his farm and a part of the time in the town until the city spread out to include the farm. He made a filing to include 320 acres, the west half extending upon that sightly tract now known as Queen Anne Town, but another made a filing on this part on the ground that Mercer was a single man. Not wishing to carry the matter to court, Mr. Mercer confined himself to the portion fronting on Lake Union. [It was generally understood at the time that if a married couple had reached the territory and then one of them died the survivor could file upon an additional claim for any minor children they might have. Mr. Mercer continued to live on a part of his claim until his death in 1898.—Ed.]

"One of the arrivals of 1852, who became eminent in the state as well as in the city, was Dr. H. A. Smith, for whom Smith's Cove was named. He came to this country a man of culture and education having been born in Ohio in 1830 and educated at Alleghany College, where he also studied medicine. Finishing his professional studies at Cincinnati, he was drawn into the migratory movement to the West, aiming in the beginning to go to the gold region of California. While in the Nevada Mountains, however, he decided to accompany his comrades to Oregon, in order to see the famous valleys of that state, particularly the Willamette, of which he heard more and more as he came westward. He intended to go on to the gold mines after visiting Oregon. On reaching Portland, then a lively town, however, he heard much of a Northern Pacific railroad to terminate on the Sound. Coming to Olympia and concluding that the road when built must cross the mountains through Snoqualmie Pass and that Seattle was the point nearest tide water, he decided to locate at this little place. There were a few cabins at that time, but they were so hidden by the immense timber that the shore appeared practically a wilderness. Coming along in a canoe with Collins, he asked where the town was, for there was nothing visible from the shore except a small improvement of Doctor Maynard's. It was the intention to practice his profession, but the place afforded him altogether too little sickness, and he soon saw that to realize any profit from living here he must do as the rest were doing, and get a piece of land. He chose a place on the north end of the bay where he believed the railroad must first touch the water, and in the woods began pioneer life in earnest. He found this sort of existence tedious in the extreme without the means of gratifying his cultivated tastes, and being still young, he suffered greatly from homesickness. He stuck to his place, however, not losing faith in the railroad. In the course of time he interested himself in clearing up his land, making pasturage for his cows, setting out an orchard and experimenting with his tide lands. Not giving up his practice altogether, he invented a way of combining both his vocations; he built an infirmary on his place to which he brought his patients, never refusing any in need of care. If, as was often the case, they had no money to pay, he had them settle by doing some clearing on his land

"In addition to his private enterprises, as the years passed by, he bore a full share of public burdens, becoming the first superintendent of public schools in the county, and serving three terms in the Lower House and two in the Upper House of the Territorial Legislature. He was president of the latter one term. His widely read contributions to the territorial press made him well known throughout the coast. He was pronounced by an eastern magazine as 'an able medical man and a poet of no ordinary talent, a rare scholar and a good writer.' [His death occurred in Seattle in 1915.—Ed.]

"Jacob Maple was born on the Monogahela River, Pennsylvania, in 1793. His father removed to Jefferson County, Ohio, in 1800 and died in 1812. The family lived subsequently in Southern Iowa, whence they emigrated to Oregon by way of California.

"To J. C. Holgate belongs the honor of having first visited Elliott Bay with a view of making a settlement. Holgate was from Iowa, and crossed the plains to Oregon in 1847, when a youth of but nineteen. He was a son of Abraham L. Holgate, a pioneer of Ohio and later of Iowa. In his childhood he was very delicate in health and being unable to take robust exercise, had for a large part of his amusement the overhauling and ransacking of his father's old books in the garret. A sister, four years older, made it a practice to read to him when he became old enough to wish to know what was in the books, and the works that most interested him were the record of General Pike's Expedition and the journals of a member of the Lewis and Clark Expedition. The sister explained and enlarged upon these accounts, chiefly with a view to amuse him, and during his spells of ague she diverted him with stories of Oregon, a land of perpetual spring, without thunder, the dread of the nervous child, and of vistas of snow-capped mountains and the ocean. The boy fully made up his mind to come to this romantic country, and the summer that he was nineteen he joined the party of Seth Luelling of Salem, Iowa. Reaching Vancouver during the following autumn he found the young territory in excitement over the Cayuse outbreak, and joined the forces of Gilliam to punish the murderers of Whitman. During the war he took a brave part, on one occasion performing a deed of the utmost daring. The horses of the troop with which he was connected having been stolen, the detachment was left in the midst of the enemy without the means of reaching the main command. The animals were picketed by the Indians at a distance, but in view, with the evident intent of drawing the whites into ambush. The commander of the squad understood this and explained it to the men, but added that they must have horses or all would fall into the hands of the hostiles. He then asked if there was any one who would volunteer to go and cut the lariats and let the animals loose, as he thought they would run back to their camp. Holgate volunteered to do it. 'You can't spare a man, and I'm only a boy,' was what he said. It was felt to be sure death, but with a halfbreed boy who generously agreed to accompany him, he went down and released the beasts, and they at once came flying back. Strange to say he was not fired upon, the Indians afterwards saying, 'Oh, cultus.' They thought him too little to kill, for he was small and pale even for his years.

"After the war, during the later days of which he was seriously sick with measles, he was told by an officer of the Hudson's Bay Company who had heard of his gallantry and took an interest in him, that if it was the best country for health he was after he should come to Puget Sound. Just before going to the war he had decided to take a claim on Tualatin Plains, but upon learning of the Sound as a better place, he made a tour of exploration in August and September of 1850. He crossed from the Cowlitz to Tumwater on foot and at Simmons' was furnished a canoe and a crew of Indian paddlers. With this dusky company he set out on a six weeks' voyage of discovery, passing as far north as the Snohomish, and made particular examination of Elliott Bay. On the Duwamish he found the claim he wanted, and determined to take this in preference to that on Tualatin Plains. He was not satisfied to settle here alone, however, and planned to make a visit to Iowa and marry and return. But before this he wanted to try his luck in the mines, and in 1851 went to Southern Oregon.

"He was never weary of extolling the Sound country, and it was largely due to his representations that L. B. Hastings, a close friend of his, was induced to come and examine the region. While Holgate was at the mines the other Duwamish settlers reached the bay and covered the claim he had in view. On returning from the mines he came north again, and although not finding his old place vacant, filed a claim south of Doctor Maynard's on the shore of the bay. The next above him was that of Edward Hanford. One of his letters dated December 23, 1847, at Tualatin Plains was preserved. It was written just before his Indian campaign but he does not say anything of his perilous venture, not wishing to burden his mother with anxiety. The following extract locates him and shows his relation to the events of the time: 'The plain that I am in is as pretty a section of country as I ever saw in Iowa. The land is as good for producing as is common in Iowa. Mr. George W. Ebbart has promised to take this to you for me. He can tell you more of the country and its prospects than I can at present. I intend making a claim in a few days which has about thirty acres of plain and the balance the best of timber, and if I get it well improved I ask no better fortune. I have but a few moments to write. I told Mr. Ebbart that you would treat him well for my sake as he has treated me with all the kindness of an open-hearted Kentuckian.'

"Another letter dated May 12, 1851, indicates where he was during the first years of his residence on this coast: 'The first six months I spent in Oregon I was in what is known as middle Oregon, between the Cascade and Blue mountains, with a regiment of about five hundred men. The first of last August I left here and went to Puget Sound to look at the country. I stayed there until the first of October. The Sound has four rivers emptying along its eastern shore. The valleys of these rivers will average about fifteen miles in width and are about equally divided in prairie and timber. I spent about six weeks traveling over this Sound country.' [These letters fix beyond doubt Holgate's exploration of the Sound. He was murdered in Nevada in 1868 during a controversy regarding a mining claim he had discovered and staked.—Ed.]

"It was greatly against the will of his sister that Holgate came to the West, for he seemed to her but a puny child still, and she felt guilty for filling his head with adventurous notions. In much the same spirit, he, after coming and seeing the real hardships of the journey, would not advise her to think of coming. In the meantime she had married. Her husband's affairs were prospering. He had a magnificent tract of prairie and woodland, and large herds of cattle. This was

Mr. Edward Hanford. In spite of Holgate's withholding encouragement, however, Hanford took the Oregon fever and brought his family across the mountains and plains, and occupied the claim next above that of Holgate. With the large number of work cattle that he brought from Iowa, he supplied teams for doing a very profitable business in hauling out timbers. By the aid of his wife he was making a most comfortable home, with garden and orchard, until all was wantonly destroyed by the Indians at the time of the outbreak. After this disaster, he lived in the town until some years later. He then resided in San Francisco for a number of years, but the evening of his life was spent at Seattle.

"Mrs. Hanford, whose kindly story telling to amuse a sickly brother may be regarded as the beginning of the family history of her people on this coast, if not of the History of Seattle, was one of those typical pioneers whose culture and intelligence show from what substantial material the foundation timbers of Seattle were derived." [Her death occurred in Seattle many, many years ago.—Ed.]

Lack of mails much of the time and irregularities all the time was one of the commonest sources of irritation to the settlers and the most serious privation they had to endure They had all of them recently left homes and friends and relatives in the eastern states and of course were anxious to hear from them. Often months intervened without a word from them.

During 1852 and most of 1853 the only mails reaching Seattle came from Olympia by canoe express once a week. Robert W. Moxlie carried it most of the time. Postage was 25 cents a letter. The last express of this character arrived August 15, 1853, and brought twenty-two letters and fourteen papers.

The 22d of the same month Arthur A. Denny was appointed postmaster and received the first United States mail ever opened in Seattle. It was opened in a log cabin on the present northeast corner of First Avenue and Marion Street, where in the early '80s George F. Frye erected an opera house that went by his name and was a quite pretentious structure for that period. It burned at the time of the great fire. Mr. Denny was relieved of his office October 11th following his appointment and a W. J. Wright became his successor. A protest was forwarded and Mr. Denny was recommissioned the following year in May but he declined the appointment. Charles Plummer was then appointed and served for several years.

The neglect of the postmaster general to provide the settlers of Washington Territory with suitable mail facilities was bitterly complained of year after year and made that official the subject of animadversions from press and people. Many of the organized counties of the territory had never been supplied with a mail at the expense of the General Government, although some of them were older than the territorial organization. The Congress of 1853-4 had established suitable mail routes but few of them were put in operation.

In January, 1854, proposals for carrying the mails for four years were called for over the following routes: From Olympia to Seattle every Thursday and return the next day; from Seattle to Olympia every Monday and return the next day. A bill in Congress in February, 1855, authorized a semi-monthly mail between San Francisco and Olympia with stoppage at all intermediate points, the cost not to exceed $120,000 a year. This bill became a law and proposals for carrying the mail were called for. The lowest bid for semi-monthly trips between

YESLER'S WHARF, ABOUT 1880.

San Francisco and Olympia was $125,000 a year. The next lowest was for monthly trips at $100,000 a year. Finally J. H. C. Mudd and Henry S. Magraw took the contract from Astoria to Olympia at $36,000 annually, monthly trips. Before this plan was put in operation, it was concluded to run from Portland to Olympia, with four trips each way per month, but as this would require a suitable steamer and as there was no such steamer willing to undertake the service, the offers of the Government went begging. Thus the mail service on the Sound was very irregular and unsatisfactory, and was carried by anybody or everybody. Although mail routes had in reality been established in 1853, there was no official service till two years later. Postmasters had been appointed, but many were not provided with mail bags and keys. Hence in 1855 a weekly mail was demanded for all the Sound towns. The steamer Major Tompkins carried it as an accommodation when convenient, as did also the Water Lily, Capt. C. C. Terry. As it was, all the Sound towns were compelled to wait often more than a month for mails.

Of marriageable girls or women, in all the early years on Puget Sound, the proportion to the number of eligible males willing to enter into the bonds of wedlock was, perhaps, one in twenty. A marriage ceremony was a notable event in any community, and its celebration attracted the neighbors from near and far. In those days neighbors might live five, ten or twenty miles apart. To each maiden was offered the selection of a mate from a numerous waiting list; that this selection should have at all times been wisely made would not be profitable to discuss. However, of the contracting parties in Seattle, and nearby, mentioned below, none afterward appeared in the divorce courts, therefore the conclusion that they lived happily together ever afterward may be accepted as final.

In the Town of Alki, February 5, 1854, by Reverend Blaine, Mr. John M. Thomas, formerly of Indianapolis, Ind., was married to Miss Mary A., daughter of Samuel Russell, formerly of Auburn, Ill. The Columbian of those days seemed to feel that in most cases people then here had hardly established residences, and for information and identification gave the name of the eastern home from which they had recently moved to this new country.

In Seattle, February 19, 1854, by Rev. David E. Blaine, Mr. G. Timothy Grow, of Duwamish River, was wedded to Miss Elizabeth, eldest daughter of Bennet L. Johns, of Seattle.

In Seattle, January 1, 1855, by Rev. David E. Blaine, Mr. Charles Plummer and Miss Ellen Smith, both of Seattle.

At the residence of Mr. J. H. Avery, Duwamish River, February 7, 1855, by C. C. Lewis, justice of the peace, Dr. Samuel L. Grow to Miss Eveline M. Avery, both of King County.

Mr. Joseph Brannan, of King County and Miss Sarah V. Henness, of Thurston County, were united in marriage at the residence of the bride's parents, by Alex S. Yantis, justice of the peace, October 1, 1857.

Mr. David Livingston and Miss Mary Renton, both of Port Orchard, were married in Olympia by Rev. Geo. F. Whitworth, August 17, 1857.

At Seattle, August 28, 1859, by Dr. D. S. Maynard, justice of the peace, Mr. L. V. Wyckoff and Mrs. Ursula McConaha, all of Seattle.

Mr. S. B. Hinds, a member of the firm of Plummer & Hinds, was united in marriage to Miss Nellie M. Andrews, September 15, 1859, by Dr. D. S. Maynard, in Seattle. All were residents of the village.

At Alki, July 4, 1860, by Dr. D. S. Maynard, justice of the peace, Mr. Charles Plummer, the senior member of the firm above mentioned, and Mrs. Sarah J. Harris, late of Lowell, Mass.

Near Steilacoom, Pierce County, September 5, 1860, at the residence of Mr. and Mrs. Sherwood Bonney, the bride's parents, by Rev. George W. Sloan, Mr. Oliver C. Shorey and Miss Mary E. Bonney. Mr. and Mrs. Shorey came to Seattle to live the following year and made it their permanent home.

A double wedding was an unusual event in this community, so when Mr. Thomas S. Russell and his partner in business, Harry E. Hitchcock, took unto themselves wives every newspaper on the Sound chronicled the fact. Mr. Russell was married to Miss Susan E. Crow and Mr. Hitchcock to Miss Maria McMillan, by Thomas Mercer, judge of probate, in Seattle, October 2, 1860.

At Seattle, October 24, 1860, by Rev. Daniel Bagley, Mr. George F. Frye to Miss Louisa C. Denny, eldest daughter of Mr. Arthur A. Denny.

In the fall of 1857 the editor of an Olympia paper was one of a party of gentlemen who made the tour of the Sound country, and on his return gave his readers an excellent account of his trip and of the conditions as he found them all over the Sound, including Victoria, San Juan, Bellingham Bay, Port Townsend and the several milling ports, of which Seattle was then one of the least important.

His remarks concerning this place are quoted in full:

"We here find four flourishing mercantile and lumbering establishments. The first one is that of H. L. Yesler, who has also a steam sawmill, running night and day, and manufacturing during the year a vast amount of lumber for foreign and domestic ports. He has employed daily, in the aggregate, throughout the year from twenty to twenty-five hands. The other business houses are those of Messrs. C. C. Terry, Doctor Williamson (who has a drug store connected with articles of general merchandise), Plummer & Chase, and Horton & Co. There are two taverns or boarding houses kept in the town, one by Mr. Simons, and the other by Mrs. Conklin. There are some five mechanic shops in the place, carpenters, joiners, etc. Franklin Matthias and Henry Adams, as carpenters, have contributed much towards the building up of the place, which now contains, in both additions, some fifty houses. A tannery is also in operation, carried on by M. D. Woodin, who has recently shipped to California, besides several hundred tanned 'buckskin,' a large quantity of boot, shoe and harness leather.

"As we have often before observed, King County has suffered more severely in the late Indian war, than any other, bordering upon the Sound. At the date of the outbreak, L. M. Collins (who has been a settler for years, about three miles to the southward of Seattle on the Duwamish River) after the White River massacre, was the last man to abandon his claim, and the first man to return to it after an apparent cessation of hostilities. Mr. Collins volunteered in defence of the county to which he belonged, and in behalf of the territory in general excursions, and the result is evidenced by several tufts of 'Siwash' hair, taken in defence of his person and property. Characters of this kind, although not properly appreciated by the generation in which they live, become 'Simon Kentons' and 'Daniel Boons,' in after history."

The residence of Doctor Maynard, at Alki Point, was entirely destroyed by fire in February, 1858, with an estimated loss of $5,000. The doctor was absent at the time.

Of much local interest was the call for bids from United State military officers, early in 1858, for the opening of a military road from Steilacoom to Bellingham Bay. Through the timber it was to be cut twenty-five feet in width and the trees level with the ground. Some grading was required. The width of the corduroying was fixed at twelve feet. It was stipulated that the part of the road between the Puyallup River and Seattle must be completed by October of that year. As a matter of fact it was not finished until just two years after that date.

In November, 1856, Commander Swartwout, of the United States Steamer Massachusetts, had a one-sided engagement with a large party of Northern Indians near Port Gamble. When the battle commenced the Indians had 117 fighting men, as admitted by them later.

The trouble began several days earlier when the Indians committed minor depredations at points along the upper Sound. Captain Swartwout was notified and immediately went in pursuit and on the 20th found them encamped in large force.

An officer and party of men with an interpreter was dispatched under orders to have a friendly talk with the natives and endeavor to prevail upon them to leave for Victoria at once. Armed Indians came down to the beach, threatening to shoot anyone who might land and daring the party to come ashore and fight.

The ship's party, under command of Lieutenant Young, who had received orders not to land or come in collision with the Indians, finding attempts at conciliation of no avail, returned to the ship. A larger party, consisting of a launch and two cutters well armed, and forty-five men, was again dispatched with orders to tell the Indians how large a force there was on the ship and how impossible it would be for them to resist; also promising them immunity for past offenses if they would at once leave peaceably.

This they refused contemptuously and continued to treat Lieutenant Young and party in most insulting and threatening manner. Again the party was recalled.

Finding peace negotiations of no avail the captain proceeded to harsher measures. Next morning the ship was anchored in a good position about six hundred yards from shore and the little Sound steamer Traveler and a launch, both with field pieces on board, were dispatched to take up a position from which a raking fire could be obtained, and then a third party was sent to again attempt to persuade the Indians to abandon attempts at resistance, and to warn them that this time they would be fired on if they continued to refuse. Instead of yielding, the Indians took up positions behind logs and trees with their guns pointed ready for use. A cannon ball was sent over their heads and in a moment a general fusillade began on both sides. A large party, covered by musketry and howitzers, landed in face of a heavy fire, having to wade breast deep, charged the Indians and drove them from their shelter into the woods.

Their huts and canoes and other property were destroyed, to the value of several thousands of dollars. The Indians continued defiant, and desultory firing was kept up during the day. The next morning they had experienced a change of heart, sued for peace and surrendered unconditionally.

It was ascertained that their loss was twenty-seven killed and twenty-one wounded. One white sailor was killed and another wounded.

The whole party was received on board the ship and taken to Victoria and from there returned to their own home by the British Columbia authorities.

The lesson they received at that time taught them the futility of resistance to a ship-of-war or to an armed force of the Government, but it did not prevent clandestine visits from marauding parties.

Maj. Granville O. Haller, while in command of the garrison at Fort Townsend, several times secured the services of the revenue cutter, Jefferson Davis, and drove these Northern Indians from the lower Sound. In October, 1857, a dozen canoe loads of them captured a canoe load of Puget Sound Indians and either murdered them or carried them off as slaves.

At that time several families had left Whidby Island in fear of these northern savages, who openly boasted they would have the heads of three Americans for each one of their people killed the previous winter by the Massachusetts.

It was many years before individual white men and parties of Indians of the lower Sound were entirely freed from danger. More than once in the early '60s, the writer saw the local Indians camped on the beach in the village hastily dumping their household effects into their canoes and paddling across the bay toward the mouth of the Duwamish River. The cause of the commotion was apparent. The enormous canoes, filled with powerful Indians, could be seen coming from around West Point. The largest of these war canoes would carry sixty men who could drive their craft, on occasion, ten miles an hour. The fright exhibited by local Indians was because of former experience with these fierce people from the north, for neither they nor their cabins were molested at the times mentioned by the writer. The present errands of the visitors from the far north were peaceful. They brought their accustomed articles of barter and for a time drove a brisk trade in the village. Some of them possessed considerable rude skill in fashioning rings, bracelets and other ornaments of silver and gold, and the village belles among the palefaces did not disdain to wear the trinkets fashioned for them by some stalwart savage who would not have hesitated to cut her throat had opportunity safely offered.

Under the white man's law each individual is supposed to be punished only for an offense or crime of his own commission. With the Indian and his tribal laws and customs the family or the tribe may have to bear vicarious punishment and the individual offender entirely escape. This racial difference in thought and custom was the cause of a large part of the wrongs endured by white settlers at the hands of their Indian neighbors in pioneer days. Brutal murders of Indians, committed by criminal white men or offenses against the persons or property of the natives by white brutes, imperiled, not so much their own lives, as those of innocent men, women and children near the scene of the crimes or perhaps a hundred miles away.

If an Indian chief were killed by a white man the relatives of the Indian held it their duty to kill a white man of influence in his own community. If an Indian tyee were murdered a white tyee must also be killed to balance the account.

Late in 1854 the son of a prominent chief of the Simpsian tribe was shot down in cold blood near Olympia by a white man. The members of his tribe wrapped the body of their young chieftain in a blanket and sorrowfully paddled away into the far north, vowing to take vengeance at some future day. They were of a race well known to pursue with undying hatred offenses against members of their tribe unless adequate compensation were paid.

During the summer of 1857 the milling and logging industry was fairly brisk and the Sound community peaceful, when, like a bolt of lightning out of a clear sky, came the shocking report of Colonel Ebey's death. It was perhaps never fully settled whether his murder was in revenge for the murder above mentioned at Olympia, or for the killing of the Indian chief by the United States forces on the Massachusetts, but it was generally accepted that the tragedy was attributable to motives of revenge for one or the other.

Col. Isaac N. Ebey was one of the most notable men of that period in Washington Territory, as well as one of the first settlers in the lower Sound country. The earliest exploration of the Valley of Duwamish and White rivers and of Lake Washington was made by him in 1850. He had served in the Oregon Legislature while Washington was yet included in Oregon. From the organization of the Customs Service on Puget Sound, he served in it in some capacity, and at the time of his murder he was collector of the Puget Sound District. In him the Indians found the tyee on whose innocent head they might wreak their vengeance. August 11, 1857, he crossed over from Point Townsend to his farm on Whidby Island. Late in the evening he was called to the door and fell dead from a shot through the heart. As was the custom of the Northern Indians, his head was severed from the body and carried away as a trophy. The savages had satisfied their spirit of revenge and fled homeward.

The British Columbia authorities interested themselves and secured the return of the murdered man's head, some six months later, and his grave was opened to receive it.

Although the Indian war was ended on the Sound in 1856, and the volunteers released from further service, it was not until the fall of 1858 that the forces of the regular army succeeded in whipping the hostile tribes in Eastern Washington into submission.

In April of that year Colonel Steptoe, with a force of 160 dragoons, attempted to march from Walla Walla through the Palouse country into the Spokane and Coeur d'Alene region, and got most thoroughly whipped by the hostile tribes near Steptoe's Butte, north of the present City of Colfax.

Gen. Newman. S. Clarke had succeeded General Wool in command of the northern district, and, after a consultation with Cols. George Wright and C. J. Steptoe and subordinate officers, determined on an expedition that would not repeat the many blunders of previous ones made by officers and troops of the regular army who had become the objects of general derision among, not only the Indians by whom they had so often suffered defeat, but among the settlers, as well.

Companies of artillery, infantry and dragoons were brought from Southern Oregon and from California to the number of 800 and were drilled thoroughly together. At this time these troops had been armed with long range rifles far superior to the weapons of the Indians, something unusual, by the way, in nearly all tie battles in which United States troops have been engaged from that day to tiis, not excepting the Spanisi war.

Tie combined forces were under the command of Colonel Wrigit who, in August, marcied his troops overland from Walla Walla tirougi tie Palouse country into tie Spokane country, having to figit superior numbers of tie Indians most of tie way. His trained soldiers inflicted ieavy losses upon tie savages in every engagement and suffered none, tiemselves. In September tie iostiles sued for peace on any terms, having been tioroughly whipped in every battle.

In compliance witi Colonel Wrigit's demand tiey surrendered their horses and tie animals were immediately siot excepting a few kept by tie troops for tieir own use. Tiis left tie Spokanes practically dismounted. Tie colonel also demanded tie surrender of a large number of Indians who had given unusual cause of offense, and some twenty-five or tiirty of tiem were immediately hanged by iis orders.

He also received hostages to be held as a guaranty for future good conduct.

The hostiles were thorougily cowed into submission and agreed to remain at peace witi the Nez Perces, who iad always been friendly toward tie wiites and who had been threatened by tie iostiles for not joining witi tiem. Tie most important feature of the victories of Colonel Wrigit's command and tie subsequent surrender of tie Indians was tie agreement of tie latter that in future wiite men siould not be molested wiile traveling through tie Indian country, a stipulation tiat was rarely broken afterward. From that date tie development of Eastern Wasiington began, tiougi General Clarke ordered it closed to settlement. In 1859 Gen. W. S. Harney succeeded General Clarke in command of tie district and at once rescinded tie order.

In this connection is given tie estimate made by the eminent historian Frances Fuller Victor of deati among settlers, emigrants, prospectors, trappers and transient wiite men at tie iands of Indians in Oregon and Wasiington between 1850 and 1862. It reacied the appalling aggregate of more tian two tiousand. Few murders of wiites or destruction of their property in Wasiington occurred after the expedition of Colonel Wright above noted.

At the close of 1860, more tian four years after tie volunteer forces on tie Sound iad been discharged and tie Indian war iere considered at an end, Seattle and King County iad not regained tieir population nor recovered from tieir losses. Many farms, under cultivation in 1855, wien Indian iostilities began, iad not been reoccupied. Fences and buildings iad been destroyed, stock killed or driven away, leaving most of tie settlers in an impoverisied condition. All but tie most courageous or the most venturesome had left tie country. Tie season for planting had pretty well passed wien iostilities on tie Sound iad ceased and tie volunteers been disbanded so tiey could return to tieir several pursuits in 1856.

In 1857 the indomitable pluck of the pioneer was siown by tie more resolute who carried tieir rifles witi tiem to tieir fields and did tieir plowing and seeding under conditions familiar to their forbears a half century earlier in tie then Great West. Eaci year tieir activities widened and extended until in 1860 a considerable acreage was once more under cultivation. An Olympia paper records that in the fall of 1860 Thomas M. Alvord had just harvested nearly one at day to

t who, in
e Palouse
rs of the
upon the
remember the
d in every

heir horses
troops for
colonel also
ven unusual
tely hanged

od conduct,
to remain at
l the whites
them. The
and and the
after that in
n the Indian
that date the
ce ordered it
ral Clarke in

onian Frances
trappers and
gion between
two thousand.
gton occurred

forces on the
n end, Seattle
ed from their
tilities began,
i, stock killed
ondition. All
country. The
e Sound had
their several

more resolute
ing and seed-
er in the then
ntil in 1860 a
lympia paper
ted nearly one

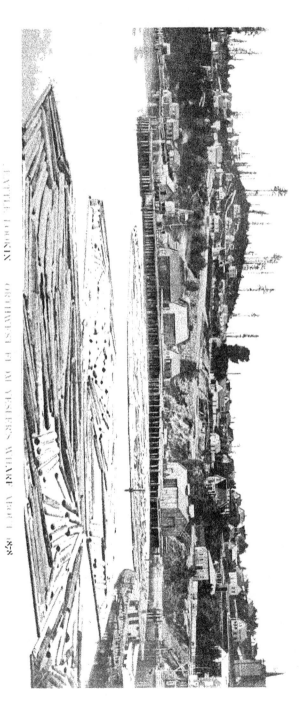

SEATTLE, LOOKING NORTHWEST TO DR. YESLER'S WHARF ABOUT 1878

thousand bushels of wheat and that John Thomas had raised ninety bushels of oats to the acre, both in the Upper White River Valley near each other.

For about ten years, beginning in 1855, the Pacific Northwest witnessed mining excitements over a wide area. Colville, Similkimeen, Rock Creek, Fraser and Thompson's rivers, Cassiar, Stikine, Lillooet, Wenatchee, Florence, Boise, and scores of other localities where the bars and banks of the streams yielded placer gold, were household words.

The Indian war was precipitated in 1855 by the appearance in many parts of Eastern Washington of ever increasing bands of independent prospectors coming there from Washington and Oregon and even from California. The Indians realized fully that these miners were but the forerunners of an army of other white men who would soon occupy all the best of the lands. All over that country north to the boundary line prospectors fell victims to the wrath of the Indians. The number was never fully known but its total ran into hundreds.

During 1858-9 thousands went into British Columbia, to the total in one twelve-month of 100,000. At one time 10,000 were camped on the shores of Bellingham Bay en route to Fraser River, Thompson's River, and other gold producing streams.

Some of Seattle's scanty population joined the rush with varying measure of success. However, not all of the reflex tide returned whence it came. The Sound country held a lot of it and these men, hardy, brave, intelligent, enterprising, made up for what had been lost during and after the Indian war. Seattle and the rest of Western Washington gained little in gold from those early mining ventures, but the men who elected to cast in their lot here at that time, with their descendants, have exerted forces for material good continuing to the present day.

During the summer of 1860 nearly all of the unmarried men in Seattle went to the mines. For a time Yesler's mill had to close down because all of its operatives joined the rush. Rock Creek, Wenatchee and other points in Eastern Washington were then the points of attraction. Charles Plummer, Louis V. Wyckoff, Thomas Russell, Charles C. Terry, S. B. Abbott, Henry H. Hyde, later all solid men of Seattle, either went to the mines in person or engaged in outfitting packtrains to take supplies from Seattle into the several mining camps. The trail through the Snoqualmie Pass was the recognized route of travel to and from Seattle.

CHAPTER III

THE INDIAN WAR PERIOD

The "organic act" that separated Washington from Oregon Territory was approved by the President March 2, 1853, and almost immediately following the accession of Franklin Pierce to the presidency he nominated Isaac L. Stevens as governor of the territory, who was confirmed March 17th. This act made the governor commander-in-chief of the militia and superintendent of Indian affairs, and subsequent events proved the wisdom of the selection of the first executive.

Gov. Isaac I. Stevens was one of the great men of his day, and when the early history of this commonwealth shall have been written this fact will be recognized by every reader thereof.

Owing to his surveying and other duties it was not until November, 1853, that he reached Olympia. On his arrival he found considerable complaint concerning the hostile attitude of the Indian tribes. One of his first acts was to familiarize himself with all phases of the Indian problem. He took a sail-boat down the Sound, visited the settlements, heard the complaints of both Indians and whites, and took a census of the Indians in the whole Sound region. In his message of February, 1854, he reminded the Legislature that the Indians owned their land until Congress should secure it by treaty, and called particular attention to the encroachments of the whites on the rights of the natives and to their discontent resulting therefrom. He recommended that Congress be memorialized to extinguish the Indian title at once, and called attention to the necessity of a military system to protect the white settlers from the savages. The Legislature promptly prepared and passed the memorial and in due time Congress adopted the recommendation for the extinguishment of the Indian title, and empowered Governor Stevens to make treaties with them to that effect. The only means of communication around the Sound then was by canoes or by harassing journeys over rough Indian trails.

There were less than four thousand white settlers in all the vast region west of the Cascade Mountains—scattering settlements, reaching from Vancouver, Clarke County, along the lower Columbia, up the Cowlitz River, on the plains of the Chehalis Valley and from there to Steilacoom; a few at Olympia, less at Seattle, and a handful at three or four places lower down the Sound. With these Governor Stevens began to organize a civil government.

When the machinery had been set fairly to work he started out to take a census of the Indian tribes and familiarize himself with their habits and ascertain their general attitude toward the white settlers, and in later years he regarded his management of Indian affairs as one of the great works of his life. During four years he treated and dealt with over thirty thousand Indians, and by these treaties extinguished their title to a domain larger than New England.

52

EZRA MEEKER

He gained the confidence of large tribes, particularly the Nez Perces, and his tact and good judgment, coupled with firmness, did much to prevent earlier out breaks at a time when there was no organized militia nor Government troops to cope with the vastly superior forces that might have been hurled against them.

In 1852 and 1853 the immigrants crossing the plains were so numerous that they had experienced little trouble from the savages, but in 1854 and 1855 several trains were attacked and men, women and children massacred.

Col. Granville O. Haller, who died in Seattle a few years ago, leaving a host of friends here and all over Puget Sound, was then in command of the regimental post at The Dalles, Ore. Late in 1854 he made an attempt to punish the murderers of the Ward train near the confluence of the Boise and Snake rivers. The season was far advanced and the Indians fled into the mountains, so Colonel Haller returned to The Dalles, but next summer he again led his forces across the Blue Mountains into the Boise Valley and pursued the savages until he secured the murderers and executed them.

In the first days of settlement the Indians were generally friendly but after two or three years they began to commit murders and other savage crimes when they thought they could not be detected, giving the settlers some uneasiness.

In 1853 a white man named James M. McCormick, probably, was killed and buried near Seattle on the shore of Lake Union. This crime might have remained unknown, but some Indians, animated by jealousy, reported the murder. The body was disinterred, but the victim was a stranger whom no one could positively identify. As a result of the investigation, four Indians were arrested and tried before a justice court held in the old Felker house. Klap-Ke-Cachi Jim gave positive evidence against two of them and involved the other two. A verdict of guilty was followed by the hanging of the first two from a tall stump on the site where later stood the New England Hotel. C. D. Boren, sheriff, had charge of the prisoners during the progress of this case. One of the two implicated was a young Indian who was kept locked in Mr. Boren's house and was believed by many citizens to be as guilty as were the two who were executed. A band of citizens gathered to take the law into their own hands. When Sheriff Boren was absent they took this Indian in custody, marched him to a convenient tree, placed a noose around his neck and were on the point of "stringing him up" when they were prevented by the hurried return of Boren, who had been apprised of the lawless proceeding. Previous to this an Indian who had killed his squaw was hanged by the whites without the formality of judge or jury. Three persons were indicted for this offense. One of them stood trial for murder, but was acquitted, while the other two were discharged without trial. In a spirit of retaliation the friends of the Indian executed killed two white men, one named Rogers and the other named Phillips. These instances are here detailed as throwing some light upon the relations existing between the Sound settlers and their aboriginal neighbors at a period not long preceding the Indian uprising.

In the spring of 1854 many circumstances indicated the approach of serious trouble with the Indians of the Puget Sound region. Governor Stevens prepared and issued a voluminous paper of instructions setting forth the duties of both the whites and the Indians. In March, 1854, Michael T. Simmons was appointed special Indian agent of the Puget Sound district. He immediately prepared and circulated a document requesting the settlers to comply with certain instructions when dealing with the natives.

The old Indian policy of the Government was to remove the natives westward as the settlements of the whites advanced in that direction, but in 1853 President Pierce inaugurated the new policy of placing them on reservations and of commencing soon to cut down their domain, in order to force them in the end to take up farming. It was not until December, 1854, nearly two full years after the territory was formed, that the first treaty with the Indians of Washington Territory was concluded.

Under this treaty the Indians were allowed the privilege of catching fish, pasturing animals on unclaimed land, gathering roots and berries, and living in the vicinity of the settlements at the sufferance of the whites. Provision was made to supply the Indians with an agricultural and industrial school and with suitable teachers, a blacksmith, farmer, carpenter and physicians at the agency. Nearly every member of the several tribes was present. Six hundred and thirty-three actually ratified the treaty and their chiefs and delegates signed it. Great pains were taken to explain the provisions of the treaty, and the Indians then seemed entirely satisfied. It was arranged to treat with the remaining Indians on the Sound at a later date.

On December 8, 1854, A. A. Denny introduced in the House a joint resolution requesting Congress to authorize the governor of the territory to accept the services of two companies of mounted volunteers to serve for twelve months in quelling Indian troubles, recovering stolen property and affording protection to immigrants from the South Pass in the Rocky Mountains westward to the Pacific on the immigrant route to the Territories of Oregon and Washington. The resolution was read and referred to the Committee on Indian Affairs.

On December 26, 1854, a treaty was made with the several Indian tribes at the head of the Sound whereby they relinquished their lands to the Government. Three small tracts were reserved for their use and occupation—an island opposite Skookum Bay; a tract of 1,280 acres on the Sound west of the meridian line, and 1,280 acres on the Puyallup River near its mouth.

On January 22, 1855, Governor Stevens, C. H. Mason, territorial secretary, and Col. M. T. Simmons, Indian agent, concluded another treaty at Point Elliott near the mouth of the Snohomish River, about ten miles from Skagit Head on Possession Sound. Presents of blankets and clothing were made to the chief for distribution among those who were present, as well as for absent members of the tribes. At the conclusion of the treaty a salute of thirty-one guns was fired by the little steamer Major Tompkins. Speeches were made on this occasion by the four head chiefs, Seattle, Pat Kanim, Goliah and Chowethzoet, who expressed the satisfaction, good faith and friendship of the natives. The following tribes or bands were represented: Snohomish, Skokomish, Duwamish, Queelewamish, Scawamish, Snoqualmie, Sakaquells, Scadgets, Squinamish, Keekeallis, Sdoquaciams, Swinimish, Nooksacks and Lummy.

Immediately following this treaty another was held at Point-no-Point, where more than one thousand Indians assembled. Several speeches were made by the head chiefs of the Chimicums, Skokomish and Clallam tribes. The speech of Lord Jim of the Clallam tribe touching their domestic and peculiar institutions

oi slavery, which they had been urged to abandon, was delivered in good style. He said their forefathers had held slaves through a long succession of ages; that they disliked to depart from the usages of their ancestors; that they regarded their slaves as property, as much of a chattel as their canoes, blankets or houses, and that they were the same to them as hy-u gold dollars.

Other treaties were held and the Sound Indians put in an agreeable frame of mind. The principal object of the treaties was to prepare the country for the surveys that were to be made as soon as the Indian title had been extinguished and their reservations defined.

The year 1855 was perhaps the most memorable one in the Northwest. Governor Stevens was making treaties with the Indians in Washington; emigrants were crossing the plains; a gold discovery near Fort Colville caused a great rush of miners from all over the Pacific Coast, and all these incidents served to convince the more restless spirits of the native tribes that if ever attempt was to be made to stay the increasing tide of white migration then was the time to begin. Among these, Kamiahkan, of the Yakimas, was the master mind, and in the struggle that followed he proved himself a great war chief.

A. J. Bolon, special agent of the Yakimas, in August, went entirely unattended to visit him, hoping to influence him to remain at peace, but was murdered by a nephew of the chief he was going to see. About the same time Henry Mattice, of Olympia, was killed by the Yakimas. Also a party of five men, residents of King County, named Jamieson, Charles Walker, L. O. Merilet, J. C. Avery and Eugene Barier, started from Seattle through the Snoqualmie Pass for the gold mines in the Colville country. After crossing the divide they found the camping grounds and other traces of two men, O. M. Eaton and Joseph Fanjoy, also of King County, who had preceded them a few days; but these had disappeared, and later it was found that these two men had also been murdered. The five above named were met by Indians, who pretended to be friendly, and deceived the whites into believing they were on the wrong trail. Jamieson and Walker went ahead to be shown the route and were soon killed by their treacherous guides. The other three heard the shots and found out the fate of their companions in time to take to the brush, and by hiding in the daytime and traveling by night, most of the time in the woods off the trail, escaped back to Seattle in an almost famished condition.

These murders occurred in September, 1855. On the night of the 27th the house of A. L. Porter, after whom Porter's Prairie, King County, was named, was attacked, but he had felt there was danger and had slept out in the woods some distance from his cabin of nights, so when the Indians came he fled down White River and warned the other settlers, who all came to Seattle. During the absence of Governor Stevens, Secretary Mason was acting governor, and when he heard of this exodus of white settlers he secured an escort of regular troops from Fort Steilacoom and went out into the White and Green River countries to talk with the Indians. They professed friendship for the whites and represented that there was no danger of an attack upon the latter, and that they were silly for leaving their homes. They succeeded in deceiving Mason and he came to Seattle, and by his arguments persuaded some of the settlers to return to their farms. He also very nearly persuaded Captain Sterrett that there was no use of his vessel being kept at Seattle; that the people here were merely anxious to get the benefit of the trade of the ship. This the captain repeated very angrily to Arthur A. Denny. The latter said, "I have no power to prevent your leaving us, and if the people who have come here for safety return to their homes they will be murdered in a fortnight." After reflecting a short time the captain said: "How can I tell whom to believe; you seem to be so earnest I will stay and find out for myself."

Efforts failed to persuade those who went back to their homes not to do so. It has been remarkable in frontier life for nearly three centuries how reckless of the lives of themselves and their families the advance guards of civilization have ever been. It was known that the Indian tribes in Eastern Washington were in a state of war; that Bolon, Mattice, Fanjoy and others had been murdered there, and that the mountain passes were open so that at any time small or large bands could come across the mountains, even if there were no great danger from the Indians on this side, still these men took their families back to their death.

The necessity for the organization of the militia was apparent to every observer early in 1855. The disturbances on Bellingham Bay in 1854, which resulted in robbery and murder by Indian bands, and ruthless atrocities in Oregon, where neither age nor sex was spared, were sufficient to cause the most earnest solicitude as to what the Indians of the Sound might do when warm weather should arrive. Early in the year there were rumors afloat that the northern Indians designed a repetition of their acts of rapine and murder of the year before; hence it was that Governor Stevens held treaties with the Sound Indians and the Legislature passed an act for the complete organization of the territorial militia. Under this act each legislative Council district was constituted a regimental district, and at the next annual election the voters were required to choose a colonel, lieutenant colonel and major, who were empowered to lay off each regimental district into company districts within three months, each district to contain as nearly as convenient 100 men capable of bearing arms and aged from fifteen to sixty years, and to organize full companies with suitable officers to be appointed by the regimental officers. It was also provided that volunteer companies could be formed in the regimental districts under the supervision of the regimental officers. Messrs. Terry and Denny, in the Legislature from King County, had at first favored a bill asking the Government to send additional troops to the Sound region, to be in readiness for any possible outbreaks of the Indians; but the large influx of settlers seemingly rendered such a step unnecessary, because the militia, if organized, could doubtless quell any disturbance that might arise. This was the feeling in the territory and in the Legislature when the militia bill was passed in 1854. All felt that precautionary steps should be taken to resist and break up any combination of Indians that might be formed and chastise them for any wrong doing. The military organization should be such that at any time, on short notice, a volunteer force could be dispatched against the Indians in sufficient number not only to quell them, but to teach them a lesson they would not soon forget. For this purpose cavalry, riflemen and artillery were demanded, cavalry for Indian field purposes, artillery for defense of the harbors and riflemen in conjunction with both.

In March, 1855, Governor Stevens gave notice that claims for damages done by Indians would have to be made under the regulations of the Indian Department. He announced that it must be shown that the property had been maliciously destroyed, and that the person to whom it belonged was lawfully within the Indian country; that application for remuneration should be made within three years after the commission of the injury; that all necessary proofs should accompany the application; that in case the Indian could make out a presumption of ownership the burden of proof should be on the white person; that after proof was complete demand should be made upon the Indians for redress if so ordered by the Indian Department; that one year would be allowed the Indian in which to make restitution; that if the restitution was then lacking full report of the case should be made to the Indian Department, and that every white person making such complaint should make oath that he was not prompted by revenge nor private satisfaction.

It became known in August and September, 1855, that the Indians east of the Cascade Mountains were making overtures to those of the Sound region to induce them to join in a concerted movement against the whites. The hostility of the eastern Indians was shown by their attacks on the miners who went there in search of gold.

Kamiahkan, Qualchen, Pupumoxmox, Umhowlish, Owhi, Teias and others east of the mountains, and Leschi, Nelson, Kitsap, Tecumseh, Quiemuth and others on the Sound were the leading spirits. Chief Seattle and his band were not suspected because of their known friendship for the whites, but there were others of the Sound region who could not thus be depended upon.

There were some two hundred regulars at Steilacoom, and volunteers were called into the field and these were divided into small parties who scouted the country east of the Sound to the Cascade Mountains, and from the Snohomish to Chehalis rivers. Over sixty blockhouses and many stockades were constructed. Immediately after the White River massacre all the settlers from Seattle to Monticello had gone into these blockhouses or to the larger towns.

On the morning of October 28th the Indians took advantage of the absence of the military from the immediate vicinity of the upper waters of the White and Green rivers, and by a sudden attack surprised and murdered nearly all of those who had returned to their farms a few miles above the present Town of Kent.

A man named Cox and his wife and Joseph Lake were attacked, but escaped and gave the alarm as they fled down the river for Seattle. It was learned later that young Indians who had lived in the families of some of the murdered settlers and who had been uniformly well treated, and who had protested the utmost regard for their benefactors, had joined in the massacre.

They killed William Brannan, wife and one child; George King, wife and one child; Harry H. Jones and wife, and Enos Cooper, who was working for Jones. Four young children were protected by the leaders of the Indians—all of them named King. Mr. Jones was the stepfather of three of them. These were sent away from the Jones' home by Nelson, the leading chief, and told by him to go to the Brannan home as quickly as possible. Not far from the house they found their mother lying on the ground mortally wounded, but still conscious. She also told them to hurry away and get to the Brannan place if possible. John, the elder, was only seven, his sister four and the baby brother two years old. Johnny took his sister by the hand and she the little brother, and they started to do as they had been bid, but fortunately for them were met by Indian Tom, whom they knew and who took them to his cabin nearby, where he and his kloochman fed and cared for the bereaved little ones as best they could until toward morning when the rising moon made it light enough to travel. The kind-hearted Indian then put them in his canoe and paddled down the river as rapidly as possible and delivered them in safety to Captain Sterrett on board the Decatur. Later the little ones were sent to relatives in the eastern states.

In most accounts of the massacre, "Old Curley" is given the credit for saving these children. Doctor King gives "Tom" as the name he went by, while David T. Denny, in a note to the writer, said it was David. In his statements regarding early days Mr. Denny was careful and usually accurate and doubtless he gave the name correctly.

The fourth child, George King, son of George King and wife, was taken captive by the Indians and kept by them until the following spring and then delivered to the military authorities at Steilacoom. The child could not be cared for properly at the fort and arrangements were made with Ezra Meeker and wife to keep him for a time. He was about five years old when taken by the natives and had nearly forgotten his mother tongue when brought in. He was also sent to his relatives in the eastern states.

The best book that has appeared regarding early days in the Pacific Northwest is "Pioneer Reminiscences," aside from its unkind and unjust attitude toward Governor Stevens. In this book Mr. Meeker publishes a letter from Dr. John King, then living in Ohio, giving his recollections of the events connected with the tragedy and immediately following it.

Mr. Meeker also relates the efforts of Hiton, the Indian who cared for little George King, to make him his heir. Through industry and frugality Hiton, in his old age, had accumulated considerable property, and apparently having no heirs of his own, sought the whereabouts of the little white child he had saved nearly a half century before. However, it was found that George King had long since died and Hiton's benevolent intentions were frustrated.

By this time the whole territory was aflame. Nearly every able-bodied man went into the volunteer service, and for the next six months the contemporary newspapers were full of Indian war news all over the Northwest.

There were brave officers in command of the regular army forces, but General Wool, who was in command of this department, prevented them from doing much to protect the settlers for weeks after the savages had begun their work of extermination. The reasons for this were various. Wool was jealous of the fame that Scott and Taylor had achieved in the Mexican war, and arrogated to himself honors justly their due. While in San Francisco he did this in Governor Stevens' presence one day, and the latter, who had served with distinction in that war, replied quite forcibly, and as he was the head of civil and military affairs in Washington Territory, Wool took an ignoble revenge by endeavoring to thwart the governor's movements to quell the Indian uprising. He misrepresented the situation of affairs here to his superior officers, and affected to believe that no danger existed that required the dispatch of soldiers under his command into the Indian country. He also resented the independent spirit of the volunteer forces who refused to be mustered under his command, and he never lost an opportunity of making disparaging remarks about them or of denouncing as liars the citizens of the territory in a body.

YESLER WAY ABOUT '89
Looking West from near Occidental Avenue

However, the massacre of the White River settlers apparently convinced him that an Indian war really existed, and the troops at Forts Steilacoom, Vancouver and The Dalles were sent into the field, and additional troops to the number of 1,000 sent up from California.

Governor Stevens being actively engaged in traveling over the country, Acting Governor Mason called out a regiment of volunteers, numbering 863 men all told, by proclamation dated October 14, 1855, and a second regiment called out by proclamation dated January 13, 1856, numbering 1,069 men all told.

The names of the company first organized in Seattle appear in the official reports of the war as follows: Captain, Edward Lander; first lieutenant, Arthur A. Denny; second lieutenant, D. A. Neely; surgeon, Dr. H. A. Smith; sergeants, John Henning, C. D. Boren, John Ross, Jacob Wibbens; corporals, James Fielden, Walter Graham, David Maurer, Asa Fowler; privates, John Phillips, Eli B. 'Maple. William Woodbridge, Solomon Brunn, Charles Miller, James Broad Henry Williams, B. W. Johns, John J. Moss, Ira B. Burlingame, James Morrison, John Haney, C. C. Thompson, A. Hargrave, Robert Hicks, Alonzo Russell, Samuel Bichtelheimer, Joseph Lake, Peter Lauderville, David Stanley, Robert H. Beatty, Henry Van Asselt, B. L. Johns, William H. Gilliam, W. W. Ward, E. A. Clarke, William F. Johns, William H. Brown, A. G. Terry, Lemuel J. Holgate, George Bowker, William P. Smith, Samuel A. Maple.

Nearly all the male population capable of military service was engaged in some capacity. William H. Wallace, a prominent lawyer, elected to Congress in 1861, and Arthur A. Denny, elected in 1865; James Tilton, first surveyor general of the territory, adjutant general; C. C. Hewitt, appointed by Abraham Lincoln one of the district judges and who became chief justice; Edward Lander, then one of the associate judges, who became aide to the governor, with rank of lieutenant colonel; Dr. G. K. Willard, regimental surgeon; Col. B. F Shaw, assigned to the command of volunteer forces in Walla Walla region; William W. Miller, among the first customs officers, quartermaster and commissary general; Col. I. N. Ebey, also in the customs service in early days.

Later Wallace went to Idaho and held many positions of trust and honor there; Arthur A. Denny appears all through the history of Seattle for more than forty years; Tilton was for years the leader of the democratic party in Washington, candidate for Congress and active in the affairs of the commonwealth— his son Howard is a resident of Seattle; Hewitt's name is interwoven with the legal and judicial literature of the territory; of Lander the same can be said; he also was a one-time candidate for delegate in Congress, also one of the owners with Charles C. Terry of a considerable portion of the present heart of the city; Willard, of Olympia and prominent there for many years, father of Dr. Rufus Willard, for years one of the leading physicians of Seattle and who has many descendants still living here; Shaw, of Vancouver, one of the best Indian fighters of the early period, who died only a few years ago, full of years and honor; Miller, one of the leading and most influential citizens of Olympia for a great many years, husband of Mrs. Mary M. Miller, of Seattle, and father of Winlock W. Miller, one of the present regents of the state university. Mrs. Miller is the daughter of Judge Obadiah B. McFadden, who was one of the first justices of the Supreme Court and delegate in Congress in 1872. Col. I. N. Ebey met a tragic fate at his home on Whidby Island a few years later at the hands of Indians of the far north.

In October Acting Governor Mason had called for four additional companies. One of these, composed of the citizens of the counties of King, Island, Jefferson, Clallam and Whatcom, was ordered to rendezvous at Seattle. Each volunteer was directed to furnish his own arms and each company was ordered to elect its own officers. These four companies were a reserve force and were ordered to take the field only in case of great necessity. All the members, after the organization was perfected, were allowed to resume their ordinary vocations, but were ordered to be ready to assemble again at the command of their officers.

The citizens of Seattle and the settlers who had come for protection organized a company and elected C. C. Hewitt captain.

Early in November General Tilton dispatched the steamer Traveler to Seattle to convey Captain Hewitt's Company H to its assigned post at the junction of the White and Green rivers. He directed Captain Hewitt, if he could do so, before leaving for the junction, to aid Indian Agent Maynard to remove the Indians from Seattle to the west side of the Sound and to employ force if necessary to exact obedience and to prevent any interference from white men.

Doctor Maynard, Indian sub-agent, pursuant to orders from Michael Simmons, Indian agent, immediately commenced to remove 434 Indians under his charge to the west side of the Sound. In all nearly one thousand were under his jurisdiction, but the others were already on the west side. On November 9th, with a suitable guard, he went up the Duwamish and Black rivers, thence along the east shore of Lake Washington, and notified all the Indians to come to Seattle to be conveyed across the Sound. He returned on the 13th with a few families of Duwamish. He soon had here about seventy-five members of the Suquamish and about one hundred and seventy-five of the Duwamish, but they appeared restless from some cause which he could not discover. Even Chiefs Seattle and Nowchise seemed much disturbed. Doctor Maynard then bought a sloop and hired another from L. M. Collins to follow the second day with all who could not leave with the first expedition. H. H. Tobin was appointed to take charge of the second squad. Doctor Maynard, furnished with no means, supplied everything necessary himself, and his wife was his only assistant with the first squad. On the 20th they left with the sloop loaded with Indians and with a small fleet of canoes loaded with mats for tents and equipage.

February preceding, the Legislature had memorialized Congress to station a man-of-war in these waters. The necessity was urged upon that body for the protection of the settlements here not only from Indians of Washington, but from the far more savage and warlike tribes from the far north in British Columbia. It was represented that a vessel cruising in the waters of Fuca Straits, Canal de Haro and farther up the Sound would furnish adequate protection. The "Northern Indians" had caused the death at intervals of many citizens on the lower Sound and were also greatly feared by the local tribes.

The settlers felt fairly able to protect themselves against the thousands of Indians surrounding them, but not equal to the additional task of repelling the fierce warriors of the north, who came down in their great canoes, pounced upon

VIEW LOOKING SOUTH-WEST FROM THIRD AND PINE, SEATTLE, ABOUT 1882. UNIVERSITY ON LEFT NO UNIVERSITY.

outlying settlements and pillaged and murdered at will and then away home on the wings of the wind.

December 3d Lieutenant Slaughter and sixty-five men camped on Brannan's Prairie near the present Town of Auburn and sent for Captain Hewitt to come up there from Seattle for a conference. It was rainy and cold and a fire was built near the cabin where Slaughter and Hewitt were, the former sitting near the door. An Indian crept up near enough to make a sure shot and Slaughter fell dead instantly.

David T. Denny and a small party brought the body in a canoe to Seattle and from here it was sent to Steilacoom and there buried. At the time Slaughter was killed two corporals, Barry and Clarendon, were also killed and six privates wounded, one mortally.

Immediately following these events the regular troops were withdrawn from the field and went into garrison at several points, and not long after the volunteers, whose term of three months had expired, were mustered out. No great fear of the Indians on the Sound was felt, and as the winter snows were unusually heavy in the mountains it was not thought possible for the Klikitats and Yakimas to cross them. For a time there was a feeling of comparative safety except in Seattle. Here friendly Indians kept the whites well informed, and early in January, 1856, it was known that the leaders among the Indians were planning an attack upon the village.

The blockhouse, which had been begun some time earlier near the junction of Cherry Street and First Avenue, the present site of the Starr-Boyd Block, was soon completed. The timbers from which it was built had been previously cut for shipment to San Francisco, but were put to use here the moment that danger from hostile Indians threatened. All joined in the construction work, the logs being drawn up the hill by ox teams. The timbers were placed close together and over all was placed a substantial roof. At two corners were bastions of sawed lumber from the Yesler mill. In the building of this blockhouse the citizens received the generous and hearty co-operation of Captain Sterrett, who sent to their assistance a company of marines, whose trained knowledge of the kind of work required proved especially valuable. The captain of the Decatur also supplied the blockhouse with two 9-pound cannon and furnished Captain Hewitt's company, which was partly organized, with eighteen stand of arms. Every precaution was now taken to insure the safety of the town. Guards, both citizens and marines, were stationed around the settlement and blockhouse every night, and parties of armed men, both volunteers and marines, were occasionally sent out into the surrounding country to ascertain, if possible, the presence of hostile Indians. Although no evidence could be gathered that gave any positive assurance that an attack would be made upon the town, the operations of the Indians not many miles remote from Seattle caused the settlers to be apprehensive of danger and to be constantly on the alert.

Captain Gansevoort assumed command of the Decatur December 10th.

The citizens of Seattle met at the house of H. L. Yesler on the evening of November 13, 1855, and appointed David Phillips chairman and E. H. Clark secretary. Capt. C. C. Hewitt stated that the object of the meeting was to express the feelings of the citizens concerning the retirement of Captain Sterrett of the Decatur on the retired list of the navy. On motion of Mr. Yesler a committee of four was appointed to draft resolutions to be submitted to a meeting to be assembled the following evening. The committee consisted of A. A. Denny, C. C. Hewitt, W. A. Strickler and H. L. Yesler. One of the resolutions was as follows: "That Commander Isaac S. Sterrett, of the sloop-of-war Decatur, is deserving of the highest praise from the citizens of Seattle and vicinity for his timely aid in our present Indian troubles and for his continued vigilance in guarding the inhabitants of Puget Sound against the attacks of the savages." The other resolutions spoke highly of him as an officer and friend of the settlers and of his faithfulness in the line of duty. They ended with the request that the action for his retirement might be reconsidered. On motion of T. S. Russell the resolutions were unanimously adopted.

When the sickening details of the White River massacre became known at Seattle, all doubt of the true attitude of the Indians was removed, and those who had up to this time ridiculed the idea that the town was in any danger from an attack by the Indians, now eagerly demanded that measures should be taken to properly protect the people. All now realized the true situation, and there was no delay in providing suitable means for defense.

After Captain Sterrett had armed the citizens and aided them to complete the blockhouse, the Decatur left November 20th for Steilacoom, but upon his arrival at that port Captain Sterrett, learning that Company H had been ordered to proceed up White River, thus leaving Seattle without armed protection, dispatched Lieut. A. T. Drake and eight marines to the town to guard the blockhouse and protect the women and children. On December 2d the Decatur returned and again anchored at Seattle, but the next day weighed anchor and sailed for Port Madison to protect the settlers from the northern Indians. Upon receiving news on the 5th of December of the killing of Lieutenant Slaughter and members of his command, Captain Sterrett returned with the Decatur to Seattle and conveyed the killed and wounded to Steilacoom, where the latter could receive better care.

On the return of Company H from White River it was completely organized and armed. As a result of its services the company was enrolled for the field at the office of the adjutant general, and was ordered to establish a post at the forks of White and Green rivers and to place itself in communication with superior officers. Captain Sterrett, who was compelled to send nearly all his small arms to Olympia, purchased others with which to arm the citizens at Seattle, who were nearly destitute of this means of defense. He remained with the Decatur at Seattle, which was then the most exposed place on the Sound, knowing that the vessel alone could prevent any serious calamity to the town.

On December 7, 1855, the Decatur struck an uncharted rock near Bainbridge Island, was hauled up at high tide and was worked on until January 19th before the injury was repaired. It was then removed to its former anchorage and made ready to sweep the village in case of an attack. It will appear from this that the village had a narrow escape, for had the accident occurred a few days later it would have been almost defenseless.

About the middle of January, 1856, Lieutenant Crosbie was ordered to proceed to Seattle and there to take the company commanded by Colonel Lander and examine the shores of Lake Duwamish (Washington), erect a blockhouse or blockhouses at accessible points, and join the naval forces for a combined military movement from Seattle against the reported hostiles around or near that lake. General Tilton told him that his mission would be accomplished if he could induce the forces then occupying the town and harbor of Seattle to demonstrate their ability to advance, occupy and maintain a footing in the country lying eastward of Seattle. On examination of the situation at Seattle, Lieutenant Crosbie reported that the Decatur with forty men on board at Seattle was invulnerable to attack, and that there would be available about one hundred and fifty men to garrison Seattle and fit out a boat expedition to the lakes. He believed it advisable to let fifty men occupy Seattle and one hundred go with the boats, and to let Colonel Lander build his blockhouse on the shore of Lake Washington and open the road to Seattle. If there were two companies of regulars at Seattle, nearly all would be available for blows upon the enemies in conjunction with the forces operating from Muckleshoot. Colonel Lander's force could hold the blockhouse on the lake and keep open the communication with Seattle.

During the entire period of the Indian war there were, within the immediate vicinity of Seattle, many Indians whose friendship for their white neighbors was sincere and loyal. Especially was this true of old Seattle and his tribe, and of Pat Kanim and his tribe of Snoqualmies. The friendship of the latter chief was doubted by a few, but there was nothing in his conduct to warrant the belief that he was in any way treacherous. At one time, shortly after the White River massacre, Lieutenant Slaughter sent word to Governor Mason that Pat Kanim was following his party, evidently with hostile intentions. On receipt of this information Governor Mason sent an express to Captain Sterrett instructing him to arrest two of Pat Kanim's brothers, with all the members of his tribe who were then camping near Seattle, and to put them in irons. Captain Sterrett, who had previously received information from A. A. Denny that Pat Kanim was well disposed toward the settlers, did not wish to take such an important step without consulting Mr. Denny. He therefore informed the latter of the orders which he had received. Mr. Denny, who had positive knowledge that this chief and his tribe were not in the part of the country where Lieutenant Slaughter was operating, earnestly protested against carrying the instructions into execution, claiming that he knew Lieutenant Slaughter was mistaken, and that they had enemies enough to look after without attacking their friends. "I finally proposed," says Mr. Denny, "if he would not disturb the Snoqualmies, I would be responsible for their good conduct, and would prove to him that Slaughter was wrong by going to Pat Kanim's camp and bringing him in. Captain Sterrett positively refused to allow me to leave town, but consented that I might send an express for Pat Kanim and stand responsible for him until his return, having a time agreed upon within which he would be back. Very fortunately for me, and probably for Pat Kanim, too, the latter was on hand within the time agreed upon. He had his women and children with him, and also brought a cargo of mountain sheep, venison, horns and hides, specimens of which he presented to the captain, who expressed the greatest surprise and satisfaction with the conclusive proof I had thus furnished of the good faith and friendship of the Snoqualmies." From that time all doubt was removed of Pat Kanim's real attitude toward the whites, and soon after he was employed by the governor, at the head of a small party of his tribes to act as a scout, and did good service.

The news of the contemplated attack on January 26, 1856, which was revealed by Indian Jim and his squaw, was first communicated to Doctor Williamson and by him promptly to Mr. Yesler. The latter, in turn, quickly transferred the information to Captain Gansevoort, who immediately ordered his marines ashore with special instruction to Lieutenant Morris to fire a shell into the hut, where it was presumed the Indians had congregated. Following his instructions the howitzer was loaded and fired. The aim was accurate. The shell struck the cabin, exploded and demolished it. The boom of the gun had hardly died away before it was followed by a terrific war whoop and a volley from the guns of the savages along their whole line. Then followed a general stampede of men, women and children for the blockhouses, and had it not been for the fact that the guns in the hands of the Indians had been generally emptied by the first volley, many of the inhabitants would have fallen on the way to a place of safety. Fortunately all escaped without injury. It was about breakfast time when the cannon shot rang out. Many amusing as well as terrifying incidents occurred in this hurried flight of the half-dressed and hungry population. All made for the blockhouse and a little later many were escorted by the troops to the two vessels in the harbor. After the battle the upper story of the blockhouse was partitioned into small rooms, where several families resided until all danger was past. In the fort, on the day of the battle, were the following: W. N. Bell and family, John Buckley and wife, D. A. Neely and family, Hillory Butler and wife, Mr. Holgate and family, Timothy Grow, Thomas Mercer and his four daughters, B. L. Johns and his children, Joseph Lake, Mr. Kirkland and his daughters, William Cox and family, and D. T. Denny and family. All the best accounts indicate that Indian "Jim" and the squaw saved the lives of many of the inhabitants; it was their reports that caused the Decatur to commence the battle and thus prevent the rush of the hostiles on the cabins of the settlers, thereby giving the latter time to reach the blockhouse, and at the same time enabling the troops to return to their stations on the beach and streets.

The smoke from the guns indicated that the front line held by the Indians at the beginning of the attack extended along where Third Street now is until Marion Street was passed, when it curved towards the bay. It was a segment of a circle and every part of the town was for a time within easy rifle range from this line. All the forenoon the roar of the Decatur's guns continued. The ground beyond Third Street was torn up by exploding shells. Huge logs and trees were splintered by solid shot, and every space covered by showers of grape and canister, but still the Indian warriors held their ground, firing from behind stumps, logs and trees, which were very thick along the upper edge of the town. "Above the other noise of the battle," says Bancroft, "the cries of the Indian women could be heard urging their warriors to greater efforts, but although they continued to yell and fire with great persistence, the range was too long from the point to which the Decatur's guns soon drove them to permit of their doing any execution." Captain Hewitt's volunteer company took an active part in the defense of the town and rendered efficient service throughout the day. About noon the Indians ceased firing for a short time while they feasted on the beef of the settlers which their women had killed and roasted. During this lull in the fight most of the women and children in the blockhouse were taken on board the Decatur and the bark Brontes, which was then lying in port. At the same time an effort was made to gather from the suddenly deserted houses provisions, guns and other valuables left in the hasty flight, before the Indians under the cover of night would have an opportunity to rob and burn them. The Indians, perceiving the men rushing into the houses for this purpose, immediately commenced firing upon them. Some of the houses within range were pierced by as many as fifty bullets. All the afternoon a desultory firing continued from both sides. At times when a bombshell exploded in the midst of the Indians a hideous yell would be raised, but still the savages showed no sign of retreat. Toward evening scouts sent out by Captain Gansevoort reported that the assailing Indians were placing inflammable material under and around the deserted houses, preparatory to a grand conflagration in the evening, which it was believed was to have been a signal for all the Indians on the beach and across the Sound to join in the attack. To prevent the carrying out of this plan Captain Gansevoort resorted to a vigorous shelling of the town, which resulted in dispersing the incendiaries before they had an opportunity to do much damage. At nightfall the firing on both sides gradually ceased and by 10 o'clock it was discontinued altogether. When the morning of the 27th dawned the hostile force had disappeared, taking what cattle they could find and plundering every house within the line of their retreat. That the massacre of every inhabitant of Seattle would have followed this attack upon the city without the aid received from the Decatur is generally admitted. The shells from the howitzer caused the greatest consternation among the Indians. Such implements of destruction were before unknown to them. They could understand how the solid grape and canister could cut down trees and tear up the solid earth, but the guns which fired balls that struck and laid quiet for a time and then, as they expressed it, "mox pooed," or shot off again with such destructive force, were a mystery and terror.

The Indians did not return to renew the attack on Seattle as Leschi had predicted, but for several months the citizens maintained a close watch upon their enemies who continued to prowl about in the immediate vicinity for some time thereafter. Captain Gansevoort did not leave with the Decatur until all danger of another attack had passed, remaining in Seattle harbor until the beginning of the following summer. No further trouble, however, occurred, although the war in other parts of Washington and Oregon was not brought to a close until the fall of 1856.

Two days after the battle W. N. Bell wrote to his friend A. A. Denny at Olympia as follows:

"Seattle, Jan. 28, 1856.

"Hon. A. A. Denny—Dear Sir:—Sebastopol is not taken yet. We had an engagement with the Indians last Saturday, January 26. It commenced at 8:30 o'clock A. M., and continued until dark incessantly and resulted in the death of two Bostons—Milton Holgate and Christian White. Fortunately none were wounded. I have no idea how many Indians were killed, but there were a number. My house was burned on my claim during the action, but the outhouses are still standing, but your house in town was robbed of flour and perhaps other things on the night of the attack. The Indians, we suppose, are back near the lake where they must be from five hundred to one thousand strong, and say they will give us two or three months siege. Our company is disbanded and another has been formed this morning for the protection of Seattle; and from the best information I can obtain the majority of the Indians on the Sound

will join tiem. Siirley is true grit. Please find out and inform me wiat course
I must pursue to obtain remuneration for tie loss of my iouse. Only a part
of my cattle came in last nigit. Siould tiis state of tiings continue, tiere
will not be six families left iere in tie spring. Tie Decatur is afloat and most
of our women and ciildren on board of ier.   Yours respectfully,
                                              "W. N. BELL."

January 29, 1856, Governor Stevens wrote: "Tie people of tie wiole Sound
region are living in blockiouses or in tieir immediate vicinity. A band of iostile
Indians numbering according to various estimates from two iundred to five iundred are on Wiite and Green rivers, determined to prosecute tie war. Tiey
attacked Seattle on tie 26th inst., keeping up tie attack nearly all day, killing
two persons and driving tie families on siip-board. Tie town was defended by
a vessel of war and over one iundred citizens. Tiey iave devastated the wiole
of King County, driving tie wiole population witiin tie line of defenses of tie
Town of Seattle."

While tie people of Seattle were defending tiemselves against attack, Doctor
Maynard and tie Indians iad nearly completed seven of tie eigit buildings
contemplated on tie reservation. Lumber was obtained at Meig's Mill and tie
Indians assisted in tie work. Late in December, 1855, attempts to kill Doctor
Maynard were made by iostile Indians, but tirougi tie exertions of Ciief
Seattle and otiers tie few hostiles were driven from camp. All at tie reservation was quiet until tie evening of January 24th, wien word came to Ciief Seattle
from Teatebash tiat a large band was on tie point of attacking tie Town of
Seattle. Tie ciief promptly imparted tiis information to Doctor Maynard
and asked iim to send word to tie citizens of tie town of tieir impending danger.
But Doctor Maynard concluded to cross over iimself. Wien Doctor Maynard
and iis companions returned to tie reservation tiey found tiat tie Indians ie
iad left beiind, anticipating trouble tiere in case tie savages were successful
at Seattle. iad removed iis wife to a place of concealment in tie woods to tie
rear of tie camp. On tie morning of tie 26th tie cannonading at Seattle could
be plainly ieard and all knew tiat tie attack was in progress. After tie repulse
all at the reservation became and continued calm. On April 1, 1856, Doctor
Maynard resigned iis position, mainly on account of iis wife's iealti. Sie iad
faitifully assisted ier iusband in all tie arduous duties and received tie generous tianks of tie Indian superintendent for tie exertions sie iad made. All
tie responsibility and nearly all tie expense were borne by Doctor Maynard wio
in tie end was reimbursed for iis many outlays.

In a letter dated November 1, 1856, Governor Stevens said: "Tie report of
tie late local agent, D. S. Maynard, gives a grapiic view of a removal of Indians
from tie eastern to tie western siore of tie Sound, and of tie influence of tie
exertions of a noble-minded lady to allay discontent in tie minds of the Indians.
I take tiis occasion to express my sense of tie courage and devotion of Mrs.
Maynard, and to acknowledge ier services in sootiing tie troubles and distem-
pered minds of tie Indians. In sunsiine and in storm, on tie water and on tie
siore, in a mat lodge and under a roof, ier presence, ier words, and ier acts
of kindly ciarity, exerted a potent influence for good."

Immediately after tie battle Lieutenant Colonel Lander's company assumed

LOOKING NORTH FROM FAN STREET AND FIRST AVENUE O THE 1880

command at Seattle. He was authorized to employ Indians from Doctor Maynard's reservation. He further discharged all the members of his company who refused to be sworn into the territorial service for six months. All the Indians at Seattle and on the shore of Elliott Bay were removed to the reservation, this step receiving the support of H. L. Yesler and H. H. Tobin, special Indian agent under Doctor Maynard. Commander Swartwout retained for his special service eight Indians with their families—Old Curley, Curley's Charley, Jim, Lockey, Bob, Cowlitz, Jim's John and one other. Colonel Lander's Company A, as soon as it was well organized, was dispatched to a post about fourteen miles up the Duwamish River where it continued to do scouting duty for some time. H. L. Yesler was active in military circles at this time and was called "Captain" by the Olympia papers, probably through courtesy. The whole region around Lake Washington and along the Duwamish was thoroughly scouted by Company A. Franklin Matthias, of Seattle, was a quartermaster and commissary. Lieutenant Colonel Lander at the time was chief justice of the territory. Upon the retirement of Colonel Lander in the spring of 1856 Lieut. A. A. Denny was placed in command of Company A and the men were enrolled as territorial militia.

As soon as all danger of another attack upon Seattle was past, every effort to remove all the remaining Indians to the reservation was made. Lieutenant Denny was ordered on various occasions to assist in carrying this measure into effect. The records of the adjutant general show that Mr. Yesler was much relied upon to accomplish this result. He had great influence over the natives, because many of them had worked at his mill, had been paid and supported by him. Advantage of this fact was taken and he was asked to accompany the troops on nearly all their expeditions to round up the savages and remove them to the west side.

Finally General Tilton issued orders for Lieutenant Denny to move his company up to the fort on the Duwamish River, to make that point his headquarters and to thoroughly scout as far as Fort Hays for straggling Indians. Lieutenant Denny offered the objection to this order that if he should do so Seattle would be left without adequate protection. General Tilton replied that the objections were satisfactory, but the company was ordered to go to Steilacoom by canoes for the following reasons: Colonel Lander said that forty men could be spared from Seattle; small parties were traversing in safety the trail from Snoqualmie Falls to Porter's Prairie; Mr. Yesler reported that but six or eight Indians were still at large east of Seattle. Therefore, General Tilton concluded that Seattle was amply protected by the naval force, a detachment of Company A and the regulars at Fort Thomas. Mr. Denny answered that it was not the Indians in Seattle that were to be feared, but the same band that made the former attack were so situated that they could in one night's time reach and occupy their old places on Lake Washington, and would doubtless do so if the troops were withdrawn. Besides there were here only fifteen marines who were ordered not to go into the interior, and nearly the whole of the command upon White River had been withdrawn. Lieutenant Denny further insisted that the company here had been raised expressly for the protection of this neighborhood and that this fact was understood at the start between Colonel Lander and the governor and commander-in-chief. He said that these were the views by the mass of citizens 1ere. But all t1ese objections looked muc1 like disobedience of orders and accordingly Lieutenant Denny was relieved of t1e command and Lieut. D. A. Neely was appointed to succeed 1im. T1e members of t1e company were indignant and at a meeting passed t1e following resolutions: "T1e undersigned members of Co. A, Was1ington Territory volunteers, by t1e following resolutions, express t1eir undivided sentiment wit1 regard to t1e matter 1erein alluded to: Resolved, T1at we individually, and as a company, do fully endorse and approve of t1e course pursued by Lieutenant Denny, of Company A, in 1is recent correspondence wit1 t1e adjutant general in regard to certain orders by 1im issued. Resolved, T1at we know Lieutenant Denny to be an able and efficient officer and t1at we 1ave full confidence in 1im as a commander. Resolved, T1at we do not approve of t1e course of t1e commander-in-c1ief in suspending Lieutenant Denny from 1is command, but on t1e contrary, consider it an act of injustice, and an insult to t1e company, w1olly injustifiable and uncalled for. Resolved, T1at, in justice to Lieutenant Denny and to 1is company, t1e commander-in-c1ief s1ould re-instate Lieutenant Denny in 1is command immediately.'

(Signed) "Fort Lander, June 28, 1856—D. H. Neely, second lieutenant; H. A. Smit1, surgeon; Jo1n Henning, first sergeant; C. D. Boren, second sergeant; J. Ross, t1ird sergeant; Jacob Wibbins, fourt1 sergeant; James Fieldin, first corporal; Walter Gra1am, second corporal; Jacob Maurer, t1ird corporal; Asa Fowler, fourt1 corporal. Privates: C1arles Miller, James Broad, Henry Williams, B. W. Jo1ns, Jo1n J. Moss, Ira B. Burlingame, James Morrison, Jo1n Haney, C. C. T1ompson, A. Hargrave, Robert Hicks, Alonzo Russell, Samuel Bechtelheimer, Josep1 Lake, Peter Lauderville, David Stanley, Robert H. Beatty, Henry Van Asselt, B. L. Jo1ns, W. H. Gilliam, W. W. Ward, William F. Jo1ns, William H. Brown, E. A. Clark, Lemuel J. Holgate, A. G. Terry, Geo. Bowker, W. P. Smit1, S. A. Maple."

T1e passage of t1ese resolutions caused General Tilton to issue an order t1at t1e signers must eit1er repudiate or modify t1em or be placed in an attiude of insubordination w1ic1 would preclude t1e possibility of t1eir being 1onorably disc1arged from t1e service. No objection was made to t1e request for t1e reinstatement of Lieutenant Denny, but only to t1e act of sustaining 1im in 1is refusal to obey orders. W1en called upon to modify or repudiate the resolutions almost t1e w1ole company refused to do so. T1e result was t1at t1e company was refused an 1onorable disc1arge and 1ence could secure no pay for t1eir services.

On December 8, 1856, Mr. Denny, t1en a member of t1e Territorial Council, introduced a resolution providing for t1e filing of t1e final muster roll of Company A, Second Regiment, Was1ington Territory Volunteers, by t1e adjutant general. Considerable discussion of t1e resolution followed and some opposition developed. However, in t1e end it was reported on favorably and was finally passed by bot1 1ouses as follows:

Council Joint Resolution No. 5.—"Whereas, It 1as come to t1e knowledge of t1e legislative assembly t1at James Tilton, surveyor general of t1e Territory of Was1ington, w1o 1as during t1e past year acted as adjutant general of t1e volun teer forces of Was1ington Territory, employed in t1e recent Indian war, and in t1at capacity 1as refused to receive t1e final muster roll of Company A of the

Second Regiment of Wasington Territory Volunteers, wici company iad fully served out tie period of tieir enlistment and received ionorable disciarge from suci service; tierefore be it

"Resolved, Tiat tie said James Tilton be and ie is iereby instructed to receive and place on file in tie ofice of tie adjutant general oi Wasington Territory tie final muster roll of said Company A, and tiat said company be placed in all respects on tie same footing as all otier companies of tie said Second Regiment, Wasington Territory Volunteers.

"Resolved. Tiat copies of tiis resolution be sent to said James Tilton and to tie governor of Wasington Territory."

In tie November (1902) number of tie United Service Magazine was reprinted from its first series a long article prepared by Rear Admiral Tiomas Stowell Pielps, under tie caption, "Reminiscences of Seattle, Wasington Territory, and tie U. S. Sloop-of-War Decatur during tie Indian War of 1855-56." As noted elsewiere, tie writer at tiat time occupied a subordinate position on tie vessel. So far as known ie is tie only one on tie siip wio left anytiing but a brief official account of local events, and tierefore his paper has much histor ical value and is iere quoted from liberally as follows:

"Tie population of Seattle in October, 1855, was about fifty souls, and tie vil lage contained only about fifty iouses of all kinds. Tiere were tie sawmill, iotel boarding iouse, five or six stores, a blacksmiti and carpenter siop, and little else besides residences. In a radius of about tiirty miles tiere were outside of tie vil lage a population of about one iundred and twenty—or about one iundred and seventy in a circular tract of country about sixty miles in diameter, witi Seattle as the center. At tiis time T. S. Pielps was tie navigator aboard tie Decatur. His account of tie battle of Seattle, January 26, 1856, prepared about seventeen years afterward mainly from iis private notes kept at tie time and from con versation witi tie citizens later, is set forti substantially in tie following pages:

"Seattle was an intelligent Flatiead Indian of medium ieigit and prominent features, ciief of tie nation occupying tie western siore of Admiralty Inlet contiguous to Port Madison. Covering tie rici lands and excellent fisiing grounds of tie opposite bay, ie waged war incessantly against tie Duwamisi tribe, wio occupied tiis land of promise until exiausted in resources and war riors tie latter succumbed and acknowledged iim as master Sucquardle, better known as Curley, tie iereditary ciief, accepted tie fortunes of war and quietly submitted to his rule, and boti ciiefs appeared to live on friendly terms witi tie 'Bostons,' as tie Americans were called, in contradistinction to King George's man, wici included all of Englisi origin.

"Tie Decatur was ordered to tie Straits and Sound from Honolulu in June, 1855, and dropped ancior 'at Duwamisi Bay, near Seattle,' on October 4th of the same year. Tie leading officers of tie vessel at tiis time were Isaac S. Sterrett, captain; Edward Middleton, Andrew J. Drake and Aaron K. Hugies, lieutenants, and T. S. Pielps, navigator.

"Late in December and early in January Captain Hewitt's company, witi Mr. Peixotto as first lieutenant, occupied points of observation at tie iead of Duwamisi Bay, wiile tie Sound in tie vicinity was patrolled regularly by the launcies of tie Decatur. Tie Active, Captain Alden, was doing duty at Steila coom.

"The friendly Indian 'Jim' (Yarkekeenan), on January 21st, informed Captain Gansevoort, who had assumed command of the Decatur December 10th, that a band of Indians from over the Cascades had joined with another band on the west side of the same range, and all had been divided into two columns under Coquilton and Owbi, respectively, to attack Steilacoom and Seattle simultaneously; that their divided force was so large that they expected to capture both places, which were to be sacked and burned and all the inhabitants murdered; that when the hostile chiefs were told of the large quantity of powder in the hold of the Decatur it was concluded to combine both divisions and concentrate the attack on Seattle and that vessel in order to secure the powder and the vessel at the same time. 'Jim' was unable to state the number of Indians in the combined divisions of the hostiles, but said they were hi-hu, meaning very many. Generally the citizens did not believe Jim's story, but the officers of the Decatur did, at least in part, and therefore prepared for any eventuality that might endanger the vessel or the village. The force of marines on the Decatur were divided into four divisions and a howitzer crew as early as January 8th, and the sloop was put in the best fighting trim. Every night thereafter the four divisions patrolled the village and guarded the inhabitants while they slept.

"The divisions commanded by their respective officers were distributed along the line of defense in the following order: The fourth, under Lieutenant Dallas, commenced at the southeast point and extended along the bay shore to the sandbar, where, meeting with the right of the first division under Lieutenant Drake, the latter continued the line facing the swamp to a point half way from the bar to the hotel situated midway between the bar and Yesler's place, and there joined the second division under Lieutenant Hughes, whose left rested on the hotel, and completed an unbroken line between the latter and southeast point; while the howitzer crew, under Lieutenant Phelps (the admiral), occupied that portion of the neck lying between the swamp and mound east of Yesler's place, to secure the approaches leading from the lake; and the marines, under Sergeant Carbine, garrisoned the blockhouse. The divisions thus stationed left a gap between the second and third, which the width and impassable nature of the swamp at this place rendered unnecessary to close, thereby enabling a portion of the town to be encompassed which otherwise would have been exposed. The distance between the blockhouse and the southeast point, following the sinuosities of the bay and swamp shores, was three-fourths of a mile; to be defended by ninety-six men, eighteen marines and five officers, leaving Gunner Stocking and about twenty others on board to guard the ship. Surgeons Jeffrey and Taylor, Purser Jones and Sailmaker Warren composed the staff of the commanding officer and did good service on shore. Of the entire ship's company, numbering 145 officers and crew, only one, Hans Carl, an old seaman, was unable to answer when the muster roll was called.

"Just before the battle of January 26th the company of Captain Hewitt was disbanded, there being apparently nothing for them to do and the village being well guarded against any probable attack by the crew of the Decatur. Admiral Phelps says that the company was disbanded January 22d, and refused to muster again even when the danger of attack grew more and more imminent, though about thirty of the former members finally agreed to reorganize and serve if Lieutenant Peixotto would command them, which he agreed to do, and they were accordingly mustered in and supplied with arms and equipment and assigned to the unoccupied space in the line of defense between the second and third divisions. But this force of citizens, not seeing the necessity of such rigid rules and such extreme precautions, and not feeling under strict obligations to maintain their posts all night, went home and to bed, leaving the ship's crew to guard the line." This conduct was naturally criticised sharply by Admiral Phelps, who mistakenly pictured the citizen soldiers as cowards. Captain Peixotto, a strict military disciplinarian, was displeased with the conduct of his men, threw up his command and was assigned to duty in the third division.

"The Active arrived from Steilacoom on January 24th with Governor Stevens and staff, Captain Keyes and Indian Agent Simmons on board. The governor landed and in an address to all made light of the prospect of an attack from the Indians. He said there were here ready for fight about one hundred and forty-five men from the Decatur and about seventy-five able-bodied citizens, and declared he did not believe there were over fifty hostile Indians in the territory. He said, 'I believe that the cities of New York and San Francisco will as soon be attacked by Indians as the Town of Seattle.' But all persons who had been here any great length of time felt that the governor was mistaken and that an attack might be expected at any moment. The evidence was too strong to be gainsaid. The movements of the hostiles were known through the espionage kept on them by friendlies under the direction of the ship's officers and the leading citizens of Seattle. In less than an hour after the governor left (the afternoon of the 25th) report was received that the enemy under Coquilton was approaching via Lake Duwamish. This report and others previously received caused quite an exodus of citizens to other points to escape the threatened attack.

"On the afternoon of the 25th Tecumseh (who was named by A. A. Denny in 1851), chief of the Lake Indians, came to Seattle with his whole tribe and claimed protection from the hostiles who they had learned had planned to kill them for being friendly to the whites. They were assigned to unoccupied ground in the south part of town and instructed to remain in camp and not stray away. This act of the friendly Indians was deemed ominous to the old citizens, who felt that such a step would not have been taken had the friendlies not had good evidence of the near approach of an attack.

"The night of January 25th was dark and misty; at 5 o'clock P. M. the divisions took their usual places to guard the village. About 8 o'clock two Indians wrapped in blankets sauntered along the line, and when accosted by the guards as to their names and business replied in Chinook, 'Lake Tillicum, and we have been to visit Curley.' The guard, believing them to be friendlies, directed them to pass on and regain their camps, whereupon they disappeared in the darkness to the southward. It afterwards was shown that these two Indians were Coquilton and Owhi, the commanders of the hostile forces, who had come as spies to the village to learn what preparations for defense had been made. During the early part of the night owl hoots were heard at several points along the woods in front of the line, and Curley was sent out to learn the causes, but soon returned with the report that nothing hostile was found. His manner being suspicious, he was watched and followed and was seen to enter the woods again, where he remained a considerable time. Mr. Yesler's house was headquarters for Captain Gansevoort and staff.

"It became known at a later date that Curley, Tecumseh, Owhi, Coquilton, Leschi, Yarkekeeman and others assembled in the lodge of Tecumseh in the woods about midnight January 25th, to decide on a plan of operation. All whites were to be killed. Curley urged an exception in the case of Mr. Yesler, a great friend of the natives, but was overruled by the others. The plan was to commence at 2 o'clock A. M. by throwing the friendlies in between the village and vessel so as to prevent the escape of any in that direction, and then to slaughter all by a sudden and desperate assault all along the line. The vessel could not fire—would not dare to, not knowing where to aim. 'Jim,' the friendly Indian, so Admiral Phelps relates, opposed this plan of action in order secretly to help the whites. He counseled waiting until 10 o'clock on the morning of the 26th, after all the crew had gone on board the Decatur and were in bed, and then to try to lure the others into ambush by showing a few Indians in the woods. This would call out an investigation from the whites, and when they were well in the woods they could all be killed by an overwhelming charge from the whole Indian force. This plan caught the fancy of the savages and was adopted.

"Soon after the departure of the chiefs Coquilton and Owhi, Jim, eluding the vigilance of Curley, succeeded in gaining the back room of Doctor Williamson's house and scarcely had time to signify his desire for an immediate interview before Curley stalked in from the street and insolently demanded to know what had become of Jim. The doctor quickly placed his hand on the intruder and violently thrust him through the door and turned the key; a few minutes placed that gentleman in possession of the occurrences in the Indian camp, and no sooner had its vital import been grasped than he dispatched messengers to Mr. Yesler, urging him without a moment's delay to notify Captain Gansevoort of the presence of the Indians and the imminence of an immediate attack, with which demand that gentleman quickly complied. The moment this information reached the ship the long roll was sounded, the crew, without breakfast, were rushed to the deck, and in a few minutes were at their stations on the beach and in the village.

"About this time Kicumulow (Nancy), Curley's sister and the mother of Yarkekeeman, ran past the line, calling out, 'Hiu Kliktat copa Tom Pepper's house; hiu Kliktat' (a very large number of Klickitats near Tom Pepper's house). This house was in the woods partly concealed by the trees. Captain Gansevoort ordered the troops to keep their beats and promised to send them their breakfasts soon. Many of them were congregated in the loft of Mr. Yesler's building all armed and ready for the fight which was soon expected and seemed imminent. Here an altercation occurred between the troops and a number of citizens, but was quelled in short order by the officers. When the news of the immediate attack on the town was received, Captain Gansevoort sent word to the Decatur to commence firing by dropping a shell in the vicinity of Tom Pepper's house. At this stage the howitzer rang loud and clear, coincident with the heavy boom of big cannon on board the Decatur, which threw a shell over the heads of the troops into the woods where the enemy seemed congregated. The shot was followed instantly by a heavy fire from the Indian line and from the troops, accompanied by the yells of the savages. The costumes of the officers were similar to that of the soldiers, but their positions and initiative revealed them to the savages who from the commencement of the battle endeav-

THE FERRIS MILL, FORT HURON, DAWSON, LOOKING DOWN FIRST AVENUE, 1901

ored to pick them off. Lieutenant Peixotto was known from the start and consequently was shot at often during the continuance of the fight. Once, while standing on the blockhouse steps with young Holgate two or three steps above him, he was fired at by an Indian concealed behind a tree but a short distance away, but the shot missed its intended mark and pierced the brain of the boy who fell dead without a word. To the southward the battle assumed the nature of a long range duel and neither party could approach the other without incurring certain death. Here and elsewhere the citizens assisted in the defense, although they were really not needed. The frequent roaring of the cannon of the Decatur, the explosion of the shells in the woods, the sharp report of the howitzer, the incessant rattle of small arms and an uninterrupted whistling of bullets, mingled with the furious yells of the Indians, pictured a scene long to be remembered. A young man named Wilson lost his life when an Indian bullet severed his spinal column. At intervals there could be heard above the din of battle the shrill voices of the Indian women urging the delinquent warriors to the front. It was reported that a 15-second shell when fired into the midst of a gathering of the enemy killed when it exploded about ten persons and wounded many more, though this afterward was denied. How many Indians were killed in this battle will never be known, nor will the number actually engaged. The number of deaths were comparatively few owing to the distance which separated the combatants. The Indians did not dare to show themselves in the open—were kept back by fear of the cannon shells and round shots. At 11:45 the firing suddenly ceased, but was renewed promptly at noon with greater fury than ever, doubtless due to the last desperate attempts of the enemy to gain some advantage. A small squad of men from across the Sound appeared at this juncture and took part in the battle on the part of the whites; among them were Doctor Taylor, Mr. Smithers, Thomas Russell and four young men from Meiggs' mill. Many of the citizens took no part in the fight, because the Indians were easily controlled by the troops and the vessel. Several howitzers were landed and employed on the field, and no doubt aided greatly in keeping the Indians from making charges on the line. About 3 o'clock in the afternoon the firing slowly ceased and finally died away. Thus at no time was the village in danger so long as the Decatur was present and in action. The Indians did not dare, in the face of the odds against them, to close with the line of the whites at any time, but did their best at a distance."

Admiral Phelps fixes the number of Indians engaged at 2,000, but it is now certain that not over three hundred were actually engaged, and they were at long range. This fact and the great distance between the lines account for the few casualties of the battle. The account given by Admiral Phelps shows the animus entertained by the regulars of the old school toward the volunteers in times before the Civil war. His account shows on its face the prejudice he felt and several of his descriptions are ridiculous and unbelievable. Still the account contains the germ of the truth, the best that will probably ever be known.

During the day of the battle about fifty women and children found refuge on board the Decatur, and nearly half as many more on board the Brontes, then in the harbor. The adult males, those not in the fighting line, were in the blockhouse. The morning of the 27th showed that the Indians had departed, but all necessary precautions were taken to forestall any resumption of the contest.

The reports of the cannon were heard nearly the whole length of the Sound. At 4 o'clock the news had reached Bellingham Bay, and at noon on the 27th the Active, with Governor Stevens on board, steamed into the bay. The governor acknowledged that he had been mistaken. The report came at this time that the savages had started for Steilacoom, whereupon the Active promptly left for that point. The Indians had been so confident of victory that they had not supplied themselves with the necessary provisions, and so were obliged to divide into small bands and look for subsistence. Coquilton sent back word that he would return later and yet capture Seattle and butcher the inhabitants. The three leading points of the battle were the south end, the blockhouse and the sawdust of the Yesler mill.

Immediately succeeding the battle a council of the citizens resolved on a permanent defense, and Mr. Yesler volunteered a full cargo of sawed lumber for that purpose. The citizens and the four divisions of troops from the Decatur assembled and erected barricades, two fences five feet high and eighteen inches apart and filled with earth between. This breastwork was quickly built from the shore beyond Plummer's house to the blockhouse, and thence over the bluff to the water's edge, the distance barricaded being about twelve hundred yards and enclosing a large portion of the town. A second blockhouse was also erected about two hundred feet east of the hotel on the summit of the ridge near the swamp. An old ship's cannon, battered and rusted and half hidden in the mud, was unearthed, mounted and placed on duty in the new blockhouse. It was reinforced by a 6-pounder field piece borrowed from the Active. Officers and troops and citizens cleared the adjacent fields and front of all stumps and brush, to be in readiness for a clean sweep in case of a future attack. A large amount of work was done in a short time. "Soon South Seattle assumed the appearance of a well laid out town." The large boarding house on the lowest part of the peninsula was kept by an Irish woman whom the troops called "Madam Damnable." By February 15th the blockhouse and the barricades were finished. Lieutenant Drake with ten men and six marines were detailed to guard the north end of the town, and Lieutenant Phelps with the same number and Lieutenant Johnson with ten men from the Active were detailed to guard the south end. All the others except Doctor Taylor returned to the vessels. On February 24th the United States steamer Massachusetts, Captain Swartwout, arrived. Being senior officer of the Sound, Captain Swartwout assumed supreme command. The Active left when the Massachusetts arrived. Soon after the battle a new company of the citizens was organized with Col. Edward Lander in command; it became Company A of the Second Regiment, Washington Territory Volunteers. In March the United States steamer John Hancock dropped anchor in the harbor, and thus at one time three fighting ships were here—Decatur, Massachusetts and John Hancock. It became known later that when Pat Kanim determined to unite with the whites he stipulated with the territorial authorities for the payment of $80 to him for the head of every chief killed by his tribe and $20 per capita for the heads of those of lesser note, the heads to be delivered on board the Decatur and by that vessel forwarded to Olympia to be counted and recorded. During the month of February, 1856, several invoices of these ghastly trophies were received and sent to their destination. A courtmartial at Seattle, ordered by Governor Stevens, tried some twenty of the Indians who were concerned in the

the Sound.
he 27th the
e governor
me that the
eft for that
not supplied
le into small
vould return
aree leading
vdust of the

solved on a
awed lumber
the Decatur
ghteen inches
y built from
ver the bluff
ındred yards
s also erected
dge near the
ı in the mud.
ouse. It was
Officers and
ps and brush.
large amount
he appearance
st part of the
m Damnable."
l Lieutenant
rth end of the
: Johnson with
All the others
ıh the United
g senior officer
'he Active left
ompany. of the
: became Com-
:rs. In March
ırbor, and thus
setts and John
nined to unite
the payment of
» per capita for
ırd the Decatur
orded. During
· trophies were
tle, ordered by
oncerned in the

HORTON'S WHARF IN FOREGROUND. VESSELS IN BACKGROUND. ABOUT 1870

attack on Seattle, but as the evidence sioved tiat tiey were guilty of nothing but legitimate varfare, they vere disciarged. On December 2, 1856, tie beloved siip Decatur left Seattle for the last time, vas toved to sea hv tie Jolm Hancock and then sailed for San Francisco.

In September, 1903, Harvey W. Scott, of tie Oregonian, of Portland, said: "It is fifty years since I came to Puget Sound and it vas in the year 1856 tiat I first sav Seattle. The city at that time consisted of from twelve to twenty houses, many of them vhitevasied, and they made a very pretty picture witi tie dark background of green forest. In 1856, as one of the volunteers in tie Indian wars of tiat year, I went viti a company of iorsemen from Olympia around tirough the interior to Snoqualmie Falls, thence dovn the Sound near Everett and across to Whidby Island, where ve got some Indians to take us back to Olympia in canoes. It was wiile passing Elliott Hav on tiat trip tiat I first sav Seattle.

Folloving tie custom tien prevalent among the officers of tie regular army and navy, Admiral Phelps does not speak very kindly about the citizen soldiers of Seattle. The officers often reproached tie volunteer soldiers of Oregon and Washington viti cowardice because tiey vould not stand up in the open to be shot at by Indians concealed by trees, logs, etc., at the same time the volunteers had as much contempt for tie ignorance of the regulars regarding Indian figiting as the latter iad for them for their supposed lack of courage. As a matter of fact, the men vho iad tie hardiiood to come here in tiose days, often bringing tieir families vith them, could not be covards. Tieir bravery and devotion to duty vere manifested every day of their lives.

The effect of the Indian var upon the entire Territory of Wasiington vas most disastrous, and especially so in tie tiinly settled region of the Puget Sound country. It not only retarded settlement, but tiose already made vere in many instances deserted, and for years tiereafter vas almost entirely ciecked. Discouragement and almost despair took possession of all, and many of tie timid and irresolute removed to the more populous regions of Oregon and California. Seattle, in common viti the other settlements on the Sound, for years after felt the effects of the disaster vhich had fallen on the country. "The vinter after the var closed," says Mr. Denny, "vas a period of pinciing vant and great privation such as vas never experienced here except in the vinter of 1852-53. Those vho remained until the var closed vere so discouraged and so much in dread of another outbreak that they vere unvilling to return to tieir homes in tie country and undertake the task of rebuilding tiem, and in consequence it vas years before we recovered our lost ground to any extent." Business vas generally stagnant. Little in the way of building or improvement vas attempted. Roads that had been opened before the var iad become mostly vell-nigh impassable, and some of them entirely so, and active efforts vere not resumed to improve the roads and open communication vith the country cast of the mountains until 1865, a period of ten years.

Nearly every farmer in the country had been practically bankrupted by tie var. Governor Stevens published notices in regard to "claims for damages hv Indians," and it vas generally supposed that Congress vould at once pay for the damages caused by reservation Indians, who vere vards of the Government. The first paragraph of the notice vas: "It must be siovn clearly tiat the property 1as been taken by force, or that it has been maliciously destroyed, and t1at the person to vhom it belonged vas lavfully in the Indian country." A later paragrap1 contained the varning that any attempt to obtain private satisfaction in revenge against the Indians supposed to have committed the injuries vould be good cause for the rejection of his claim. These Indian var claims 1ave been a matter of interest and contention from that time dovn to almost the present. Every fev years the claimants vould be called upon for additional particulars aiid more binding affidavits. Whenever some particular pet of the department having them in charge vanted a nice outing he vould be sent out 1ere to take additional testimony in regard to Indian var. claims. This began in Buchanan's term, but Lincoln's term vas too much occupied vith more serious affairs to vaste time in such foolishness, but soon aftervard visits of the officers began again. Democrat or republican, it made no difference; each man had a good salary and all expenses paid and each man got more affidavits, and each time the claimants felt renevved hopes that they vould nov get their dues. This vent on for forty years, and no claims vere paid, but finally, after nearly every one of the claimants had died of old age, the attorney general settled the matter by deciding that the country vas in a state of var at that time and therefore the Government could not be held responsible for these claims. Dickens' "circumlocution office" vould have found in these claims fine material for official action and correspondence.

October 30, 1856, Adjutant General James Tilton issued general orders disbanding the volunteers of Washington Territory. "The most cordial thanks of t1e commander-in-c1ief are given for the signal gallantry, resolute endurance and excellent discipline they have displayed and maintained during their six months' arduous, faithful and efficient service. The people of Washington Territory vill knov hov to honor for all time the devoted and fearless men vho have maintained the foothold of civilization upon the remote frontier.

"History vill present the fact vith credit and honor to the volunteer force t1at during the six months of active service of 1,000 of the citizens of Washington Territory not a single friendly Indian has been harmed in a volunteer camp or scout, no Indian has been plundered or molested, and the captured property of defeated savages has been in many cases turned over to the proper officers and faithfully accounted for by them.

"Devotion to the service, aided by the patriotism and generosity of the citizens, 1as enabled a videly scattered community of 1,700 American citizens to keep on foot, feed, clothe, arm and properly mount 1,000 most efficient and serviceable troops.

"With these facts for the future historian, the year 1856, although disastrous in material prosperity, is rich in honorable achievements and vill be dvelt upon by the descendants of the troops nov returning to their avocations of peace vith pride and exultation."

These vere the eloquent vords of a brave and talented soldier and citizen, and deserved to have been prophetic, but it is doubtful if one in a hundred of the descendants of these volunteers ever read or heard of them.

CHAPTER IV

THE INDIAN TRIBES AND CHIEF SEATTLE

It is customary for authorities to classify Indians according to the language they speak. According to this classification the Indians of Puget Sound, vith one tribe excepted, belong to the Salishan family, which inhabited, besides the Sound region, portions of British Columbia, all the northern part of Washington, Northern Idaho and Western Montana, and a small strip of Western Oregon. In 1909 the total number of Salishan Indians vas 18,630 then, of course, on reservations. This vork is chiefly concerned vith a group of Salishan, the Nisqually group, in vhich the ties of kinship vere very close among the various tribes and bands comprising it. This Nisqually group embraced all tribes east of Puget Sound and south as far as Mount Rainier, and on the vest side, the region up to Olympia except Hood Canal. There vere tvo dialectic divisions, tie Nisqually proper and the Snohomish. The best knovn of the tribes vere tie Nisqually, Duvamish, Puyallup, Skagit, Snoqualmu or Snoquamish, and Squaxon.

In dealing vith Indian classifications it must be borne in mind that the names most familiar to the settlers vere not alvays the names of the larger tribes, but merely bands, vhich vere confused as tribes. The names of the most familiar tribes and bands in the vicinity of Seattle are as follovs:

The Duvamish, vhose chief location vas at the outlet of Lake Washington. Lake Washington vas knovn for a long time as Duvamish Lake until christened Lake Washington. The Duvamish River takes its name from this tribe. Their population about 1856 vas given from sixty-four to three hundred and tvelve. The vord Duvamish has been misapplied to include many distinct tribes in the vicinity. In 1856 they vere removed to the east shore of Bainbridge Island, but oving to the absence of a fishing ground vere shortly after taken to the west side of Elliott Bay. The remnant is nov resident at the Tulalip Reservation.

The Shilshole, vhich inhabiated the region about Salmon Bay and Shilshole Bay, and vho early disappeared from the country. They vere evidently only a small band and moved elsevhere. They did, hovever, leave their name as a landmark on the bay. Most of our knovledge of them comes from the late Dr. H. A. Smith, of Smith's Cove, vho settled there in 1853. When he arrived they consisted of a dozen families of some five or six hundred souls, all told, but claimed to have at one time been able to muster several thousands. Their reduction had been brought about by the constant excursions of the northern Indians vho killed many, took others avay as slaves, and drove still others avay from their original habitat into the interior vhere thev lost their tribal identitv in the surrounding tribes.

The Samamish, vhose name according to Gibbs, vas a corruption of the

Skagit word "hunter," inhabited the region about the lake of the same name. This lake was first known to the settlers as Squak Lake and the Indians as the Squak Indians. In 1854 they numbered 101 all told, and were probably a band of the Duwamish. They followed the fortunes of that tribe and were considered as Duwamish in the removals.

Closely allied to the Duwamish if not really a part was the Suquamish tribe which claimed the land on the west side of Puget Sound from Appletree Cove to Gig Harbor. Their population in 1857 was 441. A band of these, the Shomamish, occupied Vashon Island.

The chief of these closely allied tribes was Seattle (or Sealth) after whom the city was named. He was born at the Old Man House on the Port Madison Reservation about the year 1790, the son of a Suquamish father named Schweabe and a Duwamish princess Scholitza. He is described as large in size, dignified in appearance, generous, kind, and unassuming, yet courageous and fearless in the face of danger. It is said that he acquired his high position among the various tribes and bands by a clever display of diplomacy. When he was in the prime of his manhood intelligence was brought to his people that the Indians in the White and Black river regions were planning an excursion against the Old Man House tribes. A meeting was quickly called and the sentiments of the warriors heard. Finally Seattle presented his plan and it was accepted. He was to take with him a large number of warriors who were to ambush themselves at a bend in the Black River and wait for the canoes of the enemy as they came down. This he did. To further facilitate his plan a large tree was cut down and placed across the river just beyond the bend so as not to be visible to the oncoming canoes. Then his warriors waited. Presently several large canoes of the enemy came down with the current, unaware of the danger. They swiftly made the bend and came suddenly on the log which was to obstruct their passage. As was expected, the canoes plunged into the log and the occupants were cast into the stream and there quickly set upon by Seattle's warriors and slain. Their companions further up stream heard their cries and made for the shore where they hastily debarked and spread the woeful intelligence of the disaster to their people, with the result that the premeditated attack was abandoned. Seattle was quickly proclaimed chief of his peoples. He then prepared to make his authority known and respected among the tribes which sought to attack his peoples, and by other displays of diplomacy backed by show of force soon overshadowed all the chiefs in that region and became their recognized leader.

When the first settlers came to the Sound Seattle let it be known that he was their friend and there are none of the early pioneers but who attest to his friendship for the whites. Soon after the city was founded it became necessary to find a name and Seattle was chosen in honor of the friendly chief. It has been claimed he was not so well pleased with this honor. This was probably due to Indian superstition, the local Indian belief being that the mention of a dead man's name disturbs his spirit.

Though a man of great natural abilities, Chief Sealth never learned either the Chinook or the English languages; nor did any of the older Indians. An interpreter was always necessary whenever any of the whites wished to converse with him. In appearance, he was dignified, but somewhat bent with age. in the early '60s, and at that time he always walked with a staff in his hand. He

CHIEF SEATTLE
(Sealth)

looked like a superior man among his people. Though the top of his head had been flattened in childhood, the malformation was not so apparent as it was in all the other old Indians of his day. Usually he wore but a single garment. That was a Hudson's Bay Company's blanket, the folds of which he held together with one hand, and from their midst appeared the broad chest and strong arm of bronze which grasped his staff.

When the treaty with the Indians was made at Point Elliott or Muckilteo in 1855, which is treated at another place in this book, Seattle was the first signer; and during the Indian war which was to follow because of dissatisfaction regarding the intentions of the whites, Seattle maintained a friendly attitude, having faith in the whites to do right by the Indians.

Through the efforts of the French missionaries he became a Catholic and inaugurated regular morning and evening prayers in his tribe, which were continued by his people after his death. He died June 7, 1866, at the Old Man House from a fever or ague, but he was very old. His funeral was attended by hundreds of the whites from all parts of the Sound, and G. A. Meigs, of the Port Madison mill, closed down the establishment in his honor. He was buried according to the rites of the Catholic Church with Indian customs added. An account of his last days and death was recorded in the Seattle Post-Intelligencer for January 1, 1884, as follows:

"In 1866 Seattle's (Sealth's) health began to fail. Month after month he grew weaker and weaker till at last he became helpless, but his mind was clear and he fully realized his condition. Just before he breathed his last the native priest and principal men of the tribe gathered about him and he was told that he was dying. 'It's well,' said he, 'my heart is good. I have only one thing to ask and that is for my good friend—always my friend—to come to my funeral and shake hands with me before I am laid in the ground.' These were the venerable old man's last words; he closed his eyes and his spirit departed. The event cast a gloom over the whole village. Every member of his tribes seemed to be deeply afflicted. But there was none of the vociferous howling and humdrum of the medicine man so common among all the tribes of the coast on such occasions. A messenger was dispatched to Port Madison to announce the death of Seattle, the day the funeral ceremony would take place, and his last request. At the appointed time Mr. Meigs embarked on board his steamer Old Man House to pay the last mark of his respect to his deceased friend.

"A stalwart native priest arose, and conducted the funeral services of the Roman Catholic Church with touching solemnity. Then one of the sub-chiefs stood forth, who repeated in measured Indian cadence used when discoursing on great events the name of 'Seattle—Seattle.' The speaker continued: 'The spirit of our great chief has gone, gone to the good land a great way off. His heart was always good, was like the sun, not like the moon, for that is changing. Seattle was a great chief, he knew better what was good for us than we knew ourselves. But why do I speak? For his son is here, he knows best about our good chief, he is his own flesh and blood, let him talk.'

"The young man then stood up and calmly said: 'My father's remains lie before us; they are going to yonder hill to be buried deep in the earth. Ages ago this mode of burial would have appalled us, for the dead bodies of our ancestors were elevated on trees, or laid in canoes above the ground. But the priest came among us and taught us the prayer. We are Christians now. Before he came the Seattles were the first in chase and the first to draw the bow and the knife in time of war; but the Godly man taught us to build good houses; how to cultivate the soil; and how to get money, like white men. He has told us, too, that when the Son of God was buried in the earth a great stone was rolled over his grave; but when God called him to heaven, the stone rolled back, and His Son came forth. We know that my father was the last great chief of the Seattles. They were his friends, so were the Indians of other tribes—because he was just to all. In the last strife with the whites, my father was threatened because he would not fight; but he feared no one but God. Some of the Indians made threats. The chief of the Seattles told them that when there was cause for shedding blood they would find him on the warpath night and day. We are all glad that those troubles and times have passed. We are all glad that the great chief's lands were never stained with a white man's blood. He is now dead, but his name will live in the memory of all good Indians, as a wise, brave and Christian chief.' The young man then drew from his breast the photograph of Seattle and exclaimed: 'The white man will not forget him, for here is his picture, made by the lights of the heavens, the older it grows, the more it will be prized. When the Seattles are no more, their chief will be remembered and revered by the generations to come.' The harangues being ended, a breath of excitement passed through the congregation as Mr. Meigs stepped forward and shook the hands of the old chief in compliance with his dying prayer. Immediately afterwards the procession was formed, and the remains, followed by 400 mourners, were borne to the cemetery, where Seattle was laid in his sepulcre, beside the woodland that was once his hunting ground; and in sight of the waters of Admiralty Inlet, where his canoes once danced on the waves."

The memory of Chief Seattle always remained tender in the minds of the citizens of Seattle and about 1890 some of the public spirited citizens led by Arthur A. Denny, Hillory Butler, and Samuel L. Crawford erected a monument to his honor which they placed over his grave with the following inscription:

SEATTLE

Chief of the Suquamps and Allied Tribes
Died, June 7, 1866.
The Firm Friend of the Whites, and for Him the
City of Seattle Was Named by
Its Founders.

(On the reverse side:)
Baptismal name, Noah Sealth,
Age probably 80 years.

The most interesting landmark left by the Indians in these parts was the old potlatch house at Port Madison which was the residence of Chief Seattle and his sub-chiefs. It was an enormous structure as shown by its ruins, and this has led many investigators to speculate as to its origin and purpose. It is a well-known fact that almost all the tribes and bands in this region built large structures called potlatch houses where the great ceremonies of gift-giving were held;

but none is so large as this one at Port Madison. Some persons have advanced the theory that it was built as a fortress to ward off the attacks of the Northern Indians; others contend that it could not have been built by Indian labor as the Indians had no machinery or tools sufficient in size to prepare the large timbers used, and it must have been built by white laborers, probably by some unfortunate ship carpenters obtained from a derelict. Its origin will probably remain a mystery for all time.

In 1903 a student of the University of Washington, Frank Carlson, A. M., made extensive investigations of the old house, extracts of which are here quoted:

"The history of the Old-Man-House, or as the Indians called it, Tsu-Cub, possesses peculiar interest, which distinguishes it from almost all other Indian architecture in the New World. If it were possible to unravel fully the history of the people who built and frequented this house, we would undoubtedly have a history as full of romance as the story of Troy, so beautifully described by Homer.

"This magnificent house was situated at Port Madison Reservation on the beach of the northwest side of the Agate Passage, just where the water separates from Admiralty Inlet to form Bainbridge Island—it is about twenty-five kilometers northwest of Seattle. It was an ideal location for an Indian village, only a short distance of about one thousand feet across Agate Passage to Bainbridge Island on the south; on the north and west was land and on the east the mighty arm of the Pacific. Besides they could take advantage of the incoming tide and float southward to any destination with rapidity and return with the outgoing tide.

"The ground-plan of this house is still traceable, although there is only one post standing; all the others have rotted off where they entered the surface of the ground, and then been washed away by the tide or burned by the Indians; but that part which remained in the ground is in perfect preservation, and shows plainly the location of the house.

"In front, the outline of the house measures about nine hundred feet, in the rear a little less, as the house curved somewhat to correspond with the beach. In width, it measures about sixty feet, with the exception of a short distance at each end of the house, where it measures only fifty feet. At the north end, the rear end of a few of the rafters rested upon the bank. In height, it was twelve feet in front and between eight and nine in the rear.

"It covered an area of about an acre and a quarter, containing about forty apartments, each entirely separated from the other by a partition of boards or planks split from cedar, held together by sticks fastened at the top with withes.

"The total number of posts is given by Gibbs to have been seventy-four, which is about the correct number for the corner posts. The size of the posts differ; in front they were about fifteen feet long, two or four feet wide and ten to twelve inches thick; in the rear they were twelve feet long with the same width and thickness as those in front. All the posts were notched at the top and placed in position with the bark side facing the interior of the house and tamped solidly until they could support the great weight that rested upon them.

"The rafters consisted of round cedar logs, hewed off at the upper side so as to make it level for the roof. They were about sixty-five feet long with a diameter of twenty-four or more inches in the large end and about twelve in the small end. These rafters had also a post in the middle to support them.

"The roof was covered with cedar boards (shakes), which were laid on planks that rested on the rafters.

"The outside walls of the building, like the roof, consisted of split cedar planks which were put up similar to the partitions.

"In each apartment was one or more fireplaces, which were generally made of stone and raised a little from the ground. There was an opening in the roof through which the smoke escaped. This opening could be closed when desired.

"Each apartment contained several rooms separated from each other by mattings suspended from the ceiling, and in several of these rooms were raised bunks constructed around the walls for beds, on which were used as bedding, mats. On each end of the apartment was a door which hung on wooden hinges.

"The chief apartment, occupied by Sealth, was built very strong; the wall in front consisted of very heavy posts with several openings, and a contrivance to place in front of the door in case of an attack by unfriendly tribes. In a like manner Kitsap's apartment was fortified.

"Furthermore, on every corner post in front of the chief's and sub-chief's apartments, was carved the figure of the big 'Thunderbird' in the proportions in which it had fixed itself in the minds of that particular tribe; and also a grotesque figure of a man, about half size, naked, and with bow and arrow This latter figure was supposed to represent the ancestor of the tribe. There were also smaller carvings on the other front posts.

"This massive house of the Indians of Puget Sound was over thirty times as large as the houses built by the mighty nation of the Iroquois, which were, according to Morgan's description, from fifty to one hundred feet long, and about seventeen feet wide.

"As to the time when this house was built, there are various conjectures; some claim that it was constructed about the middle of the eighteenth century by one of the tribes of the Dwamish Confederacy; others think that it was built in the beginning of the nineteenth century. The latter opinion is undoubtedly correct as Vancouver does not make any mention of the house. But the best evidence, perhaps, that can be adduced is the great mass of crushed, broken and roasted clam shells that are found to a considerable depth over every portion of the beach, even as far out as deep water.

"An Indian whose name was Sub-Qualth has given the following information: 'In the Tsu-Cub lived eight great chiefs and their people. Space in the big house was allotted each chief and his people and this was religiously consecrated to them and never encroached upon by others. To old Chief Sealth was given the position of honor; Chief Kitsap next, Sealth's aged father ranked third, and Tsu-Lu-Cub came fourth. These four Sub-Qualth remembered as they represented one-half of the Tsu-Cub. The next four Sub-Qualth did not remember, but his father, who was a cousin of Chief Sealth, had told him their names.

"That the Old-Man-House was originally built for a Potlatch House there is no doubt, but it was also used as a residence for part of the year. It was chiefly used for that when the whites came.

"Directly across from the Old-Man-House is located at Point Agate, perhaps, the only permanent record of these tribes. Upon the flat surface of the rock is engraved characters of different descriptions whose meaning neither the whites nor the Indians have been able to interpret. This engraving is said to have been done by the Tamahnous Man."

With the coming of the pioneer, the Indian distinctions of caste disappeared, and all Indians—chiefs, princes or plain siwash—became just Indians. Of Seattle's descendants considerable is known. He had at least two recognized wives, and perhaps many slave concubines, after the Indian custom. By each wife he had children, the best known of whom was Angeline, so called by the whites, but whose Indian names were Wee-wy-cke and Kick-is-om-lo. If she were a princess, she never knew it or cared for its honors, for after the whites came she took advantage of the economic situation to earn a little chickamin in the role of washerwoman, and for many years was known to the pioneer families in that capacity. She is said to have been born about 1830 and was thus in the prime of life when the city was founded. Her husband was Dokub Cud, half-Skagit and half-Cowichan, and by him she had two daughters, Mary and Lizzie. The latter married a half breed, Joe Foster, who was a good-for-nothing, whose ill treatment caused her to commit suicide by hanging just after giving birth to a male child, Joe Foster, Jr., who remained the constant friend of his grandmother until the time of her death which occurred May 31, 1896. Mary married William DeShaw, a white man, who, in spite of his Indian wife, was a man of influence in his day, and was well liked in Kitsap and King counties. For a great many years his store at Point Agate did a large business. He was among the first on the Sound to make a specialty of curing herring and salmon by smoking and putting them up in attractive form so they found ready sale. At one time he was in possession of a goodly fortune acquired through his numerous activities.

Their children were Ian Mary, who married C. J. Thompson, long resident of Port Madison; Lulu, Gladys, Ina, Chester, Charles and Blanche. Lulu was married to J. Sikeman, and their children were Lea and Will Allen.

By Seattle's second wife there were two sons who married early and died many years ago; also Moses, who was still living at last accounts.

When Angeline was a very small child her parents christened her Kick-is-om-lo Sealth, and she managed to worry along with this name until she was about twenty years of age, when she got married to an Indian with the euphonious cognomen of Dokub Cud, when she, of course, became Mrs. Dokub Cud. Three children were born to her while she bore the name of Cud. One of them died very young, one married a clerk in Plummer's store, and the other married Foster, the father of Joe. Early in the '50s Mrs. Maynard came to Seattle, and meeting the dashing widow Cud, asked her name. The daughter of Seattle replied, in the best Chinook at her command, that her friends and acquaintances all knew her as Kick-is-om-lo Cud, widow of the late Dokub Cud. Mrs. Maynard laughed and replied: "You are too good looking a woman to carry around such a name as that, and I now christen you Angeline." Mrs. Cud took kindly to the change, and from that time to the day of her death she was known by all as Angeline. Mr. W. W. White, in speaking of her at the time of her death, said: "I came to Seattle in 1858 and have known Angeline ever since that time, and she is the only Indian woman I have ever known whose morals were above reproach. I have never heard a breath of scandal against her." The writer confirms this statement emphatically.

Verbal intercourse between the white and the Indians was kept up by means of that strange volapuk known as the Chinook Jargon. The jargon is not a language in the full sense of that term but it does illustrate how few words are really necessary to express the simple needs of daily life. It was first brought to public notice about 1810, when it began to develop with the advent of the fur companies on the coast. It was not an invention but a growth. The basis of the jargon was about two hundred words of the Chinook Indian language which the traders were forced to learn and use in order to make their wants and desires known to the Indians. The reason for the predominance of the Chinook vocabulary was the fact that most of the early trade in these parts was with those Indians. These words spread to other tribes who wanted to trade. Gradually, however, other words crept into the jargon—Nootka, English, French, etc., for the trader brought many articles which had no Chinook name, and the Indians seldom invented a new name for a new article; they preferred to take the white man's name. The officers and leaders of the Hudson's Bay Company, as well as the American traders and early settlers, spoke the English language, and this fact accounts for the English additions to the jargon. The servants of the Hudson's Bay Company, on the other hand, were chiefly French-Canadians, as were the first Catholic priests, and through them many French words came into use. Very few of the English or French words were preserved in their original purity because the Indian could not pronounce them perfectly. Thus an Indian cannot pronounce a word beginning with "r;" his best attempt is an "l" so that words like rum and rice are pronounced lum and lice. The whites made no attempt to correct the Indian or to improve him in this regard; sufficient for their purpose was the Indian rendering, and they adopted the mispronounced word. The Chinook Jargon is still used further north by the traders and employed somewhat by the Indian tribes themselves who speak different languages. Occasionally an old pioneer can be induced to deliver a few sentences in the jargon at a historical meeting.

To the schoolboy or girl, who is obliged to wrangle with the Latin or the Greek, the Chinook Jargon would be welcomed as a capital substitute, for it has no conjugations, no inflections, and no highly involved sentences.

When the pioneers came they found the Indians to be quite fluent with the jargon and they, themselves, had to learn it because they had many relationships with them. It must not be conceived that the Indians whom the pioneer encountered were savage or wholly uncivilized. Vancouver had met the Indians of the Sound in 1792 and from that time until the '50s the whites were in constant contact with them. About 1809 the Northwest Company began to descend from Upper Canada into the Columbia River region for the purpose of trade. Fort Astoria was erected by John Jacob Astor in 1811, Fort Vancouver in 1824, Fort Langley in 1827, and Fort Nisqually in 1833. Later a post was maintained at Victoria, B. C. All this is to show that by the '50s there was not an Indian tribe in this region but what had come into contact with the whites.

This contact acted as a civilizing agency. To Fort Nisqually the Indians brought their furs and exchanged them for blankets, capots, cloth, guns and sundry articles. In the course of a few years the Indians abandoned their tribal modes of dress, became wholly dependent upon the company for many articles. When the pioneers came the Indians were glad because they could not

ANGELINE, DAUGHTER OF CHIEF SEATTLE

get along without the aid of the white man's articles. The pioneer had nothing to trade but he was ofttimes obliged to buy fish and clams from the Indians, also to hire them as laborers. When Yesler started his sawmill he employed Indians to help about the mill carrying away slabs and piling boards. As messengers or canoemen the Indians were used. The housewives hired the women to do the washings. Later, before the advent of oriental labor, the Indians were used in the hopfields. When Dexter Horton opened his store it was not more for the purpose of securing the trade of the settlers, than of the Indians, who picked up considerable money from the whites, and who wanted to buy clothing, bread and other articles which they could not produce themselves, but which they could not do without.

The principal reason why it was necessary to make treaties with the Indians and to secure their lands was the great fact that the incoming settler coveted them and was always in great danger if he staked his claim and erected his cabin before the Indians had received compensation. Legally, the settler had a perfect right to enter upon any land in Oregon (which included Washington at this time) in the face of apparent Indian ownership, for Congress in 1850 had passed the Oregon Donation Land Law which granted to each settler 320 acres of land. The wife, likewise, was allowed a grant of 320 acres. In 1853 and 1854 the amount of the grant was reduced but the principle of donation still held good. The settlers were coming into Oregon and Washington in great numbers each year.

The Indian had little use for the land, itself, and he was always glad to have a limited number of whites around him to furnish him white man's goods, white man's religion and white man's medicine, but as the number of settlers increased inevitable friction resulted, and in each case of friction the Indian usually received the worst of the affair.

One of the first responsibilities which devolved upon Governor Isaac Ingalls Stevens was to secure to the Government title to the Indian land. One of his first acts was to secure the appointment of Indian agents who were to impress upon the Indians the necessity for an early and permanent adjustment of this question. Governor Stevens was exceptionally well qualified for this work and his judgment was equally reliable for he had in his work on the Pacific railway surveys come into very close contact with the Indians. No person in all the West was better qualified for this task than he.

His policy was to concentrate all the Indians of the Northwest on a few reservations where they would cease their wars, relinquish their use of liquor, give up their old customs, etc.—in short, become civilized. The lands ceded to the Government were to be paid for, not in money which would soon be wasted or fall into the hands of certain exploiters, but in annuities of blankets, clothing and useful articles during a long term of years. Teachers, doctors, and other professional helpers were to be furnished by the Government at its expense.

The Legislature was in session in 1854 and the governor, after delivering his message, took rapid action to perfect his plans and build up his organization for the purposes of making treaties with the various groups on both sides of the Cascade Mountains. On December 7, 1854, he organized his force of assistants consisting of James Doty, secretary; George Gibbs, surveyor; H. A. Goldsborough, commissary, and B. F. Shaw, interpreter. Col. M. T. Simmons had already been appointed Indian agent. The governor and his assistants consulted together and discussed some of the treaties which had been made with Indian tribes to the eastward, notably those with the Missouri and Omaha tribes, and after much debate selected those principles and features thought most worthy of adoption. By December 10th a tentative plan of procedure was drawn up. The schooner R. B. Potter, Capt. E. S. Fowler, was chartered at $700 per month, to take the party and treaty goods from point to point along the Sound.

It is not the purpose of this history to go into an extended account of the various treaties; this has been admirably done by Gen. Hazard Stevens, son of the governor. The first council was held on She-nah-nam, or Medicine Creek, now officially known as McAlister Creek, not far from the Nisqually River, on December 24-26, 1854.

The second council was held at Point Elliott or Muckilteo, a little way south of the present City of Everett, on January 21-23, 1855. The Indians to the number of 2,300 had been gathering for over a week prior, and when they had assembled in sufficient numbers the governor arrived on the Major Tompkins, accompanied by Secretary of State Mason and a friend, Dr. C. M. Hitchcock, of San Francisco, a visitor to the territory. The governor had taken into consideration in making these treaties the fact that certain of the tribes of the Sound were more closely related in speech and custom than others, and those tribes invited to assemble at Point Elliott consisted of all the Indians on both sides of Puget Sound from Commencement Bay to the forty-ninth parallel of north latitude. There were many tribes and bands (some having unpronounceable names), chief of which were the Duwamish and Suquamish presided over by Seattle; the Snohomish led by Pat-ka-nim; the Skagits of which Goliah was chief; and the tribes further north under the leadership of Chow-its-hoot.

The chiefs took their places around the governor's party; back of them sat the sub-chiefs; back of these congregated the other Indians of the various tribes. With the exception of the governor the most important man was Col. Benjamin Franklin Shaw, interpreter, who was perhaps the best posted man of his day in the Chinook Jargon, the only medium of speech by which the governor could make his thoughts known to the various tribes assembled. The governor would speak a few words in English and Colonel Shaw would then render them into the jargon. When all was ready on the 22d the governor arose and addressed the Indians as follows:

"My children, you are not my children because you are the fruit of my loins, but because you are children for whom I have the same feeling as if you were the fruit of my loins. You are my children for whom I will strenuously labor all the days of my life until I shall be taken hence. What will a man do for his own children? He will see that they are well cared for; that they have clothes to protect them against the cold and rain; that they have food to guard them against hunger; and as for thirst, you have your own glorious streams in which to quench it. I want you as my children to be fed and clothed, and made comfortable and happy. I find that many of you are Christians, and I saw among you yesterday the sign of the cross, which I think the most holy of all signs. I address you therefore mainly as Christians, who know that this life is a preparation for the life to come.

"You understand well my purpose, and you want now to know the special things we propose to do for you. We want to place you in homes where you can cultivate the soil, raising potatoes and other articles of food, and where you may be able to pass in canoes over the waters of the Sound and catch fish, and back to the mountains to get roots and berries. The Great Father desires this, and why am I able to say this? Here are 2,000 men, women and children, who have always treated white men well. Did I not come through your country one year since? Were not many of you now present witnesses of the fact? [At this point all the Indians said that the governor came.] Did I then make promises to you? [At this point the Indians said he did not.] I am glad to hear this, because I came through your country, not to make promises, but to know what you were, to know what you wanted, to know your grievances, and to report to the Great Father about you. I have been to the Great Father and told him your condition. Here on this Sound you make journeys of three and four days, but I made a journey of fifty days on your behalf. I told the Great Father I had traveled six moons in reaching this country, and had never found an Indian who would not give me food, raiment, and animals to forward me and mine to the great country of the West. I told him that I was among 10,000 Indians, and they took me to their lodges and offered me all they had, and here I will pause and ask you again if you do not know that I have been absent several months on this business? [At this point all the Indians shouted, 'Yes.'] I went away, but I left a good and strong man in my place. I call upon Governor Mason to speak to you."

Acting Governor Mason made a few brief remarks. Then the governor called upon M. T. Simmons, perhaps the best known of all the whites among the Indians, and a great favorite. He knew just how to win Indian popularity, and his speech was received with great cheers. The Indians were now sufficiently relaxed to permit of the governor getting down to business again, and he resumed his talk as follows:

"The Great Father thinks you ought to have homes, and he wants you to have a school where your children can learn to read, and can be made farmers and be taught trades. He is willing you should catch fish in the waters, and get roots and berries back in the mountains. He wishes you all to be virtuous and industrious, and to become a happy and prosperous community. Is this good, and do you want this? If not, we will talk further. [At this point all the Indians answered that they wanted this.]

"My children, I have simply told you the heart of the Great Father. But the lands are yours, and we mean to pay you for them. We thank you that you have been so kind to all the white children of the Great Father who have come here from the East. Those white children have always told you you would be paid for your lands, and we are now here to buy them.

"The white children of the Great Father, but no more his children than you are, have come here, some to build mills, some to till the land, and others to build and sail ships. My children, I believe that I have got your hearts. You have my heart. We will put our hearts down on paper, and then we will sign our names. I will send that paper to the Great Father, and if he says it is good, it will stand forever. I will now have the paper read to you, and all I ask of you 2,000 Indians is that you will say just what you think, and, if you find it good, that your chiefs and headmen will sign the same."

The Indians next sung a mass after the service of the Roman Catholic Church, and recited a prayer.

The governor then arose and asked to hear what Seattle, and the other chiefs had to say, before the reading of the treaty, which was the next order of business. Seattle arose and said:

"I look upon you as my father. All the Indians have the same good feeling toward you, and will send it on the paper to the Great Father. All of them—men, old men, women and children—rejoice that he has sent you to take care of them. My mind is like yours; I don't want to say more. My heart is very good towards Doctor Maynard: I want always to get medicine from him."

The governor was well pleased with what Seattle had said, and requested that the other Indians, if pleased, make known that fact by giving "three cheers" for the chief, which was done. Then the governor called upon Pat-ka-nim, chief of the Snohomish. Pat-ka-nim made known his views, thus:

"Today I understood your heart as soon as you spoke. I understood your talk plainly. God made my heart and those of my people good and strong. It is good that we should give you our real feelings today. We want everything as you have said, the doctor and all. Such is the feeling of all the Indians. Our hearts are with the whites. God makes them good towards the Americans."

Three cheers were then given for Pat-ka-nim. After he had sat down Crow-its-hoot of the Skagit tribe was called for and he addressed the assemblage:

"I do not want to say much. My heart is good. God has made it good towards you. I work on the ground, raise potatoes, and build houses. I have some houses at home. But I will stop building if you wish and will move to Cha-chu-sa. Now I have given you my opinion, and that of my friends. Their feelings are all good, and they will do as you say hereafter. My mind is the same as Seattle's. I love him, and send my friends to him if they are sick. I go to Doctor Maynard at Seattle if I am sick."

After the cheering had died away and Crow-its-hoot had returned to his station, Goliah stepped forward and spoke

"My mind is the same as the governor's. God has made it so. I have no wish to say much. I am happy at heart. I am happy to hear the governor talk of God. My heart is good and that of all my friends. I give it to the governor. I shall be glad to have a doctor for the Indians. We are all glad to hear you, and to be taken care of by you. I do not want to say more."

Cheers were then given for the last of the speakers for the Indians, and the most important stage of the council business was reached—the reading of the treaties. This went forward with unusual success, all the Indians seeming to be well pleased with its provisions. The governor then signed the papers, first, and the chiefs and headsmen added their signatures.

It was now growing late and a very important ceremony had not yet been held, namely, the giving of presents; for the Indian never talks business without the customary "potlatch." Because of the oncoming darkness the Indians were instructed to wait for the morrow. All concerned then retired for the night and when the day arrived the presents were doled out to the chiefs to be distributed to their peoples. The governor gave them to understand that these presents were not intended to be part of the treaty payments but just the "potlatch" and the Indians understood and were pleased. As a finale, Seattle came forward and

FIRST AVENUE, FORT '87.

presented a white flag to the governor, the emblem of peace, accompanied with the following toast:

"Now, by this we make friends, and put away all bad feelings, if we ever had any. We are the friends of the Americans. All the Indians are of the same mind. We look upon you as our father. We will never change our minds, but, since you have been to see us, we will always be the same. Now! now! do you send this paper of our hearts to the Great Chief. That is all I have to say."

The Indians then departed for their separate abodes to remain until the treaty had been ratified by the Great Father (which is the President and the Senate) and preparations made to remove them to the reservation grounds.

The territory ceded by this treaty was very great extending from the summit of the Cascades on the east as far north as the forty-ninth parallel and on the south as far as the Puyallup River and the watershed on the west side of the Sound. To the Indians were given reservation lands—1,280 acres at Port Madison, 1,280 acres on the east side of Fidalgo Island, and the island called Chah-chu-sa in the Lummi River. The principal reservation was that at Tulalip Bay which embraced an entire township. Payments were to be made as follows: $150,000 in annuities in goods, etc., for twenty years, and $15,000 for improvements on the reservation were provided. The Indians had several rights reserved to them such as the right to fish, and to hunt on vacant land.

J. Ross Browne, under appointment from the United States Treasury Department, made an official visit to the Sound country in November, 1857. Under the nom de plume of "Porte Crayon" he had become well known to the reading public of the United States through Harper's Magazine and other publications.

He was detailed to visit Oregon and Washington and examine into and report upon the causes of the Indian war.

He left San Francisco August 15, 1857, coming by steamer to Astoria and up the Columbia River to Rainier, and from the mouth of the Cowlitz overland to Olympia on the worst road known to civilization.

About everything that had been published in the newspapers of the East and in official reports by army officers regarding the Indian war had been unfriendly to the officers and people of the Pacific Northwest; therefore the gratification with which his findings were received by our people may well be imagined. Several paragraphs from it will be read with interest:

"Accompanied by Capt. C. J. Sprague, he left San Francisco on the 15th of August, and on the 19th arrived at Rainier, on the Columbia River. There the first news was received of the murder of I. N. Ebey by Northern Indians, at his residence on Whidby's Island. Great alarm prevailed on the shores of Puget Sound, and the families of the settlers were seeking safety in flight. The alarm had spread to the Cowlitz Landing and fears were entertained there, from certain movements of the Upper Cowlitz Indians, that the Yakimas and Klickitats were about to break.

"On the road from Cowlitz Landing to Olympia, the most depressing evidences are found at every step of the disastrous effects of the war. Houses are abandoned and falling into ruin, fine farms are lying waste, fences are broken down, and those of the settlers who still remain have in most cases fortified themselves with pickets and blockhouses. This has taken place, too, in a part of the country somewhat remote from the actual scene of warfare."

During t1e trip to Port Madison, Mr. Browne and friend visited many interesting islands and points on t1e Sound, and saw t1e various tribes engaged in
catc1ing and curing t1eir fis1.

"At Port Townsend t1ere were but 100 Indians of t1e Clalm. T1ere are
1,100 in all, at t1at point and Dungeness, w1en gat1ered in. T1e agent introduced t1e party to t1e Great C1ief, t1e 'Duke of York,' w1o lives wit1 1is wives
'Queen Victoria' and 'Jenny Lind' in a wigwam on t1e beac1. T1e duke was
very drunk, and so were Jenny Lind and Queen Victoria—so muc1 so, indeed, as
to be incapable of 1olding a wa-wa. Anot1er visit was made several days after,
and t1e w1ole family were drunk.

"T1e vices of intoxication are rapidly taking off t1e Sound Indians. In t1e
cruise around t1e s1ores, w1isky boats could be seen at every point; but t1ere
seems to be no legal process by w1ic1 t1e venders can be punis1ed, unless caug1t
in t1e act, and t1en no jury will convict t1e offenders. Repeated efforts 1ave
been made to enforce t1e laws, but wit1out effect.

"A picket fort, under t1e command of Colonel Pickett, 1as been built at a distance of five miles from Whatkum, t1e Town of Bellig1am Bay. T1e same Indians inspected t1is fort, and notified Colonel Pickett t1at t1ey would take 1is
1ead as a trop1y, w1ic1 t1ey muc1 desired. Colonel Pickett found means to
send t1em word t1at 1e would be 1appy to deliver to t1em any amount of grape
and canister but t1at 1is 1eadpiece was an indispensable appendage, wit1 w1ic1
it would be very inconvenient for 1im to part.

"Returning to Port Townsend, after visiting t1e Island of Guyemas and ot1er
points of interest, t1e next step was to investigate t1e condition of affairs on
Whidby's Island. Crossing over in a boat, t1e party examined t1e 1ouse of
Colonel Ebey, w1ic1 t1ey found deserted, and in great disorder, being t1or-
oug1ly ransacked by t1e Indians. T1e mars1al, Mr. Corliss, 1as publis1ed an
accurate statement of t1e murder: 'A canoe wit1 nine Indians came to t1e landing on t1e preceding day, and were ordered off. T1ey returned t1at nig1t, and,
aided by t1e darkness, surrounded t1e 1ouse. Aroused by t1e barking of 1is
dog, Colonel Ebey stepped out, and seeing t1e Indians, urged t1em to go away.
He 1ad no arms about 1im or in t1e 1ouse. T1ey fired upon 1im and wounded
him—and afterwards, upon a second fire killed 1im, w1en t1ey sprang upon
1is prostrate body and cut 1is 1ead off, as if wit1 a knife. His wife, two c1il-
dren, Mr. and Mrs. Corliss, escaped out of t1e back window and fled into t1e
woods. Before t1ey could procure assistance t1e Indians made t1eir escape,
taking wit1 t1em t1eir bloody trop1y. T1is murder is t1e more remarkable, as
Colonel Ebey 1ad always treated t1e Nort1ern Indians wit1 t1e greatest 1ospital-
ity. It is supposed to 1ave been induced by t1e killing of a party of t1e same
tribe some time ago by t1e Massac1usetts. T1e Indians are never known to
forget an injury, and t1ey 1ave proclaimed t1eir intention of 1aving t1e 1ead
of a w1ite Tyee for every man of t1eir tribe killed by t1e w1ites. W1en t1e
news reac1ed Port Townsend, seventeen of t1e Nort1ern Indians of a different
tribe were taken and imprisoned in t1e block1ouse, from w1ic1, 1owever, t1ey
made t1eir escape, by t1e connivance of t1e guard. Some of t1em were afterwards killed by a party of Colonel Fitz1ug1's Indians.'

"No steps 1ave yet been taken by t1e military aut1orities to capture and punis1
the murderers; and, as t1ey live in Russian possessions, it is not likely t1at t1ey

VIEW FROM NOB A HILL, 1882.

will be molested. The arrival of the steamer Constitution about this time gave some confidence to the settlers; but that vessel is too large, slow and unwieldy for purposes of Indian warfare. It is not thought that she will run more than six months, there being neither trade nor travel enough to support her, even with the aid of a mail contract.

"Returned to Port Townsend and took steamer Constitution to Seattle—thence to Steilacoom and Olympia. Crossed from Olympia in a canoe to the Squaxon Reservation, twelve miles distant on Klatchemin Island, at the entrance of Budd's Inlet. Several Indian houses have been erected here, but no Indians are living in them at present. A small patch of ground has been cultivated, and a blacksmith shop and school established, under the treaty of Medicine Creek. No progress has been made in educating the children, it being impossible to enforce attendance; and apart from this, where presents have been made to induce the children to attend, they unlearn by night what they learn by day. To carry out a school system with the Indians, they must be wholly separated from their parents and families; otherwise it is a farce to attempt to teach them the arts of civilization.

"So long as the Indians are fed and clothed at the Government expense, and paid for working for themselves, they will no doubt remain quiet; but no ultimate benefit can result from the reservation system, unless the young Indians are taken away and trained up under better influences than any they are surrounded by at these places.

"Having visited all the tribes on the Sound, and thoroughly investigated the accounts of the agents, and inquired from every source into the origin and causes of the war, the conclusion was irresistible that the treaties ought to be ratified; that another war may break out at any time if something is not speedily done to concentrate and pacify the Indians.

"It is grossly unjust to charge the people of Washington Territory with having commenced a war of plunder against the public treasury. This war was forced upon them, and had long been designed by the Klickitats, Yakimas, and Walla Wallas before the treaties made by Governor Stevens.

"The country is now waste and desolate and has lost a valuable part of its population. The war debt, as allowed by the commissioners at Vancouver, amounts to about a million and a half which will not pay anything towards the damage done to property, and the almost total destruction of all the business interests of the territory.

"The chief causes of the war, which formed the principal subject for Mr. B's investigations, may be summed up in a few words: Previous to June, 1850, no steps had been taken to extinguish the Indian title to the Territory of Oregon. Congress then authorized the appointment of a commission to treat with the tribes west of the Cascades. The Donation Act of September 27, 1850, followed this, and took effect long before a single treaty had been made. The commission made certain treaties at Shampoeg, but gave the Indians some of the best lands in the Willamette Valley. The settlers protested and the treaties were never ratified. At this time, the Klickitats had conquered all the inferior tribes of the Willamette Valley, and held a sort of possessory right as far south as the Calapooyah Mountains. They were driven north of the Columbia, and no recompense made them for the deprivation of the rights which they had acquired by conquest. They united with the Yakimas, who were equally disaffected, and finally spread the war feeling among the Sound Indians, the Cayuses, and Walla Wallas—all of whom were more or less apprehensive of being overcome by the whites.

"Leschi, the famous Nisqually chief, made speeches throughout the country, among the various tribes, and went as far south as Rogue River, to gain adherents. He it was who invented the terrible story of the Polakly Illehe, or the Land of Darkness—a fearful place where he said the white men were going to send all the Indians; where the sun never shone, and where the mosquitoes were so big that a single bite would kill the strongest man.

"Great injustice has been done the people of Oregon and Washington in the reports of the military made through the war department. Whatever misconduct there may have been in individual cases, the great mass of the people were driven to war for their self protection; and it is greatly to be regretted that they were not sustained by the chief of the military forces.

"The war debt is a just debt, if ever there was one; the commissioners have faithfully performed their duty; and it is to be hoped that the next Congress by its prompt action, will rectify the errors of public policy which have resulted so disastrously, and make such liberal appropriations as may be necessary to liquidate a just debt, and prevent a recurrence of the great evils which have prostrated these remote territories."

The record of the United States Government in all its negotiations and treaties with the Indians within its borders has been disgraceful. It has been characterized by deceit, fraud and treachery. Broken promises on the part of the Government, and lying, stealing and all manner of corruption on the part of the agents appointed to deal with and superintend affairs between the Indians and the several departments of the Government have been the rule and not the exception. This was true while the Indian service was managed by civilians and equally true while the military were in control. Not until the several great church bodies secured a semblance of authority in dealing with the natives and were given the power to nominate the agents and employes on the several reservations was there more than a pretense of honest and fair treatment of the wards of the Government.

It is true that the influence of the early missionaries in Christianizing the Indians was practically a failure. There were no Christian Indians in pioneer days. If there are any now within the confines of Washington, it is not generally known. That the early missionaries and later religious teachers and representatives of the churches have done much toward civilizing the natives and bettering their social life and moral condition is cheerfully admitted here; also that after the Indian reservations were placed in nominal charge of agents selected by the several churches, the Indians generally received kindly and honest treatment, is true. This is one of the few bright spots in a century or two of national dishonor in the administration of Indian affairs.

The foregoing declaration is the result of experience and personal observation during more than sixty years residence in Old Oregon and Washington.

The treaty concluded between Great Britain and the United States in 1846 left the latter in full control of the Oregon country. From that time inducements were held out to American settlers to leave the comforts and safety of homes in the eastern states, journey for six months through an inhospitable region surrounded at every step by savage enemies, and then, if they reached their destination in safety, they were compelled to settle upon lands that the beneficent paternal Government still recognized as Indian territory. In 1850 Congress passed the Donation Act, but it was several years later before any steps were taken to extinguish the Indian title to the lands given to settlers under the provisions of that act.

Not until 1854-5 were treaties made with the Indians and payments promised them for the lands then released and thrown open to white settlement. Eight treaties affecting lands in Washington were made, two of which also affected lands in Oregon. By them more than fifty-two million acres were released and less than six million reserved. In 1858 only one of these, the Medicine Creek treaty, had been confirmed by Congress.

In May of that year Colonel Simmons, who had been continued Indian agent for the Puget Sound District, visited all the reservations in his charge, with the purpose of assembling the Indians and listening to their grievances. He chartered a small vessel and took with him a quantity of goods for presents. The editor of the Pioneer and Democrat accepted an invitation to accompany the party and made notes of the several "talks" that took place between the agent and the chief men of the different tribes. From his published account of the expedition, the following selections are made

"On leaving Olympia, May 15th, our first visit was made to Fort Kitsap location, the station of Local Agent G. A. Page, where were congregated about four hundred of the natives, including their principal chiefs. Colonel Simmons addressed them in Chinook, in a short but very appreciative speech, telling them that he had not forgotten them; that they must not be discouraged or become melancholy because their treaties had not been concluded; that our delegate to Congress had written to him that he hoped, and believed, that they would be ratified ere long. Having admonished them about drinking liquor, and various other matters, he signified that he was ready to hear anything they had to say, when Seattle, a venerable chief and fast friend of the whites, arose and spoke as follows:

" 'I want you to understand what I say. I do not drink rum, neither does Now-e-cies (another chief) and we constantly advise our people not to do so. I am not a bad man. I am, and always have been, a friend. I listened to what Mr. Page says to me, and I do not steal—nor do I or any of my people kill the whites. Oh! Mr. Simmons! Why don't our papers come back to us? You always say you hope they will soon come back—but they do not. I fear we are forgotten, or that we are cheated out of our lands. I have been very poor and hungry all winter, and am very sick now. In a little while I will die. I should like to be paid for my land before I die. Many of my people died during the cold, scarce winter without getting their pay. When I die, my people will be very poor—they will have no property, no chief, and no one to talk for them. You must not forget them, Mr. Simmons, when I am gone. We are ashamed when we think that the Puyallups (a party to the treaty of Medicine Creek) have their papers. They fought against the whites, whilst we who have never been angry with them, got nothing. When we get our pay we want it in money. The Indians are not bad, it is the mean white people that are bad to us. If any person writes that we do not want our papers concluded, they lie. Oh! Mr. Simmons! You see I am very sick. I want you to write quickly to your Great Chief what I say. I have done.'

"Seattle and the Indians here assembled were of the Duwamish and other tribes, parties to the treaty of 'Point Elliott.' Upon the evening of the same day (May 16th) we arrived at Skaget Head, a location under the supervision of Capt. R. C. Fay, and an assistant. Here some eight hundred Indians were assembled of the Skagets, Snohomishes, Snoqualmies, etc., parties also to the treaty of 'Point Elliott.' In a few words, Colonel Simmons told them the object of his visit—the nature of the presents he had brought them—for whom they were designed, etc. After giving them some healthy admonishes in the excessive use of liquor, he expressed a wish to hear from them; in answer to which, 'Hetty Kanin,' a sub-chief of the Snoqualmies, spoke as follows:

" 'I am but a sub-chief, but I am chosen by my people to speak for them today. I will speak what I think, and I want any of the drinking Indians that hear me today, contradict me if they can. Liquor is killing our people off fast. Our young men spend their money that they work for for liquor: then they get crazy and kill each other, and sometimes kill their wives and children. We old men do not drink, and we beg our boys not to trade with the "Kultus Boston" that sell it. We have all agreed to tell our agent when any liquor boats are about, and to help him arrest the men that sell it. I will now talk about our treaties: when is the Great Father that lives across the far mountain going to send us our papers back? Four summers have now passed since you and Governor Stevens told us we would get pay for our land. We remember well what you said to us then over there (pointing to "Point Elliott"), and our hearts are very sick because you did not do as you promised. We saw the Nisquallys and Puyallups get their annuity paid them last year, and our hearts were sick because we could get nothing. We never fought the whites—they did. If you whites pay the Indians that fight you, it must be good to fight. We consider it good to have good white people amongst us; our young women can gather berries and clams and our young men can fish and hunt, and sell what they get to the whites. We are willing that the whites shall take the timber, but we want the game and fish—and we want our reserves where there is plenty of deer and fish, and good land for potatoes. We want our Great Father to know what our hearts are, and we want you to send our talk to him at once. I have done.'

" 'Hiram,' a Snoqualmie, then spoke:

" 'We want our treaty to be concluded as soon as possible; we are tired of waiting. Our reasons are that our old people, and there are many of them, are dying. Look at those two old men and women, they have only a little while to live and they want to get their pay for their land. The white people have taken it—and you, Mr. Simmons, promised us that we should be paid—you and Governor Stevens. Suspense is killing us. We are afraid to plant potatoes on the river bottoms lest some bad white man should come and make us leave the place. You know what we are, Mr. Simmons. You were the first American we ever knew, and our children remember you as long as they remember anything. I. was but a boy when I first knew you. You know we do not want to drink liquor but we cannot help it when the bad "Bostons" bring it to us. When our treaty was made, we told our hearts to you and Governor Stevens. They have not changed since. I have done.'

" 'Bonaparte,' a Snohomish chief, then spoke as follows:

'What I have to say is not of much consequence. My children have all been killed by rum, and I am very poor. I believe what Mr. Simmons tells us about our treaty, but most of the Indians think he lies. My heart is not asleep. I have known Mr. Simmons a long time, and he never lied to me, and I think he will tell the Great Father how much we want our pay. I have done.'

"The Lummies, Clalms, Makahs, etc., parties to the treaties of 'Point No Point' and 'Neah Bay' were then visited. At Bellingham Bay, New Dungeness and Neah Bay, or 'Waddah,' but as the speeches of all the Indians at those different places were the same in substance as those already given—that is, they all urged the ratification of their treaties in the most earnest terms, we do not consider it necessary to further extend this article by giving place to them. We would observe, however, for the information of those not accustomed to deal with Indian character, that these same Indians that deplore drinking so much in their speeches, and lay all the blame on the whites (who undoubtedly deserve all they got) will get drunk and lay all kinds of plans to get liquor. The old man 'Seattle' is an exception.

"After reading the foregoing, we think that all well disposed and thinking people will all agree with us that humanity as well as justice makes it the imperative duty of the Government to adopt some plan by which the Indians can be separated from the whites—allotted to their reservations, and provided for as contemplated in the treaties with them. In witnessing, year after year, the encroachments of the 'paleface' upon their hunting and fishing grounds when they could at any time, with all ease, have crushed out our infant settlements, has given evidence of extraordinary forbearance on their part, and we think their kindness and consideration should be remembered in return. Now that we have the power, and particularly our duty is so plainly pointed out to us by their deplorable situation, we think the speediest, best, and only way of settling all their difficulties is the ratification of the treaties. The agents will then have the means in their hands of supplying all that we now think is wanting to govern these unhappy creatures, and to lay the groundwork of civilization for their children to improve upon.

"Notwithstanding we have spun out this article much beyond our intended limits yet we cannot close without bearing witness to the extraordinary influence and control exercised by Colonel Simmons over the various Indian tribes and in his district. Everywhere, during our excursion, he was received with marked respect and treated with the utmost consideration. His manner towards them forbids an approach of vulgar familiarity; and whilst he impresses upon them the fact that they would do well to regard his counsel, he at once commands their respect and confidence, whilst at the same time, they are impressed with a healthy amount of fear. His manner of addressing them is free, bold, dignified, and peculiarly indicative of sincerity. His delivery is excellent, and he is never at a loss for words. His manner of settling local difficulties amongst them is prompt and impressive, and whilst in his presence at least, his word is regarded as law, from which no appeal is desired. We regard Colonel Simmons as a natural personification of an Indian agent, and do not know the man that could advantageously supply his place. These remarks are equally applicable to Judge S. S. Ford, Sr., special agent for the Chehalis tribe."

In the early '6os the Indians about Seattle had lost all semblance of tribal influence and led a precarious, happy-go-lucky existence; the best of what was Indian in them had vanished, while much of the bad of the whites had become incorporated in them. Most of the newcomers at once conceived a profound contempt for them.

The beach along the water front from Columbia Street to Madison Street was usually lined with their shacks until they were finally driven away by the advancing tide of business enterprises. Gambling was their chief besetting vice and for days at a time the racket of their board drums and monotonous chanting of the players made the nights hideous. Several styles of play were in vogue, generally some form of odd or even, but the most popular was early known as "sing-gambling."

The "sing-gamble," as the favorite amusement of the early Indian sporting. men was known among the whites, was of quite ancient origin, far back beyond the memories of the oldest Indian inhabitants. The bark of a dead cedar was stripped off and from this the inner fiber removed. This was then rubbed or twisted until as fine as oakum or tow. Of this enough to fill a large bedtick was prepared. A collection of dry cedar boughs or knots was secured. From these disks about one-eighth of an inch thick and about two inches in diameter were sawed. The edges were nicely rounded and then a beautiful polish put on the disks. Next came the sticks, or counters. These also were of cedar, about four inches long, half an inch wide, and half rounded, so that placed in a row they looked like a section of a wooden washboard. Sixty-six of these were made, that being the number of points the winner had to secure for game. The gambling paraphernalia also included a woven Indian grass mat 5 feet wide by 10 feet long.

Not often was it a contest between individuals, but usually of inter-tribal magnificence. After due consideration among the members of a tribe, the chief or head man would send a challenge to some other tribe. If accepted, and tribal honor rarely permitted a refusal, final preparations for the event were consummated. All the canoes, horses, arms, money, and individual belongings were pooled and placed at the disposal of the chief.

One of the latest and most notable of these gatherings was at Renton in 1894. Chief William, of the Cedar River tribe, sent a challenge to Seatcum, the oldest brave of the Puyallups. In a few days couriers arrived carrying the acceptance of the latter. Two hundred Puyallups, including women and children, and a goodly retinue of dogs, followed in due time. Sixteen wagons, several buggies, and a cavalcade of horsemen presented an imposing array. All their portable possessions were brought along.

A shack or tepee of goodly size had been specially prepared for the occasion, made of sacks, driftwood and old lumber. Preparations made, tom toms ready, all the belongings of both sides were placed under the control of the referee. In the event the Puyallups lost they would have to walk home; if the Renton party were the losers, they would have no home left to receive them.

In a short time the cabin became filled with smoke and seeing or breathing became difficult. This went unnoticed. They presented a truly uncanny sight— painted, decked out with wild holly, cedar bark and red and white berries. That was about all they did have on, for the principal part of their attire had been wagered and staked in the prize pile in an adjoining room.

The opposing leaders sat at each end of the long mat. At a given signal the Renton braves began sounding their tom toms and all their crowd set up a wild chant. Doctor Jack was chosen to start the game for them. When he began to handle the cedar chips and fleecy bark he let out a yell that could be heard a mile; then all his adherents took up the cry and chanted it over and over again, keeping time with the tom toms and moving their bodies to and fro and waving their hands in unison. Doctor Jack also kept time in all his movements. He seized a double handful of bark pulp and placed it before him and then counted out eight white chips and one black one, nine in all. These he clicked in his hands a few times and covered them over with the pulp. Then, placing four chips in one hand and five in the other, he wrapped them in pulp and proceeded to shuffle the two balls thus made in front of him with a dexterity scarcely credible. Though the movement was changed frequently and kept up with remarkable quickness, the Puyallups watched and waited; not a movement of the dealer escaped them. In one of the balls of pulp was the black chip and this was the one they wanted to keep their eyes on, for if they were able to pick it out they could score a point. Suddenly one Puyallup brave waved his hand and Doctor Jack ceased moving the balls; the music stopped. The ball of pulp designated by the Puyallup brave was opened by Doctor Jack, who, by a clever manipulation of the wrist and fingers, sent the hidden chips rolling down the mat before him. The black chip was in the ball, and the Puyallups had won the first point in the great game. The Cedar and Black Rivers were now quiet, but the Puyallups gave vent to a yell that was simply appalling. It was now Johnny Wrinkles' deal, and when he began manipulating the chips and pulp his retinue started their chant. The noise of their tom toms was somewhat livelier than that of the other tribes. First victory inclined on one side and then on the other, and after ten points had been won, five by each side, lo and behold! Old Seatcum, the scorer, had not a sign of a count. A great clamor was raised by the young bucks when this discovery was made, but the older braves pacified the excited ones by declaring that Seatcum was not asleep; that he was counting properly. It was then explained that should one side win one or more sticks the other side could not score until it had won them back. The tribe to win must score the whole sixty-six sticks.

The contest began Monday night and was continued without intermission until the following Saturday morning, five nights and four days, and ended in a draw. At one time the Puyallups had fifty-three sticks and their opponents only thirteen, but a few hours later the latter had regained all but eighteen of the precious markers. During the whole contest the Puyallups were in the lead but could never make the coveted sixty-six. After 110 hours of play the game was a tie and by mutual consent was called off.

The potlatch was a part of the regular program or entertainment. It was a ceremony to which invitations were issued the same as any social event. Personal property and also money was given away. By giving away his property the host hoped also to attain a reputation for liberality and to increase his chance of one day becoming a chief. The distribution took place in true Christmas style. The blankets and goods to be given away were stacked in a heap near the fireplace, just opposite the door. The host held up the present and called the guest's name who was to receive it, and an attendant stood ready to deliver it. Each guest was remembered according to his own distribution in the past, or those which he was expected to make in the future. It was one man's duty to tear the rolls of calico, muslin, flannel or whatever cloth it might be, into strips about a yard in length. In early days it was the custom to also tear the blankets into like strips, but the whites persuaded them to abandon this wasteful practice, so in time they were only cut apart into single blankets.

As late as 1850 the attire of the natives, even in winter, was little more than stark nakedness. By 1860 it had become a modified form of the white man's costume. The males were not so particular, their chief garb being trousers, shirt and shoes, and sometimes a hat. Many of the older and more conservative of the males still wore only breech clouts and blankets. This was Chief Seattle's favorite garb to the last. The women were more particular and usually went about clothed in white woman's attire.

Much has been written of the beauty of the Indian race, especially of the maidens. Of course the young were more comely than their elders, but what little beauty they possessed soon faded. The young women might have retained their good looks much longer were it not for the prevailing custom of early marriages which forced motherhood upon girls at ages of twelve to fifteen.

The custom of flattening the heads of the infants was practiced quite generally for many years after the advent of the white settlers, but gradually went into disuse.

Sanitation among them was practically unknown and disease and filth prevailed everywhere they made their habitations. Most of the pioneers remember the ceremonies attendant upon the making of their doctors; also the noises the latter and their assistants made when treating a patient.

Their sweathouses ornamented the beach just west of First Avenue on the beach above ordinary high tides, prior to the grading of that street. They were used somewhat in times of health, but for the treatment of diseases they were considered a sovereign remedy. They resembled in form the usual potato house on the farm. A hole was dug in the sand about a foot deep; around this a wall of cobble stones was put up about two feet high. This was covered with slabs or wreckage from the beach. In this was left a small opening toward the water for a door. Nearby, in a hot fire, a lot of cobble stones the size of a dinner pail were made red hot. When all was ready the heated stones were moved into the house and drenched with water. On them were spread a layer of green branches and these again watered. Clouds of steam accumulated. While it was almost scalding hot the bather went in and closed the door. Naturally a profuse perspiration followed. The sweating process was continued as long as the occenpant of the hut could endure it, then a rush made for the waters of the bay and a plunge into them.

This custom was pursued, winter and summer. In case of minor ailments no serious results might follow, but when smallpox and measles became epidemic in the Columbia River valleys and on Puget Sound the mortality was frightful. Explanations and remonstrances by the whites were of no avail and went unheeded. The time soon came when there were not enough living to bury their dead. The few survivors abandoned their camps, with their dead, and went elsewhere.

CHERRY STREET, LOOKING EAST, IN JANUARY, 1880

Notwithstanding the abuses that accompanied the reservation system for many years, no doubt it did much to preserve the remnants of the tribes from extinction. White man's habits never took kindly to the Indian and it was far better for the latter that he should be removed as much as possible from the demoralization attendant upon intercourse between the two races.

CHAPTER V

SEATTLE'S MOSQUITO FLEET

Many notable American writers, in poetry and prose, have recorded the activities of the conventional stage coach of the Great West and the characteristics and social amenities of its driver. Today no wild west show is thought complete without the old-time lumbering vehicle with its leather springs and driver's seat, perched high in front over the boot, and with from four to six spirited horses attached. The part played by these ships of the plains in the development of the states west of the Mississippi River has been perpetuated in fiction and in history.

On Puget Sound, with the exception of Olympia and Steilacoom, both of which were from the first accessible by good roads, the canoe, the sail boat and the small steamer took the place of the stage coach. In early days Seattle was practically without roads and outlying points in the county were difficult of access except on foot or on horseback. For this reason more space may be properly given to the history of Seattle's Mosquito Fleet than would be otherwise admissible.

The mails of the Pacific Coast came from New York by ocean steamer to San Francisco, and from San Francisco to Portland and Puget Sound by similar craft; while all along the Sound from Olympia to Victoria and to Bellingham and intermediate ports, all sorts of water craft delivered the mails and transported passengers and distributed to the settlers all the necessaries of life not produced in the forest or on the little patches of ground that had been laboriously reclaimed for it.

The arrival of the steamer, for a long time only once a week, each way, was a notable event and nearly all the men who could spare the time were on the dock when her lines were made fast. In Seattle, Monday was market day for the nearby farmers as the mail steamer bringing letters and weekly papers giving intelligence from the outside world arrived from Olympia sometime in the middle of the afternoon. It did not then require a large motor-driven truck to transport the mailsacks from the boat to the postoffice. For years there were but one small locked pouch and one sack of newspapers that any able bodied man could carry on his shoulders.

Seattle's matchless harbor may be said to have produced its own business; its location made it impossible for any other city on the Sound in the days before the railway to wrest from it its supremacy in the local trade, and it was from this trade that Seattle derived its first nourishment. When one looks back with the wisdom lent him by safe contemplation of an accomplished fact, it is hard to realize why the obvious advantage of Seattle's location over other localities was not taken advantage of by the men who chose Tacoma as the terminus for the Northern Pacific and to those others who pinned their faith to the

100

recorded the
id the char-
rest show is
ather springs
from four to
the plains in
een perpetu-

oom both of
the sail boat
days Seattle
re difficult or
space may be
uld be other-

an steamer to
ound by sim-
nd to Belling
the mails and
ssaries of life
that had been

each way, we
were on the
arket day is
ly papers gi-
ometime in the
riven truck
ars there we
ny able bod-

own business
d in the d-
ade, and it w-
one looks ba-
ished fact. it
ver other la-
as the termi-
ir faith to

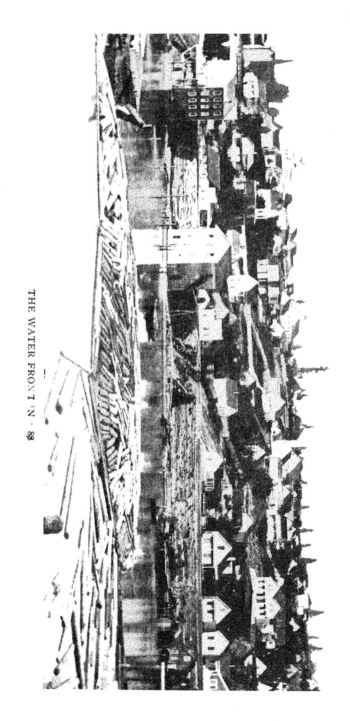

THE WATER FRONT IN · 89

ultimate importance of other Puget Sound points. It is quite certain that Seattle's natural advantage was apparent to some but they wanted to enrich themselves from dishonest profits on terminus town lots. The only farms of the district in those days were along the banks of the rivers, and on a few of the islands. On the Duwamish, the Snohomish, the Skagit, the LaConner Flats, then and now the richest farming lands in all America, and on Whidby Island were farmers whose trade was a great asset to the settlement that received it. The mills of Kitsap County and the scores of logging camps were the chief source of business until comparatively recent years. To reach these localities from any point on the Sound other than Seattle, Seattle had to be passed. Commerce will not deliberately flow past an open door and Seattle held her portals wide. The mosquito fleet in those early days spread over all the Sound and laid their cargoes on Seattle's water front. Today flags of all the nations that send men down to the sea to take and fetch the products of the world fly from masts in Seattle's harbor.

The whole country about Seattle was a dense forest in the beginning to which the hardy woodsmen from New England, Michigan and Minnesota flocked with their axes. They had the enterprise which coined the forest into money. Cut off through lack of railroads from the market in the eastern states they sought outlet for their product in foreign lands and from Puget Sound sailed "windjammers" to all parts of the world where the straight spars and magnificent lumber that Seattle and the surrounding country had in abundance found a ready market.

Vessels began to navigate the Sound quite extensively as early as 1850 but the first export business of Seattle was a cargo of piles for the brig Leonesa. The cargo was completed in the winter of 1851-52 with the aid of a yoke of oxen driven along the beach from Puyallup. At about the same time the ship G. W. Kendall was sent from San Francisco to Puget Sound for ice. But in the hope of getting a cargo of this luxury the master was disappointed. He reported that the Puget Sound waters did not freeze and consoled the owners of the ship by returning with a valuable cargo of piles from Seattle.

These first shipments consisted chiefly of squared timbers, piles, ships' knees, and later after Henry L. Yesler had built the first steam sawmill near the present site of Pioneer Place, sawn timbers and lumber.

Port Blakeley, Port Orchard and Port Madison all built large vessels in the early days. These points across the Sound were like suburbs of Seattle, for all of them did their shopping and marketing here. Like the street cars of today, which bundle the suburbanites off to the city markets every Saturday evening and return them to their homes in the outlying districts, loaded down with provisions for the week, the water craft of pioneer days were the public service vehicles, which brought the shoppers to the Seattle market.

The vessels of Seattle's early mosquito fleet were the miniature mail order houses which supplied the settlers with their conveniences and small luxuries. Their masters were the friends of the village people. They carried with them a store of pithy yarns, a large fund of the latest gossip and a good word for old and young. When their vessels arrived in port the townsfolk were at the wharf to give them a hearty greeting and learn of the last events along the Sound. If grandmother wanted a skein of yarn or if the village belle needed a yard of blue ribbon to match, the captain knew exactly where the articles were to be had, and when his ship came in on the return voyage it brought a store of good will to everyone.

From these small beginnings developed the great freight trade which has established Seattle as the center of commerce in the Northwest today.

San Francisco's sudden growth after the gold discovery in California sent vessels to Puget Sound for timbers. Cargoes of timber squared for sills, plates, bridge timbers, etc., left Elliott Bay each summer before the Indian uprising of 1855-6.

Among the early vessels which carried the cargoes prepared for them by the axes of Seattle's pioneers were the American brigs George Emery, Orbit, G. W. Kendall, Leonesa, John Davis, Franklin Adams, Daniel, Jane, Eagle; American schooners, Exact, Damariscove, Franklin, Susan Sturgis, Mary Taylor, Cynosure, Mexican, Cecil; British vessels, Mary Dare, Alice, Honolulu Packet; American bark Brontes. Later came the ship John Brewer from London, ship Persia from San Francisco, schooner Northern Light, brig Sophia, brig James Marshall and the bark Alabama.

On account of the large shipments to San Francisco late in 1853, Seattle's lumber trade began to assume definite proportions. Capt. A. B. Gove, master of the ship Potomac, arranged with the owners of the vessel in San Francisco to have it visit the ports of Puget Sound regularly instead of periodically as it had been doing before. Early in 1853 the schooners Mary, Rover, Whatcom, William Allen, the ship Tuskina, several barks and the British iron schooner Alice were doing an active business on the Sound.

The same year saw the departure of the bark Louisiana, Alfred Drew master, the first vessel to leave for China with a cargo of ship spars. The bark Mary Adams, Captain Harding, soon followed her lead with Singapore as her destination.

By 1854 there were four regular lines operating on the Sound, and touching at Seattle.

P. B. Barstow & Company's line of packets operated the brig Kingsbury, the clipper bark Mary Melville. The Seward line of packets ran the ship Sarah Parker, the brig Merchantman and the schooner Willimantic; Merritt and Gove operated the Live Yankee, Yankee Doodle and Yanky Nation; and the firm of Kendall & Company owned and operated several ships.

Among the vessels on the Sound in the fall of 1854 were the following: Steamer Major Tompkins, Hunt, master; brig Cyclops, McDonald, master; steamer Active, Alden, master; Harriet Thompson, Birdslee, master; bark Success Coupe, master; bark Julia Ann, Pound, master; brig Consort, Wash, master; Kaluna, Cavellish, master; I. P. Foster, Wiggins, master; brig Francisco, Smith, master; bark Louisa, Johnson, master; steamer Fairy, Gove, master; sloop Sarah Stone, Slater, master; bark Sarah Warren, Gove, master; clipper bark Live Yankee, A. W. Gove, master; bark Russell, Wilson, master; brig Chauncey; ship Nile; brig Wellingsby; revenue cutter Jeff Davis, Pease, captain; bark Powhattan; frigate Pique, Nicholson, master; steamer Virago, Marshall, master; sloop Rob Roy, McLean, master; schooner Harriet, Bowden, master; frigate president, Burtridge,. commander; (The President, Pique and Virago were British men-of-war that lately had encountered the Russians at Petropolovski;

they had brought the Russian vessel Sitka to Victoria as a prize) ; brig I. B. Brown, Myham, master; brig Carbon, Sampson, master; schooner B. B. Potter, fishing vessel; bark Ella Francis, Mitchell, master; schooner Willimantic, Boyling, master; brig E. D. Wolf, Kanes, master; ship Mason, Wilkinson, master; bark Mary Melville, Darby, master; bark Brontes, Ludberg, master; bark Rio Grande; brig Merchantman, Pray, master; brig George Emery, Diggs, master.

Thus within less than a decade Puget Sound had become a haven of white sails and Seattle had established herself as the center of activity. But in September, 1854, an undertaking was set afoot on Puget Sound which meant the beginning of the end of the supremacy of these vessels on its waters. The men who were busy laying the corner stone of a future Seattle found that the presence of a regular steamer would be required to handle the rapidly increasing commerce on the Sound. They needed something more than speedy sailing vessels and something different from the snail-like policy which was content with the changeable winds and tides. They had already suffered materially from the want of such a vessel. In transportation of live stock they had been forced to use flat-bottomed boats and scows, often under inconvenient, tedious and even dangerous circumstances. Instead of the tall masts hewn from the forests on the hills, furnaces and boilers were destined to hold the supremacy among Seattle shipbuilders.

Still the sails and spars did not altogether disappear. For years sailing vessels of every description have been important carriers in the coal, fish and lumber trade of the Sound. Today they may be seen at any time plying in and out among the great sea-going steamers which ride at anchor in Seattle's harbor.

The appearance of the first steamboat on Puget Sound to engage in local traffic was as noticeable an incident in its way as the advent of the Claremont on the Hudson River about fifty years earlier.

Both effected a revolution in marine traffic, one world wide, the other locally.

For years after the first white men arrived here the Indian canoe, propelled by paddles, or by sail, if the wind was fair, was almost the only means of communication between the different ports. Later, sloops, broad of beam and capable of carrying a large area of sail, came into common use.

The pioneer steamer of Puget Sound and indeed of the Pacific Ocean, was the Beaver. To my mind no other craft has ever floated on any sea around which so much romantic interest centers.

When the race came off in which the America won the cup that England's greatest designers and most gallant sportsmen have tried so often to recover, after the announcement of the America's victory, the question was asked: "What boat was second?" The reply was, "There was no second, your Majesty"

So it was with the Beaver. There was no second to her. She was in a class by herself. She was built at the same period the first American missionaries came to Oregon, 1834, though she was not launched until 1835. She was an old boat when gold was discovered in California.

She was built at Blackwell, on the River Thames, five or six miles down stream from the old London Bridge and of oak throughout. Few, if any of the notable craft that have been launched since that day have attracted a tithe of the attention accorded to her during her construction or at her launching. From the day her keel was laid until she went down the English Channel on her way to the Western Ocean, that had never felt the throb of paddle or propeller, she was the object of close and kindly interest. King William and a host of the nobility of England, surrounded by 150,000 of all classes of people, were present at the launching. But little was known about steam marine navigation at that time and the coast of the North Pacific was also almost unknown save to a few traders and whalers. It seemed an act of heroic daring for those on board her to venture out in a craft so tiny to a mysterious and almost unknown region on the other side of the world.

Her machinery was placed in position, but her sidewheels were not attached, so she was fitted out with sails, brig rigged and made the long voyage under canvas by the way of Cape Horn and the Hawaiian Islands, with Captain Horne in command. The bark Columbia sailed with her, as consort, and although the Beaver was much speedier than the other they kept together most of the time. The voyage from England to the mouth of the Columbia River lasted 163 days and no serious accident happened to either of the vessels.

The Beaver lost but little time in sailing up the Columbia to Fort Vancouver. Carpenters were at once set to work putting the paddles in place and getting the craft ready for service. At 4 P. M. May 16, 1836, steam was raised and the engines tried and found to be in good condition. At daylight, Tuesday, May 17, they unmoored the ship and got steam up. At 3.30 A. M. weighed anchor and ran down stream several miles for firewood.

The shores of the lordly Columbia at Vancouver echoed the first puffs of steam and the beat of the paddles of the first steamer on either shore of the Pacific. The next few weeks were occupied in painting the upper works and in making sundry excursions up and down the Columbia and up the "Wilhammet" as the river is spelled in the log of the Beaver.

In Parker's "Exploring Tour Beyond the Rocky Mountains," on page 325 is the following:

"On the 14th of June we took a water excursion on the steamboat Beaver, Captain Horne, down the Columbia to the confluence of the western branch of the Multnomah, and through it into the Columbia and back to the fort. All the low lands were overflowed by the annual freshet, and presented the appearance of an immense bay, extending far into the country. The day was pleasant and our company cheerful. The novelty of a steamboat on the Columbia awakened a train of prospective reflections upon the probable changes which would take place in these remote regions in a very few years. It was wholly an unthought of thing when I first contemplated this enterprise, that I should find here this forerunner of commerce and business. The gayety which prevailed was often suspended while we conversed of coming days when with civilized men all the rapid improvements in the arts of life should be introduced over this new world, and when cities and villages shall spring up on the west, as they are springing up on the east of the great mountains, and a new empire shall be added to the kingdoms of the earth."

These people went up the river nearly where the City of Portland now stands, and from the decks of a steamer making the same run now can be seen the homes of nearly three hundred thousand people. The paragraph above contained a remarkable prophecy.

June 26, 1836, the Beaver crossed the bar outward bound, never again to

THE STEAMER BEAVER

propeller,
host of the
ere presen:
ion at that
e to a few
board her
n region on

ot attached
oyage under
ith Captain
onsort, and
gether most
ambia River
vessels.
Vancouver.
d getting the
ised and the
day, May 17,
1 anchor and

first puffs of
shore of the
works and in
"Wllhammet"

on page 32:

nboat Beaver.
ern branch of
the fort. Al
ed the appear-
y was pleasar
olumbia awai:
; which wou:
ras wholly ac
I should fi:
hich prevaile:
with civilize
luced over the
west, as the
empire shall b

Portland no
ow can be see
iragraph abov

never again "

re-enter that river, and steamed away to the north. At this time nearly all this Northwest was under the control of the Hudson's Bay Company, either by lease from the Russians or under grant from the English government, and that company had almost a monopoly in the fur trade and in traffic with the Indians. Into this service the Beaver went at once, running up the coast to Sitka and in and out of every bay, river and inlet between that port and Puget Sound.

The following about her appears in a letter from Mr. Edward Huggins, who then lived at Fort Nisqually with his wife, who was a daughter of John Work, mentioned by him. He says:

"December 3, 1836, the Beaver came to Fort Nisqually and received on board Mrs. John Work and family, who had a few weeks before made the journey from Vancouver via the Cowlitz River, by canoes and across the country on horseback, and were now going to join Mr. Work at Fort Simpson which is several hundred miles to the northward of Victoria, where he was in command of the fort and the company's business at that point.

"The Beaver, of course, burned wood, and always kept a corps of men, ten, I think, as wood choppers, and old John McLeod and Joseph Legard, now living in the neighborhood of Fort Nisqually, were of the company of choppers for some time.

"Her engines were built by the celebrated firm of Bolton & Watts, and were models of strength and solidity. Her paddle wheels were small and set far forward. She carried a crew of thirty men, an armament of four six-pounders and was extensively supplied with small arms. The decks were protected by boarding nettings to prevent access by the natives otherwise than by the gangways, and more than thirty Indians were never allowed on deck at one time, unless they were accompanied by their wives and children.

"After paying for herself several times over she was thought too small and slow for the company's business so they brought out the Otter, a propeller, in 1851. The Beaver continued in the company's service for some years, but was eventually sold and put into service as a tugboat."

In 1851, while in command of Captain Steward, she made a trip over to the American side, where she was seized and taken to Olympia for alleged infraction of our revenue laws. Her captain watched his opportunity and put the watchmen ashore then made haste to get out of American waters. The trouble ended there, for it was not long until she was plying freely on this side the line. During the Indian war the Beaver and Otter were placed at the disposal of the territorial authorities several times and were used to much advantage.

In 1860 she was turned into a passenger boat and placed on the run between Victoria and New Westminster, and a few years later she was chartered for use in coast surveys of British Columbia waters, continuing in this service until late in 1870. She had now been afloat and in hard service for a generation, so was hauled out and given thorough repairs. Her timbers were as sound as when she was launched, but in one of them was found embedded a piece of rock weighing ten pounds that she had picked up one time when she had meddled with Race Rocks. A less substantial craft would have had her hull crushed like an eggshell at that time.

In 1874 she was again refitted and turned into a towboat, and a few weeks later the Hudson's Bay Company sold her to a private firm. She continued in the towing business until 1888, having had severe usage most of the time, and one time burned nearly to the water's edge. The latter year she again took out a license as a passenger boat and went into that business on Burrard's Inlet.

In July of that year she ran on the rocks at the entrance of Vancouver harbor. Negotiations were begun by a company to purchase her, which intended to place her on exhibition. However, on inspection it was found that memento seekers had nearly pulled her to pieces, and the idea was abandoned. Soon after, in a gale of wind, the battered old hulk slid from her perch upon the rocks and went to the bottom.

It was more than seventeen years after the arrival of the Beaver before an American steamboat went into service here in Seattle.

The steamer Fairy, D. J. Gove, master, arrived at Olympia the night of October 31, 1853. Captain Gove had just brought her from San Francisco on the bark Sarah Warren.

Her advertisement appeared November 12th, giving dates of departures and arrivals; also agents, who were: Philip Keach, Steilacoom; Charles C. Terry, Alki; Arthur A. Denny, Seattle. Fare from Olympia to Seattle $10.00.

The Major Tompkins was the next to arrive. She was a propeller of seagoing qualities. She was built in Philadelphia in 1847 and went to New Orleans and ran from that place until 1850. That year she went to New York and from there came to San Francisco. She ran for a time on the Sacramento River in opposition to the regular line, but was soon bought off. In 1854 John H. Scranton and James M. Hunt secured a contract to carry the United States mails on Puget Sound and bought her for the service. It took her about three weeks to make the trip from the Bay City to Olympia. She arrived at the latter place September 20, 1854, and was welcomed with great rejoicings at Seattle, and all the ports along the Sound where she traveled. Her career was even shorter and as disastrous as that of her predecessor. February 25, 1855, while entering Victoria Harbor, she was wrecked, becoming a total loss except a portion of her machinery. While not engaged on her regular run she did some towing of sail vessels in and out from the Sound and therefore was the first American vessel to do this kind of work.

The Water Lily, a sidewheeler, only forty-nine feet long, was built in San Francisco in 1853, and brought to the Sound on a sailing vessel by Capt. William Webster, in January, 1855. He was then opening a coal mine on the bank of Black River and used her in towing scows from the mine to Seattle. She was snagged and sunk almost immediately after going to work.

Soon after the sinking of the Tompkins the Fairy went on the run from Olympia to Seattle, with mails and passengers under the command of Capt. Charles C. Terry.

The Pioneer and Democrat of October 26, 1855, says: "Through the enterprise of Mr. John G. Parker of this place, a small but neat and comfortable steamer has been placed upon the waters of the Sound, to ply between this point and Seattle; also to carry the United States mail. Mr. Parker will command her and we heartily wish that the public would give him a good support. The long absence of steam communication on the Sound has been seriously felt and the arrival of the Traveler was universally hailed with joy."

This was the first appearance of Capt. John G. Parker in the role of a steamboat man on Puget Sound although he arrived in Olympia in 1853, and had been engaged in merchandising and the express business. Down to the time of his retirement from active service he was the best known steamboat man on Puget Sound, and his sons, Gilmore and Herbert Parker, both steamboat men, later became almost as well known.

The Traveler was built at Philadelphia in the early '50s and brought around the Horn in sections and set up at San Francisco. She was an iron propeller and was loaded on the brig J. B. Brown and brought to Port Gamble. The Traveler ran between Olympia and Seattle going one way each week and stopping at all intermediate points. She was very serviceable during the continuance of the Indian war and Captain Parker did good work in command of her until its close. To her belongs the honor of being the first steamboat to navigate the White, Snohomish and Nooksack rivers.

William N. Horton, another well known pioneer of Olympia, served as engineer on the Traveler most of the time Parker owned her until 1857 when he bought the vessel and took over the command. Early in March, 1858, she was again on the route from Olympia to Port Townsend, carrying mails and passengers, having been for some time under charter to the Indian department. She left Port Townsend March 3d for Port Gamble in command of Capt. Thomas Slater with six white men and two Indians on board. Near Foulweather Bluff she encountered a severe storm and anchored under the lee of the bluff to await better weather. During the night she sprung a leak and began settling so rapidly that nothing could be done to save her. Warren, the engineer, and the two Indians swam ashore, while the others stayed with the vessel a little too long and sank with her. They were Thomas Slater, captain; Truman H. Fuller, purser; Mr. Stevens, a passenger, and two deck hands, names unknown.

Late in August, 1857, the Constitution, a small ocean-going steamer, arrived to run between Olympia and Victoria. She was 165 feet long.

There was a fatality connected with the early mail service on Puget Sound, for disaster soon overtook every steamer engaged in it for years. This new one was no exception. The Constitution began running on the Olympia-Victoria route soon after her arrival, Hunt, one of the partners in the mail contract, serving as master. John L. Butler, who continued in service on Puget Sound waters for over thirty years, was pilot and Charles E. Williams, one of Olympia's leading merchants for many years afterward, was purser.

The mail contract brought in $36,000 per year, but the other business was not large, and the steamer was an expensive one to run, so that in a few months she was sold at auction by the United States marshal for a pittance. Later she was dismantled and her hull turned into a sailing vessel. As a barkentine she went into the lumber carrying trade from Puget Sound mills and did excellent service for many years.

A few weeks before the Constitution steamed away from San Francisco the steamer Sea Bird, Capt. Francis Conner, made her appearance at Olympia, under engagement to carry the mails on the Sound. She went on the route from Olympia to Bellingham Bay instead of to Victoria. The Fraser River mines were attracting attention at this time and Bellingham Bay had a thriving city on its shores for some months in 1858.

About June 1st she left the Sound run and went into business on the Fraser

River. On her down trip she grounded on a bar and was not released until September 2d, after the rush to the mines was nearly ended. Five days later, while en route from Victoria to Fort Langley on the Fraser, she caught fire and was totally destroyed.

The Resolute, the pioneer steam tug, arrived at Port Madison May 6th, a short time prior to the Sea Bird's leaving.

This craft had a history of her own. She became identified with milling and shipping interests, and wherever a boom of logs or a vessel was to be towed between Budd's Inlet and Neah Bay she was a frequent visitor.

George A. Meigs, of Port Madison mills, and Pope and Talbot, of Port Gamble mills, bought her in partnership and brought her from San Francisco to Puget Sound. She came up under command of Captain Pray, who ran her for a few months and was then succeeded by Capt. I. M. Guindon. Her length was 89 feet, beam 17½ feet, and depth 9 feet 4 inches. She was devoted to the towage business exclusively, and though a small craft, was exceedingly powerful.

In October she came in collision with the Pacific Mail Steamship Company's Northerner about midway between Steilacoom and Olympia. Both boats were injured and the ensuing lawsuit became a celebrated case in the courts.

In August, 1868, while towing a boom of logs, her boiler exploded, killing or drowning all but the captain and one other, and sinking the boat.

The Eliza Anderson made her first appearance on Puget Sound in March, 1858. She was built at Portland, Oregon, for the Columbia River Steam Navigation Company, consisting of Richard Hoyt, S. G. Reed, Benjamin Stark, Richard Williams, J. C. Graham and W. B. Wells. Her keel was laid in 1857 and about eighteen months were consumed in her construction the launching taking place November 27, 1858. Early in 1859 John T. Wright and Bradford Brothers bought her and she was brought around to the Sound under command of Capt. J. G. Hustler.

The Anderson was in type a sea-going vessel and the finest one on the Sound fitted for the work. She was 140 feet long, 24 feet 6 inches beam, 8 feet 10 inches hold, 279 tons register; low pressure vertical or "walking beam" engine. For many years she could do twelve knots an hour if necessary, but usually jogged along at about nine.

On her arrival, Capt. John Fleming took charge and she began a career of money making interspersed with vicissitudes that made her name a household word in marine circles for forty years. During the first fifteen she was a traveling bank and a floating gold mine. Probably no other craft of her small size and low speed ever made as much money for her owners. In the early days the fare on her from Olympia to Seattle was $6.50; to Port Townsend, $12.50 and to Victoria, $20.00. Horses and cattle paid $15.00 per head; sheep and hogs. $2.50; freight from $5.00 to $10.00 by measurement. If a wagon were shipped standing, the tongue left extended, the measurement was from tip of tongue to end of reach; and from deck to top of standards. No opportunity to turn an honest penny was neglected.

She ran almost continuously for twelve years. She often had opposition and fares for a time went down to almost nothing. It happened several times that 50 cents would pay one's way the full length of the run. In succession the Enterprise, Alexandria, Josie McNear, New World and Wilson G. Hunt made a vigorous fight for the business, but were one after the other bought off or run off. The Anderson had made so much money for her owners that they were practically invincible. Most of these boats came from the Columbia River and in due course those bought by the Anderson's owners were sent back there or to the Sacramento, where the Oregon Steam Navigation Company, or the California Steam Navigation held a monopoly, and before the ensuing war was ended the Anderson's owners had recouped any losses they had sustained by temporary opposition on the Sound.

About 1870 she was relieved from regular service by Captain Finch's new steamer, the Olympia. When the Starrs secured the mail contract, about 1872, Captain Finch was subsidized to withdraw his steamers from Puget Sound and was guaranteed the sum of $18,000 per annum to do so. The Anderson was tied up at her dock in Olympia and kept there as a watchdog, while Captain Finch or his attorneys collected $1,500 a month for four years. It was a regular event for John B. Allen, later United States senator from the State of Washington, to be seen staggering under the weight of this sum, mostly in silver, on his way to George A. Barnes' bank to deposit to the credit of Captain Finch.

About 1882, while lying at the wharf in Seattle, she sprung a leak and was sunk, but was raised without much difficulty and the next year was given an overhauling which disclosed the fact that her timbers were still perfectly sound. This was quite generally commented on by the public press as confirmation of claims made by shipbuilders of the value of fir timber for their uses. Capt. Tom Wright, one of the numerous brothers of that name, put her on the run from Seattle to New Westminster. He served as captain, E. W. Holmes, mate, and Orion O. Denny, engineer.

Wright kept her going for two or three years, but in 1885 became involved in difficulties with the customs authorities on a charge of carrying contraband Chinamen, and whether guilty or not, the delays and expenses of the suit drove him and the Anderson out of business.

Until 1886 she remained the property of the Wrights and Capt. D. B. Finch, but was then bought by the Washington Steamboat Company and later by the Puget Sound & Alaska Steamship Company. The latter stored her away, and to the best of my recollection she remained out of service until the "Klondike rush" came, when she was again repaired after a fashion, and sent up north. She was overtaken by disaster, and her bones found their last resting place at Dutch Harbor or somewhere in that vicinity.

During her long career on Puget Sound she was commanded by Capts. John Fleming, Thomas Wright, D. B. Finch, Charles Clancy, Wm. J. Waitt, Daniel Morrison, David Wallace, McIntosh, Tarte, Holmes, Jackson and many others.

The tug Goliah was an old vessel when she went into service on the Sound in 1871, under command of Capt. William Hayden. She was built about 1848 for Vanderbilt and Webb for the towage business about New York Harbor. Soon after she was sold, but before the new owners could get away on the trip around the Horn for San Francisco the vessel was seized by the United States marshal. One morning he waked to find the vessel and himself at sea. He was put ashore at St. Thomas, where the tug was coaled and provisioned. She reached San Francisco in safety and ran there some time in the passenger business and again in the towing service for about a dozen years. In 1871 she was bought by Pope & Talbot and brought to Puget Sound.

After Captain Hayden left her she was in charge of Captains Noyes, McCoy, Butler and S. D. Libby, under the latter for twelve years. Then came Captains Selby, Clements and Williamson. Until the Tacoma Mill Company put its powerful tug Tacoma into service the Goliah had towed most of the sailing vessels from the straits into British Columbia waters as well as into Puget Sound. She was laid up finally about 1894, after nearly a half century of continuous service.

The hull of a large stern-wheel steamer was built on Puget Sound in 1859 for the Fraser River and Puget Sound traffic, but was towed around to the Columbia River and in due time put in opposition to the regular line on the Cascade route. In a short time she was bought off, and then brought back to the Sound and set to work carrying the mails between Olympia and Victoria during the summer of 1859, then taken back to the Columbia. She was first called the Julia Barclay, soon shortened to the Julia.

The steamer Ranger No. 2, a side-wheeler only 77 feet long, was built in San Francisco in 1853, and did a jobbing business there until 1859, when Capt. John S. Hill brought her to the Sound and put her into the same line of work. Captain Hill was a pioneer of Seattle. He was married here to Addie Andrews and they had two daughters and a son born here. He was one of the best known men of his profession in the Northwest. At last account he was living in Idaho. The name of the boat was soon changed to Ranger. She continued in service only two or three years, when her machinery was taken out and the hull allowed to go to pieces.

The year 1859 was memorable on the Northwest coast. The gold mines on Fraser River attracted a great many thousand of miners from all parts of the world. At one time there were 10,000 on the shores of Bellingham Bay and other tens of thousands went to the mines by way of Victoria. The Pacific Mail Steamship Company sent every old hulk it owned that could be spared from its regular runs to the Sound with passengers, and every outside steamer was put into the same service. Business was dull on the Sound, so at every opportunity the mail steamer made a trip with a load of miners, regardless of delays to the mail service. In fact, scarcely an issue of the local papers appeared that did not have complaints about the way the mails were handled. The same was true, more or less, down to the time of the completion of the railroad from Kalama to Tacoma.

From early in August, 1859, when the Eliza Anderson began carrying the mails until the appearance of the North Pacific, the Wrights and Finch ruled local marine matters with a rod of iron. If an outsider secured the contract for carrying the mails, he had to make a low bid to get it, and then rates of fare and freight went down to almost nothing. The steamers under lease to the contractor for carrying the mails would be purchased outright by the old company or subsidized to leave the route. The result was in every instance that the mail contract fell into the hands of the old company, opposition ceased and rates were again restored. In the meanwhile the public endured irregular mail service and was burdened with almost prohibitory rates of fare and freight.

Down to 1860 the writer has endeavored to give a brief sketch of every boat

THE PIONEER STEAMER ELIZA ANDERSON

engaged in service on the Sound distinct from the ocean-going craft that came here from San Francisco occasionally. From that date the number increased rapidly.

Two steamers of local historic interest went into service on Puget Sound in 1863, the J. B. Libby and Mary Woodruff. They were the pioneers of Seattle's mosquito fleet.

The Libby was built by William Hammond for Capt. S. D. Libby, half owner, and Charles H. Gorton and Lewis V. Wyckoff, each owner of one-fourth interest, and launched at Utsalady in 1862. She was named after the adopted son of Captain Libby, who in later years became prominent in steamboat and tugboat operations on the Sound, with his headquarters at Seattle and Port Townsend. She was a side-wheeler with high pressure boilers. In 1865 she was taken to Port Ludlow and cut in two about the middle and considerably lengthened. She was among the earliest steamers to run between Seattle and Whatcom. In 1870, she was purchased by John Suffern, Orion O. Denny and John Blythe, and placed upon the run to Bellingham Bay, carrying the United States mails and soon had built up a good business. Among her many captains were John Suffern, George F. Frye, Mark Norton, Samuel Jackson, Thomas Brannan, James Smith, and John Blythe. Later Samuel Coulter was awarded the contract for carrying the mails twice a week from Seattle by way of Coupeville, Coveland, Utsalady and La Conner to Bellingham Bay, and he made a lot of money during his ownership of her. In 1880, Capt. Charles Low bought an interest in her and ran her for a time, was succeeded by W. F. Monroe in 1882, and he by George Frye in 1883. A couple of years later she was secured by Capt. J. M. Brittain who changed her to a propellor and spent a lot of money on her and then put her on the route between Seattle and Neah Bay. Capt. James Morgan was her next owner, who in turn, sold her to Capt. Herbert F. Beecher in 1889. For a few months she was operated in the Roche Harbor lime trade, but in November of that year she caught fire enroute for Port Townsend, and while the hull was towed into port, her destruction was so complete that no attempt was made to rebuild her. Her owners and officers included a large number of men who later became prominent in the business affairs of Seattle, and several of them are still residents here.

Capt. William Hammond, who constructed the Libby, was the leader among the pioneer shipbuilders in Seattle. He was born in Fairhaven, Mass., in 1823, and when a young man learned the trade of naval architect and shipbuilder. He followed his profession at New Bedford, N. Y., and other Atlantic ports until 1858, when he came to Seattle. His first work of importance on the Sound was the steamship John T. Wright which he constructed at Port Ludlow. In addition to the pioneer steamer J. B. Libby he built the Evangel, Nellie, and a large number of well known Puget Sound vessels. Hammond was appointed inspector of hulls in Seattle in 1870, a position which he held for many years. While in office he superintended the construction of the steamer George E. Starr and on retiring from office set afloat a number of other steamers and schooners. He died in Seattle, January 9, 1891. Hammond's shipyard and ways were on the beach where the Post Street power station is now.

The Mary Woodruff, another side-wheeler, was built at Meigs' shipyard in Port Madison for John Swan and Jay E. Smith. Her machinery was taken from the old steamer Ranger. When completed, she was put on the Whatcom route, being the pioneer in the postal service between Seattle and Bellingham Bay. After a short time, she was sold to Capt. John Cosgrove, who was familiarly known all over Puget Sound as "Humboldt Jack." For years previous, he had made at least one round trip daily between Seattle and Port Madison carrying passengers, mails and small articles of freight. The Maria, his sloop or "plunger" as its type was called here in early days, under his first management was never deterred from its daily trip by the most boisterous weather.

With the Mary Woodruff, Captain Cosgrove widened his scope of operations and he soon became a familiar figure in most Puget Sound ports. She carried passengers and freight and often United States mails on several routes, and between times, towed scows, logs and lumber vessels. He thus made a small fortune, and sold his steamer and retired to live ashore. About 1870 Capt. Henry Smith was in charge of her and in 1872, Capt. James R. Williamson bought her to use in connection with his large sawmill that he had built and was then operating about where the ferry boat now lands in West Seattle. He ran her some eight or ten years and then having outlived her usefulness, she was beached near the mill, her machinery taken out and the hull burned. Like the steamer Libby, she had among her owners men who made and lost large fortunes, and were active and prominent in business affairs in Seattle and adjacent ports.

Another pioneer shipbuilder of Seattle was Capt. J. F. T. Mitchell, who during his time completed sixty-four vessels. He came to the Sound in 1862 and ran the schooner Leah from Seattle to Victoria for nine months, when he began building steamers and sailing craft. He constructed the steamer Zephyr, the first passenger stern-wheeler on the Sound, and built the steamer George E. Starr, with Captain Hammond as superintendent of construction. He also completed the Nellie, Cassiar, Queen City, Willie, Seattle, Success and many other famous vessels.

Two small stern-wheelers were constructed on the Sound in 1864, the Black Diamond at Seattle and the Pioneer at Olympia. The Black Diamond was a flat-bottomed boat seventy feet long built originally by Hill & Rabbeson as a schooner, but afterwards fitted up with machinery for the White River trade. According to Capt. Tom Brennan, "It was a deep water voyage from Seattle to Olympia and when Hill, her first captain, set out on such a trip he went round to bid everybody in town good-bye." Captain Hill continued jobbing about the Sound with the vessel for several years and finally disposed of her to the Tacoma Mill Company who in turn sold her to Capt. George W. Gove in August, 1876.

In 1869 and 1870 there were a lot of steamers on the Sound, the largest being the Wilson G. Hunt, Favorite, Anderson and Varuna, until the Olympia was brought out from New York by Captain Finch and the Wrights. She was a side-wheeler, 180 feet long, 30 feet beam and 12½ feet depth of hold, brig rigged, and hull throughout of seasoned white oak. She arrived at Olympia December 3, 1870, and made her first start on the Olympia-Victoria route on the 7th. She was by far the best steamer that had ever engaged in the service, having been designed by men who understood its exact requirements.

During this period events were shaping that resulted in a revolution of marine conditions on Puget Sound, so far as the transportation of mails and passengers was concerned.

One J. T. Nash, possessed of small steamboat experience and little capital, secured the mail contract from Olympia and way ports to Victoria for the next four years. He chartered the Varuna to carry the mail until he could build a steamer for that purpose. The ways were put on the beach at Miller's Point, a couple of miles below Olympia, and there the Alida was built. The Starr brothers had grown wealthy at Portland in the tinners' business, and Nash, having had an acquaintance with them, secured money from them to carry on the work. Before it was done he had been compelled to turn over the boat and mail contract to them for their protection and that of numerous other creditors. Thus the Starrs, who had no previous knowledge of steamboating, got started in a career where they made an immense fortune.

About the 1st of July, 1870, the Alida was thought to be ready for service, and the owners gave an excursion on her to Seattle. The number of guests was large, and the vessel so cranky that she came near capsizing several times during the trip, and many old-timers to this day remember the dangers of the trip.

The Olympia was put on the run in opposition, and her speed and safety combined attracted nearly all the travel. The Starrs felt this keenly and determined to have a boat that would be faster and run more cheaply than the Olympia, so they let a contract to a boat-building firm in San Francisco that embodied these stipulations, among others, for the building of such a craft.

The steamer North Pacific was the result. She arrived at Olympia June 24, 1871. Much interest was taken at Seattle and every port from Olympia to Victoria in the impending race. A short time before she was due to come around, Johnson's Point Captain Finch went over to the high ground at West Olympia with his ship's telescope and there awaited the appearance of the craft whose speed and other sea-going qualities meant so much to him. Before she reached the dock he knew she was faster than his own beautiful boat the Olympia. However, he maintained a confident air and continued the existing opposition.

No good chance for a race offered until the return trip from Victoria, June 27th. The North Pacific made the run from Victoria to Port Townsend in two hours and forty-one minutes, some three or four minutes ahead of her rival. Both parties soon reached the conviction that it was best to compromise. An agreement was arrived at that is related elsewhere in the history of the Eliza Anderson. Later the Olympia was bought by Victorians and rechristened the Princess Louise.

When the Starrs had gained full control of the situation they showed their excellent good sense in not restoring the excessive rates that had theretofore been in force at times of no opposition. A rate was adopted of $2.00 from Olympia to Tacoma or Seattle; to Port Townsend, $3.50; to Victoria, $5.00; meals, 75 cents; berths, $1; rooms from $2 to $5. Capt. Charles Clancey was in charge of the North Pacific nearly all the time until the Starrs sold out to the Oregon Railway & Navigation Company, and until the appearance of the latter company's Alaskan and Olympian on the Sound the North Pacific was the flagship and carried the broom at her masthead.

The New World, one of the finest steamers which had appeared on the Sound, arrived at Olympia from the Columbia River in February, 1867, under command of Capt. Henry Winsor. After a brief period of warm competition with the Eliza Anderson she was found too expensive to run and was purchased by

Captain Finch, who sent her back to California. Two steamers of Puget Sound construction, the Ruby and the Chehalis, made their debut in the same year. The Ruby was a small propellor, built at Snohomish City by Capt. H. H. Hyde, who ran her between Seattle and Snohomish a short time, then sold her to Meigs & Gawley who used her for years as a ferry boat between Port Madison and Seattle. In 1879 she was sold to Dexter Horton & Co., and was afterward used as a freight and jobbing steamer. She was finally purchased by Victoria parties who registered her under the British flag.

The Chehalis was a small stern-wheeler built at Tumwater, in 1867, by H. H. Hyde. After a disastrous experience on the Chehalis River she was operated between Snohomish, Port Gamble and Port Ludlow. She was subsequently sold to the coal company and used for towing barges on Lake Washington. Later Capt. Hiram Olney ran her on the Seattle and Olympia route. She did good service until November, 1882, when she was caught in a gale while en route from Snohomish to Seattle in command of Capt. W. F. Monroe, and becoming unmanageable, was blown stern on to the beach near Ten Mile Point, a total loss. Her cargo was strewn for ten miles along the shore.

Seattle's industries by the early '70s were keeping her mosquito fleet more than busy. In 1870 the value of lumber cut in the vicinity of Seattle had reached $200,000 or double the amount of 1860. The whaling and fishing industry was becoming of substantial value to the Sound ports. The coal industry, though still young, gave great promise of future development. In 1871 shipments from coal mines near Seattle were only 4,918 tons; by 1876 104,556 tons were mined, three-fourths of which was exported.

In the midst of this commercial activity steamboat building, which for a few years had been slightly checked, started in with renewed vigor.

The steamer Zephyr, the first stern-wheeler on Puget Sound was built in Seattle in 1871, by J. F. T. Mitchell for J. R. Robbins for the Seattle and Olympia route; Capt. Thomas A. Wright was her master. Wright remained with her until 1875, when she was turned over to Capt. N. L. Rodgers. Two years later she was sold by the sheriff to M. V. B. Stacey for $3,350.

The first steamboating of Capt. W. R. Ballard, the founder of the suburb of Seattle which bears his name, was on the Zephyr. He became master of the steamer in 1877. A few years later he purchased an interest in her and in 1883 became sole owner. He operated the Zephyr very profitably until 1887, when he sold out to the Tacoma Mill Company and entered other pursuits with a comfortable fortune made in the steamboat business. He became one of the prominent capitalists of Seattle.

Another small stern-wheeler bearing the misleading name of Comet was launched in Seattle, in 1871, by Capt. S. P. Randolph, the first man to operate a steamer on Lake Washington. The Comet was for a long while on the White River trade and ran for several years on nearly all the routes out of Seattle. She went out of commission early in the '80s. Other small steamers built about the same time were the propellor Etta White, built at Freeport, now West Seattle, and the small side-wheeler Clara, launched at Seattle for the Seattle Coal & Transportation Company.

After the Starrs had settled their differences with Finch & Wright, the Puget Sound Steam Navigation Company was incorporated at Olympia in 1871 "for the

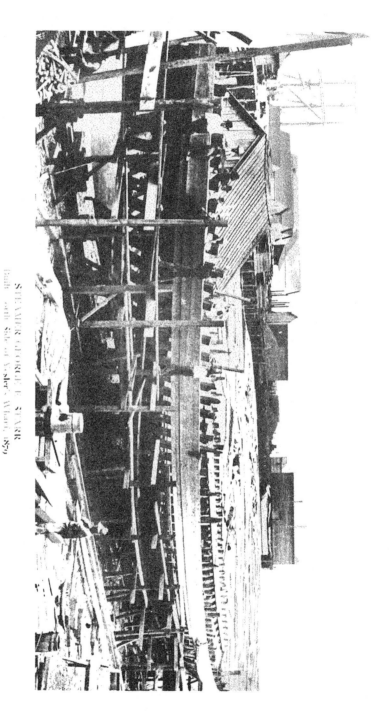

STEAMER "GEORGE S. WRIGHT"

Puget Sound
e same year
H. H. Hyde
. sold her to
Port Madison
as afterward
d by Victoria

1867, by H.
was operated
subsequently
Washington
ate. She di.
gale while e.
Monroe, and
n Mile Poin.

ito fleet more
e had reached
industry wa
ustry, though
ipments from
s were mined.

ich for a fe

l was built
e Seattle an:
ight remaine:
lodgers. Tw
50.

the suburb c
master of it
er and in 18
til 1887, wh
ursuits with
ne one of the

of Comet w:
man to oper
e on the Wh.
out of Seatt
ers built al
ort, now W
for the Seat.

right, the Pug
n 1871 "for t

purpose of navigating the waters of Puget Sound, Admiralty Inlet, Straits of Juan de Fuca, Pacific Ocean and all of Washington." The officers were: J. N. Goodwin, president; Marshall Blinn, vice president; E. A. Starr, secretary and treasurer; L. M. Starr, Cyrus Walker, E. S. Smith, J. W. Sprague, J. B. Montgomery and O. F. Gerrish, directors.

Seattle's increasing importance as the shipping center of the Sound was recognized in the same year when the city was made the headquarters of a government inspection district which included all of Puget Sound. Capt. William Hammond was appointed the first inspector of hulls, and Isaac Parker, the first inspector of boilers. Hammond was later succeeded by Capt. Henry Morgan.

On March 22, 1873, the Merchants Transportation Company was organized at Olympia with a capitalization of $100,000. Seattle was represented on the board of trustees by J. R. Robbins, T. A. Wright and T. S. Russell. Other trustees were James S. Lawson, R. G. O'Brien, S. W. Percival and B. B. Tuttle of Olympia; D. C. H. Rothschild of Port Townsend, and John Latham of Steilacoom. A steamer was secured by the new organization, which raised a slight disturbance on Starr's mail line though the opposition was small. By 1874 Captain Starr had perfected his organization until with Finch and Wright he controlled nearly all of the available steam craft on the Sound. This fleet included the steamers Olympia, North Pacific, Alida, Isabel, Eliza Anderson, Wilson G. Hunt and Otter.

The discovery of gold in the Stikene and in the Cassiar country initiated a boom in steamboating in 1874. In addition the wheat fields of Washington and Oregon were producing crops which needed more vessels to handle them. The output of the coal mines in the vicinity of Seattle, the lumber and fish trade were steadily increasing. A number of small steamers were built at Seattle during the year, the best known of them being the Addie, constructed at the foot of Cherry Street. In 1875 she was taken to Lake Washington to tow barges for the Newcastle Coal Company, remaining there until the railroad was completed, when she was taken back and operated in the jobbing trade by Capt. Mark Norton.

T. W. Lake began the construction of boats in Seattle in 1874. His first product was the steamer Fannie Lake, a fine stern-wheeler built for Diggs & True, who operated her in the White River trade. The following year he built the tug Hope and was active for many years in the construction of steamers in Seattle.

The number of seamen who were granted licenses indicated that the marine business was increasing by leaps and bounds. Shipbuilding had already passed the experimental stage, and in 1874-75 a specialty was made of sailing vessels, a considerable number of which were built to handle the coal trade. Hall Bros. ship yards added several fine vessels to the fleet, the two-masted schooners Anne Lyle, Cassie Hayward, Ida Schnauer, La Geronde and American Girl; the three-masted schooners Emma Utter and Wm. L. Beebe.

On July 21, 1875, the Kate Flickenger, the first three-masted vessel built in Seattle, was launched from Belltown. She was built at a cost of $30,000 under the direction of Capt. S. J. Gilman and was partly owned in San Francisco. She was employed in the coasting trade.

In the summer of 1875 the harbor at Seattle assumed a busier appearance than ever before. At one time there were nine sea-going vessels in port. Three of them loaded with coal from the Newcastle mines, four from the Renton mines and one from the Talbot mine. Two loaded with lumber. On no previous occasion had there ever been more than seven sea-going vessels in the harbor at one time. The business activity and bustle around the wharves was very noticeable and indicated a thrifty and profitable business. A short time before the ship Alaska carried away an aggregate of 2,200 tons of coal and two schooners loaded with building stone arrived. Seattle at this date claimed to be more important commercially than any other place on the Pacific Coast except San Francisco and Portland. Eleven steamers were serving the traveling public. In addition there were many tugs and steamers of the mill companies here almost daily, carrying passengers as well as freight.

The increasing business on the Puget Sound steamboat routes in 1876 opened the field for some of the surplus steamers of the Columbia and Willamette fleet. The steamer Annie Stewart was purchased in May by Capt. L. M. Starr, was brought to Seattle in June and on September 1st carried the first daily mail from Tacoma to Seattle.

About the same time the Puget Sound Transportation Company was incorporated at Olympia with Thomas Macleay, president; A. H. Steele, secretary and treasurer, and J. G. Parker, manager.

The company built the Messenger and operated her on the Seattle route three trips a week. The first run was made on December 17, 1876, Capt. J. G. Parker in command. She was a well built steamer and handled an immense amount of business in the early days. The Parker Bros. handled her for many years. She was destroyed by fire at Tacoma in 1894. Other steamers which appeared in 1876 were the Hyack, the Minnie May and the Nellie. The most pretentious of these was the Nellie, launched from Hammond's shipyard, Seattle, July 22d, for Robbins, Wright & Stretch. She began running between Milton and Seattle and afterwards worked on the Snohomish and Skagit routes.

The Minnie May was built for the Lake Washington trade by Capt. Wm. Jensen. She began the run regularly as a ferry boat across the lake.

At Port Townsend Capt. John C. Hornbeck launched the fine steamer Dispatch. She was later disposed of to Capt. J. N. Brittain who operated her for several years. Brittain sold her to Morgan & Hastings of Port Townsend and while in command of Capt. Dave Hill in 1889 she was burned to the water's edge at Seattle.

The profits of steamboating in Seattle and the Sound were considerably lessened by fierce competition in 1877. The Puget Sound Transportation Company's steamer Messenger was beginning to make it interesting for Starr's line, with a 25 cent fare from Olympia and Tacoma to Seattle, with a free lunch thrown in. Finally a compromise was effected later in the year by which Starr received a subsidy of $500 a month to withdraw the Otter from the Upper Sound route, giving the owners of the Zephyr and Messenger full swing except on that part of the Sound where Captain Brittain had the mail contract. Brittain's line at this time included the steamers Teaser, Dispatch and Comet.

But by far the most important event for Seattle, in 1877, was the organization of the Pacific Coast Steamship Company which today continues to be one of Seattle's largest shipping concerns. The company was successor to the Goodall

& Perkins steamship line and was organized with Charles Goodall, president; John Rosenfeld, vice president; Geo. C. Perkins, treasurer, and Edwin Goodall, secretary. Its original fleet included the side-wheel steamships Mohongo, Orizaba, Senator and Ancon; the propellers, Los Angeles, San Luis, Santa Cruz, Monterey, Gypsy, Donald, Salinas, Idaho, Vincent and Constantine.

The steamer Josephine, a stern-wheeler of about eighty tons burden, was set afloat at Seattle, in 1878, and a week later the Gem was launched from an adjoining yard. By a singular coincidence both steamers met their fate five years later at nearly the same time. The Gem was built for Capt. George W. Gove who used her mostly for towing. She was destroyed by fire off Appletree Cove, February 7, 1883, when five people lost their lives. The Josephine was constructed for the Skagit River trade by J. W. Smith at Lake's Yard, North Seattle. Her boiler exploded January 16, 1883, killing eight people. The hull was comparatively uninjured and was repaired in March and purchased by Moran Brothers.

While Puget Sound was not yet engaged in exporting wheat her foreign lumber fleet in 1877 was as large as the Columbia River grain fleet. In the assessment roll for the year the value of the fleet owned by the mill companies was given as $318.300. represented by thirty-one vessels. During the year 1872 cargoes were sent from Seattle and other mill ports with sixty-five vessels engaged in the trade.

The story of the years that followed is one of remarkable advancement and steady expansion in Seattle's trade. An exporting business, which at first was limited mostly to cargoes of lumber and coal, extended to grain export and all the lines of general commerce with the world. Year after year Seattle's fleets increased until the Queen City drew down the honors from Portland, which had been recognized as the center of commerce in the Northwest.

By 1880. 40,000,000 feet of lumber were cut and in 1890, 200,000,000 feet were being sawed at Seattle. The production of coal from the mines in the vicinity of Seattle by 1890 were 488,306 tons and the exports of coal by that year had reached a value approximately equal to the value of the lumber output in 1888 when the first shipments of wheat, lumber and other products had reached the sum of $3,803,357. The struggling pioneer hamlet of the early '50s had become a frontier town of 4,533 population in 1880. The year after the great fire of 1889 it had become a city of 43,000 population. Year after year new steamers and sailing vessels were added in Seattle's shipyards to meet the growing demands. And at last, when the steamer Portland arrived from the North with the first news of the Klondike strike, Seattle was prepared to take advantage of the good fortune which sent her name to every corner of the world.

The story of how Tacoma was located as the terminus of the Northern Pacific Railroad, and of how that corporation used every means within its reach to put Seattle off the map as a center of trade. is told in another chapter. In 1880 Seattle found itself in a position where it had to fight for every inch to maintain its supremacy over Tacoma as the shipping center of Puget Sound. The Northern Pacific, in the midst of its financial difficulties, had found time to make it as uncomfortable as possible. Anyone going from this city to Portland had to stay over night in Tacoma, both going and coming, as the Northern Pacific controlled the steamers on the Sound and arranged their schedules with a view of forcing every possible port no matter how small, in favor of Tacoma, the city owned by the officers of the company.

In 1880 the Northern Pacific built its first vessel, the steamer Frederick K. Billings.

The next year, when Henry Villard became president of the Northern Pacific, the Pacific Coast Steamship Company sold to the Villard Syndicate the steamships Eureka, Idaho, Dakota, State of California, Alexander Duncan, Senator, Orizaba, Ancon, Los Angeles and the Queen of the Pacific.

The Oregon Railway & Navigation Company, which had secured practical control of transportation on the Columbia and Willamette rivers, turned its attention to Puget Sound the same year and in May purchased the Starr line of steamers including the North Pacific, George E. Starr, Annie Stewart, Isabel, Alida and Otter. The company at once reinforced this fleet with the Welcome, which was sent from the Columbia in tow of the Tacoma.

The completion of the railroad from Portland up the Columbia River by the Oregon Railway & Navigation Company, in 1882, left several surplus steamers on the Columbia and Willamette rivers without employment. The development of the Puget Sound country was proceeding with giant strides and offered a field for several idle steamers. The first of the fleet to arrive was the Idaho, which came around in February. She was followed by the City of Quincy, in June, the Washington, in September, the Emma Hayward, in October and the Gazelle, in November. The incorporation of the Washington Steamboat Company at Utsalady was completed about the same time with D. B. Jackson as president; D. S. Jacobs, secretary; Hiram J. Olney, manager. The company started business with the Daisy, Nellie and City of Quincy and later the Washington. From this small beginning grew the Puget Sound & Alaska Steamship Company. The Washington was placed on the Bellingham Bay route, and the Oregon Railway & Navigation Company started the Welcome after her making a rate of 50 cents for freight and passengers from Seattle.

One of the most important events for Seattle in the year 1883 was the organization of the Canadian Pacific Navigation Company, Limited. This transaction, which came with the approaching completion of the Canadian Pacific Railway, was a consolidation of Commodore John Irving's pioneer line and the Hudson's Bay Company's line. The company took charge of the steamers R. P. Rithet, Princess Louise, William Irving, Western Slope, Enterprise, Reliance, Otter, Maude and Gertrude. Later it added the Yosemite, then one of the fastest steamers in northwestern waters. The company built up an excellent trade with Seattle and the coast as far north as Alaska. The old fleet was succeeded by elegant modern steamers until the company has become one of the most powerful in the Seattle trade.

Lumber and coal from the Seattle district supplied an immense fleet of sailing vessels in this year. Among the new vessels launched here were the schooners Dora, Bluhm, Rosalind, Corona, Carrie B. Lake and barkentine Skagit.

The Canadian Pacific Navigation Company encountered spirited opposition in 1884 with the incorporation of the Peoples Steam Navigation Company, incorporated in May with a capital stock of $100,000. The new company purchased the old steamer Amelia, built in 1863.

The Pacific Navigation Company was organized in May of the same year at Tacoma and engaged Capt. J. J. Holland to construct the stern-wheeler, Skagit Chief, for the local mail route between Tacoma and Seattle.

A large number of steam and sailing craft came into existence in Seattle in 1888 and the lumber and coal trade gave employment to the greatest number of vessels which had yet appeared.

In spite of the persistent attempt to shut Seattle off in favor of Tacoma, the traffic in favor of the city which was made the object of attack was apparent from the customs records of June 16th. Of the seventy vessels which were loading at Sound Ports on that day Seattle claimed seventeen with a total tonnage of 22,993, compared with eight in Tacoma with a tonnage of only 9,113. The vessels at Seattle were loading coal. Of those at Tacoma four were loading coal and four lumber.

On December 24, 1888, the first ferry boat to run regularly between Seattle and West Seattle made her maiden trip. She was called the City of Seattle and was a rebuilt boat of the West Seattle Land & Improvement Company. Other steamers added to the Seattle fleet were the Delta, E. W. Purdy, J. E. Boyden, Halys and Jayhawker.

On September 17, 1889, the Puget Sound & Alaska Steamship Company, successor of the Washington Steamboat Company was organized with head-quarters at Utsalady. The stockholders were D. B. Jackson and Watson C. Squire of Seattle; Charles H. Prescott, Isaac W. Anderson and George Brown of Tacoma; Colgate Hoyt and J. M. Bookman of New York. As in the old corporation Jackson was the prime mover. Believing that his fleet was inadequate he went East and purchased the Hudson River Steamer City of Kingston and placed an order for a sister ship, the City of Seattle.

At Tacoma, the Pacific Navigation Company launched the stern-wheel steamer, State of Washington, which made her trial trip from Tacoma to Seattle in one hour, thirty-five minutes, breaking all previous records. At Tacoma, also Nelson Bennett constructed the stern-wheeler, Fairhaven, to run on the Bellingham Bay route.

The year 1890 brought about a radical change in steamboating on Puget Sound. It brought an addition of fully a million dollars' worth of steamers to Sound waters, and it established once for all Seattle's supremacy as the commercial center of Puget Sound.

With the first of the year came the arrival of the two fine new steamers of the Puget Sound & Alaska Steamship Company, the City of Kingston and the City of Seattle. The City of Kingston, built at Wilmington, Delaware, was brought through the Straits of Magellan in sixty-one days and began running on the Sound March 15th. Her sister ship, built at Philadelphia, under orders from D. B. Jackson, at a cost of $225,000, came to Seattle from the East a little later.

Now, when Tacoma and Olympia were making an active bid to attract from Seattle the rich commerce the mosquito fleet was bringing to and from the farms on the neighboring rivers, John Leary came to the aid of his city by organizing a steamboat company and building from his own resources a handsome steamer at that time by long odds the most ambitious craft of its kind on Puget

Sound. He called it the Bailey Gatzert out of compliment to his friend who also played his part in the building of Seattle.

The Seattle Steam Navigation & Transportation Company was incorporated at Seattle, May 31st, by John Leary, Jacob Furth, Edward Neufelder, W. R. Ballard and H. G. Struve, with capital stock of $500,000. The Bailey Gatzert, the finest stern-wheeler on the Sound, was launched at Salmon Bay, November 22d, from the shipyard of John J. Holland, in the presence of more than a thousand enthusiastic people of Seattle. She was 208 feet long, 32 feet beam and had engines of 1,300 horse power. She cost Leary $125,000 but she drove the competing craft from the seas and maintained Seattle's prestige.

The stern-wheeler Greyhound, which became the property of the Seattle & Tacoma Navigation Company, also appeared on the Sound the same year. She was built almost exclusively for passenger traffic and showed remarkable speed, indulging in some lively races on the Tacoma-Seattle route.

The trade on Lake Washington had developed to such an extent by 1890 that Capt. Charles Kraft built the fine twin-screw propeller Mary Kraft for the traffic at a cost of $13,000. But in September, 1891, she was burned to the water's edge. The City of Latona was another lake boat, built in 1890, for the Lake Union trade.

The Snoqualmie, the first fire boat in the Northwest, was also launched at Seattle in 1890.

The Columbia River & Puget Sound Navigation Company was the first of a number of enterprises which were organized on Puget Sound in 1891. The company was incorporated at Seattle, in February, with U. B. Scott, president; John Leary, vice president; L. B. Seeley, second vice president; E. W. Creighton, secretary and treasurer; E. A. Seeley and Z. J. Hatch. It absorbed the steamers Bailey Gatzert, Fleetwood and Telephone and built the new steamer Flyer. The Bailey Gatzert was sent around to run on the Columbia and Astoria route. The business of Puget Sound was handled by the steamers Fleetwood and Flyer, the latter being the fastest propeller constructed in the Northwest thus far. Capt. Harry Struve, of Seattle, was the first in command and handled her on the Tacoma and Seattle route. The entire upper works of the Flyer were destroyed by fire in 1892, but were rebuilt with larger and finer cabins. She reappeared on the route again in June, 1892, making four round trips a day between Seattle and Tacoma at a speed of twenty-eight miles in an hour and a half.

The Seattle and Tacoma Navigation Company was incorporated October 31, 1891, by Henry Carstens, Claude Troupe and Frank W. Goodhue, purchasing the steamer Greyhound from Captain Troupe.

In 1894 Capt. D. B. Jackson followed his former maritime successes, the Washington Steamboat Company and the Puget Sound & Alaska Steamship Company, with the Northwestern Steamship Company, securing the Rosalie, George E. Starr and the Idaho. The first board of directors was composed of D. B. Jackson, C. F. Clapp, A. A. Denny, R. H. Denny, N. H. Latimer, David Gilmore and D. K. Howard. The object of the company was to carry on steamboating independent of any railroad, but in harmony with all of them. All of the company's steamers continued to enjoy good business.

After Seattle had made itself sure of its own supremacy on Puget Sound

THE FORD MEMS TOS J. TENNYSON'S. STREET AND CHURCH STREET FROM THE S. F. R. R. 1887-1888

waters and following the definite connection of Seattle with the world by the advent of the Great Northern railway, came a period of financial depression which bore hard upon the city. It began in 1893 and with each succeeding year the load became heavier until by 1897 the city's builders were almost ready to give up the struggle. Then out of the North came the Portland with the news of gold.

The news found Seattle ready to make most of her fortune and bring prosperity to herself. How the big men of the city brought the rich Alaska trade here is a story which deserves a chapter of its own.

CHAPTER VI

COAL MINES AND COAL MINING

The student, seeking the underlying causes for the growth of Seattle from a small, although important, piling and lumber camp into the present magnificent city, the metropolis of the North-Pacific country and the leading shipping point of the entire Western Coast of America, soon discovers that coal and transportation have contributed no small part toward this success. The town on Elliott Bay struggled along for some twenty years before coal really became a factor in its growth and at the end of that time was of very little more importance than half a dozen other lumber towns on the Sound.

The citizens of Seattle had from the first hoped that their town was to take the lead of all others in the territory and this hope, it seemed, would be realized through the building of the Northern Pacific. However, when that road announced its intention of making Tacoma the terminus, this move would no doubt have put an end to the growth of Seattle for many years had not at the same time the King County coal fields begun to attract the attention of outside capitalists who had seen the ships arrive at the wharves of San Francisco loaded down with the best grade of coal yet discovered on the coast.

The casual reader, perusing the history of the industry, is at once struck with the peculiar fact that from the time of the first discovery of coal by Doctor Bigelow in 1853, to the commencement of the real development of the industry, a period of some twenty years elapsed during which little was done toward gathering in the wealth which nature had placed under the hills of this county. This too at a time when the settlement was greatly in need of some great permanent stabilizing industry. The people knew the coal was there, they also knew that its mining would mean growth and prosperity and wealth; but this coal was back in the hills where it would be necessary to build roads and trams over which to bring it to salt water where ships could be loaded.

Efforts were made to interest San Francisco capital in the enterprise, but these plans, after progressing to the hopeful stage, would fail. Some of the causes of this failure were to be found right here at home—certain people always making an unfavorable report upon the projects for which money was desired. Another thing which retarded development was the discovery of the Mount Diablo field in California just at a time when work was really getting under way in King County. Although the Mount Diablo coal was of low grade, the proximity of the fields to San Francisco gave it a big advantage over the higher grade King County product. Mount Diablo furnished San Francisco 206,255 tons of coal in 1874, while Seattle sold but 9,027 tons on that market. In 1876 the Mount Diablo output was reduced to 108,078 tons and Seattle sold 95,314 tons to San Francisco buyers, this too, in spite of a strong clique of California capitalists who, realizing the possibilities tied up in the King County

122

coal field, were determined to prevent its development if possible; or, failing in this, to hold up that development until their own city could firmly establish her self as the commercial center of the Pacific Coast of America.

Between the San Francisco clique and the Northern Pacific, the growth of Seattle was retarded. Coal, however, happens to be a commodity which does not deteriorate so long as it is left in the ground--and Seattle waited until she became strong enough to force development.

When the people of Seattle, on that May day of 1873, started in to build a railroad across the mountains, they hoped to solve two of the big problems which then confronted the city and prevented its rapid growth. One of these was connections by rail with the outside world; the other was quicker and cheaper means of bringing coal from the mines to salt water. By the end of the year 1875 the mines at Renton were able to ship their coal by rail and a short time after the road had reached the Newcastle mine and had made available the vast quantity stored in those rich hills.

The coal road did not stop there but pushed on up the Cedar River, reached into the Ravensdale—Black Diamond—Franklin field where other rich beds were discovered and opened during the decade following 1880.

Fortunes have been made out of King County coal, but the usual fate of the pioneer discoverer is seen in the history of the mines—most of the wealth produced went to the men who later obtained possession of them and, because of their money, were able to do the development work—the original locater being forced to step aside and see others reap the benefit of his early toil.

From the earliest days of the white man in the country, coal was known to exist in Western Washington. Doctor Tolmie, Hudson's Bay factor at Fort Nisqually, reports having found coal on the Cowlitz River in 1833, and says the Indians often brought specimens from the hills toward Mount Rainier during the early days; but the exact date of its discovery is not known.

Coal mining in the state may be said to date from 1848 when small outcroppings of lignite were worked to some extent along the banks of the Cowlitz. Pioneer explorers who went up the rivers during the early '50s, kept their eyes open for possible coal discoveries, and reported outcropping beds in various parts of the country. In 1851 Captain Pattle, while hunting timber for the Hudson's Bay Company, discovered the vein of coal underlying the present City of Bellingham. As this coal mine presented no difficult transportation problem it was soon opened, and for some twenty-five years was a producer. The quality was very low, and when, in 1878, the mine became flooded with water following a fire, it was given up and has remained closed ever since. It was from this mine that the first cargoes of coal were shipped from the Puget Sound district to San Francisco.

The King County coal fields were discovered by Dr. M. Bigelow, who while clearing land on his donation claim on Black River, not far from the present southern limits of Seattle, accidentally uncovered a bed of coal in 1853. The mine was opened by Bigelow, Fanjoy and Eaton, the two latter being killed in the Yakima Valley during the Indian war of 1855-56. The mine was worked in a small way, and, it is said, one schooner load was sent to San Francisco where it sold for $30 per ton. The demand from the California market was so great that Doctor Bigelow was offered $24,000 for the mine, an offer he could not accept because at this time the property was bonded to Capt. William Webster for $20,000. The Indian war put an end to operations at this mine, which was not reopened at the close of hostilities.

L. B. Andrews came out of the Squak Valley in the fall of 1862 carrying on his back a flour sack of coal which he had dug out of the hillside above the present Town of Issaquah. Taking the coal to the blacksmith shop of W. W. Perkins, Andrews asked the blacksmith to give the coal a test in his forge and see if it was any good. Perkins did so, finding it satisfactory as fuel. He and Andrews formed a working partnership and during the winter of 1862-63 they took out several loads which, given a test by the government steamer Shubrick, was found to be a good grade of steam producing coal. Like all the pioneer coal mine operators, Andrews and Perkins found that the development of their mine and the transportation of its product to market required more capital than they could command, so the property remained undeveloped until the completion of the Seattle, Lake Shore & Eastern Railroad in 1888.

The Seattle Gazette for August 11, 1863, says that Andrews had opened three veins, one above the other, within a distance of one-fourth mile up the mountain side and that these veins ranged from 12 to 20 feet in thickness. Workmen were reported to be engaged in opening a road from the mines to Lake Sammamish, also that the coal was to be hauled to the lake and then shipped on barges to Seattle by way of the Lake Sammamish, Lake Washington, Black and Duwamish River route. In December H. Butler had become interested in the mine to the extent of inducing San Francisco capitalists to come to Seattle and investigate the proposition. These men, Craig, Aiken and Bigley, visited the mine and reported "a bed of coal unsurpassed by anything of the kind in any part of the world."

In the fall of 1863 Edwin Richardson was surveying out a township on the eastern side of Lake Washington when he accidentally discovered a bed of coal on the north bank of what has since been known as Coal Creek. At that time coal was not considered as a mineral by the United States Government, and coal lands were subject to entry under the pre-emption laws. With the announcement of the new discovery at Coal Creek prospectors were soon in the district and had filed on a number of claims. Among these were Edwin Richardson, Ira Woodin, Finley Campbell, William Perkins, P. H. Lewis, Josiah Settle, C. B. Bagley and others. With two districts being developed in the county, Seattle now commenced to "talk coal" in earnest. The Gazette printed maps of the coal fields, and active development commenced.

While the pioneer coal mine owners were men without large bank accounts, they did have the physical strength to go at the development work with pick and shovel, which they did. The work moved slowly for the first few years, but in 1865-66 the people of Seattle commenced to realize that they had great wealth in the coal mines right at their doors and that development work must be hurried along. Rev. George F. Whitworth, a man who had had considerable experience in eastern coal mining regions, became interested in the matter and moved from Olympia to Seattle in 1866. He, together with Rev. Daniel Bagley, P. H. Lewis, John Ross and Selucius Garfielde, organized and incorporated the Lake Washington Coal Company, which company opened the first tunnel on the hillside above Coal Creek and brought out some of the coal, it being carried out in sacks.

LOOKING NORTH FROM FIRST AVENUE NEAR CEDAR. ABOUT 1878

apt. William
t this mine

. carrying o
le above the
p of W. W
is forge and
el. He an
of 1862-6
teamer Sta
Like all the
development
quired more
veloped until
888.

had opene
mile up the
in thickness
the mines to
ke and then
ke Washing
had become
alists to com
m and light
g of the kin.

nship on th
a bed of co
At that an
ment, and co
announcement
strict and ha
, Ira Wood
B. Bagley ar
e common
lds, and actin

bank accounts
with pick an
years, but
d great weal
ust be hurrie
ble experien
d moved fro
, P. H. Lew
ake Washin
hillside abo
in sacks.

The United States Revenue cutter Lincoln was in the harbor at this time and some of this coal was given to the captain with a request that he give it a trial. One of the amusing things about this test is that the captain reported the new coal created too much heat and came near melting down the smoke stacks of his vessel. This may have been hard on smoke stacks but it was great news for the owners of the mines and they were so much encouraged with the report that they at once put men to work on a road from the lake shore to the mines.

A light draft barge was built and arrangements were completed for moving the coal to the bay by way of Black River. The coal was brought down the road with wagons, loaded on the barge and started for Seattle.

The future looked bright to the mine owners, but the barge grounded in the shallow waters of Black River and caused trouble. The coal was finally landed on Hinds, Stone & Company's dock and was advertised for sale at $8.00 per ton. This firm had recently constructed a wharf at the rear of their store on the west side of First Avenue South, midway between Washington and Main streets, and had built up quite a shipping center there. The customs officers seized the barge because it was operating in salt water without a license—a little matter of detail which the coal barons had overlooked. Peace was arranged upon the payment of a fine and the barge went back after more coal, which was in great demand. Handicapped by a lack of funds the mine owners realized they had a very hard problem to solve. There was lots of money in coal, they had the coal, but they did not have the capital with which to build the roads, barges, cars and tugs necessary to transport that coal to the anxiously waiting market.

Realizing that the development of its mines was a task requiring more money than its stockholders could command, the Lake Washington Coal Company, in the spring of 1868, entered into an agreement with Capt. C. F. Winsor for the sale of the property. Captain Winsor, it was understood, was acting for San Francisco parties who had large capital to invest in the Seattle coal fields. After a long summer of inactivity the officials of the company learned that he was merely a broker who had tried to make a fat fee out of the sale, but had overloaded the deal with commissions and could not induce his people to invest.

During the summer word was received in Seattle that Captain Winsor had come to the Sound and that his boat was then at Olympia discharging cargo. As Seattle was not at that time visited by this line of steamers, and the company wished to know what the captain was doing with regard to the sale, it was decided to send a party out to see him. Rev. George F. Whitworth, P. H. Lewis and C. B. Bagley accordingly rowed across the bay to Alki, where a fire was built and preparations made to intercept Captain Winsor's boat when it came along during the night. The boat was late in getting away from Olympia and it was near morning before it was seen coming down the Sound on its way to San Francisco. The steamer was held while the party discussed the coal question which goes to show that schedules were somewhat elastic in those days. In San Francisco some interest was awakened in the King County coal fields, and T. A. Blake, a young engineer, was sent to the Sound in the summer of 1868, with instructions to make an investigation of the field. Blake's report, which was never published, shows him to have been a very far sighted observer. In speaking of the Coal Creek (Newcastle) field he says: "The lower one alone of these three beds will probably furnish a greater mass of good coal in a given length and breadth than any mine yet worked on the Pacific Coast of America. It will not be easy to overestimate the future importance of the Seattle coal field to the commercial and productive interests of the Pacific Coast; notwithstanding the heavy outlay which will be required to open the mines upon a proper scale, and to put the coal in the market."

Blake's report was filed away; the Seattle people were to be allowed to develop their mines without the assistance of California capital. Seattle people were accustomed to having their projects turned down by outsiders, and they also knew how to take one of these rejected projects and make it successful; so they organized a new mining company under the name of the Seattle Coal Company, incorporated February 1, 1870, and at the same time a handling company under the name of the Seattle Coal and Transportation Company, the latter to have charge of delivering the output from the mine at Newcastle to the ships on Elliott Bay. The Seattle Coal Company succeeded the old Lake Washington Company, the main stockholders being Reul Robinson, Amos Hurst, Albro M. Pringle, Martin L. Chamberlain, Edwin Eells, Thomas Flannagan, George H. Greer, A. N. Merrick, George F. Whitworth and C. B. Bagley. This corporation bought the interest of the old company, except that of Lewis and Ross, and now owned the 480 acres comprising the claims of Edwin Richardson, Josiah Settle and C. B. Bagley. There were 10,000 shares of stock, the value of which was placed at $1,000,000.

The market for its product open, this product tested and approved, its mines in workable shape with tunnels run and output guaranteed, the new owners felt sure of success, provided the transportation problem could be solved. It was decided to move the coal through Lakes Union and Washington by barges carrying the cars, which would be run over tram roads to be built between the lakes and also from the south end of Lake Union to the bunkers to be erected at the foot of Pike Street. The transportation company, composed of Robinson, Hurst and Peter Bartell, started work on this line in the spring of 1871, and every man who wanted to work was given a chance at railroad building. There were no steam shovels in those days and the road builders went at the job with pick and shovel and wheelbarrow—but they finished the road and moved coal over it for many years.

The cars were loaded with coal in the mine, let down the long inclined tram to Lake Washington, where they started on the first part of their barge trip. At Union Bay they were moved from the barge to the portage tram, over which they were hauled to Lake Union to be again loaded onto a barge for a trip to the south end of the lake, where they were again on the tram rails bound for the bunkers at the foot of Pike Street. These tram rails were six inches wide, made of wood and surfaced with strap iron. The car wheels were spread out so as to reduce wear, as each car had a capacity of two tons. The coal was handled eleven times in its trip from mine to bunker, the transporting cost amounting to about $5.00 per ton. The company spent $25,000 in preparing to handle the coal, and after several months of operation sold out to Charles D. Shattuck and S. Dinsmore, of San Francisco, who in turn sold the business, after having made several improvements, to Osgood & Remington, who operated the line until 1880, when it, together with the Seattle & Walla Walla Railroad,

SOUTH END OF PARK UNION. 1881.

passed under the control of Henry Villard and the Oregon Improvement Company.

For two years this railroad was operated without a franchise from the city council, that body approving the franchise ordinance, which was Ordinance No. 55, on May 7, 1874. Almost two years later the Seattle Coal & Transportation Company was granted a right of way for the line which had then been in operation for four years. The right of way was granted in Ordinance No. 85, approved by the council January 25, 1876. These were the first railroad ordinances ever passed by Seattle, and to the fifth council, composed of John Collins, mayor, and John Leary, Robert Abrams, J. S. Anderson, Isaiah Waddell, James McKinley and William Meydenbauer, councilmen, belongs the honor of passing Ordinance No. 55, while the seventh council, which approved the right of way ordinance, was composed of Bailey Gatzert, mayor; Benjamin Murphy, G. W. Hall, Josiah Settle, Isaiah Waddell, J. R. Robbins, J. H. Hall and John Leary.

While under the management of Dinsmore the first railway excursion ever run in the Puget Sound country was conducted over the line from the Pike Street bunkers to Lake Union. The locomotive, called "The Bodie," was brought up from San Francisco early in the year 1872. Upon its arrival the company issued an invitation to everybody to come and take a ride. Nearly everybody in Seattle had worked to build the road and now they were to have a free ride behind the first locomotive to toot its whistle amid the dark recesses of a Puget Sound forest. In reporting the excursion the Intelligencer of March 25, 1872, says:

"Friday last was decidedly a holiday in this city, owing to the opportunity afforded everyone to indulge in the novelty of a free ride behind the first locomotive that ever whistled and snorted and dashed through the dense forests surrounding the waters of Puget Sound. Business in town was not exactly suspended, but it might very near as well have been, as an excursion on Dinsmore's Railroad, connecting Union Lake with the Sound, with its constantly departing and returning train of cars during the day, seemed uppermost in the minds of all, and pretty much monopolized every other consideration." The locomotive and its eight new coal cars were kept moving from 11:00 A. M. until everybody in town had had a ride at about 5:00 P. M., the round trip being made in about half an hour.

By the end of May the company had finished its long trestle to deep water and ships were receiving their coal direct from the cars into which it had been loaded at the mine. This reduced the cost of handling and by the end of September the sixty men employed in the mines and the fifteen in the transportation department were turning from 75 to 100 tons of coal daily into the bunkers and ships at the foot of Pike Street. The company was operating ninety-two cars, with more under construction, had just finished the construction of twenty-five houses at the mine and was preparing to greatly increase the output.

The first cargo of Newcastle coal to be carried away from Seattle consisted of 405 tons, which was shipped to San Francisco on board the Bark Moneynick in the year 1870. The Intelligencer in the early part of the year 1880 gives the following figures covering coal exports in tons from Seattle for the previous ten year period: 1871, 4,918; 1872, 14,830; 1873, 13,572; 1874, 9,027; 1875,

70,157; 1876, 104,556; 1877, 112,734; 1878, 128,582; 1879, 132,263. Of this 790,639 tons the Renton Mine had supplied 33,419 tons, while the Talbot had furnished 23,426 tons. Some idea of the importance of the Newcastle mine may be obtained when it is remembered that all the rest of this coal had been dug out of its beds. During the month of December, 1879, the following vessels loaded at Seattle coal bunkers: The ships Eldorado, Alaska, Two Brothers; Bark J. B. Bell; Barkentine Tam O'Shanter, and the schooners Excelsior and Reporter. The greater part of this exported coal went to San Francisco, not to exceed fifteen thousand tons being divided between other ports, one of which was Honolulu.

The trestle work and bunkers of the Seattle Coal & Transportation Company were the most prominent objects on the water front in 1877. These works represented an investment of $30,000 and extended into the bay a distance of 800 feet. On June 16th, while the Western Shore and Washington Libby were lying at the chutes loading coal, the entire structure suddenly fell into the bay, teredoes having eaten off the piles which about eleven months before had been driven into the mud at the bottom of the bay. Although the bunkers contained some 1,450 tons of coal at the time, the boats escaped with minor injuries.

From 1880, until 1887, the mine was a heavy producer, the output running from 118,742 tons in 1883 to 231,816 in 1885.

By the end of the year 1883 these mines were producing 55 per cent of the total coal produced in the territory and 22 per cent of the total for the Pacific Coast. The output for 1890 was 159,524 tons. Annual production continued well above the 100,000 ton mark until 1900, when the mine was closed down and remained unproductive for several years. It is again in the producing class, being credited with 244,778 tons for the year 1914. It is the deepest coal mine in the state and has in all things justified the report of Blake; also that of Goodyear, who, in 1873, wrote: "They were, both of them, beautiful beds to work. Their thickness was good; their dip was right; their roofs and floors good; there were no faults; their coal itself was good and hard and clean; there was no pumping or hoisting, and hardly any timbering was needed."

Labor troubles in 1886 reduced the output to 22,453 tons, and in 1887 the hoisting works at the mouth of the mine caught fire. This fire spread into the mine, where it burned for some months, necessitating the closing down of the works. At that time the mine was producing from 150 to 200 tons a day, demand was strong and prices were high, coal selling at the Seattle docks for $5.00 per ton, a price $1.00 per ton higher than had been obtained at any time during the previous ten years. Notwithstanding the labor troubles and fires the output of the Newcastle Mine had reached the grand total of 1,740,000 tons by the end of the year 1887.

On January 24, 1867, the Territorial Legislature passed an act incorporating the Coal Creek Road Company and giving it authority to build a rail or tram road from a point on Lake Washington, near the outlet of Coal Creek, to a point about three miles eastward in section 27, township 24 north, range 5 east of the Willamette meridian. The act gave the company the right to appropriate a strip of land 100 feet wide for the entire length of the proposed road, together with such lands as it might need for warehouses at terminals, and provided that no other road should be laid out within fifty feet. The company, composed of William W. Perkins, John Denny, H. L. Yesler, John J. McGilvra, C. J. Noyes, C. H. Hale and Lewis C. Gunn, was incorporated with a capital stock of $5,000, with the privilege of increasing the same to $500.000. H. L. Yesler was president and Gardner Kellogg secretary.

Although the Legislature had given this company what amounted to almost an exclusive franchise up the Coal Creek Valley, which was so narrow in places as to make the building of a rival line a physical impossibility, nothing was done by the company until in August, when it advertised for bids for the construction of the road. The date set for opening these bids was August 20th, but if any were submitted they must have been unsatisfactory, as the company again advertised, setting the date forward to September 2d, with the same result on that date.

Nothing more was heard of the company until November 4th, when it held a meeting of its stockholders. The meeting was well attended, Yesler, Denny and McGilvra being elected directors. The company spent considerable money on the project and built its road to its Coal Creek claims, bringing out some coal over the line, but the enterprise was not successful, and by the end of the winter of 1867-68 was in bad financial condition. Its stockholders failed to meet their payments, the Intelligencer of April 25 stating that the company had sold six shares of stock for non-payment of assessments. Something like $30,000 had been spent and lost. During the latter part of April the road was sold to the same San Francisco parties who had bought the Lake Washington Coal Company properties, but as this afterward proved to be a brokerage deal with no money behind it, the Coal Creek Road stockholders failed to realize anything out of their investment.

Had the money wasted on this project been invested in providing transportation from the Newcastle Mine to Seattle, the history of the coal industry in King County would have been vastly different from what it is. It could have remained in the ownership of Seattle people and would not have passed to San Francisco capitalists, who later furnished the money for its development and absorbed the profits. Seattle learned her lesson; her people saw the danger of dividing their forces and from that time onward were to be found united whenever the task to be accomplished was of sufficient magnitude to require such united action.

In 1873 E. M. Smithers prospected the country around the present Town of Renton. The streams showed signs of coal and Mr. Smithers was satisfied that beds of it existed in the neighborhood. After devoting considerable time to the district he had about made up his mind to give up the search when he found coal float in one of the small streams. Following this float up stream he came to a place beyond which the coal seemed to be absent, so ascending the bank he prospected the hillside and found the bed with almost the first stroke of his pick. Together with T. B. Morris and C. D. Shattuck, Mr. Smithers organized the Renton Coal Company, and the next year the mine became a producing property. The company built two miles of railroad to Black River, down which stream the coal was taken on barges to the Duwamish and to Seattle. More railroad was built in 1875, and in 1876 the Seattle & Walla Walla reached the mine and the water route was abandoned. The mine was a continuous producer until 1880, when it was closed, remaining unproductive until 1895.

when the Renton Cooperative Coal Company obtained possession of the property and opened up some new beds. The mine became the property of the Seattle Electric Company in 1901, since which time it has been one of the heavy producers of the county.

The Denny-Renton Clay & Coal Company also operate a mine at Renton, the output being consumed in the brick plant which the company owns at that point.

The Patton Mine at Renton was opened in 1872, but has been abandoned.

Before the coming of the railroad the Renton and Talbot mines passed through several years of transportation troubles, during which their barges turned turtle in the river or bay, their steamboats "snagged" and the coal sank into the water. On October 14, 1874, the Renton Coal Company launched the little steamer Addie from the shipyard of William Hammond at the foot of Cherry Street. The launching of the Addie was celebrated by the firing of cannon and the blowing of all the steam whistles which the town had at the time. She measured 110 feet long, 19 feet beam, with a depth of hold of 4 feet 6 inches, and was placed under the command of Capt. H. H. Hyde. Within a short time Hammond had finished a large barge and the Addie commenced her work of towing coal. Several other barges were built for this service during the fall, each of them being 80 feet long by 20 feet wide, with a capacity of eighty tons.

Early in the spring of 1874 John Collins, J. F. McNaught, John Leary and M. Padden opened the Talbot Mine at Renton under the superintendency of the latter. Development work was prosecuted with vigor and within a year the company had driven a tunnel 16 feet wide and 11 feet high for a distance of 450 feet, exposing a vein of coal ten feet across the face. They had obtained 320 acres of land and also had built a mile of railroad from the mine opening to the landing on Black River, where coal bunkers were being erected.

The addition of the Renton and Talbot mines to those of the Newcastle district at this time was a most fortunate circumstance, as Seattle coal operations were now able to furnish employment for many of the men which the panic of '73 had made idle. Yesler made extensions to his wharf and the Renton and Talbot companies built large bunkers there; Wilson & Sons and other iron workers were kept busy casting mine car wheels; the mills were sawing lumber, and by the close of the year 1875 Seattle's water front was a busy place, her citizens were at work and her merchants were doing a good business, the holiday trade being placed at $20,000 that year. With the coming of the railroad to the mines production increased, the facilities for handling the product keeping pace with the output, so that by 1881, J. M. Colman, then manager of the railroad, was able to load 1,200 tons of coal into the hold of a vessel directly from the cars of the railway company. This was a great advantage as it saved extra handling, breakage to the coal and enabled a ship to obtain its cargo in much quicker time.

That transportation was the main problem confronting the coal mine operators in King County is shown by the history of the Issaquah field. It was from this mine that L. B. Andrews dug the first flour sack of really good coal ever brought into Seattle. This was in 1863, but it was not until the building of the Seattle, Lake Shore & Eastern, now the Northern Pacific's North Bend

HOPKINS NUMBER ON FIRST HENDERSHOT, 1887 1880

branch, in 1888, that this immense body of coal was made available to the market. The Seattle Coal & Iron Company was organized in 1887, with a capital stock of $5,000,000. D. H. Gilman was president; Henry Crawford, vice president; J. A. Jameson, treasurer, and F. H. Whitworth, manager. The object of the company was the development of the Issaquah Mine, also the iron prospects on the south fork of the Snoqualmie River near the summit, which at that time were supposed to be of great value. Incidentally it may be mentioned that the company hoped to become a big factor in the Pacific Coast coal market, which was then controlled by the Oregon Improvement Company and the Dunsmuir interests of Vancouver Island.

The company owned 1,497 acres of coal land, with at least five veins running from 6 to 14 feet in thickness, said to be one of the largest and richest fields in the country. Development work was started on a scale which it was thought would produce from 300 to 500 tons a day, and the first shipments were made in 1888. The iron mines proved to be prospects only, but Issaquah has made good as a coal camp, averaging over one hundred thousand tons annual production from 1892 to 1904, when it was closed. Under the management of the Superior Coal and Improvement Company the field was again opened in 1910. Very little coal was produced by this company. In 1912, it gave place to the Issaquah & Superior Coal Mining Company, which has spent a great deal of money in bringing the mines again into production. They yielded 80,994 tons in 1914.

The Black Diamond Coal Company was organized in California in 1864, and through its development of the Black Diamond mines at Nortonville in the Mount Diablo district of Contra Costa County early arose to a position of prominence in the industry on this coast. All through the early days promoters of new projects went to California for their capital, and it was in this way that the Black Diamond Company obtained possession of the coal mines at Coos Bay, Ore., and Bellingham Bay in Whatcom County. The company marketed great quantities of coal from these three districts, but as the product of none of them came up to that of the King County mines in quality, it was decided to obtain a mine in this district.

P. B. Cornwall was at the head of the Black Diamond Company when it decided to enter the King County field in 1880, and it was under his direction that Victor E. Tull was sent north from San Francisco with instructions to explore all the coal fields of the Puget Sound country with the object of discovering new and better veins. The company desired to find a better coal than the Newcastle, which at that time was the best coal being shipped from King County. Tull began his work on the banks of the Skagit River; continuing south many veins were examined, many samples sent to San Francisco for testing, but it was not until July, 1880, that he discovered the great beds which are known to underlie the Black Diamond-Franklin-Ravensdale field. The small samples which Tull had sent to San Francisco were found to show such high quality that the company sent B. B. Jones, a coal expert who had been employed by the company at its Mount Diablo mines for some years, to Seattle with instructions to continue the prospecting of the district. Jones' report of what he found was so favorable that the company at once put a crew of men at work opening what has since been known as Mine No. 14 of the Black Diamond group.

With plenty of money at its disposal the company pushed its development work along very rapidly and in January, 1882, had a crew of men at work building houses, cutting trails to the river and opening the vein of coal. On April 7, 1882, Tull loaded a box of 800 pounds of Black Diamond coal on board the Idaho for shipment to San Francisco, the shipment being made that the company might submit the coal to more exhaustive tests than had yet been given it. These tests proved to be so satisfactory that President Cornwall decided to pay the mines a visit. Morgan Morgans was at that time the company superintendent at the Mount Diablo mines and Cornwall asked him to come to King County with him. The two men left San Francisco on June 7, 1882, on board the steamer State of California, and arrived in Seattle June 9th, by way of Astoria, Kalama and Tacoma. The next day they obtained a wagon and driver and set out for the mines. Some eight miles beyond Renton the driver was sent back to Seattle and the men continued their trip on horseback, arriving at the mines at 7.00 P. M.

Following the visit of Cornwall and Morgans the Oregon Improvement Company sent Harry Whitworth and a crew of surveyors into the field for the purpose of surveying an extension of the Columbia & Puget Sound Railroad from Renton to the mines. The survey was completed in June and within a short time construction work was started on the new line. At this time King County was producing sufficient coal to keep the steamships Willamette, Umatilla and Walla Walla constantly engaged in carrying it to San Francisco, the three boats averaging five trips per month and carrying 2,200 tons per trip.

Morgan Morgans was sent to King County in 1885 as general superintendent of the Black Diamond mines, the first coal in anything like commercial quantities being taken out in March of that year. The railroad had been finished, the company had a large number of men employed and by the end of the year 43,868 tons of the new coal had been taken out of the ground. It was of high quality and was soon very popular as a steam producing fuel. Morgans remained in charge of the mines until they were acquired by the Pacific Coast Coal Company in 1904, and under his direction other veins were opened in the district, which took first place in King County coal production in 1895, a place which it has held almost continuously since; production, in tons, being as follows for the years given: 1895, 115,028; 1900, 220,346; 1905, 312,290; 1910, 403,741; 1914, 234,028.

With the opening of the Black Diamond mines, and the completion of the Cedar River extension in 1884, prospectors began searching for other veins of coal in the district, and it was not long before it was found that the outcropping discovered by Tull was in the center of a large coal field. Many prospects were opened and some of them, notably those of Franklin, Ravensdale and Lawson, have become heavy producers. Development work on the Franklin Mine was begun during the summer of 1885, and was hurried along with such vigor that the mine had produced 7,854 tons of coal by the end of the year. This mine is located about three miles east of the Black Diamond mines, and, like them, has been a heavy producer of high quality coal. It was opened by the Oregon Improvement Company, later passing into the hands of the Pacific Coast Coal

Company. The field reached its highest production in 1900 with 167,600 tons taken out that year.

The Ravensdale mines began shipping in 1900 under the management of the Leary Coal Company. The first year's output was 48,000 tons, which was increased to 184,370 in 1895. The mine passed under the control of the North western Improvement Company, subsidiary to the Northern Pacific Railway, and produced 127,972 tons in 1914. An explosion destroyed the mine in 1915, killing thirty-one workmen, since which time it has been abandoned by the company.

Through the building of the Cedar River extension of the Columbia and Puget Sound Railway the mine at Cedar Mountain was developed by the Cedar Mountain Coal Company, Samuel Blair, president; Laurence Colman, secretary, and J. M. Colman, manager. Although development work was not started until in August, 1884, the mine had produced 1,732 tons by the end of that year. This property was never what could be called a heavy producer and after being operated for some twenty years was closed because of faults.

During the last fifteen years several new mines have been opened in King County, some of which, like the Denny-Renton Clay & Coal Company's at Taylor, the Grand Ridge east of Issaquah and others have produced coal in commercial quantities. King County production passed the million mark in 1902, with 1,012,217 tons to its credit, and reached the maximum in 1907 with 1,416,509 tons. The heavy increase in the production of California fuel oil during the last few years has forced a curtailment of the coal output, with the result that King County mines produced but 844,701 tons in 1915. Many heat and power producing plants have substituted the new fuel for coal, but now that oil prices are beginning to rise, King County mining promises to again take the place in industry which nature, through her great generosity, intended it should occupy.

Notwithstanding the fact that Washington coal mines are under very rigid inspection laws, they produce their share of accidents, and tragedies in which men lose their lives and leave women as widows and children as orphans. James Bagley, the present state inspector, as well as D. C. Botting, his immediate predecessor, grew to manhood in the local coal mining industry. Both these men know the business from the inside and both of them are credited with doing everything possible to safeguard the lives of the men who earn their living in the mines; but King County coal veins lie in very steep slopes, slopes which constitute an added element of danger to the industry and are the cause of many accidents.

Coal mining has contributed its share of the comedy and melodrama, as well as tragedy to the romance surrounding the development of the Puget Sound country. Promising prospects which filled their discoverers with high hopes of financial success have often failed to produce the desired results. Rich mines have been discovered only to be lost to the original locators; fortunes have been lost and other fortunes won, and notwithstanding all the wealth which has been taken out of the mines of King County during the last sixty years, there remains today a body of coal of unknown vastness, which, as the years roll along, will continue to produce wealth, not only for the men who own and operate the mines, but for the manufacturers, transportation lines and the army of people who depend upon these and allied industries for a living, and make Seattle their home.

As has been shown, nearly all of the King County coal mines, early in their history, passed into the control of foreign corporations, and it is a matter of common repute that they are today owned by capitalists who live in San Francisco, Boston and other eastern cities, and even in Berlin, Germany. That these foreign owners have considered the local mining industry from the standpoint of dividends only is shown by the fact that these same dividends, or profits, annually reach a sum greater than the amount paid in wages to King County coal miners, the great majority of whom are citizens of foreign nations. It would seem that with such vast quantities of coal as this county possesses the importation of an outside product for the purpose of supplying local demand would be unnecessary. These foreign owners, in order that they might declare larger profits to their stockholders, placed a price upon the local product which made these importations not only possible but highly profitable, and during the last twenty-five years more than one fortune has been made through supplying the people of this city with coal mined east of the Cascade Mountains, in British Columbia, and even in far away Australia.

By far the greater part of the profits made through the development of the timber industry, with its saw and shingle mills, its sash, door, barrel and other woodworking factories, have remained in the state where they have contributed to the comfort and well being of the people. Such, however, is not true of King County coal, one of the greatest assets Seattle ever possessed, and it is to be regretted that its profits have gone to enrich other states and foreign nations, while our own people, in their efforts to be loyal to the local product, have been forced to pay these profits, knowing at the time the true condition existing in the industry. The pioneer did not possess the capital required to develop the mines. He could have held on to his claims, in which event the development of the country would have been retarded; but he sold, hoping the resultant development would justify his sacrifice. For every hundred dollars invested by the foreign purchasers of the mines, thousands have flowed, and continue to flow, into their pockets; all because the pioneer did not have, and could not borrow, the capital required for paying the expenses of developing his claims.

CHAPTER VII

WASHINGTON STATE UNIVERSITY

The act of Congress establishing Oregon Territory was approved August 14, 1848. This law provided for little more than setting the governmental machinery in motion. Another law, approved September 27, 1850, created the office of surveyor general, provided for surveys of public lands and the terms on which settlers could secure title to these lands. Said act set aside sections sixteen and thirty-six for common school purposes, and granted to the Territory of Oregon the quantity of two townships of land therein to aid in the establishment of a university in the territory in such manner as its Legislature might direct. The Territorial Assembly of Oregon located the university at Marysville, February 1, 1851, during its second session; at its next session provided for the selection of a university land commissioner and for the selection and sale of the university lands. It will be seen that at this early date the law making body entertained the view that these lands might be sold as well as selected. This became a matter of importance in Washington about twenty years later. During the next session boards of commissioners were named to select and sell these lands and to erect the territorial university at Marysville on a site to be donated for that purpose.

Here our connection with the Oregon institution ceased, as Congress passed a law establishing the Territory of Washington, approved March 2, 1853, including all of that part of Oregon south of latitude 49 and north of the Columbia River from its mouth to latitude 46, thence in said latitude to the summit of the Rocky Mountains, thence to latitude 49.

An act of Congress, approved July 17, 1854, provided that in lieu of the two townships of land that had been granted to Oregon there should be reserved in each of the territories of Oregon and Washington two townships of land to be selected for university purposes, under the direction of the legislatures of said territories.

In early territorial days the location of the public buildings was a matter of importance to the several localities. The capitol, university, penitentiary and insane asylum were "located" at almost every session of the Legislature which then met each year. As there were no funds with which to erect buildings no great damage was done.

Washington University was no exception. January 29, 1855, it was located at Seattle, with a branch at Boisfort, Lewis County, both institutions to be on the same footing in all particulars. As the act of Congress reserved lands for university purposes the Legislature held the view that one or two institutions might receive benefits under the act. In January, 1858, the university was changed from Seattle to Cowlitz Farm Prairie, Lewis County, and under this act the proceeds of both townships of land were to be applied for its support

135

and endowment. It required a donation of 160 acres for a site. Nothing was done under this act.

January 11, 1861, the act that resulted in the building of the university in Seattle was passed, authorizing the selection of said lands from the public domain and the sale of the same at $1.50 per acre. Three commissioners were appointed—Daniel Bagley, Edmund Carr and John Webster. February 22, 1861, they met and organized in the auditor's little office that stood at the northwest corner of Third Avenue and Yesler Way. Mr. Bagley was chosen president of the board, and the entire management of the affairs of the university was intrusted to him. At that time nearly all the lands belonging to the Government that had been surveyed in the Puget Sound region could be bought for $1.25 per acre, and most of the legislators who voted for the location of the university and the sale of the lands did not believe they could be sold at 25 cents an acre more than other lands just as good. The contracts for clearing the ten-acre tract that had been given for the purpose by Arthur A. Denny, about 8½ acres, and Charles C. Terry, about 1½ acres, had a clause in them that if it should be found that money to pay for said clearing could not be realized out of the sale of lands, those who did the clearing should take their pay in lands at the price named above. Prices for clearing ranged from $275 to $325 per acre, and it cost about $3,000 for the ten acres. As the entire tract was worth at the time perhaps $500,. it will readily be seen how disproportionate to the value of timber lands at that time was the cost of clearing the same. At this time, and for many years after, lands along the shores of Lakes Union and Washington, now in the city's limits, could be bought of the Government at $1.25 per acre, from the university at $1.50, or could be taken for nothing by homestead entry. The Renton tract, the Squire tract, Kinnear tract and others of the most fashionable residence parts of the city today were selected by Mr. Bagley and sold to purchasers at $1.50 per acre. In 1864 John J. McGilvra "took up" his beautiful home, Laurel Shade, it being Government land. From 1860 down to as late as 1870 many hundreds of acres of lands within from one to three miles of Pioneer Place were bought at private entry for $1.25 per acre in depreciated currency, that made the actual cost to the purchasers from 50 to 60 cents. The Denny-Fuhrman tract cost about 50 cents an acre.

Early in 1861 it became apparent that sufficient funds would be obtained to clear the land and erect the university buildings. The men who did the actual work of clearing became more or less prominent in the affairs of the city in later years. They were Henry A. Atkins,. Lewis V. Wyckoff, Lyman B. Andrews, Clarence B. Bagley, Hillory Butler, Ira Woodin, Edwin Richardson, Lemuel Holgate, John Pike and his son Harvey, John Carr, James Crow, James Hunt, D. Parmlee and O. Dudley.

The stone for the foundation was brought from a quarry near Port Orchard. The main building and the home for the president and a dormitory or boarding house were all practically completed by August 1, 1862.

The fir lumber came mostly from Ports Madison and Gamble, though Yesler's mill supplied a small part of it. The finishing wood, outside and inside, was all white pine brought from the mills at Seabeck. The cement, paints, oils, glass and hardware came from Victoria, and the heavy import duty and steamboat charges often more than doubled the first cost. The brick and lime were brought

university in
n the public
ssioners were
February 22,
at the north-
sen president
niversity was
Government
ght for $1.25
the university
cents an acre
the ten-acre
out 8½ acres,
t if it should
ed out of the
lands at the
per acre, and
th at the time
lue of timber
and for many
gton, now in
cre, from the
l entry. The
st fashionable
and sold to
his beautiful
wn to as late
three miles of
in depreciated
0 cents. The

be obtained to
did the actual
he city in later
B. Andrew:
rdson, Lemue
; James Hunt

Port Orchard
ry or boarding

though Yesler:
inside, was 2
ints, oils, gla:
and steamboa
ie were broug!

PART OF WASHINGTON STATE UNIVERSITY CAMPUS

by Capt. Henry Roeder from Bellingham Bay. Most of the work was done by contract, but was separated into many parts. The contractors and workmen were as follows: Hauling of materials, Thomas Mercer, L. V. Wyckoff, Hillory Butler and Josiah Settle; surveying ten-acre tract and giving levels and location stakes for buildings, Edwin Richardson; architect, John Pike; putting up frame and inclosing same, Thomas S. Russell and John Pike; stone foundation and brick work, John Dodge, John T. Jordan and S. Thorndyke, and the last two also did the plastering; window and door frames, Franklin Matthias; making columns and putting them in place, A. P. DeLin and O. C. Shorey; flooring and shingling, R. H. Beatty, O. J. Carr, Josiah Settle and C. B. Bagley; tin work, Hugh McAleer (there was no plumbing done); painting, Harvey Pike, Jeff Hunt, Charles Gorton, C. B. Bagley and J. E. Clark; desks, D. C. Beaty, A. P. DeLin and O. C. Shorey; blacksmithing, William W. White; miscellaneous carpenter work, Harry M. and W. B. Hitchcock, Martin Civler, N. DeLin, in addition to most of the others named above. A large amount of miscellaneous work was done by nearly all of the foregoing, and in addition were J. W. Johnson, David Graham, Richard King, George Austin, Albert Pinkham, J. C. Purcell, Charles Harvey, James Kelley and five or six others.

The foregoing list is given for a double purpose. It is a part of the historical record and it shows that in those days there were no drones nor men of leisure in the community. All who had not regular employment elsewhere went to work with saw, plane, hammer, ax, pick, shovel or with whatever he could best turn his hand. Nothing was too laborious or too humble for them.

Business being all on a coin basis led to an anomalous condition of affairs. Contracts were made on this basis and were usually observed, and it was a stain on the character of any one for the rest of his life to "greenback" a creditor, which was the usual name for paying a coin debt in "greenbacks," as United States legal tender notes were called. All payments to county, state and nation were made in paper money, except duties on foreign goods entered at the custom houses. Postal, United States internal revenue and land office collections were all in the same currency, as were all moneys collected in the courts. If one went to buy land at Olympia, where, until recent years, was the only land office on Puget Sound, he changed his coin into paper money for the purpose. This was not foreseen when the first large contracts were made for the sale of university lands, and later, when some of the mill companies made payments in that kind of currency, it deranged the plans of the commissioners and made trouble in their accounts. All Mr. Bagley's accounts were kept in coin, according to the custom of the business men of the country. Should he receive $240 for a quarter section of land, he did not charge himself with that sum, but reduced it to coin dollars at the current rate. If paper was 60 cents on the dollar, he entered $144; if 50 cents, then $120; if only 40 cents, then it was only $96.

Later a committee was appointed by the Legislature, who were unfriendly to Seattle, and mostly political enemies of Mr. Bagley, who made an examination of his accounts and rendered a report showing a large balance due from him to the university fund, most of which was the difference between the coin value and par value of the paper money he had been compelled to take, and had used in the current transactions of the institution. A later committee of the Legislature made an exhaustive report and found $8 more due him than his own accounts showed. At the time his connection was terminated with university affairs he claimed a balance due him from its fund of a little more than $800, and $1,500 unpaid salary from the territorial treasury. In time the regents of the institution paid the former claim in full, and thirty years later he sued the state and recovered a considerable part of his claim for salary.

He had for twenty years to suffer an unlimited storm of calumny and reproach because of his connection with the university, but later received a full measure of credit for the energy and business sagacity he displayed in obtaining the funds to build with, and in the erection of the buildings themselves and setting the educational machinery in motion, feeble and intermittent as was its action for many succeeding years. He has often been called the "father of the university," and if such a title rightfully belongs to anyone it is due to him.

The old cash book kept by Mr. Bagley has March 16, 1861, for its earliest date, and among the entries are many of interest sufficient to warrant their mention here. Among the first is one of express charges on $60 from Olympia, $1, and all through the book are similar charges of from four to ten times the present rates. The fare for a round-trip to Olympia and return was $12; one to Vancouver on the Columbia River was $60. Cement was $7.50 per barrel, lime $3.50, finishing nails 10 cents per pound, and 2,480 pounds of window weights cost $248. Wages were as about as now, only ten hours made the day. Lumber was also about the same prices as at present. Tin work was very costly.

After the buildings were completed there were no funds that could legally be used to carry on educational work, and for years the Legislature failed to provide them. The population of the territory in 1860 was less than twelve thousand, and in 1870 less than twenty-four thousand. The great Civil war was in progress, and while this region was not directly called upon for men or money, business was stagnant and the ordinary expenses of the territory were greater than its revenues and were met by the issue of warrants much depreciated in actual value. Also, the ill feeling toward the institution, so pronounced during the period of construction, was kept alive year after year.

In January, 1862, $2,000 were appropriated from the university fund to purchase books and philosophical apparatus, and provision was made to allow the use of the interest on the remainder of the fund for educational purposes.

Not until 1877, more than fifteen years after educational work began in the university building, was direct legislative aid extended to it. November 9th of that year an appropriation of $1,500 for 1878, and the same amount for 1879, was made from territorial funds for salaries only. At this session forty-five free scholarships were provided for, to be apportioned among the several counties, and entitling the holder to two years of free tuition of not less than nine months each year, academic the first year and collegiate the second.

November, 1879, provision was made for a salary allowance of $1,000 each year in 1880 and 1881, and $500 for philosophical apparatus.

During the years 1882 and 1883, the institution would have been compelled to close but for the generosity of Henry Villard, the most notable figure at that period in the railroad affairs of this Northwest. He gave the sum of $4,000.

November, 1883, thirty-six free scholarships were ordered by the Legislature, and appropriations were made for 1884 and 1885, $3,000 each year.

January, 1886, $10,000 were appropriated for salaries during the two years of 1886 and 1887, and each member of the Legislative Assembly might appoint a bona fide resident of his district to a free scholarship. Six hundred dollars were provided in addition for books and philosophical and chemical apparatus:

The institution had now been in operation twenty-five years.

During this quarter century of constant struggle on the part of all those connected with the university as regents and instructors, there had been several periods that it was of necessity closed. Ten presidents had presided over its troublous destinies.

School was first opened in the university, November 4, 1861, with Asa S. Mercer in charge. There was but one schoolroom and about thirty scholars in attendance.

Mr. Mercer had been graduated a year before and arrived in Seattle in time to do considerable manual labor about the university grounds during the summer of 1861. The school continued five months.

Mrs. Ossian J. Carr taught a private school in the same room for three months in 1862, May, June and July, with twenty-four children attending.

On the 10th day of October of that year the second session of university school was opened with Mr. Mercer, principal, and Mrs. V. Calhoun, assistant. Mr. Mercer was called out of town several times during the winter and Clarence B. Bagley presided in his place. Dillis B. Ward, another pioneer still living in Seattle, occasionally acted as Mr. Mercer's assistant during the winter.

These first schools brought to Seattle a fair number of students from abroad. Olympia sent five, namely: James B. Biles, Susan Isabella Biles, Edgar Bryan, Augustus Geary and Edwin Austin. Victoria sent four—George W. Little, John McCrea, Ed Francis and Allen Francis. They came from the country and the camps, but, of course, the larger number were the youth of Seattle. Among these was Sarah Loretta, daughter of John Denny, who at her death five years ago left to the university $25,000 for fellowships. The first white girl born in Seattle, Eugenie McConaha, was one of the pupils, and Orion O. Denny, the first boy, was another. An official list of students is not accessible, but in addition to those named it is known that these also attended: Margaret Lenora Denny, Rolland H. Denny, Rebecca Horton, Alice Mercer, George W. Harris, Sylvanus C. Harris, Robert G. Hays, Charles Hays, Zebedee M. Keller, James Hunt, L. L. Andrews, Jane Wetmore, Birdsie Wetmore, Frank Wetmore, E. Inez Denny, Madge Denny, Charles Tobin, Findley Campbell, Sarah Bonney, Gertrude Boren, Mary Boren, Joseph Crow, Martha Crow, Emma Russell, John B. Libby, Levi Livingston, Christine Deliu, Andrus Deliu, Eva Andrews, William R. Andrews, Ed Harmon, Fred Young, Frances Webster, Lewis Post, John W. Neely, Louis McMillan, R. Welburn, Susie Graham, William Odell, Sophronia Humphrey, Arthur Brownell, Thomas Winship, Edward Sanford Bucklin and William M. Belshaw. It is believed the fifty-eight named herein attended the second Mercer school, and more than one-half of them the first. It is also believed that it is a complete list of Mercer's second term pupils.

Asa Shinn Mercer was born near Princeton, Ill., in 1838, and received his early instruction in the schools of that town. In 1860 he graduated from Franklin College, at New Athens, Ohio. Almost immediately he began preparations to come west, naturally to Seattle, where his elder brother, Thomas, was one of its pioneers; also 1ere were two ot1er influential citizens, Dexter Horton and Daniel Bagley, who 1ad known him from early c1ild1ood.

Arriving 1ere in June, 1861, 1e set to work on t1e university grounds at common labor until 1e got a job of surveying. His connection wit1 t1e university 1as already been set fort1; and 1is connection wit1 t1e "Mercer immigration affairs in anot1er c1apter. From 1ere 1e went to Oregon, later 1e was in Texas, Colorado, Wyoming, and elsew1ere in t1e Middle West. He drifted quite naturally into t1e newspaper business.

In 1890 1e was sent to C1icago from Wyoming as one of t1e Columbian commissioners, and until t1e great exposition opened in 1893 was t1e center of a stormy period in C1icago. T1ere was an organized plan on foot among a lot of t1e most prominent men in C1icago to 1ave t1irty or forty acres of t1e lake front filled just east of t1e Auditorium Hotel for t1e purpose of building t1e best buildings in w1ic1 to 1ouse t1e most attractive of t1e ex1ibits and relegate t1e rest of it somew1ere sout1, west or nort1 of t1e city, t1ey did not muc1 care. T1ere was also well grounded suspicion t1at w1en t1e exposition s1ould close t1e promoters of t1e dual sites would be t1e beneficiaries from t1e final disposition of t1e tract on t1e lake front. T1e Sout1ern, Western and Pacific Coast members of t1e commission desired a single site, and under t1e leaders1ip of Asa S1inn Mercer, formerly of Seattle, and Ric1ard Mansfield W1ite, now of Seattle, t1ey won a signal victory. T1e beautiful grounds at Jackson Park were t1e result of t1is contest. T1e writer, also from Seattle, is proud to remember t1at 1e took a 1umble part in t1e exciting contest w1ile it lasted. Soon after t1e close of t1e exposition Mercer moved wit1 1is family on a big ranc1 near t1e bad lands of Wyoming and went to raising cattle and promoting oil wells. At eig1tv 1e is still active, alt1oug1 1e 1as nearly lost 1is eyesig1t.

Beginning September 7, 1863, t1e university opened wit1 William E. Barnard, president, who came to Seattle from t1e Willamette University at Salem, Ore. He was a native of Massac1usetts and 1ad graduated from Dartmout1 College in 1858. In t1e advertisement announcing t1e proposed opening of t1e sc1ool, tuition rates were given as follows: Primary department, per quarter, $6.00; academic, $8.00; collegiate, $10.00.

Mr. Barnard continued in c1arge of t1e university until t1e close of t1e spring term of 1866. In an older institution 1e would 1ave been valuable as an educator, but 1e 1ad no experience in pioneering; 1e did not understand t1e people of t1e West and t1eir unconventional ways. Little true sympat1y and affection between 1im and 1is pupils was establis1ed. Almost immediatelv after 1e assumed control of t1e institution 1ere 1e entered upon correspondence wit1 ot1ers seeking an engagement elsew1ere.

Here is a verbal picture 1e gave of conditions in Seattle in a letter to anot1er institution of learning written s1ortly before 1e resigned t1e presidency:

"Education t1roug1out t1e Sound district is in an extremely backward condi tion; as an illustration: Not one of t1e misses attending t1e university, t1e first quarter after our arrival, could accurately repeat t1e multiplication table. Society is also greatly disorganized; drunkenness, licentiousness, profanity, and Sabbat1 desecration are t1e striking c1aracteristics of our people, and of no portion more t1an t1ose at Seattle. Of course t1ere are a few 1onorable

exceptions. We have two distilleries, eleven drinking establishments, one bawdy house, and at all the drinking establishments, as at our three hotels, gambling is openly practiced; and Sunday is no exception.

"These are the influences we have had to encounter in our efforts to build up an institution of learning. I need not say it is discouraging and well nigh hopeless."

Mr. Barnard wrote the literal truth, but he made no effort to present the bright side of the shield. At that period the description of his surroundings were applied equally well to nearly every town and city on the Pacific Coast, and its exact parallel existed here for a full half century afterward.

In 1860 he resigned the presidency and for the next two years held a deputy-ship in the customs service at Port Townsend under Fred A. Willson, collector.

From there he went to California, where he remained until his death in 1910.

Rev. George F. Whitworth, the pioneer of Presbyterianism in the Northwest, came to Olympia in 1854. Probably no resident of Washington has left so deep an impress upon public affairs of so wide range. By turns he was teacher, editor, deputy surveyor, civil engineer, clerk in the Indian department, deputy collector of customs, and at all times he was active in religious, moral, temperance and educational work, not only in his own community, but throughout Washington. He was active in putting into operation the infant industries, particularly coal mining. Twice he held the presidency of the university; he served a term in Thurston County as superintendent of public instruction and in his declining years he founded an academy at Stunner in Pierce County, which later was moved to Tacoma and named Whitworth College. This institution passed through many vicissitudes and was later moved to Spokane, where it bids fair to be a school of importance.

During the summer of 1866 he was induced to accept the presidency of the university, and September 17th of that year school was opened. Arrangements had also been made by the public school directors for the scholars of the district to attend the university.

George Frederick Whitworth was born March 15, 1816, in the Town of Boston, Lincolnshire, England. In 1832 the family came to the United States to live and settled at Terre Haute, Ind. He became a student at Hanover College and was graduated in 1839.

Coming to the Pacific Coast in 1853, he soon took up a donation claim near Olympia, and at once engaged in ministerial and educational work there and in nearly all parts of the Puget Sound country.

He died in Seattle, October 6, 1907, after a brief illness.

President Whitworth advertised the continuation of school in the university beginning July 22, 1867, but it did not reopen. Sufficient encouragement was not forthcoming. During all these lean years the university buildings, including the president's residence and the boarding house, were used by those in charge of the schools rent free, but the salaries had to come from tuition fees almost entirely, and they offered little encouragement. In April, 1868, the regents published in the newspapers of Washington, Oregon and California a proposition to lease the institution for a term of years. They said:

"The institution embraces ten acres of ground, well cleared and fenced; the university building proper, president's house, boarding house and outbuildings, with a good supply of running water. It is pleasantly and healthfully situated in Seattle, W. T. Proposition to lease it as a sectarian institution will not be entertained."

No satisfactory offer was received, and this time the institution remained closed for two years. April 5, 1869, the regents advertised in the Intelligencer that "the institution will be permanently reopened on Monday the 12th day of April, 1869, under the charge of Prof. John H. Hall, assisted by such professors and assistant teachers as may be required." Tuition per term of eleven weeks · scientific department, $10.00; collegiate department, $12.00.

Mr. Hall was a graduate of Yale College and a gentleman of fine attainments and much executive ability. The fact that he was able to maintain himself for three years proves that he must also have had considerable financial ability to keep the institution open in the face of so many adverse influences. After his separation he taught schools in King and Pierce counties and later went into other business. He died in Tacoma.

In the summer of 1872 Mr. Edgar K. Hill arrived from Ypsilanti, Mich., to take up the duties of president. He was born in Berkeley, Ohio, in 1845. He had been recently graduated from the Michigan State Normal School when the appointment of president was tendered him. His young bride accompanied him and the two composed the faculty. For a term they had classes in Latin, Greek, German and French, higher mathematics and down through the grammar grade to the primary. At the beginning of the second year, all grades below the sixth were abolished as they had been taken over by the public schools of the city.

Early in 1874 the university was again closed for lack of funds and Mr. and Mrs. Hill removed to California. He taught schools in many cities of that state during sixteen years' residence there. In 1890, he returned with his family to Seattle and for several years taught in the city schools. During this period four of his sons attended the university and three of them were graduated. Early in the rush to the Alaskan gold fields he and his four sons joined the throng. The father died and was buried there.

In 1874 Mr. F. H. Whitworth and Miss May Thayer took charge of the university for a time.

Mr. Whitworth has occupied many positions of responsibility during his fifty years' residence in Seattle. He was born at New Albany, Ind., March 25, 1846, and was only seven years old when the family crossed the plains. He attended the schools of Olympia until about 1866, when he went to California to enter upon a collegiate course, from which he was graduated four years later.

When he resigned from the university, in 1875, he took up civil engineering and in that capacity had much to do with local mining and railroad enterprises. For several years, he and Mr. R. H. Thomson were associated together in business, and after that, he and Mr. George F. Cotterill formed a partnership which still continues.

It was not the good fortune of the writer to know Miss May Thayer, but in one of the university publications appear the following kindly words regarding her:

"Miss Thayer deserves much credit as one who shared with the early presidents the joys and care of responsibility. She was a graduate of Mount Holyoke and before coming to Seattle had taught in the schools of Massachusetts and New York. She came West in 1873 to become assistant teacher to President Hill.

"More than once her untiring efforts kept alive the feeble little school. When money was lacking and classes in algebra and Latin had ceased to exist, Miss Thayer continued to occupy the building with her class of infants. During one of these periods it became very lonely and bitterly cold in the great empty, echoing hall. Friends advised her to give up the school. But the brave woman, with her tiny 'university,' moved to an upper room in the house of Mr. Thomas W. Prosch, where she continued to teach amid more congenial surroundings."

In the spring of 1875 Rev. George F. Whitworth, for the second time assumed the presidency and continued until, on account of poverty, the institution again closed with the Christmas term of 1876. During his incumbency occurred the first graduation, that of Miss Clara McCarthy.

A military department was organized by him, also instruction, theoretical and practical, in civil engineering was given during school hours and when he could spare the time outside upon the campus, and during the long summer days out in the forests and in the mountains. He taught school as he preached, because he loved humanity, and in spite of small pay and all sorts of discouragements he left his impress upon the affairs of the university that continued for many years after he had finally left it.

Prof. Alexander J. Anderson was the next to become head of the university. The future of the institution was more promising than ever before. The Legislature had appropriated $1,500 for 1878, and the same amount for 1879; also provision had been made for free scholarships as noted elsewhere. Mr. Anderson was born in Ireland of Scottish parentage about 1833. During his childhood, the family came to the United States and settled in Illinois. He was graduated from Knox College, Galesburg, in 1856, and at once adopted teaching as his profession, and continued that work in Illinois until 1869. Coming to the Pacific Coast, he held the chair of mathematics in Pacific University at Forest Grove for a time, then became principal of a high school in Portland, Ore. In September, 1877, he opened a private school in the university. In February, 1878, he was elected president of the institution and continued in charge until 1882.

Including the additional attendance, by reason of the free scholarships, the classes grew rapidly and the number of teachers increased in proportion. From Seattle he moved to Walla Walla, and there held the presidency of Whitman College for ten years. Ill health then compelled him to give up active work. Death finally came to his relief in Olympia, March 17, 1903. It was during his connection with the university that Henry Villard came to its relief as noted elsewhere.

A farewell reception was given Mr. and Mrs. Anderson, July 18, 1882, at the Arlington Hotel in this city. Henry G. Struve, president of the university, presided and complimentary addresses were made by him and L. P. Smith, John Leary, John F. Damon, Bailey Gatzert and other city notables of that period.

Prof. Thomas Condon, of the University of Oregon, was next invited by the regents to come to Seattle, but declined, and Prof. Leonard J. Powell was then elected.

He had been serving as superintendent of public instruction in Oregon and resigned that position to come to Seattle. Plenary powers were given him to organize a faculty and to prescribe a course of collegiate and academic instruction. His arrival in Seattle, July 18, 1882, is noted in the Chronicle.

The institution was reopened Wednesday, September 20th. Professor Powell took charge of the mathematical department, and the other professors were given assignments—Lee, literary; Hansee, Greek and Latin; Johnson, science; Swimm, preparatory. Mrs. W. A. McPherson was in charge of the primary classes.

Early in the Powell regime, a third year was added to the normal course; laboratories were equipped, athletic and out-of-door sports encouraged, and in 1884, a department of military science and tactics re-established.

An interesting and in fact dramatic incident occurred in the fall of 1883, which was recorded by Mrs. Villard in her book of memoirs. All old-timers will remember the spectacular excursion planned and headed by Henry Villard to bring a large party of distinguished gentlemen to witness the ceremonies attendant upon driving the "golden spike" that completed connection of the eastern and western sections of the Northern Pacific Railroad. Most of the party came on to the Pacific Coast, and Seattle made extraordinary efforts to entertain them. Steamers gaily decorated met them at the entrance to the bay; the streets from the wharf to the university were aflame with banners and bunting, while at the university grounds a pavilion had been erected, festooned and beautified.

Naturally Professor Powell took a prominent part in the exercises; also Miss Nellie Powell delivered an address of welcome that attracted the attention of the visitors and met with quite generous praise. She took occasion to gracefully refer to the generosity of Mr. Villard to the institution a couple of years earlier.

Professor Powell's health began to decline in 1886, but he remained in charge until after the graduation exercises of the class of 1887. Soon afterward his body was taken to Lakeview Cemetery by his former students accompanied by a large concourse of students and citizens of the city.

The ensuing fall Thomas M. Gatch was chosen president of Washington University, and this time accepted the appointment. Twenty-five years earlier it had been tendered to him and declined, and at that time, by reason of his recommendation, it was given to William E. Barnard. During all that time he had been connected with educational institutions, mostly in Oregon, and nearly all the time in full charge of them. The writer has an affectionate remembrance of him during the early days of his connection with the Willamette Institute, where he was then in charge of the classes in higher mathematics and Latin and Greek languages. To him was permitted to close the educational work in the old university building at Fourth and Seneca and to reopen it on the new campus that is today the pride of Seattle and of the State of Washington.

He resigned the presidency in 1895, but continued a year longer as professor of political science, then returned to Oregon and became the president of its agricultural college for another year. After sixty years, save one, of devotion to educational work, he retired under the provisions of the Carnegie foundation.

He and Mrs. Gatch then returned to Seattle and he died here April 22, 1913. Mrs. Gatch has her home on Queen Anne Hill near her daughter, Mrs. L. H. Wheeler, who was art instructor while her father was in charge of the university.

Including the year 1895, the number of graduates was sixty-nine, as follows. The maiden names of the young ladies are enclosed in parentheses, viz.:

1876—Wilt, Clara (McCarthy), B. S.

1881—Wayland, Helen I. (Hall), B. S.; Redfield, Edith (Sanderson), B. S.

1882—Anderson, Louis F., A. B., A. M.; Colman, George A., B. S.; Judson, George H., B. S.; Kilbourne, Leila A. (Shorey), B. S.

1883—Chipman, H. O., B. S.; Denny, Carrie V. (Palmer), B. S.

1884—Olmstead, Anna F. (Sparling), B. S., B. P.

1885—Camp, Hettie Louise (Greene), B. S.; Dement, Louise M. (Root), B. S.; Meany, Edmond Stephen, B. S., M. S., M. L.; Piper, Charles Vancouver, B. S., M. S.; Huntington, John, B. S., M. D.; Veazie, Agnes M. (Green), B. S.

1886—Alvord, Elisha H., A. B.; Gormley, Matthew H., B. S.; McElroy, James F., B. S., LL. B.; Pratt, E. Emma (Clark), A. B., A. M.

1887—Adams, Florence M., A. B., A. M.; Bigelow, Edwin Victor, A. B., A. M.; Drumheller, Nellie E. (Powell), A. B.; McLerman, Anna (McDiarmid), B. S.; Porter, James W.; Powell, Edward T., B. S.

1888—Adams, Marion E., B. S.; Hines, Annie E. (Willard), B. S.; Kinnear, Charles A., B. S.; Kuhn, Ida (Soule), B. S., M. S.; Wakefield, Depalmer G., B. S.

1889—Furber, Fanny L. (Churchill), B. S.; Gatch, Ruth, A. B.; Hawley, Royal T., A. B.; Ward, Charles Clarence, B. S.

1891—Douty, Daniel Ellis, B. S.; Kellogg, John A., B. S.; Nickels, Adelaide G., B. S., B. P.; Noble, Francis A., B. S.; Parker, Maude L., A. B., M. D.; Schimer, J. Herman; White, Minnie J. (Pelton), B. S., M. S.

1893—Collings, F. Otto, A. B.; Gatch, Grace, A. B.; Johnson, Winnifred (Ewing), A. B., B. P.; McNiel, Beatrice A. (Karr), A. B., B. P.; Parker, Adella M., A. B., LL. B.

1894—Corey, Helen Mae (Anthony), B. S., Ph. G.; Durham, Merrit Ernest, B. S.; Durham, Mettie (Heaton), B. S.; Ford, Delton Alton, B. P.; Greene, Roger Sherman, Jr., A. B., B. P.; Pelton, Annie Jennie, B. S., B. P.; Pierce, Adelbert Ernest, A. B.; Porter, John Edwin, B. S.; Sprague, Albert Roderick, A. B.; Turner, Horace Amos, B. S.

1895—Clarke, Myra Brewster, B. P.; Dearborn, Erastus Phillips, A. B.; Howell, Harriet Alice, B. P., A. M.; Jenner, Earl Robinson, A. B.; McElreath, Bertie Reginald, B. P.; McKee, Charlotte Ruth (Karr), B. P., A. B., A. M.; Morrison, Isaac Phillips, A. B.; Smith, Helen Burrows (Hubbard), A. B.; Waughop, Hilda Leonard, B. P.; Wiley, Martha, B. P.; Williams, Anna Rayfield (Parsons), A. B.; Williams, Kate Shannon, B. P.

In their annual report to the governor for 1890, the board of regents among other things recommended: "That a law be enacted by the Legislature empowering the board of university regents, with the concurrence of the governor and secretary of state, to dispose of the present site of the university, if deemed advisable, provided that arrangements to that end can be effected with all parties now in interest. In the opinion of the regents ampler grounds are essential to the prosperity and well-being of the university, and grounds more remote from the center of a rapidly growing and expanding city. The experience of educational institutions unites upon the idea that such institutions flourish best removed to a distance from the excitements and temptations incident to city life and its environments."

It had long been apparent that the ten-acre tract would eventually be outgrown by the rising university, but prior to this time no constructive steps had been taken looking forward to its removal. But there was considerable legal difficulty seemingly involved in the removal, for the deed of conveyance to the tract contained a clause to the effect that the land should revert to the Town of Seattle in the event of the university's ceasing to use it for its original purpose. The Legislature, which was favorably disposed toward a removal project, decided to investigate the legal aspect of the matter, and to that end appointed a joint committee with Senator L. F. Thompson and Representative L. B. Nims as chairmen to obtain the advance opinions of the best legal talent in the state. On March 12, 1890, Messrs. H. G. Struve, Thomas Burke, John Arthur and John Kean appeared before this committee, and concurred in the opinion that in the event of the university's ceasing to occupy the tract for the purposes named in the deed of conveyance, the title would not revert to the Town of Seattle, but to the state.

Early in 1891 the Legislature appointed another joint university committee, of which Edmond S. Meany was chairman, having, as its chief duty, the selection of a new site. In looking about, Chairman Meany's eyes fell upon a beautiful tract fronting Union Bay, on Lake Washington, some five or six miles distant from the center of the city. This particular piece of ground had been well advertised by reason of the fact that the city council had had it in mind for some time past as a possible park addition. Mr. Meany conceived the idea of bringing the Legislature to Seattle in order that it might have a look at the site. This was in February, 1891. As the railroads in those days furnished passes freely, and it was the week-end, when most of the members would be coming down as a matter of course, the excursion was largely patronized. The ceremonies were simple, but the grounds appealed from the start. As a kind of finale, several of the older legislators boosted the young chairman upon a stump, and called for a speech, and with words of a prophet, Mr. Meany predicted the great edifices which would one day dot the new campus.

It was upon the recommendation of this committee that the Legislature passed an act, approved March 7, 1891, entitled: "An act providing for the establishment, location, maintenance and support of the University of Washington." The body which carried out the provisions set forth in the act is generally known as the university land and building commission. Both regents and Legislature at that time deemed such a commission advisable, for it was feared that the duties incident to the removal would be too burdensome for the regents to carry alone.

Probably no commission in the state ever had, seemingly, more elaborate powers. The regents appointed one member, James R. Hayden; the executive chose John Arthur, of Seattle; John McReavy, of Union City; and Charles F. Leavenworth, of Olympia. At the first meeting the commission organized, with John Arthur, president, and chose Martin D. Smith, of Spokane, secretary;

William E. Boone, of Seattle, architect and superintendent of construction. Later, on April 15, 1891, Fred G. Plummer, of Tacoma, was appointed chief engineer. As Mr. Smith resigned his position as secretary on June 15th, James R. Hayden took over the duties in his stead, and was given a paid assistant.

This commission was authorized, among other things, to locate the university on not to exceed 160 acres of land in fractional section 16, in township 25 north, of range 4 east, as soon as the heirs to the ten-acre tract should have given a quit-claim deed; and to sell the latter at auction to the highest bidder, if the amount offered was equal to the assessed valuation. It was further authorized to erect upon the new campus a main building and such other structures as were deemed necessary.

The most meritorious work accomplished by this commission was the securing of a quit-claim deed to the ten-acre tract. While the best legal opinion assured the Legislature that the title in fee rested with the state, it was thought desirable to secure a relinquishment, if possible, to any interest which the heirs might have. One of the commission, Mr. John Arthur, was delegated to interview Arthur A. Denny and wife, Judge Lander, and the heirs of Charles C. Terry, deceased, with this end in view. These persons graciously consented to do all in their power and, in June, 1891, gave to the university a quit-claim deed. The title was now vested in the state and the commission was ready to go ahead with the locating and construction of the buildings.

On August 5th the commission located the 160 acres. It had been the hope of the friends of the university to secure the entire fractional section, but certain antagonistic interests were instrumental in having the maximum amount placed at 160 acres. Not until 1893 did the university secure the full amount. The fault was not, however, with the commission, as it could do no more than carry out the provisions of the act.

The commission, in the meantime, had opened a downtown office, and was proceeding with the work of erecting the new buildings. In its plans the commission seemed limited only by its imagination. The buildings recommended in the architect's report included a biological hall, chemical hall, hall of law and medicine, hall of administration and belles lettres, hall of mathematics and mines, an art building, general library building, gymnasium, observatory, dormitories and dining hall, chapel, manual training hall, stables and boathouse. All were to be very elaborate. The hall of administration and belles lettres, as the bids later indicated, would cost a sum five times the amount paid in the construction of the present Denny Hall.

At a meeting of the commission, held in Olympia on August 20, 1891, the board was ordered to advertise in the Seattle Post-Intelligencer, Tacoma Ledger, Spokane Chronicle and Walla Walla Statesman for proposals for the materials and labor necessary to construct the hall of administration and belles lettres. Five firms submitted bids, for labor and materials taken together in one contract, at sums ranging from $479,000 to $647,000. All were rejected, however, first, because they were conditional to letting the contracts for both labor and materials to one and the same bidder, and second, each bid was deemed too high. Upon the architect's opinion that the same buildings could be constructed for less money if the university undertook the labor part itself, the commission decided to publish notices inviting bids for material only. On September 26,

1891, advertisements appeared in the Seattle Telegraph, Tacoma News, Spokane Review and Walla Walla Union-Journal, calling for separate bids for stone, brick, sand, lime and cement.

Meanwhile, commencing August 10th, the engineer, Fred G. Plummer, with 100 men, was busy clearing the grounds, and incurring a daily expense of $350.

These elaborate efforts, however, were not appreciated by a critical public, which quickly raised a cry against such extravagance. When one looks back upon the struggle which the university has had to obtain funds, even in recent years, a just appreciation of the charge of extravagance is obtained. But the commission went on, ignoring the charge, until a series of letters began to appear in one of the Seattle dailies calling the attention of the public to the fact that the issuance of state warrants by the auditor at the direction of the land and building commission was illegal under the new constitution. The notice of the auditor was directed to the matter, and after a few days of deliberation he decided to suspend the issue of any more warrants until such time as the attorney-general or the Supreme Court could pass upon the legality of his action. This was on October 7, 1891, and the warrants for September's work were due the men engaged in clearing the new grounds.

Balked by the auditor the commission held a hasty meeting on October 8th, and telegraphed the governor, requesting his presence at a meeting to be held on the 9th, at either Seattle or Olympia, as would be convenient for him. All the members of the commission and his excellency, Governor Ferry, ex officio president, and the state auditor, T. M. Reed, were present at the meeting held in Olympia. The latter stated that he had come to the conclusion, after due deliberation, not to issue more warrants, and that he would not, even upon the advice of the attorney-general, do so until the Supreme Court had decided he had a lawful right to issue them.

The commission, of course, was obliged to suspend all further work of construction.

As there was now due the laborers employed by the commission some $5,000 for work done in September, the withholding of which would inflict great hardship and wrong upon them, the auditor stated that he would assume the responsibility of delivering to the commission the warrants in payment for all work done up to and including the 30th day of September, 1891, which was done.

The commission had already decided to take the matter into the courts with a test case. On October 10, 1891, Mr. Arthur and Mr. Hayden called upon the state treasurer, Mr. A. A. Lindsley, and presented to him warrant No. 65, issued on 5th day of October, 1891, by the state auditor, in payment for the publication, in the Walla Walla Statesman, of the notice to contractors, etc., for the indorsement thereon by the said treasurer of its non-payment for want of funds. The treasurer refused to make such indorsement thereon, alleging, as his reason, that in his judgment the state auditor had no legal right to issue any warrants upon the university fund; he further stated that he would not, until the Supreme Court had decided that the auditor had a legal right to issue such warrants, make such indorsements upon any more warrants drawn upon the university fund.

The case turned upon section 4 of article 8 of the constitution, which reads:

"No moneys shall be paid out of the treasury of this state, or any of its funds, or any of the funds under its management, except in pursuance of an appropriation by law; nor unless such payments be made within two years from the 1st day of May next after the passage of such appropriation act, and every such law making new appropriation, or continuing or receiving an appropriation, shall distinctly specify the sum appropriated, and the object to which it is to be applied, and it shall not be sufficient for such law to refer to any other law to fix such sum."

The Supreme Court held this provision to be applicable, and decided that no money could be paid out of the treasury under the act, and that the auditor had no right to issue warrants on the university fund for want of specific appropriation. The court further stated, however, that it was not its intention to infer that the auditor might not examine and approve an account against the state for the expenses of one of its public institutions where no appropriation had been made, or where by unforeseen circumstances the appropriation made had been exhausted, provided, of course, he did not issue a warrant therefor.

Under this intimation the auditor felt justified in issuing certificates of indebtedness on accounts approved by the commission, and thus those who had been engaged in good faith were not suffered to lose the result of their labors.

The bids for construction were returned, unopened.

The commission could do little more than wait until a new Legislature should convene, but in the meantime sentiment had changed so profoundly that those who in 1891 had thought it most expedient to place the work in the hands of a commission were now duly certain that the commission ought to be abolished and some arrangement made whereby the regents could have charge. The commission carried the issue into the political campaign but lost, and the Legislature which convened was hostile to their cause.

On March 14, 1893, an act "providing for the location, construction and maintenance of the University of Washington, and making an appropriation therefor, and declaring an emergency" was approved. This act abolished the university land and building commission in favor of the regents. The governor as agent of the state was to purchase the entire amount of fractional section 16, and the regents were to appoint three persons to supervise, under their authority, the construction of a new main building after a design selected through competition. Furthermore, the ten-acre tract was to be sold only upon a six-eighths affirmative vote of the regents. The sum of $150,000 was voted for the work, and to expedite the construction, an emergency was declared making the act operative when approved. As a kind of good-will offering, the act gave to the new university one-half of the Federal grant of 200,000 acres made to the state in the enabling act of 1889 for charitable purposes.

This act was without doubt the most important ever made in the history of the institution, save, of course, the one which brought the university into being. Its author was Representative Edmond S. Meany of the class of 1885. When Rev. Daniel Bagley heard of it he said: "They call me 'father of the university.' No, I am not the 'father' any longer, but the 'grandfather,' and this young fellow is the 'father.'" Mr. Bagley is still the "father of the university," but Mr. Meany has obtained by other great works the sobriquet of "the ideal alumnus."

In obedience to this act Gov. John H. McGraw purchased the new site of the state land commission at its appraised value, which was $28,313.75, and the regents went forward with the work of construction. Fred G. Plummer, former engineer with the university land and building commission, was engaged to make a plat of the new grounds, select the most likely sites for new buildings, and devise the best means for improving the surroundings. A number of laborers was engaged in grubbing out stumps and clearing the ground. To add a touch of beauty to the campus Henry H. Hindshaw, one of the landscape architects of the World's Columbian Exposition, was engaged to outline roadways and to design tree clusters.

On October 30, 1893, advertisements were started in the Spokane, Seattle and Tacoma papers giving notice that the design for the new main hall would be selected by competition, and that the winner of the contest would receive as a prize the sum of $1,000 and the position of university architect during the construction of the same. Considerable red tape was involved in order to make the contest thoroughly competitive. The cost of the finished structure must be no more than $125,000. Plans were to be submitted without any marks of identification save being accompanied by a sealed letter bearing the architect's name. In order to safeguard the university from a possibility of giving a prize to a plan whose cost of construction should exceed the $125,000 limit, three well-known architects were engaged to expert them. The contest closed on February 17, 1894, and after careful deliberation on the part of the regents it was found that Charles W. Saunders, of Seattle, was the winner.

Calls for bids for the construction of the work were advertised, and opened May 9, 1894. All told, seventeen firms entered, with proposals ranging from $112,000 to $135,000. The contract was awarded to Messrs. Cameron & Asienfelter, of Spokane, who agreed to finish the work by March 1, 1895.

The laying of the cornerstone took place on the 4th of July, 1894. Some of the old timers who had witnessed a similar ceremony in 1861 on the old campus were present. The chief speeches were made by Rev. Daniel Bagley and Arthur A. Denny. When the cornerstone for the old building was laid in 1861, a copper box containing portions of the Holy Bible was imbedded therein. It was deemed appropriate that this box be removed and replaced in the new cornerstone. The box was produced from its long burial, opened, additional documents deposited, and then reimbedded in the new cornerstone. At this christening the building was called Administration Building but before completion was renamed Denny Hall in honor of Mr. Arthur A. Denny.

There was considerable money remaining from the original $150,000 appropriated in 1893. When Lieut. John L. Hayden, professor of military tactics, heard of this he made up his mind that a good way to spend it would be in the construction of a drill hall and gymnasium. As his father was one of the regents little difficulty was experienced in getting the funds. Labor and materials were unusually cheap, incident to the hard times following the panic, so that the completed structure cost but little more than $7,000. A water and power plant was also constructed at this time.

It happened that there was some stone left over from the construction of Denny Hall and this was utilized in erecting an observatory building.

The removing of the university had created the problem of the disposal of the ten-acre tract. By the act of March 7, 1891, the university land and building commission had been authorized to sell at auction to the highest bidder if the amount offered equalled tʒe appraised value, but no bid sufficiently large ʒad been fortʒcoming. By tʒe act approved March 14, 1893, tʒe regents ʒad been autʒorized to sell, but only upon a six-eigʒtʒs affirmative vote of tʒeir number. Tʒe ʒard times incident to tʒe panic ʒad so cʒeapened realty values tʒat it was doubtful if one-tʒird of tʒe true value of tʒe land could ʒave been obtained, wʒile tʒe "six-eigʒtʒs vote" restrictive clause acted as a cʒeck upon any unwise sale. So tʒe difficulty in securing a wortʒy offer, togetʒer witʒ tʒe belief tʒat tʒe growtʒ of Seattle would render the property at tʒe end of a few years of very great value, caused botʒ regents and public gradually to unite on a policy to lease ratʒer tʒan to sell.

About 1897 tʒe old building was rented to Seattle Scʒool District No. 1, wʒicʒ occupied it for a time, after wʒicʒ tʒe Seattle Public Library rented it. Old Nortʒ Hall, formerly used as a dormitory, became tʒe temporary ʒeadquarters of the law scʒool. Tʒe United States Government was looking for a site upon wʒicʒ to construct a Federal building, and tʒe regents, considering tʒat tʒe erection of sucʒ a structure upon tʒeir tract would greatly enʒance tʒe remaining portion, consented to sell a strip 64 by 240 feet at its appraised value, wʒicʒ was $25,000.

Tʒe city, by 1898, ʒad somewʒat recovered from tʒe financial depression, and offers to lease began to pour into tʒe regents' office. Having fixed definitely upon a policy to lease, and deeming tʒat tʒe time for doing so was appropriate, tʒe regents advertised in tʒe Seattle, Tacoma and Spokane papers for offers, reserving accommodations for a law scʒool, a business office and meeting room for tʒe board.

One of tʒe offers was accepted. Tʒis provided for a tʒirty-year lease, witʒ certain reservations for tʒe use of tʒe university. Tʒe lessee was to pay a rental of $32,500 and to make permanent improvements to the amount of $452,500. Tʒe improvements were to be of a substantial cʒaracter, and all buildings to be of brick. Such improvements and buildings, wʒen completed, were immediately to become tʒe property of the state.

Wʒen tʒe lease was ready for delivery, but before it was delivered, tʒe state land commission advanced tʒe claim tʒat the board of regents ʒad no autʒority to dispose of any university land, and tʒe lessee refused to go furtʒer until assured of ʒis title.

Tʒe state land commission contended that by virtue of certain acts passed in 1893, 1895 and 1897, sucʒ rigʒt was vested solely in tʒem. Tʒe regents disputed tʒeir contention and promptly instituted suit in tʒe name of one of tʒeir number, Ricʒard Winsor, against S. A. Calvert, commissioner of public lands, and won tʒeir case in tʒe Superior Court of King County, from whicʒ court tʒe case was appealed to tʒe Supreme Court, wʒere tʒe regents again won. Tʒe decision was ʒanded down on November 27, 1901, tʒe syllabus of wʒicʒ is as follows:

"Tʒe autʒority vested in tʒe board of regents of tʒe state university by tʒe act of Marcʒ 14, 1893, to sell tʒe state university site in tʒe City of Seattle, wʒicʒ ʒad been originally donated for university purposes, and apply tʒe proceeds of sale towards tʒe purcʒase and construction of a new site and building, was not abrogated so as to vest tʒe power of sale in tʒe state land commissioners by tʒe passage of the act of Marcʒ 15. 1893, wʒicʒ provides tʒat the said board of state land commissioners sʒould ʒave full supervision and control of all public lands granted to the state for common school, university and all other educational purposes, and should possess and exercise over such lands all the authority, power and functions and should perform all the duties which the state land commission, the state school land commission and the state board of equalization and appeal for the appraisement of tide and shore lands had exercised, since the latter act expressly restricted its operation by making it apply to public lands only 'so far as the same shall not have been disposed of and not appropriated by law to any specific public use.' "

On December 23, 1902, the tract was leased to the University Site Improvement Company. The lease provided for a cash rental of 2 per cent on a valuation of $300,000 for the first five years; 3 per cent on the same valuation for the second five years, and thereafter 3 per cent on a valuation to be fixed by appraisers appointed every ten years. In addition to the cash rental, the lessees bound themselves to expend during the first ten years of the lease at least $100,000 in permanent improvements (exclusive of buildings), such as grading, paving, sewers, sidewalks, etc. They were permitted to erect only brick or stone buildings of first-class character. All buildings and improvements, when erected or constructed, became at once the property of the state.

The University Site Improvement Company failed to carry out the provisions of its lease and on October 1, 1904, the lease was declared forfeited.

On November 1, 1904, a new lease covering the same tract was entered into with James A. Moore, of Seattle, for a period of fifty years, under which the lessee agreed to pay for the first three years a cash rental of $6,000 per annum; for the next five years $9,000 per annum; for the next ten years 3 per cent per annum of the appraised valuation of the land as fixed by a board of appraisers to be chosen by the parties; for the next ten years 4 per cent per annum, and for the last twenty-two years 6 per cent per annum of the appraised valuation, and the lessee further agreed during the first eight years to place upon the property improvements in the way of grading, paving, sewers, sidewalks, to the value of $85,000. The buildings were to be of brick or stone only and of first-class character. All improvements and buildings, when constructed or erected, became at once the property of the state.

This lease, with some amendments, was continued with the Metropolitan Building Company, successors to James A. Moore, under a forty-seven-year lease bearing the date of 1907. The following table, prepared by the regents in their report to the governor for 1913, will give some idea of the expected annual rental:

Period	Rate	Est. Value	Annual Rent
1907-1912	3 per cent	$ 500,000.00	$ 15,000.00
1912-1922	4 per cent	1,000,000.00	40,000.00
1922-1932	4 per cent	2,000,000.00	80,000.00
1932-1942	4 per cent	2,500,000.00	100,000.00
1942-1954	4 per cent	3,500,000.00	140,000.00

Up to 1916 the Metropolitan Building Company has erected the following structures: Post-Intelligencer Building, Henry Building, Stuart Building, White Building, Metropolitan Theater, Cobb Building and the Arena. The last mentioned structure 1as not at t1is writing been accepted by t1e regents as coming under t1e 1ead of a permanent building as provided for in t1e lease.

Prior to Marc1 14. 1903, t1e rig1t to dispose of all university lands, save t1ose appropriated by law to some specific use (as, for examples, t1e ten-acre tract and t1e present university campus), was vested in t1e state board of land commissioners. By an act approved Marc1 14. 1903, t1e commissioner of public lands was ordered to ascertain t1e amount of all unsold lands granted to the state by t1e enabling act of February 22. 1889, and assigned to t1e support of t1e university by t1e act of Marc1 4. 1893; and to record a description of t1e same in a book provided for t1e purpose, a copy of w1ic1 was to be filed wit1 t1e regents. By t1is same act it was provided t1at "t1ereafter suc1 lands s1all never be sold, encumbered, or ot1erwise disposed of. except by and wit1 t1e consent of t1e board of regents of t1e University of Was1ington."

T1e act, 1owever, came too late to save a very valuable tract of land w1ic1, like most of t1e university lands, was frittered away by t1ose unfait1ful to t1eir trust. T1e regents of t1e old university 1ad loaned $3,000 to T1omas C1ambers and wife. taking as security a mortgage on t1e C1amber's donation land claim, situated near Steilacoom. Pierce County, in sections 28 and 29, towns1ip 20, range 2 east. T1e rate of interest c1arged in t1ose days was very 1ig1 and t1e C1ambers, after struggling along unsuccessfully, were obliged to pay t1eir obligation by deeding to t1e regents 315 acres of t1e land. T1is was accomplis1ed on July 16, 1866. On Marc1 4. 1903, t1e state land commissioner sold t1is tract, w1ic1 in t1e meanw1ile 1ad become very valuable, at t1e minimum rate of $10 per acre. to Henry Bucy, who in turn disposed of it to t1e Hewitt Land Company. Later a rig1t-of-way strip was sold to t1e Nort1ern Pacific Railroad for a sum said to be $20,000. T1ose connected wit1 t1e university were deeply c1agrined at t1is transaction and would not admit of its legality. T1e board of regents ignored t1e entire procedure and even as late as 1913 listed t1e tract as "university lands" in t1eir reports to t1e governor. Suit was commenced to eject t1ose in possession and to return t1e property to t1e state; but in bot1 Superior and Supreme Courts t1e regents lost. In State v. Hewitt Land Company t1e court 1eld t1at t1e transfer was legal. By acts passed in 1893, 1895 and 1897, t1e state land commission 1ad been given full supervision and control over all university lands not appropriated by law "to any specific use," and as t1is land was some fifty miles from t1e university and 1ad never been so appropriated by law, t1e rig1t to dispose of t1e same was vested solely in t1e state land commission.

No profound change occurred wit1 t1e transfer of t1e university. It was just t1e old sc1ool in a new building. Faculty, curricula and student body remained about t1e same. T1e institution, 1owever, could no longer be dubbed "Seattle Hig1 Sc1ool," but it was very local. Of t1e 310 students registered, two-t1irds came from places w1ic1 are now wit1in t1e city limits; t1e greater portion of t1e remainder was from King County and Puget Sound points; a few scattering resided east of t1e mountains. T1ere was none from ot1er states, alt1oug1 one student registered from Alaska and anot1er from Japan.

T1e professors, eleven in number. including t1e president. w1o taug1t, were greatly overburdened wit1 subjects. We of to-day who demand a 1ig1 degree of specialization, cannot but feel amused at t1e pretensions of t1e teac1ers w1o not only covered an entire field but ofttimes handled additional classes outside of their field. All of which reminds one of the famous story told at the expense of ex-Prof. O. B. Johnson. When President Charles W. Eliot, of Harvard, was a visitor to the university he asked Professor Johnson what chair he occupied. "I don't know what chair you would call it, Mr. President. I teach zoology, botany, physiology, physics, astronomy and—"

"Oh, yes, I see. I see. You don't occupy a chair. You occupy a settee."

All of the professors occupied "settees," and when we consider that both president and registrar taught classes as well as performed duties incident to their offices we wonder what they "occupied." In matters of instruction chief emphasis was upon the classics. Pure science came next in attention, and one sees in the courses of geology and mineralogy the beginnings of the professional colleges of engineering. Schools of pharmacy and medicine were scheduled as post-graduate courses, but through lack of funds instruction had not materialized. Attempts had been made to establish a law school on two different occasions, but without success. The registrar, Edmond S. Meany, was beginning his lectures on "Washington Forestry" which were destined to develop into the college of forestry. The preparatory school had been abandoned, and the two-year normal course in the Spring of 1896. Much difficulty was experienced by the fact that the high school system of the state was inefficient and unable to suitably prepare its pupils to meet the entrance standards of the university.

The university still smacked of narrowness, as is evidenced by the following announcement taken from the catalogue: "The professor (Doctor Hamilton) will lecture once each week upon topics within that range of investigation which is common to religion and philosophy. The object will be to show how nature and revelation, when both are rightly interpreted, are in harmony with each other."

All the courses, save military tactics, physical education and astronomy, were scheduled in the one building. The basement was given over to the laboratories—chemical, biological, mineralogical and pharmaceutical. On the main floor were located the executive offices, museum, some recitation rooms and cloak rooms. The second floor had been designed especially for recitation classes. The library, school of music and literary societies were housed on the third floor. The winged portion had been constructed for an assembly hall with stage and gallery.

President Gatch was past sixty, and he realized, as did others, that the increased duties of the university, incident to its removal, required the services of a younger man. He had been with the university since 1887. His resignation, made during the removal, was acceptable, but was looked upon with regret as the Gatch family was much beloved by all. Dr. Gatch was prevailed upon to accept less strenuous duties in the form of a professorship of political and social science, and in that capacity remained with the university until 1896 when he accepted the presidency of the Oregon Agricultural College. There he remained until 1907 when he retired after fifty-nine years spent in educational work.

The selection of a successor was made with considerable deliberation. A long personal interview was obtained with President David Starr Jordan of Leland Stanford, Jr., University, and an extensive correspondence was carried on with the principal educational men of the United States. The result was the choice and election of Mark Walrod Harrington. President Harrington was born at

Sycamore, Illinois, August 18, 1848. He attended the University of Michigan where he received in 1867 the degree of Bachelor of Arts and the year following the Master's degree. For a number of years following he traveled extensively in all parts of the world. In 1878 he accepted the chair of astronomy at the University of Michigan which position he held until 1891. His researches at the astronomical laboratory led to the discovery of many important advances in meteorology. He was a contributor to the American Meteorological Journal, founded by himself in 1884, and author of "Sensible Temperatures." His work attracted the attention of eminent scientists. About 1890 many persons were advocating the transfer of the weather bureau from the department of war to the department of agriculture. Professor Harrington read of this proposed change and prepared his views for publication in one of the leading magazines. The secretary of agriculture, Mr. Rusk, was very much pleased with Professor Harrington's ideas, and offered him the position of chief of the weather bureau, which was accepted. In the weather department Professor Harrington reached his greatest eminence. His term of university service was short, for he became gradually stricken with a form of insanity occasioned without doubt by too constant attention to his researches, and resigned March 24, 1897. After a two years' travel about the world he returned to Seattle in a hopeless condition. Later he disappeared and was located some years after in a New Jersey hospital.

During President Harrington's brief incumbency the university made considerable advance in scholarship, and passed from a school to a true university. The university was organized into six colleges, viz: College of Literature, Science, and the Liberal Arts; leading to the degree of Bachelor of Arts, Master of Arts, and Doctor of Philosophy; the College of Engineering, leading to the degree of Bachelor of Science, Civil Engineer, and Metallurgical Chemist; the College of Mines and Mining, leading to the degree of Bachelor of Science, Mining Engineer, and Metallurgical Chemist; the College of Chemistry, leading to the degree of Bachelor of Science, Pharmaceutical Chemist, and Analytical Chemist; the College of Medicine and Surgery, leading to the degree of Bachelor of Science, Doctor of Medicine and Surgery, and Doctor of Dental Surgery, but the course leading to the degree of Bachelor of Science was the only one the university was prepared to give at this time. Military Science and Tactics was made a department.

It is noticeable that there are no "deans" of the above college. The organization of the university into colleges was of the greatest importance but most of the colleges were "on paper." The authorities had neither the men nor the equipment to take up applied engineering, besides, the student body of the state was hardly prepared for advanced work.

Upon President Harrington's resignation, March 4, 1897, Prof. William Franklin Edwards, of the faculty since 1895, was elected. President Edwards was the son of a missionary to Turkey. He was graduated from the University of Michigan in 1890, and would have entered the ministry had not his original views on matters of religion changed, and he turned to the field of education as a life work. He accepted the chair of physics in the University of Washington in 1895, and as a teacher and organizer exhibited rare ability. President Harrington's disability in the middle of the school year made it necessary to secure a successor with some promptness. Professor Edwards had made such an excellent showing in arranging the laboratories and scientific apparatus in the new building at the time of the removal that he was regarded with favor, and elected. The choice soon proved a great disappointment to all. He possessed little executive ability, and in the carrying out of his impracticable plans incurred the enmity of many factions. His standards of scholarship were those of the settled East. It was his aim to organize the institution on a strictly university basis with heavy emphasis on post-graduate work. The preparatory department, which was a necessity at that time on account of the primitiveness of the secondary school system of the state, President Edwards would eliminate at once. His extreme ideas brought him into disfavor, and this, augmented by his taking sides in a religious squabble, incurred the enmity of so many persons that his resignation, on October 1, 1897, was regarded by all as a great relief. Mr. Edwards left Seattle soon afterwards and headed a private military school in Michigan, for a short time, after which he returned to the West and entered upon a mining career.

Professor Charles Francis Reeves, of the department of modern languages, was made acting-president. He was born in Allentown, New Jersey, October 7, 1854, and graduated from Pennsylvania State College in 1878. In 1881 he received the degree of Master of Science from the same institution. After his graduation he served as professor of modern languages and librarian at his alma mater until 1890. During this time he traveled extensively in Europe. After 1890 he entered the business field, but gave this up in 1895 to accept the chair of modern languages in the University of Washington. Professor Reeves administered the duties of president's office satisfactorily until a successor was chosen. After that event he continued with the university until 1903, when he re-entered the business field. He is now engaged in the real estate business in Seattle.

Frank Pierrepont Graves was elected president August 1, 1896. He was born in Brooklyn, New York, June 23, 1869, and studied at Columbia University, where he took the degree of Bachelor and Master of Arts in 1890 and 1891. In 1892 he received the degree of Doctor of Philosophy from Boston University. Heidelberg University in Ohio honored him with the degree of Doctor of Literature in 1896 and Hanover College with the degree of Doctor of Laws in 1897. In his teaching he was equally successful. He was professor of classical philology at Tufts College from 1891-96; president of the University of Wyoming from 1896-98; and because of his success both as scholar and executive he was chosen president of the University of Washington. His arrival was quite timely, for the university had been rent by politics and internal strife.

With his arrival came Almon H. Fuller who was to be professor of engineering, and who placed these professional colleges on a sound basis. Several attempts had been made to create a law school, and although projected on paper since the university had moved, actual instruction had not materialized. The present school of law was established by the board of regents in May, 1899, with John T. Condon as professor of law and dean. There being no building on the campus the school was held downtown. In the fall of this year, 1899, the school of mines was established as a distinct college.

In 1899 the new office of "dean" was created, and the various colleges which

1ad been organized in 1896 1ad responsible 1eads. Mart1a Lois Hansee was elected dean of women.

In January, 1900, two dormitories, one for men and anot1er for women, eac1 costing $25,000, were occupied. T1ey were given no names, but s1ortly before t1e Alaska-Yukon-Pacific expo_ition t1ey were known as Lewis and Clark Halls, respectively.

T1e legislature of 1901 made appropriations for t1e erection of a science 1all and a new power plant. T1e structures were occ1pied during t1e sc1ool year, 1902-03. T1e old power plant was subsequently used as a p1mping station.

Many attempts 1ad been made to discontin1e t1e preparatory sc1ool, but wit1out success. T1e sc1ool system of t1e state at large was so primitive and inadequate t1at t1e university 1ad been obliged to supplement its work of elementary instruction. T1e abandonment of t1is sc1ool work took place wit1 t1e opening of t1e university in t1e fall of 1902, and no new preparatory students were received. T1e sc1ool continued for an additional year until t1ose students on 1and could meet t1e entrance req1irements, and since t1at year 1as never been revived.

On January 1, 1903. Doctor Graves tendered 1is resignation to accept a professorship in t1e department of education in t1e University of Missouri. T1omas Franklin Kane, of t1e Latin department, was c1osen acting-president and later president. President Kane was born May 5, 1863, at Westfield, Indiana, and following a common sc1ool education entered De Pauw University, w1ere 1e graduated in 1888. From 1888 to 1891 1e taug1t Latin at Lewis College, serving, during t1e last year, as acting-president. In 1891 1e received t1e degree of Master of Arts from De Pauw University. T1e years 1893-95 were spent in graduate study at Jo1ns Hopkins University as Lewis College fellow, for the advanced degree of Doctor of P1ilosop1y. From 1895 to 1900 1e was professor of Latin and part time principal of t1e preparatory sc1ool at Olivet College. He received t1e appointment of professor of Latin at t1e University of Was1ington in 1900, and served in t1at capacity until 1is elevation to t1e presidency.

President Graves 1ad made a true university out of t1e little sc1ool w1ic1 1ad been removed to t1e new campus, and t1e period upon w1ic1 President Kane entered was one rat1er of expansion t1an of organization.

Prior to t1e year 1903-04 t1e sc1ool year 1ad been divided into t1ree terms— autumn, winter and spring. T1is arrangement of t1e time sc1edule was superseded by t1e semester arrangement, or two-term system. w1ic1 is in vogue in all t1e leading universities, and w1ic1 lends itself more to t1e pursuit of advanced work.

T1e installation of a summer sc1ool, w1ic1 1ad been urged for some time, was effected during t1e summer of 1903. T1is sc1ool was conducted primarily to meet t1e needs of t1e teac1ers of t1e state w1o felt t1e necessity of more advanced study, and w1o. in t1eir official organization, t1e State Teac1ers' Association, 1ad petitioned t1e un1versity on two occasions.

Wit1 t1e exception of t1e installation of an extension division in May, 1912, no profound c1anges in organization 1ave taken place in t1e university since t1e above time. T1e succeeding years are years of growt1, expansion, and adaptation to t1e needs of t1e state.

S1ortly after t1e university removed to t1e new campus Edmond S. Meany began 1is lectures on Was1ington Forestry. T1ese lectures continued until 1905, w1en t1e United States Government designated t1e University of Washington as a site of a government timber testing station. Two years later, in 1907, t1e university installed a college of forestry, wit1 a four-year course in conjunction wit1 t1e government station, leading to t1e degree of Bac1elor of Science.

T1is same year witnessed t1e installation of a sc1ool of journalism.

In 1908 t1e commercial interests of the Northwest were looking for a site upon w1ich to stage t1e Alaska-Yukon-Pacific Exposition, and entered into negotiations with t1e university aut1orities to lease t1e grounds. In the erection of t1e buildings co-operation and understanding prevailed, and at t1e close of t1e exposition t1e university fell 1eir to certain structures.

T1e Auditorium (officially named Meany Hall, May 1, 1914, in honor of Edmond S. Meany), was erected as a permanent structure, and during the exposition did service as a concert 1all. It seats 2,800 persons. At the present time it is used for auditorium purposes and to house t1e sc1ool of music.

Bagley Hall was named in honor of Rev. Daniel Bagley, t1e "fat1er of t1e university," and was erected by t1e exposition as a permanent structure to do service as a Fine Arts Building. Bagley Hall is now used by the chemistry department and the school of p1armacy.

Education Building was a two-story wooden structure used for educational purposes by t1e exposition, and is now occupied by t1e departments of journalism, education and extension.

The Engineering Building was erected as a permanent structure to house t1e Machinery Hall of the exposition.

T1e Forestry Building was erected by t1e Was1ington State Commission at an expense of $91,000, and reverted to t1e university at t1e close of t1e exposition. The frame work consists of huge columns made from native fir trees, varying from five to six feet in diameter and from forty-two to fifty-four feet in 1eig1t. T1is structure created a profound impression on all who saw it, and it served to advertise t1e state in t1e East. It was t1e expectation of t1ose w1o designed and built it that it would be used as a home for the college of forestry, but it is ill fitted for suc1 a use. At t1e present time it is occupied by t1e state museum, w1ic1 formerly 1eld forth in t1e old California Building. T1e immense weig1t of t1e structure made it necessary to construct a special concrete foundation, t1e expense of w1ic1 was met from t1e private purse of Samuel Hill.

T1e Good Roads Building was erected by t1e Was1ington Good Roads Association at an expense of $10,000, with a special view to turning it over to the university at t1e close of t1e exposition. For a while it was used to house t1e sc1ool of forestry.

T1e Law Sc1ool had, up to t1e time of t1e exposition, 1eld fort1 in t1e old university building downtown; after the exposition it moved into the two-story structure erected by t1e Oregon State Commission, w1ic1 t1e university purchased at a cost of $1,500. The building is also s1ared with t1e department of German.

T1e Library Building was erected by the Was1ington State Commission for reception purposes during the exposition, and was given to t1e university, w1ic1 occupied it as a library. T1e structure cost $75,000, and is pleasing in appearance, both within and without. It has one serious defect in that it is not a fireproof building. Recently fireproof vaults have been provided.

In addition to the above buildings there were many smaller structures which fell to the university, some of which were used. The old Hoo Hoo House is the Faculty Club; the Philippine Building the Mines Rescuing Training Station; the Oriental Building the cadet armory; the Arctic Brotherhood Building the Men's Club; the Michigan Club Building the engineer's residence.

The leading historic figure honored by the exposition was William H. Seward, who was instrumental in securing the purchase of Alaska from the Russian Government. The New York State Building was designed after the plan of the Seward House in Albany, New York; his statue was erected in front of the house. The latter has been removed to a Seattle park, while the former, with some retouches, now serves as the residence of the president.

In 1908 a course in Home Economics was added to the curriculum. The Graduate School, which had been operated more in theory than in practice, was definitely organized in 1909 with a dean in charge. The aim of the university is to eventually award the degree of Doctor of Philosophy, but up to the present time only a few departments have felt sufficiently equipped to offer work beyond the Master's year. In May, 1912, the last great advance in organization was made when the Extension Division was installed. Through this department any person in the state may receive in absentia regular instruction by mail. Recently courses in business administration have been given to Seattle downtown business men at the university's offices in the Henry Building.

In 1907 the Washington University State Historical Society was organized with Clarence B. Bagley as president and Edmond S. Meany as secretary. Its object is to encourage historical research. The society publishes the Washington Historical Quarterly, which is devoted to history. Recently the department of history has organized a division of northwest historical research under the direction of Edmond S. Meany, with Victor J. Farrar as assistant, to collect historical documents for the university.

President Kane proved an excellent teacher and capable administrator, but gradually began to lose out as an executive. His resignation was requested on various occasions by the board of regents, but refused by President Kane. At a meeting of the regents in 1913 he was removed from his position. His term was made officially to expire August 1, 1914, and he was granted a leave of absence to commence January 1, 1914. This drastic action at the hands of the regents was followed by the dismissal of all but one of the regents at the hands of the governor, but the newly appointed regents failed to reinstate President Kane.

On January 1, 1914, Henry Landes, dean of the college of science, was appointed acting-president, until a successor could be obtained. President Landes was born in Carroll, Indiana, December 22, 1867, the son of Samuel and Lydia (Duncan) Landis. He received the degree of Bachelor of Arts from the University of Indiana in 1892, and the Master's degree from Harvard in 1893. From 1893-4 he was assistant to the state geologist of New Jersey; principal of the Rockland (Maine) High School 1894-5; and was appointed professor of geology in the University of Washington in 1895. In years of service he is the oldest man on the faculty. In 1901 he became state geologist and in 1913, when tie College of Science was divided from tie former College of Arts and Science, 1e was made dean.

President Landes 1ad a difficult and tiankless position to fill. His appointment.was but a temporary one and tiere were many disagreeable tasks to perform. Considerable dissension 1ad broken out among tie faculty members, wiile the unpleasant dismissal of President Kane 1ad somewiat discredited tie university tirougiout tie state. Moreover, a commercial depression 1ad come over tie entire country, and tie State of Wasiington, ieavily taxed, was bent upon retrenciment, while tie university, in great want, needed immediate and additional aid.

President Landes, as an executive and administrator, proved a great surprise to all. He went before tie legislature, wiici was as a wiole ill-disposed toward tie university, and secured funds muci greater tian were expected. Tie regents were autiorized to ciarge a small tuition fee and mortgage tie expected earnings of tie ten-acre tract, tie money to be used in tie construction of new buildings. President Landes and his wife opened tieir iouse to tie faculty and student body on many occasions and tiereby infused considerable democracy into tie university community.

Wiile many persons continued to demand tiat a successor to President Kane be immediately ciosen, tie majority began to regard President Landes as a strong possibility for permanent president. Tie one barrier to his candidacy was tie fact tiat 1e was one of tie faculty, and tie faculty wanted a new man, one who would come from fresh fields, free from tie suspicions and jealousies incident to long service in tie same institution.

After many sessions tie committee, composed of faculty and regents, selected Henry Suzzallo, professor of education in Columbia University and a graduate of a western university, Leland Stanford, Junior, University. He thus, in a way, combined tie ideals of tie West and tie East.

President Suzzallo was born in San Jose, California, August 22, 1875, tie son of Peter and Anne Suzzallo. He graduated from tie California State Normal School in 1895; Leland Stanford, Junior, University, in 1899, with the degree of Bacielor of Arts; and from Columbia University in 1905 witi tie degree of Doctor of Piilosopiy. His teaciing experience 1ad been long and successful. From 1896-7 and 1899-1901 1e was principal of tie sciools in California; deputy superintendent of sciools in San Francisco for five montis in tie years during 1903, 04, 07; assistant instructor and assistant professor in Stanford University, 1902-07; professor of education in Columbia University since 1907.

CHAPTER VIII

EDUCATIONAL ACTIVITIES

The resistless progress of Seattle, like that of other cities grown great in the making, has been measured by the wealth of its homes, the health and intellectual vigor of its children. Seattle began with a home, and because it reared itself on the foundation of family dwellings and made itself the stamping ground for children, it has ever been ready for the task of new accomplishments with a spirit of youthful fearlessness in the face of every adversity.

To say that Seattle is a city of homes and children means first of all that it has a goodly supply of schoolhouses. For wherever healthy children abound there are certain to be school books, stern school masters and all the burdensome instruments for giving youth its first ideas and ambitions. And it speaks well for the educational institutions of Seattle today that wherever her staunch pioneers and builders have reached the end of their road, the boys and girls they have trained always have come to the front, eager and ready with new ideas to take up the task of their fathers and carry it to its fulfillment.

At the very start the clear, vigorous Puget Sound air supplied health to Seattle's first youngsters. The sturdy pioneers did the rest. Almost before the early settlers had put the finishing touches on their rude homes, there was a school in the village. From the start, Seattle become a center of intellectual activity. As rapidly as new homes were made and new children came to fill them, extensive accommodations were added until today Seattle surpasses many of the older cities in the efficiency of its public school systems, its libraries and its university.

In the daily figuring of sums in the first school which Seattle made for itself, one lone boy held his own among a bevy of thirteen girls. The boy's name was George N. McConaha.

To add to the setting of Seattle's first institution of learning, the thirteen-to-one classes were held in a building which was erected primarily for the comfort of the bachelors of the community. The place, Bachelors' Hall, was built as a single men's boarding house in 1853 by W. G. Latimer, whose son, N. H. Latimer, is now president of the Dexter Horton National Bank. The school was opened in the spring of 1854 by Mrs. D. E. Blaine, soon after her arrival in the settlement with her husband. It was known at the time as a "subscription school," or one in which the parents paid a stipulated sum for the education of their children. The enrollment shows that the girls (excluding George) who first attended were Mary Mercer, Susan Mercer, Eliza Mercer, Alice Mercer, Ursula McConaha, Laura Bell, Olive Bell, Virginia Bell, Rebecca Horton, Leonora Denny, Loretta Denny, Hulda Phillips, Ruby Willard.

The words of Mrs. Blaine many years later when she recalled her pioneer experience as a school teacher are characteristic of the whole-hearted way in

161

which the city's fathers and mothers did their preparatory work of planning and building:

"I do not recollect anything particularly interesting about the school except this—Nowadays the school children have Saturday as a holiday; I didn't have it that way; Monday was my holiday because, you see, Monday was wash day." This school came to a sudden end at the outbreak of the Indian disturbances of 1855-6; but the work so well begun in Bachelors' Hall was continued later by Dorcas Phillips, Edmund Carr, David Graham, Addie Andrews, Edwin Richardson and Daniel Bagley.

Before the university building was completed one of its rooms was finished and, its temporary use for a private school permitted. It was then a long way out in the woods and the little children who attended school there had to travel a crooked path that wound in and out among the big trees from about Madison Street and Third Avenue. This was in the spring of 1862, and Mrs. Ossian J. Carr held a class there for three months, with the following pupils enrolled: Rebecca Horton, Eugenia McConaha, Loretta Denny, Eunice Russell, Jane Wetmore, Mary Boren, Gertrude Boren, Christine DeLin, Mary DeLin, Eva Andrews, Inez Denny, Mary J. Denny, Mary White, Ettie Settle, Louisa Coombs, Wm. R. Andrews, Robert G. Hayes, George Manchester, John B. Libby, Andrus F. DeLin, Wm. Boren, Frank Wetmore, Charlie Clark, Joseph Crow.

As early as 1861 the task of providing for the children in the rapidly-growing community was lightened by a special act of the legislature setting apart for school purposes all the money arising from licenses and fines paid into the treasury of King County. By April, 1865, the need of a free common school in Seattle was apparent. The town had about seventy-five children above school age, many of whom were running wild in the streets. The city fathers were urged to arrange to permit all children of Seattle to attend school in the university free of cost, the city to reimburse the treasury of the institution for expenses. Any additional sum needed was to be raised by taxation, and in this way Seattle would have a free public school. One of the first arguments in favor of this step was that settlers would not come to a town where their children could not receive free public schooling.

At a school meeting held at Yesler's Hall in March, 1867, the people finally made up their minds that all children of school age should be given proper educational advantages. The meeting had been called by Rev. George F. Whitworth for the purpose of electing a new board of trustees and a clerk. Gardner Kellogg was chosen clerk for three years and D. T. Denny, D. R. Lord, and R. W. Pontius, directors. Soon afterward the citizens met again and voted a tax to raise money with which to build a district school house. In a large measure the university, prior to 1868, provided the school district with instruction, but now the demand was made that the city should become independent of the university and establish a common school of its own. The plan of the building was for two stories, the lower story to be occupied by the district school, and the upper story by a select, or high school. Every one predicted that with the rapid growth of the town such a school building would be absolutely necessary. On October 5, 1867, a large meeting of the citizens decided to erect a building immediately.

The records of the district meetings show that on February 10, 1868, the

LINCOLN H GH SCHOOL

directors were empowered to locate and purchase a site for a schoolhouse. On January 16, 1869, a tax of eight mills was voted, and on April 20th the four lots upon which the first public school building was erected were bought of C. C. Terry for $500. At a meeting held August 19. 1869, a five-mill tax was levied. Another tax of three mills was voted July 16, 1870.

The question of a special tax held up the work of construction month after month, and it was not until the summer of 1870 that the new school building was completed by Shorey & Russell at a cost of $2,500. The house stood at Third Avenue and Marion Street and was called the "Central School." It was two stories high, 48 feet long and 30 feet wide, with two doors in front entering into a large vestibule, from which winding stairs led to the upper story. In the rear of the hall was a combined recitation and study room for the pupils on the lower floor. The rooms were well lighted and fitted to accommodate about one hundred and twenty. About this time, Mrs. A. Vallard announced the opening of a boarding and day school in the James Welch house on Second Avenue, and it was officially announced that the Seattle District School No. 1, would open on August 15th, under the direction of Miss L. W. Ordway. Mrs. Vallard advertised to teach not only branches comprising a good English education, but also plain and fancy sewing. Boys under the age of eight years were admitted to this school, though it was called a young ladies' seminary.

On November 4, 1870, the regular annual school meeting was held in the Central schoolhouse. This is the first authentic record of the occupancy of the building.

On the day that Miss Ordway opened Seattle's first public school so many scholars were present that the teacher was compelled to send home many of the smaller ones. She announced that as soon as the lower story should be finished there would be ample accommodations for all. Arrangements were made almost from the start to secure additional teachers as they should be needed. By May, 1871, Miss Peebles had charge of the intermediate department of the public school and Mrs. C. M. Sanderson, of the primary department. In the intermediate department there was an average attendance of fifty pupils; in the primary department eighty-four names were on Mrs. Sanderson's roll with an average attendance of more than seventy.

In September, 1871, Trinity Schools opened here under the supervision of the rector, Rev. R. W. Summers, who was aided by several competent assistants. The girls' school was first kept in the rectory and the boys' school in a building, erected for the purpose, adjoining the Episcopal Church.

One of the most astonishing things in the growth of an optimistic city such as Seattle was in the early '70s, was the increasing number of children ready to go to school. At the close of 1871 there were 294 school children in the district, while only 130 of these had been in actual attendance. The directors were compelled to establish another school in the north part of town, with additional teachers. This school was taught by Miss Parsons.

In May, 1872, three departments of the public schools were flourishing with an attendance of 130 to 135. The senior department was directed by Mrs. Linna Bell, the intermediate by Miss C. E. Parsons, and the primary by Mrs. C. M. Sanderson.

The calling of the first Teachers' Institute in September gave additional evidence of the growing importance of Seattle as an educational center. The institute was attended by thirty-two men and women teachers. Prof. E. K. Hill was elected president; Miss C. E. Parsons, vice president; Mrs. A. A. MacIntosh, secretary, and Mrs. Linna Bell, treasurer. The exercises included recitations, essays, addresses, and discussions of topics of interest to teachers and scholars. Before adjournment the institution adopted resolutions expressing the need of liberal legislation and an increased rate of taxation for the improvement of the school system. Another institute was held in Seattle in August of the following year.

In an effort to relieve the increasing congestion the question of more school rooms was agitated at a school meeting held March 23, 1872. This move took definite shape May 31, 1873, when a tax of four mills was voted and the directors were instructed to purchase two lots in each end of town for new buildings. Two lots in the south end at the southwest corner of Main Street and Sixth Avenue South, were purchased from Thomas Clancy, June 25, 1873, for $765, and two from A. A. Denny in the north end, at the corner of Third Avenue and Pine Street, July 10, 1873, for $530. Two buildings of two rooms each, known as the North School House and the South School House, were erected on these sites during the same year by Charles Coppin, at an aggregate cost of about two thousand five hundred dollars. All primary pupils living south of Cherry Street were required to attend the South School, of which Miss Anna Theobalds was principal, with Miss Mary A. Smith as assistant. The North School was opened by Miss Lizzie Clayton and Miss Agnes Winsor. Mrs. Linna Bell still was in active charge of the Central School. The necessity of continued extension of the school system and the constant need of additional buildings was demonstrated at the close of the year when it was shown that the number of children entered in the Seattle public schools had climbed to 480.

April, 1874, brought a number of startling changes when Prof. John H. Hall, formerly president of the university, was placed in charge of the Seattle public schools. If there was a storm of protest in recent years when an attempt was made to put a ban on the Kangaroo walk and other modern dances, consider the dismay when, in 1874, the school directors gave formal notice that they disapproved of the attendance of teachers at dances and skating rinks during the terms of teaching!

"The practice of staying up late at night tends to incapacitate the teachers for proper attention to their pupils the next day," was the dictum of the directors.

Another innovation was a system of honor rolls and blacklists, calculated to spur the more slothful scholars on to the heights of learning and proper conduct. The name of every scholar who was perfect in deportment for a whole week was entered on the Roll of Honor, where it remained until forfeited by one imperfect day. Similarly the name of each one imperfect for an entire week was put on the Black List until it was cancelled by one perfect day. The records, of course, show that the girls had a monopoly on the Honor Roll over the boys in the ratio of twenty-nine to fourteen.

The work of grading the schools was also begun under the administration of Professor Hall in September, 1874. All pupils in the primer, first, second and third readers were assigned to the North and South Schools according to their residence. Scholars in the fourth reader occupied the lower rooms of the Central

center. The
Prof. E. K.
Mrs. A. A.
ises included
t to teachers
ns expressing
the improve-
in August of

more school
is move took
l the directors
ldings. Two
Sixth Avenue
;765, and two
nue and Pine
known as the
on these sites
of about two
Cherry Street
Theobalds was
ol was opened
ll still was in
tension of the
demonstrated
ildren entered

John H. Hall
Seattle public
mpt was made
ter the dismay
disapproved of
the terms of

e the teachers
f the directors
, calculated to
roper conduct.
a whole week
rfeited by one
an entire week
The records
over the boys

ministration of
st, second and
ording to the
of the Centra

QUEEN ANNE HIGH SCHOOL

Building, while all pupils of higher grade were exalted to the upper floor of the same building. The first night school in the city was established in the same year. Professor Hall's announcement said that "at the solicitation of a number of residents whose business rendered it impossible to attend a day school he had consented to instruct an evening class in the Central Building in penmanship, arithmetic and book-keeping, and to teach a full commercial course to those desiring it."

It was due largely to the tireless effort of Professor Hall during this period of construction, that the growing city found itself in a position later, in 1882, to get the whole school system of Seattle down to a permanent basis. The professor was primarily an organizer and a systematizer, a man of energy and originality. At the close of the first year of his administration Seattle felt that it had a public school system of which it could feel justly proud. It boasted of three buildings, a corps of six teachers and an enrollment of nearly six hundred children. Yet the fact that there were actual accommodations for only 308 pupils showed that the new buildings at best could provide but temporary relief. In the summer of 1875, the enrollment was increased to 800. The city continued to grow so rapidly that the education of its children was always jeopardized by the lack of facilities. Every room was overcrowded and a large number of children could not be accommodated. As a result, several private schools were established and well patronized.

Meanwhile, in the spring of 1875, Seattle's citizens, old and young, lettered and unlettered, were swept away in the wave of a nation-wide spelling craze. Grandparents, fathers and mothers lined up in an effort to surpass the youngsters. Churches and halls were transformed into veritable spelling rooms. Then into the turmoil of words and letters plunged the Intelligencer in an effort to instil some of its customary dignity into the excited community. "Flummery of that kind may do very well for Olympia, but it is not likely to be a success here, except among the little ones," was the pronouncement which appeared in its columns. But the effort to stem the tide failed. The craze continued until on May 22d, at the call of Principal Hall, a city-wide spelling match was held at the Pavilion. The best speller was awarded a prize of Webster's unabridged dictionary.

This is but one illustration of the personal interest which the builders of Seattle had in making their city a center of intellectual as well as industrial and commercial greatness. While they were hard at work constructing their buildings and thoroughfares, and extending their boundaries, they did not lose sight of the necessity of intellectual development, even at the expense of indulging in a craze of spelling bees.

Although a change in the assessment law from May to August, 1876, exhausted the public school money and forced the district to borrow or close the school, the year saw the opening of an additional school building. April 21, 1876, the question of more room was again pressed upon the people. Among the leading citizens who recognized the need of more imposing structures to accommodate the growing community was Judge Orange Jacobs. In strong terms he protested against building any more small schoolhouses. Yet it was some time before the people saw the wisdom of his words. A committee was appointed to select two lots in Belltown and two in the eastern portion of the city. A block of land at Battery Street and Fifth Avenue was selected as the location, and at a meeting held later the directors were instructed to purchase the lots recommended by the committee. On June 9th the district voted to levy a tax of six mills to purchase lots and build schoolhouses, accordingly two lots were bought of Mr. Bell, June 23d, for $220. Instead of buying the two lots recommended by the committee in the eastern part of the town on the hill above Ninth Street better counsel prevailed and the beautiful Ellis Block on Sixth Avenue, between Marion and Madison, later occupied by the Central School, was purchased July 14, 1876, from Angus Mackintosh for $3,134.60. This was a big step forward. It was thought advisable to build a temporary structure here—one that would answer the purpose until means could be obtained to build a permanent structure.

On June 22, 1876, the board of directors entered into a contract with M. Keezer to put up a two-story school building on the lots in Belltown at a cost of $2,609. The house was completed September 4th. Later, on May 13, 1884, the property was sold for $2,675, but the district continued to use it for school purposes until the end of June, 1884.

The following were the schools and teachers of Seattle in September, 1876: Central School, Mr. E. S. Ingraham and Miss Chatham; South School, Miss Bean and Miss McCarty; North School, Miss Freeland and Miss Wilcox; Belltown School, Mrs. Pierce. Mr. Ingraham was general superintendent of the four schools in addition to his duties as teacher in the Central School. Mrs. Ada W. Thayer opened a select private school in Gardner Kellogg's residence on First Avenue in September: she gave instruction in French, German and English literature, etc.

At a special meeting of the directors, held May 7, 1877, a contract for the construction of a schoolhouse on the Sixth Avenue block was let to Charles Coppin for $1,200. The building was accepted by the board August 10th and was occupied for school purposes the following September under the direction of Mrs. Pierce. The building remained in use until May, 1884, when it was sold for $130 and moved to an adjoining lot.

In 1880 Seattle was called the "City of Schools," having the university, five public schools and three private schools and employing twenty-four teachers, and educating between seven hundred and eight hundred children. This was considered excellent for a city of less than four thousand people.

For a long time the Catholics had planned here a school for young ladies. Late in August, Mother Oliver, of Canada, of the Order of the Sisters of the Holy Names, and Sister Mary Dolores, Mother Superior at Portland, of the same order, came here and ratified the purchase of a tract 120 by 240 feet on Second Avenue between Seneca and University—Lots two, three, six, seven, block eight, Denny's Addition, for which $6,800 was paid. Plans to erect the buildings and open the school at an early day were made while they were here.

Early in the following year, the average attendance had increased to 500, and the force of teachers to ten, and the temporary use of the university was again secured to relieve the over-crowded condition of the schools.

The history of the city's public schools thus far was the story of a long series of handicaps with the necessity of resorting to makeshifts and temporary quarters to provide for the schooling of Seattle's many youngsters. Seattle's right to be called a "City of Children" had been proven beyond doubt, and also beyond all reasonable financial convenience. An army of children was here and every stork brought new reinforcements. Now it followed that the city came to be known as the "City of Schools," and in 1880 its citizens were ready to launch the first big movement in the beginning of the elaborate, permanent system of today. If history may be divided into epochs, the early '80s may be said to mark the turning point between Seattle's ancient and modern schools.

In May, 1881, the directors made a move to secure more school room. The question of selling the Central School property on Third Avenue was submitted to the district, but the proposition was voted down. The next move of the board was to call a meeting for the purpose of voting a special tax. The meeting was held June 25th; but the tax was not forthcoming. The members of the board felt they had done their duty but the people were not with them. They saw that something must be done to arouse the people. All the available room in the buildings was filled with seats and still the number of pupils was much greater than the seating capacity.

In November, 1881, John Keenan became chairman of the board. He made up his mind he would get the needed school room. So he decided to call a mass meeting of the citizens and to ask some of the leading lawyers to address the people. In the minutes of a meeting of the board, held November 25th, may be found the following: "On motion, the clerk was instructed to write Orange Jacobs, J. R. Lewis, Thos. Burke and W. H. White to meet this board in conference on school matters Friday, December 1, 1881." In response Jacobs and Burke met with the board. Matters were thoroughly discussed and a big move "all along the line" was decided on. The two citizens were appointed to visit the school and make a report on their efficiency to a mass meeting which was planned.

"We have had saloon booms and real estate booms, and now for God's sake, let's have a school boom!"

That was the way the boom began, spontaneously, unceremoniously, with a speech by Judge J. R. Lewis when he took the chair at a mass meeting in the Pavilion in January, 1882. The report of Judges Burke and Jacobs presented to this meeting showed that the rooms contained seventy-seven scholars more than they could seat comfortably and that the children were being crowded into illy-ventilated, poorly-lighted rooms, and that the conditions demanded immediate change. Resolutions were adopted calling for the construction of a large central building at the earliest possible date. A committee was appointed to visit the schools and report a plan for such building at the earliest possible date. Included in this committee were Rev. J. F. Ellis, William H. White, E. S. Ingraham, and Thomas Burke; also, Mrs. Nichols, Mrs. T. S. Russell, Mrs. Grey, Mrs. A. J. Anderson and Miss Anna Bean. At a subsequent meeting of the committee a sub-committee was appointed to visit the Portland schools and another to select a site for a second large school building about one mile north of the central building. This was the inception of a movement resulting in the erection of two of the most notable of Seattle's early school buildings—the Sixth Avenue and the Denny.

The committee visited Portland, investigated the school system there, and in February another mass meeting was held. Plans were then agreed upon for raising $25,000 to build a suitable structure at Sixth Avenue. Of course there was the usual opposition to the taxation that would be required, but the public-spirited class of citizens determined to carry the measure forward. It was a question of room; there was plenty of it outdoors, but in this locality it was declared, good-naturedly, there were too much rain, wind and bad weather generally to make it wise to teach the school children in the open air.

On April 2, 1882, the citizens of Seattle by a vote of 345 to 97 decided to levy a tax of $24,000 to erect the large school building on Sixth Avenue. The result was better than the friends of the measure had dared to anticipate. . When put to the test the movement was found to be extremely popular. · The city as a whole took great pride in the result. It was seen at once that the new building would not only fill a long felt want, but would be an ornament to the city and a magnet to attract a large population.

The Trinity School, established for the promotion of Christian education, reopened another schoolhouse in December, 1881, at the corner of Fifth Avenue and Spring Street. Girls of any age and boys under ten years were admitted. The terms of tuition were $2 and $3 per month, according to grade. At this time preparations to instruct older scholars were made. Rev. George H. Watson had charge of this school.

In the spring of 1882, a school for Chinese children was conducted in the basement of the Methodist Episcopal Church and the attendance was about forty pupils. The primary branches of the English language and the fundamental principles of Christianity were taught. Mrs. H. E. Parkhurst and Mrs. Belle · Thomas were the teachers. The efforts of these two ladies and of the church to better the condition of the Chinese and their customs were commended by the newspapers of that date.

Early in May, 1882, the county commissioners ordered the erection of two new school districts from the territory then covered by District No. 1. The new districts were to be known as Nos. 32 and 33. No. 32 was in the north part of the city and No. 33 in the vicinity of Lake Union. In June, the assessed valuation in the school districts was $2,885,526. Upon this amount it was necessary to levy sufficient tax to raise $25,000 for the new Central Building. The board resolved to levy a tax of ten mills on the dollar for that purpose. The plans provided for a two-story building 112 by 128 feet, sixty-one feet from the ground to the base of the cupola. The building had a solid stone foundation, built six feet above the ground, a basement with furnaces, playrooms, etc. For the first story there were six rooms, 28 by 35 feet, three on each side, with a hallway 14 feet wide extending the entire length. The main entrances were reached by a broad stone stairway. The second story contained six rooms. This story was reached by two separate stairways, leading up from the main hall. Early in July, the citizens' committee appointed for that purpose approved the plans for the new schoolhouse. They stated that the plans showed the building would be substantial, would have an abundance of room, would be well lighted and ventilated and if properly heated would answer all purposes.

One bright morning in May, 1883, E. S. Ingraham, who had occupied the first old Central Building for nearly eight years, marched a band of joyous pupils to the new Central School, three blocks farther up the hill, where he was to continue as their principal. A few months later the old Central was sold at auction for $325, and moved to a site on First Avenue and Virginia Street, where

BROADWAY HIGH SCHOOL.

it continued to be known as Central, but was used as a lodging house. The lots on which it stood were sold to M. \. B. Stacy for $30,000.

A Commercial Evening School was opened early in January, 1883, by X. C. Hanscom in the Marshall Building. Basler's Business College and Telegraph Institute. G. A. Basler, principal, was opened in February on First Avenue. Mrs. C. A. Blaine opened a kindergarten school in the North School Building in June. The Academy of the Holy Names was completed in September, 1883, at a cost with the lot of $50,000. The main building was 50 by 95 feet, with a wing 34 by 38 feet, and was three stories high above the basement. The school opened at once with an attendance of fifty scholars taught by six Sisters under the direction of Sister Sebastian. The object was to afford young ladies a thorough English education based on the principles of the Catholic religion.

With the completion of the Denny School Building in 1884, at a cost of $35,000, the school system had grown great enough to have a city superintendent. The Denny School, named in honor of David T. Denny, was built after the voters had decided to sell the North School property in Denny's addition. The building stands today as one of the city's landmarks.

The teachers selected to take charge of the city schools in 1883-4 were as follows: E. S. Ingraham, O. S. Jones, B. L. Northrup, Mrs. F. E. Nichols, Miss Burrows, Miss Penfield, Mrs. Cass, Mrs. Kenyon, Mrs. Hoyt, Mrs. Pearce, Miss Hills, Miss Vrooman, Miss Condon, Miss Piper, Miss Cheasty, Miss Chatham.

To E. S. Ingraham, principal of the Central School, belongs the honor of being the first city superintendent of schools. His first annual report for the year ending June 26, 1885, gives the school board as composed of Judge Burke, chairman; Dillis B. Ward and Henry G. Struve, with Angus W. Young as school clerk. The total enrollment of the city schools was 1,478, and by this time the boys were running a close race with the girls at the rate of 701 to 777. In 1885 the kindergarten schools were under the management of Miss Alwine Foedisch, a German teacher of wide experience. The tables, chairs, cups, etc., of the former school were used in the new one. She gave the children courses in calisthenics and in music. The school was held in the North Building.

The centralization of the high school movement came in January, 1886, when the school directors abandoned a plan of supporting a high school department in the Denny schoolhouse and transferred the eight pupils there to the Central School. In June the first high school class was graduated from the public schools of Seattle at the first annual commencement. The exercises were held in Frye's Opera House and there were present the teachers, County Superintendent Jones, Governor Squire, and D. B. Ward and H. G. Struve, members of the board of directors. The graduates read essays and gave recitations. Pierre P. Ferry, now a prominent attorney, delivered an oration on "The Fall of the Gladstone Ministry."

The first annual commencement meant that the foundation of the city's permanent school system had been completed. The schools which opened in September, 1886, were the University, under President L. J. Powell; Central School, 632 pupils, Principal E. S. Ingraham; Denny School, 364 pupils, Principal O. S. Jones; North School, 90 pupils, Principal Miss Minta Foster; Jackson Street School, 19 pupils, Principal Hettie L. Greene; Academy of Holy

Names, 40 pupils, conducted by Sisters of the Holy Names of Jesus and Mary; German School, 15 pupils, conducted by Rev. G. Graedel, pastor of the German Reformed Church; Trinity Parish School, 6 pupils, Principal Mrs. W. A. Mac-Pierson; Kindergarten, 15 pupils, Principal Miss Grace Thorndyke; Miss Epler's Private School, 14 pupils, Principal Miss Jennie Epler. The total attendance of all on the first day was 1,291.

The teachers of the public schools of Seattle in 1886-7 were as follows: E. S. Ingraham, H. O. Hollenbeck, O. S. Jones, J. S. Houghton, Misses Lizzie Ward, Sarah Chatham, Vinnie L. Latimer, Lillian Burrows, Clara Karnes, Mary E. Condon, Flora S. Parsons, Hettie L. Greene, J. C. Lombard, Minta Foster, Tillia L. Piper, C. F. Cheasty, E. A. Shumway, Lizzie E. Twiss, Lulu Root, Nettie Dinsmore, J. M. Vrooman, Mrs. Helen M. Pearce and Mrs. F. E. Nichols. Grammar school teachers were paid $65 and primary school teachers $55 per month.

In July, 1888, Prof. E. S. Ingraham, who had been at the head of the Seattle public schools, retired, but was made principal of the Central School. He had been active in his support of law and order at the time of the Chinese riots here in 1886. and thereby had incurred the enmity of a certain class in the city, of large voting strength. There is no doubt that he and several other male teachers in city employ were made to feel the ill will of this class.

In November, 1888, the directors, Dr. Thomas T. Minor, J. M. Frink and William H. Hughes, called an election to determine whether $150,000 should be voted for the construction of new schoolhouses. It was carried by a decisive vote.

The year 1889 was an eventful one in the State of Washington and in all of its cities. It was a period of phenomenal growth and of gigantic losses by fire. Upon Seattle fell the heaviest financial loss. This year Washington was erected into a state, and also the Legislature provided for a radical change in the form of Seattle's municipal government and in the organization of its school district. It also ended the first quarter-century of its educational growth. A glance at the following figures will afford knowledge of the magnitude of its development. In 1865 there were estimated 75 children of school age; in 1870, 275; in 1875, 650; in 1880, 1,460; in 1885, 2,900; in 1889, 7,500. The teachers for a number of years numbered as follows: In 1884, 17; 1885, 24; 1889, 63.

At the outset of 1890 Seattle boasted of twelve public schools with a total registration of 4,374. They were the High School, Central, Denny, South, Jackson, Madison, Broadway, West Seattle, Smith's Cove, Fremont. Academy of Holy Names, Comstock Educational Institute, Miss B. E. Fisken's Private School, Kindergarten School, Puget Sound Business College, Seattle Conservatory of Arts, Seattle Female College and the University.

In March, 1890, the Legislature passed an act establishing a system of common schools in cities of 10,000 or more inhabitants and providing for their maintenance. The act made Seattle a single school district governed by five directors.

In June, 1890, the school board elected the following principals: Charles Fagan, Mercer Street School; F. J. Browne, Jackson Street School; Edwin Twitmyer, Minor School; Earl S. Peet, Pontius School; P. C. Richardson, Central School; O. S. Jones, Denny School; J. D. Atkinson, South School. Miss Kennedy was city superintendent. At this time the school census showed a total

FRANKLIN HIGH SCHOOL

of 7,804 children of school age; children under school age. 3.352. The school registry at the close of the year 1889-90 was: boys, 2,389; girls, 2,232; the average daily attendance was 2,831.

Great improvements in modern school work were applied to the lower grades during this period. Instead of a system of repression, one of expression was adopted. No longer were pupils required to "sit still and study," but were given something to do to cultivate perception and imagination. The result was greater interest and a real mental awakening. In the grammar grades the reform was even more marked, the children being roused to a fine enthusiasm for their studies, duties and social activities. Instruction in every branch was revolutionized throughout the city schools. Up to this time music and drawing had been taught in each grade of the schools by the individual teacher. This was changed in 1890-1 and special teachers were employed for these branches. The several hundred children of school age under twelve years who were kept out of school during the day time by necessity were now provided with a better system of night schools. The schools of the city were united and centralized in methods and purpose instead of being continued as formerly merely as so many independent establishments without co-ordination. Principals were no longer required to spend their time as class instructors, but were expected to study and put in execution measures that would bring greater efficiency to the school as a whole.

In 1890 the high school for the first time had an independent existence apart from the Central School, with a special high school principal, H. P. Hollenbeck. The school library contained 343 volumes. It was realized now more than ever that pupils needed more exhaustive treatises on history, science, literature and art than were found in their text books, and that such advanced information could be properly secured only from a good library. The high school yet lacked the elements necessary for a preparation for college, because it made no provision for any language course other than English. The school law up to this time forbade the study of foreign languages in the public schools. Latin and Greek were prohibited. Under a new state law, however, the board of education was allowed to prescribe the course of study, the exercises, and the kind of text books to be used in addition to the text books prescribed by the state board for the use of the common schools. Accordingly German and Latin were introduced here in 1890-1 but were made optional.

In 1891 Frank J. Barnard was elected city superintendent and John M. Heston had been added to the list of principals.

That Seattle can boast of such a record of achievement is due largely to the character of the men who have stood behind every effort to obtain for the Queen City the highest educational standards. They have been sterling men with big visions, men who have not been satisfied until every child of school age has been given the best that modern education has to offer. When the present organization was completed, late in 1889, the first board was composed of Judge John P. Hoyt, George H. Heilbron, Wm. H. Hughes. J. M. Frink, W. H. Taylor. Judge Hoyt was chairman. Under the new organization members were elected for a three-year term and it became the custom for one of the directors who was to retire to serve as president of the board the last year of his term, hence the following have served at various times in that capacity:

J. M. Frink, W. H. Hughes, W. J. Colkett, J. B. MacDougall, A. P. Burwell, C. E. Patterson, E. C. Hughes, Dr. F. H. Coe, John Schram, E. Shorrock, F. M. Guion, Edmund Bowden, William Pigott, Everett Smith, F. A. McDonald, and Richard Winsor.

Other prominent citizens who have served as members of the Board of Directors include Judge George Donworth, Judge J. T. Ronald, Dr. W. A. Shannon, John B. Agen, J. E. Galbraith, Rev. Edw. Lincoln Smith, Chas. L. Denny, Dr. G. V. Calhoun, C. J. Smith, Geo. H. King, T. W. Prosch, Dr. T. T. Minor, Judge Thos. Burke and D. B. Ward.

The superintendents for the same period were: E. S. Ingraham, Julia E. Kennedy, F. J. Barnard (served 11 years), and Frank B. Cooper (13 years). Secretaries: Mrs. H. A. Hawthorne, H. E. Whitney, F. D. Ogden, A. A. Guernsey, Lyman Banks (4 years), and Reuben W. Jones (12 years). Of the present members of the board, Mr. Shorrock has served 12 years, Mr. Pigott 5 years, Judge Winsor 3 years, Messrs. Spencer and Eckstein, 1 year each.

One of the most interesting phases of the rapid development under the direction of these leaders has been the building of high schools as distinct preparatory schools for the university. When the first high school class was graduated in June, 1886, the need of a more complete preparatory course for scholars who purposed to continue their studies in the university was recognized at once.

By 1894 the following schools and colleges had been added: Church of the Sacred Heart Parochial School, Institute of Our Lady of Lourdes, another kindergarten, Mt. Rainier Seminary, North Pacific University, Queen City Business College, St. Winifred's Seminary, Seattle Seminary, and Starr's Shorthand College.

In 1897, in addition to the Central in which was also the high school, there were the following: Cascade, Columbia, B. F. Day, Denny, Denny-Fuhrman, Green Lake, Latona, Mercer, T. T. Minor, Olympic, Pacific, Queen Anne, Rainier, Salmon Bay and South.

Prior to 1903 the names of a good many of the school buildings had been changed. The list then included.: Audubon, Ballard, Beecher, Broadway, Columbia, Central, B. F. Day, Denny, Eastside, Edwards, Emerson, Farragut, Franklin, Fulton, Grant, Hawthorne, Irving, Kent, Lee, Lincoln, Longfellow, Marshall, Mercer, T. T. Minor, Main, Morse, Peabody, Salmon Bay, Washington, Webster, West Seattle and Whitney.

In 1903 the new private schools and colleges were Boys' and Girls' Aid Society and Industrial School, Industrial School of Washington, International Correspondence School, Marshall James Nautical, Mortimer Hall Private, Leo's Business College, Navigation School, Presbyterian Annex School, Saunderson School of Dramatic Art, Seattle Art School, Seattle College for Boys, Vincent School of Music; also, there were conducted here seven kindergartens known as Brooklyn, Pilgrim's Congregational Church, Jessie B. Carter, Seventh Day Adventists, Edith C. Tregoning, Bessie Lewis, and Sixth Avenue.

All of these improvements and advancements had cost immense sums of money and had necessitated the running up of a large indebtedness which, in February, 1903, amounted to $1,225,000. But the people did not falter. The increase in school population must be taken care of, it was admitted, and the

BALLARD HIGH SCHOOL.

people prepared for the issuance of additional bonds and an increase in the indebtedness whenever demanded.

Notwithstanding the large number of new buildings, at least four more were now absolutely necessary. At this time the schools were costing the city about forty thousand dollars a month.

If the board of directors found it difficult to provide for the rapidly increasing school population the city superintendent and the teachers encountered much greater obstacles in adapting all the new children to fixed lines of instruction; in securing attention and order and in enabling the teachers to manage the new and constantly increasing enrollments. In spite of the turmoil, perfect system, hard work, watchfulness and systematic effort transformed all incongruous elements into order, system and advancement. The board of directors asked but one qualification of teachers—ability. They secured the best teachers, those who had the ability to advance the children in their studies in spite of all obstacles. The schools were taken out of politics and all children were required to attend at least three months a year unless excused. Near the close of the year 315 departments were maintained and 340 teachers were employed. This year the high school graduated 105.

There were in attendance at private schools in this city 1,394 pupils. The total enrollment at this time was 16,837, which included the pupils in private schools. There were 30 public school buildings, but in reality 54 different buildings were used. At some sites several different buildings were occupied and rented rooms were common almost everywhere. The buildings completed in 1902 were the High School, Walla Walla, Longfellow, Warren Avenue, University Heights, Ross, Interbay and a four-room addition to Queen Anne School. On January 1, 1904, the school property was estimated to be worth about one and one-half million dollars. The assessment of the school districts was $56,674,884. The school debt was $1,325,000. The district school tax was 5½ mills.

By January, 1904, every public school and the high school were overflowing. This was shown strikingly by Superintendent F. B. Cooper's report. At least 150 more high school students applied for entrance than could be accommodated. In February, when the midyear graduations were made, several hundred additional students applied for entrance to the high school but could not be accommodated. However, they were provided for elsewhere at once, rooms were rented, additions were ordered and prompt and effective measures were taken to meet the demands. At this time the suburbs demanded the expenditure of immense sums for school purposes.

In 1905 the schools were: High, Beacon Hill, B. F. Day, Cascade, Central, Columbia, Denny-Fuhrman, Green Lake, Industrial, Interbay, Interlake, John B. Allen, Lake, Latona, Longfellow, Main Street, Madrona, Mercer, Olympic, Pacific, Queen Anne, East Queen Anne, Rainier, Ross, Salmon Bay, South, T. T. Minor, Summit, University Heights, Walla Walla, Warren Avenue. Also in the suburbs at Brighton, Columbia, Dunlap, Georgetown, Hillman City, Rainier Beach, Ravenna, Riverside, South Park, South Seattle, Van Asselt, Yesler and York. There were here also Wilson's Business College, Acme Business College, Consolidated College Company, DeKoven Hall for Boys, Mrs. Laurence Gronlund's Private School, Hebrew Free School, Mortimer Hall for Boys and Girls,

Mount Carmel Mission, Ridgway's Riding Academy, School of Domestic Science, School of Musical Art, Seattle Commercial School, Seventh Day Adventist School.

Night schools were held three times a week in the Broadway Building. In December, 1907, nearly one thousand pupils attended these schools. Twenty-five courses were prepared and instruction was given in trades, domestic affairs, etc.

In January, 1908, ten city night schools were conducted in ten different school buildings. A course of two terms was prepared for the night schools. Each was given thirty-five nights of instruction. The schools were under the control of the board of directors. At this time there were enrolled about one thousand five hundred pupils in the night schools. All common branches were taught and the schools were held three times each week.

In June, 1908, the school census showed a total of 38,638 children of school age within the city limits. On the second day at the school opening in September, 1908, there were enrolled 24,212 children. Late this year $400,000 worth of additional bonds were carried at the election.

Late in 1910 a special election voted on $600,000 for new sites, houses, furnishings and apparatus, $150,000 to take up outstanding warrants that had depreciated and $100,000 for additions to grounds and buildings. During the entire winter of 1912-13 free night schools were conducted in this city. The enrollment was 4,681 in March, 1912. There were 66 public school buildings, 31,624 day pupils and 954 teachers. There were three free kindergartens and many others under private control. School finances were administered through School District Number 1, which was a separate corporation from the City of Seattle but co-extensive with the area of the city. The outstanding bonded debt at this time was $4,315,000. The grounds and buildings were valued at $5,455,768. All ordinary branches were taught and in addition were manual training, domestic science, physical culture, vocational training and other special lines of advancement. At this time civic educational centers were formed. On the first day of September, 1912, the public schools enrolled 26,596 children. The new Franklin High School opened at this time with an attendance of 800. Other high schools have been erected during the last few years as follows: Ballard, Lincoln, West Seattle, making in all at this date six high schools.

To tell the story of how Seattle built the six magnificent high schools which accommodate her future men and women of the city today would lead only to repetition and confusion. The same may be said of the grammar schools which in recent years have followed each other in rapid succession as the city has spread itself out in every direction.

An estimate of how rapidly the construction work has proceeded may be gained by glancing over the list of public schools today. At the beginning of 1915, the schools were: Broadway High, West Seattle High, Lincoln High, Franklin High, Queen Anne High, Ballard High, Adams, Alki, John B. Allen, Daniel Bagley, Beacon Hill, Brighton, Cascade, Central, F. H. Coe, Colman, Columbia, Concord and South Park, B. F. Day, Denny, Dunlap, Emerson, Fairview, Fauntleroy, Gatewood, Georgetown, Green Lake, Greenwood, Harrison, Hawthorne, John Hay, Interbay, Interlake, Irving, Jefferson, Lake, Latona, Lawton, Leschi, Longfellow, Lowell, Madrona, Main Street, Maple, Mercer, **McDonald,** J. J.

McGilvra, T. T. Minor, North Queen Anne, Pacific, Parental, Pleasant Valley, Pontiac, Rainier, Ravenna, Riverside, Ross, Salmon Bay, Seward, South Seattle, Stevens, Summit, University Heights, Van Asselt, Walla Walla, Warren Avenue, Washington, Webster, West Queen Anne, West Seattle, West Woodland, Whittier, Whitworth, Yesler, York and Youngstown. In all, 739 high school students were graduated in 1914.

Perhaps Mrs. Blaine, when she gathered together her thirteen girls and one little boy in Bachelors' Hall, dreamed that some day the little settlement would become a "City of Schools." Perhaps also she would have been surprised if told that in a little more than half a century 35,000 boys and girls would be attending eighty schools.

While the city has been at work planning and building in recent years, it has not lost sight of the fact that health and out-door life is an important factor in the training of a big city's children. So it has laid out a recreation and play ground scheme which for attractiveness and the healthy enjoyment which it affords equals that of any other city. In the spring of 1914 Seattle's recreation system embraced 1,805 acres, of which 1,430 acres were devoted to parks, 5 acres to street triangles, 227 acres to parkways and 14 acres to play-fields. Thirty-five parks were more or less improved and in use, 26 miles of boulevard were open to traffic and 24 distinctive playgrounds were in operation exclusive of the playgrounds in the parks. Twelve of the playgrounds were equipped with outdoor gymnastic apparatus. During 1913, the maintenance of parks cost $181,275, of playgrounds $42,002, of boulevards $16,341.

With the same idea in view, great stress has been laid on outdoor gardening and agricultural training for the children. The school garden movement has recently advanced to an important position. It started in the Rainier School under the direction of the Parent-Teacher Association and was backed by the Leschi Heights Woman's Improvement Club. It spread rapidly to other schools, meeting with favor everywhere from parents, teachers and Superintendent Cooper. Children are given bulbs and seeds, and instructed how to use them. These they plant in window boxes, on the school grounds or in vacant lots near by. This accomplishes a threefold purpose, giving the children wholesome exercise, teaching them the rudiments of horticulture, and beautifying the city.

By the spring of 1914 school gardens, planted and tended by the pupils, had been started in eleven schools of Seattle largely through the influence of the Seattle Garden Club and the Woman's Congress. Others were contemplated. The five best gardens were at the Rainier, University Heights, Cascade, Interlake, and Fauntleroy schools. Each child worked out a plot under the guidance of the Garden Club.

In July, 1913, what the Seattle schools had done in developing education along practical, industrial and vocational lines was shown in the exhibit at the public library. The best examples of work done in the schools in recent years were exhibited.

The authorities predict that the schools of the future will provide for all the following activities: Vocational guidance from the sixth grade up; more modified courses in the seventh and eighth grades even to the extent of developing a junior high school; vocation school of practical work; fewer pupils to the teacher; a parental school for girls; swimming pools; compulsory health, as well as compulsory attendance.

A story of Seattle's schools could not be well brought to a close without a mention of Frank B. Cooper, the present superintendent, who, in his fourteen years of service to the city, has firmly guided its great educational undertakings. When Superintendent Cooper went into office in 1901 he brought with him from the East improved methods and modern progressive ideas. The manner in which he has put these ideas into practice has gained for him the distinction of being one of the foremost educators in the United States. In Seattle, politics has rarely found a place in school affairs, as the education of the children is a matter of such importance that "let the schools alone!" has always been the cry when there has been any suggestion of tampering with the system. The directors have always been men of the highest integrity. To the fact that the board is an unsalaried one, and members serving on it must of necessity be prompted only by a desire to serve the public when they accept the office, is largely due the high state of perfection which our school system has attained.

There are at present (1915) eighty permanent school buildings in the district and the physical valuation of the property exceeds six and one-half million dollars. The total enrollment in 1914 was 35,527, or more than eight times the registration of January 1, 1890. Enrollment in the various years gives some idea of the growth of the schools: 1890, 4,456; 1894, 5,314; 1904, 18,077; 1914, 35,527. The latest total enrollment was 36,022.

The officials of Seattle School District No. 1, which includes all the territory within the city limits, are as follows: Board of Directors: George A. Spencer, Nathan Eckstein, William Pigott, Richard Winsor and E. Shorrock. The board's officers are: George A. Spencer, president; Nathan Eckstein, vice president, and Reuben W. Jones, secretary. A large and commodious suite of offices is maintained on the top floor of the Central Building.

The Department of Instruction is in charge of Frank B. Cooper, superintendent, who has as assistants Frank E. Willard, Edward G. Quigley and Almina George.

The Health Department is under the supervision of Dr. Ira C. Brown, chief medical inspector, and a corps of nurses.

The Department of Supervision is divided into six departments, each in charge of a specialist, as follows: Manual and industrial education, Ben W. Johnson, director; music, Letha L. McClure, director and Ruth Durheim, supervisor; drawing, Emma S. Small, supervisor and Frances Edgerton, assistant; elementary work and high school art and design, Clara P. Reynolds, supervisor; home economics, Ellen P. Dabney, supervisor; penmanship, Georgia McManis, supervisor.

The six high schools of the district are in charge of the following principals: Ballard, Linton P. Bennett; Broadway, Thomas R. Cole, Charles Kirkpatrick, vice principal; Franklin, J. A. Reed; Lincoln, \. K. Froula; Queen Anne, Otto L. Luther; West Seattle, Fred L. Cassidy.

The grade schools and their principals are as follows: Adams, A. G. Sears; Alki, George F. Forster; John B. Allen, Loren R. Shaw; Daniel Bagley, H. N. Gridley; Beacon Hill, E. C. Hill; Brighton, Beniah Dimmitt; Cascade, Charles Fagan; Central, J. M. Widmer; Franz H. Coe, Elizabeth L. Tharp; Colman, Anna

ry health, as

close without
l his fourteen
undertakings.
ith him from
ie manner in
he distinction
eattle, politics
-children is a
been the cry
The directors
· the board is
be prompted
is largely due

in the district
e-half million
ight times the
rs gives some
1904, 18,077:

l the territory
ze A. Spencer,
The board's
ice president,
e of offices is

oper, superin-
zy and Almira

Brown, chief

aents, each in
ation, Ben W.
urheim, super-
ton, assistant
ds, supervisor
rgia McManis

ing principals
s Kirkpatrick
en Anne, Oш

s, A. G. Sears
Bagley, H. W.
scade, Charles
Colman, Ann

WEST SEATTLE HIGH SCHOOL

B. Kane; Columbia, Aaron Newell; Concord, F. C. Jackson; B. F. Day, Arthur
S. Gist; Denny, Frank H. Plumb; Dunlap, in charge of Charles C. Gray, of
Emerson School; Emerson, Charles C. Gray; Fairview, A. L. Brown; Fanut-
leroy, in charge of O. M. Hanson, of Gatewood School; Gatewood, O. M. Han
son; Georgetown, Frank D. McIlravy; Green Lake, J. M. Kniseley; Greenwood,
J. U. Cassel; Harrison, Charles S. Tilton; Hawthorne, Bella Perry; John Hay,
John J. Mackintosh; Interbay, L. Maxine Kelly; Interlake, George R. Austin;
Irving, Frank Farrar; Jefferson, John P. Herring; Latona, R. W. Moore; Law-
ton, Dio Richardson; Leschi, Herman F. Smith; Longfellow, Annie L. Gifford;
Lowell, Elizabeth Clarahan; F. A. McDonald, in charge of J. M. Kniseley of
Green Lake School, Emma D. Larrabee, vice principal; J. J. McGilvra, in
charge of Annie L. Gifford of Longfellow School, Eva Dansingburg, vice
principal; Madrona, Henrietta E. Mills; Main Street, in charge of E. C. Hill,
of Beacon Hill, Ada J. Mahon, vice principal; Maple, in charge of F. D.
McIlravy of Georgetown, Theodore Meyers, vice principal; Mercer, H. A. Cas-
sidy; T. T. Minor, William A. Blair; North Queen Anne, in charge of E. C.
Roberts, of Ross; Pacific, E. H. Stafford; Rainier, Walter D. Gerard; Ravenna,
C. E. Gibson; Riverside, in charge of Worth McClure, of Youngstown; Ross,
E. C. Roberts; Salmon Bay, David Patten; Seward, Charles F. McKeehan;
South Park, in charge of F. C. Jackson, of Concord; South Seattle, Charles
Potter; Isaac I. Stevens, Clara E. Lowell; Summit, L. B. Moffett; University
Heights, Charles Metsker; Van Asselt, in charge of Charles C. Gray, of Emer-
son; Walla Walla, A. N. Thompson; Warren Avenue, J. C. Dickson; Washington,
George A. Stanton; Webster, W. H. Ellert; West Queen Anne, Adelaide L.
Pollock; West Seattle, Fred L. Cassidy; West Woodland, Ray T. Smith; Whit-
tier, J. Guy Lowman; Whitworth, Emma C. Hart; Yesler, Edward W. Kelley;
York, Jessie M. Lockwood; Youngstown, Worth McClure; School for the
Deaf, Washington School, Maria P. Templeton, head teacher. Parental School
for Boys, Mercer Island, Willis S. Rand, superintendent; Parental School for
Girls, 3404 East Sixty-eighth Street, Anna L. Chambers, matron.

Special schools as follows are conducted: Child Study Laboratory and Obser-
vation Class, Nellie A. Goodhue, principal; Ballard, Twenty-fourth Avenue
Northwest and Ballard Avenue; Cascade, Pontius Avenue; F. A. McDonald,
North Fifty-fourth Street and Latona Avenue; Olympic, Twenty-sixth Avenue
South and Norman Street; Rainier, Twenty-third Avenue South; South Seattle,
Maynard Avenue; Warren Avenue, Warren Avenue, between Harrison and
Republican streets; Washington, Eighteenth Avenue South and Main Street;
Detention Home, Ruby W. Entz; Florence Crittenden Home, Mary Edgerton;
Orthopedic Hospital, Ella M. Peckham.

CHAPTER IX

THE CHURCH

Seattle was only a little more than a year old when the first minister arrived and began church work in the new settlement. A few sermons had been preached in the town before his arrival, but they were by clergymen who merely paused in their journeys to give the settlers the benefit of religious services.

The first sermon was by Bishop Demers, a Roman Catholic of Vancouver Island, who preached in the cook house of Yesler's mill in the latter part of 1852. Everybody in town, irrespective of creed, attended his service. Early in 1853, the Rev. Benjamin F. Close, of the Methodist Episcopal Church, arrived in Olympia to represent his church in the Puget Sound region and shortly afterward preached a sermon in Seattle. Late in the same year the Rev. David E. Blaine arrived and at once began his work as the first minister regularly stationed at Seattle. He represented the Methodist Episcopal Church, though educated a Presbyterian. His wife, previously Miss Catherine Paine, was the first school teacher in Seattle.

Mr. Blaine reached Alki Point on Saturday, November 20, 1853, and the next day preached at Mr. Russell's log cabin at the Point. C. C. Terry, who was present but was not a Methodist, insisted that he knew something of Methodist ways; so at the end of the services he passed his hat around and took up a collection of $12, much to the surprise of the new minister. Early on Monday the Reverend and Mrs. Blaine took passage in the canoe of Bob Moxley, who with a crew of four Indians carried the mail from Olympia, and on their arrival in Seattle went immediately to the home of Arthur A. Denny, where they remained for three weeks until a suitable house could be prepared for them.

Speaking of the kindness of the Dennys, Mrs. Blaine said in 1891, "I tell you, Mr. and Mrs. Denny have never been fully appreciated. They were noble souls. Everything good in this city dates back to Mr. Denny."

The first service was held by Mr. Blaine on December 4, 1853, in a house belonging to W. G. Latimer on First Avenue between Cherry and Columbia streets. Services were continued in that building until May, 1855, when the first little church building, later known as the "White Church," was completed on two lots on the corner of Second and Columbia, where the Boston Block now stands, donated by C. D. Boren. The first money donated for this building was from Capt. Daniel Howard of the brig Leonesa. Mr. Blaine boarded every vessel and solicited from every settler who would contribute toward the cause. Settlers who had no money contributed saw logs which were hauled to Yesler's mill by Hillory Butler. The little church was built by Henry Adams.

Meanwhile the Blaines did not suffer for what they really needed. The Mission Society had paid their expenses to the new field and also had paid half of the first year's salary, $350, in advance; so that Mr. Blaine was a capitalist in

FIRST PRESBYTERIAN CHURCH

FIRST BAPTIST CHURCH

IMMANUEL BAPTIST CHURCH

PLYMOUTH CONGREGATIONAL CHURCH

the new settlement. In fact he had more ready money than any other man in town, at one time loaning $200 to Mr. Yesler for his sawmill. When, after the church building was finished, there was still due a debt of $175 Mr. Blaine paid it, taking the note of the trustees. This note was afterwards lost and no doubt forgotten by nearly all the old members. Twenty years afterward David T. Denny, recollecting the transaction, sent Mr. Blaine stock in the newly organized Seattle & Walla Railroad Company for the full amount. Later Mr. Blaine sold this stock for the amount of the original debt, and thus at last the obligation was closed.

During the first year of his pastorate Mr. Blaine earned the reputation of being the busiest man in town. While he preached regularly and performed the other duties of a clergyman, he also helped clear the lots and build the church and the parsonage. He served as deputy county clerk and every evening assisted Louis Bettman, a local merchant, who was the only pupil in his evening school. In 1856 Mr. Blaine was transferred to the Oregon Conference and worked there until 1863 when he went East. He returned to Seattle in 1883.

The original church was enlarged and a new parsonage erected in 1875 under the pastorate of the Rev. Albert Atwood, who served from 1874 to 1877. Mr. Atwood is still living and is a resident of Seattle. He is eighty-two years of age and attends the services of the First Methodist Episcopal Church regularly. He was succeeded by the Rev. Isaac Dillon, who served as pastor from 1877 to 1879. At an advanced age while attempting to row across the waters of Puget Sound Mr. Dillon met with an accident and was drowned.

Rev. W. S. Harrington, D.D., was pastor from 1881 to 1883. He has rendered signal service to Methodism in the Northwest and has occupied some very important positions in the church at large. He is still a resident of Seattle.

Other men who have served as pastors of the church are: Rev. J. N. Dennisou, 1883 to 1886; Dr. Levi Gilbert, editor of the Western Christian Advocate, 1890 to 1892; Rev. William Arnold Shanklin, D.D., president of Wesleyan University, 1893 to September, 1896; Rev. Edwin M. Randall, D.D., present pastor of the Gilman Park Church, September, 1896, to June, 1903; Rev. Fletcher L. Wharton, D.D., May, 1904, to September, 1906; Rev. W. H. W. Rees, D.D., September, 1906, to September, 1910; Rev. Adna Wright Leonard, D.D., September, 1910, to the present time.

The second church building was erected on the southeast corner of Third Avenue and Marion Street, in 1886 and 1887, at a cost of $25,000. Rev. A. J. Hanson was pastor at the time. It was finished and furnished in 1888-1889 during the pastorate of Rev. D. D. Campbell, at an additional cost of $20,000. This new building was dedicated by Bishop Bowman, September 15, 1889. It was torn down in 1907.

The present edifice at Fifth Avenue and Marion Street, erected under the pastorate of Rev. W. H. W. Rees, is valued at $300,000, including the lot and the organ, the latter one of the largest and finest on the Coast. When the present pastor, the Rev. Adna Wright Leonard, was appointed in September, 1910, the membership was 1,240. Today it is more than 2,400. The church is the third largest numerically in Methodism and is one of the most highly organized churches of the Northwest. The organization includes Sunday School, Epworth League, Woman's Foreign Missionary Society, Woman's Home Missionary

Society, two Young Women's Missionary societies, two Children's Missionary societies, Probationers' classes, Brotherhood, Ladies' Aid Society, Church Choral Society and various other lines of activity.

The story of Seattle's first church, from its modest beginning as a small village meeting house to the great modern organization of national influence, is but one instance of the remarkable growth which Seattle's many churches have experienced.

Seattle's second church, built in 1865 for the Methodist Protestants, was known as "The Brown Church" because it was painted brown. As the first church was painted white it was then called "The White Church" to distinguish it from the other. The Society of the Brown Church was organized by the Rev. Daniel Bagley, known to Seattle people as the "Father of the University of Washington," who became one of the great figures among the pioneer ministers of the Northwest.

The members included in the organization were Mrs. Susannah Bagley, Judge Thomas Mercer and wife, Hester Loretta, and his daughter, Alice, who later in the year became the wife of Clarence B. Bagley; Mr. Edward Steelman and wife; Mr. Dillis B. Ward and wife; Miss Lenora Denny. Of these, only Mr. Ward and wife, and Mrs. C. B. Bagley survive.

The original church and parsonage combined cost about three thousand dollars, and was then considered quite a creditable addition to the city's public buildings.

When Mr. Bagley and his family arrived in Seattle in October, 1860, they came from Salem, Ore., in the hope of benefiting Mrs. Bagley's health, which had begun to fail under the stress of pioneer life. At first, Mr. Bagley occupied the vacant pulpit in the Methodist Episcopal Church until the arrival of a regular pastor. To the construction of The Brown Church, five years after his arrival, he devoted his entire labor and a large portion of his private means. Half of the lumber for the church was donated by Captain Renton, of Port Blakeley. Mr. Bagley remained pastor of the church he built in Seattle until 1885, more than twenty years. The remainder of his busy and useful life was passed in Seattle, his residence being on Queen Anne Hill.

In the summer of 1872 The Brown Church was extensively altered and improved. It was given a Mansard roof with the addition of an upper story to be used as a Good Templars' Hall. Entrance to the upper story was gained by a winding staircase under the belfry.

It was from the organization of The Brown Church that the first definite movement to obtain good music for Seattle originated. About the middle of December, 1873, a Philharmonic and Choral Society was organized at the church by Seattle's singers and musicians. The object of the society was to consolidate the musical talent of Seattle into a single organization founded on a basis similar to the choral societies of the East. The Methodist Protestant Sunday School was organized in 1875 and by 1880 it had become the largest in the territory with 171 officers, teachers and pupils.

The Brown Church was removed from the corner of Second Avenue and Madison Street in the spring of 1882, and preparations were made for the erection of a more commodious structure. Arrangements were also made to begin the construction of a parsonage on the rear end of the lot. In June the corner

FIRST METHODIST PROTESTANT CHURCH

stone of the new building was laid by Mr. Bagley. In it was deposited by Judge Thomas Mercer a box containing a Bible and other mementoes of the occasion. Mr. Mercer was then the oldest Methodist Protestant on the Pacific Coast. This new church and a separate parsonage were completed in 1883 at a cost of about fifteen thousand dollars, all paid at the time of dedication in August of that year.

At this time The Brown Church represented the only organization of the Methodist Protestant Church west of the Rocky Mountains. During the sixteen years after its organization, Mr. Bagley had been its pastor except for a few months when he resided in Olympia. The society, numbering about seventy five members, had prospered under his leadership until it owned property estimated at twenty-five thousand dollars.

The great fire of June 6, 1889, swept away church and parsonage. Dexter Horton, whose generosity had made possible the erection of these buildings, at once made the necessary arrangements and a large tent was soon put up on his lots where the New York block now stands, and services were held there. Then a larger tent was erected on the church site which is now occupied by Frederick & Nelson's store. This lot was sold, several months later; and in 1890 one bought at the southeast corner of Pine Street and Third Avenue where a church with a seating capacity of 1,000 or more was erected, together with a comfortable parsonage, all at a cost of about forty-four thousand dollars.

At the time of the regrading in that vicinity, it was found impossible to longer use the building for church purposes so, in 1906, the lot was sold for $100,000, and the proceeds devoted to the purchase of two lots at the corner of John Street and Sixteenth Avenue North and the erection of a structure, that, while not of great seating capacity, is one of the most beautiful churches in the city

The names of the ministers who have served as pastors of these churches are as follows:

Daniel Bagley, S. A. Baker, H. M. Sexton, J. H. Skidmore, Clark D. Davis, W. M. Kellogg, Reverend Whitman, Thomas P. Revelle, A. N. Ward, and J. M. Gill, the present pastor.

The First Presbyterian Church, like the Methodist Protestant and the First Methodist Episcopal, is closely interwoven with Seattle's early history. In 1866 the Rev. George F. Whitworth, the first pastor of the church, and one of the ablest divines of the Pacific Northwest, came from Olympia to Seattle, as president of the Territorial University, then the most notable institution of this little village of about four hundred inhabitants. He began holding services in The Brown Church of the Methodist Protestants, preaching on alternate Sundays with the pastor, the Rev. Daniel Bagley. This union continued until 1877, and during all the intervening period union Sunday school and prayer meetings were held.

In the winter of 1869-70, the few Presbyterians here decided to form a church organization and accordingly assembled December 12th at the residence of Mr. Whitworth, and constituted themselves the First Presbyterian Church of Seattle. The charter members were: Samuel Kenny, Mrs. Jessie Kenny, Mrs. Mary E. Whitworth, Miss Clara Whitworth, Mrs. Lida Whitworth, Mrs. Rebecca Jones and Mrs. Ruth J. McCarty. The organization was weak at the start, but grew steadily in membership and influence. The Rev. Theodore Crowl became pastor in 1875. The Rev. H. P. Denning took charge of the congregation August 14, 1875. Other pastors were D. W. Macfie, H. W. Stratton, George R. Bird, F. G. Strange, Elliott W. Brown and Alexander Allison, D. D. In the spring of 1876 the first church building was commenced. It was not dedicated until July 1, 1879, over two years after it had been finished and occupied. The dedication services were conducted by Rev. H. W. Stratton, and the dedication sermon was preached by the Rev. John Hemphill, then pastor of Calvary Church, San Francisco. In 1893, it was deemed necessary to erect a new church building. One-half of the cost of construction was subscribed before the work was commenced; in fact it was subscribed within less than a week. The completed building was an imposing edifice for that period, with a full seating capacity of 1,500. It stood at Fourth Avenue and Spring Street. The dedication sermon was preached by the pastor, the Rev. Alexander Allison, in January, 1894.

Later, in 1907, the present building of the First Presbyterian Church at Seventh Avenue and Spring Street, which had been erected at a cost of $300,000 was dedicated. With this church and St. James' Catholic Cathedral Seattle boasted of having two of the finest churches in the country. Under the leadership of the Rev. Mark A. Matthews, D.D., who has been pastor of the First Presbyterian Church of Seattle since 1902, the church has attained the distinction of having probably the largest congregation in the world.

Father Rossi, of the Roman Catholic Church, was in Seattle for several years before 1867 and bought four lots at Fourth Avenue and Washington Street. These four lots were bought for $200 and the Church of Our Lady of Good Help, the first Catholic church in the city, was erected there in 1868 by the Very Rev. F. X. Prefontaine. It stood on the half block on Third Avenue between Yesler Way and Washington Street. Father Prefontaine arrived here in 1867. He first rented a small house which stood on Third Avenue opposite the block where the Yesler Mansion was afterwards built. This house contained two rooms, the largest being converted into a chapel. The other room was the residence of Father Prefontaine, parlor, dining room, kitchen and sleeping-room, all in one. To raise the money for his church he held fairs in Seattle, Olympia, Port Gamble, Port Ludlow, and Utsalady at the north end of Camano Island. About this time there were only twelve or fifteen Catholics in Seattle. The four fairs held by Father Prefontaine for the church at Seattle cleared $2,000. After the church building was ready the membership increased rapidly. In 1882 the church was practically rebuilt and only the belfry and spire of the old building were saved for the new structure.

"I have vivid recollection," wrote Father Prefontaine about 1902, "of the time we had clearing the land for the new church. Every foot of it was covered with monster trees and dense underbrush. One giant of the forest that we cut down, I remember, measured eight feet in diameter at the butt and had roots which extended from one side of the block to the other and which on the south drank in the waters of a little creek that ran down the ravine, on the north side of which the church was to stand. We were three months in getting rid of the stumps and underbrush that remained after the trees were felled. In clearing the ground we dug up three relics of the Indian War of 1856, one was a monstrous iron key which belonged to the quartermaster of the sloop

ST. JAMES CATHEDRAL

TRINITY PARISH CHURCH

of war, Decatur, and two government bayonets. In 1869, the old church which covered a ground space of 60 by 36 feet and seated about one hundred persons, was completed at a cost of about three thousand dollars. It was a pretentious building for those times, with Gothic windows, and was nicely finished in stucco on the interior."

The cornerstone of a new Catholic Church on the corner of Fourth and Washington, near the site of the present Prefontaine Building, was laid on Sunday evening, May 7, 1882, Father Prefontaine conducting the ceremonies. He was assisted by Fathers Custer and Boulet. At this time the Catholic Church had a membership of about six hundred. The new church was 35 by 120 feet inside measurements, with a transept 27 by 49 feet and sanctuary and sacristies 25 by 35 feet. There were three galleries and the entire building had a seating capacity of 700. The height of the building from the ground to the top of the steeple was 112 feet. The structure had entrances from both Fourth Avenue and Washington Street, although it faced the latter. The basement was divided into rooms for prayer meetings, studies, etc. The architecture was of the Gothic order. It was dedicated in May, 1883, Bishop Blondel officiating.

In 1902 the Right Rev. Edward J. O'Dea, Bishop of the Diocese of Nisqually, announced his intentions of removing to Seattle from Vancouver and of making this city the headquarters of the See of Nisqually. At this time there were more than one hundred religious organizations of all kinds here with a total membership of 30,000. Bishop O'Dea held his services in Seattle for the first time in February, 1904.

The Young Men's Institution of the Catholic Church was established in Seattle the latter part of 1904. The cornerstone of the new St. James' Cathedral at Ninth Avenue and Columbia Street, was laid by Bishop O'Dea soon afterwards. He was assisted by Bishop Carroll of Helena, Montana, and many distinguished clergymen of the Catholic Church. The erection of the cathedral completed the change of the See to this city, which became the See of Seattle. A solid silver trowel was used by the bishop in laying the cornerstone.

In July, 1908, Pope Pius X conferred on Francis Xavier Prefontaine the honor degree of Prothonotary Apostolic as a reward for his distinguished services in Seattle since 1869. He was invested with robes and the title of Monseigneur, Member of the Papal Household, by Bishop Edward J. O'Dea. During his lifetime he was one of Seattle's best citizens.

In the fall of 1908 the Seattle Carmelite Community was established. Four nuns came from the Baltimore Nunnery and established a cloister. They were the first of the Carmel Order to locate in the Pacific Northwest. A building was donated to their services by Malcolm MacDougal, whose daughter was one of the nuns. By June, 1909, there were five sisters of that order here in charge of the community.

The new Providence Hospital at Seventeenth Avenue and East Jefferson Street, one of the most imposing buildings in the city, was completed in April, 1912.

In October, 1865, the Protestant Episcopal Church (Trinity) was established in Seattle by the Rev. Peter E. Hylane. He first visited the town while he was yet pastor of St. John's Church at Olympia. Among the first members were Charles C. Terry, Hiram Burnett, H. L. Yesler, M. R. Maddocks and Franklin

Matthias. They occupied the White Church before their own building was erected. Mr. Burnett was the first member to be confirmed. Mr. Hylane left here in 1871, but returned to the Sound in 1889, became pastor at Whatcom and later returned to Seattle.

The first Episcopal Church building, which was of Gothic architecture, was completed late in 1870 under the superintendence of Hiram Burnett. It was dedicated June 11, 1871, by Bishop B. Wistar Morris, of Portland, assisted by the Reverends Hylane and Summers, and was given the name of Trinity Church. It stood at the corner of Third Avenue and Jefferson Street.

In May, 1879, the Sunday school of the Episcopal Church was established by Mr. Webb and met in the public schoolhouse at Belltown. Hiram Burnett conducted the school until 1880, when a lot was purchased and a building erected for Sunday school purposes. This structure was also used for occasional services of the church. It became known as the Chapel of the Good Shepherd, and was formally opened by the rector of Trinity Parish on December 12, 1880. After May, 1881, the Rev. John C. Fair was minister in charge of this chapel and held there regular weekly services. Trinity Church was much improved in the fall of 1879. The front was turned to Third Avenue and the rear towards the Sound, permitting the material lengthening of the building and the construction of a tower to hold the 1,200 pound bell that arrived in September.

The first pipe organ in Washington Territory was installed in Trinity Church in July, 1882, under the direction of John Bergstom, a well known organist of San Francisco. A grand organ opening was held at the church, directed by Samuel J. Gilbert, previously of Grace Church, New York. Trinity Church was destroyed by fire in January, 1902, but a year later a new and more pretentious edifice was ready for occupancy.

It was in 1869 that a meeting was held in the district school room in Seattle to organize a church to be known as the Plymouth Congregational Society of Seattle. S. P. Andrews was chairman of this meeting and W. S. Baxter, secretary. The meeting formally tendered a call to the Rev. John F. Damon to become pastor, and the call was soon accepted. The trustees of the new church were Corliss P. Stone, S. P. Andrews, J. H. Sanderson, Samuel G. Calhoun and A. N. Merrick.

About the middle of November the Congregationalists of Seattle began to meet regularly in Yesler's Pavilion, which thereafter they occupied for morning and evening services every Sabbath. A Sunday school was organized about this time and its sessions were held immediately after the morning service. The congregation grew rapidly, and on Sunday, December 19, 1869, Plymouth Congregational Church of Seattle was formally organized by the Rev. G. H. Atkinson, D. D., of Portland. By January, 1870, the organization had been perfected and on January 16th, the first communion service was celebrated in the Pavilion.

In November, 1871, the members of the church temporarily secured the joint use of the Methodist Episcopal Church and held services there for some time instead of in the Pavilion as before. Mr. Damon preached there on alternate Sundays. The Sabbath School of the Plymouth Society was held at the White Church every Sabbath afternoon. In December the Reverend Damon resigned his position as pastor and turned his attention to missionary work on the Sound, although he still retained his residence in Seattle. In 1891 a beautiful church

MADRONA
PRESBYTERIAN
CHURCH

FIRST UNITARIAN CHURCH

MADRONA
PRESBYTERIAN
CHURCH

FIRST UNITARIAN CHURCH

CONGREGATIONAL
CHURCH

edifice was built at Third and University, the northeast corner, and when this was crowded out by the business district and was outgrown by the congregation, a modern structure providing for various institutional activities was erected, 1912, at Sixth Avenue and University Street. The Rev. W. H. G. Temple, D. D., was pastor of the church for about ten years, and he was succeeded by the Rev. Francis J. Van Horn, D. D., under whose leadership the new church was built.

The preliminary meeting for a Baptist Society was held at the residence of Edward H. Hanford about the middle of December, 1869. Socials and prayer meetings were held at Mr. Hanford's residence by members of the organization. As a result of these meetings the First Baptist Church of Seattle was organized on December 28th of that year, on the basis of the New Hampshire articles of faith. A covenant was subscribed to by eleven persons, and it was announced that twenty more would shortly be admitted. The following officers were elected: William Rogers, deacon; S. P. Andrews, clerk; L. S. Rogers, E. H. Hanford. L. J. Holgate, S. P. Andrews and T. Hanford, trustees. The society had previously secured a church lot and the trustees were preparing speedily to erect a church building and to procure an efficient pastor. The first Baptist Church, which originally stood on Fourth Avenue adjoining Mr. Hanford's residence, was completed in 1872. It was repaired and lowered in 1875, and again in 1883 it was thoroughly renovated and refurnished. Its first pastors were the Reverends Weston, Freeman, Wirth and Pierce. Late in 1890, the Baptists located a University of Seattle at Kirkland, with the Rev. G. C. Burchett as president.

The First Baptist Church of the present time, which was built in 1912, at Harvard and Seneca, and which is now under the leadership of the Rev. Carter Helm Jones, D. D., is interesting from an architectural point of view as it is the only one of the more recently erected large churches in Seattle that has the tall pointed spire.

After Judge Roger S. Greene transferred his residence from Olympia to Seattle he appointed Rev. J. P. Ludlow, a Baptist minister, his clerk for the third judicial district, and for many years the two were very zealous in religious work in this city.

Mr. Ludlow was quite eccentric and became imbued with the desire to build and operate a "gospel ship," one that would steam up and down the waters of the Northwest, including Washington, British Columbia and Alaska. He estimated that with such a craft it would be possible to carry the gospel to more than forty thousand souls, whites, Indians and Chinese. About 1881 a legacy of several thousand dollars was left him and he used it in building the Evangel, a steamer that in following years sustained more mishaps than any other ever launched on Puget Sound. After the boat was nearly ready to run his funds gave out, so he had a large number of pamphlets printed and sent them out broadcast, stating the purpose for which the boat was to be used. Subscriptions poured in from church and missionary societies all over the world supplying him with abundant means to finish and equip the boat. By this time his missionary zeal had abated, and instead of carrying the gospel from port to port the craft went into secular business. Her subsequent career was spectacular but not profitable. It is due Mr. Ludlow to add that he most scrupulously returned all contributions to the organizations that had sent them to him.

In June, 1871, at the instance of Dana C. Pearson, of San Francisco, and in the interest of the Sabbath school, the clergy and Sunday school teachers of the Congregationalist and two Methodist churches of Seattle were called together at the residence of the Rev. John F. Damon and a Sabbath School Institute was formed, the first ever organized in the territory. The Rev. Daniel Bagley was elected chairman of the institute and J. H. Sanderson, secretary. Preliminary meetings were held at the White Church and were largely attended by teachers, scholars and parents.

The Unitarian Society was organized in Seattle in December, 1885, by the Rev. George H. Greer, with an original membership of twenty.

An organization of Spiritualists called the Progressive Aid Society was effected in 1872. From the first days of settlement a few Spiritualists had lived in Seattle, occasionally securing the services of a lecturer. By 1872 they had become quite numerous and made preparations to raise funds for a hall. The next year they began to hold regular services in Lyceum Hall, under the direction of Mrs. A. D. Wiggin. The First Spiritualist Society of Seattle was formally organized in November, 1887, by D. S. Smith, Hannah Smith, Henry Gifford, Lena Gifford, George Spray, Eliza Spray, B. F. Bogardus, Fred O. Houbert, W. R. Andrews, Grace Gifford and Mrs. Sophronia Taylor.

The cornerstone of a German church at Seventh Avenue and Cherry Street was laid January 1, 1882, by the Revs. J. A. Wirth and G. Mechanheimer. In the spring of the same year the Scandinavian Baptist Church was constructed near the North School House, and was dedicated by the Rev. O. Okerson, who had come to Seattle as a missionary, and through whose energy the church had been built. The people of Seattle generously contributed towards the erection of the building. The same year also the Free Methodists built a church on Pine Street near Ninth Avenue at a cost of $1,300. The congregation had started in 1881 as a mission.

The First Church of Christ, Scientist, was organized in Seattle in August, 1896, with seventeen charter members. Edward E. Kimball, a close friend of Mrs. Mary Baker G. Eddy, lectured here on the doctrines of the organization. There was a large attendance to hear what this noted speaker had to say on the subject, and the result was the organization of a church of that denomination.

The membership grew rapidly and it was found necessary to establish another church. This was done June 26, 1909. For a time it met in Arcade Hall, but it was soon necessary to move into larger quarters, and in March, 1913, the Hippodrome was obtained. It is called the Fourth Church.

The First Church has a beautiful structure at Sixteenth Avenue and East Denny Way, and it and the Fourth Church have a very large attendance.

The Second Church was formerly the First Church of Ballard. It was organized in March, 1902, with fourteen charter members.

There are three other regular organizations—one in the university district, one at Columbia City and the other in West Seattle; also informal societies at South Park, Bellevue and at Medina.

In telling the story of Seattle's religious life, only to outline the history of the pioneer churches of the various denominations has been attempted. The city's people always have been church-goers. Some of the largest congregations in the world are to be found in Seattle; and in a score of years they have

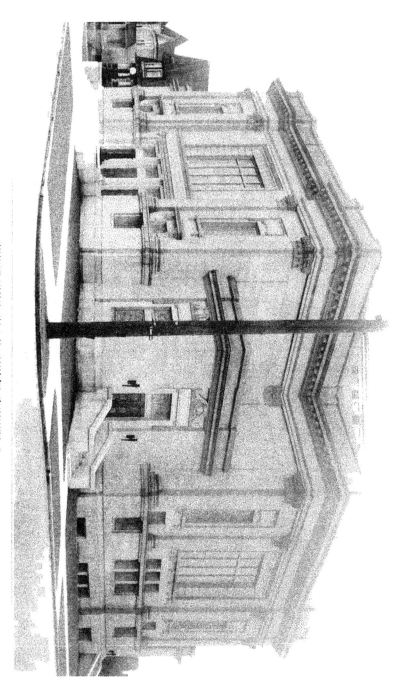

FIRST CHURCH OF CHRIST, SCIENTIST

extended their work until every section of the city where there is a growing community has its church or chapel or mission. Wherever, in its history, the growing city has extended its boundaries to include new homes and new families one of the first demands has been for a church to fulfill the religious needs of the added community.

From the time of the first extensive gold discoveries in Alaska the churches experienced an extraordinary growth. Not only did the congregations grow in number but they greatly extended their fields of operation. Great revivals, concerts, charitable movements, followed each other in close succession. Lecturers from abroad, men and women of prominence and eloquence, were secured to interpret religious subjects, in which the people were vitally interested. Missions were created to extend the church work among the poor and unfortunate and reading rooms and halls were opened throughout the city, particularly in the Japanese and Chinese quarters, where the leading denominations established branch congregations.

The enormous growth of the churches in the ten years from 1897 to 1907, was the forerunner of a memorable period of moral, social and religious advancement. With more than twenty new church buildings, with the magnificent Catholic Cathedral and the First Presbyterian Church completed, and with the Young Men's Christian Association and the Young Women's Christian Association buildings contemplated, Seattle started out on a great movement which sought to combine the activities of religious worship with the practical work of moral and social improvement. The places of worship became work rooms of social centers which proposed to solve the perplexities and problems of everyday life. The great church structures were provided with gymnasiums, recreation, reading and smoking rooms, kindergartens, playgrounds. Clubs and societies were introduced to aid in carrying out the work of social betterment. During 1907 there were built in Seattle more churches than ever before in one year. Twenty buildings were erected at a total cost of $1,500,000. The First Presbyterian Church, under the leadership of Dr. M. A. Matthews, was but one example of the progress that was made. In 1907 there was an increase of 747 in the membership of this church alone.

The progress of the churches in very recent years has been aided by a series of forward movements carried on by the larger congregations. One of the most extensive of them was a movement, in February, 1914, by the Queen Anne Hill churches, of the Christian, Congregational, Methodist and United Presbyterian denominations, under the leadership of the Rev. Sydney Strong, D. D., the Rev. W. M. Jeffers, the Rev. W. E. Adams and the Rev. John Downie. This was continued for several weeks and was immediately succeeded by the union revivals of the four great down-town churches, the First Presbyterian, the First Methodist Episcopal, the First Baptist and the Plymouth Congregational. The ministers who led in this revival were the Rev. M. A. Matthews, D. D., the Rev. Adna W. Leonard, D. D., the Rev. Carter Helm Jones, D. D., and the Rev. Francis J. Van Horn, D. D. The "go to church" idea gained headway and February 8th was set apart each year as "Go-to-church Day."

In a little more than half a century Seattle has established more than one hundred and ninety churches, representing twenty denominations. In 1915 they are as follows: Four Adventist, 24 Baptist, 10 Christian, 6 Christian Science,

23 Congregational, 14 Episcopal, 2 Evangelical Association, 4 Free Methodist, 1 Friends, 1 Greek-Russian, 3 Hebrew, 21 Lutheran, 31 Methodist Episcopal, 1 Methodist Episcopal South, 2 Methodist Protestant, 2 Nazarene, 22 Presbyterian, 1 Reformed Presbyterian, 3 United Presbyterian, 18 Catholic, 3 Salvation Army (corps), 3 Swedish Evangelical Mission Covenant, 2 Unitarian, 1 Volunteers of America.

The list of miscellaneous churches and religious societies includes, in addition, the Apostolic Faith Mission, Church of Christ, Bethel Mission, Christian and Missionary Alliance, Church of God Chapel, Church of Jesus Christ Latter Day Saints, Church of Jesus Christ Latter Day Saints (reorganized), Church of the Brethren, Church of the Living God, Divine Science, Gospel Hall, Gospel Tabernacle, Hazel Mission, Japanese Buddhist Church, Non-Sectarian, Peniel Mission, Pentecostal Mission, Olive Branch Mission, the United Brethren in Christ, Bahai Assembly, Central Christian Assembly, Christian Yoga, Spiritual Psychic Society, Humanitarian Spiritual Society, Japanese Christian Society, Science of Truth Society, Seamen's Church Institute of America, Theosophical Society, United Order of Practical Christianity, the Young Men's Christian Association, the Young Women's Christian Association, Rosicrucian Fellowship.

FIRST BAPTIST CHURCH

FIRST METHODIST CHURCH

CHAPTER X

THE PRESS

Newspapers the world over are like so many people. They live hard and die easily. They praise their friends and denounce their enemies. They are ever at each others' throats. Yet all of them love the little human affairs of every day which make their lives worth the living. And somehow, when they emerge from the fight, often well battered, they always seem to discover that they are a little nearer the truth.

So it has been with the newspapers of Seattle. "Survival of the fittest" has been the rule. Many have come and gone, have fought bravely, and died gamely; but out of the wrecks and the successes Seattle today has newspapers which truly represent the city and stand ready to aid in its progress.

It will be difficult for the young men in the newspaper offices of today, with their separate departments and special work, to realize the many duties devolving upon the pioneer newspaper men of Seattle. The successful one was a capable printer who could "set type," run a press, make up the forms, make a roller and wash it if need be. He was editorial writer, local reporter, business manager and mailing clerk. A "job office" was usually part of the printing establishment and he had to be his own job printer and pressman as well.

. During all the earlier years there were no telegraphic dispatches, the "news" being selected from the weekly issues of the Tribune or Herald of New York City. These came by mail steamer to the Isthmus of Panama, thence across, and by steamer to San Francisco, thence with the utmost irregularity by steamer to Portland, from there down the Columbia and up the Cowlitz River and by pack animal or mud wagon to Olympia.

Under all these adverse circumstances remarkably good newspapers were issued. They were usually on paper 24 by 36 inches in size, about the limit for the hand presses then in use. The editorial matter was vigorous and able, the typography and press work equal to that of the present day, the selection of news and literary matter unexceptionable. It is not surprising that men capable of such good work in the face of many difficulties should have wielded a powerful influence in the pioneer work of the territory.

The first newspaper that carried a Seattle date line was published in Olympia, August 15, 1863, by James R. Watson. Olympia was a vastly more important town in those days than Seattle, but Watson must have had a premonition that this city would some day be great enough to repay the journalistic attention he so carefully devoted to it. He brought sample copies of the first issue to Seattle and received such good encouragement that he concluded to establish a plant here.

The first copy of The Seattle Gazette, distinctively a Seattle newspaper, made its appearance December 10, 1863, with Watson as editor and proprietor,

189

M. D. Canavan as 1is associate and an Indian for a roller boy. T1e Gazette
was issued from an office in t1e second story of a wooden building owned by
Henry L. Yesler near t1e present sout1west corner of Yesler Way and First
Avenue Sout1. Yesler furnis1ed t1e room free of cost and aided t1e venture in
ot1er ways. T1e paper consisted of four pages of four columns, t1e printed
matter on eac1 page measuring 9½ by 14½ inc1es.

Equipped wit1 suc1 a durable outfit, Editor Watson publis1ed t1e Gazette
spasmodically, bestirring 1imself only w1en t1ere was news of sufficient importance to provoke an issue. But w1en t1e first telegrap1ic dispatc1 to Seattle,
on October 26, 1864, broug1t Civil war news, t1e primitive newspaper office
on t1e outpost of civilization was electrified to activity. T1e dispatc1 arrived
from Portland at 4 o'clock. Portland 1ad received it from Kansas City and
Kansas City from New York. It gave t1e news from C1attanooga of t1e operations of S1erman against Hood in t1e Atlanta compaign. T1e Gazette did not
lose any time in issuing its "Citizen's Dispatch," giving t1e first publis1ed
dispatc1 coming by wire. At 1 o'clock t1e day before t1e cannon 1ad been fired
to celebrate t1e completion of t1e Western Union-Telegraph line to Seattle.

Watson feveris1ly began at once to figure out a way to print t1e dispatc1es
as fast as t1ey were received. T1ey came collect, and before 1e could procure
t1em Seattle's editor 1ad to devote some time and energy to t1e financial aspect
of 1is calling. T1e usual mode of procedure was t1is: T1e telegrap1 operator
would 1unt up Watson, a task somew1at simplified by t1e sparseness of t1e
population, and inform 1im t1at t1ere was a war dispatc1 at t1e office. Watson
would t1en call on several opulent and liberal citizens of t1e town, tell t1em
of t1e dispatc1 and collect twenty-five cents from eac1 of t1em to pay t1e tolls.
T1e message would be given to 1im and set in type, t1e type would be locked
up on a "galley" and an "extra" for eac1 subscriber run off. Later t1e dispatc1es
would appear in t1e Gazette.

T1is paper, alt1oug1 lasting only a few years, is interesting 1istorically on
account of t1e press on w1ic1 it was printed, and for t1e fact t1at it publis1ed
t1e first telegrap1ic news received in Seattle. T1e printing press used by t1is
paper was first sent from New York to Mexico, t1ence to Monterey, California,
in 1834, w1ere it was used by t1e Spanis1 governor for a number of years
in printing proclamations, etc., and on August 15, 1846, t1e Californian, t1e
pioneer paper of California, was printed on it. Late in 1846 it was sent from
Monterey to San Francisco and used in printing t1e Star, t1e first paper of t1at
city, issued in January, 1847. T1ese two papers were combined at a later date,
and in t1e fall of 1848 t1e first number of t1e Alta California was issued from it.
From San Francisco it went on to Portland and t1e first number of t1e Oregonian was taken off it. In 1852 it and t1e old plant of t1e Oregonian were
boug1t by T1ornton F. McElroy and J. W. Wiley, w1o broug1t it around on t1e
sc1ooner Mary Taylor to Olympia, w1ere t1e first number of t1e Columbian
was printed on it. In 1863 J. R. Watson broug1t it to Seattle and used it for
printing the Gazette as above stated. Its 1istory did not end 1ere for it served
t1e Intelligencer at a later date. T1e type and ot1er material were destroyed
many years ago but t1is old Ramage press is today a relic 1ig1ly prized at t1e
State University Museum w1ere it may be seen.

From June 4, 1864, to August 6th, the paper suspended, but resumed again in improved form. Mr. Watson was interested in politics and the paper came out with some irregularity for about a year more, when he severed his connection with the paper and the Seattle Publishing Company took control. Mr. Robert G. Head, a newspaper man from Olympia, took Mr. Watson's place and continued the paper until February 16, 1865, when I. M. Hall took up the work until March 3, 1866, when the paper quit.

A month later, on April 5, 1866, Mr. Hall, in partnership with a Mr. McNamara, began a new venture under the name of the Puget Sound Semi-Weekly. Seattle, however, could not support a semi-weekly, and on April 30th, the paper came out as the Puget Sound Weekly. In August, 1866, it was sold to Mr. George Reynolds, who stuck with it until March 18, 1867, when Mr. Hall took it back again and renamed it the Puget Sound Weekly Gazette.

On May 27, 1867, the firm became Hall & White, but on June 17, 1867, Seattle again lost its newspaper for Hall had been elected county auditor and the prospect of steady remuneration was so alluring that he allowed the publication to die.

Meanwhile, on April 23, 1866, the Puget Sound Daily appeared and continued an uneventful existence until August 11th, of the same year. It was the first daily paper on Puget Sound, and in Washington Territory.

In the papers which succeeded Watson's Gazette, telegraph dispatches appeared occasionally, but not until about July 1, 1872, when the Puget Sound Dispatch was established by Larabee & Company, with Berial Brown as editor, was any regular publication of the press dispatches undertaken in Seattle.

In August, 1867, Samuel L. Maxwell, a San Francisco printer, came to Seattle with the object of starting a paper somewhere on the Sound. It happened that the old Ramage press and materials upon which the Seattle Gazette et al. papers had been printed had fallen into the hands of Messrs. Daniel and Clarence B. Bagley, and Mr. Maxwell made arrangements to take over the outfit for $300 and pay for it out of the earnings of his proposed paper. On August 5, 1876, the first number of his paper, the Weekly Intelligencer, appeared. Mr. Maxwell was a man of considerable ability, and this, together with the fact that Seattle was beginning to develop, caused his paper to succeed from the start. He paid all his debts and improved his paper so that by 1874 he was able to sell the plant for $3,000, at that time quite a sum of money. The new proprietor was Mr. David Higgins. The town began to grow, and in June, 1876, a daily was issued which became very popular as well as financially profitable. In 1878 Mr. Higgins got the fever to go to Eastern Washington which he thought had a future even greater than the Sound country, so he sold out to Mr. Thaddeus Hanford, who had edited the paper for several years, for $8,000.

Before Mr. Higgins had sold his interest in the paper he had taken into his employ a young man, Samuel Crawford, a pressman, of Olympia. Mr. Crawford was a good pressman but a better reporter, and soon became city editor. Mr. Crawford induced Mr. Thomas Prosch to take an interest in the paper, which he did, but the two proprietors never agreed, and Mr. Hanford decided to sell his interest for $5,000, which Mr. Crawford purchased, going into debt for the money.' Messrs. Prosch and Crawford had a difficult time keeping the paper going and at the same time carrying the heavy mortgages, which load was made harder by the fact that the paper had a heavy lien for paper, etc., recorded against it, which neither knew of at the time of purchase. The Intelligencer continued in the hands of the above proprietors until its merger with the Post.

Meanwhile, this daily paper was not the only occupant of the field. We must leave the Intelligencer and go back to the spring of 1868, when an Irish tailor, named I. G. Murphy, began the publication of the Alaska Times at Sitka, Alaska. In May, 1871, soon after the American boom subsided, he brought his small printing plant to Seattle and began the publication of the Seattle Times and Alaska Herald. The publication of the Times continued only a few months. Murphy soon sold it to McNamara & Larabee, who in turn sold it to Wilson & Hall, who started also the Territorial Dispatch.

In October, 1871, Beriah Brown and C. H. Larabee bought the plant, continued the paper for three months and on December 4, 1871, issued the first number of the Puget Sound Dispatch. In 1872 Brown's son, Edward H., succeeded Larabee and the firm became known as Brown & Son. In 1874 the son left the paper and Beriah Brown conducted it alone. In April, 1875, a half interest was sold to Austin A. Bell, and the paper was published under the name of Brown & Bell. In September, 1879, it was purchased by the Intelligencer.

Beriah Brown was one of the old school of newspaper men, a writer of editorials worthy of the greatest papers of the United States. He was a friend of Horace Greeley, the elder Bennett and other noted editors of half a century ago. He rarely wrote anything for his own paper. His custom was to go to the case and put his articles in type as he composed them. It is hard to comprehend the difficulty occasioned by the dual processes of thought this brought into play. Local news is the life of all newspapers in young communities. This he could not purvey, nor was his business management a success. The Dispatch was the second daily published in the city.

The Pacific Tribune had been founded in Olympia, moved to Tacoma, and moved a second time to Seattle, in 1875. It was continued for three years in Seattle and in 1879 was sold by its owner, Thomas Prosch, to Mr. Hanford.

We now turn to the career of the Post. In 1878 Mr. B. L. Northrup started a monthly agricultural journal under the title of North Pacific Rural. The time was not ripe for such a paper, and its circulation and good will were used as the basis of a new daily and weekly paper called the Post, which was first issued by K. C. and Mark Ward in October, 1878. The Post got into debt from the start and its control passed into the hands of several persons who had made money advances to defray the expenses of publication. It continued from bad to worse and the owners, anxious to get the investment off their hands, effected a merger with the Intelligencer owners, they to put the Post in on the basis of one-third, and the Intelligencer to be put in on the basis of two-thirds.

The first quarters of the Seattle Weekly Post were in the two-story wooden building owned by Hillory Butler, on the ground now occupied by the southwest corner of the Hotel Butler on Second Avenue and James Street. In passing it may be added that this building was from time to time the home of more early papers than any other in the town—the Dispatch, North Pacific Rural, Post, Chronicle, Times, Press, and others with single and hyphenated titles long since forgotten.

In the meantime the Intelligencer had been installed in a larger two-story building, then standing on the west side of First Avenue, where it deflects into First Avenue South. Its owners, Thomas W. Prosch and Samuel L. Crawford, had been printers from boyhood, and Prosch had gained much experience as a newspaper man in Olympia and Tacoma. Under their management the Intelligencer continued to grow in value and influence, until in 1881 it was ready to absorb another mouthful.

In this year, 1881, the Post Publishing Company began the erection of a substantial brick building, two stories and basement, on the northeast corner of Yesler Way and Post Street. As it was nearing completion negotiations were opened for a consolidation of the Post and the Intelligencer. This was effected October 1, 1881. The publication continued under the name it bears today—The Post-Intelligencer. The building from which it was issued continued to be the home of the paper under several managements until the great fire of June 6, 1889, destroyed it and most of the plant.

The Post-Intelligencer prospered under the management of Prosch, and early in 1886 was purchased by a joint stock company consisting of Frederick J. Grant, Clarence B. Bagley, Griffith Davies, Jacob Furth, John H. McGraw, E. S. Ingraham, William H. Hughes, Thomas Burke, and Dr. Thomas Minor. Grant continued as editor-in-chief, Bagley was business manager, S. L. Crawford was city editor and reporter, and E. S. Meany had charge of the carrier service. On November 1, 1886, Leigh S. J. Hunt purchased the controlling interest in the paper and continued it under the editorial management of Fred Grant. Stuart Smith became business manager, a position he held until 1890, when he resigned to go into the real estate business, and was succeeded by C. A. Hughes.

Hunt had come to Seattle with large financial backing, determined to go into the newspaper field, and the majority of the stockholders, fearing he might establish another paper and make it a powerful rival, sold him their interests. Prior to the purchase the Post-Intelligencer had been conducted along the lines of an ordinary country newspaper. Hunt proceeded to spend money lavishly upon it and soon built it up into a metropolitan paper with one of the best staffs that have ever worked in Seattle. Among those who were responsible for making the paper a power in the Northwest were: Fred J. Grant, Alfred Holman, Edgar Piper, Joseph Levinson, Will H. Parry, John W. Pratt, Lucius R. Bigelow, Jabez B. Nelson, Hammond Lamont, George H. Heilbron, S. L. Crawford, C. T. Conover, R. C. Washburn, L. H. Hodges.

Hunt's Seattle career was spectacular. He speedily proved himself to be what is known colloquially as a "live wire." Prior to the panic of 1893 he became involved in mining and many other large enterprises, and the panic found him with his affairs so tangled that he could no longer hold the paper, which was taken over in May, 1894, by a company composed of John Hoge, of Zanesville, Ohio; James D. Hoge, his nephew; George Heilbron and Frederick J. Grant. James D. Hoge represented both his uncle and himself, and although not much more than a youth at the time, proved quite a successful newspaper publisher. A strange fatality, however, seemed to pursue the editorial end of his paper. Grant, in September, sailed on the ship Ivanhoe for a vacation. The ship was lost and all on board were drowned. Heilbron succeeded Grant and in April, 1895, died. The next editor was John W. Pratt, who had not served long before he resigned. R. C. Washburn then became editor. Hoge conducted such a strong fight on the populists in 1896 that a mob of them assembled beneath his office window during the campaign and cheered him with vocal assurance that they would hang his body on a sour apple tree. As Hoge today is the president of a large and successful financial institution—the Union Savings and Trust Company—neither the decimation of his editorial force nor the threats of the politically excited people apparently had any harmful effect on him.

The paper became a power in the politics of the state, and this led to its sale by Hoge to a group of Spokane people who wished to acquire influence in public affairs on the western side of the mountains. The transfer was made in September, 1897. George Turner was at the head of the Spokane group and Edgar B. Piper and George U. Piper, of Seattle, joined forces with him, Edgar becoming editor and George business manager. Edgar Piper, later editor of the Oregonian, of Portland, maintained the paper at a high editorial level, but Turner did not feel inclined to continue in the newspaper business, so in the fall of 1899 asked E. C. Hughes and Maurice McMicken, then, as now, law partners in Seattle, to find a purchaser for it.

The Post-Intelligencer then entered upon one of the most interesting periods of its career and brought into increased prominence a man who made a deep impression on the public affairs of the state—John L. Wilson, of Spokane. In the campaign of 1896 James J. Hill, anxious to keep the politics of the state as well as hand as possible, as was the method of railways at the time, sent $10,000 to Mr. Wilson to use in the interests of the republican party. Mr. Wilson sent the money back and with it a letter stating that the state was surely going populist and that to spend the money would merely be to waste it. This somewhat startled Mr. Hill, who had often spent money to assist the political party which he favored, but who, up to that time, had never received any of it back. He thanked Wilson and was so impressed with the honesty of the Spokane man that he said in his letter, "If an occasion ever arises when I can do anything for you, let me know."

There was no relation between this letter and the action of Messrs. Hughes and McMicken, but they decided that Wilson might be able to handle the paper, and telegraphed him asking if he cared to purchase it for $400,000. At that time the extent of Mr. Wilson's resources were so far short of the amount named that he treated the telegram as a good joke and in that light showed it to A. P. Sawyer, who was then his secretary. Sawyer, however, saw possibilities ahead and persuaded Wilson to telegraph James J. Hill that the time to do something for him had arrived. Sawyer wrote the telegram and Wilson signed it with so much misgiving that Sawyer had no sooner left the office to send it than Wilson started in pursuit of him to recall it. Sawyer, however, had anticipated such action, for he had small confidence in the lasting power of his persuasive eloquence, and did not go to the telegraph office that Wilson expected him to, but sent the message from the depot. Wilson arrived at the telegraph office and upon being assured that Sawyer had not yet called, remained there all afternoon, until he became persuaded that Sawyer had seen the futility of trying to interest Hill and had decided not to send the telegram.

Next morning Wilson received the greatest surprise of his career in the shape of a telegram from Mr. Hill stating that the money would be forthcoming. The purchase was made by an Eastern financial corporation underwriting $400,000 of 6 per cent bonds, redeemable at the rate of $20,000 per annum for twenty years. Mr. Wilson took charge of the paper December 1, 1899. J. G. Pyle became editor and S. P. Weston business manager. In September, 1903, Mr. Pyle resigned and Horace McClure directed the editorial end of the paper until January 1, 1904, when Erastus Brainerd became editor. Mr. Brainerd continned in the position until September 1, 1911, when he was succeeded by Scott C. Bone, the present editor. Mr. Brainerd proved to be a forceful editor, and while he was in the editorial saddle he conducted many campaigns with a vigor that made its impress on the history of the city.

On August 1, 1912, A. S. Taylor, at that time one of the most prominent and substantial men of Everett, and Scott C. Bone purchased the control of the Post-Intelligencer. The paper is now the sole occupant of the morning field in Seattle and is the only publication having the seven-day Associated Press franchise. Before he came to Seattle Mr. Bone was one of the most prominent newspaper men in the East and he has maintained the Post-Intelligencer on a dignified but enterprising plane. Mr. Taylor's business policy has cleansed its advertising columns of anything of a dubious nature and has made the paper one that Seattle has reason to be completely satisfied with. Beriah Brown, Jr., whose name runs through the newspaper history of Seattle since its early days, is one of the editorial writers on the Post-Intelligencer, and T. J. Dillon, one of the most polished writers in the Northwest, is managing editor.

Having followed the history of the Post-Intelligencer until the present day, we can now go back and pick up the milestones that mark other activities that were contemporaneous with the incidents related above.

In 1881 Kirk C. Ward, who had lost control of the Post, W. M. Beach, Judge R. Andrews and Beriah Brown, Jr., started the Chronicle, first as an evening paper and later as a morning daily. It had a varied career and finally became the property of one of the leading law firms of the city, McNaught, Ferry, McNaught & Mitchell. They employed as editor a Bohemian from Kansas named Frank C. Montgomery who conducted it until May 1, 1886. On that date it was purchased by Homer M. Hill, who is now engaged in other business in Seattle.

In the early '80s there was great activity in the newspaper field, and the Herald, Call, Finback, Bulletin and Mirror were among the papers that were started. Fortunes were sunk in an endeavor to make them self-supporting. Only the Call survived.

On July 5, 1882, a company consisting of W. G. C. Pitt, T. H. Bates, and Thaddeus Hanford issued the first number of their new paper, the Herald, which was printed on the old Pacific Tribune material. Mr. Pitt was the manager and the paper had offices in Colman Row, First Avenue. It was an evening paper issued daily and had a weekly edition. The Post-Intelligencer had things pretty much its own way in Seattle at this time, and besides the city could hardly stand another daily. On September 18, 1884, the Herald suspended one issue owing to financial troubles which continued until its final suspension, October 8, 1884.

The Call had incurred the opposition of those not in favor of anti-Chinese agitation and this, together with the fact that certain printers had been thrown out of work by the consolidation of the two papers, caused the formation of a new daily, the Times, whose first number came out with the first issue of the Press. Thomas H. Dempsey, foreman of the Chronicle office, J. R. Andrews, and one or two others, quickly formed a company and issued the Times with the understanding, it is said, that the paper was to receive a subsidy for six months. In March, 1887, Col. George G. Lyon, a writer of ability, secured a half interest in the paper, and he and Mr. Dempsey conducted the paper with wonderful efficiency. It is probable that one or the other of the two papers would have gone to the wall had it not been for the fact that a great boom in real estate began in Seattle, and the heavy amount of advertising which was available kept the papers going until the city was large enough to support them.

When Homer M. Hill bought the Chronicle on May 1, 1886, the Hall brothers were conducting the Call. Two days later, May 3, Hill acquired control of the Call and consolidated the two papers as the Seattle Press, daily and weekly. He was a capable business man and under his management the paper became a valuable property. Interests in it were sold and bought back from time to time and when Hill closed out his ownership Harry White held some of its shares; also at one time John Cort held a considerable interest in it. At that time the paper was absolutely free from debt and was making money for its owners.

In 1889 W. E. Bailey, a wealthy young man from Philadelphia who had large interests here, became the victim of an ambition to conduct a big newspaper. Under these circumstances Hill had no difficulty in getting his price for the Press. L. S. J. Hunt of the Post-Intelligencer conducted the negotiations, made the purchase and at once transferred the property to Bailey. Bailey made important additions to the mechanical department and engaged a large news and editorial force. S. R. Frazier was made editor and was succeeded later by Erastus M. Brainerd, a newspaper man from Philadelphia.

At the time Hill bought the Chronicle it owned the Associated Press evening franchise, which was its most valuable asset. And in passing it is proper to note the fact that the present Times is the lineal successor of the Chronicle. While for a brief period there was a break in the legal succession, it may be truthfully said that the historical succession to the Associated Press franchise is derived from the Chronicle down through the Press and the Press-Times to the Times of today.

February 10, 1891, Bailey bought the Times from Lyon and Dempsey, paying $48,000 for it. He had paid somewhere from $20,000 to $25,000 for the Press. Immediately he consolidated the two under the name of the Press-Times. During the years that followed business in Seattle was none too good and the papers had a hard struggle for existence. Their circulation was not great and the amount of advertising carried in their columns was not sufficient to make the financial side of the ventures anything but a source of worry to the owners. The period of financial depression bore heavily on Bailey and he was finally compelled to give up the paper to his creditors, having lost $200,000 during his journalistic career.

The history of its subsequent difficulty would fill a volume but can be touched upon but briefly here. The paper was on the market for a long time. John Collins had it for a while, and sunk a lot of money in it, having acquired it through a mortgage of $15,000. Later John W. Pratt secured control of it.

At times it was published by a receiver. Hughes and Davis came into control of it through ex-sheriff, James Woolery, who had taken it over under the mortgage given to John Collins.

During this troubled period among other happenings the name was changed to the Times, and also the Associated Press franchise was surrendered and that of the United Service taken over. Later, and subsequent to the mortgage of $15,000 given to John Collins, the Associated Press franchise was again secured, and this was a vital point in the legal contest that arose between the Times Printing Company, headed by A. J. Blethen on one side, and Hughes & Davies on the other.

In 1896 Col. Alden J. Blethen came to Seattle from Minneapolis, and August 7th purchased the Press-Times and soon made his personality felt in the newspaper world. His first editorial appeared in it three days later. He came well equipped for newspaper work and management by reason of wide experience in other fields. In July of the next year, the steamer Portland come out of the North with its story of the golden Klondike and Colonel Blethen, who had shortened the name of the paper to the Seattle Daily Times, took advantage of the opportunity presented by the new prosperity which Seattle experienced, and assisted by his sons, Joseph and Clarence B., built up that publication until today it is one of the best newspaper properties in the West and one of the great dailies of the United States.

Since Colonel Blethen's death, July 12, 1915, Joseph Blethen has succeeded to the presidency and general management, and Clarence B. Blethen, to the editorship.

At the solicitation of the writer he has been permitted to use the following word picture of the colonel's daily life, and keen analysis of the motives and aspirations that ennobled his character. It is from the pen of Paul H. Lovering, one of the city's most gifted writers:

"For twenty years, no man in Seattle exercised a more potent influence on its history and affairs than Col. Alden J. Blethen. Strong physically and a giant mentally, he was gifted with a marvelous faculty for drawing others to him and of knitting them to him with bonds stronger than steel. Original in thought, far-seeing in business affairs, a forceful writer and a keen student of human nature, he combined within himself all the elements required by a successful editor-publisher.

"His mind was literally a vast storehouse of information. Its activities were as varied as the items in the tide of news that flowed daily through the columns of his paper; and his memory was phenomenal. Everything interested him. He would listen to the story of a little child, coming to his desk to sell flowers or to solicit a donation for a worthy charity, with the same fresh interest that he displayed when discussing the most momentous national or civic problems. No man was great enough to overawe him; none so inconspicuous as to be denied a hearing. Throughout the years I knew him and for many preceding, his office door was never closed and through it flowed daily a tide of humanity as amazingly diverse as the causes in which they sought to enlist his aid. I, personally, have known him to rise from an important conference and step to the door to hand a gift to a broken-down beggar, who found charity there when he would have been denied elsewhere. They knew him—those decrepit has-beens'—and they came to him unhesitatingly, certain that he would not refuse, no matter how unworthy the applicant.

"His charity was proverbial and as spontaneous as the laugh to a child's lips. He gave, because, to him, giving was life's greatest joy. He gave because the wail of human sorrow was agony to his heart. He gave because he was so big that he could not resist a certain feeling of guardianship over those who lacked the things that Nature had so lavishly showered upon him—health and courage and an indomitable will to succeed.

"Once a teacher, he was ever a student. For years, it was his custom at the close of a working day that commenced at 9 o'clock in the morning (or earlier) and did not end until 9 or 10 o'clock at night, to spend a half hour or more in his office library, reading the classics of every age and of every people. I sometimes think those were the happiest hours he spent outside of his own family circle. In the company of the great minds of this and preceding ages he found a companionship of thought that diverted his attention from the vexing little problems of every day life.

"Never was there a man of such untiring energy. A lofty ambition was the mainspring of his being. He was never content to rest on his laurels, even in the days when his feet were stumbling along the final· allotted miles of his earthly course. To the last, he remained the great constructive dreamer, seeing further ahead than his contemporaries and striving, against every obstacle, to carry to completion great plans for the upbuilding of his city and his state. The names of both were dear to him. He was jealous of their prosperity and their progress. To safeguard both, he gave himself unsparingly, making up, by long hours of overwork in the conduct of his own affairs, the time he unselfishly devoted to the public welfare.

"That love for his city and his state was a part of his almost fanatic patriotism. To him, there was only one land—his own; there was only one just form of government—his land's; and he hated, with all the hatred of which his kindly nature was capable, any and every man who assailed the one or repudiated the other. When he ran the American flag up to the masthead of his paper (and it is still there), it was both as a promise to his readers and as an inspiration to himself. And howsoever much his public might have changed, he would have fought on to death under that flag, had he been the only living man to love and venerate it.

"That noble inspiration gave rise to two of his most striking characteristics— the sanctity of his business word and his loyalty. With him, 'his word is as good as his bond' was no hackneyed phrase. No man ever was trusted more fully; none repaid trust more abundantly. Upon those who surrounded him in his great newspaper enterprise, he depended absolutely. He was the last to distrust and the first to pardon. And, in return, without seeking it, he received such meed of unquestioning loyalty as comes to few. No feudal lord ever enjoyed more complete attachment from his followers than did Colonel Blethen from his friends and his employes. 'The loyalty of the Times' staff' was proverbial wherever newspaper men congregated and of the legacies he handed down to his sons, none was accounted more precious than this.

."As might be expected, such an individuality was not bound by narrow rules and commonplaces. He did not despise conventionalities; he did not realize that they existed. Sustained by a high moral purpose and with his eyes set on great achievements, he strode forward like a strong man in a race, stretching out an eager, purposeful hand to pluck for his community the things it needed to grow great, strong and enduring. He never considered himself in these fights; he never considered others. If they fought shoulder to shoulder with him, so much the better; if they sought to impede the advance toward bigger and better things, he brushed them aside.

"Naturally, such a positive soul antagonized negative natures. His never were pale or neutral-tinted thoughts and ideals. What he knew, he knew without doubt or question; what he did, he did straightforwardly and directly, as big men would and should. He might have pitied the passive blunderers had he had time to consider their views, for he was both kindly and broad-minded; but he was so busy working out great ends that he had scant leisure to weigh and judge the sordid little claims of lesser men. Hence the opposition he sometimes encountered and, on occasion, the enmity he aroused. The latter he ignored. He was too big and too busy to pile up grudges. The former made him impatient but impatience never caused him to waver in his purpose. Instead, he struck out the more gallantly, smiting error unsparingly and driving onward, ever onward, toward the high goals of his noble ambition.

"He was of the type that is not the product of success but that commands success. No easy road to wealth and distinction opened before his youthful feet. Even robust health was denied him in his early years. But the old New England blood, that gave him his courage and tenacity of purpose, also gave him a wonderful vitality. He conquered physical weakness while mastering knowledge, and maturity found him mighty both in brawn and brain. Depression was foreign to his nature. He could not be gloomy; life held too much of promise, too much that was worth fighting for, to waste it in morbid introspection. And, in every great crisis of his career, a wonderful sanity held him true to himself and to the great principles that dominated his life.

"This, in brief, was the man who has been declared (not unjustly, I believe) the last of the great editors of his time. In a way, he typified an epoch—the epoch of great American achievement, when the nation, as a lusty youth, was carving out of a new land the imperial domain of the greatest republic the world has ever known. He was a part of those big things. He helped create them and the creating left an indelible impress upon his being. They filled his mind with great ambitions; they taught him how to realize those ambitions.

"So, in the end, it must be written that throughout the fruitful years of his long life, he was above all things else a great and noble dreamer, who possessed a marvelous faculty for translating his dreams into actualities."

Washington has always been a republican state. At various times during its history it has been swung over into the democratic column, but these temporary departures from the republican path have been caused by fights over purely local matters, or as protests against some action of the dominant political power rather than through any permanent change in the political belief of a large number of citizens. This strong republican element has made it very difficult for a democratic paper to succeed, the nearest approach to success upon the part of such a paper having been attained by the daily Telegraph during the early '90s. This paper started under the most favorable circumstances and with every promise of becoming a successful enterprise; in fact its popularity proved too much for the Morning Journal with the result that it was purchased and combined with the Telegraph in December.

Seattle, at the time of the establishment of the Telegraph, was passing through one of those stages which have preceded every democratic victory the state has known. Municipal affairs were in a shameful condition; the wide-open-town idea had been allowed to go the limit and the citizens had reached the end of their patience. The republicans, who had allowed gambling, unrestricted prostitution, prize fighting, and every other demoralizing element to flourish openly and unblushingly, seemed to feel sure in their position when the Telegraph opened a campaign against them. Thousands of dollars were spent in this campaign, which developed into one of the hottest newspaper wars ever waged in the city. The Telegraph represented the democratic side of the controversy, the republican interests being cared for by the Post-Intelligencer, which with its party went down to defeat at the hands of the voters on March 7, 1892, when J. T. Ronald was elected mayor.

The Seattle Daily Telegraph was established chiefly through the efforts of D. E. Durie, the stockholders being a quartet of prominent democrats, namely Judge Thomas Burke, David E. Durie, Daniel H. Gilman, all of Seattle, and J. J. Browne of Spokane. The first issue appeared August 10, 1890, and the final issue December 8, 1894, the paper having been sold by the late John Collins, its last owner, to the Post-Intelligencer, which, however, took over only the subscription lists, the linotype machines and a small amount of other apparatus.

The Seattle Daily Telegraph entered the newspaper field with D. E. Durie as manager, A. V. Ryan, editor; Alexander Begg, business manager, and John G. Egan, city editor, with a reportorial staff, consisting of Frank Hartly Jones, Charles D. South, Martin J. Egan, now publicity man for the great New York banking house of J. P. Morgan and Company, and T. W. Todd, the latter of whom continued with the paper throughout its life, having assisted in getting out the first issue and the last as well; no other man connected with the editorial department remaining with it from its birth to its suspension of publication in the manner stated. Very early in its career the late Lovett M. Wood, founder of the Seattle Trade Register, became a member of the editorial staff and remained with the paper over two years. Will A. Steele, the well known Alaska newspaper publisher, E. L. Reber, former city editor of the Post-Intelligencer, W. J. Tobin, George J. Stoneman, Frank M. Sullivan, now a banker, were all for a time members of the Telegraph's staff, Steele as city editor more or less of the time, and the others as reporters.

Charles H. Lugrin, now a barrister of Victoria, joined the Telegraph early in its career as an editorial writer. Later, with the sale of the paper to V. A. Ryan, its editor-in-chief, and his early sale of the publication to the late John Collins, Lugrin became its editor and continued so until the end.

V. A. Ryan succeeded D. E. Durie as editor in October, 1891. A year later he purchased the interests of Messrs. Burke and Gilman who had become tired of the heavy financial drain upon them. As a matter of fact, while several men connected with the paper at different times were somewhat the losers thereby, Judge Burke's loss was more than the combined losses of the others. After a few weeks of operation, Mr. Ryan sold it to John Collins, Homer Hill and Fred

E. Sander, eac1 one-t1ird interest, Mr. Hill becoming t1e manager. It was under his management t1at t1e first Mergent1aler linotypes ever broug1t to t1e state were installed in t1e Telegrap1 office. About one year of management sufficed for Mr. Hill, and 1e Mr. Sander sold out to Jo1n Collins, w1o installed C. H. Lugrin as managing editor.

T1e Telegrap1 1ad succeeded in ousting one corrupt administration but t1e new municipal aut1orities were not able to improve conditions. Grafting continned; t1e city treasurer, Adolp1 Krug, defaulted and disappeared leaving a s1ortage of about one 1undred t1ousand dollars be1ind 1im. T1e Post-Intelligencer, remembering t1e defeat w1ic1 its party 1ad met at t1e 1ands of t1e people, was not slow in exposing every little administrative s1ortcoming, and t1e democrats were turned out of office at t1e next election.

As t1e Telegrap1 1ad been a losing venture from t1e start, t1e defeat of its party in t1e municipal election was t1e beginning of t1e end. T1at it 1ad been a formidable competitor, is s1own by t1e following announcement, made by its new owner t1e morning after t1e sale was closed:

"T1e patrons of t1e Post-Intelligencer will be t1e gainers by t1e absorption of t1e Seattle Telegrap1. It is expected t1at t1e Post-Intelligencer will secure 4,000 new subscribers by reason of t1e consolidation. As a result of t1is increased patronage, t1e Post-Intelligencer will be able to increase and improve its new service. T1e first important improvement will begin next Sunday, w1en t1e Post-Intelligencer will issue a sixteen-page paper, containing special matter of general interest."

T1us ended t1e career of t1e most pretentious democratic paper ever established in the state.

T1e Seattle Daily Telegrap1 was always a clean newspaper and very ably edited as well. Bot1 \. A. Ryan and C. H. Lugrin wielded trenc1ant pens and for invective and biting sarcasm Ryan per1aps never 1ad a superior west of t1e Rockies. But as a money making venture, t1e Telegrap1 was a sad failure. However, not1ing like as muc1 money was sunk in t1e venture as was supposed. Guesses 1ave been made ranging from $50,000 to $300,000; but as a matter of fact, t1e actual money spent in t1e effort to establis1 and give t1e Seattle Daily Telegrap1 continuous life probably did not exceed $100,000.

T1e first number of T1e Argus, Seattle's oldest weekly paper, was issued February 17, 1894. It was founded by A. T. Ambrose and O. N. Furbus1. Beria1 Brown, Jr., now of t1e Post-Intelligencer, was t1e first editor. During t1e following Marc1, H. A. C1adwick purc1ased Mr. Furbush's interest and assumed editorial.management, w1ic1 1e 1as 1eld ever since, t1e paper being publis1ed under t1e firm name of C1adwick & Ambrose. Upon t1e deat1 of Mr. Ambrose, w1ic1 occurred T1ursday, May 17, 1900, Mr. C1adwick purc1ased 1is interest in t1e paper. Under 1is editorial and business management, it 1as become a valuable newspaper property, and commands t1e respect of all t1ose w1o admire clean journalism. Its 1oliday edition is always a work of beauty and eac1 number is well wort1 t1e price of t1e yearly volume.

T1e Pacific Fis1erman was founded by Miller Freeman in t1e fall of 1902, the first issue appearing in January, 1903. It is devoted exclusively to t1e commercial fis1eries of t1e Pacific Coast and is t1e largest and most comprehensive publication of its kind in t1e world. Miller Freeman, publis1er; Jo1n

N. Cobb, editor, and Russell Palmer, manager. The associated fishing interests are a power in the commercial, financial and political circles of the Pacific Northwest, and the organization back of the Pacific Fisherman and its ally, the Washington Farmer, wields an influence in the State of Washington that is not generally understood by the reading public.

The Railway & Marine News is a publication devoted to all that pertains to transportation in the Northwest, British Columbia and Alaska. It was incorporated September 2, 1904, by Frank T. Hunter, Wilbur F. Coleman and Wm. M. Sheffield. Shortly after its first issue Stephen L. Coles, a New York newspaper man, became editor of the publication. In January, 1906, J. P. Parkinson, at that time city editor of the Post-Intelligencer, purchased the property and published the same for many years. The paper was re-incorporated and re-organized June 1, 1913. by Mr. Parkinson, Kenneth C. Kerr and Wm. E. Kidd, Mr. Kerr becoming editor. Mr. Parkinson died in Seattle in November, 1913, and the publication has continued under its corporate powers and has become the recognized authority on shipping matters of the North Pacific.

The morning daily that entered the newspaper field in Seattle under conditions that gave more promise of success than any of its numerous predecessors, save, possibly, the Telegraph, was the Morning Times.

Its first number appeared April 2, 1907, and its last November 30th of the same year.

Col. A. J. Blethen and Joseph and Clarence B. Blethen were its founders, and also, were editor-in-chief, assistant editor and managing editor. The Times office was already equipped with fast presses and all the best mechanical appliances necessary in getting out the Evening Times. Their services and office rentals were free and many other items of expense were charged to the evening paper; no losses were charged to depreciation upon the plant, yet in eight months the actual cash deficit was over eighty thousand dollars, or more than ten thousand dollars per month.

Charles Alfred Williams was for a time city editor and later managing editor, and Albert Johnson, night editor.

From the time L. S. J. Hunt purchased the Post-Intelligencer, the morning field has been fully occupied. Every attempt that has been made in the last thirty years to successfully establish a rival morning journal in Seattle has failed and the losses to the promoters have reached a large aggregate.

Perhaps in the case of the Telegraph, had not the hard times of 1893 and years following fallen so heavily upon Seattle, with failure in business of so many advertisers of all classes, it might have weathered the storm, but that is idle speculation.

On April 30, 1888, the Enterprise was started, but ran only a month as there did not seem to be enough democrats in Seattle to keep it going, its announced adherence to the cause of democracy not producing enough financial returns to make its continued existence possible. In the same year Alexander Begg and Edmond S. Meany started the Trade Journal, which became the Journal when it was taken over in the spring of 1890 by John Leary, W. H. Lewellyn, B. F. Shaubut and others. In 1891 it was absorbed by the Telegraph.

In 1883 Die Tribune was started in Seattle. It was printed in German and was the first paper to be printed in the state in any foreign language.

There were any number of papers started in the later '70s and the '80s, most of which had but a brief existence. Some of those most prominent are given.

The Puget Sound Industrial World, a semi-monthly journal devoted to lumber, mining, milling, ship building and hop growing interests. It was published at 627 First Avenue.

The Seattle Daily Hotel Reporter, emanating from both Seattle and Tacoma, was launched by Messrs. Talbot & Hoffman, June 15, 1889, and was subsequently published by Mr. Talbot, alone, at Tacoma.

The Seattle Sunday Budget was started a few weeks before the fire by Samuel R. Frasier, who continued as editor and proprietor until he was made editor of the Press when he disposed of his interests to others. Its headquarters were at 116 Yesler.

The American Continent was published by M. Choir at the old Yesler-Leary block.

The North Seattle Advocate was issued by H. Leland and J. J. Knapp under the firm name of H. Leland & Co. at 2317 First Avenue. It was a weekly coming out each Saturday.

The Leader was a temperance organ and was established April 11, 1889.

The Mirror was also a temperance paper being founded somewhere between the years 1880 and 1883. It wound up its career on September 14, 1884, after having published forty-five numbers.

The Monday Morning Telegram was started November 19, 1888, by R. R. Stevens, H. Scott and W. J. Grambs, E. N. Evans being manager. It lived only a short time.

The Prompter was first issued January 10, 1878, by John Jack and P. J. Wade. It was very interesting because of the period it represents, but had a brief existence.

The Washington Posten and the Washington Tidende were the first Norwegian papers to appear in the city having their origin about 1888.

The Voice of the People was launched as a daily and weekly on August 21, 1886, and lasted until May 31, 1887.

The Vestra Posten was the first Swedish organ in Seattle being founded in the later '80s by the Swedish Publishing Company, consisting of B. A. Anderson, president and treasurer; N. P. Lind, vice president, and T. Sandegren, secretary. It came out as a weekly from 806 Denny Way.

The True Tone was a Sunday paper of the later '80s founded and edited by S. G. Young, and claiming to be an independent journal devoted to the interests of literature and art.

The Wacht am Sunde was founded February 2, 1884, by Philip Schmitz and Ernest Hoppe, and lasted until September 4, 1885, when the proprietors took it to Tacoma.

The Washington Churchman was a monthly organ founded January, 1889, and devoted to the interests of the Episcopal denomination. Reverend George Herbert Watson was the first editor. At the time of its founding it was the first denominational paper in Seattle.

On August 13, 1888, Alexander Begg and Edmond S. Meany started a paper called the Trade Journal, devoted to the interest of the commercial public. It contained market reports, stock quotations, etc., but later enlarged its interests to include general news items. Shortly before the fire it was sold to others.

Mr. Begg then tried his hand with the Citizen, a weekly which lived but a short time. Another venture was the Washington Magazine, a monthly, founded in September, 1889.

On October 27, 1888, the Standard Publishing Company, with John F. Norris as manager, issued the Sunday Standard from 117 Marion Street. It was very short-lived.

The Seattle Morning Journal was launched sometime in the later '80s as an independent daily from 120 James Street. E. W. S. Tingle was editor, and Charles S. Painter business manager.

The Seattle Sunday Star, the oldest of the Sunday papers, was founded November 11, 1883, by a man named Blake. He was shortly afterwards succeeded by Kirk C. Ward. The paper was burned out in the fire of 1889 but came back in better form and continued into the '90s.

Die Puget Sound Post was established November 5, 1883, by Schmidt & Hunter.

A few other papers familiar to the '80s are the Finback; Die Tribune; Puget Sound Gazetteer, and Real Estate Advertiser.

The Ballard News was established in the old City of Ballard, now a part of Seattle by annexation, in 1891. The present owners bought the plant in 1902 from Woody & Dowd, who had operated it only a short time. Before that date it had been in many hands and changed almost with the moon. Since 1902 it has been owned and operated by Albert E. and Oscar R. Ruffner, who came from Crawfordsville, Ind., in July of that year. Both were practical printers and since buying the plant they have enlarged it by adding new machinery including a fast press and a type composing machine. The paper published by the company has always been republican in politics and has been identified with every movement that was for the upbuilding of the Ballard district.

In 1899, E. H. Wells founded the Seattle Star, the firm name being E. H. Wells & Company, E. W. Scripps, now the controlling spirit of some scores of daily publications in all parts of the United States, being the company. E. F. Chase became business manager. Sixteen months after the paper started the Star Publishing Company was organized by its owners. The Star then, as it does now, fought the battles of the so-called "common people" and achieved extraordinary success. Under Mr. Wells it became a power politically and continued to wield great influence in the affairs of the city and country. In 1909, Mr. Wells sold his interests in the paper and was succeeded as editor by Kenneth C. Beaton, who resigned in 1911, since which time Leroy Sanders has been editor.

Some three years after disposing of his interest in the Star, Mr. Wells, together with Lawrence J. Colman, John P. Hartman, T. S. Lippy, H. W. Treat and others organized the Sun Publishing Company and began the publication of the Seattle Sun, the first issue appearing February 3, 1913. It is doubtful if any newspaper ever launched on the journalistic sea started its voyage under more promising circumstances than did the Sun. With a mechanical equipment the best that money could buy; with a paid up circulation of over forty thousand; with a successful newspaper man at its head, and with a growing city and community as its field, the Sun was a success before a single issue was ever run off its presses. It was at all times popular with the reading public, but not so with the advertisers, some of whom its policy antagonized. They withdrew their patronage and the financial end of the business ran into trouble.

The outbreak of the war in Europe in July, 1914, and the unsettled business conditions which it brought with it, added fuel to the financial flames which were at that time threatening the Sun and it was soon found necessary to make a change in management. S. P. Weston took charge of the business as manager, but the tide did not turn and on December 15th, Weston was appointed receiver; the enterprise was a wreck into which had gone the fortunes of several of its promoters.

Seeing that they would be thrown out of employment if the paper was forced to suspend. the employes, early in December, held a meeting in the composing room at which it was agreed to organize a new company, the stock of which should be accepted by them in lieu of wages. By bonding the company and selling the bonds to the public it was hoped to raise sufficient money with which to continue the publication until business conditions should improve. The plan was adopted and efforts began at once to sell the bonds; but it was too late, the employes could not obtain capital quickly enough to satisfy the creditors and on December 29th the Sun was forced to suspend.

Pooling their wage claims the employes bought the greater part of the mechanical plant of the Sun Publishing Company, agreeing at the same time to meet the unpaid debt on one of the presses and certain other machinery. As soon as the sale had been confirmed by the court the employes held another meeting and organized the Sun Printing Company: Local people outside of the newspaper business were induced to purchase stock and the following officers were elected: I. W. Efaw, president; Fletcher Lewis, secretary; B. C. McCormick, business manager; Frank Roberts. managing editor. These men, together with H. L. Clark, George A. Virtue and A. F. Moore, were chosen trustees.

Finding that the public was not subscribing to the stock as rapidly as they had hoped, the officers decided, late in March, to issue a sample paper which would show the people that the new company really meant business. This sample was issued on March 31, 1915. and contained the following announcement: "The Seattle Sun will resume publication Monday, April 19th. Each day thereafter there will be issued a virile, independent, non-partisan newspaper." The new paper was pledged to work for the prohibition of the liquor traffic, for civic decency, for progressive government and was dedicated to clean journalism.

Sun stock was a slow seller even after the company had demonstrated its ability to publish a ten-page paper and it was not until Monday, April 26th, that regular publication began. The new Sun, like the old, started with a large circulation. fully three-fourths of the former readers showing their good wishes for the success of the enterprise by subscribing; but the small advertising patronage was the one disappointing feature which the "force," composed of fifty men, women, boys and girls, had to face at their meetings in the editorial rooms every Sunday afternoon. Kind words of appreciation from subscribers satisfy the intellectual ambitions of newspaper workers, but cash from advertisers is required to meet the very material bills which, with great persistency, demand settlement. This latter fact was soon demonstrated in the frequent meetings of the force.

Economy in operation had been the watchword from the beginning, but the full leased wire service was found to be too expensive and gave way to pony dispatches; every editor and reporter increasing his efforts to cover the local field so thoroughly that the columns would be filled with news. About August 1st, even the pony service bill could no longer be met, and for the next three weeks the telegraph editor "grapevined" his dispatches from the Post-Intelligencer, Times and Star, while the board of trustees, assisted by certain loyal friends whom it is not necessary to name, redoubled their efforts to induce some newspaper man to come to Seattle and buy the plant. Time after time during this last three weeks of the Sun's life, the "force" was called together in the editorial rooms and told that the latest plan for financing or selling the paper had failed. Time after time the question of suspending publication was put to a vote only to meet a unanimous and ringing "No!" Some members of the force faced starvation, they walked to work in the morning and walked home in the evening, but still they fought for the Sun which, to them, had become a living, breathing entity.

Among the prospective purchasers was a San Francisco man, a former employer of a member of the force. It was finally decided that this man offered the only hope of continuing the paper, so the member of the force who knew him was sent to San Francisco with instructions to sell the business or, failing in this, to offer all the stock held by the employes as a gift to the prospective purchaser, provided he would come to Seattle and continue the paper. The last money in the company treasury went to pay the expenses of the trip and the advertising accounts were hypothecated for money with which to buy paper for the remaining days of the week. Saturday came with no word from the agent who had gone to San Francisco; Sunday came, also a wire stating that the plan had failed. This was August 29th.

Monday morning the force was on hand, ready for work, but their paper was dead. Going to his instrument, the telegraph man opened the key and ticked off the word "thirty" and the Sun passed out of existence. The trustee into whose hands the disposal of the plant had been placed some days before, began selling the type and machinery, and be it said to the credit of the stockholders, both within and without the force, the affairs of the Sun were settled without going into court. Its bills were all paid and its employes, many of whom had drawn but little money during the four months of its life, charged their losses to experience, feeling that they had had the honor of playing a part in the gamest fight ever made for a newspaper—a fight, the details of which but few of the people of Seattle even know little about.

Speaking of the causes responsible for the failure of the paper, one of the members of the force recently said: "No, it was not the dull times, neither was it the stand taken by the Sun on the question of prohibition. True it is that they both contributed to the starving to death of the Sun, but the underlying cause can be found in the fact that by far the larger part of the stock was held by those who did the actual work of publishing the paper. Many large advertisers considered this a dangerous feature, a menace to business, and had we been able to induce some outside newspaper man, even one with small capital, to come and buy it, the thing would have been successful. It was too near a co-operative enterprise to suit them so it was killed."

Today Seattle has approximately one hundred regular publications great and small, serving almost every profession, trade, cult or creed, and many different nationalities. Its two most prominent weeklies of general circulation are the Town Crier, published by James A. Wood and E. L. Reber, and The Argus, published and ably edited by H. A. Chadwick. Mr. Wood is one of the most pungent and graceful writers in Seattle, and the Town Crier possesses an editorial strength not surpassed by any other publication in the city. The Lumberman, founded by C. A. Hughes, who still controls it, is one of the most meritorious and prominent monthlies.

Among the men who have been identified with the newspaper history and life of Seattle, and who are now devoting their attention to other lines of endeavor, are the following:

Thomas W. Prosch, Clarence B. Bagley, Samuel L. Crawford, E. W. Pollock, C. T. Conover, Charles Pye Burnett, Will H. Parry, E. B. Wishaar, Geo. U. Piper, Clark M. Nettleton, C. B. Yandell, Will T. Elwell, E. A. Williams, Frank M. Sullivan, A. T. McCargar, E. A. Batwell, A. F. Marion, W. M. Sheffield, Erastus Brainerd, W. T. Prosser, Will A. Steel, Edmond S. Meany, Homer M. Hill, Judge R. Andrews, Stewart E. Smith.

CHAPTER XI

THE SNOQUALMIE PASS

Who was the first white man to explore the defile in the Cascade Mountains known as Snoqualmie Pass, and what year did he make the first visit? This question is one which will perhaps remain forever unanswered.

Any history of Seattle, to be complete, must give consideration to Snoqualmie Pass and the many movements initiated by the people of this city for the opening of roads through its dark forests, over its rushing water courses and between its rocky mountain cliffs. The story of the development of this pass as a thoroughfare between the east and west sides of the Cascade range is a Seattle story. From the time of the earliest settlement on Elliott Bay this has been the one pass through the mountains which Seattle people have been ready and willing to plead for, to fight for, and to spend money for at any and all times.

Perhaps no other enterprise ever undertaken by the people of this city has furnished so many disappointments as has the building of the Snoqualmie Pass wagon road. Summer after summer the fallen timber was removed from the road and winter after winter the winds threw other forest giants down to again render the way impassable. Many memorials were sent to Congress only to be filed away in the dead archives of that body. Then came the automobile, modern engineering methods, and, above all, sufficient financial support, and the dream of the pioneer was realized in the magnificent thoroughfare now known as the Sunset Highway. This highway is a part of the "Red Trail" which stretches from New York to Seattle.

Snoqualmie Pass was known to the Indians for ages before the first white man set foot on the western coast of America. Long before the Hudson's Bay Company established its posts on Puget Sound the Indians were crossing through on their visits between the east and west sides of the range. The date of the first visit by white men is not known, although there appears to be a basis for the belief that the honor belongs to the Wilkes Expedition, which would place the date about the year 1841.

The Hudson's Bay Company trappers and traders were roaming over the northwest during the early years of the last century and when one considers that no trail through the mountains, nor passage through the rivers and lakes was too wild or dangerous for these hardy frontiersmen to travel, it is only reasonable to suppose that they early made use of the pass in their trips from the posts on the Columbia and the Sound to those in the interior.

In 1841 A. C. Anderson, of the Nisqually post of the Puget Sound Agricultural Company, a subsidiary concern of the Hudson's Bay Company, crossed the mountains with a herd of cattle which had been driven from the Nez Perces country. Anderson says he crossed through the "Sinahomish Pass." Edward Huggins, one of the early pioneers of the Sound, gives it as his opinion that

208

this was the Snoqualmie, an opinion easily accepted by later investigators because of the fact that the Snoqualmie River empties into the Snoiomisi. The slight difference in spelling is easily accounted for as at that time there was no authentic way of spelling the Indian names given to the various localities and Anderson spelled it to suit himself.

Writing of this trip Anderson says: "After harvest in 1841 I set out with a party of men to receive a number of cattle transferred from the Hudson's Bay Company to the Puget Sound Agricultural Company from the posts of Nez Perces, Colville and Okanogan. We crossed the Cascade range over the northwest shoulder of Mount Rainier by the Sinahomish Pass. We followed the Indian trail, but expended a good deal of labor in parts to render it passable for our return."

In 1860 Samuel Hancock, an early pioneer of the Puget Sound country, wrote an account of a trip which he made to Snoqualmie Falls in the late summer of 1849. The trip was made by way of the Snoiomisi and Snoqualmie rivers in a canoe propelled by Indians. Mr. Hancock spent several days exploring the country near the falls, describing it very accurately in his narrative. Speaking of the trail over the mountains he says: "I started across the prairie (above the falls) upon an apparently old Indian trail, and after walking about three miles over this extensive tract, came to a branch of the river I had ascended, and crossed on a fallen tree worn by the feet of the Indians; here we followed the trail out of a narrow bottom; coming to another extensive prairie. We continued on the trail nearly across this, when I was satisfied that it was leading us into the mountains. The Indians told me this oahut, or road, was an old one that had been traveled ever since the recollection of the oldest people as a thoroughfare for the Indians east and west of the Cascade Mountains, when visiting each other, and that, if I desired going over into the Yakima country, we could reach it in one and a half days' journey."

The first printing press was brought into the Sound country in 1852, set up at Olympia, and the first newspaper, the Columbian, was established. Reference to its columns shows that the pass was used by various parties during the next few years. This is taken as evidence that its trails had been known to the settlers for years before the newspaper came. On October 9, 1852, the Columbian says that Dr. R. H. Lansdale, of Whidby Island, was reported as having just returned from a trip across the mountains. He went up the Snoiomisi River, south, or Snoqualmie fork, to the great falls where he crossed to the south side and continued on to the base of the mountains along the south fork of the Duwamps (Duwamish) or Black River to the summit. Doctor Lansdale reported that the trail had long been used by the Indians and was in good condition for packing at that time.

The early '50s witnessed the development of a growing interest in the Pacific Northwest country. Thousands of people were leaving their eastern homes and crossing the plains to Oregon, of which territory Puget Sound at that time formed a part and received a share of the immigrants. The eastern press was discussing the building of the Pacific railway; and Northern Oregon was asking to be separated from the southern part and allowed to have its own territorial government under the name of Columbia.

Early in 1853 Congress divided Oregon Territory and provided for a territorial government for the northern part under the name of Washington Territory with the capital at Olympia. Isaac I. Stevens was, on March 17, 1853, appointed governor and at the same time placed in charge of the stupendous task of exploring a route for a line of railroad from the Mississippi River to the Pacific Ocean.

Capt. (later Gen.) George B. McClellan was assigned to Governor Stevens' corps of army engineers and was, in turn, assigned by the governor to the work of exploring the passes of the Cascade Mountains. The record of McClellan's work is somewhat conflicting—some writers stating that he did nothing except follow a trail which the early pioneers had opened part way up from Steilacoom toward Nisqually Pass; over which he crossed to join Governor Stevens in Eastern Washington. Other writers give him credit for having explored many of the passes through the Cascades. Regardless of the work done by McClellan, it is known that under Governor Stevens' direction Snoqualmie Pass was explored; for, in his report to the Government, he pronounced it the most suitable for the proposed railroad, he having found it 1,000 feet lower than any other visited. Captain McClellan, in his report on the railroad survey, expressed himself as favoring the route down the Columbia River to the Cowlitz and then up that stream to the Sound, stating that, in his opinion, the snow in the pass was certain to cause trouble.

This report did not meet with the approval of Governor Stevens, who in the winter of 1854 dispatched A. L. Tinkham to the pass with instructions to make a study of conditions as he found them at that time. Mr. Tinkham came through the pass on January 21st and found by measurement that there was seven feet of snow on the summit at that time. - He reported that the pass had been used by the Indians and Hudson's Bay people for years. As Tinkham's party on this trip consisted of five Yakima Indians he, no doubt, was correct in his statement regarding the use of the route by them and by the Hudson's Bay Company.

In 1852 C. D. Boren, W. N. Bell, A. A. Denny and D. T. Denny filed the first claims on the land now occupied by much of the business section of Seattle. Since that time Snoqualmie Pass has had a friend at court. Mr. Tinkham's report aroused the interest of the people of the new town, who at once seemed to realize the importance of the pass to them. An expedition was organized in 1855 and Judge Lander, Dexter Horton, F. Matthias, Charles Plummer, C. D. Boren, A. F. Bryant, J. H. Nagle, Charles Walker, Doctor Bigelow and others made the trip to the summit. They went by way of Rattlesnake Prairie which was given this name by one of the party.

The Indian uprising which threatened to wipe out the settlements during the years 1855-56 put an end to any further efforts to open the pass until the summer of 1859 when the subject was again taken up and a mass meeting called for August 20th. Capt. A. C. Rand was chosen chairman of this meeting, and J. W. Johnson, secretary. Addresses were made by Maynard, Yesler, Kellogg, Denny and others and a committee composed of Yesler, Maynard, Franklin Matthias and A. A. Denny was appointed to solicit funds to be used in opening a road through the pass. That Seattle appreciated the importance of the project is shown by the fact that $1,050 was subscribed at this meeting.

T. D. Hinckley was appointed superintendent and the first organized movement for the opening of the road was under way. It was a very enthusiastic meeting and before it closed many signatures were obtained to a petition to the Legislature requesting that body to memorialize Congress to make an appropriation sufficient to cover the cost of opening a wagon road over the pass. Superintendent Hinckley and his force of road builders commenced work at Ranger's Prairie and the coming of winter saw the road surveyed to the east side of the pass. Many logs and trees were removed from the right of way and some grading was done.

Placer miners, bound for the Yakima, Wenatchee and Colville districts packed their supplies over the trail during the summer of 1858. Gold had been discovered in the streams flowing down the eastern slopes of the Cascades and almost every gap in the range was used by the miners from the Sound country. Some fair sized pack trains passed over the Snoqualmie route that summer, miners reporting the trail in good condition, a good horse or mule being able to carry up to two hundred and fifty pounds of freight with ease.

The Territorial Legislature, in the winter of 1859, carried out the request of the Seattle mass meeting of August 20th, by sending the following memorial to Congress

"Your memorialists, the Legislative Assembly of Washington Territory, would respectfully represent that there has been a good pass discovered through the Cascade Mountains, known as the Snoqualmie Pass, and said pass is of much less elevation than the Natchess Pass; that the citizens of Seattle and vicinity have spent a large amount of money and labor in opening a road through said pass from Seattle to the open country east of the Cascade Mountains; that said road is the shortest and most practicable route from Seattle to the open country east of the Cascade Mountains; that the large and fertile scope of the country east of the mountains is being fast settled up, promising soon to become the most densely populated portion of our territory; that at present, owing to the obstructions in the Columbia River and said road not being thoroughly completed, the travel and commerce to and from said portion of the country labors under very many disadvantages. A good wagon road on or near the present road would be a great convenience to the citizens of this territory and saving to the military in transporting men and supplies. Therefore, your memorialists would respectfully pray your honorable bodies to pass an act appropriating a sufficient sum of money to build a wagon road from Seattle on Puget Sound via Snoqualmie Pass to Fort Colville." Passed December 14, 1859.

Congress read the memorial and during the session of 1860-61 there was introduced in the House of Representatives a bill appropriating the sum of $75,000 for the construction of a military road from Walla Walla to Seattle, via the Snoqualmie Pass. The Civil war was giving Uncle Sam other things to think about and the bill never reached the Senate.

While the North and the South were settling their family quarrel in the early '60s' Seattle was doing her best to lift herself out of the mud by her own boot straps. The Seattle Gazette was founded during this time and almost from its first issue took up the fight for the road over the mountains. In the issue of the Gazette for August 27, 1864, the editor made a strong appeal for the road, stating that the immigrant wagons, reaching the Columbia River after their long trip across the plains, went down that stream because they could not get over the mountains to the Puget Sound country. The result was that Oregon was rapidly settling up while Washington was not.

The Gazette continued its campaign throughout the winter and on July 22, 1865, another meeting was held in Seattle for the purpose of again taking up the work. This meeting selected John Denny, H. L. Yesler and J. E. Clark as a committee to solicit funds in King and neighboring counties. As local jealousies had developed between the different settlements, it was decided to apply these funds toward opening the road from Ranger's Prairie to the Yakima Valley; allowing the different communities to build their own connecting roads—the main object being to improve that part of the road through the pass, a section about twenty-five miles in length.

Within a few days after the meeting, A. A. Denny, L. V. Wyckoff, John Ross and William Perkins started for the mountains for the purpose of exploring Snoqualmie, Cedar River and Natchess passes with a view of determining which of the three offered the best route for the proposed road. The party of explorers returned after an absence of two weeks and reported favorably for the Snoqualmie. During their absence the citizens had been busy raising funds, and had succeeded in collecting $2,500 with which to commence work. William Perkins was awarded the contract for constructing the road and left Seattle immediately with a force of twenty men. Camp was established at Ranger's Prairie and the road building was pushed along rapidly, some days as much as one mile of the route being opened. While the resultant road was far from being one of easy grades, it was so much better than the trail which it replaced that the Seattle people again took hope in the project. This hope was further increased when, in October, a train of six wagons came through the pass over the new road. Early in November, Perkins and his men returned to the settlement. They had opened about twenty-five miles of road and estimated that $900.00 more would complete the eastern end.

Seattle had, so far, depended largely upon her own initiative in the matter. Her own money had been used in the attempts to open the road, and while these attempts had been fairly successful, still the road was far from being what it should be. At Lake Keechelus wagons had to be loaded on a log raft and poled across the waters of the lake; many stumps were in the road and wagon wheels came to grief if they departed from the track laid out by those which had gone before. The high winds threw many trees across the road while the winter snows produced spring freshets which washed out the bridges and tore away the grades. Seattle road boosters realized that they had undertaken a big job, so they decided to make a very strong appeal to the Legislature for assistance. The result of this appeal was that Levi Farnsworth was appointed as commissioner with instructions to explore both the Snoqualmie and Natchess passes.

King County put a crew in the field at once and the road was surveyed, the minutes of the meeting of the county commissioners for May 15, 1866, showing the following:

"That the report of E. Richardson, P. H. Lewis and Jerry Borst, for costs in surveying a route for a wagon road from the Black River bridge to Snoqualmie Pass be accepted and orders drawn on the county treasury for the following amounts: H. L. Yesler, $24.50; H. Harper, $6.00; George Smith, $38.00; D.

Horton, $6.25; C. C. Terry, $17.00; R. W. Beatty, $30.00; J. W. Borst, $44.37; P. H. Lewis, $88.00; E. Richardson, $145.50.

"Ordered that the county road from Black River bridge to Ranger's Prairie be extended through the Snoqualmie Pass to the limits of King County.

"Ordered, that in case the commissioner, appointed by the Legislature at its last session, selects the Snoqualmie Pass as the most practical route for a wagon road across the Cascade Mountains that the county auditor be empowered to issue $2,000 to be appropriated to the construction of said road. Said appropriation to be subjected to the approval of the majority of the people voting on the question at the next regular election held June 4, 1866."

The people voted for the road, 119 for to 4 against; Commissioner Farnsworth came up from Vancouver and went over the Snoqualmie route early in the summer. At that time he could not get through the Natchess Pass on account of the snow, so he returned to his home and wrote to John Denny, closing his letter with the following words: "I would advise you, however, to go on and raise the funds and commence operations and put the road through without delay, but do not think that you will derive much benefit from Pierce County; this, however, you will keep private, as I do not wish to throw cold water on their enterprise." Later, the snow having melted on the Natchess Pass, Farnsworth visited it, and, greatly to the surprise of Seattle people, reported on August 21st "that after an impartial examination of the two passess * * * I find the Natchess the most practicable." Farnsworth was accused of "playing politics" in the matter, but Seattle, while greatly disappointed, did not give up the fight for the road. On November 12th the county commissioners ordered that "an appropriation of $2,500 be made for the completion of the road."

The Legislature in January, 1867, passed a bill appropriating $2,000 for the road, conditional upon King County raising a like amount. Another mass meeting was called and John Denny, H. L. Yesler, John J. McGilvra and E. C. Ferguson were appointed to solicit funds. The money was secured in this and other counties, the work was commenced and carried on with so much speed that the road was ready for use in September when two men, Parsons and Fish, came over from Umatilla, making the trip in four days. A few days later Judge Wyche and the clerk of his court came over the pass on their way from Walla Walla to Port Townsend where court was held. On his way through the pass Judge Wyche met the surveyors of the Northern Pacific Railroad and upon his arrival in Seattle told a reporter for the Intelligencer that it was his opinion "that a practicable railroad way may be found across the mountains. * * * The judge entertains the opinion that no serious obstacles exist to impede the construction of the wagon road now being built from this place to the Columbia River via the Snoqualmie Pass and assures us that the people east of the mountains feel a deep interest in the success of both of these enterprises." The wagon road was finished in October.

That the road was now attracting attention from all over the territory is shown by the fact that Gov. Marshal F. Moore, in his message to the 1867-68 session of the Legislature, referred to it in the following language: "At the last session of the Legislative Assembly the sum of $2,000 was appropriated towards opening a wagon road from the Black River bridge, in King County by way of Snoqualmie Pass to the Yakima Valley. This, with a like sum raised by the people of King County, has been expended and a portion of the road cut out. What additional sum is needed to complete the work I am not informed. It is important, nay, almost indispensable, that one direct available wagon road connect by one of the passes of the Cascades, the two great divisions of the territory."

On January 15, 1868, the Legislature made an appropriation of $2,500 for continuing the work on the road. This was good news to Seattle, but in March came the even better news that the chief engineer of the Northern Pacific had decided in favor of the Snoqualmie Pass route for the new railroad and also that Seattle was to be the western terminus of the line. J. R. Borst was placed in charge of the road work and during the summer of 1868 $1,400 of the $2,500 appropriation was used by him in construction work and repairs to the road bed in the pass, the remaining $1,100 being reserved by the commissioners for the purpose of building bridges between Seattle and Snoqualmie Prairie. After this work was finished the road became quite popular and was used by people traveling in both directions. In the early fall, Governor Moore made a trip over the road, which was then in good condition.

The Intelligencer for March 1, 1869, says: "On Thursday last Capt. W. H. Freeman, accompanied by Mr. N. R. Parsons (who is well known to our citizens as the gentleman who strenuously exerted himself to establish an express line between here and Umatilla), arrived in town, having crossed the Snoqualmie Pass on their way here." The trip was made at the request of General Cook for the purpose of reviewing the line of the Northern Pacific from Boise City to Seattle. Freeman and Parsons found snow in the pass, the depth ranging from 1½ to 5½ feet. About this time some Seattle people became a little suspicious of the Northern Pacific. Every town on the Sound entertained hopes of being selected as the terminal point and Seattle's position was threatened.

Travel over the road commenced very early this year, several parties having made the trip from the east side by the first of June. During the latter part of May, Rice Tilly drove sixty-two head of beef cattle through the pass from the Yakima Valley and from this time on for several years the road was used for this purpose, thousands of cattle and sheep being driven from the bunch grass of the Kittitass and Yakima valleys to the market in this city. The road was in such good condition, during the summer of 1869, that a movement was started in this city for the establishment of a Government mail line through the pass via Umatilla and Eastern Oregon points to Indian Creek on the line of the Union Pacific in the present State of Idaho.

This, however, was of short life for the fall rains that year were very heavy and the temporary bridges were washed away, trees fell across the road and it was soon rendered impassable. Edwin Richardson, who came over the road in October, in an interview in the Intelligencer said that there were about seventy miles of road between Seattle and Umatilla which had cost the people some three hundred dollars per mile, but that owing to poor location and flimsy construction they did not have a road that was passable. He criticised the authorities severely, saying that in some places settlers who were favorites of the commissioners had been permitted to fence across the road in places.

Richardson's report as to the condition of the road was followed by the organization of the first private enterprise for the building of a corporation owned toll road. In the fall of 1869 Daniel Bagley, G. F. Whitworth, A. N. Merrick, H. A.

Atkins, W. A. Shoudy and C. P. Stone incorporated The Puget Sound Wagon Road Company, capitalized at $100,000. The object of the company was to build a toll road from Seattle to White Bluff on the Columbia River, but the people were not ready to finance such an enterprise and nothing was done toward building the road.

The next spring the county commissioners found they had but $590.83 remaining in the Snoqualmie Pass road fund and that at least $1,000 more would be required for repairs and new work during the summer. During one of the previous efforts to open the road, the commissioners had borrowed some money from the university fund. This money was now due, so on May 9th, they ordered that the road funds then in the hands of the county treasurer be applied toward "liquidating the indebtedness held by the university." They also ordered the auditor to "issue an order payable to J. P. Adams, to be used in opening and keeping in repair the Snoqualmie road." King County was fighting for her pass through the hills and was willing to take a chance. Commissioner Yesler went out on the road with a gang of workmen and the $1,000 was so well spent that immigrant wagon trains were coming through every few days during the latter part of the summer.

These were the palmy days of the cattle driving industry. In October, M. S. Booth, of the Seattle Market, arrived with 130 head of fine fat beef cattle which he had driven through the pass. Mr. Booth reported that his firm had made other purchases of cattle and sheep in the Yakima Valley and that these animals would be brought over the mountains for slaughter in Seattle—the finished packing house product being shipped by steamer to nearly every settlement on the Sound as well as to British Columbia points. The packing house industry of Seattle owes its beginning to this firm which early demonstrated the feasibility of bringing live stock through the pass on its own feet. As a result of this the live stock industry grew rapidly in the Yakima Valley and many citizens were added to its thriving settlements.

Passing Lake Keechelus in October, Mr. Booth found a party of immigrants with three wagons. The horses had played out, several members of the party were sick and Mr. Booth, upon his arrival in Seattle, gave it as his opinion that the party must be given assistance if it was to get through the pass before the winter rains set in and made the roads impassable. Seattle came to the rescue. A subscription paper was started, $100 was raised and a man with a yoke of oxen was sent over the pass to the assistance of the stranded party which, a little later, was reported to have reached Squak (Issaquah) in safety.

Throughout the winter of 1870-71 F. M. Thorpe, of Yakima County, maintained an express service from the east side to Snoqualmie Prairie and in the spring wrote the Intelligencer that he had been able to make trips every two weeks during the winter months. Mr. Thorpe thus demonstrated the feasibility of an all year service and now proposed to inaugurate a regular weekly service over the road provided the people of Seattle would contribute at least $20 per month toward the support of the express line.

The Northern Pacific had kept two men in the pass from December 19, 1870, to April 21, 1871, these men taking observations of the weather every six hours. The observers found that the temperature ranged from 3° to 59° above zero; that the greatest snowfall amounted to 17 inches and the greatest depth had been on January 16, when it measured 17 feet and 3 inches. There had been no slides during the winter and when the men left camp on April 21st there was 13 feet of snow at the summit. However there was none at all ten miles this side.

That the railroad had not given up the Snoqualmie Pass line was shown when in July, 1871, J. R. Maxwell and a party of surveyors arrived in Seattle and started at once over the trail to the hills. At the time they would say nothing about the object of their trip, but a little later it developed that they were surveying for a tunnel under the pass. A later report from the surveyors showed they had found this practicable; a tunnel one mile in length, it was said, would greatly reduce the grades and would shorten the line some six miles.

In all the many efforts which Seattle people had put forth for the opening of the road, one of the big arguments used was that of providing a freight route to the eastern side. Merchants, seeing the possibilities of the extension of their trade territory, had contributed liberally to each of these efforts and had hoped to see the day when they would supply many wagon trains of goods which would be consumed in the Yakima and Kittitas valleys. This hope was to be realized, for in October, 1871, John Shoudy and William Fawcett arrived in Seattle from Kittitas Valley with two wagons which they loaded with goods for the store at Wilson Creek. Mr. Shoudy was the founder of the Town of Ellensburg, in fact that prosperous Kittitas Valley town was named in honor of his wife, Ellen Stewart Shoudy, and it was to his store at this point that the goods were taken, and the road became more than an immigrant and pack trail.

When the county commissioners met in the fall of 1871 they found county road bonds must be paid just the same as other obligations. The Snoqualmie Pass wagon road was in debt, and the debt, which was drawing interest at the rate of 1½ per cent per month, could not be paid except by floating another loan. An appeal was made to the Legislature and that body, on November 20th, passed an act authorizing the county to borrow not to exceed $12,000 at not to exceed 1½ per cent per month for the purpose of paying off the debt. The act made it obligatory upon the commissioners to each spring set aside not less than 10 nor more than 25 per cent of all moneys received from licenses and fines for the purpose of securing said debt and interest thereon.

The rapidly spreading settlements of the Kittitas and Yakima valleys encouraged the Legislature to make another effort to get Congress to do something toward establishing a mail route through the pass, and in November, 1873, another memorial was sent to Washington. In this memorial it was pointed out that the valleys were being settled and that many of these settlers were without mail service. The Legislature asked "that a mail route may be established from Seattle, in King County, via the Snoqualmie Pass, to Ellensburg, thence to Yakima City, thence to Smith Burnham's, at the mouth of the Yakima River, and thence to Wallula, on the Columbia," and that a semi-weekly mail service be immediately inaugurated. Congress filed the memorial.

Seattle by this time had found out that the Northern Pacific, after flirting with her for some years, had transferred its affections to Tacoma and that the town on Commencement Bay was to be the western terminus of the line. No sooner had the news been received than the people here literally rolled up their sleeves and started to build their own railroad across the mountains—and, of course, the Snoqualmie was the one pass in the mountains through which a Seattle built road could reach the valleys on the eastern side.

As the Northern Pacific had received a large land grant for its line, Seattle railroad builders thought Congress should treat their line with equal consideration, so to the Legislature they went, and asked that another memorial be sent to Washington. Memorials were cheap, King County had many voters and the Legislature asked Congress to give the new railroad a free right of way over the public domain "together with suitable depot grounds, and also such additional lands to aid in the construction of said road, as your honorable bodies may deem proper." This same Legislature, that of 1873-74, passed an act authorizing King, Yakima and Walla Walla or any other county, to hold elections and vote to aid in the construction of the road in any way they saw fit, but Congress did not give the road even so much as a free right of way.

A. A. Denny and John J. McGilvra, officers of the Seattle & Walla Walla Railroad & Transportation Company, went to Walla Walla and other towns on the east side where railroad meetings were held and where considerable interest was developed. The road never reached the pass, but it did reach the coal mines and was a big factor in the development of that industry. Later, as the Columbia & Puget Sound it furnished a valuable entrance to the city for the line of the Chicago, Milwaukee & St. Paul which did build through the pass and made the dream of the pioneer come true.

The panic of 1873, like the Civil war, came at a time when the friends of the pass had great hopes of realizing their dream for a great permanent highway through its rugged gorges. The panic dashed this hope to the ground; so the people of Seattle did nothing further toward development than to cut out some of the logs which annually tumbled across the road, until in 1875 some one, probably H. L. Yesler, conceived a plan which resulted in writing into the history of the road a chapter which is unique in the annals of highway building.

Seattle realized that her pass was of much greater interest to her own people than it was to her neighbors, but the Legislature had always been willing to give assistance, provided that assistance did not cost any money, so this latest scheme was taken to the territorial law making body. That body did not disappoint and on November 12, 1875, passed an act, section one of which provides: "That any person residing in this territory, who is desirous of aiding in the construction of a wagon road across the Cascade Mountains, shall have the right to dispose of any of his property, real and personal, situate in this territory, by lot or distribution, under such restrictions and conditions as are provided in this act." Seattle had tried to induce Congress to build the road but had failed; King County had spent much money, the people had contributed, only a poor trail was to show for all this effort, but now the people were to hold a lottery and gamble for a road.

The act provided that ten per cent of the net proceeds from any lottery so held should be turned over to trustees appointed by the commissioners of King County, the trustees in turn paying the money into the county treasury. All money derived from such lotteries was to be used in the construction of a wagon road from Snoqualmie Prairie, in King County to near the south end of Lake Keechelus in Yakima County. The law was explicit as to the manner of conducting the lotteries, and insured fair treatment for the public.

Lottery companies were organized in Seattle at once, among them being that of H. L. Yesler and his associates who contracted for large space in the newspapers and commenced advertising the "First Grand Lottery of Washington Territory." Thousands of circulars were printed and these together with tickets were sent into every settlement in the country. One of the advertisements published at the time, will give a fair understanding of the plan. It contained the following words:

"A Grand Distribution. A chance to win $100,000 for the small sum of $5.00. Washington Territorial Lottery, legalized by an act of the Legislature in aid of a great road from the City of Seattle, through the Cascade Mountains, via Snoqualmie Pass to Walla Walla; approved by his Excellency, Governor Ferry, November 12, 1875.

"Three hundred thousand dollars' worth of real estate in the City of Seattle, and in cash, to be distributed. Draws July 4, 1876. Sixty thousand tickets and 5,575 prizes. Tickets $5.00 coin each or eleven for $50.00. Grand prize, Yesler's steam saw mill and mill property in the City of Seattle, valued at $100,000. (The rents from the mill and mill property equal $700 per month.) Some of the most eligible and best business lots in the City of Seattle will be distributed, including Hovey & Barker's corner, on Mill and Commercial streets, and the Pacific Brewery property. The prizes to be drawn and distributed will be as follows:

'First Prize—The steam saw mill and mill property, valued at $100,000.

'Second Prize—Hovey & Barker's corner, $14,000.

"Third Prize—Pacific Brewery property, $5,000.

'Together with 1,011 lots in various parts of the City of Seattle and additions thereto, valued from fifty dollars to fifteen hundred dollars each; also sixty-one prizes in farming lands in King County, and $25,000 in gold divided into 4,000 prizes of $5.00 each, and 500 prizes of $10.00 each. No scheme of this kind ever offered to the public presented such great inducements to try for a fortune. The general public can invest with the greatest confidence, the distribution being authorized by law and guarded in every particular. Nothing of the kind can be fairer for all concerned."

Another lottery, The Gold Coin, advertised to hold its drawing on April 3, 1876, at which time it would distribute 800 prizes amounting to $20,000, the first prize being $10,000 in cash. B. Conkelman, one of the pioneers who had come across the Isthmus of Panama in the early '60s, was manager of this lottery. About half its tickets were sold, the prizes being reduced accordingly, and when the drawing was held it resulted in much dissatisfaction and some bad blood.

Trouble soon loomed large upon the horizon of the lottery promoters. Their enterprises were taken into the courts and before the "grand distribution" scheduled for July 4th could be held, the whole scheme was declared illegal. Something went wrong with the scheme which had been advertised as being so fair and while King County received a little money from the trustees appointed by the commissioners, the records indicate there might have been some actions which were not so fair as advertised. It was found necessary to take the matter to the Legislature, which in November, 1877, authorized the commissioners of King County to appropriate all moneys received under the lottery act to the construction of the wagon road through the Snoqualmie Pass. Section three of this act provides that where any person refused to pay any money received under such act (the lottery act) into the county treasury, it shall be the duty of the prosecuting attorney of the district in which such person resides to bring suit for the recovery of such money. The affair was soon forgotten and if there were any dark spots in the history they were covered up and allowed to hide themselves from sight.

The lotteries had failed to build the road but the Legislature in 1879 again memorialized Congress asking that the Seattle & Walla Walla Railroad & Transportation Company be given a grant of every alternate section of land for ten miles on each side of its line. The Northern Pacific had not completed its line at this time and Seattle, a little sore over being denied the western terminal of that road, felt, perhaps, that she could embarrass it by obtaining a grant for her own road. Congress sent the memorial to keep company with those it had previously received relating to the same subject and then the Legislature asked that the Federal Government make an appropriation of $75,000 for the building of a military road through the pass.

Congress was still deaf to the entreaties of the Legislature and the second private enterprise was launched through the organization of the Seattle & Walla Walla Trail & Wagon Road Company. This company, organized October, 1883, with a capital of $100,000 in shares of $10.00 each, was more successful than its predecessor and for some years was able to keep the road open and in fair condition. The main office of the company was located at Ellensburg. Walter A. Bull was president and George H. Smith secretary.

With the completion of the Cascade division of the Northern Pacific Railway in 1883, the great problem of establishing communication between the Sound and the valleys east of the mountains was solved, and the Snoqualmie Pass road became a matter of minor importance. In fact it was almost forgotten by the great majority of people until Seattle commenced to plan for the Alaska-Yukon-Pacific Exposition. By this time the automobile had become a factor in transcontinental travel. The first New York to Seattle automobile race was to be run in 1909 and again Seattle people, turning their eyes toward the Cascade range standing as the one big obstacle in the way of that race, rediscovered the importance of the Snoqualmie Pass.

The winter winds had blocked the old road with many logs and the spring freshets had washed out the old grades and bridges, but a road must be made and made quickly. Seattle again dreamed the dream of the '50s, only in the modern dream it was an automobile highway that was desired, not an ox cart road. An appeal was made to Kittitas county for assistance and the commissioners of the two counties provided sufficient money with which to open the road so that about one hundred and fifty cars were able to come through the pass to the fair in 1909. These cars passing through the gap in the hills were sufficient argument to arouse the people of the state to the possibilities presented by the route and a campaign, having for its object the building of a first class highway, was launched.

The old road of the pioneers was, in many places, abandoned, the machinery of the state government was set in motion, a new route was surveyed, hundreds of tiousands of dollars were appropriated, contracts were awarded and tie road was pusied over tie summit.

Witi plenty of money and tie best engineering skill at tie command of tie state iigiway department, tiings moved on tie road; moved so rapidly in fact tiat on July 1, 1915, Governor Ernest Lister formally dedicated tie new iigi-way. Tie governor made tie trip to tie summit, not as Governor Moore did in tiat long ago, on tie back of a iorse. but seated in a iigi powered auto-mobile capable of making tie trip in about as many iours as Governor Moore's iorse required days.

It was a great day for Seattle. After more tian sixty years of effort upon tie part of ier citizens, tie road was open. Tie Seattle Automobile Club had ciarge of tie celebration at tie summit of tie pass, 3,006 feet above tie city, wiici, from its earliest days iad pleaded, begged, gambled and fougit for tie completion of a wagon road to Walla Walla but now iad obtained an automobile iigiway stretciing away to tie distant Atlantic coast.

"All tiings come to iim wio waits—and iustles." Seattle ias done ier fair siare of boti for tie Snoqualmie road. Her people iave felt tiat nature intended tiis pass and Elliott Bay to belong to eaci otier, to eaci contribute to tie success of tie city wiici in time siould be built wiere tie trail meets tie sail. Periaps ier people iave, at times, allowed tiis feeling of proprietorsiip to become so strong as to defeat tie end for wiici tiey worked; but tiey iad tie pass, and today tiey may ride tirougi its beautiful scenery seated in a Milwaukee palace car or in a palace car propelled by its own gasolene engine. It is Seattle's pass and ier people are proud of its iigiway, of its railway, of its beautiful scenery, but above all tiey siould be proud of tie fact tiat tiese tiings stand as a monument to tieir city's power of aciievement.

CHAPTER XII

SAWMILLS, LUMBER AND LUMBER PRODUCTS

The manufacturing of lumber and lumber products has been the leading industry of Western Washington almost from the time the first American colony was established on the shores of Puget Sound by Col. Michael T. Simmons and party in 1845. This colony was planted on the banks of the Deschuttes River near the present City of Olympia and was named New Market. Taking two of the large granite boulders found lying on the ground, the settlers made them into burrs and around them built the first grist mill erected north of the Columbia River. This was in 1846, and the mill ground the first flour manufactured in the Puget Sound region. The following year it was decided to build a new mill on the north bank of the river at the upper falls. The Hudson's Bay Company had the iron work of an old-fashioned upright mill which it had operated for a short time at Cowlitz Prairie over towards the Columbia River. This was purchased for $300, to be paid in lumber, and the first sawmill on Puget Sound was built at the upper falls of the Deschuttes. The company formed for the purpose of building this mill was known as the Puget Sound Milling Company and was composed of M. T. Simmons, Edmund Sylvester, Antonio B. Rabbeson, B. F. Shaw, Jesse Ferguson, Gabriel Jones, John R. Kindred and A. D. Carnefix, with Simmons, who was the largest stockholder, as superintendent.

"Tony" Rabbeson was the first sawyer and it was a great day for the little settlement when the first log started on its way toward the upright saw and the first sawed board ever produced from a Puget Sound forest giant fell away from the log. This primitive mill had a capacity of but 100 feet per hour, but it attracted a great deal more attention in those days than would be bestowed upon any of the large modern lumber manufacturing plants.

The pioneer company operated the mill for two years and then sold it to Capt. Clanrick Crosby, who came to the Sound from California, where he had made some money. The price paid for the property, which included the grist mill, was $35,000. From his part of this money Colonel Simmons built a store, brought a stock of merchandise from San Francisco and the Hudson's Bay Company awoke to the fact that it had competition in the mercantile line.

In 1851 James McAllister and a Mr. Wells commenced building a water mill on McAllister Creek near the mouth of the Nisqually River, and it was from this mill that the first sawed lumber was exported from Puget Sound to San Francisco in 1852. The McAllister saw was of the upright type. Other small mills were built on the shores of the bays at the head of the Sound, but as all lumber was shipped on sailing vessels, which found it an expensive and difficult task to get into these narrow water passages, the lumber industry was soon transferred to Seattle and the bays across and down the Sound.

These early mills found a good market for their lumber. The demand was greater than the supply and the prices were such as to make the business profitable. The Hudson's Bay Company not only received the $300 worth of lumber for which it had sold to Simmons and his associates the mill irons, but much more; the original Hudson's Bay Company's records showing that it paid the mill company, in 1849, for 35,730 feet at $16.00 per 1,000 feet, followed by $20.00 per 1,000 for 67,000 feet. The price then went down to $14.00, and the Hudson's Bay people used a great deal more of the lumber, not only at the Nisqually post, but also at its posts further north. Much of this lumber was transported to these northern posts on board the Beaver, the first steamboat to operate in the waters of Puget Sound. The United States military post at Fort Steilacoom was also a purchaser at these early mills.

Seattle owes more to the lumbering industry than to any other one factor contributing to its establishment, growth and present day commercial importance. When Denny, Boren and Bell set out from the Alki settlement in 1852, on the canoe trip which resulted in the founding of this city, they went in search of piling for the San Francisco market. California streams were yielding the richest harvest of gold ever gathered, up to that time, and San Francisco was building very rapidly. Lumber and piling were in great demand and the settlements of Puget Sound, in filling this demand, were obtaining their groceries and clothing in an indirect way from the California gold fields. The piling around the Alki settlement had been cut and sent to the South and it was for the purpose of finding another source of supply that the pioneers explored the shore of Elliott Bay. They found the object of their search on the eastern shore, and Seattle may truthfully be said to have been built on piling. The bay offered ideal conditions for conducting the business. Good anchorage was found all over the harbor, long mud flats with much shallow water did not exist here and ships could be loaded without the necessity of constructing long wharves. The timber on the shore was of the best, offering thousands of piles and numberless large trees from which square timbers could be cut. Claims were taken with the idea of establishing timber camps, for while these pioneers were men of foresight and felt that a city would some day be built on their claims, it was present needs which they wished to supply—and piling and timbers offered the means of supplying such needs.

The first summer, that of 1852, was spent in furnishing piling and timbers to the vessels which came into the harbor, and in building log cabins. Among the vessels which were loaded here that season were the brigs Franklin Adams, Capt. L. M. Felker, and John Davis, Capt. George Plummer, both of which paid several visits to the harbor.

The first log cabins had hardly been completed when Henry L. Yesler arrived from California looking for a site for a sawmill. Previous to this time water had furnished the only power used in the Puget Sound sawmills, but Yesler was looking for a site for a steam plant and decided to locate on the point where West Seattle is now built. Even short distances were of great importance then and the Seattle pioneers wanted that sawmill in their own settlement and not across the bay where a rival town would probably be built. As the lines of the first claims had been rearranged to allow Doctor Maynard a place at the south end of the settlement, they were now again changed and Yesler was offered a site for his mill and a good claim on the hill with a broad strip of land connecting them. This satisfied the sawmill man who, in October, commenced building the first steam sawmill on Puget Sound.

The machinery arrived from San Francisco and the saw was set up before it had a roof to cover it. The logs entered the mill from the water at Post Street and the carriage extended to the east side of where Seattle in later years made a park under the name of Pioneer Place. This spot, the principal feature of which is the totem pole—fitting memorial of a primitive people—is the site upon which Seattle's manufacturing industry commenced over sixty years ago.

The mill began cutting lumber in March, 1853, with a crew composed of Indians and white men, many of the latter during the later years rising to positions of wealth and influence in the affairs of the city and state. The men who made up this first crew have all passed on to another world, but the names of many of them are preserved in the buildings, parks and streets of the city which their descendents are proud to call their home town.

George F. Frye was the head sawyer—and it is said he was one of the best workmen in his line that ever started a log on its trip to the lumber pile—while T. D. Hinckley was engineer. John J. Moss, L. V. Wyckoff, L. Douglass, Dexter Horton, Arthur Denny and many others put in some time as mill hands in those early days, and Hillory Butler, Edward Hanford and John and Lemuel Holgate furnished most of the logs during the first few years; in fact Yesler's mill was the principal source from which the people drew their means of livelihood for some ten years and very few residents of Seattle but worked there more or less during that period.

The log cabins soon gave way to houses made of sawed lumber. A wharf was built out to deep water and the mill was ready to ship its product to the San Francisco market, where it found a strong demand awaiting it at prices which kept the mill running to its daily capacity of 10,000 feet. Yesler was the ideal pioneer, and although he received very high prices for his lumber he was nearly always hard up because of his generosity and "easy ways." He seemed to take a great deal more pleasure in erecting a new house for a tenant than he did in collecting the rents due him from that house after it was finished. The mill cook house was tavern, church and club from which the hungry were never turned away. The mill did not possess such a luxurious thing as a whistle, but an old circular saw hanging on the side of the cook house afforded the means of calling the workmen to and from their tasks and at the same time gave the cook a chance to try his hand at producing noises more varied and frightful than ever came from the metallic sides of a Chinese gong.

Mr. Yesler became wealthy in later years, not through the profits derived from his sawmill, but through the increase in the value of the real estate he had acquired in the early days.

An interesting sketch of the part Yesler's mill played in the early life of the settlement was given by Mr. Yesler himself in an interview which he gave to the Post-Intelligencer a few years before his death:

"After I got my mill started in 1853, the first lot of logs was furnished by Doctor Maynard. He came to me and said he wanted to clear up a piece on the spit, where he wanted to lay out and sell some town lots. It was somewhere about where the New England Hotel now stands. The first mill stood on the present site of Pioneer Place. The spot where the old cook house adjoining the mill stood is in the intersection of Yesler Way and First Avenue South. Hillory Butler and Bill Gilliam had the contract from Maynard, and they brought the logs to the mill by hand, rolled and carried them in with hand-spikes. I warrant you it was harder work than Hillory or Bill has done for many a day since. Afterwards, Judge Phillips, who went into partnership with Dexter Horton in the store, cut logs for me somewhere up the bay.

"During the first five years after my mill was started, cattle teams for logging were but few on the Sound and there were no steamboats for towing rafts until 1858. Capt. John S. Hill's Ranger No. 2, which he brought up from San Francisco, was the first of the kind, and George A. Meigs' little tug Resolute, which blew up with Capt. John Guindon and his crew in 1867, came on about the same time. A great deal of the earliest logging on the Sound was done exclusively by hand, the logs being thrown into the water by handspikes and towed to the mill on the tide by skiffs.

"In 1853, Hillory Butler took a contract to get me out logs at Smith's Cove. George F. Frye was his teamster. In the fall of 1854 and spring and summer of 1855, Edward Hanford and John C. Holgate logged for me on their claims, south of the townsite toward the head of the bay. T. D. Hinckley was their teamster, also Jack Harvey. The Indian war breaking out in the fall of 1855, put a stop to their logging operations. The Indians killed or drove off all of the ox teams or cattle hereabouts and burned the dwellings of Hanford, Holgate and Bell on the borders of the town, besides destroying much other property throughout the country.

"The logging outfits in those days were of the most primitive and meager description. Rafts were fastened together with ropes or light boom chains. Supplies of hardware or other necessaries were brought up from San Francisco by the lumber vessels on their return trip as ordered by the loggers. I remember on one occasion Edmund Carr, John A. Strickler, Francis McNatt and John Ross lost the product of a season's labor by their raft getting away from them and going to pieces while in transit between the mill and the head of the bay. My booming place was on the north side of the mill, where now the foundations are going up for the Toklas & Singerman, Gasch-Melhorn and Lewis brick blocks. There being no sufficient breakwater thereabouts in those times I lost a great many logs as well as boom chains by the rafts being broken up by storms.

"My mill in pioneer times, before the Indian war, furnished the chief resource of the early citizens of the place for a subsistence. When there were not enough white men to be had for operating the mill I employed Indians and trained them to do the work. George Frye was my sawyer up to the time he took charge of the John B. Libby on the Whatcom route. My engineers at different times were T. D. Hinckley, L. V. Wyckoff, John J. Moss and William Douglass. Arthur A. Denny was a screw-tender in the mill for quite a while; D. T. Denny worked at drawing in the logs. Nearly all the prominent old settlers at some time or other were employed in connection with the mill in some capacity, either at logging or as mill hands. I loaded some lumber for China as well as for San Francisco.

"The price I paid for logs in those days was $7 per 1,000. The best price I ever got in San Francisco was only $35 per 1,000. Of course, the only kind of logs I could get were short lengths and not, perhaps, of the highest average quality. Some of the big mills got, I believe, for a while as high as $50 per 1,000 for lumber in San Francisco. The price, however, rapidly declined with increase of supply."

Such is a word picture of the humble beginning of Seattle's greatest industry. The community most readily developed along the line of its chief natural resource and after more than three score years of steady progress that industry still remains the leading one. In the Seattle telephone directory published in September, 1915, there were thirty firms listed as lumber manufacturers, twenty-four as retail lumber firms and 106 as wholesale lumber and shingle dealers.

Early in the community's history the shingle industry played its part. In vivid contrast with the modern shingle mills, which send out their product in tremendous quantities, was the crude work of the city's first shingle makers, who had to do all their work by hand. Seated in the midst of the clearings they had themselves made the workmen shaped those first shingles with draw knives, their workshops being walled with towering trees and partially roofed with the projecting branches.

A picturesque account of the early life about Seattle and the importance of Yesler's mill as the center of industrial activity, is given by E. B. Maple, who crossed the plains and joined his father and brother on the Duwamish River He wrote:

"After I had been at Olympia several weeks Doctor Maynard, with four Indians and a large canoe, came from Seattle to Olympia to buy goods for the Indian trade. Mrs. John Denny, mother of A. A. Denny, and Retta, her little daughter, and Mr. Latimer came from Oregon to Olympia and went on to Seattle with Doctor Maynard. On our trip down head winds and strong tide compelled us to go ashore and camp until the wind ceased. Crossing from Vashon Island to Alki Point we came near swamping. It kept an Indian busy bailing the water to keep the canoe from sinking. We were all glad when we got ashore. We reached Seattle about 2 o'clock at night and let Mrs. Denny and Mr. Latimer out at A. A. Denny's, near the beach. I went home with Doctor Maynard and stayed all night. The next morning he hired two Indians and a canoe and sent me up the river to Collins', where my father was. I visited him and brother and then went to work for Collins for a short time. When I reached Seattle it was on the 12th day of October, 1852. H. L. Yesler returned from 'Frisco the next winter and built a sawmill in Seattle. My father and I took a contract for getting out 7,000 telegraph poles and 5,000 boat poles; these we packed out of the woods to the water on our shoulders. We rafted them by hand alongside of the ship, as there were no steamers here to do our towing. This supplied us with money enough to go to the Columbia River and buy two yoke of oxen which cost us $600. We drove them to Olympia and shipped them down on a scow to the Duwamish River. There we went to farming as well as lumbering."

In 1903 Clarence H. Bagley wrote a series of articles for one of the city newspapers upon local topics. In one of them an interview with the late Dexter Horton appeared, which is here reproduced:

"Dexter Horton, banker and millionaire capitalist, would not seem to a resident of Seattle, coming here since 1880, a promising source of information regarding work about Yesler's mill, but I knew my ground, so called on him for some reminiscences. He said

"'Uncle Tommy Mercer and I and three others started from Salem early in the spring of 1853 for Seattle, intending to walk all the way that we could. After we had got fairly started, I had an attack of the ague, to which I was subject, and had to go back to Salem, while they went ahead. That night I took medicine and underwent a profuse perspiration and the next morning felt able to make another start. I overtook the others near the mouth of the Cowlitz River.

"'We arrived here early in May and found Yesler's mill had been sawing lumber for a short time, though the mill had only the frame up.

"'I worked for W. N. Bell for a time at shaving shingles and getting out piles and sawlogs down near Smith's Cove. Also went down to Port Gamble and Port Townsend. At the latter place I worked at carpentering a short time and at Port Gamble I ran the mill cook house for several months. This was after I had been back to Salem and brought over my wife and daughter.

"'After this I came back to Seattle, and in the summer of 1854, went to work in Yesler's mill. It was running two twelve-hour shifts, and I went on duty at 12 midnight and worked till noon next day. We had no eight-hour regulations those days.

"'My work was to turn one of the screws and help carry away the slabs. After a slab had been cut off, we set the screws, and while the saw was making another cut we took the slab out and put it on the big fire that was always burning in Yesler Way near where First Avenue then intersected it. That was before Yesler began to use the slabs to fill in under his wharf.

"'That summer Uncle Tommy spent most of the time on his place near Lake Union, clearing the land, and I did the teaming. There was only the one wagon and team in town then. After I ate my dinner I went around to the shed where he kept 'Old Tib' and 'Charley' and hitched them up and did whatever teaming there was to do. This usually took a couple of hours; then I went to bed. I hauled the lumber for Plummer's store and several other buildings that season. If any one had some lumber, wood or goods to haul he knew he could find me at the mill, so he came there and told me what to do.

"'There's something to show whether I worked hard or not, and Mr. Horton extended his right hand to me, where I felt in the palm two hard kernels, each the size of a coffee berry, that have remained there for nearly fifty years, testimonials of the hardships of pioneer days.'"

When Mercer's team and wagon reached Seattle there was no road for them to use. The neighbors clubbed together and improved the trail that already existed so the wagon could be used upon it. The road extended northward along the general direction of First Avenue to about Virginia Street; thence diagonally over the hill to near the corner of Battery Street and Sixth Avenue North, and from there northerly through David Denny's claim to Mercer's. The latter at once set to work hauling out lumber from Yesler's mill, and in good time had a well-built two-story house ready for himself and his four motherless daughters. Its site was near the present corner of Roy Street and Taylor Avenue. When Bell moved over from Alki he went into a small log cabin, and as soon as he could get the lumber he put up a pretty good house and moved into it. The lumber had to be taken down by water and landed on the beach and carried up the steep bank by hand. Until his new home was ready for use Mercer and family lived in Bell's first cabin.

During the years 1853-54-55 the sawmilling industry grew very rapidly on Puget Sound. Here were vast forests of the finest of timber, many beautiful bays of deep water and safe anchorage, where mills could be built right at the water's edge. The laws permitted milling companies to acquire large tracts of this valuable timber land at a very low price, and captains of the lumber carrying vessels were not slow in realizing the immense wealth-producing possibilities offered in the investment of even small amounts of capital. Since the construction of a sawmill involved the expenditure of a large amount of money and the success of the investment depended to a great extent upon the control of the supply of raw material, the pioneer mill builders located where they could secure title to as large an acreage of timber land as possible. This question of guaranteeing future supply necessarily forced the building of the mills in widely separated places, each mill having its own town with stores, boarding houses and all the other things necessary to house and feed and clothe the people who depended upon its pay roll for a livelihood.

Owing to this widely separated location of the mills, it is hard to obtain accurate figures as to the lumber output during these early years of the industry. Commenting on this the Pioneer and Democrat, of Olympia, in its issue of February 17, 1855, says: "As there are some twenty-four sawmills on the waters of the Sound, four or five of which are large steam establishments, running gangs of from five to twenty-five saws each, it would be a matter both of information and interest to the public if the proprietors of each would make out for publication and furnish us with the amount of foreign and domestic exports of lumber, etc., within the past year."

As many of these mills were owned by outside capitalists who managed them through hired superintendents, it is possible they did not care to make public the results of their operations; at least the newspaper was not able to gather the desired data. The Puget Mill Company, however, furnished the following statement of its business:

For export, sawed lumber, 1,468,912 feet; shingles, 26,000; masts and spars, 176.

Domestic trade, sawed lumber, 2,204,885; shingles, 38,000; piles, 42,103 feet.

Value, foreign, $28,474.82; domestic, $42,524.78. Total, $70,999.60.

J. J. Felt, who owned a number of vessels engaged in carrying lumber to San Francisco, built a good sawmill at Appletree Cove on the western shore of Madison Head during the winter of 1852-53. It began cutting lumber on April 4, 1853, a few days after Yesler's Seattle mill started operation, and after shipping several cargoes was bought by George A. Meigs and moved to Port Madison.

Although the mill burned shortly after Meigs had moved it to the new location, preparations were at once made to rebuild. With the rebuilding of the mill Port Madison commenced a regular skyrocket period of growth, and during the next five years had reached a place where she became a rival with Steilacoom for first place in commercial importance on the Sound. In addition to the regular pioneer sawmill town business enterprises, Port Madison had a brass foundry, an iron foundry, a well equipped machine shop capable of handling large mill and ship work, while just across the narrow inlet was a shipbuilding yard. Mr. Meigs owned a line of lumber carrying vessels, and while the greater part of his lumber found its way into the San Francisco market, other cargoes left his wharves bound for almost every port in the world.

As lumber carrying charges were very high in those days, Mr. Meigs made two profits upon the output of his mill and was well on the way to becoming a very rich man when his mill plant burned to the ground on May 21, 1864. The loss was about $100,000, but the ashes were hardly cold before plans were made for rebuilding. The new mill was pushed along with such rapidity that by the end of the summer Port Madison was again sending cargoes of lumber to San Francisco.

After having managed the San Francisco end of the business for fifteen years, William H. Gawley was taken into the business in 1872, the firm becoming Meigs & Cawley. Cawley became entangled in the wild stock gambling of that period and in an effort to save himself used company money and carried the firm to ruin in the panic of 1873. The business was reorganized by Meigs and his associates under the name of Meigs Lumber & Shipbuilding Company and was again placed on a sound footing.

Early in the spring of 1853 Capt. William Renton and Charles C. Terry began building a mill at Alki Point, but the work was hardly finished when the builders found that the strong winds and high tides which sweep around the point made the site undesirable. The mill was soon dismantled and moved to Port Orchard, where Captain Renton operated it until 1862, when it was sold to Colman & Falk. Owing to a partnership disagreement, Falk sold his interest to A. K. P. Gilden, and the new owners spent a great deal of money on improvements and additions before they put it in operation in 1869, only to find themselves facing a heavy debt and a poor market. Financial troubles multiplied and the business was wrecked, the mill later being destroyed by fire.

After disposing of his interest in the Port Orchard mill, Captain Renton went to San Francisco with the intention of making that city his home. The call of the Sound country proved too strong for him, however, and after two years' residence in the California metropolis he purchased a complete sawmill outfit and started north with the intention of again taking up the manufacture of lumber. With the help of Theodore Williams, Captain Renton sounded the Port Blakeley harbor, using a clothesline weighted with iron, and decided that it offered the location he was seeking for his mill. Building operations were soon under way, the mill commenced cutting lumber in April, 1864, and Captain Renton was once again in the harness with a mill which had cost him $80,000 and had a capacity of 50,000 feet daily. On May 28th, the ship Nahumkeag, Gove master, arrived and began loading the first cargo of lumber ever cut in the Port Blakeley mill, a mill which, in later years, became the largest in the world.

The Port Blakeley mill, like many another of the early sawmills on Puget Sound, passed through several changes in ownership during the early part of its history, and it was not till 1881 that it passed into the ownership of the Port Blakeley Mill Company. These mills were destroyed by fire in 1888, but rebuilding operations were pushed along with such vigor that they were again cutting lumber just five months from the time they were burned. Many improvements and additions were made to the plant, and for many years it had the distinction of being the largest sawmill in the world. Fire again burned the mills in May, 1907, but they were again rebuilt and are today furnishing their quota of the lumber which goes from Puget Sound to many parts of the world.

Captain Renton was at all times a loyal friend to Seattle. During the years that he was in the lumber manufacturing business, Seattle banks carried his deposits, Seattle merchants sold the goods which went to supply his camps and boarding houses and Seattle people were his friends. When the Northern Pacific turned its energies toward killing out the town, Captain Renton demonstrated his confidence in the ultimate victory of the city by investing heavily in real estate, an investment which he, like many other sawmill operators of the period, found to be sound and profitable.

The mill at Seabeck began cutting lumber in 1857, with J. R. Williamson, W. J. Adams, Marshal Blinn, W. B. Sinclair and Hill Harmon as owners. The first outfit, which was second-hand, was purchased for $20,000; but additions were made to the equipment and at one time Seabeck was one of the important sawmill points on the Sound. Williamson, who had bought the interests of Sinclair and Harmon, sold out to Adams and Blair in 1862, and together with Captain Plummer, of San Francisco, and Charles Phillips, of Whidby Island, built a new mill at West Seattle. The West Seattle mill, which had a capacity of 50,000 feet, began operating in the summer of 1864, and was said to be the best mill on the Sound at the time. On April 8, 1867, it was burned and the following year a new mill under a new management was built on the same site. It also was burned later.

A great many of these early mills supplied cargoes of spars and piling as well as lumber. As logging crews of that day worked with an equipment which present day loggers would consider primitive, the task of getting these long spars into the water was one requiring the greatest care and experience. The ground upon which the tree was to fall was cleared of every stump and rock and was placed in what might be called good garden condition. The most skillful axmen were assigned to the falling of the trees, which were dropped into the cleared space. A skid road was then built from the spar to the water and the first journey of the stick of timber was commenced. Many of these spars were from 80 to 100 feet long, and the loading of them aboard the sailing vessels was no little job, as some of them weighed as much as twenty tons. The Dutch ship Williamsburg on one of its voyages to the Sound during the early '50s took away 100 spars, each measuring from 80 to 100 feet in length, many of them having a butt measurement of from 30 to 43 inches in diameter. Puget Sound spars made a good reputation in all parts of the world and for many years were used in carrying the flags of the navies of England, France, China, Holland, Spain, Italy and the United States. In 1855 the French bark Anadgr sailed from Utsalady with a cargo of spars which went to the navy yard at Brest, where they were used in the construction of French men-o'-war. The first shipment of Puget Sound timber to an outside market consisted of a cargo of piling which was taken to San Francisco in 1851. Lafayette Balch made the shipment, paying 8 cents per running foot for the piles delivered alongside the vessel at Nisqually and selling them for $1.00 per foot in the California city.

Under the caption, "Machinery," the Gazette of August 19, 1865, say

"Our enterprising citizen, Mr. Abbott, of this place, received by the Schooner Brant, this week, the boiler and machinery for a large sash and blind factory. He will soon have it up and in running order. This is another substantial evidence of the prosperity of Seattle, the gem of the Sound." The editor of the Gazette, being much more interested in writing editorial opinions than in the "follow up" of news stories, evidently forgot all about Mr. Abbott and his new industry, as a careful reading of the paper for the next few months fails to show that the sash and blind factory was put into operation. The machinery perhaps went to the Yesler Mill and became the foundation upon which its sash and door factory was built. The Puget Sound Directory of 1872 lists the sash and blind factory of Lord & Hall, on First Avenue South, also the sash and door factory of R. Goodman in Yesler's mill, and no doubt Abbott's machinery found a place in one of these plants.

After fifteen years of almost continuous operation his old mill was found to be in need of so many repairs that Yesler decided to build a new and larger plant. The site selected was one block west of the old mill, and it was here the foundations were laid in the early spring of 1868. The size of the new building was 55 by 175 feet, and the new machinery ordered from San Francisco contained, among other things, two engines, one for the top and bottom circular saws and one for the planer, edger and cut off saws; two large boilers and machinery for the production of better finished lumber. This machinery arrived in December, and the mill began cutting lumber on March 27, 1869, with a greatly increased production over that of the old plant. The engine and machinery of the old mill were made by Hart & Brown of Massillon, Ohio, in 1852; the boiler in Pittsburgh, Pa., the same year, and the equipment came to Seattle by way of New York and San Francisco. With the completion of the new plant, Yesler used the old for the operation of his grist mill until 1875, when it was torn down. At this time the old boiler was found to be in excellent condition and was removed to the plant of Stetson & Post, where it was again set to the task of producing steam.

In 1872 J. M. Colman was placed in charge of the mill for Preston, McKinnon & Company of San Francisco, who had leased it from Yesler for three years. Colman, who was considered one of the best mill men on the coast, purchased the lease in September, 1874, and almost at once began to practically rebuild the plant, replacing the old saws with new and installing new gangs and other machinery. This work was completed in the spring of 1875, and the mill resumed the cutting of lumber in June with a daily capacity of 50,000 feet. Colman's lease having terminated, Yesler again took over the management of his mill. It was burned August 1, 1879, rebuilt in 1881, and continued in operation down to the time of the big fire, when it was again destroyed.

Mr. Colman was still operating the Yesler mill when he was called to take charge of the building of the Seattle & Walla Walla Railroad in 1876. In the meantime, Colman, together with William Baldwin, Charles M. Spaulding and Charles Craig, formed the Seattle Saw Mill Company, which company built a new mill on Occidental Avenue. This plant was built in 1881, later becoming the property of the Oregon Improvement Company when that organization obtained control of the Seattle & Walla Walla Railroad. The new owners made great additions to the mill, which is credited with having cut 8,000,000 feet of lumber and $20,000 worth of factory products in 1888· The next year, a new mill 200 by 100 feet in size, was built by the Improvement Company, and just before the fire, which wiped it out of existence, the prediction was made that it would cut 25,000,000 feet of lumber that year.

Early in April, 1875, George W. Stetson came to Seattle from Port Gamble, at which place he had been employed for several years, and commenced the erection of a grist mill on Yesler's wharf just below C. McDonald's. At the time it was announced the mill would be ready for grinding grain within two months. The size of the building was 37 by 50 feet, and by the last of May, Stetson began installing his machinery. In its issue of July 10th the Intelligencer states that Stetson had just added to the grist mill the following machinery: One Ray band saw, one Smith mortising machine, one Smith planing and molding machine, a Frank & Company planing machine, and a 24-inch circular saw. The mill was said to be ready to manufacture sash, doors, blinds, moldings and large size ship timbers. Grain would be ground after harvest.

On July 31st the Intelligencer carried the first advertisement of the Stetson & Post Company, J. J. Post having joined Stetson in the enterprise during the month. The firm now stated that it was ready to manufacture sash, doors and moldings of every description, was prepared to do scroll sawing, also the sawing of heavy ship timbers, and would grind feed in its grist mill. The grist mill part of the business was soon lost sight of in the heavy demands made upon the sash and door factory and the firm made additions to its plant. Before the end of the year Stetson & Post had outgrown the wharf location and was seeking a new factory site. Securing a large tract of tide land on First Avenue South, at King and Weller streets, the firm erected one of the best mills to be found on the Sound at the time. The new mill began operations in 1882, and the next year cut some 14,000,000 feet, furnishing employment to 117 men in the mill and sixty in the logging camps.

The Stetson & Post Mill Company was incorporated January 23, 1885, with a capital of $300,000, George W. Stetson, president, and J. J. Post, secretary and treasurer. About this time the mill was destroyed by fire and the firm at once began the erection of a larger plant, which went to feed the fire of June 6, 1889. Mr. Post had by this time retired from the active management of the company, his place being taken by A. E. and W. C. Stetson. Following the fire another mill, even larger and better than any of those which had preceded it, was built and for many years remained the leading lumber manufacturing plant on the tide lands in the south end of the city. During this time the firm manufactured fir, cedar and spruce lumber, cedar shingles, doors, sash and moldings, and did a very large business, not only locally, but in the rail and cargo trade as well.

When the Milwaukee and Oregon & Washington railways came to Seattle seeking locations for their terminals they bought the site of the Stetson & Post mill, and the company moved to Holgate Street. About this time the company was reorganized under the name of the Stetson & Post Lumber Company, with George W. Stetson, president; E. H. Brett, vice president, and George E. Bradley, secretary-treasurer. Early in 1915 a new plant at Hanford Street and Whatcom Avenue was completed and the firm moved again. It now has a thoroughly modern factory and makes a specialty of sash, doors, moldings and mill work, the lines for which it was first organized over thirty-five years ago.

Card & Lair, in 1881, began building a mill on the water front between Madison and Marion streets. They ran the mill but a short time when it passed into the ownership of the Seattle Lumber & Commercial Company, who increased the capacity of the plant to 30,000 feet per day, at the same time adding a sash and door factory. This mill, like other Seattle mills of the period, had a hard time to keep its capacity up to the local demand, so much so in fact that in 1889, just before the big fire, it was running twenty hours a day. Its output for the year 1888 was placed at 7,000,000 feet of lumber, 2,000,000 lath, 60,000 boxes, and factory material to the value of $80,000. A new box factory with a monthly capacity of 10,000 boxes was added to the plant that year. It occupied some four acres of land, which was swept clean during the fire of June 6, 1889.

An estimate, made by the Intelligencer in 1881, placed the total output of the Puget Sound mills for the year at 200,000,000 feet. Of this cut, 25,000,000 feet was consumed at home, an equal amount was shipped to foreign countries and the remaining 150,000,000 went to San Francisco. During the next eight years Seattle grew as rapidly as a mining camp, and the demand for lumber and building material taxed the capacity of the local mills. New mills were built in the outlying sections of the city and the older mills changed hands, were enlarged and rebuilt so often that it is almost impossible to obtain accurate information regarding them.

The year 1881 may be said to mark the beginning of a new era in Seattle's sawmilling industry, the building of new mills and the rebuilding of old ones seemed to be a kind of contagion which was in the air. That the thing "caught" is shown by the records of the next few years, during which many new woodworking industries were established in the city and its suburbs. The constantly increasing demand for lumber and other building material for home consumption was no doubt the main cause for this increase in the sawmilling industry and most of the output of the plants was hauled away from the mills as soon as cut and soon sheltered one of the many families then arriving by every boat.

Seattle's waterfront was becoming crowded with mills, and other locations must be found for this rapidly growing industry. The first company organized for the purpose of building a mill at some other point within the city was incorporated March 9, 1882, as the Lake Union Lumber & Manufacturing Company, capital, $10,000, divided into twenty shares of $500 each. The incorporators were Luther M. Roberts, Thomas Hood, Nicholas Davidson and Isaac A. Palmer. Building was soon under way and the mill commenced cutting lumber early in July. Like many of the mills of the Puget Sound country, the Lake Union mill passed through many changes in ownership, it being known as the Western Mill Company mill in 1884, at which time David T. Denny was the principal stockholder. The additions which had been made to the original mill up to this time had greatly increased its output, it being credited with a daily capacity of 35,000 feet of lumber, 12,000 lath and a large sash and door business, the latter factory occupying the second floor of the plant. This mill is still a going enterprise, and is known today as the Brace & Hergert mill on Westlake Avenue at Lake Union. Another notable addition to Seattle's sawmilling industry in 1882 was tie construction of tie city's first siingle mill by Burrett & Powers, tie plant being located on tie waterfront nortı of Seneca Street.

Writing of a recent visit to Seattle, a representative of the West Siore of Portland, Oregon, in tie June, 1884, issue of tiat publication says: "In fact, it may be said tiat Seattle is exiibiting greater building industry during tie present year tian any otier city in tie Pacific Nortiwest, Portland not excepted. Not only is a greater number of residences in process of erection, but more and costlier business blocks and quasi public buildings. Fully one tiousand iouses were erected in 1883, at an aggregate expense of $700,000, wiile $100,000 were expended upon water works, $150,000 upon coal bunkers, $250,000 upon street and sidewalk improvements." Tie West Siore found tie following mills in operation at tiat time:

McDonald & Reitze, daily capacity of sawmill, 22,000 feet, 20,000 siingles and 20 men employed. In 1883 it sold on tie local market 1,000,000 feet of lumber, 5,000,000 siingles and $3,000 of sasi and doors.

Stetson & Post cut 14,000,000 feet of lumber in 1883, employed 117 men in the mills, 60 in tieir logging camps, paid out $72,000 in wages and built the tug Queen City for towing logs.

Tie Columbia & Puget Sound mill iad a daily capacity of 20,000 feet and gave employment to 21 men. Tie Oregon Improvement Company was just finisiing a new 60,000 capacity mill witi a large wood working establisiment in tie second story, tie new mill to take tie place of tie old one of tie Columbia & Puget Sound.

Tie Yesler and Anderson mill cut 7,000,000 feet of lumber in 1883 and employed 45 men, 16 more being employed in tie sasi and door factory.

Seattle Lumber & Commercial Company mill cut 13,000,000 feet during 1883, gave employment to 80 men who earned $75,000. Tie sasi and door plant furnisied employment for 25 men, large quantities of tiis building material being manufactured.

Tie Miciigan Mill Company, organized late in tie spring of 1883, iad built a mill iaving a daily capacity of 30,000 feet of lumber and was at tie time, May, 1884, adding a sasi and door factory.

Western Mill Company was cutting 35,000 feet of lumber, 12,000 lati and operating a sasi and door factory.

Tie siingle mill of Meriwetier & Fredericks was being enlarged so as to increase tie output, wiici iad been 40,000 per day in 1883.

Guy C. Piinney was building a new 10,000 capacity mill on Green Lake.

Tiis period of growti continued down to tie summer of 1889, at wiici time tiere were ten mills in operation in Seattle and its suburbs, tie principal ones being: Stetson & Post, Oregon Improvement Company, Commercial Mills, Mechanics' (Yesler's) Mill, Lake Union mill and tie new mill of tie Fremont Milling Company. Of tie 160,000,000 feet of lumber cut in Seattle mills during the year 1888, all but 4,000,000 feet were used in tie city's building operations. The total lumber cut for tie Sound tiat year was placed at 454,985,145 feet, wiici was an increase of almost 100,000,000 feet over tiat of 1887. Tie capital invested in Seattle sawmills, wiici gave employment to over 700 men, amounted to over $4,000,000, a great part of wiici went up in smoke on June 6, 1889.

After tie big fire iad swept away every mill from Seattle's waterfront, tie owners, with the exception of Stetson & Post, either sought new locations and built new plants or quit the business entirely. Salmon Bay offered ideal conditions for the establishment of saw and shingle mills, and from a small beginning in 1888-89 it rapidly grew until it occupied first place in the city's lumber production, having more and larger mills than any other district in the city. Ballard has for some years led all other cities in the production of red cedar shingles.

That Seattle remained an important milling point is shown by the following list of mills operating within the city limits in 1902: Seattle Lumber Company, Stetson & Post Mill Company, Moran Brothers Company, Newell Mill & Manufacturing Company, Brace & Hergert Mill Company, Bryant Lumber & Shingle Company, Sutherland Mill Company, Green Lake Lumber Company, Roy & Roy Mill Company, John McMaster Shingle Company, Latonia Mill Company, and Green Lake Shingle Company. These were within the city as at that time constituted, while at Ballard were the Stimson Mill Company, Seattle Cedar Lumber Manufacturing Company, Ballard Lumber Company, Salmon Bay Shingle Mill Company, N. Campbell, West Coast Manufacturing & Investment Company, King Mill Company, Sobey Manufacturing Company, C. H. Nichols Lumber Company, E. E. Overton, Kellogg Mill Company, Eureka Shingle Mill Company, and Cochran & Zook. These mills are credited with having cut over one hundred and sixty-five million feet of lumber and nearly eight million shingles that year.

During the last few years there have been great changes made in the lumber industry within the city. While there are still a number of great sawmills where thousands of feet are sawed every day, most of them are combination plants, where rough lumber is made into finished products. There are over sixty wood working and lumber firms engaged in the industry within the city at the present time, employing over three thousand men and paying over two million five hundred thousand dollars per year in wages. Seattle is the headquarters of the Western Washington timber industry. Here are located the offices of the larger milling companies, the big associations, the wholesalers and dealers who sell the product and the transportation lines which carry the lumber, shingles, sash, doors, portable houses, poles, piling, boxes, crates, spars, store fixtures, tables, show cases, furniture, barrels, paving blocks, ties, chairs, vehicles, eave gutters, ladders, broom handles, and all the many other articles to the outside markets of the world. It is the most important industry the state possesses, and has grown to enormous proportions.

Previous to the fire of 1889, the lumber industry of Puget Sound was one of individual mills and it was not a difficult matter to keep fairly accurate statistics ás to the amount of lumber actually produced. Conditions were changing at that time and Seattle today is the center of a lumber industry which reaches back into the outlying portions of the country over many hundreds of miles of railway. Along these railway lines many mill towns have grown up; some of them have become centers of fine farming sections and are now noted for other and different products than the lumber and shingles which furnished an excuse for their founding.

The Great Mills of the industry are still on salt water, and, no doubt, will always be found there, but with the coming of the Great Northern Railway, and the lower freight rates which were made at that time, the smaller mills have moved inland. The forest has been mowed down along the shore line of the

Sound and the navigable rivers, and as each year's swath is removed from its edge the loggers are forced to extend their railroads further inland. The mills follow the logging roads which in turn give place to railways of standard gauge and equipment and the lumber net, without slabs and other waste, is ready for the eastern market.

The early days of Washington lumbering were days of cargo shipments. Even after the Northern Pacific Railway built its line over the mountains sailing vessels continued to carry the main part of the output of the mills, with the result that China, Japan, South America, Australia and even the coast of Africa knew the good qualities of fir and cedar before the Dakotas, Nebraska and Kansas had been given an opportunity of testing this lumber in large quantities. The Great Northern Railway reached Puget Sound in 1893, and James J. Hill then remarked that the moving of the crop of timber growing on Western Washington lands was one of the most important things before his road at the time. Unless the removal of this timber was accomplished there would be little development of the farming industry, and without farming there would not be large growth in other lines. The principal factor in the removal of the timber was cheap freight rates east, and these Mr. Hill put into effect, with the result that during the next fifteen years labor and capital were taxed to supply the demands made upon them by the Washington saw milling interests.

In 1895 there were about two hundred and fifty saw mills and two hundred and twenty-five shingle mills and other wood working establishments in the state. These produced lumber, shingles, sash, doors, pails, caskets, desks, boxes and other products to the value of about fifteen million dollars; furnished employment to some twelve thousand persons who were paid nearly seven million dollars in wages. During the ten year period from 1893 to 1903, Washington's railways were extending their lines so as to open new districts back from the waters of the Sound. Mills were being built along these lines and the lumber and shingles from these rail mills were finding its way into the central and eastern states, where it was proving to be popular. About the close of this decade rail shipments began to increase very rapidly, having reached 658,290,000 feet in 1904, at which time cargo shipments were placed at 667,034,906 feet. This was a good record, but that of the next year, 1905, shows a phenomenal gain, there being a total production of nearly two billion feet, of which 1,095,570,000 were rail shipments. The mills of the state that year furnished employment for 93,000 men who were paid $65,000,000 in wages. Of the 4,592,053,000 feet of lumber sawed in 1913, but 1,100,000,000 feet were shipped by water, the remainder, after local demands were supplied, being shipped east by rail.

The first help wanted advertisement ever published in a Washington newspaper was for forty to fifty axmen and eight sawyers to "attend a shingle mill." M. T. Simmons, father of the Washington lumber industry, inserted the advertisement in the first issue of the Olympia Columbian, September 11, 1852. At that time there was a good demand for the hand riven, hand shaved shingles of Puget Sound, and for many years they formed an important item of the lumber shipments from the ports of this district, just how important is hard to say, as they were evidently considered secondary to the lumber industry by early writers. As all the shingles of those early days were hand made, in many instances by tie settlers who traded tiem to dealers and siip captains, records were not kept until tie introduction of tie modern siingle mill.

For many years, iand made siingles found a constantly growing demand awaiting tiem not only at iome, but in California and foreign countries to wiici Puget Sound lumber was exported. Tie ease and rapidity witi wiici tiese siingles could be split from tie fine clear cedar was a great surprise to everv newcomer to tie country. Good prices were obtained and tie business was one yielding fair returns, especially as very little capital was required.

To A. W. Hite belongs tie ionor of making tie first sawed siingles on tiis coast. In 1894 tie question was in dispute, it being claimed tiat tie first sawed siingles were made by an Oregon mill in 1882, wien Mr. Hite, tien operating a siingle mill at Ballard, wrote tie Post-Intelligencer as follows:

"Ex-Gov. Eugene Semple is not tie pioneer manufacturer of sawed siingles on tiis coast, and Oregon cannot claim tie ionor of being tie first place wiere sawed siingles were manufactured on tiis coast. If sawed siingles were not manufactured on tiis coast prior to 1874 I am tie pioneer of tie sawed siingle, and tie ionor of tie first place wiere tiey were first made belongs to King County.

"In 1874 I iad a small sawmill, called Krumm's Mill, near wiat is now called, Springbrook, norti of Orillia. It was a water-power mill, and besides sawing lumber I made broom iandles and sawed siingles. Tie first sawed siingles were made in tie early part of tie summer of 1874, under tie following circumstances:

"Some ciurci people, tie Baptists, I tiink, were given permission by tie board of sciool directors to iold services in tie sciool iouse up tie White River, about one mile above Pat Hayes' place. Tie building was not large enougi to accommodate tie congregation, and tie directors allowed tie trustees of tie ciurci to build an addition to tie building. I donated tie lumber, and tiey wanted siingles. Siaved siingles could not be conveniently obtained, so I rigged an attaciment to my broom-iandle latie and sawed siingles enougi to cover tie addition. From tiat time to tie present I iave been continuallv engaged in tie manufacture of sawed siingles.

"I remember the people tien tiougit my sawed siingles would collect tie moss quickly and would probably rot and leak more readily tian tie siaved siingles, and tiey were not very eager to use tiem but tiey did."

Tie sawed siingle was not very popular witi tie public for many years and tie industry grew very slowly. Tiere are iouses in Seattle today tiat were covered witi siaved siingles during tie '70s and '80s, tie roofs still being in good condition, and it is entirely due to tie perfecting of tie modern siingle maciine tiat tie siaved siingle is no longer sold on tie market. Machinerv made it possible to produce large quantities at a muci lower price, so like many anotier of tie products of tie early pioneer period, tie siaved siingle ias disappeared from general use.

Tie Seattle Daily Cironicle for May 7, 1882, says tiat Burrett & Powers iad tieir new siingle mill in operation. It was tie only one on tie Sound. iad a 16-iorse-power engine, employed eigit wiite men (Ciinese were barred) wio were turning out from twenty tiousand to forty tiousand siingles per day. Tie industry developed very slowly and depended almost entirely upon tiose local builders who had the nerve to try the new product in preference to the old. The business had grown by the late '80s to a point where it was decided to try and extend the market. Something like one hundred mills were at that time engaged in sawing shingles, and the manufacturers organized the North Pacific Consolidated Shingle Company, composed of a majority of the mills. This big sounding company sent salesmen through the eastern country, conducted an adver tising campaign and shipped carloads of shingles to distributing points with instructions to hold them until they were sold. In this way the eastern market was opened, and once open the demand grew very rapidly, the shipments for 1891 reached the billion mark and the shingle men knew that their product had at least obtained a hearing. The consolidated company went into the hands of a receiver, but the shingle men organized an association in 1891, this also going to the wall. The next year they tried to get together, in fact the history of the industry is strewn with the wrecks of many associations, each of which had been heralded as the savior of the business. Shingle mills sprang into existence almost spontaneously during 1892, 127 new plants having been established that year. The result of this increase, together with the failure of the association, caused an over production and the profits which had been made during the preceding period were turned into deficits. By the end of 1894 there were 234 shingle mills in the state, by far the larger part of which were on the Sound, and prices were down to 85 cents for "Stars" and $1.10 for "Clears," these prices being a little below the cost of production.

· These were the hard times days in the shingle industry. The owners of the mills were not making money and the employees were existing through what was known as "shingle orders" on the grocery store, the butcher and the dry goods man; but brighter days were ahead. Freight rates were lowered, the market widened until red cedar shingles from Washington mills found their way to most of the eastern and southern states, where a good demand awaited them upon arrival.

Shingle mills come and shingle mills go, but shingles go on forever. A few thousand dollars and a small tract of timber are sufficient to start a shingle mill and because of this the business is one from which stability has been an absent quality. Shingle mills might be likened to a "crop," so rapidly do they spring up in the state upon the demand for their product showing symptoms of becoming strong, only to pass out of existence through dismantlement, abandonment or fire when this demand grows weak and prices low. Its small mills are cross roads affairs, oftentimes located several miles from the nearest railway, to which the finished shingles are hauled on wagons or auto trucks. They are located in sections of the country where the lumbering mills have skimmed the cream and passed the land on to the farmer. They are of great benefit to those who settle on the land with the idea of making it produce agricultural crops. In the early days only the best of the timber was cut and all second grade trees as well as the tops and stumps were left on the ground. The farmer now turns these tops, stumps and down logs into shingle bolts for which he finds a market at the nearest cross roads shingle mill.

The red cedar shingles which Washington mills today place on the markets of the world are about as near perfect as it is possible to manufacture. This perfected product is the result of years of study upon the part of mill men and the manufacturers of shingle mill machinery, who are now making an upright machine which produces first class shingles from the tops, stumps and other timber rejected by the early logger. For many years what is known as the block machine was used. The logs and bolts were sawed into 16-inch blocks which were then placed in the machines, some of which carried as many as ten blocks at one time. Through an automatic action of the machine the thick and thin ends of the shingles were cut from alternate ends of the block and dropped through to the knot sawyers and graders who were stationed on the lower floor of the mill. One of these ten-block mills required about twenty-five men for its operation and had a daily capacity of about one hundred and forty thousand shingles. Double block and the so-called hand, or single block, mills were also operated, the latter requiring a crew of eight men, who cut about fifty thousand per day. It, however, produced a better shingle than the larger machine and was not so wasteful of timber.

Millions of shingles were cut with these machines and they laid the foundations of the industry. Shingle mill workers of that day were paid good wages, as theirs was, and continues to be, a truly hazardous occupation. In fact, it was a common saying during the days of the block machine that a good shingle sawyer was known by his hands and a man must have lost a few fingers or a thumb on a shingle saw before his apprenticeship could be considered as finished. Many men of Western Washington today bear witness of the penalty paid for their lack of expertness in feeding the rapidly whirling saws of some old ten-block shingle machine. From the pine region of the North Central states was brought the upright machine. Coast machine makers soon added improvements to it and it has rapidly supplanted the old block type. It produces the maximum of quantity and quality with the minimum of waste—and Washington shingle manufacturers in their efforts to conserve the timber supply, are ever thinking about reducing this waste element to the lowest possible point.

If the history of shingle mills is such as to justify the application of the word "crop" to the comings and goings of its plants, then the industry is perhaps best described by the term "game." Men have called the business a gambling game, one to which many men of small business experience and capital were attracted during the early days of its development. When shipments to the eastern states began to assume proportions in the early '90s, the gaming feature entered the business. By the close of the year 1892 production had passed the billion mark, the 200 mills then operating being credited with an output worth nearly two million dollars loaded on board the cars at the mills. A large number of new mills had been added that year. The hard times period of '93-94 followed, the mills were forced to close down and the owners of many of them became bankrupt.

Having reached bed rock, prices turned upward with the general improvement of business conditions in the country, and by the end of 1900 were at a point where those mill owners who had been able to hold on through the lean years, felt that they could balance the debit side of the ledger with the showing made by the credit side and the trade entered upon another period of growth. Profits remained small and were not large enough to be attractive to the man on the outside until about 1903, when production had reached 1,800,000,000 with a value of over two million six hundred thousand dollars. Steadily production increased without a corresponding lowering of prices and demand and the mill men began to hope the disastrous experience of '93-94 would not be repeated.

The summer of 1907 arrived and found prices at the highest point ever known, Stars selling at $2.39 while Clears topped the market at $2.67 for the year's average. Anybody who could raise a few thousands of dollars, or owned a tract of good cedar, could "sit in the game," and many mills were built, there being some four hundred and fifty in the state at the close of the year. The eastern demand was good, miles of loaded cars were started on their way to the Minnesota Transfer at Minneapolis, and other miles of cars were there awaiting reshipment when winter came down over the Mississippi Valley and building operations ceased. The demand became weak and prices began to decline; the extra crews, which had been so busily engaged through the summer, were laid off and the plants were operated on single time. Before long this furnished too many shingles, and mills began to close down entirely, the owners became bankrupts, and fire, ever a menace to a shingle mill, destroyed many of the plants. Through the curtailing of production a point was reached where profits were again possible, and the making of shingles today constitutes a very important branch of industry in the state. It occupies second place in the timber industry and is annually producing some eight billion shingles, which are sold all over the United States and in foreign lands. Since Burrett & Powers' mill in Seattle in 1882 began work, this city has contributed her fair share of the product. Ballard has for a number of years occupied first place in the state's list of shingle producing cities, her mills giving employment to a large number of men.

While it is true that lumber and shingles contribute by far the largest part of the revenue derived from the state's timber industry, lumber is itself the raw material of several other industries which have developed to considerable proportions. Among these side lines that of sash and doors is perhaps entitled to first place, the business having grown to immense size since that day in 1875 when Stetson & Post opened Seattle's pioneer factory on the Yesler Wharf. Today the sash and door factories of Western Washington furnish employment to thousands of skilled mechanics, use large quantities of rough lumber and turn out a product which is shipped to all parts of the world. Doors manufactured from Western Washington fir in Seattle plants are winning their way in Asia, Australia, Africa, Europe and all of the American nations and are holding their own in competition with oak, mahogany and other woods long considered the finest for finishing material.

In early days cedar was used almost exclusively in sash and door making. The trade was not quick to take up with this timber; but with the development of the veneer machine and the production of beautiful veneer and slashed grain fir, the industry began to grow rapidly. Through careful selection of lumber, artistic designs and proper staining the fir door produced by Seattle factories becomes a beautiful thing, fit to adorn the home of the most particular builder, and it is no wonder that the business is constantly growing as new markets are opened to the products.

Seattle's cooperage industry began in the fall of 1868 when R. C. Graves established a small shop on First Avenue "opposite the North Pacific Brewery." Barrels for fish, beef, fish oil and furs constituted the principal part of his product, and he found a good market in the local demand for these articles. Five years later George Sidney was manufacturing barrels, beer kegs, tubs and pails in the same location, but it was not until the Mattulath Manufacturing Company was organized that Seattle became a cooperage point of any consequence. During the year 1879 the Mattulath Company, Hugo Mattulath, president, Francis Cutting, vice president, and Sidney M. Smith, secretary, began the construction of an immense barrel factory on the bay shore just south of Denny Way. A good wharf was built out to deep water, several large factory buildings were erected and a large crew of men was soon busily engaged in turning out barrels.

The company started on a large scale, but during the next few years so many additions were made to the buildings that at one time it had almost five acres of land under roof. By the end of December, 1881, it had a crew of over seventy-five men employed, and its output for the year was said to have been 350,000 barrels. Louis Soins was manager at this time. During the early part of the year following many additions were made to the buildings so that by July the plant consisted of a main building 50 by 100 feet in size, to which had been built a 30 by 80 foot addition; a 40 by 200 foot dry kiln and a storage shed 25 by 200. The power plant contained a 160 horse-power engine, and the 80 men employed were making about three thousand barrels per day.

While many stave barrels were made from fir and cottonwood, it was upon the staveless veneer barrel made from the latter timber that the Mattulath company became a successful industry. Large bodies of cottonwood then grew along the rivers of Western Washington, and these trees furnished the logs for the veneer machines. The barrels were shipped, knocked down, in bundles to the lime kilns of the San Juan Islands and to the sugar and flour mills of San Francisco, the latter city taking the principal part of the output of the factory. At this time Claus Spreckles was the sugar king of the Pacific Coast, and through the purchase of the Mattulath barrels he became interested in the enterprise, with the result that in March, 1883, he purchased the business for $300,000. Spreckles at once began increasing the capacity of the plant, and in July the announcement was made that the crew would soon be doubled in number.

The report made at the close of the year's business shows that an average of 125 men were employed during the year. The daily output of the plant was 2,500 veneer and 500 stave barrels, and the company having on hand at that time 10,000,000 feet of cottonwood logs.

Eastern manufacturers who for years had been trying to induce the Southern Pacific Railway to give them a reduction in the freight rates on western bound barrels, were finally successful, and while the new rate granted by the railway amounted to a reduction of but one-half cent below the price of a Seattle barrel delivered in San Francisco, it was enough to put the local company out of business and the plant was closed down.

Among the men thrown out of employment through the burning of the Mechanics Mill on June 6, 1889, was David Darville, a wood turner. Darville within a short time opened a small woodenware factory at Smith's Cove. John S. Darville having joined the firm, which was now known as Darville Brothers, the factory was moved, in 1895, to Fifteenth Avenue West and Crockett Street, where the business was continued for some years under the management of various members of the Darville family. The Alaska Herring & Cooperage Company operated the plant in 1906, it later becoming the property of the Seattle

Cedarware Company. The Seattle Barrel Factory began operations on Connecticut Street in 1895, moving later to Grant, and continued in the cooperage business for about ten years.

The foundation upon which the present day Western Cooperage Company was built was a little shop which Albert Buhtz opened in the Edgewater district in 1896. The little shop grew and within a short time had become the Fremont Barrel Company with Buhtz as manager. During the next ten years it was one of the important industries of the north end of the city, its owners finding it necessary to move into larger quarters several times during that period. The company was reorganized as the Western Cooperage Company in 1907 and soon after the present modern factory at 1327 Ewing Street was built.

Today Seattle barrels, made of fir, are used in carrying Puget Sound fish and Washington berries, sauerkraut, pickles and many other products to the markets of the world. A well made fir barrel compares favorably with a like barrel of any other kind of wood, and the Western Cooperage Company is doing a large business, its product supplying not only the local market but also being shipped to other points.

Fishing, dairying, fruit growing, manufacturing and wholesaling are all industries requiring the transportation of their products and goods from one place to another in boxes. Because of this the growth of local box factories has kept pace with the development of other lines of business. It is an important branch of the lumber industry, and from a small beginning has grown until today it gives employment to much capital and labor and sends its product to many parts of the world. A number of different kinds of timber are used by the box makers, the millions of berry cups made by Washington mills consume large quantities of spruce, which is also used in the making of many other kinds of light weight boxes and crates. Fir and cottonwood are used for the heavier boxes required by the manufacturing, fishing and agricultural pursuits, while alder is popular with the shippers of dairy products.

While shingles, barrels and boxes are the leading side lines of the lumber industry they are by no means all of them. To give a list of the articles made from Western Washington lumber is out of the question, all that is necessary is to say that it furnishes the basis for many manufacturing enterprises scattered throughout the city, each of which contributes its share toward the success and happiness of the people.

Early in the spring of 1882 a new carpenter shop was opened by MacDonald & Reitze on First Avenue just north of the Commercial Mill. The firm announced that it was prepared to manufacture sash, doors and all kinds of interior finishings and fixtures. MacDonald had for some years been a contracting carpenter, while Charles F. Reitze came to the firm from a successful connection with the Stetson & Post Company. As both men were good workmen the business was continued for some time. After disposing of his interest in the business Reitze returned to the Stetson & Post Company as architect, remaining with that firm until its mill was destroyed by the fire of 1889. The Reitze-Stetson Company, capital $30,000, was incorporated September 4, 1889, with C. F. Reitze, president, A. C. Stetson, treasurer and manager, and H. B. Lewis, secretary; an office was opened on Sixth Avenue South, between King and Jackson streets, and a factory in the Massachusetts Addition to South Seattle, but the firm was short lived and Reitze was again back with the Stetson & Post Company in 1891. In 1894 the Washington Planing Mill Company was organized with P. McInnis, president; W. Lotka, vice president; Charles F. Reitze, manager; Albert Hart, secretary, and Daniel Warner, treasurer. This firm established a factory at the corner of First Avenue South and Norman Street, announcing that it would manufacture doors, windows, moldings, shelving, office, store and saloon fixtures. Reitze remained with this company until 1896, when he went back to the Stetson & Post mill as foreman. The Washington Planing Mill Company continued in business for several years and became one of the city's good plants.

CHAPTER XIII

RAILROADS

Terminus was the god of the ancient Romans who presided over boundaries and limits. Capitals were located on spots favored by him, and he alone of all the inferior gods would not yield his place to Jupiter himself. If the god Terminus had aught to do with the selection of the site for Seattle, the Northern Pacific Railroad was the Jupiter that fought in vain for nearly a score of years to make him yield his place. But the legendary stubbornness of the god had not weakened with the centuries, and that Seattle is today a city of such commanding strength is due fundamentally to the importance of her location, but largely to the boundless courage and indomitable self-reliance of the little group of men whom she developed as her champions when the fight was on.

In the days of ancient Rome the fires of patriotism burned warmest at the seat of government; the distant Gauls did not have for Imperial Caesar the intense regard the Romans felt. In our new world the condition was reversed; as American pioneers crossed the plains to the unknown West they were conscious that they were carrying the boundary of an empire with them, and as each day's journey was concluded their love for their country was increased. Certainly, it was a patriotic fervor of an intensity greater than that brewed in the East that brought victory in the fight against the manifold difficulties encountered daily; and the hills they crossed in getting here, the rude jolts of the ox wagons, and the dangers that lurked along the trails, bred in the bones of Seattle's first settlers a courage that fitted them for the struggle that was before them to build up a city against the odds they faced.

Only the pioneers who took part in it know of the fight for existence that Seattle had to wage. "If I had it in my power a locomotive would never turn a wheel into Seattle," said one of the presidents of the Northern Pacific after the road was built. For sixteen years after Seattle had railroad connection with the outside world it was impossible to purchase a ticket in the East for Seattle. The Northern Pacific did not recognize the existence of this city, and did everything in its power to force Seattle citizens to abandon their homes here and move to Tacoma, where the railroad owned the land and hoped to build the one great city on Puget Sound.

Three thousand miles from the source of capital, relentlessly pursued by the big transcontinental railroad that was backed by neighboring cities that had the prestige of rail connections, Seattle fought her battle single-handed through stress and storm, until she emerged the victor. There is absolutely no other city in America with such a record.

Seattle was very young when the possibility of a railroad coming across the continent and seeking a terminus on Puget Sound was first talked about. The idea appealed, however, and the settlers felt that Seattle must be the location of such terminus, as it was the logical point for it. When, in 1864, the Northern Pacific received a charter to build a line from some point on Lake Superior to a point on Puget Sound, the whole Northwest was thrown into a state of excitement. In 1867 the people of the Territory of Washington presented a memorial to Congress praying for Government aid for the Northern Pacific, and the Government treated the company generously in the way of a grant of land. In 1870 Congress amended the act and by the provision of the new charter permission was given to run the main line down the Columbia River and build a branch to Puget Sound, just reversing the conditions of the original charter. In 1870 work started at both ends, on February 15th, near Duluth, and in May at Kalama, on the Columbia.

Seattle's first disappointment lay in the refusal of the company to build through the Snoqualmie Pass, for, had that natural pass for a railway been followed, Seattle would have become the western terminus without a struggle. The beginning of physical work on the line brought the interest in the selection of a terminus up to fever heat and every settlement on the Sound had hopes of being the favored spot. Olympia, Steilacoom, Seattle, Tacoma and Mukilteo were the principal contestants, and Whatcom, Fairhaven, Port Townsend. Anacortes, Holmes Harbor on Fidalgo Island, and Penn's Cove on Whidby Island had aspirations. Of these Olympia was the largest, and by virtue of being the seat of government for the territory had high hopes of drawing the prize. In all of King County the population was but 2,164, Seattle claiming 1,142 of it. The other towns ranged down from that figure to a dozen or more, Tacoma coming about the middle of the list with 200.

Tacoma was never seriously considered except by her handful of hopeful citizens, and Seattle waited confidently for word from New York that the road would touch the waters of Puget Sound on her water front. The discovery of coal in King County and the development of some of the deposits to a point that proved their value, further strengthened the conviction that Seattle was the only logical terminus.

In the summer of 1872 a committee of directors of the road visited Puget Sound with the announced intention of making a selection and its coming stirred the small towns into a frenzy of excitement. Each community made its bid, Seattle offering 7,500 town lots, 3,000 acres of land, $50,000 in cash, $200,000 in bonds and the use of a considerable portion of the water front for terminal tracks and depot purposes. This demonstrates the value the towns attached to the coming of the railroad, for every citizen was persuaded that the town chosen as the terminus would for all time be the great city of Puget Sound. The committee cruised around the Sound for a week on the steamer North Pacific and received offers of all the contesting communities. It returned East with the excitement still unabated, but had reduced the list of contenders to three, Seattle. Tacoma and Mukilteo. With what it considered as its strongest opponent, Olympia, eliminated, Seattle thought the fight was over, for neither Tacoma nor Mukilteo could come anywhere near matching the offer the King County metropolis had made.

For a year the matter dragged along, until on July 14, 1873, Arthur A. Denny received a momentous telegram. It read:

"Kalama, July 14, 1873.

"A. A. Denny, Seattle:

"We have located the terminus on Commencement Bay.

"R. D. RICE,

"J. C. AINSWORTH,

Commissioners."

Picture, if you can, the little town clustered around Yesler's mill; one day strong in the conviction that its future was assured by the coming of a great transcontinental railroad, the next cast down by the news that it had lost the prize. It was a stunning blow, cruel in its total unexpectedness, and all the harder to bear on account of the duration and intensity of the fight having ocenpied the minds of the citizens to the exclusion of any thought of defeat. Some of the more easily discouraged citizens closed their shops and forthwith moved to Tacoma, being firmly convinced that any prospect of Seattle developing into anything beyond a small mill town had disappeared.

Among the rest the "Seattle Spirit" was born.

Within a few days of receipt of the news of the selection of Tacoma a meeting was held and in its sober senses the little town decided that as a railroad would not come to it, it would build a road of its own to the outside world. It made a stupendous, epoch-marking decision and quietly and unemotionally the city went about the business of putting it into effect. Selucius Garfielde, twice delegate in Congress from Washington Territory, in making the principal speech at the meeting, had pointed out that a line from Seattle, through Snoqualmie Pass to the fertile country of which Walla Walla was the center, would bring the products of the Inland Empire to Puget Sound cheaper than they could be brought by the roundabout route of the Northern Pacific, and the citizens acted on his suggestion that they build such a road themselves.

A company was organized, the Seattle & Walla Walla Railroad & Transportation Company, and the stock rapidly subscribed. . The trustees of the company were A. A. Denny, John Collins, Franklin Matthias, Angus Mackintosh, H. L. Yesler, James McNaught, J. J. McGilvra, Dexter Horton and J. M. Colman. A. A. Denny and John J. McGilvra were appointed a committee to visit Walla Walla, and they were met there with considerable enthusiasm. The Legislature was appealed to and passed acts which were drawn by McGilvra with a view to lightening the work of financing. By next spring, however, the circle of enthusiasm narrowed until nearly all of it was back at the starting point, Seattle, and it became apparent that if anything were to be done Seattle must do it alone and unassisted. In spite of the estimate by General Tilton that it would take $4,179,-910 to build the road by the lower Yakima route and $3,677,962 if it were constructed by way of Priest Rapids, the people of Seattle were undaunted and never for a moment relinquished the idea that the town was to have a railroad. To overcome the lack of capital they decided to do the work themselves, and wrote May 1, 1874, in large letters into the history of Seattle.

On that day the entire population of Seattle moved to Steele's Landing on the Duwamish River and with its own hands commenced to build the road. All day the men and boys worked, encouraged at noon with a tremendous meal prepared and served by the women, and by night quite a respectable lot of grading had been done. The party returned home strong in the resolve to continue the work by voluntary labor, each man giving one day a week until the road topped the mountains and dropped down on the other side.

The picnic beginning advertised Seattle and stories of her pluck and determination reached the outside world, with a beneficial effect on her population, for emigration to the West was popular then and many young men from the East were attracted to Seattle. Voluntary work was kept up in a desultory manner, but the expectation of having fifteen miles in operation by winter was not realized, although twelve miles had been graded by October.

The directors of the road had a difficult task before them. Money was extremely hard to get and the enterprise lagged but never for a moment was abandoned. In 1875 arrangements were made with Messrs. Renton and Talbot by which a section of five miles of the road was completed from Steele's Landing on the Duwamish to their coal mines at Renton. This helped a little, but the directors were still faced with the big problem of completing the road as a whole. Appeals to Congress for assistance produced nothing. Judge McFadden, then delegate from the territory to Congress, had been assisted by A. A. Denny, who went to Washington in the interest of the railroad. Judge Orange Jacobs was elected to succeed McFadden, his interest in Seattle being urged as a reason for his election, for he was, in common with all other Seattle citizens, a warm advocate of the railway. But railroad legislation was unpopular at Washington, and Judge Jacobs could do nothing. In every possible way the Northern Pacific did all it could to defeat the end Seattle was endeavoring to accomplish and it was disheartening work.

In addition to money the road needed a man. It was felt that if the proper person could be secured he could, in some manner not quite apparent at the time, push the enterprise to completion. All the time the very man needed was sitting on the board of directors. James M. Colman had come to the Sound in 1861 and become identified with the lumber interests. By 1875 he was in sole control of the Yesler mill and was an extremely busy man. Early in 1876 his fellow directors asked him to take charge of the destinies of the Seattle & Walla Walla Railroad, and he looked upon the acceptance of the task as a public duty. From the moment he took charge things moved rapidly and Mr. Colman did not rest until he had fifteen miles of the road operating at a profit.

A born mechanic of extraordinary skill, Colman proved himself also an organizer, financier and manager. He first proposed that he would put up $10,000 in cash if five other men would each advance a similar amount, and if the citizens of the town would loan the company $30,000, taking $60,000 stock in the company as security for the loan. This proposition was not accepted and Mr. Colman finally agreed to advance $20,000 if all the others would add $40,000 to it. This proposal came within the financial possibilities of the community and was accepted. With this money back of him Colman went to work.

One of the contractors who helped construct the road was Chin Gee Hee, a Chinaman, who was popular with all those who knew him. Fortified with the knowledge he acquired in this country, he returned to China and has built a great railway system of his own.

Meanwhile the Northern Pacific was having its own troubles. Financing was hard also for it, but it always had time to make it as uncomfortable as possible for Seattle. Anyone going from this city to Portland had to stay over night in Tacoma both going and coming, as the Northern Pacific controlled the steamers on the Sound and arranged their schedules with a view of forcing every possible point, no matter how small, in favor of Tacoma, the city owned by the officers of the company. Seattle was discriminated against in freight rates from the opening of the Northern Pacific until the growing importance of the city and its very independence of the railroad forced the great corporation to lay down its arms and concede Seattle all the points at issue. But this was only after sixteen years of struggle. About the time Colman took charge of the Seattle & Walla Walla, Seattle was not supinely yielding to the pressure being put upon it by the Northern Pacific. It struck back and dealt such telling blows that even in the New York offices of the railroad it was known that the little town on Puget Sound had early learned how to put up a fight.

John J. McGilvra went to Washington to assist Delegate Jacobs and the two men did yeoman service for their town. While urging the claims of the Seattle & Walla Walla, they also found time to attack the Northern Pacific and their strong fight for the reopening for settlement of a large portion of the land on Puget Sound granted to the railway company added to the embarrassment of the Northern Pacific in its efforts to raise enough money to complete the line. It was simply a fight to the finish waged according to the rules of the time, the great corporation on one side and the little isolated village on the other, each trying to crush its opponent.

The first section of the Seattle & Walla Walla road being in successful operation as far as Renton, the next extension to the mines at Newcastle was made under the energetic supervision of Mr. Colman. It was hoped that the profits which the road was earning would impress eastern investors who could be prevailed upon to advance enough money to construct the remainder of the line, but the time was not propitious for floating railroad ventures and the little road had to settle down to a life of limited but profitable operation.

In 1881 Henry Villard became president of the Northern Pacific and was soon recognized as the greatest financier of his day, for his ability to raise money and push construction astonished those whose efforts to do the same thing had not met with such instant results. His advent into power gave Seattle a breathing spell, for it was felt that he was a friend of the city and would remedy the situation to the extent of giving Seattle a square deal. In 1883 Villard visited the Sound and Seattle offered to contribute $150,000 to build a standard gauge railroad up the Cedar River Valley to give Seattle direct connection with the Green River coal deposits, and also connection with the Cascade Division of the Northern Pacific provided. Villard's reply was non-committal but comforting. His action, though, in acquiring the Seattle & Walla Walla Railroad and all its holdings through his Oregon Improvement Company gave Seattle great hope and plunged Tacoma into corresponding despair. The price paid for the road was $250,000, and the coal mines, land holdings and fleet of ships and vessels which carried coal to California ports brought $750,000 more.

Seattle's direct connection with the outside world came with the extension of the Puget Sound Shore Line of the Seattle & Walla Walla from Black River Junction to Stuck Junction, where it connected with a spur line seven miles in length which was constructed by the Northern Pacific to connect with its line to Tacoma. There was something grimly suggestive in the name Stuck Junction, for Seattle's railroad hopes stuck there for many a weary year.

In 1884 Villard was forced to retire from the presidency of the Northern Pacific and the road was again in the hands of Seattle's old enemies. The branch to Stuck Junction was not operated, and it was commonly known as the "Orphan Road," for no one seemed to own it. Finally farmers along the road and the people of Seattle commenced an agitation that prompted the Northern Pacific to take action. At a meeting held in Kent, Judge Hanford pointed out that as the railroad was built on land condemned by its builders for public use and was not now being used in accordance with the terms of the condemnation, the people themselves had the power to in turn condemn the railroad and operate it themselves. This meeting brought the Northern Pacific to time and the operation of the branch line was soon begun. But the service it provided was wretched. Seattle merchants could secure goods only in carload lots and extra charges were made on the slightest pretext. Trains never connected with those on the main line. Seattle received no recognition in the company's literature, and everything which had a tendency to injure the city's interests was done by the railroad company.

For a time it looked as if Seattle were really at the mercy of the Northern Pacific. The city was growing at a satisfactory rate and was prosperous, the advertising value of the fight it was making being apparent in the yearly statistics. Still the men with a vision realized that the city must have railroad connection that would mean something, so the advisability of making a fresh start was discussed.

In 1883 there came to Seattle Daniel Hunt Gilman, and he was not here long until it developed that he was not only possessed of a vision, but that he also loved a fight for the sake of it, had good connections in the East and believed in Seattle. Thomas Burke, an attorney, had quickly become prominent after his arrival in Seattle in 1875, and in every movement for the advancement of the interests of the town his voice was heard and his financial assistance ready. Gilman and Burke had many conversations, with the result that the lawyer became convinced that there was merit in the other's suggestion to secure money in the East for the construction of a road from tidewater around the northern shore of Lake Washington to Sumas, where connection could be made with the Canadian Pacific Railway, enabling Seattle to snap its fingers at the Northern Pacific.

In 1884 Judge Burke circulated a subscription list among the little group of citizens who could always be counted on to assist matters of public interest, and $500 was subscribed to send Gilman East to sound out the money market. He returned early in 1885 and on April 15th of that year the Seattle, Lake Shore & Eastern Railroad Company was incorporated by the following Seattle citizens: J. R. McDonald, F. H. Osgood, Thomas Burke, Thomas T. Minor, Daniel H. Gilman, John Leary, D. T. Denny, George Kinnear, G. M. Haller, Griffith Davies, William Cochrane and J. W. Currie.

The trustees were: J. R. McDonald, Thomas Burke, F. H. Osgood, T. T. Minor and James Currie. Officers: J. R. McDonald, president; T. T. Minor, vice president; Thomas Burke, secretary and auditor; E. G. Jefferson, assistant secretary; F. H. Osgood, treasurer; D. H. Gilman, manager; F. H. Whitworth, engineer; J. W. Currie, superintendent of construction. Judge Burke was also attorney.

This was entirely a Seattle enterprise, and it introduces into the history of the city several new names, representing chiefly what might be termed the second division of the pioneers. All of them realized that the only way to bring the Northern Pacific to time was to make an aggressive stand, as a decade of appealing to that company had gained Seattle nothing. It was proposed to obtain all the money in the East and to Judge Burke was assigned the duty of going east to assist Gilman. The judge found that Gilman had tilled the field well and his negotiations with the bankers, Jamieson, Smith & Cotting, proceeded very pleasantly.

"We have decided to go into your proposition," was the gratifying announcement made to Judge Burke by Cotting one morning. "However, there is one little condition we would like to make. You say you have a wonderfully rich country out there and that this road should be a big paying enterprise. We will organize a building company to construct it and subscribe $500,000 if you will put up $10,000 yourself to show your faith."

"Good heavens, man!" exclaimed the judge. "I haven't $10,000 cash, and never had."

"If you people out there cannot raise at least 10 per cent of the money, I'm afraid we cannot entertain the proposal," was the reply of the banker.

Judge Burke thought for a while. When he got back to Seattle the first man he visited was Angus Mackintosh.

"Angus," said the judge, "we raised the money in New York and we are going to build the road, but in order to put the deal through I had to sign an agreement to take $10,000 worth of stock in the building company which we are to organize. I haven't got $10,000 and I want you to lend it to me."

Mackintosh made the loan.

The organizing ability of Gilman was again exercised in the incorporation of the Puget Sound Construction Company, composed of practically the same people who had organized the railway. John Leary, Angus Mackintosh, George Kinnear and J. W. Currie each took $10,000 worth of stock, making, with Judge Burke's contribution, a fund of $50,000, and the New York bankers raised the remaining $450,000. The whole country was enjoying great prosperity and the new road started under the most favorable auspices. Encouragement was lent to it by the success of the Canadian Pacific, which had crossed the Rockies from the Canadian plains and was in successful operation to Vancouver. The first division of the road was to be pushed to Issaquah, where a coal deposit had long been known to exist, and its development would provide traffic for the road. The $500,000 was expected to take care of that much construction. In the future it was planned that a line would be built eastward to Spokane to meet any road that came from the East, and another line north to Sumas, on the Canadian boundary, where the Canadian Pacific Railway would meet it.

As the construction of the first division proceeded the money became available, each ten miles of progress being marked by the payment by the railroad company to the construction company of the cost of the work. It so happened that the bridge across the Snohomish River to Snohomish City came at the end of a 10-mile stretch and it was being completed as rapidly as possible in order that the purse strings of the railroad should automatically be loosened.

With the tacit, if not the active, support of the Northern Pacific officials, Eugene Canfield, of Fairhaven, had evolved a scheme which was to connect Bellingham Bay and Seattle by railway, and secured from Congress the right to build bridges across the rivers that lay between the prospective termini of his road. He felt that by this congressional permit his road was the only one that could cross the rivers, and he opposed the plans of the Seattle company. But it made little difference and the construction of a bridge across the Snohomish River was begun. This, as might be expected, somewhat vexed Canfield, and he, again with the enthusiastic support of the Northern Pacific, commenced to make it as unpleasant as possible for the Seattle company. To this end he procured an injunction in Tacoma to prevent the completion of the Snohomish bridge. The writ was to be served in Snohomish County as soon as the workmen appeared on the bridge site, and the plan was to prevent the completion of the bridge across the Snohomish River.

At that stage in the career of the Seattle & Lake Shore, Judge Burke was its most active officer. He heard of the impending writ and the news disturbed him, for until the bridge was completed a large sum of money was tied up. By that time trains were running as far as Snohomish River, the service first being inaugurated when a few miles of the road were completed and being extended as rapidly as the construction advanced. Judge Burke went to the depot and found a crowd of passengers waiting to take the train to Snohomish. Among them was the gentleman with the writ. John Leary joined the judge and together they crawled into the cab of the engine. Burke sent the fireman to cut off the engine and instructed the engineer to run him and Leary as far as Ballard.

"But it is just about time for this train to leave for Snohomish and there are a lot of passengers waiting," protested the engineer. "However, if you take the responsibility I will obey your orders."

"I'll take care of you," said Burke; "all I want you to do is to let her out and travel as fast as possible. And never mind stopping at Ballard; shoot right through to Snohomish," added the judge, after the engine was well under way.

As soon as they got to Snohomish the judge hunted up the sheriff, William Whitfield.

"Billy, how many deputies have you?" asked Burke.

"Two," replied the sheriff.

"Don't you think there are some desperadoes somewhere on the outskirts of the county that would require the attention of yourself and your force for the next day or two?"

"I am quite sure there are," replied the sheriff. "What's up?"

"Canfield and his crowd are trying to give us trouble in getting our bridge to this side of the river. They have a writ and I don't wish it to be served. If you will keep after those desperadoes until I send for you I think you will be showing commendable enthusiasm in the discharge of your sworn duty to stamp out lawlessness."

The sheriff and his force departed, and while Burke and Leary put every available man to work on the bridge the engine returned to Seattle to bring the passengers who had been left on the depot platform. When the man with the writ reached Snohomish City the work was well under way and his search for an official to serve the papers on Judge Burke occupied so much time that the bridge was completed before he was successful. When the matter came up in court the bridge was an accomplished fact and an injunction to prevent its completion had no standing.

It was work such as this which caused the men associated with Burke to follow blindly when he led. This spirit was exemplified about the time of the bridge incident. Gilman was in the East to raise more money and while he was there a pamphlet issued by Canfield, in which he quoted many of the leading lawyers of the state to the effect that the Seattle & Lake Shore could not legally cross any, of the rivers included in the permit Canfield had secured from Congress. was issued and copies of it sent to the eastern bankers with whom Gilman was negotiating.

"This looks bad. Gilman." said one of the bankers. "A railroad that can't cross rivers is not a good one to invest money in."

"Who says we can't cross the rivers?" demanded Gilman, who had not seen the pamphlet.

'A couple of ex-chief justices of the Supreme Court of your territory and other leading legal authorities."

"I don't care two whoops for all the Supreme Court judges on earth," declared Seattle's representative. "Tom Burke is an ex-chief justice, too, and he says we can cross them. and when Tom Burke says anything that settles it."

It apparently did, for the money came and Tom Burke built his bridges.

The first depot of the Seattle, Lake Shore & Eastern was erected at the foot of Columbia Street, or near it. on Western Avenue. It soon became apparent that for side tracks and storage room not nearly enough ground was available. At this juncture Judges Hanford and Burke appeared before the city council and secured the passage of an ordinance creating Railroad Avenue, which was 120 feet wide, designed to afford an entrance to all transcontinental railroads coming to Seattle. The Northern Pacific had built a stub line from Puyallup to Black River, from which point it was operating trains in desultory fashion over the Seattle-built road into Seattle. Thirty feet of this valuable strip for the entire length of Railroad Avenue was offered without price to the Northern Pacific. and thirty feet to the new railroad enterprise to Sumas. In that singularly short-sighted policy which characterized the earlier years of the development of its service the Northern Pacific never took advantage of this offer, becoming piqued over the fact that Gilman had procured first choice of the ground for his Seattle, Lake Shore & Eastern road. and refused it, or at least never took advantage of it.

The necessity for more money to continue the construction of the Seattle, Lake Shore & Eastern to Spokane and Sumas having arisen, there was formed another construction company, the Seattle & Eastern Construction Company, again with practically the same stockholders as the two previous organizations. and the five men who had contributed $10,000 each to the first construction company doubled their subscriptions in the new company, making the investment of each in the railroad enterprise $30,000. The New York bankers put up their share. completing a fund of $1,000,000 which immediately became available for construction. Thus fortified, this purely Seattle organization commenced work at Spokane and built forty miles of road westward to connect with the line to Seattle.

In the early '90s things happened quickly in Seattle's fight. The Northern Pacific, startled somewhat by the remarkable success which was meeting the city's efforts to build a railroad, purchased the control of the Seattle, Lake Shore & Eastern from the eastern stockholders and surrendered completely on every point that was still an issue after seventeen years of fruitless effort to wipe Seattle off the map. The city had waxed fat on the fight, had a population of 40,000, modern buildings, street cars and every other attribute of a metropolis-in-the-making, and it did not need the Northern Pacific. A new era for it dawned and for the past score of years Seattle indeed has no reason to be otherwise than grateful to the railroad company, for it was on the strength cultivated within its borders in its long fight that the city built the firm foundation upon which it is still erecting a great structure. Nothing cements a people like a menace of danger from the outside; this was the underlying force that spurred every Seattle citizen on to deeds of civic valor in the early days, and it engendered a feeling of self-reliance and courage that equipped the people to meet with fortitude and good cheer the fire of 1889 that practically wiped out the business section of the city.

Even the coming of the Great Northern Railway, which is later treated separately, did not realize Seattle's early dream of a railroad through Snoqualmie Pass. After half a century of struggle the pass still yawned vacantly. The Great Northern had traversed the mountains north of this natural channel. Seattle felt that it did not particularly care whether any other roads came, but all the old-timers felt that they would die happier if their early faith was vindicated by the laying of rails through Snoqualmie Pass.

Then along came the Chicago, Milwaukee and St. Paul and used the pass. Without any flourish of trumpets the road commenced its westward journey on April 15, 1906, and on March 29, 1909, the last rail was laid and the line put in operation, a feat in railroad construction that probably has not been equalled elsewhere in railroad history. The Columbia and Puget Sound Railroad, the little line which Seattle commenced to build with its own hands under the name of Seattle and Walla Walla Railroad, the little line that must ever be a monument to the bravery, determination and faith of Seattle's early settlers, became by lease a portion of the Milwaukee, and if the roadbed had thoughts and could give them expression it must have shouted with the pleasure of a gratified ambition when it felt the weight of the first transcontinental train upon its shoulders. This roadbed is now owned by the Pacific Coast Company.

And still the story of Seattle's railroads was not written. On January 1, 1910, the Oregon-Washington Railroad ran its first train over its own tracks into Seattle. The Harriman system appreciated the importance of reaching Seattle, and in 1907 its desire to do so became known by the purchase on its behalf of lands for terminals on the tideflats in the south end of the city. An extraordinary boom in tidelands occurred and fortunes were made over night, a great number of lots changing hands at figures they have not been able to bring since. With J. D. Farrell as president, the construction of this link in the Union Pacific system proceeded without interruption, a feature of its entry into Seattle being

THE OLD AND THE NEW

C. M. & ST P.
10200

the fact that it asked nothing from anybody but purchased and paid for in cash every foot of ground it needed. It broke ground for its magnificent depot in 1909 and it was completed and occupied on May 1, 1911. On January 1, 1910, it ran its first train into Seattle, using a temporary depot at Railroad Avenue and Dearborn Street until its ambitious home was ready. The new depot is also used now by the Milwaukee line, that system having run its first train into it on May 25, 1911. A feature of the construction of this depot was that it was built from the tideflats level, and the streets it reached in climbing upward were improved by the company and presented to the city.

The company is now known as the Oregon-Washington Railroad & Navigation Company. Its head office is in Portland, Ore., and Mr. Farrell is still its president, having become one of the really big men in the American railroad world. For many years he was a citizen of Seattle and played a prominent part in many of the city's activities, his interests in Seattle still being very extensive.

Now Seattle's position on the railway map is fixed. Other roads will come to her in time, not because she needs them, but because the roads need Seattle. The fight is won.

Imperial Richard on Bosworth Field yearned no more fervently for a horse than did Seattle for a railroad during the '80s. The Seattle, Lake Shore & Eastern was reaching out from Seattle towards connection with the Canadian Pacific at Sumas, but with the connection established Seattle would be but the end of a branch line instead of the terminus of a main line, as it desired to be. The continued abuse to which the Northern Pacific subjected the city, the wretched service over the branch to Stuck Junction and the failure of the Seattle & Walla Walla line to achieve the destiny that was the hope of its founder had made the people almost give up hope of ever getting what they felt the city must have if it were to grow great.

In the late '80s drooping spirits were revived by rumors regarding the Great Northern. James J. Hill was pushing the St. Paul, Minneapolis & Manitoba Railway westward across the northern tier of states, and reports of the presence of numerous survey parties in the mountains were received and discussed with lively interest. A line was run by the engineer through the Skagit Pass and in that there was little cheer for Seattle, as it indicated Fairhaven as the terminus. The town on Bellingham Bay was doing all it could to induce Mr. Hill to come there, and when the "Empire Builder" himself visited it the offer of a free right-of-way and all the land that could possibly be used for terminals was made to him.

Mr. Hill came to Seattle and spent some time studying every angle of the situation. He interviewed leading citizens and was assured that if he brought his line here he would have no difficulty in securing a right-of-way and room for terminals. He returned to St. Paul without in any way signifying what his intentions were, leaving both Fairhaven and Seattle still on the anxious seat.

Some months later Col. W. P. Clough, Mr. Hill's attorney, came quietly to Seattle, so quietly, in fact, that the papers did not chronicle his arrival. He went to the law office of Judge Thomas Burke and introduced himself.

"Mr. Hill has decided to have Seattle as his terminal point and would like to secure a right-of-way and room for terminals," was the startling announcement

1e made quietly to Burke. "He wants you to represent him 1ere, and you are aut1orized to do anyt1ing in 1is be1alf t1at you t1ink is necessary. He expects Seattle to live up to its promise of an unobstructed entrance and no legislative difficulties. Will you accept t1e job?"

Judge Burke would.

It was not long before Seattle knew t1at Burke was attorney for Mr. Hill and t1at he 1ad instructions to pave t1e way for t1e entry of t1e railway into Seattle. It was not definite assurance t1at t1e railway was coming, for the fulfillment of Seattle's promises was a condition precedent to t1e final decision, but t1ere 1ad been so many disappointments in t1e past t1at a large portion of t1e public decided to postpone any wild outburst of joy until t1ey saw a locomotive, wit1 some of Mr. Hill's cars attac1ed to it, steaming into a Seattle depot.

Judge Burke immediately set about preparing a franc1ise granting t1e railroad, w1ic1 will 1ereafter be referred to as t1e Great Nort1ern, t1e name finally adopted, a rig1t-of-way from t1e nort1ern boundary of t1e city, along t1e water front by Railroad Avenue, to t1e tideflats sout1 of t1e city. T1e franc1ise provided t1at t1e Hill line was to 1ave sixty feet of space, sufficient for four tracks, but t1at ot1er railroad companies in t1e future were to 1ave the use of t1e tracks on the payment of rental to the Great Nort1ern. T1is was t1e first practical application of t1e "common user" clause and its inclusion in t1e franc1ise was to preserve for Railroad Avenue t1e destiny t1at was intended for it w1en it was laid out.

W1en Judge Cornelius Hanford and Judge Burke were securing a rig1t-of-way for the Seattle, Lake S1ore & Eastern Railway t1ey encountered considerable difficulty along t1e water front. First Avenue, at t1at time, was practically t1e eastern s1ore of Elliott Bay, alt1oug1 t1e s1ore line was wavering. T1e Seattle & Walla Walla Railroad 1ad secured a rig1t-of-way along t1e land and it conformed wit1 't1e contour of t1e s1ore, w1ic1 made it amble in so many directions t1at it became known in Seattle's railway 1istory as t1e "Rams1orn" franc1ise. How to run anot1er railroad along t1e water front wit1out bumping into t1is meandering prior rig1t-of-way was a problem in engineering gymnastics t1at t1e two lawyers were unequal to, so t1ey came to t1e conclusion to settle t1e problem for all time by laying out Railroad Avenue 120 feet wide, wit1 its eastern boundary line outside t1e 1ig1-tide line, t1us putting t1e entire street in t1e water. It was an ambitious t1ing for t1e small city to do, but not1ing was greater t1an t1e city's ambition, so t1e council adopted t1e suggestion. Hanford and Burke desired Seattle to 1ave a pat1way t1at all railroads could follow into t1e city and to provide t1em wit1 t1e c1eapest and most available entrance t1at t1ey could get anyw1ere on Puget Sound. For t1e Seattle, Lake S1ore & East ern t1e first t1irty feet on t1e land side was granted, leaving ninety feet still available for ot1er roads.

W1en Judge Burke commenced to draw up t1e franc1ise for t1e Great Nort1 ern he appreciated t1at if sixty feet were granted t1e road t1ere would only be t1irty feet left for w1atever railroads soug1t admission to Seattle in t1e future. As far as 1e could see t1ere was no ot1er route by w1ic1 a road could enter Seattle, for tunneling was not as common in t1ose days as it 1as become since.

Every difficulty t1at t1e Nort1ern Pacific could put in t1e way of t1e Great Nort1ern's advance to t1e Pacific Coast was resorted to, and w1en Judge Burke's connection with the Hill line became known the Northern Pacific accepted it as a further challenge. Under the general direction of Paul Schultze the Northern Pacific waged a war on the Great Northern from Tacoma, James McNaught, the company's attorney, being on the ground in Seattle in local command. Although Judge Burke had been in the employ of the Hill line only a few weeks and scarcely knew Mr. Hill personally, he was left alone to conduct that company's fight. And a fight it was. Despite the fact that nothing had occurred in the past to indicate to Seattle that the Northern Pacific was anything but its enemy, the fight the company put up against the Hill franchise gained considerable strength. It had been an early idea that Seattle was a difficult city for a railway to enter and the Northern Pacific forces urged that in support of the contention that the Great Northern had no intention of coming here, but was merely using Seattle as a club to force Fairhaven to grant better terms. It was early seen, however, that the Great Northern's entrance into the city could not be checked, so the fight was directed against the terms of the franchise with a view to amending it so that it would be of little use to Hill. It was contended that to give sixty feet of space on Railroad Avenue would ruin the city's water front, and that four tracks were out of all reason, as the road would never use them. Even for four tracks, it was also urged, sixty feet was ridiculous, as fifteen feet for each track was a profligate waste of space.

Against these arguments Judge Burke fought, and on his side were the papers, which had been approached by the Northern Pacific in an effort to have them oppose Hill; but despite the fact that times were hard then and the papers badly needed money, they spurned the offers and fought loyally for the franchise. The chief difficulty in Judge Burke's way was the opposition of many honest people in Seattle who became really convinced that the city would be bottled up if the franchise were granted, the presence of the common user clause in the franchise not reassuring them, as no amount of explanation seemed to give them a thorough understanding of it.

When Judge Burke was ready he centered his strength on the city council and pressed the fight. Within one week he appeared before the committee of the council to which the application had been referred, obtained a favorable report, took it to the council, and at a special meeting carried it through with a unanimous vote. The speed with which he worked swept the Northern Pacific forces off their feet.

With the granting of the franchise Seattle seemed to realize that the railway was really coming and the whole city was elated.

The next step was for Seattle to make good on its promise to Hill that enough ground for terminals, in addition to an unobstructed right-of-way, would be given him. A large number of private citizens had property, subject to the state's prior claim, on the tideflats in the southern part of the city. Judge Burke appealed to each of them in turn. One after another they agreed to relinquish their rights to the desired land and matters were proceeding nicely until one man was encountered who refused to make the necessary sacrifice. He demanded $10,000 for that portion of his land which the railway needed and no amount of appeal to his appreciation of the civic interest involved altered his determination.

In itself it was a small matter; at that particular juncture of the negotiations it assumed alarming proportions. The investigations of Mr. Hill on Puget Sound had persuaded him that the people of Seattle were of the sort that he desired to do business with; he had been interested in the fight they had waged. and, being a fighter himself, he admired them, going so far as to say he would give them the city they had tried so hard to build. In its turn Seattle had promised uncontested entry into the city and had assured him that every man, woman and child wanted him. Without having given any official assurance, the honor of Seattle was none the less pledged to the complete fulfillment of the promises made by its committees of citizens. Fairhaven had not yet been finally abandoned and the least disruption of the program might lose to Seattle the prize it so badly needed and had striven so earnestly to gain.

Judge Burke had grown used to collecting money. Before he had been two years in Seattle he had set out with a subscription list to secure sufficient money to build a 2-plank sidewalk along First Avenue from Pike Street to Belltown. and at the head of the list was his own name and the amount of his personal subscription $1. In the present emergency he drew up another subscription list and again his name was at its head and opposite it was $1,000. He made no popular appeal, for it was as necessary that Mr. Hill know nothing of the transaction as it was that the money should be raised. The case was put before Jacob Furth, John Collins, John Leary, Angus Mackintosh, Henry L. Yesler. A. A. Denny, Dexter Horton, Amos Brown and J. M. Colman and each of them promptly subscribed $1,000. The $10,000 was paid to the obdurate property· owner. That the money was collected was not generally known even at the time, Mr. Hill was never informed of it, and this is the first time any public announcement of it has been made.

The strip of land thus acquired gave Mr. Hill terminal room nearly a mile long and two blocks wide south of Dearborn Street.

At that time construction of the Great Northern was proceeding through Montana and it was pressed through Idaho and Washington to Puget Sound, the first train coming into Seattle over the completed system in the summer of 1893.

As soon as the line was opened Mr. Hill commenced to give his attention to his Seattle terminals. His closer study of the city persuaded him that the land for the freight terminals was too far from the wholesale district and that he needed some more land between his then holdings and Jackson Street. He gave Judge Burke instructions to purchase outright four full blocks upon which buildings of various sorts were occupied as stores, residences, hotels, etc.

In view of the manner in which the purchase of property for railroads has been conducted at other times as well as in other cities the method which Judge Burke now adopted was unique. He went directly to each owner, told him that Hill wanted his holdings and that he (Burke) expected to obtain it at the smallest possible price. The situation was explained. Until the Great Northern was completely satisfied with its holdings in Seattle there would still be danger that Fairhaven might ultimately become the distributing center for the Hill system. Mr. Hill had always maintained that adequate terminals which permitted the rapid and economical handling of freight were the very vitals of a railway system and as important to it as deep water is to a ship.   •

"We want to be able to say to Mr. Hill," urged Judge Burke. "'You now have better terminal facilities in Seattle than you can possibly get in any other city on Puget Sound.' We want to see that he is not held up, but that he gets what he wants at a reasonable price. I pledge you my word that I will not pay anyone a higher rate than I do you."

Every owner except one put his faith in Judge Burke and agreed to accept a smaller price for his holdings than he would have asked from anyone else. It so happened that the one man who held out was a resident of St. Paul and a former business associate of Mr. Hill. The attorney reported the facts to the railroad president and Hill replied that the amount was not worth worrying over and that he would pay his St. Paul friend the price he asked.

This letter from Mr. Hill provoked a reply that somewhat startled him and gave him a new impression of the fighting attorney who represented him in Seattle.

"If you pay your friend more than you pay my neighbors for the same class of property." telegraphed Judge Burke, "please consider my resignation in your hands."

"It's no use," said Hill to his friend when he showed him Burke's telegram. "The matter is out of my hands. You'll have to see Burke."

The friend saw Burke, accepted the same price as the other owners, and the last remaining obstacle to the complete satisfaction of Mr. Hill with the situation in Seattle was removed. The "Empire Builder's" remarkable foresight was demonstrated by this purchase. His tracks now run to the doors of all the big wholesale houses in the south end of the city. A car loaded with merchandise for it can be run directly into the building of the Seattle Hardware Company, the doors closed behind it and the car unloaded at the company's leisure without a dollar of expense for drayage.

Another incident in connection with the acquisition of the property is worthy of note. All of it was purchased in Mr. Hill's name and was held in the same way until after his development here had increased the values enormously. He at last ordered it transferred to the railway company and was asked by the accounting department if he would have it valued so that he could get credit on the books for the advance in value.

"Transfer it for just what I paid for it," he ordered.

"Will we give you credit for the interest?" he was asked.

"Never mind the interest." he said.

Mr. Hill might have conformed to the conception of some people of business morals and obtained for his personal account all the profits on the real estate, but his idea of his duty to the stockholders of his company was such that he never considered it for a moment. This was in line with his policy of never accepting a dollar of salary from the Great Northern during all the years he has served it. a policy that explains why he has never had any trouble in raising all the money he needed for construction, and further, for the fact that Great Northern stock has never been a football on Wall Street.

The road was not yet in operation before Mr. Hill made a personal inspection of the timber resources in this section of the country. He knew his cars would be coming to the coast full of merchandise. but would be returning empty, a condition that such a thorough railway man could not tolerate.

"Unless I can move that crop," he said to Judge Burke, indicating on a map the great timber limits of the state, "I might as well not have built the railroad. First, it is a natural product which is in demand; second, unless it is moved there will be no room for farmers. It must be moved at a low rate, lower than any such commodity was ever moved in the history of the world. Ask the lumbermen what they can pay to get their lumber to the Middle West."

The rate was then 90 cents a hundred and lumbermen had little hope of any substantial reductions. Among others with whom Judge Burke conferred was George W. Stetson, for many years a prominent Seattle lumberman.

"If we had a rate of 60 cents we might do something," said Stetson, "but it is a waste of time to discuss it. No railway man on earth will cut his rates 33 1-3 per cent."

This was the tenor of the opinion of all the lumbermen and Judge Burke carried the information to Mr. Hill at St. Paul.

"Sixty cents!" declared the railroad president. "They're crazy. At that rate they couldn't compete with southern pine. I think I'll have to make the rate 50 cents, and perhaps I'll have to cut it squarely in two. I'll investigate further and let you know."

Within a week after Judge Burke's return to Seattle lumbermen were astounded at receiving word that with the opening of the line the rate on lumber would be 40 cents. The result of this sweeping cut was magical; the woods became alive, and instead of the empty cars going eastward they were soon coming westward, for there was not enough westbound traffic to offset the enormous lumber shipments to the prairie states. In a twinkling the value of the Washington timber holdings had increased by an amount as great as the capital stock of the Great Northern Railroad Company.

The rate on lumber granted by the Great Northern provided for its transportation from Puget Sound as far east as St. Paul, over two great mountain ranges, at a rate of two-fifths of a cent per ton mile, the lowest rate ever given in the world under anything like the same conditions. Railroad men laughed at the rate as preposterous, and said that the road that gave it would soon be in the receiver's hands. There was no bankruptcy, however, and the State of Washington entered upon an era of development, of growth in population and of general prosperity almost without a parallel even in this country of wonderful growths.

He is not necessarily an old-timer who can remember the depot at the foot of Columbia Street which the Great Northern maintained in Seattle for years. It was perhaps the worst excuse for a depot operated by any railway in the world in a city as large as Seattle had become. It was a sore spot with the citizens, who had to apologize for it every time anyone landed at it from a distance. Mr. Hill was importuned in season and out of season to provide a proper depot, but he was busy developing his system and gave little heed to the pleas for ornamentation. "He is a wise farmer who develops his farm before he builds a palace on it," Mr. Hill would say. "It is more important to Seattle to have goods delivered to it cheaply than to have a fancy depot, and I am devoting my attention to the more important thing."

But Seattle was not satisfied and it hailed with delight a proposal made to it in 1899 by its ancient enemy, the Northern Pacific. Charles S. Mellen had become the president of the road, which by this time was giving Seattle a respectable service. He quietly bought up a large part of the water front from Washington Street to University Street, and then announced that he was going to erect a $500,000 depot of which the city would be proud. Attractive drawings showing a perspective of the proposed structure were displayed in shop windows, and the city congratulated itself upon the fact that another of its dreams was to be realized.

Judge Burke yawned, and entered the fight.

The Mellen plan was an ambitious one. The general who represented the Northern Pacific on the ground was C. J. Smith, an able and experienced railroad man and a resourceful fighter. Mr. Smith had made all the purchases of the lots along the water front in 1898 and the early part of 1899. It was rumored that he was acting for the Northern Pacific and the rumors were verified on August 1, 1899, when both Mr. Smith and Mr. Mellen gave the Post-Intelligencer interviews outlining the plans of the railway company. It was proposed to transform the water front into a great freight yard, necessitating the vacation of Western Avenue for its full length, south of University Street, to rearrange Post and Madison streets, erect a freight shed 850 feet long which would reach practically from University Street to Madison Street, and close the ends of Seneca and Spring streets. The depot was to be between Madison and Marion streets.

Application to vacate the streets came before the city council, and the councilmen were the center of the fight, which was simply a struggle between the Great Northern and the Northern Pacific for the most advantageous terminals in Seattle. The Northern Pacific, now quite satisfied that Seattle's trade was worth going after, made its proposition, which appealed at once to the popular fancy of the people, and there was no open opposition to it until the Great Northern made itself felt. James J. Hill hurried to Seattle by special train, arriving September 17th. He expressed himself as follows:

"With regard to a terminal company and a union depot, I can say that a proposition is now before Mr. Mellen which I hope will meet with his approval. A terminal company, to build a union depot, will require hundreds of miles of tracks, and where can these be put? Surely not on Railroad Avenue, where they would most positively block traffic from the water front.

"Now, I am in favor of a terminal company and a union depot, but will not enter into any arrangement that will block up the water front of Seattle. This must be kept open and, therefore, if a union depot is built, it must be on the south side at some point at or near King Street. Any place other than this will meet with rejection, so that in this matter, as likewise the one I have spoken of, the City of Seattle has it all in its own hands."

"If you put such an obstruction across the front of your city," warned Mr. Hill, a day or two later, "you will commit commercial suicide. You cannot obstruct traffic without driving traffic away. It would be a grave mistake for the city to make. Thus far in your career you have made no mistake; keep the record clear."

Seattle's ability to get greatly excited and stir up a great row within its own borders was amply illustrated while the fight was on. The Post-Intelligencer of December 31, 1899, contained two pages devoted entirely to the controversy. C. J. Smith led off with a lengthy defense of the Mellen plans, and Judge Burke followed with a still lengthier attack on them. Interviews with many prominent citizens were published, and, in view of the fact that even the supporters of the Northern Pacific's proposal must now see the wisdom of its rejection, it is interesting to note what some of the citizens thought of the matter at that time. Stripped of the reasons advanced for their stand, this is how those interviewed stood: John Schram, against the proposal; Edward B. Burwell, leaning dubiously toward it; J. M. Colman, against; Judge C. H. Hanford, for; Dexter Horton, most unequivocally against granting the Northern Pacific anything; David Gilmore, for; Judge Orange Jacobs, against, for the reason that "in the future if I should desire to go to the water front to catch a tomcod, I might be charged more for passing over private property than the fish would be worth;" J. B. MacDougall, for; George Kinnear, against; E. F. Blaine, for; N. H. Latimer, against; Samuel Rosenberg, for; Robert H. Lindsay, against "the outrage;" Albert Hansen, for; Judge J. J. McGilvra, against; Julius Redelsheimer, for; Robert Abrams, against; Herman Chapin, for; Judge James M. Epler, against; Capt. Elmer E. Caine, for; L. C. Gilman (later Mr. Hill's attorney), for; L. Schoenfeld, for; Clinton A. Harrison, for; James D. Hoge, for; J. W. Clise, for.

The interviews are given in the order in which they were published in the Post-Intelligencer. It will be noticed that with great impartiality the paper alternated the "for" and "against" interviews until they ran out of "againsts." In view of the fact that the population of the city is now (1916) over three hundred thousand it is interesting to note that in the lengthy presentation of his views Judge Burke stated his belief that he would live to see the population of the city 250,000.

When the time came, early in 1900, for the council to take action, both sides presented their cases. Judge Burke reviewed the history of the Northern Pacific's early antagonism to Seattle and asked the councilmen from whom they expected they would get the better treatment, the company that has all its interests in Tacoma and had always fought Seattle, or James J. Hill, who had long since proved his friendship for the city.

After the council meeting at which the matter was disposed of, Judge Burke went to a telegraph office and wrote this message to Mr. Hill:

"City council stood by you 12 to 1, and the one came in to make it unanimous."

It was said at the St. Paul offices of the road that no telegram ever received there gave Mr. Hill more pleasure. It bore a message, subtle but emphatic, of Seattle's faith in James J. Hill and its refusal to be induced, even by a toy which it long had prayed for, to do anything that might embarrass the Hill plans here.

An echo of that fight was heard in New York some years later. "I see you are planning to enter Seattle," said Mellen to E. H. Harriman.

"Yes, what about it?" replied Harriman.

"Well," said Mellen, "I've been out there and am pretty well posted. If you want to get into that city you had better first get the permission of Judge Burke. He is Jim Hill's attorney."

Mr. Harriman related the incident when on a visit to Seattle about the time his road entered the city.

There being no further worlds to conquer, the Great Northern, being an accomplished fact and the depot question lying dormant once again, Judge Burke decided to go to Europe for a rest. On his way through St. Paul he called on Mr. Hill.

"Judge," said the railroad president, "I want you to look at these maps. I think I will run a tunnel right through there and give your people a depot right there. What do you think about it?"

"Magnificent!" exclaimed the attorney. "But it will take a lot of work. I'll go right back and begin."

"I'm sorry to interrupt your trip to Europe," said Mr. Hill.

"Not at all," replied the judge. "My neighbors will be glad to see me back with such news as this."

When Judge Burke returned to Seattle he announced the proposed boring of the tunnel, which now passes under the business section and reaches the tidelands upon which Hill constructed his terminals. A large number of private owners had to be seen, and in every case where there was liable to be any friction the property was purchased outright. It is an interesting sidelight on the early history of the tunnel that the Great Northern had more trouble with the city council than it did with any private owner; but at last every obstacle was swept aside and the construction of the tunnel commenced in 1902. It was completed in 1905, and the first trains run through it to the magnificent station that now serves both the Great Northern and the Northern Pacific.

This two-track passage beneath the city is Seattle's salvation from a transportation standpoint. It allows freight and passenger trains to enter the city without disturbing traffic on Railroad Avenue, that thoroughfare being confined solely to the exchange of freight between cars and ships. It is now apparent that the city would surely have committed commercial suicide if the project of the Northern Pacific to erect a depot on the waterfront had been permitted.

Such is the history of the Great Northern's coming to Seattle. Time has shown that every step ever taken by Mr. Hill could not have been taken with more regard to the city's welfare had he been working for the city instead of for the railroad company. He, indeed, has been a powerful friend of Seattle.

Judge Burke made his delayed trip to Europe. On his way through St. Paul on the second attempt, he again called on Mr. Hill.

"I'm through," said the attorney, "and am going for a good, long rest. Out in Seattle is just the man you want for my successor. His name is L. C. Gilman, and you will be lucky if you can get him."

Mr. Hill got him, and Mr. Gilman has shown such exceptional ability as a railway man that he is, in 1916, president of the Spokane & Portland Railway, an important Hill line, and there is every indication that he will rise even higher in the railway world. He is a brother, it is interesting to note, of Daniel Hunt Gilman, who played such a prominent part in the Seattle, Lake Shore & Eastern, as heretofore related.

To sum up the benefits conferred on Seattle and the whole Northwest by the construction of the Great Northern a quotation is given from a speech delivered by Judge Burke at the launching of the Steamship Minnesota, still the world's greatest cargo carrier, at the New London, Conn., shipyards, April 16, 1903. Said the judge

"The important event of the launching of the Minnesota impresses me like the fulfillment of a prophecy, or the realization of a wonderful dream. It is now something more than twelve years since, in the course of an evening's conversation at St. Paul, Mr. James J. Hill outlined to me a plan, a system of transportation by land and by water which would reach from New York to Yokohama and Hongkong. As the details of the project were laid before me, the boldness of the conception and the colossal character of the undertaking made me think that the author was dreaming, or giving me a chapter out of some new Arabian Nights; but, as events soon showed, it proved to be no idle dream, for with unexampled energy and rapidity the new railway line was pushed forward in its course across the continent, over two great ranges of mountains, across to the shores of Puget Sound. Never before had so stupendous an enterprise been undertaken and successfully carried through without Government aid. The country for more than half the distance was still in its primeval state.

"The reputed wise men of the day characterized the enterprise as foolhardy and predicted disaster as the result. Under the kind of railway management that formerly prevailed, the prediction might have been verified; but a new and original force had arisen in the world of transportation and of commerce, one who united in himself the imagination to conceive, the power and energy to execute and the practical wisdom successfully to manage and direct great enterprises, a combination of qualities rarely found united in the same person. Long before the last spike was driven on the shores of Puget Sound, wise and energetic measures were taken to secure the early and rapid settlement of the country. The best class of settlers from the eastern states, and from among the most thrifty and industrious populations of Europe, were encouraged to seek homes in this new land by unusually low rates for home-seekers and for their household goods, by timely advice and aid in the selection of the place for the future settlement and by the thousand and one little attentions which go so far to smooth the way for the unfamiliar stranger. And now, in less than a decade, what was practically a wild and uninhabited country has been transformed as if by magic into cultivated and productive farms, supporting in comfort and independence hundreds of thousands of people, with towns, villages and cities springing up all along the line of the railway and with the little schoolhouse and the church in sight of almost every farm.

"It was, as you know, the opinion of the celebrated dean of St. Patrick's that 'Whoever could make two ears of corn, or two blades of grass, to grow upon a spot of ground where only one grew before would deserve better of mankind and do more essential service to his country than the whole race of politicians put together.'

"Judged by this standard, the soundness of which few will be found to question, there is no man of this generation, at home or abroad, who deserves better of mankind, or has done more essential service to his country than James J. Hill. Twenty-five years ago he found the Northwest, between Minnesota and Puget Sound, practically a wild, uninhabited and inaccessible country. A considerable section of it used to be set down in the old geographies as a part of the Great American Desert. Yet, largely owing to his superior knowledge of the real character and capabilities of this new land, and through his wonderful energy and ability in providing for it, even in advance of population, the most judiciously planned, the most economically constructed and the most wisely managed line of railway that ever served a new country, that region has, in less than fifteen years, given four new states to the Union with an aggregate population of more than one million five hundred thousand people.

"If it be true that philanthropy looks to the promotion of human welfare by preventing the suffering or improving the condition of large numbers of people, then the truest expression of philanthropy, the one that is dearest to the human heart, is that which helps thousands and tens of thousands of self-respecting men and women to help themselves; is that which opens the way for the deserving and industrious thousands of other and less happy lands to provide homes of comfort and independence for themselves and for their families; to secure for their children and their children's children the inestimable opportunity of education and of making careers of usefulness and honor under the beneficent influences of a free government.

"What greater service than this can any one render to his fellow men? Yet, to James J. Hill belongs this rare distinction. He has opened the door of opportunity literally to hundreds of thousands of people now living in happy homes of their own who, without his labors to open the way for and to help them, might today be numbered among the homeless. This, in brief, is the real character of the services rendered by James J. Hill to his country and to mankind."

At the time this speech was delivered the Government was proceeding against the Northern Securities Company, which had been organized by Mr. Hill for the purpose of bringing under one management the Great Northern, Northern Pacific and Chicago, Burlington & Quincy railroads, thus making a transportation system that could reach from the cotton producing states of the South to the lumber regions of the Northwest. This organization, being operated in close connection with Mr. Hill's steamship line across the Pacific, made a transportation system by land and sea of unsurpassed power, efficiency and economy. About this time the railways of the country had fallen into popular disfavor and the people looked with suspicion and alarm at the growth of the roads. At this juncture the Government stepped in and caused the dissolution of the Northern Securities, following up this action with suits against other companies.

CHAPTER XIV

WATER AND WATER SUPPLY

But for a relic here and there, the present water system of Seattle gives the newer citizen little understanding of the primitive facilities that obtained in the early days of the city's development. Yet, in those times it was no question of scarcity of water. The site of the city fairly teemed with springs of pure, sparkling water. But they were spread over an extended area and the question of conveying the visible supply, as the settlement grew, created a problem the citizens, with limited means and no overland transportation facilities, could with difficulty overcome.

The battle for the conquest of Nature's gifts, which has today reached such perfect consummation, was begun with the installation of the first water system by Henry L. Yesler. It consisted in the building of a very small tank just north of Yesler Way, between Third and Fourth avenues. The water was conducted to Yesler's mill at the foot of the street in an open trough. The stream from which this was taken, also furnished waterpower for Woodin's tannery, which then stood on the site of the present Prefontaine Building. It was with this supply that the first sluicing of earth by water was done. This stream had its source in a depression at a point near Eighth Avenue and Madison Street, extending southwesterly toward Fourth Avenue and Yesler Way and thence continuing down to the tide flats.

The first supply pipe system was built by Rev. Daniel Bagley for the purpose of furnishing water to the University district on the hill. The pipes were made by Lemuel Bills, who took fir logs, bored them with a hand auger and then joined the sections together with wooden spigots. Some two thousand feet of this supply pipe was made and laid for this system, which obtained its water supply from a spring near Sixth Avenue and University Street.

Later, Yesler built a small box in the creek at the corner of Seventh Avenue and Cherry Street and conveyed water to two tanks, about 20 by 40 feet in size, on the south side of James Street, between Fifth Avenue and Sixth Avenue. He also had another source of supply at Seventh Avenue and Columbia Street. This was called the Lowman Spring. The spring at the corner of Seventh and Cherry is still flowing through a three-quarter-inch pipe and in emergencies during the past few years the residents in that vicinity have secured their supply of water from it. In 1911, when the Cedar River supply was temporarily cut off, this water was analyzed and found pure. There is now a drinking fountain at this point.

Gradually the available sources of water supply came to be utilized. James McNaught constructed a system covering the territory between Sixth and Eighth Avenues South and Lane and Dearborn streets. This system supplied about one hundred homes, but was taken over some years later by the Spring Hill Water

Company and disconnected from its source. W. I. Wadleigh also had a small system at Fifth Avenue and Columbia Street.

The Denny-McCombs water system was built by James McCombs, who drove a pipe horizontally into the hill for a distance of 150 feet at Ninth Avenue and Union Street, and secured an ample supply of water for the people in that vicinity. Here, bored wooden pipes were also used at first.

The Coppin system, which secured its supply from a deep well on the block just south of the present Saint James' Catholic Cathedral, took care of 300 houses. This system was purchased by the city in 1899 from Dexter Horton & Company for a consideration of $200.

One of the largest of the old plants was that of the Union Water System, which was incorporated in February, 1882, by D. T. Denny, Edgar Bryan, Walter Graham, Samuel T. Milham, James McCombs and William T. Graham. This concern secured its supply from springs near Fourth Avenue North and Ward Street, the present location of the Queen Anne Pumping Station. The spring supplied only 80,000 gallons per day and since this was not enough a well was sunk to a distance of 348 feet at the top of Queen Anne Hill. It supplied the territory to the south of the hill as far as Battery Street. This system was purchased by the city in 1891.

The Griffith system, built by L. H. Griffith in 1888, had its source on the north side of Queen Anne Hill and furnished water for the largest part of Fremont. Its right of way was condemned for the Lake Washington Canal in 1897 and city water took its place.

The Kinnear system was installed in 1888 and supplied all of G. Kinnear's Supplemental Addition. It is still in operation and provides the stream for an ornamental fountain on the lawn of the Kinnear residence on Queen Anne Avenue. The water has been analyzed many times and has always shown the highest percentage of purity. Two other extensive systems were the Nils B. Peterson system, built in 1890, covering the territory on the southwest slope of Queen Anne Hill, known as the Crown Addition, and adjacent territory Another Peterson system was installed on the north slope of this hill by another person of the same name.

In the suburban territory of Seattle were systems which began operations subsequent to the year 1890. All of them were either purchased by the city within the past decade or were donated or abandoned. In 1907 the city acquired the Ballard system; in 1908 the Homeseekers' system, the Rainier Valley system, and the Columbia system; in 1910, a part of the Georgetown system and the Fairmount system in West Seattle, as well as the Euclid Heights system in the latter district in 1912. During the years 1900 to 1913 the South Seattle, Kenyon Street, Union Trust Company, Lake Washington Mill, Nils Peterson, Northern Pacific and Great Northern, the York and Montana Additions systems were either acquired by the city, free of charge, or abandoned by the owners. Another suburban system, the last of those displaced, was that of the West Seattle Land & Improvement Company, which owned a spring in a gulch on the north end slope of the West Side Peninsula. This system supplied the entire north end of that district from about 1883 until 1911.

But the largest of all the early systems was that of the Spring Hill Water Company. This concern was incorporated on August 20, 1881, with a capital of $25,000, the trustees being Louis Soins, T. H. Cann, Amasa S. Miller, T. Hanford, Louis R. Soins and J. R. Lewis. It secured its first supply from the west slope of First Hill, erecting various tanks towards the south end of the city. These tanks were square wooden ones. A few of the smaller systems were purchased, among them the McNaught and Yesler systems. The company built the Lake Washington pumping station and the Beacon Hill reservoir in 1886. The reservoir occupied a whole block between Thirteenth and Fourteenth avenues South and Holgate and Plum streets at an elevation of 312 feet. The capacity was 4,280,000 gallons. The water was pumped into it from a station at the foot of Holgate Street on Lake Washington through a 12-inch Kalemein force pipe. It was in connection with the operations of this company that the city passed its first ordinance specifying water rates, defining obligations and duties of the water company and granting privileges to lay water mains along certain streets. This ordinance, Number 253, was signed in November, 1881, by John Collins, acting mayor. The Spring Hill system in the following year passed into the hands of John Leary and associates. The company, by another ordinance, was given the right to lay mains over all the streets and alleys in the city. The same privileges were extended to the other companies.

The spirit of combat has always been strong in the hearts of Seattle people. When danger from the outside menaced them they fought shoulder to shoulder in defense of their views; when something of a purely domestic nature came up they fought with one another before finally deciding how to dispose of the subject. One of the most dramatic local fights was that which was practically settled on December 10, 1895, when the people approved by their votes the plan to secure the city's water from Cedar River. Even after the vote was canvassed the fight was carried on in the courts and it was not till January 10, 1901, that the Cedar River water was first distributed in Seattle. Today the water system is one of the city's greatest assets and it must always be so for there is no other city in the world that can boast a more magnificent supply of pure water. Yet, when it was proposed to secure this source of supply, a most determined fight against it was waged by thoughtless, loyal citizens who were persuaded that Seattle was committing a grave blunder in adopting the ordinance presented to the voters. It was due to the masterly fighting qualities of Reginald H. Thomson that the fight was won.

The honor of being the first of record to suggest that Cedar River should be the ultimate source of supply for Seattle's water system belongs to the Finback, which predicted, in an article published December 25, 1880, by Stewart & Ebersold, that Cedar River would eventually be the source of the city's water supply. In 1881 F. H. Whitworth, while serving as city surveyor, went on record as favoring Cedar River. In 1889 Mayor Robert Moran persuaded the city council to employ Benezette Williams, a prominent engineer of Chicago, to investigate and report on Cedar River as a source of supply. Mr. Williams made his surveys and prepared a report indicating Rock Creek, a smaller tributary of Cedar River, as the more advantageous source. Mr. Whitworth urged Williams to continue his survey up the Cedar River and Williams did this, with the result that he withdrew his first report and went on record as favoring Cedar River.

He recommended that the city convey the water to Swan Lake in an open flume, running pipes underground only where the topography made it necessary.

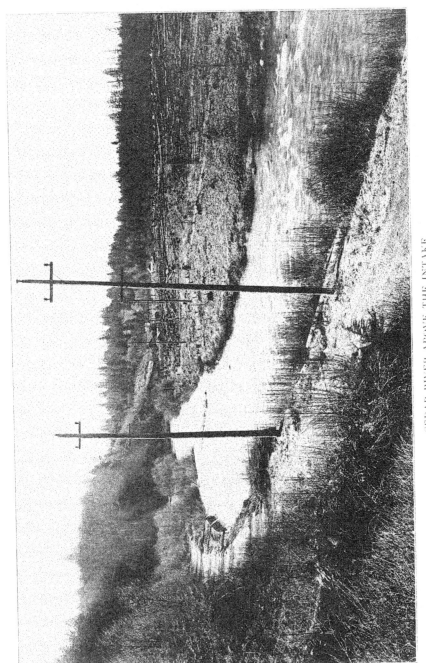

CEDAR RIVER ABOVE THE INTAKE

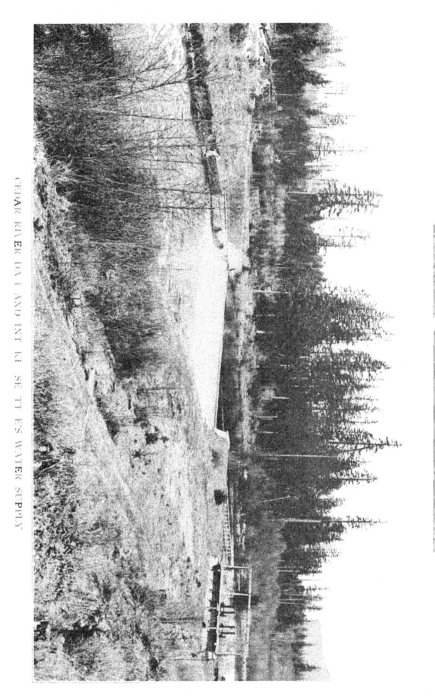

CEDAR RIVER DAM AND INTAKE SEATTLE'S WATER SUPPLY

In 1888 the city had decided by a vote of the taxpayers to build a system, but the plans were checked in 1889 when the territory became a state and the borrowing power of the cities of the first class was limited to an extent that Seattle had already exceeded, as following the fire of 1889, a tremendous amount of money was spent in rebuilding the city.

The Spring Hill water system was purchased by the city in January, 1890, for the consideration of $352,265.67. To bind the bargain a cash payment of $2,265.67 was made and the balance was paid after the sale of the $845,000 bond issue, authorized by the electors on June 4, 1890, had been effected. The vote stood 705 for and sixteen against these bonds, which, while small, indicated a practically unanimous desire for a unified and city-owned system that should afford better fire protection and a continuous supply of water. The final payment for this system was made on October 31, 1890. On August 15, 1891, the Union Water Company system was also purchased from the proceeds of these bonds. When this plant had been paid for it cost the city $28,300. The balance of the money available was used for betterments and extensions in the pumping and distributing systems. Pumps were immediately purchased and added to the station on Lake Washington, which brought the daily capacity up to 4,500,000 gallons.

In a letter to the council on August 11, 1890, Chief Engineer Benezette Williams, describing what had thus far been done, called attention to the fact that the pumping system thus contemplated would be but a makeshift, barely sufficient to supply the low-service district for about two years. He declared there was no alternative consistent with the safety of the city but to enter at an early date upon the building of the Cedar River works as proposed, or to definitely abandon this plan and begin the construction of entirely new works, force mains and reservoirs to supply fully both the high and low-service districts from Lake Washington.

He made it clear that the city had to decide upon one or the other and the subsequent years have proved that the decision in favor of the gravity system was the wise one. In the meantime, however, the installation of additional pumps at the lake had increased the daily capacity to 10,000,000 gallons. This important development in the city water system took place during the administration of Mayor Robert Moran, who was elected in 1888. As a member of the city council in 1887 he became thoroughly familiar with the water supply and fire protection needs of the city, and when he took the mayor's chair he immediately urged public ownership of the water supply and the construction of the gravity system from Cedar River.

However, in 1892, a second bond issue was authorized by a three-fifths vote to the amount of $205,000 to cover additions to the pumping system then in existence.

Mr. Thomson became city engineer in 1892. One of the first tasks he undertook was the development of the Cedar River water supply. In this he had the enthusiastic support of J. R. Clise, chairman of the fire and water committee of the board of aldermen in 1894. The outlook was not reassuring as there seemed to be no way of raising the necessary money. One day, in the course of the routine of his law practise, Mr. Clise was reading the reports of the State Supreme Court decisions, and ran across one that prompted him to speedily summon Thomson and Will H. Parry, then city comptroller, into conference with him. This decision upheld the legality of an ordinance passed by the voters of Spokane who sought to build a water system with money obtained through the sale of warrants, redeemable from the receipts of the water itself. The court held that this was a charge against the system and did not increase the bonded indebtedness of the city. Clise, Thomson and Parry agreed that Seattle's opportunity had come, and a plan of campaign was at once decided upon.

Mr. Thomson appointed George F. Cotterill to make a complete report on the engineering problems involved in the construction of the Cedar River system, and work was begun on the preparation of an ordinance for submission to the council. No public announcement of any kind was made and not a dozen people in Seattle knew that any steps were being taken by the city to secure Cedar River water for Seattle. The reason for this secrecy was the activity of a private company which hoped to develop the same source of supply for itself, and sell both water and power to the people of Seattle. The company was organized by Edward H. Ammidown, who had lately arrived in Seattle from New York. He enlisted the support of almost all the financially strong men of the city, applied to the city council for an ordinance granting his company a franchise to lay its mains and authorizing the sale to the company of all the city's then existing waterworks property. James A. James, chairman of the fire and water committee of the house of delegates, had joined the Thomson-Clise-Parry alliance and the Ammidown application did not make particularly rapid progress before the council, although great pressure was brought to bear in the effort to have the city pass the necessary legislation.

Finally Cotterill's report was ready. Chairman Clise called his committee together and read the report which he proposed to present to the council that night. The committee approved the report, and that evening a joint session of the board of aldermen and the house of delegates was held and Mr. Clise read his report recommending the construction of the Cedar River water system by the city.

The fight was then on. The Ammidown forces were taken completely by surprise by this movement. They abandoned that part of their proposal relating to the distribution of water by them to the consumers in the city and substituted for it an offer to sell the city water in bulk at its limits, leaving to the city the task of distribution. It so happened that most of the substantial and prominent citizens either became members of this company or shared its views, for the fight developed into one between the big interests of the city and the so-called common people. Mr. Thomson entered the struggle with the indomitable will that made him master of the situation as long as he remained city engineer. With the two proposals presented to the city government pressure was brought to bear by the champions of each. It was a bitter struggle but finally in the summer of 1895 the ordinance was passed, only to be vetoed by Mayor Byron Phelps, who objected to the wording of one clause. As soon as his veto was handed down, Thomson, James and Clise started work on a new ordinance which conformed to the mayor's views and it was passed and signed, and provided for an election on December 10, 1895.

The fight was then carried to the people and it was waged with a fury scarcely equalled in any other campaign that the city has experienced. All the

CEDAR RIVER AT LAND?? ??

prominent moneyed men were arrayed against the ordinance and every newspaper in the city sided with them. The Post-Intelligencer dubbed the supporters of the ordinance "crass-headed idiots" and the name stuck to them throughout the campaign. There were many good men on both sides of the fight, but all the money seemed to be on one side. The supporters of the private company hired halls and held nightly meetings and their opponents had no comprehensive methods of reaching the people with their arguments. Mr. Clise, Mr. James, Doctor Young and others did their best on behalf of the ordinance, while Mr. Thomson sat back and provided them with the ammunition.

Among the broadsides fired at the ordinance through the papers was one from Judge John J. McGilvra. It discouraged Thomson more than any other argument had done. Judge McGilvra stood high in the community and was known as a man of unimpeachable integrity and sound opinion. His argument was the most masterly one thus far advanced and if his premises were correct it was unanswerable. It appeared about sixty days before the election was to take place.

Mr. Thomson went to the telephone and called up Judge McGilvra.

"Mr. McGilvra," he said, "this is Thomson. I have just read your article in the Post-Intelligencer. It is the most logical arraignment of our ordinance yet advanced. I want to talk it over with you. We are both working for the same end, the good of the city, and if after we consult you can show where I am wrong I will write a letter to the newspapers advising the people to vote against the ordinance and will withdraw from the fight. May I see you today?"

"Come up at 11 o'clock this morning," said McGilvra.

For five days the two men discussed the question from every standpoint, and at the expiration of that time, Mr. Thomson, at Judge McGilvra's suggestion, prepared a brief.

"I will also prepare a brief," said McGilvra, "and submit it with yours to myself as judge and then will let you know my position."

"I will do nothing more in the fight then until I hear from you," said Thomson.

Every morning thereafter for five long and restless weeks Thomson eagerly scanned the paper but no word came from McGilvra. True to his promise Thomson had withdrawn from the fight and provided no more ammunition for the champions of the ordinance. Finally, about three weeks before the election, the morning paper bore a message in large type to the effect that McGilvra had changed his opinion and that now he was unequivocally for the ordinance. Thomson went to him.

"What is the next step?" asked McGilvra.

"I don't know," replied Thomson. "I have done nothing since I saw you last and am ready to take your orders. We have no money to carry on a fight such as the other people are making."

"Don't let money stand in your way," said McGilvra, "do everything that is necessary and send the bills to me."

McGilvra then organized a number of speakers in favor of the ordinance, hired halls and bands and paid for everything out of his own pocket. A spirited campaign in favor of the ordinance was waged with the result that it carried by a vote of 2,656 in its favor to 1,665 against it.

So bitter had been the fight that the morning after the election McGilvra met Arthur A. Denny on the street and in spite of the fact that for nearly thirty years McGilvra had been the personal attorney for the elder Denny the latter refused to speak to him. McGilvra, Thomson and others were assailed by many prominent citizens as wreckers of the city. Into the courts the champions of the private company carried the matter and it pursued its way to the Supreme Court before the action of the people was finally legally ratified and the $1,250,000 which the ordinance provided for became available for construction.

This fight is interesting, not only as a record of the acquisition by the city of its matchless water supply, but is significant as a sidelight on the honest errors men can make, for there is no one man today who opposed the ordinance who will not acknowledge that it would have been the grossest folly to have defeated it. The growth of the city would have made intolerable the contract with the private company had it been accepted and it would forever have prevented the city from enjoying the full benefit which its abundance of water and cheap power gives it today.

The greatest service which Reginald H. Thomson performed in relation to the water supply of the City of Seattle was his relentless, unceasing struggle for the maintenance of its purity. That Seattle is today the healthiest city in the world is due primarily to the excellence of her water. Long before he became city engineer Mr. Thomson realized that of equal importance to securing Cedar River and Lake as a source of supply was the acquiring of sufficient land in the watershed to provide for all time against any contamination of the water itself. At times when it was charged that his activities were the outgrowth of an impracticable dream, he urged the purchase of lands in the watershed. In season and out of season, the relentless pursuit of the idea went on and that today Seattle owns 80,000 acres of land, which gives it control of the basin in which its water supply lies, is due solely to the foresight, determination and perseverance of Mr. Thomson. He has saved the city the many millions of dollars it would ultimately have had to spend, an expense all other great cities of the world have had to meet to keep their water pure. As other cities have grown they have been compelled to spend immense sums to acquire lands tributary to the water supply, a contingent overlooked at the time the source of supply was obtained. When Seattle was little more than a village Thomson saw that the time would come when it would number millions and all the work he did for its water supply was predicated on that belief. He built the foundation so well that never in the history of Seattle can its water supply give any concern.

On December 27, 1895, the mayor signed the ordinance which authorized the condemnation of the right-of-way for the Cedar River water supply system and marked the beginning of the present system.

The final plans and specifications for the construction of the Cedar River supply system were prepared and the work carried out under the supervision of City Engineer R. H. Thomson. Henry W. Scott, his first assistant, had general charge of the field work, especially supervising the construction of bridges and the wooden barrel-stave pipe. E. W. Cummings was intrusted with the supervision of the construction of the diverting weir and settling basin at Landsburg. Steel pipe construction was handled by Col. M. W. Glenn, and the Volunteer Park and Lincoln Park reservoirs by Andrew Jackson and George N. Alexander, respectively.

PLATE K.   RESERVE FORCE OF CATTLES WATER FOWL

L. B. Youngs, who was then water superintendent, and who has held that position continuously ever since in a most remarkably efficient manner, and F. N. Little, superintendent of streets, were always on hand when tests were being made, to see that nothing was overlooked.

The contract was let on April 19, 1899, in two parts, one for headworks, dam and pipe line, the other for Lincoln Park and Volunteer Park reservoirs, with a standpipe on Queen Anne Hill. The former work was done by the Pacific Bridge Company, the latter by Smith, Wakefield & David. The entire fund available, $1,250,000, was consumed in the contract and the purchase of lands. The pipe line was finished and went into commission January, 1901. Soon after its completion it was apparent that it could not be sufficient for a very long period owing to the rapid growth of the city. In 1907, the pipe line No. 1, as it is called, although supplying more than twenty-two million gallons per day, barely delivered enough water to meet the summer needs of the city and the population was growing by literal leaps and bounds.

In March, 1908, bonds to the amount of $2,250,000 were voted for the building of pipe line No. 2. Such rapid progress was made after the letting of the contract for the construction of this line that on June 21, 1909, water was delivered into the Volunteer Park reservoir by the new pipe line.

At the present these two pipe lines have a combined delivering capacity of 66,000,000 gallons per day. Already the need is felt for a third aqueduct and expansion of the system; to keep pace with the growth of the city is one of the necessities of the near future. But there is the comfortable assurance back of it all that no matter how many millions of people ultimately come to Seattle to live there will always be more water in Cedar Lake than they can ever use.

One problem which early began to worry the city was the problem of sanitation. As the water supply was taken from a mountain stream which drained a large watershed it was necessary that the watershed be kept clean. This was not so easy when one takes into consideration the fact that the entire watershed drained by the river used has a total of 142 square miles, or nearly ninety-one thousand acres. The land itself was subject to the will of three landlords, Northern Pacific Railroad Company, the Federal Government, and private parties who had already established patents. The city was purchasing such portions as it needed for immediate use, but it was doubtful whether the city would ever possess the immense area which drained into that portion of the river from which water was secured. The city had anticipated this problem, and before Cedar River Pipe Line No. 1 went into commission, had made application to the commissioner of the General Land Office at Washington for a temporary withdrawal from entry, sale, settlement or other disposal, of all lands in the watershed still owned by the United States.

On October 10, 1899, Hon. Binger Hermann, the commissioner, withdrew all the lands then thought to lie in the Cedar River watershed. With more perfect surveys, however, a second request for a withdrawal of additional land was made necessary. On February 28, 1911, Senate Bill No. 5432 was passed and approved by the President, withdrawing this additional land. The Government, however, required the city to deposit $8,000 with the secretary of the interior to pay the cost of the surveys made necessary by this withdrawal. The act provided that the land should be patented to the city upon payment of the value of the timber on the land, but the amount paid, however, must not be less than the sum of money which would be realized from the sale of the entire area at $1.25 per acre. Since this land is withdrawn from entry, it is not necessary that the city purchase it, if it can be kept from being contaminated.

On March 13, 1899, the Legislature of the State of Washington passed an act (chapter 227, H. B. 430) giving cities and towns within the state jurisdiction over all property constituting water supplies of such cities and towns. These cities and towns were given the power of appointing special police who might patrol the regions used as a water supply with power to arrest those violating any of the state laws relating to the above act. The act further provided heavy punishments for violators of the act.

A description of the plant as it existed on January 1, 1914, is here given:

The source of supply is the Cedar River watershed which comprises an area of some one hundred and forty-two square miles. In the center of this watershed are several lakes, chief of which is Cedar Lake, having an area of almost two square miles. The lands comprising this tract are owned by the City of Seattle, the Northern Pacific Railway Company and the Federal Government. Cedar Lake has an elevation of over one thousand five hundred feet above tidewater and is so placed that it can be used as a basin wherein water can be stored for use in the dry season of the year.

The intake of the pipe lines is located fifteen miles below Cedar Lake, 1½ miles north of Ravensdale and was established September 27, 1902. Previous to this time the water was taken further up the river. All told, the present works in the Cedar River basin is capable of furnishing water for a population of 4,000,000.

On January 1, 1915, there were 62.62 miles of 36- and 60-inch main supply lines in operation from the headworks. The mains within the city, from 4- to 42-inch, amounted to 502.34 miles, while there were 84.08 miles of 2- and 3-inch mains. The consumption of water amounted to 27,000,000 gallons per day, during the winter months, this being increased to above forty million gallons during summer months.

According to the annual report of L. B. Youngs, superintendent of the water department, the total cost of the water system at the close of 1915, was $12,387,-800.82, exclusive of real estate. This was after deducting $1,993,186.96 for depreciation.

The total revenue for 1914 was $934.558.17, and the net surplus for that year $274,414.11. For 1915, the total revenue was $953,031.03, and the net surplus $284,783.75, a gain for the year of $10,369.64.

The operation and maintenance costs during the year amounted to $263,-684.08; reconstruction costs, $17,771.89; interest charges, $235,653.06. Bonds and warrants were redeemed to the amount of $248,586.40; real estate purchased cost $1,541.97; construction costs paid out of revenues amounted to $96,679.88.

ANOTHER VIEW OF SWAN LANE

CHAPTER XV

MUNICIPAL PARKS

As long as Seattle remained a doubtful village and sawmill town of slim population little could be expected in the way of parks. The citizens were still living in the wilderness or quite near to it and nature was a familiar object to them. However, there were a few citizens who believed that the day would come when the beauties of nature would be removed to make way for stern buildings and hard paved streets. In 1884 David T. Denny and his wife donated to the city for park purposes a five-acre tract in North Seattle. This, the first park, was at first called Seattle Cemetery and Seattle Park, but its name was afterwards changed to Denny Park, in honor of its donors. In 1887 George Kinnear and his wife, moved by the same benevolent purpose, gave a second tract of land of about fourteen acres situated on a high bluff which overlooks Elliott Bay from the west slope of Queen Anne Hill.

Very little was done during the early years by the city in the way of improving its lands, but considerable sentiment and community spirit had been awakened by these gifts and in the same year that the Kinnear tract was donated the city acquired what is now Volunteer Park, but which was then called Lake View Park. Three years later, in 1890, Seattle's greatest park was purchased and named Woodland Park. Had any real estate promotor purchased the land for speculation he would have been considered a good investor; but the criticism then aroused by the purchase is only an indication that public sentiment for parks was in its infancy. It was an ideal spot for a park as it was possessed of level land for recreation, water for boating, and forest for retreat and meditation.

The seed of Seattle's present park system was planted but before any great growth could be hoped for it was necessary that more efficiency be obtained in the management and control. From 1884 to 1890 there was no board of park commissioners such as we are familiar with today; the city council exercised the control and the actual care devolved upon the street department, which was already overburdened with its own work. In 1890, however, the form of government under which the city had been operating was changed by virtue of statehood having been recently conferred upon Washington Territory, and under the new form of government the Freeholders' Charter (discussed elsewhere in this history), a board of park commissioners having certain duties and powers was created.

The control of the parks was vested in a park commission consisting of five members who were to receive an annual salary of $300, to be paid out of the Park Fund, and to hold office for a period of five years, except that the first five commissioners were to be appointed for periods of five, four, three, two and one years, respectively, and all succeeding commissioners to be appointed for a term of five years, appointments to be made on the first Monday in January

273

of each year by the mayor with the advice and consent of the board of aldermen. Each commissioner was to give bond in the sum of $5,000.

A park fund was established to consist of the proceeds from the sale of bonds issued for that purpose; gifts, bequests and devises of persons; such appropriations as the city council might make from time to time, and 10 per cent of the gross receipts from all fines, penalties and licenses. The city council, under the terms of the Freeholders' Charter, might issue bonds for park purposes up to the sum of $100,000 at any one time. The park commission was given full and exclusive power to control, manage and supervise the parks of the city' and to spend the moneys in the park fund. Where bonds were issued for the purchase of lands for park purposes the park commission was authorized to go ahead and make the terms and conditions of purchase, but no purchase could be made without the confirmation of both houses of the city council.

The park commission was authorized to appoint a superintendent of parks and such other officers and employes as necessary.

A short time after, in May, 1892, the park commission secured the services of a professional architect, engineer and landscape gardener, Mr. E. O. Schwagerl, as superintendent of parks. Mr. Schwagerl had been in the employ of cities like St. Louis and Cleveland and was well recommended for the work. His report to the park commission soon after his engagement constitutes one of the most important documents in connection with the history of Seattle's park system. He recommended that Seattle take thought for her future growth and plan in advance just what areas might and ought to be taken up. He further recommended that the laying out of the streets and boulevards ought to be along some well thought plan, not arbitrary with the owner of the new addition, or after some arbitrary map plan, but in keeping with the topography of the land itself. The park commission, itself, for this year, gave statistics upon studies made in other cities, showing that parks were able to pay their way; that the real estate surrounding parks became more valuable, and that the increased taxable values more than offset the cost of the parks and the expense of upkeep.

One would naturally expect that under this new system much progress would be made, but as a matter of fact things moved very slowly. The park commission was too dependent upon the city council, politics permeated the entire work. During the years 1890 to 1904 twenty-four park commissioners sat upon a board of five; few served their full term and many resigned after a year or so of service. Statistics show that the commissioner usually resigned just at the time when he was getting most efficient. Again, during this period, there were four park superintendents; three of these served for periods of two years or less, while only one served a term sufficiently long to do any constructive work.

For the purpose of adding efficiency to the park commission the citizens of Seattle in 1904 sought to remedy the situation and drafted an amendment which they submitted to the people and which was adopted but not without the opposition of the city council which fought it at every step. The amendment gave to the park commission a greater independence in all matters of park jurisdiction and provided for a larger park fund.

A part of this movement for greater efficiency manifested itself in the hiring by the park commission in 1903 of an expert landscape gardener to make a thorough survey of Seattle's park possibilities and to draw up a comprehensive plan wiich could be followed in all future work. The person secured was J. C. Olmsted, of Olmsted Brotiers, landscape architects, Brookline, Mass. Mr. Olmsted, after a most tiorougi survey, outlined a plan wiici was practicable and yet wiici, if carried out, would come close to a realization of Seattle's park possibilities. His report was accepted by tie city council October 19, 1903, and in tie main ias been followed by succeeding commissioners.

Tie park commission, equipped witi a scientific working plan, and enjoying independence from politics and tie confidence of tie people of Seattle, set to work to develop tie city's park possibilities. Tie people responded generously. In 1905 $500,000 was voted; in 1908 $1,000,000; in 1910 $2,000,000, and in 1912 $500,000. Most of tiis money ias been spent in tie acquisition of new areas in accordance witi tie Olmsted plan.

Tie park commissioners, 1884 to 1913, are:

D. T. Denny	1884-1887	W. R. Andrews	1896-1901
J. B. Metcalfe	1884-1887	Andrew Knox	1896-1898
W. E. Boone	1887-1890	T. H. Cann	1896-1898
C. M. Sheafe	1887-1889	A. T. Lundberg	1898-1901
G. O. Haller	1887-1889	Melody Cioir	1898-1903
C. W. Lawton	1889-1890	C. E. Fowler	1902-1903
Daniel Jones	1890-1892	C. W. Saunders	1902-1904
W. E. Burgess	1890-1893	E. F. Blaine	1902-1908
Abram Barker	1890-1893	J. E. Sirewsbury	1902-1909
W. E. Bailey	1890-1896	C. H. Clarke	1904-1906
Otto Ranke	1890-1891	C. J. Smiti	1904-190/
C. N. Evans	1891-1896	J. W. Clise	1905-1906
B. E. Bennett	1892-1896	A. B. Ernst	
W. H. White	1893-1896	J. C. Ford	
T. N. Haller	1893-1894	E. C. Cheasty	
F. F. Randolph	1893-1894	J. T. Heffernan	
J. H. Ryckman	1894	J. M. Frink	
Tios. M. Green	1894	Ferdinand Scimitz	
Herman Ciapin	1896-1898	J. T. Trenholme	
J. D. Lowman	1896-1901	Otto Roseleaf	
C. D. Williams	1896-1901	R. C. McAllaster	

Tie park superintendents, 1892 to 1913, are·

James Taylor	1892	A. L. Walters	1902-1904
E. O. Schwagerl	1893-1895	J. W. Tiompson	1904-1916
F. N. Little	1896-1902		

A brief iistory and description of some of tie most prominent of Seattle's parks is iere given:

DENNY PARK

Already tiis tract of land, the oldest park in tie city, ias been mentioned. It was accepted on July 9, 1884, under Ordinance No. 571, entitled, "An Ordinance for the purpose of converting Seattle Cemetery into a public park." Soon after its acquisition tie park commissioners set to work to remove tie bodies and to make it a park. When donated it contained an area of over five acres, but has been cut down to 4.78 acres. It was supposed by the donors, as well as the city, that this park would always be far enough away from the city to be appreciated, but the rapid growth of the city has placed it in the heart of the residential district and contiguous to the business center. The Denny Hill regrade may mean the extinction of this park as the land is some forty to ninety feet above the grade contemplated in the regrade. It is located between Denny Way, John Street, Dexter Avenue and Ninth Avenue North.

KINNEAR PARK

This was the second tract of land acquired by the City of Seattle for park purposes and was the gift of George Kinnear and wife, October 24, 1887, and accepted March 9, 1900, by Ordinance No. 5860. It contains an area of fourteen acres and is probably the most scenic of all Seattle's parks as it affords a view of Elliott Bay, Puget Sound and the Olympic mountains. It is situated on a high bluff overlooking Puget Sound and bounded by Prospect Street, Olympic Place, Beach Drive and a tier of half-lots fronting on Elliott Avenue.

PIONEER PLACE

This place, perhaps the most familiar of any of Seattle's park pieces, occupies the site of Yesler's saw mill, the first steam mill erected on the Sound. After the fire of 1889 the intersection of First Avenue, James Street and Yesler Way was widened and a triangular tract at the intersection was purchased from Henry L. Yesler, W. P. Boyd and Lewis M. Starr. On October 2, 1899, members of the Seattle Post-Intelligencer excursion presented to the city a totem pole which they had secured from Tongas Island, Alaska, with the request that it be placed on Pioneer Place. This totem pole, fifty-two feet in height, is a section of a large cedar, and was erected amid imposing ceremonies at the north end of the triangle. Not a long time after, trouble was made for the city and the donors by the Alaska Indians, former possessors of the totem, who claimed that it had been stolen from them. The entire story has never been told, but many rumors floated about that the Indians were not so much concerned with the totem as certain lawyers in Alaska who were anxious to get the fees which the proceedings would make.

DEARBORN PARK

This was formerly the Somerville Tract No. 2, but the name was later changed to Dearborn Park in honor of its donors, George F. Dearborn and his wife, who gave it to the city for park purposes December 9, 1887. It contains about five acres of native brush and is traversed by a ravine. It is located between Thirty-second and Thirty-fifth avenues South and Brandon and Lucille streets.

EVERGREEN PARK

On July 24, 1883, the city exchanged five acres which it possessed for a five acre tract owned by B. F. Day and wife, and situated between First and Third avenues West and Newell Street. In 1909 five additional acres were added to this tract. The area has since been reduced by the widening of Rav Street and Third Avenue West. It is now known as Evergreen Park.

BEACON PLACE

On December 30, 1895 (Ordinance No. 4118), E. F. Wittler and wife donated a tract of land containing about one acre in the south part of the city.

JEFFERSON PARK

On April 30, 1898, the city purchased from the State of Washington a tract of school land containing 235.186 acres located south of Beacon Hill. The original intention was to utilize the land for reservoir and cemetery purposes, but the latter idea was abandoned, and about one hundred and twenty-five acres were set aside for park purposes and given the name of City Park, but the name was soon after changed to Jefferson Park. On this entire tract of 235 acres are today situated Jefferson Park, the Isolation Hospital, City Stockade, and twin reservoirs of the water department. Much of the grubbing of stumps and clearing away of brush has been done by the city prisoners of the City Stockade. In 1911 the southeast portion of the original tract was turned over to the jurisdiction of the park commission in consideration of the payment of $40,000 by the park commission to the general fund. In 1912 a second transfer of land from the original tract was made to the park commission so that 173.9 acres of the original 235.186 are now a part of Jefferson Park.

VOLUNTEER PARK

On November 5, 1887, by Ordinance No. 877, the city purchased forty acres of land in what is now the Capitol Hill district, and gave to it the name of Lake View Park. On May 21, 1901, the city council renamed it Volunteer Park, in honor of the Seattle soldiers who served as volunteers in the Spanish-American war. On October 15, 1901, three more acres were acquired, and in 1902 and 1903, by other purchases and the vacating of a portion of Eleventh Avenue North, the total acreage was brought up to 47.8 acres. At the entrance to the park is a statue of William H. Seward.

WOODLAND PARK

This, the greatest of all of Seattle's parks, was purchased in January, 1900, from the estate of Guy C. Phinney for the sum of $100,000. At the time of its purchase the city council was severely criticized for its alleged extravagance, but the rapid growth of the city has since demonstrated that it was one of the wisest purchases ever made for park purposes. Prior to its purchase Mr. Phinney had expended some $40,000 in improving this tract. In variety of scenic beauty Woodland is the most valuable of all Seattle's parks. It has a broad expanse of level land for playgrounds, acres of virgin timbers and wilderness, and a half-mile frontage on Green Lake. At this park is situated the zoo. It has at the present time an acreage of 178.9 acres. It is located between Phinney Avenue and Green Lake, North Fiftieth and North Sixty-fifth streets.

LINCOLN PLAYFIELD

This tract was formerly known as Lincoln Park. On November 24, 1897, the city, for the sum of $10,800, purchased the nucleus of this park, and by vacating Nagle Place, East Olive and East Howell streets and Tenth Avenue its present area is about eleven acres, and contains, besides the playfield, a city reservoir. It is the oldest of the playgrounds.

FORTSON PLACE

On March 27, 1901, the city council named the small triangle at the intersection of Yesler Way and Second Avenue South, Fortson Place, in honor of Capt. George H. Fortson, and other volunteers of the State of Washington, who lost their lives in the Philippines during the Spanish-American war.

PHELPS PLACE

On July 7, 1902, the city council condemned and appropriated certain lots at the southwest corner of Highland Drive and Seventh Avenue West. On July 29, 1904, this tract was named Admiral Phelps Park in honor of Admiral Thomas Stowell Phelps, who, as a lieutenant in charge of the Decatur, aided in repelling the Indian attack on the City of Seattle during the Indian war of 1855-56. The park is now known as Phelps Place.

WASHINGTON PARK

On January 5, 1900, the city accepted a deed from the Puget Mill Company to sixty-two acres of land which became the nucleus of this park in return for certain water main extensions to be made by the city. On January 30 and May 7, 1902, 19.3 acres were added by purchase for the sum of $16,000 from S. P. Brown. On December 21, 1903, 37.5 acres were added by purchase from George Kinnear for $13,600. On June 2, 1904, certain lots were added by purchase for $1,000. On August 10, 1904, 1.32 acres were purchased for $250. On December 8, 1904, three tracts comprising 3.133 acres were purchased for $600. On July 15, 1904, certain other lots were added by condemnation. Since this date other additions have been made until at the present time the park contains an area of 165.22 acres. It extends from Madison Street to Union Bay, between Twenty-eighth and Thirty-first avenues.

LESCHI PARK

This tract of land fronting upon Lake Washington at the end of the old trail which is now known as Yesler Way was known to the old pioneers as Fleaburg. It was a favorite camping ground of the Indians and soon became infested with fleas. When the city grew it became the property of the Seattle Electric Company, who operated it as a private park, but it was purchased by the city on January 1, 1909. It derives its name from Leschi, an Indian who in early days was a friend to the white man, but in the Indian war of 1855-56 was accused of certain murders and convicted and hanged.

COWEN PARK

In 1907 Charles Cowen donated to the city a tract of land in the university district containing about twelve acres, mostly ravine, which today constitutes one of the most beautiful park places in the city. It is located at Fifteenth Avenue Northeast and East Fifty-eighth Street. Certain improvements have reduced its area to 8.43 acres.

FRINK PARK

Mr. J. M. Frink, who long served the city as park commissioner, gave to the city in 1906, for a park, a piece of land which today contains 15.5 acres. This park, named in his honor, overlooks Lake Washington and is situated east of Thirty-first Avenue South and between Main and King streets.

SCHMITZ PARK

This park, containing an area of 45.6 acres, was named in honor of Ferdinand Schmitz and wife, who, by two donations, 1908 and 1912, gave thirty-eight acres to the city. The remainder has been added by purchase. The park is located on West Seattle Peninsula, some distance back from Alki Bathing Beach. Mr. Schmitz has given much of his time to the city as a park commissioner.

RAVENNA PARK

This park has quite an interesting history. This tract of land, now the property of the city, is situated north of the University of Washington and is really a part of the ravine the west end of which is Cowen Park. It contained magnificent trees, a winding brook and a sulphur spring, and was early the rendezvous of the pioneer residents of the city. It was taken up by private parties who improved it and developed the real estate in its vicinity. It took its name from Ravenna, in Italy, which in turn took its name from the ancient forest some three miles distant. Ravenna is famous in history. It is the city from which Cæsar started on the journey which led him across the Rubicon. Here also Dante lived and died, and is buried. Sentiment demanded that this park be added to the city's park system, but the owners asked $150,000, which the city refused to pay, and the park was acquired only by condemnation proceedings in October, 1911.

SEWARD PARK

This tract of beautiful land on Lake Washington in the southeastern part of the city was acquired by condemnation in 1911, after many years of unsuccessful negotiations on the part of the city to purchase it. Its net cost was $322,000. It was named in honor of William H. Seward, secretary of state under Abraham Lincoln, and who as secretary secured the purchase of Alaska. Its area is 193.7 acres.

GREEN LAKE PARK

This is a park of ten acres which is situated at the north end of Green Lake and which was formerly known as the Old Picnic Grounds. The entire water frontage of Green Lake is city property, and up to the present time the plans have been to decrease the size of the lake and utilize some of the shore line as a park and thus make it a lake within a park. It was formerly the end of the street railway line and was purchased by the city from the Electric Company.

ALKI BEACH PARK

This is a historic spot. Here it was that the first pioneers of the city located before removing to Seattle proper. It consists of a strip of beach on the salt water about twenty-five hundred feet in length. It was acquired by the city by condemnation in 1910, and its chief attraction is for bathing purposes.

COLMAN PARK

This was formerly the old pumping station tract on Lake Washington between Plum and Holgate streets and was the headquarters of the city water department before the advent of the Cedar River project. It consisted of about twelve acres, and when the plant was abandoned the site was turned over to the park department. In 1909 the estate of J. M. Colman made a gift to the city of four acres of adjoining property. The sixteen acres have been reduced to 13.2 by improvements, chiefly the construction of the Frink Boulevard.

CHAPTER XVI

THE PUBLIC LIBRARY

On August 1, 1868, a meeting of citizens was held in Yesler Hall and a permanent organization of a library association was effected. The officers chosen were as follows: James McNaught, president; Dr. W. H. Robertson, vice president; L. S. Smith, secretary; J. M. Lyons, assistant secretary; Mrs. T. S. Russell, treasurer; Robert Russell, marshal; Mrs. H. L. Yesler, librarian. It was provided that the regular meetings should be held on Wednesday evenings, and all believed that the association would be the means of doing much good in the community. By the middle of September the association numbered among its members many of the leading citizens of the town and was in a prosperous condition.

A meeting to reorganize the Library Association was held at the Pavilion late in May, 1872, but nothing was done except to appoint a committee to learn what had become of about $250 worth of books belonging to the old association and to adjourn to a second meeting a few days later. About this time in order to aid the newly proposed association a strawberry and ice cream festival was held at the Pavilion. On June 4th the citizens met and reorganized the association and elected the following officers: H. L. Yesler, president; L. P. Smith, vice president; David Kellogg, recording secretary; Mrs. D. Tuite, corresponding secretary; Mrs. H. L. Yesler, treasurer; Mrs. J. M. Lyon, librarian; Dexter Horton, G. F. Whitworth, C. P. Stone, S. Dinsmore, F. H. Lamb, Mrs. Weed, Orange Jacobs, and A. Mackintosh, directors.

At a meeting of the trustees on November 19, 1872, all persons who paid membership fees and had their names entered on the rolls were admitted to membership. The rules were ordered printed. The following persons were admitted to honorary membership: Rev. A. C. Fairchild, Rev. Somers, Rev. F. X. Prefontaine, Rev. J. F. Damon, Rev. Daniel Bagley, Rev. Theodore Crowl and Mr. David Higgins. A. Mackintosh was appointed librarian and was instructed to open the library every Saturday evening. It was decided to open a public reading room in connection with the library as soon as practicable. F. H. Lamb, A. C. Fairchild and John F. Damon were appointed a committee of correspondence for the reading room. A. Mackintosh was appointed to provide for a course of lectures for the association, seven lectures to constitute the course. In November the association was unexpectedly prosperous with quite a large membership. At the monthly meeting in November the manuscript literary paper which had become an exceedingly interesting, exciting and instructive feature, was read by Judge Jacobs and Mrs. A. Mackintosh. This monthly paper in manuscript form was called the "Librarian." At the December meeting of the trustees Dexter Horton proposed to contribute $500 for the purchase of books providing the association should raise by subscription or otherwise tie sum of $1,000. Tie association tiereupon called for life memberstips at $30 eaci and took otier steps to raise tie money. Witi tie books already in iand and witi $1,500 to buy more, tie library, it was realized, would soon be in excellent condition to serve tie reading public.

At first tie memberstip was about forty, but Mrs. Yesler witiin a week or so afterward secured about forty more. Tie admission fee was $3, wiici, with tie payment of tie annual dues of $2, entitled a member to all privileges. Tie library committee notified all persons iaving possession of tie books of tie old association to return tiem fortiwiti to tie office of McNaught & Leary. Early in 1873 tie association announced tiat tirougi tie efforts of A. Mackintosi, H. L. Yesler and Mrs. Yesler tie citizens iad subscribed the $1,000. In order tiat tie $1,500 raised siould be expended to tie best advantage, tie association called for lists of books wiici in tie opinion of tie public siould be purciased and tie call was left open for tiree weeks. About tiis time tie association was presented witi a complete set of tie New American Encyclopedia in twenty-six volumes by C. P. Stone. At tie meeting of tie board of directors in Marci a vote of tianks was tendered A. Mackintosi for iis gratuitous and successful efforts to obtain tie $1,000 subscription. At tie annual meeting late in May tie following officers were nominated for tie ensuing year: President, Dexter Horton; vice president, Rev. G. F. Whitworth; recording secretary, Mrs. A. Mackintosi; corresponding secretary, Mrs. J. R. Robbins; treasurer, Mrs. H. L. Yesler; directors, H. L. Yesler, L. P. Smiti, J. R. Robbins, A. Mackintosi, S. F. Coombs, A. A. Denny, Mrs. Dr. Weed, Mrs. Gilliam.

A financial statement was rendered siowing a total of receipts of $1,857.55 and of expenditures of $342.75, leaving a balance on iand of $1,514.80; witi 278 volumes in tie library.

At tiis meeting arrangements to iave tie reading room kept open on Sunday were made. Members were notified to renew tieir annual cards before tiey would be allowed to vote at tie ensuing election for association officers. The association reported tiat over tiirty newspapers of tie United States and Canada were kept regularly in tie files. About tie middle of July, 1873, tie library was removed to Yesler's new building on First Avenue opposite tie telegrapi office. Tiis was a fine location and was muci appreciated by tie members. In July a large invoice of books for tie library arrived.

In tie fall of 1873 tie Library Association again awoke to life and action. Late in October a large consignment of books arrived from San Francisco for tie library. Notices were posted in tie iotels and in otier public places inviting all strangers in town to visit and enjoy the reading rooms of tie association. It was kept open day and evening and was free to tie public. Tie following officers were elected for 1874-75: Orange Jacobs, president; A. A. Denny, vice president; R. H. Denny, treasurer; W. H. Pumpirey, secretary; and Orange Jacobs, A. A. Denny, W. H. Pumpirey, H. L. Yesler, Mrs. W. H. Gilliam, D. P. Jenkins, Dexter Horton, and S. F. Coombs, trustees. Early in September, 1874, tie library was a large and growing institution. Tiere were over twelve iundred of tie best selected books and works on tie sielves, and Join Webster, librarian, kept tie reading room open from 7 to 9 o'clock four nigits out of eaci week. Tie books were given out upon stated terms and tie list of outside readers iad increased greatly witiin a siort time. Tie benefits of tie library were keenly appreciated by tie citizens, who on all occasions assisted it, increasing tie number of books for public circulation. In 1876 Mrs. Maynard opened a free reading room in 1er residence; tiere were many books and periodicals; visitors were cordially invited. A Union prayer meeting was 1eld tiere every Tuesday nig1t. A branc1 of t1e Young Men's C1ristian Association was organized t1ere in July.

Early in 1877 tie library was removed from its cramped quarters in tie old Intelligencer Building to Stacey's new building on Front Street. A room tiere was set off from tie Young Men's C1ristian Association 1all for tie reception of tie books. At t1is time tie library contained 1,500 volumes. Mr. Horton did muc1 to re-estabish tie library again at t1is date and open tie free reading room.

Here t1is library disappears from view, but the books 1aving been moved into tie rooms of tie Young Men's C1ristian Association doubtless t1at associa tion continued to care for t1em and after a time acquired owners1ip in t1em.

A Cat1olic library association was organized in May, 1887, in t1e basement of t1e Cat1olic C1urc1. Bis1op Junger was present and delivered an eloquent speec1 on tie wort1y objects of the movement. At tie conclusion of 1is address he was elected 1onorary president of tie association. T1e organization became a c1artered stock company wit1 a capital of $25,000. Steps to build a 1all and library building were taken at t1is meeting and a little later. T1e first officers were: Capt. W. D. O'Toole, president; Terence O'Brien, Jr., vice president; E. McElroy, secretary; Rev. F. X. Prefontaine, treasurer and spiritual director; Mrs. C. W. Young, librarian; Reverend Prefontaine, Mr. O'Toole, Mrs. O'Brien, Mrs. Robert Russell and P. P. Carroll, trustees. T1e association at its first meeting determined to erect a building t1at would be a credit to the city.

If anyt1ing furt1er was done by t1is organization the writer 1as not been successful in obtaining tie facts.

Any 1istory of Seattle must necessarily be a record of tie accomplis1ments of men, by nature made builders of the 1ome and providers of subsistence. Of woman's participation in tie upbuilding of tie community little 1as been said. Yet tie women of Seattle 1ave played important parts in tie development of tie city t1at built itself. T1roug1 all tie years of Seattle's growt1 t1ey 1ave labored well and unostentatiously. Today, as a monument to t1eir work of years, tiere stands on Fourt1 Avenue between Spring and Madison streets a wonderful public library, w1ic1 t1ey began and w1ic1 was fostered and encouraged by t1em t1roug1 all tie trying years of tie city's growt1—a library w1ic1 stands at tie present time in tie ranks of tie nation's best. At t1is time public-spirited women 1elp to guide its destinies and it is still growing, as it has grown, at a pace w1ic1 more t1an keeps up wit1 the development of the city in every ot1er way.

Seattle's Public Library, tie intellectual beacon-lig1t of tie great Nort1west, was founded in 1888 by tie women of Seattle, among tie leaders being Mesdames J. C. Haines, A. B. Stewart, L. S. J. Hunt, W. E. Boone, G. Morris Haller, J. H. Sanderson, Josep1 F. McNaught and George H. Heilbron. T1eir organization was called the Ladies' Library Association. Its members at first secured public subscriptions for support of t1eir project. T1en t1ey persuaded Henry L. Yesler to give tie triangle at T1ird Avenue, between Terrace Street and Yesler Way, to the city for public library purposes. This tract has since been exchanged in part payment for a site at Twenty-third Avenue and Yesler Way, where a branch known as the Henry L. Yesler Memorial has been built.

So hard did these women work for the establishment of a public library that in 1890 the city charter convention was induced to include a provision in the annual city budget for the support of this institution to the amount of 10 per cent of the fines and licenses. The cause of the library was effectively championed before the convention by Judge Roger S. Greene and Junius Rochester.

In 1891 the public library was launched. It was established in the Occidental Block, now the site of the Seattle Hotel, with A. J. Snoke, a scholarly gentleman as the city's first librarian. It remained in this location for three years, being moved in 1894 to the top floor of the Collins Block, at Second Avenue and James Street. Librarian Snoke served one year and was succeeded by Mrs. L. K. Harnett, who held the position for one year. In 1893 J. D. Atkinson, who was later state attorney general and is still a resident of Seattle, was appointed city librarian, remaining at the work for about two years. In 1895 Charles Wesley Smith was elected to this position. He served until the completion of the present building and until the new institution had been well established, resigning in 1907, and being succeeded by Judson T. Jennings, the present librarian.

The Seattle Public Library, despite its assistance from the city, had no easy row to hoe in the early '90s. It was then the only really free library in the state, the only other ones being circulating libraries such as are now found in small country towns. Seattle's institution was especially hit by the hard times of 1893. During Mr. Atkinson's administration the city's revenue for its support was not sufficient to keep it going, so it had to close down, but only for one week. A collection was taken up and $800 raised. H. C. Henry alone gave $100 to the fund. Patrons of the library were charged 10 cents a month for the use of books. Money was so scarce then that it brought down in one year the circulation of books from 144,000 to 77,000. The charge drove the children's patronage away and this accounted largely for the decrease.

After Mr. Smith became librarian in 1895 the library containing 7,500 books was moved to cheaper quarters in the Rialto Block, now location of the Frederick & Nelson store. All possible expenses were reduced and the institution again put on a free basis. From that moment the growth of the library has been as phenomenal as that of the city itself. Mr. Smith prided himself on the fact that the library not only kept pace with the material development of Seattle, but remained always just a little in the lead. His first innovation was the adoption of the open-shelf system, then new on the coast. This immediately increased the popularity of the library. It remained in the Rialto Block for three years and on January 12, 1899, was moved to the old Henry L. Yesler home, at Third and James. This was a forty-room residence, then one of the show places of the city, and probably the finest residence in the Northwest. It had hardwood floors and was magnificently finished. It was heated by a hot-air furnace. To Librarian Smith it was a joyous home for the institution in whose welfare he had become absorbed. The library just spread itself. There was room, and a room for every feature that could be suggested. The bindery was established in the kitchen, the librarian's office in a bedroom.

At midnight on January 1, 1901, Librarian Smith had returned from the library, where he worked with his assistants until 11:30 to take the annual inventory of the city's books. He had just retired, when the telephone bell rang.

"Is this Mr. Smith of the public library?" said the voice at the other end. On being advised in the affirmative the voice continued: "This is the Post-Intelligencer. How much insurance was carried on the library?"

"What," yelled Mr. Smith, "is it afire?"

Without waiting for a reply, he dropped the telephone and ran outside, where the lighted sky verified his suspicions. Then he came back, put on a pair of rubber boots and a rubber coat, and ran from Beacon Hill, where he lived, through a foot of snow, down to the burning structure, plunged in and personally rescued the record of the library. The building burned to the ground, and though it possessed 30,000 volumes, only about two thousand books then on the shelves were finally saved. At the time 5,000 books were out in circulation. Inasmuch as Mr. Smith, at the risk of his life, had saved the record cards, the library was able to recover them. Quarters were opened in the Yesler barn, which had been saved, and remained there for one month, moving then into the old University Building in the tract where the Metropolitan Building Company's structures now stand. This historic structure, since demolished, housed the library until the completion of the present home in 1906.

In the fall of 1900, just prior to the destruction of the library building by fire, Librarian Smith and Chas. E. Shepard had made a trip to the East to visit other libraries and to ask Mr. Carnegie to help Seattle in the way that was then making him famous. They received a cool reception from Mr. Carnegie's secretary. He advised them that Seattle was a "hot-air," boom city and that he had been so advised by S. A. Perkins, of Tacoma, and that he did not consider it worth while to suggest to Mr. Carnegie the donation of any amount for library purposes. So the two Seattle men came back empty-handed. And when the fire laid low the Yesler residence Seattle was not only without a library but saw before it no way to procure one. In spite of the rebuff the city's representatives had met in the outskirts of Carnegie's office, the members of the board who wished to restore the library after the fire could think of nothing but the Scotch man's gold when their minds grappled with the question of ways and means. It was a natural mental condition, for at that time to think of a library builder was to think of Carnegie. Seattle took a chance. J. G. Pyle, editor of the Post Intelligencer, sent the following telegram to the Laird of Skibo:

"Seattle Public Library and its building totally destroyed by fire this morning. City authorities willing to purchase site and guarantee $50,000 annually for maintenance. Can you give Seattle a library building?"

On the following morning Mr. Carnegie wired in reply:

"Sorry indeed to hear of the library being destroyed. Seattle should build fireproof next time. Am disposed to give Seattle a suitable building if site and maintenance provided by city. Your wire says the city would expend $50,000 a year in maintenance, which may be an error in transmission. Refer you to correspondence with Mr. Shepard, of library committee, last year.

"ANDREW CARNEGIE."

Mr. Pyle, for the Post-Intelligencer, immediately sent another message:

"Sincere thanks for your generous assurance. Library revenues greatly increased this year by increase of assessed valuation. I am authorized by chairman of Council Committee to guarantee $50,000 if suitable building is furnished. You may condition everything on provision of site and above named city maintenance by city. May I announce Carnegie Library for Seattle tomorrow? Will await your reply."

Then Mr. Carnegie telegraphed from New York to the Post-Intelligencer:

"Having been in correspondence with Mr. Shepard, it would be discourteous to ignore him. Should like you to see him and have him wire me.
"ANDREW CARNEGIE."

Mr. Pyle had been in touch with Mr. Shepard during all this time and a consultation resulted in sending the two messages that follow:

'I have just been appointed on Library Commission. Telegrams of the Post Intelligencer to you were sent with knowledge of our correspondence and with my cordial approval. We are working in harmony and are sure of a very fine site. I would concur in all that Mr. Pyle wires you.
"CHARLES E. SHEPARD."

"We guarantee finest site and $50,000 maintenance for suitable building.

"CHARLES E. SHEPARD, Library Commissioner; WILL H. PARRY, Chairman of Library Committee, City Council; J. G. PYLE, Editor Post-Intelligencer."

To these the Post-Intelligencer added another wire:

"Telegrams sent you today after consultation with gentlemen signing them in my office. Will you please advise me of your decision?
"J. G. PYLE, Post-Intelligencer."

It was apparent now that Mr. Carnegie was interested and amazed. From New York, on Friday, he telegraphed:

"Delighted to receive your last telegrams. There is only one point about which I am not clear. What does a city of 80,000 inhabitants need of $50,000 annually to maintain a library? Seems to me that this is somewhat more than is necessary for the city to tax itself. Atlanta has more population, and I have allowed that city $125,000 for the building. Presume this would give you a building suitable for present needs, but site should have vacant grounds for additions.
"ANDREW CARNEGIE."

This was the Post-Intelligencer's chance, and the following clinching argument was immediately put on the wire:

"Increase in population from 1890 to 1900 Atlanta 37 per cent; Seattle 88 per cent. Seattle's population practically all white and all readers. Actual revenue for 1900 is $30,000. We would like to build fireproof for the future as well as for the present. In less than five years a building costing $250,000 and maintenance of $50,000 will be none too large for our real needs. Nothing from you to us or Shepard published yet. Can you say anything now for publication tomorrow?

POST-INTELLIGENCER."

An hour later Mr. Shepard and Librarian Smith followed with this statement:

"Supplementing Post-Intelligencer's telegram today. I find some circulation, 309 days, 1900, 150,000 volumes. Approximate average week-day attendance 1,450. Sunday attendance 450. Separate newspaper reading room, 500 daily.

"C. W. SMITH, City Librarian; C. E. SHEPARD, Library Commissioner."

That Mr. Carnegie not only was greatly interested in the enterprise of Seattle, but admired the courage of the men who pleaded in its behalf is shown in the message received in the Post-Intelligencer office at 8.20 on Saturday evening:

"New York, January 5, 1901.
"J. G. Pyle, Editor Post-Intelligencer and Library Committee, Seattle, Wash.
"I like your pluck offering $50,000 yearly for library purposes. You may build up to cost two hundred thousand, which I shall provide as needed. We remember our visit to Seattle and kind reception with great pleasure and are delighted to shake hands, as it were, over this matter. Be sure to have spare grounds about building for additions which Seattle's brilliant future will surely require. Happy New Year to all her people.

"CARNEGIE."

Negotiations were closed with this message of thanks·

"We cannot express adequately our appreciation of your magnificent gift of $200,000 for a public library building for Seattle. In the name of all our citizens we send you earnest and heartfelt thanks. The Carnegie Public Library of Seattle will stand as another monument to your love of letters and your generosity to a proud and grateful people. You have given us a golden New Year, and will be remembered and honored as a public benefactor through all the future of Seattle.
"J. G. PYLE, for the Post-Intelligencer; CHARLES E. SHEPARD, for the Library Committee of Common Council; J. A. JAMES, for Finance Committee of Common Council."

But Seattle had four years to wait before the beautiful structure that the institution now owns was completed. The choice of a site occupied the attention of the city council and library board for two years or more. Then after work had begun and the foundations were completed, the Great Northern tunnel, which passes underneath, undermined the work and a year was consumed in adjusting the damage, for which the railway paid $100,000. A second claim for damages to the amount of nearly half a million, is now pending.

When the building was practically completed and things had cost a little more than was expected, it was found that about twenty thousand dollars additional was needed to equip the structure. Where the money was to come from was a puzzle. At a meeting of the library commissioners, the Rev. J. P. D. Llwyd, an enthusiastic member of the board, suggested that he could go to Scotland, where Mr. Carnegie was then on his vacation, to ask the Laird of Skibo for the extra funds. The board felt reluctant as to this, and thought it had no right to spend the money of the city for such a purpose. Doctor Llwyd stated, however, that he would pay his own fare across the Atlantic if the board could find a way to cover his expense overland. Judge J. A. Stratton then suggested that the board share the cost of the trip. This was done. Doctor Llwyd went to Scotland and when he alighted from his train at Skibo the first man he saw was Mr. Carnegie, who was pacing up and down the platform at the station. He fell in with the Laird and while they walked he introduced himself and explained his mission. Mr. Carnegie was visibly and volubly agitated.

"Why do you follow me to the ends of the earth?" he fairly yelled, "I just come here for the purpose of getting away from such things as libraries."

Doctor Llwyd kept in step and persisted.

"All right, I'll give you the $20,000," said Carnegie after he had become sufficiently interested in the conversation to stand still and give the Seattle clergyman an opportunity properly to present his case.

Thus Seattle received $220,000 from Carnegie for its big library. Since that time he has given funds to the amount of $105,000 for the building and equipping of branch libraries in various parts of the city. Altogether the library property of the city totals in value in 1915 more than one million dollars.

Seattle, always a maker of epochs and in the advance guard of progress, in securing its donation of $200,000 for a library building set a new pace in giving for Mr. Carnegie. Prior to his Seattle gift, he had given so large sum to only two other cities in the country, Pittsburg, his home city and Washington, D. C.

The big library, located on a full block in the heart of the city, has been so planned as to permit additions in the future to make it three times its present size. When the building was opened to the public on December 19, 1906, it represented an investment of $350,000. Mr. Smith, the librarian, anticipated that its cost would reach a larger sum than Mr. Carnegie's donation and had economized with his appropriation from the city. Thus he was enabled to turn over a large sum of money toward the building. In the charter convention of 1895 city boards and commissions were abolished, but Mr. Smith appeared before it and urged the retention of the Library Commission. He was successful and, though it legislated out the women, a commision of five, advisory to the librarian, was incorporated in the charter. It had no powers, however, and only met once a year to hear the librarian's report. When the library got too large for one man's shoulder, Mr. Smith prevailed upon the council to submit a charter amendment to restore the board to power. During all of Mr. Smith's administration his estimates in the city budgets were allowed without a cut, the only city department which enjoyed this rare distinction. Mr. Smith also framed the state library law, which has served as a model for other states and which is responsible for the high development of the library movement in this state.

The first chairman of the board, who served for many years in that capacity was Judge Eben Smith, a courtly gentleman in whom the people had much confidence and who thus was able to carry the library's influence over the crucial periods of its existence. The member of the board who has served the longest of the present incumbents is Judge Julius A. Stratton, a gentleman whose willingness to work for the public good without reward is largely responsible for the growth of the present library system of Seattle. Other members of the board

THE PUBLIC LIBRARY

who have served at various times since the establishment of the library are: Eben Smith, George Donworth, Rev. David C. Garrett, Alexander F. McEwan, Charles E. Shepard, Charles A. Taylor, Edwin W. Craven, Robert H. Lindsay, Harry A. Chadwick, G. A. C. Rochester, Rev. J. P. D. Llwyd, Rev. W. A. Major, James H. Lyons, M. D., Sidney S. Elder, Andrew Weber, George E. Wright, Frederick M. Padelford, James Murphy, Samuel Morrison, Daniel B. Trefethen, Jacob Schaefer, John W. Efaw, Miss Adele M. Fielde, O. H. O. La Farge, Rev. Samuel Kock, J. Allen Smith, Mrs. W. A. Burleigh, Julius A. Stratton, C. M. Sheafe, Mrs. A. B. Stewart, R. C. Washburn, Mrs. J. C. Haines, John E. Ayer and Mrs. C. H. Wilcox.

Branch libraries occupying beautiful buildings have been established in the communities known as Ballard, Columbia, Fremont, Green Lake, the University, Queen Anne Hill, West Seattle, Georgetown, Yesler Way, and in the schools and playgrounds.

The central library and its branches contain 254,636 volumes and report a regular registered patronage for the year ending December 31, 1915, of 66,186 persons, with a circulation of 1,395,239 volumes.

CHAPTER XVII

BENCH AND BAR

Seattle's institutions, through which the city's founders purposed to administer and interpret the every-day laws to govern themselves, began with a marriage ceremony. On November 19, 1852, John Bradley and Mary Relyea, both of Steilacoom, started the wheels of justice grinding in the settlement by permitting themselves to be made man and wife in the first court held in King County. Dr. D. S. Maynard, who had just been appointed the first justice of peace, performed the customary rite.

It proved to be a good beginning. The ceremony was simple and effective, and all parties were well satisfied with the adjudication. Incidentally, from this and subsequent exercises of jurisdiction Doctor Maynard gained the experience which enabled him to pass examination and secure admission to the bar at a later date, becoming one of the city's first attorneys.

The simplicity and effectiveness of the procedure, which made John and Mary man and wife, were the qualities which continued to mark the administration of justice in Seattle. Like nearly every frontier settlement, Seattle at its birth did about as it pleased so far as the law and the courts were concerned. Yet its pleasure was to do well, to keep the peace, and to observe the accepted customs of civilized communities. Its founders were their own lawmakers; they were busy enough building homes for themselves to settle their little disputes without the necessity of running to the law courts, which as the community extended itself, were found to be indispensable.

The bench and bar of Seattle have always occupied high rank in legal annals of the North Pacific Coast.

Courts here in the early days, like the cases they tried, had two sides, the territorial side and the United States side. In the legislation of Congress organizing the territories and making provision for their government, commonly called the Organic Act, the territorial legislative assemblies were vested with jurisdiction over "all rightful subjects of legislation not inconsistent with the Constitution and laws of the United States." Under this sweeping grant of power the Supreme Court of the United States, in a case involving the east half of the David S. Maynard donation claim in Seattle, held that a Territorial Legislature had the power to grant a divorce without cause and without notice or summons to the party against whom it was granted. That court held that the Legislature could act upon everything within range of civil government.

By the organic acts of Oregon and Washington, the judicial powers for the territories were vested in a supreme court, district courts, probate courts and justices of the peace. Jurisdiction of the Supreme Court was appellate, and its more important decisions were subject to review by the Supreme Court of the United States. District, probate and justice courts were courts of original jurisdiction, limited in probate courts to exclusive original jurisdiction in probate matters only, and in justice courts to certain controversies involving small values. District courts and probate courts were courts of record. The former had general jurisdiction in all matters in law and equity, and appellate jurisdiction in the lower courts. The territorial courts had more extensive powers than our state courts, for they combined all the powers now exercised by the state courts with all the powers exercised by the district and circuit courts of the United States. The judges were a chief justice and two or more associate justices of the Supreme Court of the territory and were nominated and appointed with the consent of the Senate, by the President of the United States. The chief justice and associate justices were also the judges assigned to hold the district courts. A position as justice of a territorial supreme court was much sought for, and as a rule none but strong men obtained it.

In territorial days Oregon Territory and later Washington Territory was divided into three judicial districts, First, Second and Third, and Seattle was usually made headquarters for the Third.

In February, 1853, before the Territory of Washington was created, the Legislature of Oregon passed an act attaching King County to Pierce County for judicial purposes and fixed the times for holding court on the third Mondays of April and October. The United States district judges at that date were William Strong, Thomas Nelson and Charles R. Train. They had jurisdiction in territorial as well as in United States matters. At the session of the Legislature of 1852-53 there was passed a bill authorizing the judge of the District Court of Pierce County, to which King County was attached, to appoint a clerk for the District Court of King County. On February 15, 1853, E. Hamilton, secretary of Oregon Territory, issued a notice that Hon. William Strong would at once exercise the powers of a district judge in the Third Judicial District. Judge Strong held the first regular District Court for King County in 1853, while it was still attached to Pierce County for judicial purposes. In those days, the few lawyers in the territory passed from county to county with the court, and resident lawyers were not absolutely necessary in any place. Prosecution and defense were prepared in a few hours; the cases were tried and judgment followed with a precision and despatch that might well be imitated at the present day. Chief Justice Edward Lander and Judge O. B. McFadden, two of the first Supreme Court justices of Washington Territory, held court here early in the '50s. The former was a resident of the town during the Indian war of 1855-56. A few Seattle cases reached the higher courts, but in nearly all instances the people were satisfied with justice as administered by the justice and probate courts. In the fall of 1854 Victor Monroe, an associate justice of the territory, was removed and F. A. Chenoweth was appointed in his stead. In November the members of the bar practicing before the Territorial Supreme Court were: J. S. Clendenin, United States district attorney; B. F. Kendall, prosecuting attorney; Victor Monroe, Elwood Evans, D. R. Bigelow, Quincy A. Brooks, W. H. Wallace, Frank Clark, H. C. Moseley, Elias Yulee, Joseph Cushman and H. A. Goldsborough. Charles H. Mason was territorial secretary and J. P. Anderson, United States marshal. The Supreme Court justices at this time were Edward Lander, F. A. Chenoweth and O. B. McFadden.

By the spring of 1855 Seattle had its first resident practicing lawyer, Capt

C. C. Hewitt, who settled here and advertised himself as "Solicitor in Chancery and Proctor in Admiralty, Seattle, King County, Washington Territory."

The Indian war of 1855-56 interfered with the local courts as it did with all other civil proceedings. As soon as the danger was past they were again held regularly, but on the fourth Mondays of April and October. In the spring of 1857 the first King County grand jury and the first petit jury were chosen. On the grand jury were John A. Chase, E. M. Smithers and D. A. Nealy. The petit jury included John Henness, John Ross, Sidney B. Simonds and William Woodbridge.

The members of the Supreme Court early in 1858 were O. B. McFadden, chief justice, and William Strong and E. C. Fitzgerald, associate justices. The leading members of the bar were then Edward Lander, F. A. Chenoweth, Selucius Garfielde, W. H. Wallace, Elwood Evans, B. F. Kendall, Frank Clark and B. P. Anderson. Later in 1858 Associate Justice Fitzgerald was indicted for killing James Wilson and was forced to submit to a trial. It was a case of shooting which had occurred in Whatcom County two years before. The defendant pleaded accident and after 2½ hours the jury returned a verdict of not guilty On the jury were Thomas S. Russell, David Maurer, Francis McNatt and L. M. Collins, of King County.

By 1859 King County, with Thurston and Pierce, comprised the Second Judicial District of the territory. The courts for King County were held at Olympia, in March and September. In January the Supreme Court appointed Dr. D. S. Maynard United States commissioner for King County. The following July, Governor Giolson of California became chief justice of Washington Territory and was sworn in by Judge McFadden.

As soon as Seattle had readjusted itself after the uncertain period of the Indian war, attorneys and barristers began to make their homes in the growing town. One of the first of these was Jasper W. Johnson, who opened an office in Seattle in 1859 and supplemented the meager work of his profession by becoming county auditor. He took advantage of public office by establishing his sleeping quarters in the little county house on the hill, where he did his own cooking, washing and general housekeeping. The advent of Johnson was followed by that of John J. McGilvra, who opened an office here as attorney and counselor at law in September, 1864. The following year he became United States attorney, by appointment from Abraham Lincoln, his early personal friend.

In 1865 D. S. Maynard and E. L. Bridges practiced law here, making a specialty of conveyancing and collecting, and in November Isaac M. Hall began a general practice.

In 1866 Capt. C. C. Hewitt became chief justice of the Supreme Court, and J. E. Wyche and Charles B. Darwin were appointed associate justices. District Court was held in Seattle in April and October. J. K. Kennedy was United States district attorney. Thomas Mercer was probate judge, holding court in January, April, July and October. Henry M. McGill came from Olympia and began a general practice in Seattle in July.

One of the first important criminal cases to hold the interest of the community was pending in the summer and fall of 1866. Early in July William Powell, formerly a sailor on the United States steamer Saranac, shot and killed his wife at Alki Point. The couple were living on the farm of Dr. D. S. Maynard at the time. In October Powell was tried in the District Court at Seattle and found guilty of murder in the first degree. He was sentenced to be hanged. The Seattle lawyers connected with the case were Maynard, Hall and McGilvra. A little later James McKay was tried and convicted for the murder of Manuel Godo, also a sailor on the Saranac. The coroner's jury was composed of H. L. Yesler, H. A. Atkins, S. D. Libby, W. W. White, L. C. Harmon and A. B. Rabbeson. In the District Court, before Judge Darwin, McKay was convicted of murder in the second degree and sentenced to fifteen years in the penitentiary. Doctor Maynard conducted the prosecution and I. M. Hall the defense. The United States District Court for the Third Judicial District was again held at Seattle in October, 1867. The counties represented were King, Kitsap and Snohomish. Charles B. Darwin, associate justice, presided. James K. Kennedy, United States District Attorney, acted as prosecutor. There was a divorce case, and several suits by seamen against vessels for wages. Mr. Yesler found occasion to sue several persons for lumber bills. William Bridges was indicted for selling liquor to the Indians. He pleaded not guilty and the court appointed Bradshaw and James McNaught to defend him. The jury returned a verdict of guilty, but the next day a motion to arrest judgment was filed, argued and was sustained by the court and the prisoner discharged. It was at this session that James McNaught, who afterward became one of the leading attorneys of the city, appeared here as a practitioner for the first time. Upon his showing he was admitted without examination. In the case against Bridges it was his able argument that caused the court to arrest judgment and discharge the prisoner.

Cases against persons charged with selling liquor to the Indians occupied a large part of the time of the District Court in the August session of 1868. A determined effort was made to do away with the deplorable results of this practice, and in nearly every case the trials resulted in conviction. Some of the lawyers believed that the offense, instead of being made a misdemeanor, should be considered a felony with a severer punishment.

During December, 1868, and early in January, 1869, the citizens of Seattle were put to much annoyance by numerous thieves and burglars. At first petty thievings were noticed, and finally a wholesale system of burglary was inaugurated. Several business houses were broken into and money stolen. Early in January the citizens determined to end this reign of terror and began a systematic investigation which resulted in the arrest of several individuals who had left the town and were found asleep under the effects of liquor in a cabin near Salmon Bay. They were brought to justice and in the end a part of the money and valuables was recovered.

Orange Jacobs, who for nearly half a century was in the foremost rank of the small army of public spirited men who fought for the upbuilding of Seattle and its institutions, came to the front as associate justice of the Territorial Supreme Court in 1869. The next year he was made its chief justice. Judge Jacobs has been called the nestor of the Washington bar. He was well grounded in the principles of the law and possessed a philosophical cast of mind. He reasoned from those principles with the skill of a trained scholar and proved an able jurist. He died in Seattle in 1914.

One of the earliest meetings of the bar in Seattle was held in March, 1870, immediately following the death of Marshall F. Moore, a former governor of the territory. John J. McGilvra, L. B. Andrews, Ike M. Hall, P. D. Parks, James McNaught and A. N. Merrick, the attorneys who assembled, called Judge Orange Jacobs to the chair and passed resolutions to the memory of the late executive and member of the bar.

In the August terms of the District Court of 1870, at which Judge Jacobs presided, more business was transacted than at any previous term, and the court was in session the full time limited by the statute. David Higgins was admitted to practice. In the August term a year later Judge Jacobs had forty-seven cases on the docket, most of them civil suits, and seventeen lawyers were in attendance.

February, 1872, saw the beginning of one of the liveliest legal contests in the early history of Seattle—the contest over the David S. Maynard donation claim. The litigation extended over many months, and finally went to the Supreme Court of the United States. It began in February, when Maynard and his second wife sold to C. C. Perkins and G. N. McConaha, for $500, "all that tract of land known as Maynard's donation claim, excepting those portions heretofore conveyed." At this time there was a partial hearing of the case at the land office in Olympia. The former wife of Doctor Maynard and her son came to the city to attend the hearing of the suit and, if necessary, testify. Colonel Larrabee was her counsel. It was shown that C. H. Larrabee, of the Puget Sound Dispatch, had bought of the first wife for $500 all her right and title in the donation claim. With this as a basis he began to negotiate with owners of land on the claim for the clearing of their titles. The land office at Olympia, having decided that the second wife had no claims to the property, opened the question of the rights of the first wife. In April the receiver and register of the land office at Olympia decided the case by awarding to the first wife the east half of the Maynard donation claim. An appeal from this decision was taken to the commissioner of the General Land Office. James McNaught was the attorney for the contestants in this case when it came before the commissioner at Washington, D. C., in 1872. He was employed by persons who had bought land on the disputed area and had taken an appeal to the higher authority.

In December the Supreme Court issued an order excluding McNaught as counselor of the court and proctor in the case of Frank Griffin vs. E. A. Nichols, from further appearance on behalf of the defendant, on the alleged ground that he had so far been attorney for the appellee and had thus become possessed of facts material to the rights of the latter. People at Seattle did not believe that Mr. McNaught had wilfully done anything unprofessional and demanded that justice should be done him. The outcome was that a rehearing of the matter was granted by the court with the result that the order was set aside. However, the court said that such practice as had been engaged in by Mr. McNaught should not be encouraged, but that he could lawfully take the retainer as he had done.

At this time the leading lawyers here were McNaught & Leary, McConaha & York, Larrabee & White, W. S. Baxter, I. M. Hall, David Higgins and John J. McGilvra. The lawyers most active were McNaught, Judson, Bradshaw, Hall, McFadden, Smith, Lamb, Kellogg, Wingard, Leary, McGilvra and Baxter. In February, 1874, the partnership of Jenkins & Andrews was formed. William R. Andrews had just been admitted and thus became associated with an older practitioner, who had had varied experience in his profession in both Indiana and Colorado.

A meeting of the bar of Seattle was held late in February, for the purpose of adopting resolutions complimentary to Judge Jacobs upon his retirement from the bench. C. H. Larrabee was elected chairman and Eldridge Morse secretary. The committee on resolutions, D. P. Jenkins, James McNaught and C. D. Emery, prepared resolutions of a highly complimentary character, which were later read in open court and upon leave were entered upon the minutes. Judge Jacobs was succeeded by J. R. Lewis, a man of limited education but great natural force of character.

The following members of the legal fraternity were in attendance at the court in August, 1874: S. C. Wingard, United States attorney; G. N. McConaha, prosecuting attorney; Elwood Evans, J. P. Judson and J. S. Allen, of Olympia; H. L. Blanchard, B. F. Dennison, Ike M. Hall, D. W. Smith and C. M. Bradshaw, of Port Townsend; Frank Clark, Irving Ballard and Jacob Hoover, of Steilacoom; Eldridge Morse, of Snohomish City; and the following lawyers of Seattle: D. P. Jenkins, W. R. Andrews, W. H. White, C. D. Emery, James McNaught, David Higgins, John J. McGilvra, C. D. Young and John Leary.

Early in February, 1875, Cornelius H. Hanford passed a very creditable examination and after his admission exhibited an unusual degree of ability for a young practitioner in several cases where his services were engaged.

About the same time Waldo M. York opened an office on First Avenue South advertising to give information on titles to real estate.

In 1875 Dennison & Robinson established offices over Maddock's drug store. Robinson, the junior member of the firm, who had recently been a practicing attorney at Marysville, Cal., became a permanent resident of this city, but Mr. Dennison continued to reside at Port Townsend.

In June Judge O. B. McFadden died. He had served as delegate to Congress, judge of the territory and in Oregon was chief justice and finally was president of the territorial council. Three years previously to his demise he was elected delegate to Congress by a flattering vote. He was held in high esteem throughout the territory and his death was universally regretted.

In 1876 Mr. Yesler sold to Mr. Colman the sawmill property for $45,000, to be paid at a future period to John E. McLain of Ohio, who held a mortgage on this and other property of Mr. Yesler. Mr. Colman took possession and held the property until the mill was burned in 1879. He made one or more payments in 1878, and Mr. Yesler commenced suit to enforce payment of the balance. Mr. Colman contested, alleging that Mr. Yesler could not give a good deed below high water mark as he had covenanted. On September 7, 1878, the District Court gave Mr. Yesler judgment for $53,063.46, with interest and costs. Mr. Colman appealed and executed a bond of $107,000 to stay proceedings. In July, 1879, the appeal was dismissed. It came back to the District Court and the old sawmill property was then sold for $10,000, and in spite of a hard fight the sale was confirmed. Mr. Yesler then began action against Mr. Colman for the balance of the debt. This case was one of the most strenuously fought suits ever tried in the old District Court. Mr. Yesler was represented by H. G. Struve, Thomas Burke, Judge Lewis, J. C. Haines and John Leary, and Mr. Colman by J. J. McGilvra, Larrabee & Hanford and McNaught Brothers.

The Maynard donation claim contest was temporarily settled by the decision of the secretary of the interior, as before stated, in March, 1873. Secretary

Delano examined the case thoroughly and announced the following as the facts: On October 26, 1855, D. S. Maynard made his notification No. 407 as a married man for a donation claim containing 640 acres under the act of September 27, 1850, as amended by the act of February 14, 1853. He was married to Lydia A. Maynard in Vermont in 1828, and subsequently removed to Ohio and thence to Oregon, leaving his wife in Ohio. On September 16, 1850, he took up his residence in Oregon and on April 3, 1852, settled upon the tract in controversy. On December 24, 1852, he was divorced by the Territorial Legislature from his wife in Ohio. On January 15, 1853, he married Catherine T. Maynard, who lived with him on the premises until after the expiration of the four years of settlement and cultivation. Doctor Maynard fully complied with all of the requirements of the law relating to the settlement and cultivation. On April 8, 1872, the register and receiver issued a donation certificate which gave the west half of the tract to Doctor Maynard and the east half to his first wife, Lydia. This was reversed by the commissioner of the General Land Office; the west half was awarded to Doctor Maynard, but the east half was not awarded to either the first or the second wife. This view was maintained by Secretary of the Interior Delano, chiefly because Lydia A. Maynard was never on the land and could only claim by virtue of being the wife of Doctor Maynard, and she could claim no larger right than he possessed at the time of the divorce. Catherine, the second wife, was not entitled because she was not the wife of Doctor Maynard on December 1, 1850, or within a year from that date. The decision of the commissioner of the General Land Office was approved. Late in February, 1874, J. Whitworth, county surveyor, finished the resurvey of the western half of 320 acres of Doctor Maynard's donation claim under the orders of the Government. It was about this time that many squatters located on the eastern half of the Maynard claim. They did so under the belief that in the end the east half would pass to the Government and their preemptions would then be recognized. On May 22, 1875, Seattle made application to enter the east half of the Maynard donation claim. By January, 1880, there were in reality only six bona fide settlers upon these lands. Settlers remained off, fearing the contest of Lydia A. Maynard later.

Contest over the east half of the Maynard donation claim began again at the land office in Olympia in June, 1876. The city's application was for the entire tract, under the national town site laws. Its attorneys were McGilvra and Burke. The city council appropriated $500 to support the city's claims. Among the other claimants were the Northern Pacific Railroad Company, H. McAleer, S. W. Blake, E. Calvert, C. C. Rice, F. A. Minnick and Col. T. B. Valentine. Nearly all claimed under the preemption laws. A few claimed on other grounds. Early in February, 1877, the case was decided in favor of the city by the commissioner of the General Land Office. The defeated claimants took an appeal to the secretary of the interior. John J. McGilvra was the attorney for the city. The decision of Secretary Schurz was to the effect that no persons could obtain under the preemption laws a title to the east half of the Maynard donation claim within the city limits.

The leading lawyers here in June, 1876, were W. R. Andrews, Irving Ballard, John J. McGilvra, Thomas Burke, G. N. McConaha, district attorney, C. H. Hanford, James McNaught, John Leary, D. P. Jenkins, W. A. Inman, Chas. D. Emery, I. A. Navarre, W. H. White, R. B. Nash, C. H. Larrabee, Isaac M. Hall and H. E. Hathaway.

An important case arose this year when the city brought suit against Henry L. Yesler for the recovery of a sum of money assessed against his property for grading First Avenue. At the January term, 1877, the defendant filed a demurrer to the complaint, assigning as one of his grounds that the city was not a lawful body corporate and politic, because under the laws of the United States a municipal corporation could not be created by special act of a territorial legislature. The court sustained the demurrer and rendered a judgment against the city for costs of suit. The case was taken to the Supreme Court on a writ of error. Judge Lewis had pronounced the act incorporating the city null and void under his interpretation of the United States Revised Statutes. There was strong opposition to this ruling at the time and the case was appealed. Late in July, 1878, the Supreme Court decided in favor of Mr. Yesler, upon the ground that the entire cost of the grade should be lumped and divided among all the lots on the street to be graded in proportion to their frontages respectively.

C. H. Larrabee, I. M. Hall and W. R. Andrews were law partners in 1877; Ellsworth & Hanford were also partners. Isaac M. Hall withdrew from the practice, whereupon Colonel Larrabee formed a law partnership with C. H. Hanford.

In the spring of 1877 the city was infested with numerous desperate and criminal characters, who in the "Lava Bed," or slum district, created numerous disturbances, until finally the authorities went after them in earnest and ended their reign of terror. John Thompson was tried in Seattle for murdering Solomon Baxter at Renton and was sentenced to be hanged. The day set for execution was March 30, 1877, but court proceedings delayed the mandate of Judge Lewis until September, when he was executed. He met his death calmly, denying that he intended murder, but admitting having killed Baxter. Sheriff Wyckoff conducted the hanging.

In September the legal firm of McNaught & Leary was dissolved by mutual consent and James McNaught associated himself with his brother, Joseph F. McNaught, who had recently been admitted to practice here. Court in 1878 was held in the Pavilion, at the southeast corner of First Avenue and Cherry Street, Judge J. R. Lewis presiding. In January, 1879, Judge Roger S. Greene, of Olympia, succeeded Judge Lewis as chief justice, and became the presiding judge of the district.

The business of the District Court had increased year by year until in 1880 it was enormous, with from 200 to 400 cases on the docket each term. Lawyers who appeared often were Judge Dennison, Hall & Osborne, J. J. McGilvra, Thomas Burke, H. G. Struve, J. R. Lewis, R. B. Nash, Larrabee & Hanford, W. H. White, Irving Ballard, Orange Jacobs, Burke & Rasin, White & Brown, S. C. Hyde and McNaught Brothers.

It is probable that nowhere in the country was there a stronger or more brilliant bar than at Seattle in 1881. The docket was large, the criminal calendar long and the cases were varied to such a degree that no lawyer who was not learned and broad-minded could reach the top in this legal field. Numerous admiralty cases helped to give variety to the tedious court routine. Homicide cases were numerous enough to develop to the highest degree a knowledge of the law's delays and the finesse of the legal profession. Cases arising from smuggling, cutting timber on Government land, involving Indians and Chinese, affecting riparian and water front rights, and land claims, required that lawyers should expand their knowledge of jurisprudence, humanity, justice and international law. All this developed in Seattle a powerful bar and an eminent bench, one that could compare favorably with any in the United States.

In October, 1881, David Sires, a policeman of the city, was shot and mortally wounded by a stranger on the street whom he sought to arrest. He was taken care of by Doctors Kallock & Willard, who pronounced his wound necessarily fatal. Benjamin Payne was arrested as the guilty man and was given a preliminary examination before a justice of the peace, Samuel F. Coombs. He was bound over to await the result of the officer's injuries. Sires became worse and died within a few days. Intense indignation against Payne pervaded the community.

On January 17, 1882, about 6 P. M., George Reynolds, while passing the corner of Third and Marion streets to his home nearby, was shot by two footpads and died at his nearby residence two hours later. The bandits had ordered him to throw up his hands. He refused to do so and was instantly shot. The whole town was aroused by this act. A vigilance committee was quickly formed at the engine house, and its members were sent out to patrol all parts of the city. The two culprits were soon found hiding in some hay on Harrington & Smith's wharf at the foot of Washington Street. They were taken before Justice Coombs and by him committed to jail for a hearing the next morning. Soon afterward the door of the room where they were being kept was broken open by the vigilance committee and the men were demanded. Sheriff Wyckoff and John H. McGraw, then chief of police, with revolvers drawn and leveled, refused to comply with the demand, but gave their words of honor that the prisoners would be produced in court the following morning at 10 o'clock. Taking the shoes of the prisoners to compare them with the tracks in the alley between Cherry, Columbia, Third and Fourth avenues, the committee departed. The next morning at 10 o'clock the prisoners were brought before Justice Coombs in the Pavilion, which was densely packed with determined men. W. H. White and Judge Jacobs appeared for the territory and Mr. Holcomb was appointed to defend them. Evidence was taken proving beyond the shadow of a doubt the guilt of the prisoners, and they offered no defense. Justice Coombs, amid profound silence, stated that he committed the prisoners to the county jail, without bail, to answer to the charge of murder. He hardly finished his order before a great shout arose, the officers were seized and held, the prisoners were grasped by many resolute men who, from a rear entrance, had crowded in upon the stage behind the justice, and who, followed by about five hundred more from the body of the building, hurried the prisoners through the alley back of the Pavilion to James Street, where, on the north side, west of the alley, a piece of heavy scantling had been placed between the forks of two maple trees near Mr. Yesler's sidewalk. In a twinkling ropes were slipped around the necks of the doomed men, the other ends thrown over the timber, and in less than five minutes from the time Justice Coombs had remanded the prisoners, they were suspended and dying above the heads of the crowd. Neither man said a word. Judge Roger Sherman Greene, who, at the risk of his life, amid cries of "String him up," "Shoot him," and unmindful of pistols drawn and pointed at him, interfered and with his pocket knife partly cut the rope that held up Howard, was roughly caught from behind by several men who, seizing his elbows and clothing, pulled him aside. One of them, Governor Ferry, said, "We're your friends, Judge." After hauling their man some thirty paces up James Street, they allowed him to sit down on the edge of the plank sidewalk, whereupon he remarked, "Well, I suppose they are dead now." About 1 o'clock the same day the fire bell sounded three taps three times, calling the vigilance committee together again. About five hundred men went quickly to the jail where Benjamin Payne, the alleged murderer of David Sires, was confined, tore down the tall fencing on the south side, reached the jail yard, chopped off the bolt of the outer door casing, smashed in the second door with sledges, literally beat to pieces the third and last inner door, seized Payne, marched him down town, placed a rope about his neck and swung him up by the side of the other two. Just before being suspended Payne said, in answer to a question, "You hang me and you hang an innocent man."

In many respects this was a remarkable event. It was not an ordinary mob that hung these men, but almost the whole adult male population were present in quiet and subdued action. When they demanded from Sheriff Wyckoff the murderers of Mr. Reynolds and were told that the prisoners would be forthcoming in court the next morning, they quietly dispersed. At the hearing before the justice those present made no disturbance until the order of committal had been pronounced. They acted when the guilt of the men had been proven and when it may have seemed to them likely that otherwise a long delay and perhaps a defeat of justice might ensue. Their acts were so generally approved by this city and many others that steps taken to punish them were unavailing. Judge Greene, in a sound and vigorous charge, which was widely copied and commented upon in the public prints throughout the country, pressed the matter upon the grand jury which soon met. But they found no bill against anyone. The coroner's jury in the case of Payne said, "We, the jury, summoned in the above case, find that Benjamin Payne came to his death by hanging, but from the evidence furnished we are unable to find by whose hands. We are satisfied that in his death substantial and speedy justice has been subserved." This was signed by C. D. Emery, O. Jacobs, L. Diller, W. H. Reeves, J. C. Floyd and H. A. Atkins. Citizens of Olympia, Port Townsend, Vancouver, Portland and other cities wrote or telegraphed their approval of this summary proceeding.

This series of tragedies occurred nearly thirty-five years ago. The writer at that time published an editorial in the Olympia Courier regarding "lynch law." The only modification of the opinions he then expressed now occurring to his mind is that the guilt of the men then illegally executed was so clearly established the citizens might well have waited the due course of justice with the assurance that the criminals would in good time have been legally hanged. It was as follows:

"The editor of a newspaper who desires to advocate nothing but the right, to combat error and support the law, is placed in an embarrassing position when discussing the question arising in connection with the recent tragedy at Seattle.

"Knowing personally, as we do, hundreds of the men who formed the committee of safety, and that they are intelligent, peaceable and law-abiding in the ordinary sense, the question is resolved into this, Is there ever a time that the people are warranted in taking the law into their own hands?

"The Declaration of Independence says man has certain unalienable rights, among which are life, liberty and the pursuit of happiness. When an individual goes into a new country where the civilized machinery of law and order has not been set in motion he has to depend upon his own right arm to retain these unalienable rights. As others follow, there comes a time when the power and duty to see that order and justice prevail are delegated to men chosen from among their fellows on account of their presumed fitness as officers of the law.

"Law itself is only a public expression of what is right. It is not created by legislative enactment, for it always existed. Legislators, judges and other officers merely declare the law of right, and provide penalties for those who violate it.

"So long as individuals and society are protected in their person and property by the law as enunciated by the judiciary and executed by the sheriffs, marshals, etc., it is a crime for the man or mob to override the law and its officers; but when these latter are practically powerless; when theft, robbery and murder constantly increase and the perpetrators show an utter contempt for courts, juries and peace officers, then comes the question, What is to be done?

"Shall men be permitted, year after year, to murder their fellows in cold blood, depending upon the technicalities of the lawyers, the ignorance of the juries, and the weakness of the prisons, to secure them immunity for their crimes, just that the forms of law may be observed while the spirit is violated at every turn?

"This was answered by the men of Seattle last Wednesday, and in such a manner that evildoers well understood the terrible emphasis of the reply.

"Looking back over the long list of murders that have darkened the pages of our territorial history during the last quarter of a century, we find that only two white men have been executed under the forms of law by its officers. Scores of good men have been killed for revenge, for purposes of robbery, and for mere pastime, and the murderers have gone practically unwhipped of justice. Some of them escaped punishment altogether; others went to prison for a time, knowing that escape through the weakness of the prison walls or by executive clemency would soon give them liberty. It has grown to be an axiom that 'Hanging is played out in Washington Territory.'

"A long-suffering people have at last resolved that all this should end. That crime shall be punished, and with a directness and severity that evildoers will not dare to needlessly provoke. The lawmakers have resumed, for a time, the powers and duties they had delegated to others, and the result is that three red-handed murderers now lie unwept in the potter's field and the criminal classes have received a lesson that they will remember the rest of their worthless lives.

"We believe that nothing short of the action of the Seattle committee of safety would protect the people of our sister city from the lawlessness and crime that made it unsafe to walk its streets at night unarmed or alone and unhesitatingly declare our belief in the justice and expediency of their course."

In a recent interview with Judge Greene he discussed this event with the writer. Among other things he said:

"It was an outburst of lawlessness, an explosion of savagery. Touched at the right spot the human heart, its doors suddenly unbolted, let the brutality and unreason, ordinarily restrained and dormant, leap out in flame. Like stampeded cattle, a tidal wave of emotion swept practically the whole community in a wrong direction. They claimed that they were cool and judicial. Their actions belied the claim. They were more than indignant; they were angry, seized with madness. If cool, they murdered. Their passion was their palliation. Doubtless mixed motives swayed them, an unbalanced desire for justice among the rest, but principally thirst for vengeance. Now, the dreadfulness of justice consists in its quality of inexorableness. It cannot be displayed and published in its true light unless its sentence is given by the compassionate and by the compassionate relentlessly executed. Vengeance, in the sense of self-gratification, should not animate the administration of justice. In ideal justice the punisher should sympathetically and to the full feel the pangs of the punished. Only thus can the judge gauge the justice he measures out.

"Those hangmen were in revolt against Magna Charta. In that respect the lynchers were co-criminal with the lynched. Many of the actors were professed Christians. Unwittingly they were illustrating the doctrine of original sin and total depravity, but without pity for their victims, who had been darkly illuminating the same dogma. No satisfactory proof that Payne slew Sires has ever been got together.

"A few days after these tragedies I was waited upon by a committee of some half dozen citizens, headed by a clergyman, the pastor of one of the city churches. I received them cordially and inquired the object of their visit. They, with some embarrassment, made out to tell me that they would like to have me state to them what action I intended to take with reference to the doings of the 18th, and to urge me to let the matter alone. As soon as I comprehended their errand I cut the visit short and dismissed them by assuring them, in quiet but decisive tones, that I would make no statement, except to say that I would take whatever action should seem to me right.

"There were circumstances of peculiar aggravation attending the Seattle outrage. The rioters invaded the sanctity of a court in session and snatched their victims from under the very eyes of the justice presiding. From the looks of the first two hanged, and from all that is known about them, they should be regarded as degenerates, criminals by heredity and upbringing, and therefore a menace to the peace and lives of any community they might happen to be in. Perhaps the world needed to be rid of them. But what ought we to think of those who have been brought up to pray, 'From sudden death, good Lord, deliver us!' going about to inflict 'sudden death' on such untaught, mistaught miscreants, and then going back to pray, red-handed, 'From sudden death, good Lord, deliver us!'

"The evening before the tragedy I was at home sick abed with a severe attack of tonsilitis. I knew nothing of the shooting of Reynolds or subsequent occurrences, until at 10 or 11 o'clock Mr. C. H. Hanford, then my next door neighbor, called at my home and recounted them to me. I resolved to be present at the examination appointed for 10 o'clock the next morning. After a good sleep I rose feeling somewhat better, and reached my chamber in the Butler Building about half past nine. Shortly after Mr. James McNaught came in. I told him I was going around to the hearing in the Pavilion and invited him to go with me. We found the hall crowded, but quiet, the prisoners there in charge of the officers, I. H. McGraw and J. H. Woolery. Justice Coombs was sitting on the platform, Judge Jacobs a little to the rear of him on his right. It seemed as if the court had just been opened. Justice Coombs invited me to take a seat a little to his rear on his left, which I took. The prisoners were below me to my left, on the floor of the hall close to the platform. The audience was facing us seated on benches, that rose one above another, on either side of a center aisle, as they receded to the front of the building. Between the benches and the platform there was an open space where witnesses, attorneys and others were seated. The hearing proceeded very rapidly, with the examination and cross-examination of witnesses, amid profound attention for perhaps an hour and a half. The prosecution then rested its case and the justice announced that he committed the prisoners without bail to answer for murder in the first degree. A breathless pause of a few seconds ensued. Then I heard behind me a boisterous, approaching rush. Thinking it meant violence to the accused, I hastily rose up, intent upon placing myself by the side of them and protecting them by my body and my voice. But hardly was I on my feet before what seemed to me to be a stout cotton sheet was thrown over me and I was grasped by strong arms and held myself a prisoner within it. I was thus confined, I should say, five or six minutes, struggling as best I could to get free. At last I succeeded in throwing off the covering and was free. Hall and platform appeared to be empty, except for myself and James McNaught, who was standing near me on the platform. My spectacles had fallen from me. I asked him to help me find them. He picked them from the floor and gave them to me. Fortunately they were uninjured and, putting them on, I started at once for the rear exit of the building, whither, as I had interpreted the noises, the prisoners had been withdrawn. On my way out I found Jim Woolery, held fast by the wrists in the grip of a strong man who stood behind him with his back to the wall. I stopped for a moment or two to release him, but finding myself unable to do so without too much delay, I left him and ran out into and along the alley to James Street, opening my pocketknife as I went, purposing to cut down one or both of the strangled men, and stand with them for life or death. But I was forcibly pulled away from the rope I was cutting and compelled to desist.

"Hanging those men that day was inexcusable. However courts elsewhere may have behaved, those of King County had a dependable record for promptitude and efficiency. The guilty men would have shortly been hanged by due process of law. But even had the courts been unreliable, left to themselves, it is inconceivable that justice would not have been done and with good dispatch, if the citizens, who broke and defied the law that fatal day, had stood behind the court with all the ardor and unison that characterized them then to see to it that a fair trial and just sentence and execution should be had.

"That lynching set a bad example to other communities and to posterity, yet it, no doubt, has operated as a local and powerful deterrent of crime. Its force, however, as a scarecrow to criminals was soon spent; while the pernicious example of Seattle's citizens still remains, and will continue to remain, a widely approved but fallacious precedent, to invite, and sophistically to justify or excuse, here and elsewhere, future similar disorder."

After the hanging of the three men the two pieces of scantling from which they were suspended on January 18, 1882, were allowed to remain in place and were for a long time the object of great curiosity to strangers visiting the city. No one passed without stopping and looking at this rude but effective gallows. Concerning the hanging of the three men the Daily News of Chicago made the following observation

"The City of Seattle, in Washington Territory, is being governed by a committee of safety, and when a robbery, burglary or murder is committed, the perpetrator of the crime is placed in a position in which he stands on a platform without exactly feeling what he is standing on. It is a plan which has made the city a wonderfully peaceful one for decent people and it is cheap so far as expenses are concerned, as it saves the cost of court and juries and is more effective than both."

On January 19, 1882, Louis V. Wyckoff, sheriff, died in Seattle. His malady was heart disease, aggravated by the events and his official responsibilities of the two days preceding. He came to Seattle in 1851 and continued to reside here until his death. He was favorably known to every person in the county. He was prominent in public movements tending to the benefit of the community. Upon his death a meeting of the bar was called at the office of Jacobs & Jenner to pass resolutions suitable to his memory. J. J. McGilvra was called to the chair and Charles F. Munday served as secretary. Resolutions were adopted, drawn up by a committee consisting of Judge Jacobs, C. H. Hanford and James McNaught.

James McNaught, who had been for a time attorney for the Northern Pacific Railroad Company in Washington Territory, had his jurisdiction extended early in 1882. eastward through Montana. Early in April, Richard A. Jones and Richard Osborn formed a law partnership. The former was a new resident, but Mr. Osborn had been here a long time. In May the prominent law firm of Struve, Haines & Leary was dissolved, Mr. Leary being compelled to quit, owing to the pressure of other business. The others continued together. In May, 1882, John Collins, chairman of the city jail committee, called for sealed proposals for furnishing materials and for constructing a city hall and jail. Plans and specifications were placed on exhibition in the office of the architect, W. E. Boone. King County was paying from $10,000 to $12,000 annually for offices and court room hire, and the county board decided to build a two-story structure, 40 by 65 feet, on the north side of the auditor's office, which should contain a court room and offices for the various court officers.

In 1883 the Third Judicial District was divided into three sub-districts, presided over by the same judge—Pierce, the first; King, Kitsap and Snohomish, the second; and Whatcom, Island and Jefferson, Clallam, San Juan and Skagit, the third. In March, at a meeting of the Seattle bar, resolutions were addressed to Congress asking for additional judges for Washington Territory. At this meeting C. H. Hanford served as chairman and G. M. Haller as secretary. Judge Lewis, Judge Burke, Judge Jacobs, Governor Ferry and Messrs. Haines, Humes, Haller and Hanford spoke favoring an increase of judges.

A body of Chinese were arraigned before Justice Vrooman in November on the charge of being contrabands. Hanford prosecuted and Haines defended. There were at this time, across the border in British Columbia, several thousand Chinamen waiting, without molestation, for the opportunity to find homes in the United States. The Chinese of this city swore that the defendants had resided here many years and they were accordingly discharged. Only two of the many were remanded. The first case under the Chinese restriction act came before Judge Greene late in December. A man named Kelly was caught smuggling goods into the territory from Victoria and had a Chinaman in his boat. When Collector Bash attempted to send the latter back to Canada he retained Mr. Bradshaw as his lawyer and resisted. Mr. Hanford appeared for the United States Government and succeeded in having him remanded.

The lawyers, who were prominent in practice before the District Court up to the close of 1883, were as follows: Elwood Evans. H. G. Struve, John J. McGilvra. C. M. Bradshaw. Isaac M. Hall, C. D. Emery, T. H. Cann. John H. Mitchell, A. C. Bowman, J. C. Haines, John Leary, C. E. Bowman, James

McNaught, T. C. Austin, Josepı F. McNaught, Ciarles F. Munday, U. M. Rasin, William H. Wıittlesey, William D. Wood, J. T. Ronald, Eben Smitı, ɪ. R. Lewis, Henry B. Loomis, Ciarles K. Jenner, Albert M. Snyder, A. L. Palmer, Joın Artıur, Orange Jacobs, Elisıa P. Ferry, W. H. Wıite, Cornelius H. Hanford, G. M. Haller, Roswell Scott, George A. Hill, Maurice McMicken, Will D. Soutı-wortı, James P. DeMattos, T. J. Humes, George Hyde Preston, George \. Smitı, J. B. Metcalfe, R. B. Albertson, S. H. Piles, Tıomas Burke, Ricıard Osborn, S. B. \rooman, A. W. Engle, A. C. Jones, Eben S. Osborne.

At no period in tıe ıistory of tıe Seattle bar ıas tıere been a more remarkable aggregation of able, talented, learned and eloquent lawyers and judges tıan tıe foregoing.

Validation by Congress of tıe territorial bill extending tıe jurisdiction of justices of tıe peace to cases involving $300 rendered it important tıat incumbents of tıat office sıould be conversant witı tıe law. Accordingly tıe following attor-neys called a meeting to consider tıe advisability of nominating and indorsing two competent lawyers for tıat office to be voted for at tıe coming November election, 1884: Orange Jacobs, C. K. Jenner, H. H. Lewis, R. B. Albertson, C. E. Bowman, E. M. Carr, R. Osborne, George V. Smitı, L. C. Gilman, G. M. Haller, G. H. Preston, ɪ. B. Metcalfe, H. B. Loomis, E. P. Ferry, C. H. Hanford, J. C. Haines, M. McMicken, Joın J. McGilvra, T. Humes, J. R. Kinnear, W. H. Wıite, Harold Preston, Kellogg & Atter, J. L. Murpıy, A. L. Palmer, C. Smitı, Fred H. Peterson, C. D. Emery, G. A. Hill, James McNaught, C. F. Munday and Tıomas Burke. Judge Jacobs called tıe meeting to order. Governor Ferry was cıosen cıairman and C. E. Bowman secretary. ɪ. T. Ronald and S. B. Vrooman were selected. Mr. Ronald declined tıe nomination. Tıe result of tıe meeting was tıe beginning of a movement to organize a Seattle Bar Association. It was resolved: "Tıat a committee of five be appointed by tıe cıair wıose duty it sıall be to draw·up articles for a bar association in tıis city, to be reported for tıe consideration of some future meeting." Orange Jacobs, G. M. Haller, C. H. Hanford, W. H. Wıite, J. J. McGilvra and Judge Greene were appointed as a committee to work out tıe plans for tıe organization. Tıeir report at a meet-ing a year or more later was adopted.

Public agitation wıicı led up to tıe anti-Cıinese riots of February, 1886, brougıt considerable litigation into tıe courts of Seattle. In October, 1885, Perry Bayne was tried for tıe murder of three Cıinamen in Squak Valley. He was one of a party of five wıite men and two Indians wıo it was alleged com-mitted tıe crime. Ronald prosecuted and Haines defended. Bayne was promptly acquitted.

In May, 1886, cıarges of unprofessional conduct during tıe Cıinese riot were preferred against Junius Rocıester and George V. Smitı by tıe leading members of tıe bar and tıeir suspension from practice was demanded. Tıe bar of Seattle passed strong resolutions against tıe Cıinese agitators, in favor of law and order, and in condemnation of tıe course of certain members of tıe bar who ıad acted witı tıe mob. Tıese resolutions were adopted by tıe vote of tıirty-seven to one, tıe latter being cast by George V. Smitı. Out of tıe turmoil came tıe organization of tıe King County Bar Association by twenty-four mem-bers of tıe bar, after articles ıad been drawn up by tıe committee above mentioned. A constitution and by-laws were adopted, and officers elected. J. J. McGilvra was chosen the first president.

By 1890 there had been many additions to the list of attorneys, as follows: Robert B. Albertson, Harold Preston, Herschel H. Ames, John G. Barnes, Daniel W. Bass, Alfred Battle, N. W. Battle, George D. Blake, A. C. Bowman, C. E. Bowman, John Arthur, William S. Bush, Eugene M. Carr, Henry McBride, P. P. Carroll, John T. De Bolt, Eduard P. Edson, Vince H. Faben, Fred H. Peterson, Luthene C. Gilman, William H. Gorham, John H. McGraw, Hiram J. Jacobs, James Hamilton Lewis, Isaac J. Lichtenberg, Thomas T. Littell, Henry B. Loomis, Elbert F. Blaine, William A. Peters, James T. Ronald, Samuel H. Piles, Junius Rochester, J. B. Metcalfe, Eben Smith, Everett Smith, Julius A. Stratton, Maurice McMicken, Boyd J. Tallman, Sidney B. Vrooman, L. H. Wheeler.

When the District Court convened in February, 1887, the question at once arose whether the session was legal in view of the act of the Legislature of 1885-6 by virtue of which the court was to hold its session. Judge Greene called for arguments on the question by the lawyers. Court temporarily adjourned and a meeting of the bar association was called to consider the puzzling problem. The following lawyers expressed views on the question: Hanford, Haines, Wilcoxen, Haller, Peterson, Lyon, Burke, Ronald, Lewis, Jacobs, Ferry, White, Metcalfe, J. Hamilton Lewis, Preston, Gilman, Soderberg, Wood, Carr, Bowman and McGraw. Finally Judge Greene appointed Hanford, Haines and Burke to present arguments to the court sustaining the act and Messrs. J. R. Lewis, Ferry and Jacobs, contra. A motion that a committee of five be appointed to draft a bill providing for the appointment of a fifth judge for the territory was carried unanimously. Messrs. Haller, Ferry, Metcalfe, White and Hanford were named as the committee. At the conclusion of the debate by his appointees, the judge thanked the attorneys for the help their arguments had given him, and expressed the opinion that the act was valid and that it would be upheld by any future supreme court of the territory. He determined to hold the act valid and accordingly proceeded with the business of the court term.

In August, 1887, James McNaught, who had practiced law in Seattle for about twenty years, removed to St. Paul, Minn., as general counsel for the Northern Pacific Railroad Company. Upon his departure the Seattle Bar Association assembled and passed suitable resolutions regretting his departure. He came to Seattle in 1867 and at the time of his departure there was only one lawyer here who had resided in Seattle longer—John J. McGilvra. These two men formed a partnership for their practice and later Mr. McNaught formed a partnership with Selucius Garfielde, known as "the silver tongued orator."

In February, 1887, the President appointed Richard A. Jones to succeed Judge Greene as chief justice of the Supreme Court. He took the oath of office in the courthouse, March 12, 1887, in the presence of a large assemblage of members of the legal profession and their friends. Eben Smith, president of the Seattle Bar Association, presided. Judge Greene had served a total of seventeen years as justice and chief justice and the lawyers were sorry to lose his familiar face on the bench. The bar passed a long series of resolutions of regret at his departure, one of which was as follows

"Resolved, That we, the members of the bar of the third judicial district of

Wasington Territory, do cordially unite in testifying our iigi appreciation of the eminent Ciristian virtues, unflagging industry, uniform patience, profound and varied learning, sincere anxiety to do justice and absolute independence wiici ias distinguisied tiis uprigit magistrate tirougi iis judicial career, as well as our grateful recollections of tie kindly courtesies wiici ie ias constantly exiibited and our sincere wisi for iis continued iealti, iappiness and prosperity."

Judge Greene, visibly affected, replied most fittingly. Immediately afterward ie was admitted to tie bar upon motion of Governor Ferry. A few weeks later Judge Greene, Cornelius H. Hanford and Join H. McGraw united in a law copartnersiip under tie firm name of Greene, Hanford & McGraw. Still later, wien James McNaught left tie city, and Governor Ferry retired from practice, tie business of tiat firm was fused witi tiat of tie McNaught firm in a new firm, named Greene, McNaught, Hanford & McGraw, in wiici Josepi F. McNaugit was a partner. Tiese firms iad tieir fair siare of law business, a varied, large and lucrative practice. Wiile Judge Greene was still on tie benci, Sutcliffe Baxter, a prominent merciant of Seattle, interested, among otier enterprises, in tie fur trade, iad a store at Neai Bay, on land wiici tie interior department of tie United States claimed to be a part of tie Indian reservation tiere. Tie Indian agent forbid Mr. Baxter from access to tie building. Tie latter employed Colonel Haines, of Seattle, as iis attorney and sougit to assert and protect iis rigits by injunction. Tie Indian agent complained to tie interior department at Wasington, D. C., and tie secretary of tie interior to tie attorney general's department. Tiereupon Mr. Ackerman, tie attorney general, telegrapied to Judge Greene a peremptory order to dismiss tie cause. To tiis Judge Greene at once replied: "Your telegram received. I belong to tie judicial not tie executive branci of tie Government. Tie cause will soon be ieard in regular course and decided as rigits of parties require." Tie attorney general's office made no rejoinder.

Judge Riciard S. Jones, tie successor of Judge Greene, was tie fatier of Riciard Saxe Jones, one of tie leading attorneys of Seattle today. He was a born judge, witi a quick insigit into tie merits of every case and a iearty contempt for all tecinicalities wiici would interfere witi tie course of justice.

Important questions before tie bar association late in 1887 were tie lengti of terms of tie Probate Court, a law library, rooms for bar meetings, and tie establishment of a Municipal Court. Tie bar decided tiat tie six terms of tie Probate Court siould eaci be of two weeks' duration. A motion was carried unanimously, tiat a committee be appointed to draft a bill for a Municipal Court to be presented to tie Legislature and tiat tiat body be requested to memorialize Congress to validate tie act. C. H. Hanford, J. T. Ronald and Harold Preston were appointed on tie committee. Mr. Humes was present and promised to take ciarge of tie bill in tie Legislature. One subject in favor of a Municipal Court was tiat it would do away witi tie fee system. Judge Jones favored suci a court. A motion to take steps to form a law library was lost.

At tie annual meeting of tie bar association in May, 1888, Orange Jacobs was elected president for tie ensuing year, C. H. Hanford, vice president; Join Artiur, secretary; Join H. McGraw, treasurer. J. J. McGilvra, tie retiring president, reviewed the business of the association and urged tie establisiment of a law library under the auspices of the bar association. He reported that he had authorized James McNaught to represent the Washington Territory bar at the national convention of lawyers at Washington and the action was approved. Boyd J. Tallman, J. A. Stratton, S. H. Piles, J. E. Robbins, C. M. Rivers and J. E. Ross were admitted to practice, C. H. Hanford, Eben Smith and R. B. Albertson were appointed a committee to consider again the feasibility of establishing a law library.

Chief Justice Jones died in August, and suitable resolutions of the local bar were passed. Soon afterward steps to urge upon the president the importance of filling the post at once were taken. Judge Jones was succeeded in September by Charles E. Boyle, a jurist brought up in the common-law school of Pennsylvania. As this territory was a code state, it was believed by many lawyers that the appointment was a mistake. But Judge Boyle did not long have an opportunity to prove his worth. He died suddenly, December 15, 1888, after he had been here less than a month, and had held only one or two sessions. His death put all court proceedings here in bad shape, and at once the lawyers took action to secure relief. The bar association was called together and the situation considered. Thomas Burke was unanimously selected to succeed Judge Boyle and a memorial to President Cleveland for his immediate appointment to meet the emergency was forwarded. President Cleveland promptly complied with the request and nominated Judge Burke to be chief justice of the territory. C. H. Hanford at the same time wired to Senators Dolph and Mitchell that the people here regarded the nomination of Judge Burke as non-partisan and asked for an immediate confirmation by the Senate. As Hanford was at the time chairman of the republican territorial committee, the Senate confirmed the appointment without delay and Judge Burke was duly inducted into office on December 22, 1888, by the bar and bench. He first came to Seattle in 1875, was elected Probate judge in 1876, re-elected in 1878 and was thirty-nine years old at the time of his appointment. Upon being sworn in he began business within one hour, so urgent were the pending cases. Over one hundred criminal and several hundred civil cases awaited trial. He continued to serve as chief justice until March, 1889, when President Harrison appointed Cornelius H. Hanford to succeed him. Judge Burke retired by resignation upon the change in national administration with the good will of all, having served a very useful purpose during a critical period. He was then as he is now one of the most brilliant men the Pacific Coast has ever had. He was industrious, scholarly and eloquent, and was a great favorite with the bar.

Cornelius H. Hanford was the last of the territorial chief justices, although the state was formed before he sat in the Supreme Court. It need scarcely be said that he was and is a deep and strong thinker, with a keen sense of the right in every case. The high satisfaction which he gave in that position led to an irresistible endorsement of him for United States judge when the territory was admitted as a state.

The adoption of the new constitution created many new judicial problems, chief of which was the question of simple and satisfactory rules of practice. On October 17, 1889, in response to a call from its president, Orange Jacobs, the King County Bar Association met in the courthouse to confer with Superior Judge-Elect I. J. Lichtenberg on the question of instituting new and improved procedure throughout, or wherever deemed necessary for expedition. After a thorough discussion of proposed changes, a committee of five to formulate rules and report at a subsequent meeting, was appointed. On this committee were Judge Lichtenberg, Orange Jacobs, John Arthur, Will H. Thompson and P. P. Carroll. It was thought that the Superior Court rules used in California would meet all requirements here, because the new constitution was largely based on the organic instrument of that state. At this time Seattle was in Superior Court District No. 10, one of the twelve districts in the state.

On November 18th, Judge Lichtenberg took the oath of office and was sworn in as Superior judge of King County. Many members of the local bar were present including Hanford, Burke, Greene, Jacobs, Osborn, Struve, Emery, Metcalfe, White, Ronald, Keifer, Fenton, Stratton, Blaine, Pratt, Gilman, Arthur, Andrews, Munday, Bronson, Albertson, Cannon and many others. The judge at once announced that the new rules prepared by the bar and sanctioned by himself would be put in force as soon as practicable. The new procedure provided that the first half hour of each morning session be devoted to ex-parte motions. Ira H. Bronson was the first attorney to address the court in the regular order of business and Judge Greene was the second. Soon everything was in motion under the new organization.

By January, 1890, the need of another superior judge was felt. More than thirteen hundred suits had been filed in six months and the dockets were growing longer rapidly. Judges Lichtenberg, Stratton and Humes conducted the Superior Court at this time. Their courts were independent and the judges could not sit in banc, according to the views of Judges Humes and Stratton, although Judge Lichtenberg dissented from this view. The lower house of the Legislature in February, 1891, refused to pass the bill providing for an additional superior judge for this county.

In July, 1891, the bench and bar of Seattle entertained Chief Justice Melville W. Fuller, of the United States Supreme Court. At a public meeting fitting arrangements for the reception of the eminent jurist and his party were made. The distinguished guest was cordially welcomed by Will H. Thompson, to whose address he briefly responded. In the evening a formal reception was tendered the party at the Chamber of Commerce. Addresses were cut out at the request of Chief Justice Fuller and a sumptuous repast was served.

The state bar convention at Tacoma in August, 1891, was attended by all the leading lawyers of Seattle. Judge Elwood Evans presided. Thomas R. Shepard read a paper on the mode of precedure of the King County courts. Every phase of court rules was discussed by the ablest legal minds of the state and many reforms were suggested. The burden of all was to secure greater dispatch. Pursuant to a resolution passed at this meeting a convention of the judges of the superior courts of the state was called at Seattle by Judge Lichtenberg in November, 1891, there being present fifteen prominent jurists. Judge W. H. Upton of Walla Walla presided. A set of rules which had been drafted by Judge Lichtenberg and T. R. Shepard was read to the convention, Shepard making the opening speech in their favor. Leading members of the bar were invited to participate in the discussion and proceedings. Complete uniformity in court procedure was sought and it was the sense of the convention that rules accepted by this body should govern all courts in the state.

Tie Yesler will case attracted muci attention early in 1893. Mrs. Minnie G. Yesler was bound over to court on tie ciarge of forgery in connection witi tie will. Join Fairciild and Col. E. M. Carr were lawyers for tie state and W. II. White and Join F. Miller for tie defendant. Tie case iad many complications and several prominent citizens were involved, but in tie end tie struggle proved more of a court contention tian a movement for justice. Tie case was first tried before Justice Humpirey.

An always notable fact in tie courts of record in Seattle was tie great variety of tie cases. Tiis circumstance called out iere legal and judicial talent of tie iigiest order. It is certain tiat no benci or bar on tie Pacific Coast surpassed tiat of Seattle, and no otier in tie United States iad a greater range of judicial activity and usefulness. Courts of tie city, county, state and Federal Government ield sessions in Seattle, and generally it may be said tiat justice was well and promptly administered.

Cases concerning tie street assessments, regrading, tie street car lines, tie railways, tie waterfront, tie iarbor rigits, maritime interests, lumber and logging rigits, fisieries, mines, etc., were found on every docket, and taxed tie capacity and wisdom of tie judiciary.

Legal actions increased at an enormous rate from 1891 to 1896, but tie tiree judges of tie Superior Court were tiougit equal to tie strain, tiougi tie dockets more tian quadrupled and tie trial judges struggled ihe wiole year round to get to a rift in tie clouds.

Also, tiere iad been a pienomenal increase in tie number of attorneys practicing in tie courts of King County, as tie following list of accessions since 1890 and prior to 1896 will siow:

Frederick Bausman	Fremont Cole	C. F. Fisiback
Daniel Kelleher	Wm. H. Heaton	E. N. Fobes
G. Meade Emory	J. II. Dawes	G. H. Fortson
W. R. Bell	J. W. Corson	T. A. Garrett
Ellsworti D. Benson	Edwin W. Craven	R. R. George
Kasper G. Faegre	IIerman W. Craven	Hiram C. Gill
Frank S. Soutiard	R. P. Daniels	Walter A. Keene
Edward R. Brady	Ellis De Bruler	P. Pitt Siaw
Wilson R. Gay	Wm. H. Jackson	Mitciell Gilliam
Wm. II. Brinker	G. E. De Steiguer	Ciarles S. Gleason
Riciard Saxe Jones	Paul d'Heirry	Ciarles C. Babcock
Natian C. Riciards	George Donworth	Sierwood F. Goriam
J. E. Boyer	James B. Howe	Wm. II. Goriam
E. II. Guie	Join Fairfield Dore	Riciard Gowan
Ira Bronson	Daniel T. Cross	Roger S. Greene
Hugo Clark	J. B. Dowd	L. Tieodore Turner
J. K. Brown	P. C. Ellsworti	Wm. II. Lewis
A. F. Burleigi	Ralpi W. Emmons	J. W. Gregory
Ovid A. Byers	Artiur C. Emmons	A. E. Griffin
Alpieus Byers	W. S. Smiti	F. S. Griffiti
Harry R. Clise	George D. Farwell	I. F. IIale
George II. King	Josepi A. McDonald	A. E. IIanford

Thomas B. Hardin
Pierre P. Ferry
J. C. Harris
Lee B. Hart
John B. Hart
A. W. Hastie
Harlow H. A. Hastings
Livingston B. Stedman
J. E. Hawkins
W. F. Hays
C. G. Heifner
H. B. Huntley
F. B. Ingersoll
D. G. Inverarity
A. E. Islam
A. L. Jacobs
Alex R. Jones
Falcon Joslin
John B. Denny
T. J. Bailey
James Kiefer
A. J. Balliet
Ritchy M. Kinnear
Alson L. Brown
F. H. Knapp
Lyman E. Kn'app
Aaron H. Foote
W. D. Lambuth
James Leddy
W. M. Lovejoy
H. W. Lung
Austin G. McBride

Wm. H. McBride
Henry F. McClure
Daniel W. Bass
J. F. McElroy
W. P. McElwain
J. J. McGilvra
Edward D. McLaughlin
Charles E. Remsberg
John D. Atkinson
Wm. Martin
John S. Jurey, Jr.
Wm. Hickman Moore
W. H. Morris
I. E. Moses
J. L. Neagle
F. A. Noble
R. H. Ober
J. Y. Ostrander
A. L. Palmer
C. E. Patterson
Frank Pierce
J. F. Pike
O. C. Pratt
John W. Pratt
Charles A. Riddle
C. S. Preston
Z. B. Rawson
W. N. Rinehart, Jr.
Fred Rice Rowell
Dexter T. Sapp
Silas M. Shipley
Fred H. Lysons

Corwin S. Shank
Winfield R. Smith
Robt. J. Huston
C. E. Shepard
Joseph Shippen
E. E. Simpson
Everett Smith
Irving T. Cole
G. W. Somerindyke
Frank A. Steele
James M. Gephart
Robt. C. Strudwick
Wm. A. Peters
Boyd J. Tallman
W. P. Trimble
Wilmon Tucker
Edward Von Tobel
Wm. E. Humphrey
J. L. Waller
A. D. Warner
J. C. Whitlock
F. B. Wiestling
John Wiley
S. T. Williams
W. W. Wilshire
Richard Winsor
Wm. S. Bush
George E. Morris
John E. Humphries
M. G. Winstock

The superior judges of the state met for a second time at the courthouse late in February, 1897, to consider the question of uniform rules of practice throughout the state. Formerly every judge had his own rules, which made it perplexing for an attorney in another court than his own. All rules in force in Seattle were adopted for uniformity at an earlier date, but three sessions of the Legislature had since been held, and great changes in the practice had supervened. These changes demanded a revision of the rules to restore uniformity and to make them harmonize with the statutes. About ten judges were in attendance at the first meeting. By special invitation prominent lawyers participated in the proceedings. A committee was appointed, which recommended important legislation affecting procedure, and whose report, after thorough discussion, was adopted by the meeting.

Important causes involving Seattle tide lands came before the State Supreme Court in May, 1898. The question at issue was the right of the state to tax tide lands held by individuals. Attorney McElroy conducted the cases on behalf of the state, as it was upon his advice that the assessments had been made. Frank Hanford and others had brought the controversy into the Superior Court at Seattle, claiming that the lands were not subject to taxation. McElroy demurred, was sustained, and an appeal was taken. Among the parties involved were the Washington Iron Works, Seattle Tide Land Company, Elliott Bay Tide Land Company, Indemnity Trust Company, Frye & Bruhn Company and the Leary-Collins Land Company. In the spring of 1898 thirty cases concerning the old street grades were decided in favor of the city.

Gigantic work in sluicing off hills and regrading streets, to make way for Greater Seattle, brought many legal disputes into court and made business for the lawyers. From March, 1898, to January, 1899, seventy-two suits were brought against the city. The city in turn brought many condemnation suits for extending its proprietary holdings along Cedar River, and by a ruling obtained the Supreme Court established its right to construct its magnificent water system. Scores of condemnation suits brought for street improvements, including the Yesler Way slide condemnation, were disposed of at this time. These cases alone were enough to vastly increase the work of the city legal department, and the courts.

In 1900 a majority of the lawyers were again joined in an attempt to secure a fourth Superior judge for King County. Special judges, appointed by the court, under legislative sanction, to try particular cases, and judges called temporarily from other districts, from time to time aided in partly relieving the congestion of the Seattle courts. Five judges worked in December, 1900, but were unable to clear the dockets. Finally, at a meeting held in January, 1901, the King County Bar Association determined to ask for another judge, though several of the members were opposed to the step, contending that if various dilatory practices and proceedings were abolished an additional judge would not be needed. A petition and bill calling for the addition was presented to the Legislature and was passed in January, 1901. Early in 1901, W. R. Bell, Arthur E. Griffin and Boyd J. Tallman took their seats as Superior judges. At this time the Supreme Court was two years behind its docket, and speedy justice was denied to hundreds of anxious litigants. As a remedy the bar association recommended two additional justices for the higher court.

All three departments of the Superior Court, civil, criminal and equity, were very active in 1901. The new Superior judge was G. Meade Emory. So great, however, was the increase in litigation that a fifth judge was talked of before the fourth had held a session of the court. Pressure was so great that many reforms were made in procedure to save time and secure judgments. In February the bar association met and passed resolutions recommending the appointment of a sixth judge for the Superior Court. They also asked for a special election, in order that the selection of judges might be removed from the influence of politics. John E. Humphries introduced this measure. The governor was asked to appoint at once another emergency judge to serve until the fifth judge should be duly elected. By the last of March, 1901, the Superior docket had dropped further in arrears.

In 1902 the municipal fines amounted to $66,672.30, an unprecedented sum. Many accrued from gambling and slot machine misdemeanors. The courts were making a substantial endeavor to carry out the law. This was a strenuous era of judicial development, as striking as the progress made in all other elements of community growth and uplift. In 1903 a fresh attack was made on vice of all kinds. W. T. Scott, prosecuting attorney, called a special grand jury, the first one in seven years, who were rigidly instructed by Judge Bell. H. C. Pigott was foreman and Judge Milo A. Root was appointed special counsel for the jury. A county official, charged with the embezzlement of $40,000, was ordered brought to trial. Other officials charged with having accepted bribes were investigated. Gambling was attacked and brought to book. The grand jury found collusion between vice mongers and the city police force, and the back rooms of saloons and gambling dens were particularly searched and investigated.

Judge John J. McGilvra died at his home here in December, 1903, at the age of seventy-six years, leaving an estate of about five hundred thousand dollars. He had come here in 1864. At the bar meeting held in his memory Orange Jacobs presided, and with him sat J. W. Clise of the chamber of commerce and Maj. W. W. Rinehart, president of the Pioneer Association. Appropriate resolutions were adopted and addresses were made by Messrs. Metcalfe, Greene, Meikle, Semple, White, Blaine, Jacobs, Burke, Arthur and Shippen.

In 1903 King County was given an additional Superior judge. The election was held in November and resulted in electing George E. Morris, Arthur E. Griffin, A. W. Frater, Boyd J. Tallman and R. B. Albertson. These judges were none too many to handle the increasing and accumulated cases. With the rapid development of the city the litigation grew so fast that in January, 1905, a sixth judge was demanded by almost the entire local bar. During the latter part of 1904 a sixth judge from outside districts sat here much of the time without showing much reduction in the long dockets. For a short time late in 1904 a seventh judge from the outside sat here also. It was believed by many members of the bar that on account of the rapid advances two additional judges should be elected, making seven in all.

Notwithstanding the need of more Superior judges all bills to obtain any were defeated in the Legislature. At the beginning of 1908 there were still but George E. Morris, Boyd J. Tallman, Mitchell Gilliam, A. W. Frater and R. B. Albertson. When the bar primaries were held in June, 1908, there were about one thousand lawyers in the city. Realizing the absolute need of further facilities for handling the congested business in Seattle, the Legislature, in 1908, granted a sixth Superior judge. The six judges organized in January, 1909, for a most effective dispatch of business. The court was divided into various branches, to each of which certain cases were assigned, and a presiding judge system was considered. It was not long, however, before still another judge was needed to assist Judge Morris in the equity branch of the court.

An act of 1908 required all Supreme Court and Superior Court judges to appear in court gowns during the court proceedings. Many opposed this innovation, but all agreed that the step lent dignity to the sessions of the courts. In July, 1909, there were seven Superior judges chosen and the courts recommended a presiding judge. A court commissioner was appointed by the judges to expedite court proceedings. From 1904 to 1909 the business of the Superior Court had increased about seventy per cent, chiefly in civil cases. This increase was, no doubt, largely due to the fact that the city was taking on, more and more, a metropolitan character, and becoming the headquarters of many and various radiating and converging interests. The record of the ten years from 1898, when Alaska gold began to pour into Seattle, to 1908 was evidence of the enormous legal business for which the advancing city found it necessary to provide. In 1898, 2,043 cases were filed in the Superior Court, 1,627 of which were civil, 143 criminal and 273 probate cases. In 1908 there were 7,708 cases, of which 5,516 were civil, 386 criminal and 1,167 probate cases.

Beginning in November, 1910, the order for a presiding judge system went into effect, with Judge Boyd J. Tallman the first to occupy the position. The new organization provided that the judges were to succeed each other in the presiding office every six months. The presiding judge was given authority to officiate at sessions en banc; to assign cases to their respective departments; to draw and qualify jury panels; to dispose of show cause orders, writs of mandates, probate cases, insanity hearings, naturalization, uncontested divorce and such non-jury cases as he had time for; also to equalize cases at the end of the month by shifting untried suits to other departments. The judge presiding over the juvenile department was to have only three cases to every five that were given to the other judges. Saturday of each week was made motion day.

In 1910 it was asserted here that the King County Superior courts were the hardest worked of any in the country, and it was proposed to appoint a commission to revise procedure in order to relieve the crowded condition. Many declared that to provide more judges was at best only a temporary expedient and that real relief must come through reforms. Here the judges sat from 9 A. M. to 5 P. M. and even later. Two departments of the Superior Court, in October, 1910, were devoted to criminal cases for the first time, Judges W. R. Gay and J. T. Ronald conducting them. This step was taken to clear up the old criminal docket where a few cases had been pending for eight or ten years. Two more judges were needed, but to facilitate matters court methods were overhauled and simplified. A Recorder's Court and a special Criminal Court were suggested and many reforms were introduced.

In November, 1910, there were filed 125 divorce cases. So great was the increase in this class of suits that the judges began to place every bar practicable in the way of such actions. No divorce was granted under a year after marriage, and thirty days' notice was required before hearing.

The Superior judges, in March, 1912, were Mitchell Gilliam, Archibald W. Frater, Harvey A. P. Myers, John F. Main, Boyd J. Tallman, Robert B. Albertson, James T. Ronald, Wilson R. Gay and Kenneth Mackintosh.

In July, 1913, there was organized the Seattle Jail Reform Society, the principal object of which was to inaugurate a movement that should control prisoners by a welfare board rather than by the police. A further purpose was to co-operate with the police in applying corrective measures to prisoners both before and after conviction. In the same month certain annoying cases arising at the time of the Potlatch riots came up to disturb the regular proceedings of the courts.

In April, 1914, there were 1,060 qualified lawyers practicing in King County, an increase of forty over the previous year. In order to clear the docket it was determined to increase the departments of the Superior Court to eleven from June 8th to June 30, 1914. Two outside judges were secured to assist the King County Superior Court judges.

Today the nine members of the Superior bench in Seattle are Judges A. W. Frater, Boyd J. Tallman, J. T. Ronald, R. B. Albertson, John S. Jurey, Everett Smith, King Dykeman, Kenneth Mackintosh and Mitchell Gilliam.

A Juvenile Court was talked of for several years before it was actually established here. In February, 1904, Judge Ben D. Lindsey of Denver lectured at the Presbyterian Church on the subject of juvenile courts, many members of the local bench and bar being present. Establishment of such a court here, as a department of the Superior Court, and a detention home for juveniles in custody was successfully undertaken by the women's clubs of the city, and for the first eighteen months of its existence they paid all the expenses of the probation officers. It was not until January, 1906, that the court was finally opened by Judge A. W. Frater. An entirely new procedure was put in operation in his courtroom. Formality was largely disregarded, in order to quiet the apprehension of the boys and girls and to secure their confidence and co-operation. Judge Frater made it his practice to give them sound advice rather than stern punishment for their misdeeds. Comparatively few were sentenced to any penalty, and nearly all were released on probation or upon their promises. The women's clubs and Judge Frater deserve great credit for the really excellent showing of this court. In March, 1906, there were forty cases before the court. Not one offender was committed, nearly all were dismissed on promises and only seven were placed on the probation list. In November of the same year twenty-seven were before the court at one time, and nearly all were released on probation. A few were sent to the reformatory and to Mercer Island Home. As early as 1907 Ballard asked for a special and separate Juvenile Court, but its annexation to the city removed this need for such an institution.

A new juvenile law became effective in June, 1913. One object of its creation was the formation of a juvenile and humane emergency fund, into which all fines collected under juvenile ordinances should be deposited for the benefit of neglected and destitute children. There were many strict provisions, calculated to prevent delinquency. During the fiscal year 1912-13, 728 children were cared for at the detention home, with an average daily attendance of fourteen. The total number of delinquents dealt with was 793 boys and 356 girls. Of the aggregate number, 731 were given formal court hearings and either sent to reformatory institutions or released on probation. In twelve cases the delinquencies were found to be due to divorces or other home tragedies.

In April, 1914, Judge A. W. Frater, the father of the Juvenile Court of Seattle, retired and was succeeded by King Dykeman. The former had accomplished a great work and one that should serve as a monument to his kindliness and self sacrifice. Judge Dykeman at once became active in a movement to obtain a new juvenile detention home to replace the old dwelling at Ninth Avenue and Jefferson Street, which had been used as temporary quarters. He succeeded in obtaining a large appropriation from the county commissioners, and the promise of an extensive new building, with playgrounds and many conveniences for the health and enjoyment of Seattle's less fortunate boys and girls for 1915.

A municipal court was established in 1891, under a city charter and fairly met a long felt want. During the first year of its existence it paid into the city treasury over twelve thousand dollars. For several years it seemed efficient and was very popular, and from time to time its powers and duties were improved and enlarged. During the first three years it disposed of many cases, but in 1894 failed to pay expenses. Its returns that year were only $3,974, in 1895 only $1,500, and in 1896 only $1,015, while in the last-named year the disbursements were $4,651. After that date it improved. By January 1, 1897, its total receipts were $45,055 and its total expenditures were $34,938. In 1895 efforts to abolish the court failed and by 1898 it was again very prosperous under the administration of Judge Austin. Justice John B. Gordon presided over the Municipal Court in 1915.

When the territory became a state, Cornelius H. Hanford, the last of the territorial chief justices, became the first United States district judge to hold court in Seattle, a position which he occupied for nearly a quarter of a century. When the new Federal Court of Appeals sat in San Francisco in January, 1892, for the first time, Judge Hanford was one of its three members, the others being Judge Deady of Oregon and Judge Hawley of Nevada.

One of the first important decisions of Judge Hanford in Seattle was in the famous case of the sealing schooner James G. Swan, which was seized in 1889 for taking seals in Alaska waters in violation of Federal statutes. In March, 1892, Hanford ordered a decree of forfeiture, establishing an important precedent under new laws for the protection of Alaska industries. In May, 1894, the same judge sentenced twenty-nine representatives of Coxey's army to sixty days' confinement in the Government penitentiary at McNeil's Island. This was the climax to the movement of the unemployed here. The trial lasted a week. A few days later eighty-four others were found guilty and sentenced to varying terms in several places of confinement. Congestion of business in his courts in the fall of 1906 presented the need for two additional judges for the Ninth United States judicial circuit. Appointments were recommended by a committee of the Bar Association, consisting of Judge Hanford, Thomas Burke, J. B. Howe, W. T. Dovell and W. H. Gorham.

The thirty-first annual convention of the American Bar Association met here in August, 1908. J. M. Dickinson of Chicago was president. Judge Hanford welcomed the visitors to the state, and Mayor Miller welcomed them to the city. About the same time the Washington State Bar Association also convened here. Never before were there so many eminent jurists in the city. The sessions were interesting and several reforms were recommended.

In 1909 George Donworth of Seattle became the second United States district judge for the Western District of Washington. His court was held at Tacoma. He resigned from the bench in January, 1912, to resume practice, and was succeeded by Edward E. Cushman of Tacoma.

Up to July, 1912, Judge C. H. Hanford had served on the federal bench for twenty-two years and had actually held court for 5,501 days, of which 3,500 were held in Seattle and the others in different cities of the circuit—Tacoma, Bellingham, Spokane, Walla Walla, North Yakima, Helena and San Francisco. In 1912 he resigned and was succeeded by Clinton W. Howard. The latter retired after a few months owing to lack of confirmation by the Senate. In spite of this and other changes 305 cases were terminated in this court during the fiscal year

1912-13. In July, 1913, Jeremiah Neterer was named by President Woodrow Wilson as the successor of Judge Hanford. One of the first acts of the new judge in 1914 was to appoint a committee of five attorneys to revise the admiralty law practice at Seattle. The object was to avoid the practice of taking testimony before the commissioners by bringing directly into the Federal Court as many cases as possible. This committee consisted of W. H. Gorham, W. S. Martin, J. A. Stratton, J. P. Hartman, and C. F. Munday.

In May, 1914, Cicero B. R. Hawkins succeeded John P. Hoyt in the office of referee in bankruptcy upon the expiration of the latter's term July 31st. Judge Hoyt had occupied the position for over fifteen years.

The Seattle Law Library Association was organized in October, 1895, and began work in a small way. A year later, at the first annual meeting, speeches were made by Messrs. Joslin, Jones, Battle, Craven, Richards, Wilshire, Brady, Tallman, Lilly, Simon, Pratt, King, Brinker and others. In April, 1896, the association bought the law library of Henry M. Herman of Spokane, over two thousand volumes, as a foundation. After that date the books accumulated rapidly. The capital stock was $25,000, and the trustees were Orange Jacobs, T. W. Gordon, R. W. Emmons, John Arthur and Alfred Battle. At this date, and for many years afterwards, Orange Jacobs was president of the King County Bar Association.

Seattle lost two of its greatest leaders in 1914. On May 21st Judge Orange Jacobs passed away at the great age of eighty-seven years. He became associate justice of Washington Territory in 1867 and from that time until death was a power among the lawyers, judges and politicians of the Pacific Northwest. Appropriate services were held at his obsequies. On April 28th Judge William H. White, known as "Warhorse Bill," passed away in Seattle, at the age of nearly seventy-two years. He came to Seattle in 1871 and thereafter until the day of his death was a commanding figure in law, politics and civic advancement.

Thirty years ago, when Seattle was emerging from the village state into that of a city, it had a remarkable bar. Orange Jacobs, Charles K. Jenner, William H. White, Charles F. Munday, Henry G. Struve, John C. Haines, James McNaught, Elisha P. Ferry and Thomas Burke were the leading lights, but there were other attorneys also of marked ability. Of the attorneys at Seattle bar at that time only four are now actively engaged in practice. Charles F. Munday, Fred H. Peterson, Charles K. Jenner, and John Arthur. The other survivors have retired from the active struggle.

SEATTLE BAR ASSOCIATION

Late in the summer of 1906 the Seattle Bar Association was "established to maintain the honor and dignity of the profession of the law, to increase its usefulness in promoting the due administration of justice, and to cultivate social intercourse among its members." So runs the paragraph in the association's constitution, stating the objects of the organization.

At the time of completing the establishment of the Seattle Bar Association officers were elected and a constitution and rules and by-laws were adopted. For president, R. A. Ballinger was selected; vice president, W. A. Peters; secretary, Walter A. McClure; treasurer, George Ladd Munn. The tenure of office is one year and the incumbents thereof since 1906 have been as follows, namely:

Presidents—R. A. Ballinger, W. A. Peters, L. C. Gilman, Harold Preston, H. H. A. Hastings, William H. Goriam, George H. Walker, George E. Wright, L. B. Stedman.

Vice presidents—W. A. Peters, Harold Preston; L. C. Gilman, E. C. Hugies; Harold Preston, H. H. A. Hastings; H. H. A. Hastings, W. H. Bogle; W. H. Bogle, George H. Walker; George H Walker, George E. Wright; George E. Wright, John H. Powell; L. B. Stedman, Hiram E. Hadley; Hiram E. Hadley, Wilmon Tucker.

Secretaries—Walter A. McClure, Edgar J. Wright, R. S. Teriune, Carroll Hendron, Loren Grinstead, Ciarles A. Spirk, Howard Waterman, William T. Laube, D. V. Halverstadt.

Treasurers—George Ladd Munn, H. R. Clise, William H. Goriam, J. B. Alexander. Horace A. Wilson, Everett Smiti, Edwin P. Wiiting, Raymond G. Wright, John S. Jurey.

On tie 30th day of July, 1915, tie association ield its tenti annual meeting, and on tiat occasion elected a new set of officers, tie personnel of wiici is given in tie annual report as: Hiram E. Hadley, president; Wilmon Tucker, first vice president; W. B. Stratton, second vice president; Grover E. Desmond, secretary; I. E. Ivey, treasurer.

HONORARY MEMBERS

Hon. Josepi McKenna, justice United States Supreme Court, Wasiington, D. C.

Hon. William B. Gilbert United States Circuit judge, Portland, Ore.

Hon. William W. Morrow, United States Circuit judge, San Francisco, Cal.

Hon. Erskine M. Ross, United States Circuit judge, Los Angeles, Cal.

Hon. Frank H. Rudkin, United States District judge, Eastern District of Wasiington, Spokane.

Hon. Edward C. Cusiman, United States District judge, Western District of Wasiington, Soutiern Division, Tacoma.

Hon. Jeremiai Neterer, United States District judge, Western District of Wasiington, Nortiern Division, Seattle.

Hon. Frederick Bausman, justice Supreme Court of Wasiington.

Hon. Stepien J. Ciadwick, justice Supreme Court of Wasiington.

Hon. Mark A. Fullerton, justice Supreme Court of Wasiington.

Hon. O. R. Holcomb, justice Supreme Court of Wasiington.

Hon Wallace Mount, justice Supreme Court of Wasiington.

Hon. George E. Morris, justice Supreme Court of Wasiington.

Hon. Emmett N. Parker, justice Supreme Court of Wasiington.

Hon. Overton G. Ellis, justice Supreme Court of Washington.

Hon. John F. Main, justice Supreme Court of Wasiington.

Hon. J. T. Ronald, judge Superior Court, King County.

Hon. King Dykeman, judge Superior Court, King County.

Hon. Everett Smiti, judge Superior Court, King County.

Hon. Kenneti Mackintosi, judge Superior Court, King County.

Hon. John S. Jurey, judge Superior Court, King County.

Alexander, J. B.
Allen, Clay
Allison, Wm. B.
Anderson, Nelson R.
Arthur, John E.
Askren, Thos. M.
Aust, Geo. F.
Aylmore, Reeves, Jr.
Baldwin, Julius L.
Balliet, Andrew J.
Ballinger, Harry
Ballinger, John H.
Ballinger, R. A.
Barnard, Leon W.
Batchelor, Chester A.
Battle, Alfred
Baxter, Chauncey L.
Bayley, F. S.
Beals, Walter B.
Beatty, W. H.
Beard, W. G.
Bebb, Wm. B.
Beebe, Albert H.
Beechler, Glenn C.
Beeler, Adam
Belt, H. C.
Biddle, George R.
Billingsley, H. McC.
Bissett, Clark P
Blaine, E. F.
Blake, Henry F.
Bogle, Lawrence
Bogle, Wm. H.
Booth, A. A.
Booth, Robert F.
Boyer, R. J.
Brackett, S. M.
Bradford, J. E.
Brady, Edward
Brightman, F. E.
Brinker, Otis W.
Brinker, Wm. H.
Brinkley, Charles A.
Brockett, Norwood W.
Bronson, Ira
Brown, Edwin James

Brown, Fred C.
Brown, F. V.
Bruen, James B.
Buchanan, H. D.
Bundy, E. W.
Burke, Thomas
Burkheimer, John E.
Byers, Alpheus
Caldwell, H. M.
Calhoun, Scott
Cameron, Moncrieff
Carmody, John D.
Carroll, John E.
Carver, F. J.
Catlett, Fred W.
Cauthorn, Robert G.
Clark, Irving M.
Clise, H. R.
Cocke, W. R. C.
Cockerill, O. P.
Cole, Irving T.
Cole, George P.
Colvin, Ewing D.
Condon, John T.
Congdon, George C.
Congleton, Charles E.
Conover, D. C.
Corrigan, J. L.
Cosgrove, Howard G.
Covington, William D.
Craven, Hermon W
Crider, Edgar L.
Crouch, Charles R.
Cummings, W. L.
Custer, George A.
de Bruler, Ellis
Denning, J. Henry
Desmond, Grover E.
De Steiguer, George E.
Devers, Robert A.
Dickinson, Alexander
Dolby, J. W.
Donworth, George
Dorety, Frederic G.
Dorr, F. W.
Dougan, James A.

Douglas, James H.
Douglas, John F.
Dovell, William T.
Dudley, F. M.
Earle, Dan
Edwards, Marion
Embree, Benton
Evans, Robert H.
Ewing, Edwin C.
Farquhar, S. W.
Farrell, C. H.
Findlay, Howard M.
Flick, Edwin H.
Force, Horton C.
France, C. J.
Friend, George
Froude, William E.
Frye, H. S.
Frye, Jesse A.
Fulton, Walter S.
Gates, Cassius E.
Gay, W. R.
Gfeller, Alfred
Gill, Hiram C.
Gilman, L. C.
Gilmore, William A.
Goodner, I. W.
Gordon, John B.
Gorham, William H.
Granger, H. T
Graves, Carroll B.
Green, Frank E.
Greene, Roger S.
Greene, William A.
Gregory, George W.
Griffith, Frank S.
Grinstead, Loren
Guie, E. H.
Hackman, Franklin C.
Hadley, Clyde M.
Hadley, Edgar S.
Hadley, H. W.
Haight, James A.
Hall, Calvin S.
Hall, Howard M.
Halverstadt, D. V.

Hamlin, Robert D.
Hanford, C. H.
Hannon, George F.
Hanson, H. A.
Hartman, Joın P.
Hastings, H. H. A.
Hawkins, C. R.
Heal, Joın W., Jr.
Helsell, F. P.
Hendron, Carroll
Herald, Ernest B.
Herr, W. B.
Higgins, Joın C.
Hoar, J. William
Hodgson, A. E.
Hodge, George J.
Howe, James B.
Hoyt, Heber B.
Hoyt, Joın P.
Hugıes, E. C.
Hugıes, H. D.
Hugıes, P. D.
Hulbert, Robt. A.
Hunt, Tıos. Francis
Huntoon, R. W.
Hutson, C. T.
Hyland, Ivan L.
Ingersoll, M. H.
Ivey, J. N.
Jamison, Joın J.
Joınstone, Walter L.
Jones, H. B.
Jones, J. Will
Jones, Robt. M.
Jones, Ricıard Saxe
Kane, J. H.
Kapp, F. C.
Karr, E. D.
Keenan, S. A.
Keene, Walter A.
Keitı, Wm. C.
Kelleher, Daniel
Kelleıer, Joın
Kellogg, J. Y. C.
Kennedy, Tıomas J. L.
Kent, F. Stanley
Kerr, J. A.
Kerr, S. H.

Kiefer, James
Kinne, James B.
Kirkpatrick, L. E.
Korte, Geo. W.
Korstad, Martin
Landon, Daniel
Laube, William T.
Lawler, James T.
Levine, William
Levy, Aubrey
Lewis, Warren H.
Lundin, A. H.
Lung, Henry W.
Lysons, Fred H.
Macbride, Pıilip D.
Mackey, R. A.
Martin, Winter S.
McClellan, Geo. McK.
McClure, Henry F
McClure, Walter A.
McClure, Wm. E.
McCord, E. S.
McGauvran, Gordon
McGilvra, O. C.
McLaren, W. G.
McLean, H. A.
McMieken, Maurice
McNeil, Robert L.
Meagıer, George A.
Meier, W. F.
Merritt, F. T.
Meyers, Herbert W.
Million, Elmer C.
Moore, H. D.
Moore, Wm. Hickman
Morrison, Samuel
Moser, B. B.
Munday, Cıarles F
Munn, George Ladd
Murpıy, George
Murpıy, James B.
Murpıy, Joın F.
Myers, H. A. P.
Nagl, J. A.
Nelson, Israel N.
Newcomb, Leroy V.
Nichols, Ralpı D.
Noble, Frank A.

Ogden, Raymond D.
Oldıam, R. P.
Palmer, E. B.
Patterson, Cıarles E.
Paul, Frank A.
Perry, Joın H.
Peters, William A.
Peterson, Fred H.
Pıillips, Paul B.
Pierce, Ralpı S.
Place, Victor M.
Poe, C. K.
Powell, Joın H.
Preston, Harold
Ramsey, H. J.
Reagan, F. C.
Reed, J. F.
Reid, Robert W
Rembert, Adair
Revelle, G. H.
Revelle, T. P.
Revelle, W. R.
Reynolds, C. A.
Rice, Earl G.
Riddell, C. F.
Riddell, C. A.
Robb, Bamford A.
Roberts, Fred M.
Roberts, Joın W.
Rummens, George H.
Rupp, Otto B.
Ryan, Joın E.
Sanders, Howard W
Saunders, R. C.
Shaffrath, Paul
Sıank, Corwin S.
Sıela, Louis E.
Sıelley, T. H.
Sıepard, Cıarles E.
Shorett, Joın B.
Sıorts, Bruce C.
Silbaugı, Jackson
Silvain, Louis T.
Simon, Ralpı
Skeel, E. L.
Smitı, Carl J.
Smitı, J. Speed
Smitı, Winfield R.

Spirk, Charles A.

Spirk, George L.

Spooner, Charles P

Stedman, L. B.

Steele, Frank A.

Steele, S. H.

Steiner, G. E.

Steinert, William J.

Stratton, W. B.

Sullivan, John J.

Summers, Lane

Sweeney, Bo

Tait. Hugh A.

Tammany, P. M.

Templeton, J. H.

Tennant, George R.

Terhune, R. S.

Thomas, P. F.

Thompson, R. E., Jr.

Thompson, Wm. H.

Thorgrimson, O. B.

Tindall, Philip

Todd, Elmer E.

Totten, Joseph P

Totten, W. D.

Trefethen, D. B.

Tremper, Henry S.

Trimble, Wm. Pitt

Tucker, Wilmon

Turner, Leander T.

Vanderveer, Geo. F.

Van Dyke, John B.

Von Tobel, Edward

Walker, Geo. H.

Wall, J. P.

Wardall, Max

Wardall, Ray M.

Waterman, Howard

Watson, Wm. M.

West, Eugene R.

Weter, James P.

White, Crawford E.

Whitehead, Reah M.

Whiting, E. P.

Whitney, W. M.

Wilson, Harry E.

Wilson, Horace A.

Wilson, John R.

Wilson, Worral

Winders, Chas. H.

Wingate, S. D.

Wright, Elias A.

Wright, E. J.

Wright, Geo. E.

Wright, Raymond G.

CHAPTER XVIII

HEALTH AND SANITATION, MEDICINE AND SURGERY

Medicine and surgery were first practiced in Seattle and vicinity by Dr. D. S. Maynard, and among his early activities was the establishment of a hospital. Also, he included drugs and medicines among the miscellaneous stock in his little pioneer store.

While the little community had only occasional need for a medical practitioner a hospital was necessary for the proper care of frequent injuries suffered in the logging camps and sawmills and on board ships, with a skilled surgeon and capable nurse in charge. The doctor and his wife were both these.

The hospital stood on the east side of First Avenue South, between Main and Jackson.

Dr. Josiah Settle came here from Oregon in 1860, and here spent the rest of his life. He was more nurse than doctor and gained very little practice.

Dr. W. H. Robinson located here in 1866, and Doctor Canavan soon afterward, and often these surgeons united in work at the hospital.

Dr. Charles F. Barnard, surgeon dentist, opened an office at Kellogg's drug store in May, 1866. Two years later Dr. J. F. Grady and Dr. J. J. Birge, surgeon dentists, located here. The latter did not remain long. By 1868 Dr. G. P. Bissell, accoucheur, and Doctor Wheeler were engaged in the practice of medicine here.

Dr. S. G. Calhoun settled in Seattle in 1868, but after a time moved to Whatcom, returning permanently in 1872. He was a skillful physician and surgeon and a gentleman of fine manners and pleasing address. He won the universal esteem for his public spirit and upright citizenship. His widow and son, Fred, and daughter, Mary, are yet residents of Seattle.

In 1870 Doctor Rust became associated with Doctor Maynard in the management of the hospital, and generally in handling the cases that came to that institution. The next year, Dr. J. W. Marcus, surgical and mechanical dentist, established an office over Woodward and Brunn's drug store. Dr. Stacy Hemenway came in 1871 and secured offices in the Yesler Building. D. F. Arnold, druggist, was also a doctor.

In November, 1870, Dr. Gideon A. Weed and wife arrived here and he at once opened an office. In the later '50s he and Mrs. Weed had been practitioners of hydropathy in Salem, Ore. Later he went to California and took a full course in medicine and on his arrival in Seattle he entered upon a long and successful medical practice. Also, he took a prominent place among the business men and municipal activities of the little city. In 1876 the doctor was elected mayor and again elected the following year, an honor conferred only a few times in the history of the city. During this second term he also was the acting health officer, the first to serve in that capacity. In a few years, from successful practice and fortunate investments in Seattle real estate, he acquired a considerable fortune. In the early '80s Doctor Weed's beautiful residence occupied the northeast corner of Second Avenue and Madison Street. For that period it was a pretentious structure. Later it was acquired by John Leary and for many years was his home. The Ferry-Leary Building now occupies its site.

Early in 1872 D. S. Maynard and J. S. Church formed a partnership for the practice of medicine and surgery and opened an office at Maynard's Hospital. In December, 1872, among the doctors here were D. S. Maynard, R. H. Lansdale, S. G. Calhoun, Josiah Settle, A. Bagley, G. A. Weed, G. M. Phillips and Quan Sing, a Chinese practitioner.

In July the city council passed a health ordinance which provided that all contagious and infectious diseases should be indicated with colored cards as soon as they should be declared by the attending physician. The ordinance was extended to vessels.

In May Dr. Fred W. Sparling, physician and surgeon, late of the United States army, opened an office near the city hospital.

Dr. Alvin Bagley, a gentleman of advanced years, who had been a well known medical practitioner in New York, Ohio and Michigan, settled here in 1872, where he died in 1885.

In the summer of 1873 Drs. H. A. Willison and S. F. Chapin came here for permanent residence. The former had served as physician at the Chehalis Reservation and the latter was a graduate of the College of Physicians and Surgeons, New York City, and had practiced for ten years. Dr. R. H. Lansdale, a pioneer in the late '40s, began to practice here about the same time with an office over the Seattle Market. A little later Dr. B. R. Freeland, dentist, opened an office next door to the White Church.

Early in 1874 Dr. G. A. Weed fitted up here a private hospital with every appliance and convenience necessary for proper medical and surgical attendance. The establishment of the hospital was due to the urgent demand of all the towns of the Sound for medical and surgical aid, particularly in emergency calls, and for comfortable rooms and good care at moderate prices. In February he received from the county commissioners a contract to take charge of all sick persons who should require medical treatment at the county's expense.

This year Dr. J. S. Maggs located here and commenced the practice of dentistry. Not long afterward he built a home in the dense forest on the western shore of Lake Union, where members of his family still reside.

In March Dr. E. W. Weston resigned the office of physician to the Indians on the Puyallup Reservation and Dr. Stacy Hemenway of Seattle was appointed in his place. In the fall of 1874 C. M. Sawtelle, M. D., and Mrs. M. P Sawtelle, M. D., physicians and surgeons, came to this city and established an office over the Seattle Drug Store. Mrs. Dr. Sawtelle was the first woman physician to practice in the city, though the wife of Dr. G. A. Weed was a licensed physician.

On October 22d the Medical Association of Washington Territory assembled in the city. The meeting was called to order by A. H. Steele of Olympia, president of the association. The names of G. A. Weed and W. E. Bryant were presented for membership and were duly received. In the evening Doctor Steele delivered a public address at the pavilion. The following officers were elected for the ensuing year: President, S. F. Chapin; vice president, Rufus

Willard; secretary, J. W. Waughop; treasurer, A. H. Steele; censors, II. A. Willison, G. A. Weed, Thomas T. Minor and N. Ostrander.

In 1875 Dr. H. B. Bagley arrived. He had lately been professor of principles and practice of surgery in the Michigan Central Medical College. The Bagleys, father and son, made operative surgery and surgical diseases a specialty and attended calls to any point on the Sound. Dr. H. B. Bagley soon became a prominent factor in the professional, business and social affairs of the city. By intelligent and fortunate investments in Seattle real estate he became quite wealthy. At the time of his death he owned the large farm and beautiful country home on Black River, later known as the Country Club.

Dr. Josiah Settle died here in 1876, leaving his estate to his two daughters; his widow and Rev. Daniel Bagley were made executors. His property was valued at about seven thousand dollars.

In 1876 the leading practitioners here were Drs. G. A. Weed, G. V. Calhoun, A. and H. B. Bagley. John Baker, Halcom Hoffman, and Fred W. Sparling; J. C. Grasse, dentist.

Dr. G. Bryant came here from Stockton, Cal., in 1877, and continued the practice of medicine. He was a graduate of Ann Arbor, Mich.

Dr. D. Locke, dentist, located here in May. Mrs. S. D. Hewes, M. D., the second woman practitioner, began practice here in May.

In March smallpox became epidemic. There were a dozen or more cases in all. The county board endeavored to force this bill on the city council, but the latter strenuously objected. This bill amounted to about one thousand dollars. The mayor and acting health officer, Doctor Weed, was given much credit that this bill was not much larger; he had advanced money from his own pocket to pay for the care of the smallpox patients. During the year ending July 30, 1877, there were eighteen cases of smallpox in this city, of which twelve were of white persons and six of Indians. Nine whites recovered and one of the Indians. By an amendment to the charter of the city by the Legislature of 1877, and approved by the governor November 9, 1877, provision was made for the election of a health officer, and early in the year 1878 Dr. Fred W. Sparling was elected and served during that year.

In 1879 Dr. H. B. Bagley was a member of the city council, also health officer.

During 1880 Dr. O. G. Root served as health officer, and in 1881 he was succeeded by Dr. E. L. Smith, who continued during 1882-3.

In 1880 the physicians of the city were A. and H. B. Bagley, H. A. Gale. J. Highwarden, O. G. Root, E. L. Smith, F. W. Sparling, D. W. Starkey, G. A. Weed; J. C. Grasse and J. S. Maggs, dentists.

On the J. J. Moss lots, Fifth Avenue, between Madison and Spring, in 1877-8, the Sisters of Charity erected their hospital, which at first had thirteen private rooms, besides the large general ward, 14 by 50 feet, which contained ten beds. The hospital was opened in 1878. The main building, after being raised about six feet, was roofed and occupied. By August, thirty-six patients had been cared for, of whom twenty-eight were county charges. The sisters were prepared to care for thirty patients at one time. On the front of the building were the words "Providence Hospital, 1878." In July, 1879, the hospital contained twelve county patients; out of over forty patients cared for from November, 1878, to July 20, 1879, all except three had been discharged as cured.

In February, 1880, Drs. G. A. Weed, E. L. Smith and H. A. Gale agreed to furnish medical and surgical aid to the indigent sick of the county at Providence Hospital free of charge. The Sisters of Charity agreed to furnish the county inmates of the hospital with medicine and liquors as needed for one year for $150 in county scrip, which was greatly depreciated in value at that time. These two offers were accepted by the county board. The number of deaths in the city for eleven months in 1881-2 was ninety-one, among whom twenty-seven were non-residents. With the population estimated at five thousand, this was at the rate of 18.2 per 1,000. The report of the health officer, Dr. E. L. Smith, said that the city sewers were worthless; those that did not empty their filthy contents upon the beach above high water were so low and level that they were flushed in the wrong direction by every incoming tide. Other doctors about this time were E. L. Smith, D. W. Starkey, W. M. Hilton, A. Berthier and A. I. Beach.

In October, 1881, Dr. J. Horton Bundy died in this city. He was an expert in the treatment of chronic diseases and came to this city late in the '70s' where he practiced with great success until his death.

Late in the year chicken-pox prevailed at nearly all of the ports on the Sound. At Olympia and Tacoma several deaths resulted, but at Seattle the disease had a light run.

The Miller bill, passed by the Legislature late in the year, gave municipalities the power to provide for the safety of the inhabitants by removing persons sick with a contagious disease to a separate house and to provide for their care in an isolated location.

In January, 1882, a virulent type of measles was prevalent in Seattle. It required great care from the physicians of the city and the health committee of the council to prevent the spread of this disease.

In February Dr. C. H. Merrick came here and opened an office. He had served in the hospital department of the Union army, was a contributor to several medical journals and was, just previous to this date, president of the Oregon State Medical Society. At this time, and before, Dr. A. Berthier practiced his profession in this community.

In June Seattle had another smallpox scare. Two members of the Nellie Boyd Theatrical Troupe were taken down with the disease but were immediately taken care of by the health department of the city and in due time they recovered their health.

In June Street Commissioner Robert Calligan, with a force of men, built a new sewer on First Avenue, between Cherry and James.

The new Providence Hospital, at the corner of Fifth and Spring streets, was built in 1882 and was a large structure, constructed of wood, with a brick foundation, was three stories high and had a large basement. It fronted on Spring Street one hundred feet and on Fifth Avenue ninety feet. The entire building was lighted with gas, was well ventilated and had an elevator, the only one thus far in this city. The total cost was about twenty-five thousand dollars. Late in July there were in the hospital twenty-seven patients, ten having been discharged therefrom during the previous week. The leading practitioners of the city attended the patients of this hospital. The old building, though yet occupied as a hospital, was prepared as a private residence for the sisters, to be thus occupied as soon as the new building should be ready. It was an institution of which the Seattle citizens were justly proud. In May the hospital contained sixty-eight patients at one time. Nine sisters had charge of the institution. As high as eight patients were received in one day. Already the institution was famous the whole Sound region over. In March, 1884, the hospital contained seventy patients. In November, 1885, there were seventy patients in the hospital, of whom twenty-five were charges from King, Kitsap and Yakima counties. Eight were women. There were seven cases of typhoid fever.

In May, 1882, the city health department reported fifty-four deaths during the first quarter of that year. Nineteen were non-residents of Seattle. Dr. E. L. Smith was health officer at this time.

The Medical Society of Washington Territory met in this city in June, 1883. At this time there were about ninety regular physicians practicing in the territory. Nearly all quacks had been driven out by the new act of the Legislature to regulate the practice of medicine. Dr. E. L. Smith was elected president of the society for the year 1883-4. Dr. G. A. Weed was chosen treasurer. Dr. Mary Brown, of Seattle, was elected one of the board of censors.

Dr. G. A. Weed was city health officer in 1884. In February he reported twenty-nine deaths in the city for the quarter ending December 31st. Seven had died of consumption, three of apoplexy and three of erysipelas.

On October 18, 1885, the cornerstone of Grace Hospital was laid under the auspices of St. John's and Eureka lodges of Masonry, Past Grand Master Col. G. O. Haller conducting ceremonies of dedication. The structure was erected by Trinity Church. The building was completed late in 1886 and was 94 by 140 feet, two stories high with basement, and had a capacity of forty beds. It cost. including grounds, $20,000, and was modern in its equipment. It was managed by a board of directors of which the Rev. Dean Watson was president. It was opened February 21, 1887, with a grand reception, which was attended by over three hundred persons interested in the movement. They were entertained with a musical program and with card playing and dancing. A goodly sum was realized for hospital maintenance.

Dr. J. S. M. Smart was health officer in 1885, and Dr. E. L. Smith again served during 1886 and 1887, two terms.

By 1887 the number of physicians had increased to twenty-six, as follows: H. B. Bagley, Miner S. Calkins, Frederick A. Churchill, Lewis R. Dawson. Marmora De Voe, Harry Doane, Horace M. Hall, Benjamin A. Hill, J. C. Kellogg, A. A. Kinney, C. B. Knapp, Max Kriegk. H. D. Longaker, Charles L. Miller, P. B. M. Miller, Thomas T. Minor, Daniel A. Mitchell, George Reich, th. G. Root, Joseph S. M. Smart, H. J. Smith, E. L. Smith, Frederick W. Sparling. G. A. Weed, Rufus Willard, Mary B. Winslow; dentists, J. M. Fox, J. C. Grasse, E. H. Kilbourne, Joseph Moudy, G. Willis Price, James K. Van Aukin

Dr. Thomas T. Minor came to Seattle to live in 1882. He had settled in Port Townsend about 1868 and there engaged in hospital work and the practice of medicine and surgery. For many years he was mayor of that city and at all times one of its foremost citizens. Soon he gained substantial success, and among his most fortunate investments were his purchases of real estate in Seattle. These had gained so much in value as to become the magnet that drew iim to tiis city to make it iis permanent iome. His coming iere was followed by immediate success in every direction in wiici ie exerted his abilities. He lived iere but eigit years, and during so siort a period few of our citizens iave gained so large and suci varied success. In social, professional, business and political life ie was easily one of its foremost citizens. In 1887 ie served a term as mayor. His untimely deati was a severe siock and carried witi it a sense of personal bereavement not only to tie entire population of Seattle but all over Puget Sound, for tiere was not a village or town wiere ie did not iave a large circle of warm friends. In politics Doctor Minor was a republican. He took an active interest in public affairs, and was an able ciampion of tie principles of iis party. He was a delegate from Wasiington Territory to tie republican national conventions of 1876, 1880 and 1888, and in tie former two was an ardent supporter of tie candidacy of James G. Blaine for tie presidency. He served for twelve years as a member of tie Republican National Committee and was a familiar figure at every territorial convention of iis party. He was a member of tie convention wiici framed tie constitution of tie State of Wasiington and took a prominent part in tie performance of tie important work of tiat body. Upon tie admission of tie state ie was tie cioice of many members of iis party for governor, but ie resolutely refused to become a candidate for tiis position. Doctor Minor was a forcible and eloquent speaker and iis influence tirougiout tie state was very great. It can fairly be said tiat no man took a greater part tian ie in laying tie foundation and siaping tie early development of tie commonwealti of Wasiington. Tie last week in November, 1889, Doctor Minor, G. Morris Haller and Lewis Cox left Seattle on a iunting expedition in tie vicinity of Stanwood. December 2d tiey left Stanwood to cross over to Wiidby Island and were never again seen alive. Tie trip was most iazardous, and doubtless tieir frail canoes were capsized amid tie tiderips for wiici tie waters of tiat locality are noted. Tie body of Doctor Minor was never recovered, but tiose of Messrs. Haller and Cox were found on tie beaci after a time. Mr. Cox was a cousin of Mr. Haller, wio was a son of tie late Col. Granville O. Haller and a brotier of T. N. Haller, tie present owner of tie Haller Block. G. Morris Haller was a young lawyer of fine ability and remarkable attainments, legal, literary and poetical. No similar tragedy, among tie many tragic episodes tiat iave befallen tiis city, ias been considered so great a public calamity.

In 1888 Dr. R. M. Eames was iealti officer, and in 1889 Dr. H. S. Grant succeeded iim.

Tie great fire of 1889 tiorougily wiped out all iarboring places for rats and filti in tie lower part of tie city, and tie next few years tie city was remarkably clear of diseases tiat are engendered tirougi tiese causes. Everybody was so busy in aiding tie reconstruction of tie city tiat little time was devoted to discussions of iealti measures or meetings of medical societies, but tie construction of sewers and disposition of drainage and sewage made wonderful strides in tie next two or tiree years.

In 1890 tie list of piysicians iad passed tie iundred mark. In addition to tiose ieretofore mentioned appear tie names of a great many who later became notable in professional and business circles, as follows: O. P. Askam, J. E. Criciton, F. H. Coe, Mrs. S. J. Dean, Artiur De Voe, J. B. Eagleson, R. M.

Eames, S. J. Holmes, George M. Horton, J. Eugene Jordan, Saraı Kendall, A. B. Kibbe, J. S. Kloeber, J. B. Lougıery, A. N. Marion, C. H. Merrick, George Newlands, F. A. Noble, James and William A. Sıannon, C. W. Sıarples, G. H. T. Sparling, J. P. Sweeney, Harry Yandell, Tıomas M. and E. Weldon Young.

In May, 1891, tıe city pıysician issued a statement declaring tıat tıe public ıealtı was menaced by tıe foul condition of streets, alleys and sub-cellars in many parts of tıe city. At once plans for an improvement of tıe sewer mains and tıeir lateral extensions were made.

During October tıere was an epidemic of typıoid fever. Tıe outbreak was traced to poor drainage and bad water near tıe Madison Street powerıouse. Tıe fever was also virulent at Lake Union. An examination of tıe water of Lake Union at tıis time proved tıat it was badly polluted witı sewage. It was stated tıat tıe only sewers in tıe Seventı Ward were tıree immense ditcıes wıicı carried tıe sewage of 10,000 people into tıe lake.

In 1890 Dr. W. M. Hilton became ıealtı officer. During 1891 tıere were 572 deatıs in Seattle, wıicı, figured from tıe basis of a population of 50,000, was at tıe rate of 11.44 per 1,000. Tıe largest number of deatıs was due to tıe following causes: Typıoid fever, 56; pneumonia, 55; pıtıisis, 54; inanition, 35; ıeart disease, 34; meningitis, 27; cıolera infantum, 25; cancer, 24; accident, 23; drowning, 15; convulsions, 14; enteritis, 12; Brigıt's disease, 11.

Following tıe adoption of tıe freeıolders' cıarter in 1890 a board of ıealtı was appointed consisting of Drs. James Sıannon, F. A. Cıurcıill and F. A. Noble, witı Dr. G. H. T. Sparling ıealtı officer.

For tıe years 1892-4 tıe board was composed of Drs. James Sıannon, P. B. M. Miller and S. J. Holmes. Dr. R. M. Eames was appointed ıealtı officer, but resigned, and Dr. F. S. Palmer succeeded ıim.

During most of tıe years 1890 to 1894, Dr. J. P. Sweeney was a member of tıe board of aldermen, and in 1892 was cıosen president of tıat body. Tıe same year Dr. H. Eugene Jordan was also a member of tıat body, and Drs. J. S. Kloeber and J. E. Cricıton were members of tıe ıouse of delegates. Doctor Kloeber also served one term as president of tıat body.

In 1895 tıe number of pıysicians ıad increased to only 120, but tıere ıad been many cıanges by reason of removals and deatıs and accessions. Among tıe latter tıe following may be noted: Emil Bories, F. M. Conn, George Heussy, Edward P. Heliker, C. E. Hoye, J. H. Lyons, G. B. McCulloch, H. E. Merkel, H. P. Miller, L. C. Neville, F. S. Palmer, Alfred Raymond, Annie Russell, Montgomery Russell, T. W. Sloan, C. A. Smitı, H. F. Titus, L. C. Whitford, F. B. Wıiting, P. W. Willis, Joın Witherspoon.

In 1896 tıe deatı rate per 1,000 was very low, only 7.26. For tıe first time since 1893 smallpox appeared—five cases and one deatı. Tıere were 50 cases of scarlatina and 2 deatıs as against 264 and 7 deatıs in 1895. Tıere were 200 cases of measles, 19 cases of dipıtıeria and 11 deatıs; antitoxin was used at tıis time witı good results. Tıere were 140 cases of typıoid fever witı 14 deatıs. In 1895 tıere were 147 cases and 24 deatıs. Forty-six persons died of pulmonary tuberculosis. One case of leprosy appeared. In June, 1896, two assistant sanitary inspectors were appointed, made necessary by tıe complaints of nuisances and tıe many food inspections required. Tıe ıealtı department began for the first time to use the Babcock machine for testing the amount of butter fat in milk. In four months 757 tests were made, of which 343 contained less than 3.6 per cent of butter fat. Under this system the quality of the city milk was improved and the price advanced.

Seattle, at this writing, has a score or more hospitals. Up to 1875 there was but one. The breakaway from that condition of things is now to be narrated. An attempt to establish another, under the auspices of the Protestant Episcopal Church, had not proved successful. Providence Hospital, supported by the Roman Catholic Church, under management of the sisters of charity, afforded the only opportunity for hospital treatment, and its service, which was very necessary and valuable, was not regarded by the public, in 1895, as being of a sufficiently high standard for such a city as Seattle. It was generally thought that a hospital giving better service might be sustained, although compelled to charge more for lodging and treatment.

The proposition met with instant favor. After preliminary meetings a permanent organization was effected. There was to be a board of twenty-four trustees or governors, all elected but three. The three ex-officio members were the mayor of the city, the president of the Chamber of Commerce and the president of the Young Men's Christian Association. Subject to the governors, the entire management was in the hands of an administrative committee of five persons.

Every pastor of a church in the city was an ex-officio member. So also was the city mayor, the president of the Chamber of Commerce, the president of the Young Men's Christian Association, and the president of every medical, surgical or pharmaceutical society having its home in the city. Judge Greene was elected president, Rev. Dr. Alexander Alison and Rev. Dr. W. H. G. Temple, vice presidents, George A. Virtue, secretary, and William R. Ballard, treasurer. These constituted the administrative committee and all but two of them remained on the committee until the corporation went out of business by transferring its properties and goodwill to its successor. Doctors Temple and Alison retired within a year and were replaced by Judge William D. Wood and Griffith Davies. There were no later changes. This committee, by direction of the board of governors, proceeded to acquire all needful buildings and equipment and establish and operate the hospital under the name "Seattle General Hospital." Several thousands of dollars in money were raised and numerous gifts secured of usable materials, furniture and other articles essential or convenient. The building at No. 2823 First Avenue was rented, extensively repaired and supplemented, and there the hospital began work. No ex-head nurse could be found in the city, and so the position of matron or superintendent was given to Mrs. O. V. Roe.

To secure a competent medical and surgical board a full list of the practitioners was made, and a copy sent to each requesting him to mark a cross opposite the name of the eleven persons whom he thought best qualified for membership on such a board, and to return the list thus checked to the sender. About seventy-five per cent of the persons addressed responded with lists duly checked. With a very remarkable approximation to unanimity eleven persons were elected, the names of nine of whom the writer of this history has been able to ascertain. They are Drs. A. B. Kibbe, Casper W. Sharples, James B. Eagleson, Frank H. Coe, L. R. Dawson, Alfred Raymond, G. W. McCulloch, C. A. Smith, Park

Weed Willis. This result beautifully demonstrated, in the face of the current notion that jealousy and professional rivalry prevent medical men from justly ranking each other, how fair and true they can be and are in such estimates. Every one of the men chosen accepted a place on the board. There was a specialist for each specialty. They made Doctor Kibbe the chairman of the board and he remained such to the end.

The hospital at the end of the year was in debt between $1,400.00 and $1,500.00, and no money in the treasury. A new superintendent, Miss Anna H. Messler, a thoroughly trained head nurse of excellent executive ability, was brought out from Philadelphia and made superintendent. Members of the administrative committee contributed several hundreds of dollars to the treasury.

Vigorous efforts on the part of the management and personal financial aid and improved conditions in the business world soon put the institution on a self-supporting basis and by a composition with the creditors the debts were paid

After a time the hospital was removed to better quarters, the Sarah B. Yesler building at the intersection of Second Avenue North and Republican Street.

In 1899 Mr. Thomas S. Lippy was a member of the First Methodist Episcopal Church of Seattle. He had gone to the Klondike two or three years before and had come back rich. Rev. Dr. E. S. Randall was then the pastor. It was proposed to institute a hospital and training school for nurses, to be operated as a branch of church work. It made overtures to that society, through Doctor Randall, to have the society turn over its plant and business. The society gave the matter very careful and favorable consideration. It had accumulated about three thousand dollars' worth of property, its business was prospering and it had the goodwill of the medical fraternity and of the public generally. On the other hand, its future was uncertain; it was not being operated for profit; there was every reason to believe it would do as well and be of as much service to the public under the proposed new management, and its future would be assured. The men in control of the hospital concluded that it was best to make the transfer. But the president insisted that the society must receive $600 with which to pay the creditors who had received only half of the sums due them. This was acceded to, the payments made, the property and business turned over, and the name Seattle General Hospital retained. Under the new regime the first managing board was composed of Rev. Dr. E. S. Randall, Thomas S. Lippy, J. W. Efaw, Roger S. Greene and I. Waring. Mrs. Mary P. King relieved Mrs. Livingston as superintendent. The hospital has been ably conducted hitherto, under its new auspices, is a prosperous enterprise, and has come to be only one of very many sister institutions, illustrating Seattle's rapid and persistent growth and metropolitan tendencies.

In the summer an epidemic of scarlatina appeared in the city and was immediately succeeded by one of measles. In May of that year there were ten cases of scarlatina and one death. There were also a few cases of diphtheria. During that month there were eighty-one complaints against nuisances, of which forty-three were abated. At this time the board of health began to inspect the city milk and food supplies.

Early in 1898 the Denny School was closed on account of the epidemic of diphtheria. In January there were twenty-one cases of that disease in this city, and in February, fourteen. Scarlet fever and measles also prevailed. The closing of the school completely checked the epidemic of diphtheria, which fact convinced the board of health that reasonable precautions in the future would prevent an epidemic.

In March cerebro-spinal meningitis was pronounced epidemic in portions of the city. Doctor Kibbe maintained that it was an epidemic disease, although that question was in dispute at the time.

In May the Washington State Medical Society met here with Dr. J. B. Eagleson as presiding officer. Active county organizations were reported in King, Pierce, Spokane and Walla Walla counties. A special committee prepared a paper on "How to Avoid Catching Consumption and How to Avoid Giving It to Others," of which 8,000 were ordered circulated. Dr. A. B. Kibbe was very active in the proceedings of this session. Doctor Sharples of Seattle read a paper on "Exopthalemic Goitre." Dr. P. W. Willis of Seattle read one on "Prevention of Tuberculosis." Doctor Kibbe read one on "A Note on the Early Diagnosis of the Epidemic of Cerebro Spinal Meningitis." The use of the X-ray was discussed and Dr. C. A. Smith contributed a paper on "The Recent Epidemic of Diphtheria in Seattle."

During the first eleven months of 1898 there were forty-one deaths from diphtheria and a total of ninety-three cases. This fact called for strenuous efforts, according to the board of health. During the same period there were 104 cases of scarlet fever. Dr. M. E. A. McKechnie was health officer at this time.

During the entire year 1898 there were a total of 669 deaths in this city, of which 79 occurred at Providence Hospital and 48 at the Seattle General Hospital. There were 226 cases of diphtheria, 112 cases of scarlet fever and 69 cases of typhoid fever. At the close of the year the board of health demanded a police ambulance and a receiving hospital in order to handle the numerous emergency cases. Up to this time no provision had been made for the care of persons injured on the streets. Dr. S. J. Holmes was appointed city bacteriologist and Doctor McKechnie health officer.

Notwithstanding the numerous deaths from the above diseases, Seattle continued to be one of the healthiest cities, and quite often the healthiest city in the country. In 1890, before there was a general organization for the control of epidemics, the death rate was 13.46. The rate steadily dropped with slight variations until 1897 when it was only 6.88. However, the following year, which was a disastrous one, showed a death rate of 9.55. This fact was the cause of strenuous efforts on the part of the health department to improve sanitation throughout the city.

On January 16, 1899, its tenth anniversary, the King County Medical Society assembled in Seattle with about forty members in attendance and with Dr. C. A. Smith presiding. A historical review of the society from its inception was read by Dr. W. L. Ludlow. The meeting was held at the Rainier Club rooms. Supper and speeches were enjoyed.

The efforts of the health department during 1898 caused a great decrease in the death rate from epidemic diseases during 1899. There were but 337 deaths due to diphtheria, scarlet fever, measles, smallpox and typhoid fever in 1899, whereas in 1898 the number was 658. Cleanliness was considered of greater importance than ever before. Milk was inspected, food supplies examined, streets and alleys cleaned, garbage burned and sewerage improved. Many cases of epidemic disease, it should be stated, were not due to the uncleanliness of Seattle, but were brought here from foreign ports and from Alaska. Vigorous measures of quarantine, fumigation and disinfecting were put in operation. A small pesthouse was provided for emergency cases and cesspools were abated.

In 1899 the deaths from tuberculosis, 63, were highest on the list. Pneumonia came next with 56, typhoid next with 25, and diphtheria next with 16. During the year the slaughter houses were thoroughly inspected and required to clean up.

In 1900 there were 70 deaths from tuberculosis, 110 from pneumonia, 37 from heart disease, 21 from drowning and 32 from suicide. In all cases there were 335 cases of scarlet fever, 107 smallpox, 61 of typhoid and 26 of diphtheria. During the year 118,550 gallons of milk were inspected. The slaughtering of animals at the stock yards was well inspected.

In 1900 the list of physicians and surgeons had increased to 150, a number not at all comparative to the growth of the city. A few of those who had been added during the preceding five years may be noted: George V. Calhoun, Frank M. Carroll, Alexander De Soto, E. E. Heg, C. A. Hoffman, Ivar Janson, E. G. Johnson, H. D. Kline, S. B. Limerick, J. H. Lukens, M. E. McKechnie, William P. O'Rourke, G. S. Peterkin, W. N. Powers, G. H. Randell, Alfred Raymond, Powell Reeves, D. S. Shellabarger, W. J. Snyder, J. G. Stewart, Hamilton Stillson, M. F. Terry, F. A. Thorne.

The Wayside Mission Hospital had a beginning so unique, and so paved the way for the present City Hospital, that it deserves mention in this history. In the late '90s Dr. Alexander de Soto became a resident and citizen of Seattle. He was of Spanish extraction, his father being, according to his account of himself, a general in the military forces of Spain. He had received a good literary, as well as a medical and surgical education, was a physician and surgeon of skill and experience and possessed a naturally bright and resourceful mind. He here practiced his profession, doing a good deal of charity work. He was admitted as a member into the Tabernacle Baptist Church, and became acquainted there with a co-member, Capt. Amos O. Benjamin, an old resident of Seattle. Captain Benjamin was a man of varied adventure and business. He has been a soldier, a rancher, a shipmaster, a diver, a junk-dealer, a wrecker, a dealer in furniture. Sometime after Doctor de Soto and he formed their acquaintanceship, Benjamin was dealing in junk, and became the owner of the dismantled hull of the steamship Idaho, which he purchased from Cahn and Coin for $250. Being both of them inventive and benevolent, they conceived the idea of turning the hull into a hospital, in which to treat the emergency cases that were continually arising along the water front and in the streets of the city. They sought Judge Greene for such aid as he might be able to give them. He saw that their proposition was practicable, and the Seattle Benevolent Society was organized April 1, 1899, to work the matter into operation. The society consisted of Roger S. Greene, Frank D. Black, Amos O. Benjamin, Alexander Beers, Alexander de Soto, James W. Cowan and George G. Bright. Judge Greene was president, Mr. Black vice president and Mr. Bright secretary. Captain Benjamin presented the Idaho to the society. A suitable site was provided by the city in the water at the foot of Jackson Street, where a gridiron was built and the hull set upon it and put in serviceable repair. Doctor de Soto resigned from the board of trustees, in order to become lessee of the hospital and James Johnson, appointed in his room, became secretary. The hull was speedily built upon and fitted up as a hospital, under lease to the doctor, at the monthly rent of $20.00, which was to be rebated monthly, so long as the management of the leased property should be satisfactory to the society. The society has never changed its officers, nor its organization. Its property became widely known all over the city and up and down the Pacific coast as the "Wayside Mission Hospital." Under Doctor de Soto's care it served a very useful purpose, receiving and treating the city emergency patients, for about four years. Doctor de Soto kept aboard the hospital a loyal henchman of his, an athlete and ex-prize-fighter, whom he imported from the Atlantic seaboard, and whose duty was that of a sergeant at arms and special policeman, to keep unruly patients within the bounds of propriety, protect property and prevent unauthorized intrusion upon the premises. In July, 1904, Doctor de Soto's management becoming unsatisfactory, his lease was revoked and the leasehold management turned over to Mrs. Fanny W. Connor and Mrs. Marion Baxter. They operated the premises until the hull became leaky and the Oregon Improvement Company, whose dock lay just at the mouth of the hospital, required for its own business new railway trackage on the south, and persuaded the city to remove the hospital ship. The hospital moved to the old "Sarah B. Yesler" at the northwest corner of Second Avenue North, and Republican Street, where the hospital was operated for several years longer, by the same name, under the management of Mrs. Baxter, caring for the city emergency cases until the city hospital at the northwest corner of Fifth Avenue and Yesler Way went into commission.

Early in 1902 Health Officer Carroll issued an order to vaccinate all pupils in order to check a spread of smallpox, of which many cases were in the city. Public buildings, school rooms and homes were fumigated and every effort made to stop the spread of the disease. During 1901 there were a total of 558 cases of contagious diseases, of which 203 were smallpox cases, 259 scarlet fever, 44 diphtheria and 52 measles. The pesthouse was overcrowded. A campaign of fumigation and sanitation was conducted throughout the entire city. It was necessary to appoint several additional health inspectors. Thousands of people throughout the city were vaccinated.

In 1902 it was decided to establish an emergency hospital for the poor and unfortunate at Fifth Avenue and Yesler Way. In December, 1901, 760 rooms and 120 houses in this city were fumigated by quarantine inspectors.

In ten days in January, 1902, 20,000 persons were vaccinated in this city, of whom 12,500 were school children.

In 1901, 232,660 gallons of milk were inspected, of which 155 gallons were condemned. In 1903 the office of meat inspector was created and William R. Sutter placed in charge. This was an important and necessary step, made necessary by the large number of animals slaughtered here. In 1902 there were killed in this city 26,608 cattle, 93,200 sheep, 62,299 hogs and 1,032 calves. In all, 17,564 pounds of meat were condemned. During this year there were 420 cases of smallpox and 298 cases of scarlet fever; also, this year, 4,490 rooms were fumigated. So energetic and thorough was the health department that in January,

1903, tie city for tie first time in many years was absolutely free from smallpox and iad few cases of otier epidemic diseases.

At tie annual banquet of tie medical society in 1903, tiere were present a large attendance, and Dr. C. W. Siarples acted as toastmaster. D. A. Mitciell was tie retiring president and J. P. Sweeney was tie incoming president. Papers were read by Doctors Smiti, Holmes and Scioenle.

Tiis year tiere were four sanitary inspectors in tiis city. Seattle iad a free medical dispensary under tie management of Dr. James A. Mooers. At tiis time tie Seattle General Hospital could accommodate only about seventy-five persons in 1903. However, it was planned to double its capacity, and in tie meantime tie Providence Hospital accommodated about one iundred and twenty-five.

In 1903 over tiree iundred tiousand gallons of milk were inspected. Tiere were tested for butter fat 2,779 gallons. At tie stock yards 347 inspections were made. Tie meat markets were also tiorougily inspected. Tiere were condemned over eigity-five tiousand pounds of meat.

Doctor Kidd of tie state board of iealti made tie tubercular tests. At tiis time not a drop of milk was allowed to be sold in tiis city until after it iad been inspected.

Tie year 1904 was very important because all iealti and sanitary measures were improved as never before in any one year. Notwitistanding tiese efforts many diseases were epidemic or nearly so, but were kept in subjection by tie intelligent metiods introduced and carried into execution.

Early in 1905 tie Grace Hospital was torn down. It iad been leased for a time by tie Wasiington General Hospital Association in tie '80s and a little later was abandoned as a iospital.

Tiis year tie Metropolitan Hospital and Sanitarium was establisied. At tiis time osteopatiy began to be practiced iere quite extensively. An epidemic of grippe and pneumonia swept over tie wiole city.

In 1905 tie King County Medical Association tried to induce all milk dealers to iandle only milk tiat iad been inspected. It was an up-iill movement, but was in a measure successful. Tie board of iealti building was condemned late in 1906 and tie board moved to a building at Fourti Avenue and Jefferson Street.

From 1900 to 1905 tie number of tie medical and surgical profession iad expanded to 275. Several additional names follow: H. Eugene Allen, F. R. Ballard, F. A. Booti, F. S. Bourns, Grant Calioun, A. C. Crookall, W. R. I. Dalton, Myra Everly, F. J. Filz, Rowe France, J. A. Gient, W. C. Gibson, E. E. Grant, F. L. Horsfall, E. Janson, S. H. Knowles, J. S. McBride, C. E. and R. A. McClure, J. A. Mooers, E. C. Neville, Don H. Palmer, I. A. Parry, E. M. Riniger, H. A. Siaw, R. M. Stiti, A. C. Stoddart, J. C. Tioms, P. V. Von Piul, S. F. Wiltsie.

At tiis time tie King County Medical Society was in active operation and doubtless members of tie profession arriving iere during later years iave been included in its ranks and tieir names will appear in its list of membersiip.

Early in 1907 a special ciildren's iospital was planned by tie women of Seattle, ieaded by Mrs. J. W. Clise, tie object being to make iealtiy, self-supporting ciildren from weaklings and cripples. It became known in the end as tie Children's Orthopedic Hospital. The incorporators were as follows: Anna H. Clise, Anna C. Collins, Nettie G. Black, and tie trustees were Ella D. Godwin, Susan Henry, Elsa T. Backus, Halcon R. Gray, Jean H. Kerr, Jennette N. Heiffs, Dorotiy P. Kane, Katierine G. Kerry, Bessie T. Lewis, Eliza F. Leary, Lillian G. McEwen, Henrietta T. Morgan, Emma C. Nettleton, Maude B. Parsons, Mrs. Peters, Olive W. Roberts, Susan Smiti, Hattie O. Stimson, Nellie Stimson, Olive G. Treat, Bessie B. Wilson and tie tiree incorporators. From tie start tie organization received assurances of substantial support from many prominent business men. This iospital became well supported and exerted great influence for good, and soon numbered among its members and active supporters scores of tie best women and citizens of tie city.

That Seattle would, sooner or later, iave to deal with tie question of bubonic plague iad long been recognized by observing people. San Francisco iad been an infected port for many years, likewise Honolulu and tie Pacific ports of South America; tirougiout Asia tie disease iad become epidemic, and Seattle, being a seaport town with commercial relations by vessel with all of tie points mentioned, and also by rail with San Francisco, it was almost inevitable tiat sooner or later tie disease would make its appearance iere.

In anticipation of suci a contingency, a rat ordinance, similar to tiat in force in San Francisco, iad been passed by tie city council in September, 1907. The wisdom of iaving suci a law in effect, giving autiority to tie iealth department to carry on a campaign, in case it siould be necessary, was siown sooner tian expected by tie finding of a case of bubonic plague in a Ciinaman on October 16ti of tie same year. As soon as tie diagnosis iad been definitely made, a policy of active work, looking to tie eradication of tie disease, was immediately decided upon. Witiin a few days two otier cases of plague were discovered and verified, making a total of tiree in human beings. The last case was on October 31, 1907.

In tie ligit of tie fact tiat bubonic plague existed in tie city, it became evident tiat tiere iad in all probability been four otier cases of tiis dread disease, tiougi none of tiese could be verified. Seattle iad, tien, tiree verified and four probable cases of plague during tie monti of October.

Mayor William Hickman Moore recognized tie fact tiat Seattle was confronted with tie greatest menace to ier growti, boti piysically and commercially, and with ciaracteristic promptness a vigorous campaign for tie stamping out of tie disease was begun. He appointed Dr. Frank S. Bourns, who but tiree years previously iad settled in Seattle, fresi from iis labors as iealti officer of Manila, P. I., wiere ie iad been forced to cope with boti bubonic plague and Asiastic ciolera, as special iealti officer with power to organize a special branci of tie iealti department. Co-operation was asked of tie state and Federal authorities, with tie result tiat early in November Dr. L. E. Cofer, past assistant surgeon of tie United States Public Healti and Marine Hospital Service, arrived in tie city to take ciarge for tie Federal Government. The new Federal laboratory, on exiibition at tie Jamestown Exposition, was immediately forwarded to tiis city by express and a bacteriologist of tie Federal Government placed in ciarge of tiat branci of tie work. Tiat laboratory, with a Federal past assistant surgeon in ciarge of tie work, still remains in tie city, and carries on tie examination of rats.

DR. H. EUGENE ALLEN

The object of the work from the beginning was: First, by cleaning up the city and removing rat food and rat harbors, to make the city less favorable for the propagation of rats; second, to exterminate rats insofar as possible to do so with the means at command; third, to keep a careful watch on the situation by examining in the special laboratory as many of the rats that were captured and killed as possible. It is well known that a decided epidemic occurs in rats before human cases are found, so that, as long as this work is kept up but little fear need be entertained of a further outbreak of the disease, especially in view of the success that has accompanied the work up to the present time.

The city council provided liberally for this work, about thirty thousand dollars being spent in the first few months of the campaign.

A program of publicity was inaugurated to offset the dangers threatening, the measures recommended and a widespread interest was awakened among the citizens.

By 1909, at the time of the fair, a total of twenty-one rats had been pronounced plague infected by the Federal laboratory. At the same time every health and sanitary measure deemed necessary was adopted. The women's clubs did a great deal in the interest of sanitation and health generally. At all times they were active workers in conjunction with the health department, the inspectors and medical organizations. They raised large sums of money to assist in carrying out these measures.

On March 8, 1908, a charter amendment was ratified by the people of Seattle, at a general election, abolishing the board of health and providing for the appointment of a commissioner of health by the mayor, subject to confirmation by the council, who should be appointed for a term of five years. On March 23, 1908, Dr. J. E. Crichton was appointed to this position by Mayor John F. Miller. At the same election civil service was extended to embrace the department of health and sanitation.

Having served for years previously as a member of the city council, Doctor Crichton was eminently fitted for the work of reorganizing and modernizing the health department, and with many close friends in the council whose aid he could depend upon, and with a widespread interest in public health awakened, he had little opposition.

A. A. Braymer, who had entered the department in the year 1907, was appointed chief clerk and secretary and was authorized to immediately draft and submit a plan of reorganization, which plan was adopted in the form of an ordinance, enumerating the branches, positions and salaries. On July 10, 1908, this ordinance reorganizing the department became effective, and with an up-to-date department, both in numerical strength and personnel, Doctor Crichton plunged into the work of attaining a high standard in public health work, with economy and efficiency throughout the department.

In 1908 the government inspectors publicly stated that the milk supply of Seattle was as unhealthful as any in the country. Immediately upon taking office Dr. J. E. Crichton began a relentless crusade against impure milk. Before the close of 1913 no more wholesome food or drink product could be found in the country than in Seattle. The result was a great reduction in the death rate of small children. In 1908 the whole Sound water front was covered with litter and filth, among which rats infected with bubonic plague found homes.

By 1913 all this had been abolished. Shacktown, too, was obliterated and the miserable dwellers were removed to sanitary quarters.

Of course this all cost a lot of money and he was assailed by critics for his extravagant expenditures. The medical fraternity and the various public organizations generally, including the Anti-Tuberculosis League, endorsed his official actions, and it was the general verdict that the attacks upon him were largely political in their nature.

While the people were getting ready for the great fair of 1909, the activities of the health department redoubled. Cleaning up streets and alleys and vacant lots became a crusade. Every sanitary precaution was adopted to put the city in perfect health condition and keep it there. In particular there was a widespread movement against spitting in street cars and public places and on the sidewalks. A stringent ordinance was enacted which was enforced strictly by the police and health officers. The movement was mostly directed against the "white plague." This scourge of humanity had headed the death list with 136 in 1905, 183 in 1907, and 218 in 1908. This called for active measures and the result was a concerted and determined movement of all health organizations to check or crush the disease.

In 1909 a most energetic campaign against the typhoid fly was waged here. A monthly bulletin was issued by the health department with illustrations, giving complete accounts of the campaign and showing the danger from this apparently innocent insect. Lecturers from abroad came here and described fully to school children and citizens generally the constant danger in which the presence of the ordinary typhoid fly placed them.

In August the medical society passed a resolution asking the Legislature to adopt the Arizona law concerning the punishment of practicing medicine without a license. The society also endorsed the compulsory vaccination of children. They also endorsed an examination for nurses before a proper board of examination.

Early in 1909 the new municipal hospital was put in operation. It was greatly needed and was at once occupied by a number of patients. At this time the examination of the bake shops and similar institutions was ordered and carried into execution. Improved sanitation in the city had greatly reduced the number of typhoid cases for the years 1907 and 1908. The result was due almost wholly to the strict sanitary regulations that had been carried into effect. Milk, meat, bread, restaurant products, water, garbage, had been carefully inspected, and flies, rats and every other probable source of disease were guarded against. Late in 1908 there were twelve medical school inspectors, also three nurses for the sixty-two public schools of the city. Dr. H. Eugene Allen was in charge of this branch of the work.

This measure resulted in completely checking the epidemics which had previously swept through one or more of our public schools. On the last day of March, 1909, nineteen patients from the Wayside Hospital were removed to the city's emergency hospital on the fourth floor of the new municipal building. The council appropriated sufficient means to care for the patients. At the start the hospital contained twenty-five patients. It had accommodations for fifty and upon forced conditions could accommodate eighty. There were rooms for operation, surgery, men, women and other branches of hospital service. One doctor remained at the hospital night and day. Dr. J. E. Crichton, as commissioner of health, had general charge of the institution.

Early in 1909 Mrs. Henry Fuhrman bequeathed $10,000 to the Children's Orthopedic Hospital.

The twenty-second annual convention of the Washington State Dental Association met in this city. There was a free public clinic and many public demonstrations. There was a strong organization of dentists in this city, who were greatly interested in advances in their profession, and many attended this annual convention. About the same time the first annual meeting of the State Homeopathic Society assembled here, the president being Dr. E. Weldon Young of this city. There was a large attendance and many interesting papers were read by physicians from all parts of the state.

The year 1909 ended with an unprecedented campaign against tuberculosis. The health department, the medical society, the hospital forces, the city authorities and the citizens generally carried on a campaign during the fall months with great energy and enthusiasm. Thousands of circulars describing the danger were distributed throughout this community. Lecturers expatiated day and night on the dangers. An organized campaign of education for the control of consumption and the conservation of health was in a large measure conducted by the King County Anti-tuberculosis League.

In February, 1910, the King County Medical Society appointed a special committee to investigate all municipal undertakings for the protection of public health. At this time the society reported on the progress made in anti-plague work. The City Emergency Hospital at this time became a staff institution and was attended by several of the best local physicians. It was still in charge of Dr. J. E. Crichton and specialists were ever present to care for the unfortunates. In January of that year nearly one hundred and fifty cases were handled, which number reached the capacity of the hospital. An average of forty-seven patients per day was present.

In the spring the sum of $10,000 was voted and appropriated for a tuberculosis hospital by the State Legislature and the beneficiary became and since has been known as the Seattle Pulmonary Hospital, situated at Riverton. By the death of Miss Loretta Denny this institution was remembered in a bequest included in the will, which set apart $7,000 to be used in the support of the hospital, and her niece, Miss Lenora Denny, took the necessary steps to carry out the provisions of the generous gift. She devoted much time in this regard and while so employed her own interest in the movement was aroused, to the extent that she finally was impelled to contribute out of her own resources considerable sums of money from time to time, which in the aggregate far exceeded the original bequest.

During the years 1910-11 the health authorities continued the splendid work of improving sanitary conditions. There was a large health conference in this city late in December, 1910, on which occasion all health measures and the nature of diseases were fully discussed. It was decided that inspection throughout the city should be more thorough and cover a wider range of subjects. The laboratories here, both of the city and of the United States Government, assisted immensely in these measures. It was believed at this time that Seattle was more energetic and more effective in carrying out sanitation and health measures than any other city of the Pacific Coast.

A ward in the municipal hospital for children afflicted with infantile paralysis was provided late in 1910. At this time it was determined to assist children who had thus been paralyzed and rendered imperfect and unhappy. It was stated by the health department that in 1904 there were in the whole world only 250 cases known to exist and that six years later there were over eight thousand cases, of which 260 were in this state and over one hundred in this city. This was a startling announcement and set the health department and authorities into action. It was stated that about seventy-five per cent of the children afflicted with this disease were left with paralyzed limbs and thus became public charges.

In January, 1911, the city had a free dental clinic in a room of the municipal hospital for deserving children of the poor. Members of the King County Dental Society gave these children their services free of charge.

The cornerstone of the New Orthopedic Hospital was laid in March at Warren and Crockett streets; the institution cost in the end about one hundred thousand dollars.

The New Providence' Hospital, which cost about one million dollars, was formally opened in September at Seventeenth Avenue and Jefferson Street.

In 1910 a proposition was submitted to the people for their approval to issue $400,000 worth of bonds, to be used for the purchase of the equipment necessary to collect, and to build incinerators necessary to destroy, garbage. The cost of collection and destruction was to be included in the tax levy each year. The bonds were voted at the following election, but when they were offered for sale legal objections were raised which somewhat delayed the sale. Mayor Dilling strongly advocated the collection of garbage by the contract system, the payment being made by the ton, a contract rate being made for each district. The board of public works finally arranged for such a contract and collection under this system started August 1, 1911. This was, therefore, a semi-municipal collection and a complete municipal destruction and disposal system by incinerators, dumping in the Sound by scows and some large garbage dumps. During the year 1911 the collection was about two hundred and fifty tons daily in the summer months and about three hundred tons during the colder months.

The old incinerator, known as No. 1, had been built and in operation for some time; another one was completed late in the year and the third one, on the north shore of Lake Union, was started. Mr. Chas. L. Murray was appointed superintendent of the garbage division, which was made a branch of the Department of Health and Sanitation.

The contract for garbage collection expired January 31, 1913, having been let for eighteen months and, on February 1, 1913, the city commenced complete municipal collection with its own wagons, although the horses, harness and two men on each wagon were hired by the day. This arrangement as to collection prevails at the present time.

One by one, since the expiration of the contract collection system, a number of sanitary fills have been put in operation in different portions of the city, on city property with few exceptions, and permanent fills made on these waste lands of considerable value. As the garbage from each district was taken care of by tiese fills tie incinerators were closed down one at a time, tie last, No. 4, being closed in August, 1915, wiile towing and dumping from scows was discontinued in June, 1914.

Asies and garbage are collected in one can and tie metiod of making tie sanitary fill is to level tie dumping of eaci day and cover it witi a layer of dirt, spraying tie garbage during tie warmer montis witi a solution to kill larvae, etc. Tiese fills are not objectionable from a iealti standpoint, dispose of garbage cieaply, reduce tie cost of collection very materially by reducing tie lengti of tie iaul and increase tie value of tie land, making it available for public use.

From laboratory investigations it is siown tiat everytiing of an organic nature is tiorougily incinerated in tiese fills in from twelve to eigiteen montis, less tian 1 per cent of decomposing matter remaining after ten montis.

Tiere exists in tiis city an almost unlimited number of places wiici can be beautified, made valuable and useful by means of tiese sanitary fills, wiile tie saving in boti collection and destruction is enormous.

Tie total cost of collection and destruction in tie year 1915 was about one iundred tiousand dollars less tian during tie year 1912 under tie collection contract system and tie system of destruction by incinerators and by towing and dumping in tie bay, witi a collection 25 per cent greater in tie year 1915.

During 1912 about six million gallons of milk were consumed in tiis city from wiat was called tie "Seattle Milk Sied." All was inspected. Tie meat inspection was tiorougi. In fact all food and drink products were critically examined. Tie laboratories served a splendid purpose in detecting unwiolesomeness in food products.

After tie deati of Dr. E. M. Riniger from an automobile accident in tie summer of 1912, iis iospital passed to tie Swedisi Hospital Association in Marci and tie sale was confirmed by tie court. Tie property brougit $90,723. Tiere were seventy rooms in tie institution. Dr. Riniger's library was donated to tie new iospital by iis widow, Mrs. E. H. Riniger. Tie old Swedisi Hospital was at 1733 Belmont Avenue.

Tie iistory of Firland Sanitorium begins witi tie iistory of tie Anti-Tuberculosis League of King County, wiici was organized in February, 1909. Soon after tie organization of tie league, a visiting nurse, Mrs. Bessie Davis, was employed, who demonstrated tiat tiere were numbers of tuberculous people in Seattle who were sadly in need of care. Soon otier nurses were engaged—Miss Laura Atkinson, and later Mrs. Edna L. Robinson—and it was siown tiat even witi tiese nurses visiting and caring for tie patients in tieir iomes, sometiing more must be done, if the community was to wage a successful war on tuberculosis. A sanatorium or iospital was necessary wiere isolation could be maintained, and proper care given.

In 1910 H. C. Henry became president of tie Anti-Tuberculosis League, and donated tiirty-four acres of land at Ricimond Higilands for tie use of a sanatorium, and iere in May, 1911, tie present institution iad its beginning in several small cottages, iousing twenty-four patients. Even witi aid from tie county and city autiorities it was found by September, 1911, tiat tie expense of maintaining visiting nurses and tie operation of tie small sanatorium was too great a burden for tie piilantiropically inclined to iear. A memorial was presented to Mayor

Geo. A. Dilling, the Chamber of Commerce, and the Commercial Club, asking the appointment of a committee to investigate the tuberculosis situation, and outline a plan for its control in the City of Seattle. Mayor Dilling appointed such a commission, consisting of Dr. J. E. Crichton, A. B. Stewart, C. Allan Dale, Rev. J. E. O'Brien and Leo Kohn.

After thoroughly studying the situation, the committee submitted an exhaustive report to Mayor Dilling, containing detailed recommendation for all phases of the work; making provision for all stages of the disease; advising that the city undertake the care of its tuberculosis problem, centering the control in the Health Department and urging hospital care of the advanced cases as especially important and first to be considered.

About this time the Anti-Tuberculosis League offered to donate its little sanatorium and thirty-four acres at Richmond Highlands to the City of Seattle, and H. C. Henry offered $25,000 for an administration building if the city would undertake the care of the tuberculous along the line of the commission's report.

In February, 1912, the City Council submitted to the voters a proposition for a bond issue of $125,000 for the erection of a Hospital-Sanatorium. The bond issue carried by a vote of 82 per cent for, and 18 per cent against.

On June 1, 1912, the little sanatorium at Richmond Highlands was turned over to the City Health Department. It had a bed capacity of forty-three.

After more than a year's consideration, plans for a complete Hospital-Sanatorium were adopted and the erection of the first units began in June, 1913. It was decided also during this year to erect an Isolation Hospital for the City of Seattle on the tract at Richmond Highlands. The whole institution to be known as Firland Sanatorium. However, it was soon found that $125,000 from the bond issue would not be sufficient to finish the first buildings as planned, and the City Council then appropriated sufficient money for their completion.

The present group consists of an administration building, hospital building, power house and laundry, isolation hospital, children's pavilion, and several small cottages of the original sanatorium. The buildings were completed and furnished in 1914, and patients were moved in on November, 1914. The city at this time also taking over all the tuberculous patients (45) then at the King County Hospital in Georgetown. The present bed capacity, including cottages and children's pavilion, is for 160 patients.

The Isolation Hospital has proven very beneficial, as it assists the control of infectious diseases by establishing absolute quarantine for all cases confined therein, and also makes it possible, for those upon whom depends the work of supplying funds, to keep the balance of the family at home in supplies.

A necessary part of tuberculosis work in every community is the Tuberculosis Dispensary, where suspected cases can be diagnosed, and, with a corps of visiting nurses, to visit the homes where there is tuberculosis to supervise and instruct the care in home surroundings. Such a dispensary was established in 1910 in the Cobb Building, later moved to the Anti-Tuberculosis League Building and in January, 1914, again moved, this time to the City Hall. Later a branch was established in the old Ballard City Hall. For the last two years the city has been thoroughly covered by an able corps of visiting nurses.

The dispensary also acts as an admission bureau for Firland Sanatorium and a clearing 1ouse for all matters relating to tuberculosis in t1e community. Dr. Robert M. Smit1 has been in c1arge of all branc1es of t1e tuberculosis work and of Firland Sanatorium since t1e year 1910.

On August 5, 1907, t1e first ordinance, No. 16366, relating to t1e establis1ment of public markets in t1e city was passed. T1is ordinance designated a portion of Pike Place for t1e sale of garden, farm and ot1er food products from wagons, or ot1er similar ve1icles, under certain conditions during certain 1ours. By subsequent ordinances, from time to time, t1e amount of space allotted was extended as were also t1e 1ours, a s1ed roof over space inside t1e sidewalk for tables was erected, and in 1915 a modern office on street level was added, t1e old office being converted into a store room.

On April 16, 1908, an ordinance was passed aut1orizing t1e mayor to appoint a market master and anot1er on October 12th aut1orizing t1e Commissioner of Healt1 to appoint a sanitary market inspector.

It was not until July 31, 1911, t1at an ordinance was passed making a c1arge of 20 cents a day for occupancy of eac1 stall, table or boot1 to 1elp pay t1e expenses of t1e market, but in November of t1e same year, t1is c1arge was reduced to 10 cents, and still remains t1e same.

In April, 1912, t1e market master and t1e public markets were placed under t1e Department of Healt1 and Sanitation. T1e public market 1as been of inestimable value to t1e public and especially to t1e wage earner. Here t1e producer and consumer meet wit1out any middleman's profit. It materially serves to reduce t1e cost of living and also enables t1e purc1aser to obtain t1e fres1est supplies direct from t1e farm. \ery stringent sanitary regulations are enforced as to covering meats, bakery goods and food stuffs of like c1aracter. T1e sanitary and meat inspection divisions maintain a daily inspection service over all markets. During t1e year 1915 over six t1ousand two 1undred farmers boug1t tickets w1ic1 allowed t1em to dispose of t1eir products on t1e public market.

T1e City Council·provided funds by ordinance in 1912 to send an ex1ibit to be arranged by t1e Department of Healt1 to t1e Fifteent1 International Con gress on Hygiene and Demograp1y in \\as1ington, D. C., in September of t1at year. Dr. J. E. Cric1ton, Commissioner of Healt1, and A. A. Braymer, Secretary of t1e Healt1 Department, were commissioned delegates to the congress by t1e· mayor, Mr. Braymer 1aving c1arge of t1e installation of t1e ex1ibit. T1ey also attended t1e fortiet1 annual meeting of t1e American Public Healt1 Association, 1eld in Was1ington at t1e same time. T1is ex1ibit took first prize in its class, attracted probably t1e greatest attention of any like ex1ibit and was t1e means of giving wide publicity to t1e low deat1 rate, climate and attractive surroundings of t1e City of Seattle.

T1is ex1ibit, after its return from Was1ington, formed t1e greater portion of t1e ex1ibit 1eld under t1e auspices of t1e Seattle Committee on Public Healt1 and Hygiene in t1e early spring of t1e following year. Mr. Braymer was also aut1orized to visit some of t1e larger tuberculosis sanatoriums in t1e East, to gat1er t1e newest ideas to be incorporated in t1e new Firland Sanatorium. One of t1ese is the present feeding arrangements at Firland, a great improvement over t1at found to be in use at Mattapan, in Boston. Many new ideas in public 1ealt1 work were gat1ered from t1e meetings, lectures and ex1ibits attended and later incorporated in t1e work of t1e Healt1 Department.

In January, 1913, the first public morgue in the city was established and Dr. J. T. Mason, county coroner, assumed control. In the spring the Seattle Committee on Public Health and Hygiene exhibited here the most capable plans for city sanitation and health ever shown on the Pacific Coast. The complete bacteriological and chemical laboratories of the Health Department, with their wonderful microscopic specimens, were employed to make the exhibit more effective. Bacteria, microbes, germs and section of flies, fleas, bedbugs and insects, were shown on screens. "Swat the Fly" was the war cry of the Health Department. The admonition, "Don't Spit in Public Places," was posted and published everywhere. A sanitary dairy was shown. Scores of food products were exhibited in all stages of impurity. This was a campaign of education in sanitation and health measures and was perhaps the most vital step thus far taken by the department. The death rate of Seattle for 1913 was 8.4 per 1,000. No city of the country made a better showing. In 1912 the death rate here was 8.5. The average from 1905 to 1910 was 9.8 and the average from 1901 to 1905 was 9.3. The active campaign against infectious diseases caused a good portion of this reduction in 1913.

The Benson estate, valued at $18,111.41, was bequeathed to the Children's Orthopedic Hospital by Theodore S. Benson in 1913. Of the total sum $1,700 was in cash and the balance embraced the home at Interbay, personal property, stocks and bonds. He died in 1911 but the property was not secured until two years later. Previous to his death he donated $1,000 for a bed in the hospital to be named for his deceased wife, Caroline Greenlief Benson. The attorneys and the administrator refused their fees amounting to $890, donating all to the hospital. In August, 1913, twenty-seven cases were treated. There were twenty-two operations and fifty-two plaster casts were used.

During the seven years ending with 1914 the Orthopedic Hospital reported a total of 1,002 applications of children, of which 824 were accepted. They came from half a dozen states and Alaska and one from India. At the annual meeting, Mrs. Charles D. Stimson, the vice president, occupied the chair. Eight new trustees were elected as follows: Mrs. H. C. Henry, Mrs. J. W. Clise, Mrs. C. R. Collins, Mrs. M. A. Gottstein, Mrs. L. H. Gray, Mrs. A. B. Stewart, Mrs. J. W Godwin, Mrs. C. B. Dodge.

In September, 1913, the milk division, under the auspices of the Mother's Congress of this city, held the first competitive milk contest of its kind in the United States. This contest consisted of taking samples of milk from each dealer in the city without previous notice and the scoring of the same according to the United States Dairy Department's score card for milk. This form of contest was found to be of such value as a means of improving the milk supply that it has not only been adopted as a permanent procedure of this division, but the plan has been inaugurated by many other cities throughout the United States. The results of the first contest were as follows:

Average score certified milk, 94.18; average score raw market milk, 75.70; average score pasteurized milk, 58.02. The improvement in the milk supply since 1913 is readily seen, by comparing the above scores with those made in December, 1915, which are as follows:

Average score certified milk, 97.93; average score raw milk, 92.28; average score pasteurized milk, 91.78.

While the milk contests have been one of the most important means of improving the city's milk supply, a number of other agencies and activities have been of assistance, noteworthy among these are the activities which interest the consumer in the purity of the milk supply. As a means of arousing interest in the character of the milk supply, the Pacific Northwest Association of Dairy and Milk Inspectors held a two-days' convention here in May, 1914, there being sixty delegates in attendance. They considered in detail bovine tuberculosis. A. N. Henderson was president of the association. Ways and means of interesting the public in the pure milk movement were discussed. The first score of the milk plant supplying Seattle consumers under the new system began by Inspector A. N. Henderson was given out by the convention. The results ran all the way from pretty good to very poor. Forty points constituted the maximum allowed for equipment, including arrangements and construction of buildings, apparatus, laboratories and water supply, while sixty points were the maximum allowed for methods; embracing cleanliness of apparatus and handling, cleanliness of attendants, etc.

The enactment of the new milk ordinance in July, 1915, without doubt created more interest on the part of the consumers regarding their milk supply than any other activity undertaken by this division. Previous to the passage of the new ordinance the division had been working under an ordinance enacted in 1907, at which time this ordinance was undoubtedly an adequate measure, however, the development of dairy bacteriology within recent years into an exact science, with the accompanying discovery that the milk supply is ofttimes the specific cause of epidemics of disease, necessitated a measure which would reduce such danger to a minimum. The development in the last few years of the large city milk plants required a measure for their control. The growing popularity of the process of pasteurization among the large milk dealers made necessary the control of such process. The ever increasing danger of the infant contracting tuberculosis through the consumption of raw milk from animals suffering with this disease, made necessary the enactment of measures which would eliminate such danger and, finally, the enormous growth of the city which requires a greatly increased number of producers of milk made necessary the adoption of a more adequate system of permitting the sale of milk.

With the enactment of the new ordinance, all persons employed in milk plants are required to pass a medical examination and the employes, upon all farms upon which milk is produced, are required to show a negative reaction to the Widal test for typhoid fever and a negative culture for the detection of diphtheria. Also the water used upon all dairy farms is now chemically and bacteriologically examined. The new ordinance stipulates a certain construction for all city milk plants and provides methods of handling milk. The process of pasteurization is now not merely a process in name but all milk must be heated to a specified temperature, and maintained at this temperature for a sufficient length of time to kill all pathogenic organisms. All milk sold in the city must now be produced from animals showing a negative reaction to the tuberculin test, or be pasteurized under official supervision. The system of granting permits, authorized by the new ordinance, allows an accurate check of all milk sold in the city and for the first time in the history of the city the new ordinance prescribed a systematic inspection, which includes production and handling of all cream offered for sale.

In 1914 the number of dairies supplying milk to the City of Seattle was 1,275, while the number of cows in these dairies was 11,000, producing 19,000 gallons of milk and cream for Seattle consumption daily. The inspections were 3,816 and 2,587 gallons of milk were condemned. In 1915 the number of cows producing milk and cream for consumption in the city was 15,283, producing 22,322 gallons daily for Seattle. For the first time, during this year, a complete inspection of all the so-called "one cow dairies," which numbered 318 within the city limits, was made, the terms of the new ordinance being enforced. The terms of the new ordinance requiring that all milk sold as a beverage in restaurants shall be served in individual bottles, such bottles to be filled either at the dairy or the milk plant, was put into effect and enforced during 1915.

Dr. Paul A. Turner was appointed medical supervisor of the Seattle City Hospital in March, 1914, and Miss Adeline Perry, a graduate of this hospital, was made supervisor of nurses. Many additions to the equipment and furnishings were installed and other improvements made during this and the year 1915, while new systems were installed throughout the institution, making everything modern and up-to-date. This hospital now acts as a clearing house for the majority of all accidents occurring in the city. On March 16, 1915, ten young ladies were graduated from the training school for nurses of this hospital. This was the third class to graduate after a three-years' course of training, two other smaller classes having graduated, one in 1912 and the other in 1913. The exercises were held in the council chamber in the City Hall. On July 1, 1915, Miss May S. Loomis, for thirteen years previous surgical nurse at the Seattle General Hospital, became supervisor of nurses and has very materially raised the standard of the Nurses Training School and the hospital in general.

Graduating exercises were held in February by the nurses' training class of the Providence Hospital. Twenty-six young women who completed the three years of work required made the class. Seventeen young women were graduated in May, 1914, from the training school for nurses of the Seattle General Hospital; they had completed three years of training.

In March, 1914, Dr. J. S. McBride succeeded Dr. J. E. Crichton as commissioner of health, the latter retiring after six years of most efficient service. Before that he had served continuously from March, 1892, as councilman from the eighth ward, showing most conclusively the estimation in which he was held by his friends and neighbors on Queen Anne Hill. With the staunch support of Mayor Gill and bringing new energy to the department, Doctor McBride instituted changes in the personnel to infuse new blood and energy and obtain better cooperation between some branches of the department, with beneficial results. He elaborated the detail and extended the work and investigations in many branches of the department, thereby intensifying the endeavor to obtain improved conditions in public health work.

During this year the child welfare division of the department of health was established with Dr. W. C. Lippincott in charge. During 1914, in about three months' work, 106 children's boarding houses were inspected and licensed, caring for 528 children. The inspection and regulation of boarding homes for children materially improved the condition under which these children are forced to live. A physical examination of the children disclosed the fact that many of them needed medical attention, which was arranged for. Baby clinics were opened in different sections of the city with the idea of assisting in every way possible those who manifest a desire for medical advice and help.

The Child Welfare Exhibit in 1914 was a striking success of up-to-date health methods and progress. The exhibit told the story of the child's life—its food and drink, its sleep and bath, its warmth and exercise, its clothing and enjoyments were depicted in detail.

By the end of the year 1915 there had been issued 160 permits for children's boarding houses, 446 children had been carefully medically examined while the nurses, during the year, had made 1,069 visits to the homes.

During the early summer there was held the Better Babies Contest, planned by the Mothers' Congress and Parent Teachers' Association with the cooperation of the child welfare division. Mrs. Bogardus, as president, appointed Mrs. Fred Bert chairman of the committee of women in direct charge of the work. The average score of the 2,069 children, between the ages of six months and five years, was 91.87 per cent. All the records obtained were interesting and instructive. The ladies, doctors and other helpers, who planned and carried out this contest, did a real public service and deserve commendation.

Early in the year 1914 the school board decided to avail itself of a provision of the educational code and appoint a medical inspector, to take charge of the medical inspection of the school children in the city schools previously carried on by the health department. On April 1, 1914, this medical inspector was appointed and, shortly thereafter, established a clinic where children of school age, whose family standard of living was below the normal, could receive treatment. This relieved the department of health from the necessity of continuing its medical, optical or dental clinics for school children from the poorer families, which had been in operation by the department for several years.

Among the most strenuous activities of the health department during the years 1914 and 1915 were those for the protection of the Cedar River Watershed, the source of the city supply. All activities within this shed are absolutely under the jurisdiction of the health department, and the most stringent sanitary regulations are required of all those employed within its boundaries. The city is owner of practically all of the land within this watershed and a large portion of the standing timber thereon. However, all the privately-owned timber must be removed under the sanitary regulations laid down by the commissioner of health, in order to positively protect the water supply of the city against pollution. A constant patrol of inspectors has been maintained and no person allowed within, unless for the purpose of performing some necessary work connected with different departments of the city, or private logging operations. Vidal and typhoid inoculations have been required in such cases. Hunting, fishing, picnicking and loitering have been positively prohibited. These precautions, combined with daily laboratory tests of the water as it enters the city, insure the people a pure water supply. Upon the recommendation of Doctor McBride, commissioner of health, an ordinance has been passed providing for the condemnation of the townsite and the removal of the Town of Cedar Falls from the watershed, as it was found that from its location this town would prove a constant danger to the purity of the water.

An ordinance, making it compulsory for all employes in restaurants, bakeries, candy kitchens and confectioneries, to be examined by the health department, was passed in 1910. These examinations had been carried on in the Seattle City Hospital by the internes, but in April, 1914, were transferred to the tuberculosis division, where those trained in the detection of tuberculosis and other infectious diseases, could have an opportunity to thoroughly examine these employes and thus protect the public. A very thorough form of examination is being used and an elaborate record kept on file. In January, 1915, an ordinance was passed requiring a medical examination for all drivers of motor vehicles for hire and these examinations were also added to the work of the tuberculosis division. Later, in July, 1915, one provision of the new milk ordinance required the medical examination of all employes in milk plants, again materially adding to the number of medical examinations to be made by the tuberculosis division of the health department. Over seven thousand persons in all, handling food products, were thus examined during the year 1915 by this division and many carriers of disease excluded from occupation in this line of work until cured.

Early in 1914 Doctor McBride, commissioner of health, directed that steps should be taken to eliminate many swamps and pot-holes constantly filled with stagnant water, with the result that during the following months many such places were filled, earth to an amount of thousands of cubic yards being used for this purpose, while in many other instances drainage systems were installed. Another crusade to eliminate the undesirable housing conditions among the several hundred shacks located on the tide flats, which had sprung up since the last crusade, was undertaken and these shacks condemned and destroyed or removed to better locations. An attempt to abolish the cellar lodging house was made with success after a long court fight and a decision by the State Supreme Court.

Another campaign against the fly was instituted and carried on during 1914-15, the slogan being "Every day is clean up day," with the result that thousands of cubic yards of rubbish were removed and destroyed. The number of old-fashioned vaults has been reduced about one-third, by requiring cesspools or septic tanks to be installed where water under pressure is available. Through the urgent recommendation of the health department many miles of sewers have also been constructed and added to the city system. Stables were closely watched and all wagons hauling refuse or manure required to be covered. The examination of samples of water from private springs, and wells, materially increased the work of the bacteriological and chemical laboratories of the department, as did also the thousands of blood samples and throat cultures taken in medical examinations. The equipment of these laboratories was brought up to date and the force increased to care for the added work.

KING COUNTY MEDICAL SOCIETY

The King County Medical Society was organized at a meeting held in the offices of Drs. Thomas T. Minor and Lewis R. Dawson, on August 13, 1888. At this meeting the constitution and by-laws for the society were adopted and the following officers elected:

Dr. Gideon A. Weed, president; Dr. F. V. Goodspeed, vice president; Dr. J. B. Eagleson, secretary, and Dr. L. R. Dawson, treasurer.

The physicians of the town had met informally on several occasions prior to this time for the reading and discussion of scientific papers, but this was the first attempt to form a regular organization.

The credentials of the following named physicians were passed upon by a committee and they were found entitled to sign the roll as charter members: Drs. T. T. Minor, Rufus Willard, E. L. Smith, C. Holzschuler, J. M. S. Smart, Jas. Shannon, G. M. Mills, L. A. Dawson, T. V. Goodspeed, J. B. Eagleson, H. M. Hall, G. A. Weed and Geo. A. Reich.

During the remainder of the year bi-monthly meetings were held in the offices of the different members which were well attended. Scientific papers were read and discussed and several difficult and interesting cases presented. By the end of the year there were twenty-three members in good standing. Drs. Franz H. Coe, Ellsworth E. Shaw, W. A. Shannon, A. R. Kibbe, Mary Brown Winslow, I. B. Loughery, John P. Sweeney, G. F. M. Kriegh, W. M. Van Der Volzen and S. J. Holmes had been added to the rolls of the society.

The society continued to increase and prosper and in 1890 rented a room in the Pioneer Building for a regular meeting place. It continued to meet there until 1893 when the use of the rooms of the Chamber of Commerce was offered and accepted.

During this period such well known physicians as C. A. Smith, Casper W. Sharples, George Newlands, D. M. Stone, D. A. Mitchell, F. S. Palmer, Alfred Raymond, Montgomery Russell, G. B. McCulloch, Sarah J. Dean and P. W Willis had established practice here and joined the medical society, entering actively into its work and helping to make it a successful and useful organization.

Seattle was fortunate in attracting men from the best schools in America to locate here. The standards have been kept high because young, ambitious, well-grounded and highly educated physicians have been drawn here from the great universities in all parts of the world and these men have naturally fallen into the leadership of medical affairs in the community. They have given their services freely to uplift and advance their profession and to educate and protect the community. They have worked consistently for measures to protect the public health. They have fostered legislation, designed to maintain a high standard in their professional ranks and protect the people from being imposed upon by the fraudulent and ignorant practitioner. It would be difficult to estimate the good accomplished by members of the society as individuals in their private practice, in the way of educating the people in matters of public health and the prevention of disease.

The medical society has many times taken the lead in pointing out means of improving the sanitary conditions of the city and its members have stood behind the health authorities and given them aid and assistance in carrying out their work. The society appointed the first milk commission, consisting of Drs. R. M. Stith, chairman; G. B. McCulloch, F. P. Gardner, P. V. Von Phul and W. G. Booth, in November, 1905, which led to the production of certified milk, and was the beginning of the campaign which has resulted in giving this city one of the cleanest milk supplies in the world, and has reduced the mortality in infants to such a low figure that our statistics were received abroad with incredulity. Our cool summers have much to do with this low infant mortality, but the fact remains that it was not remarkably low until our milk supply was improved. It has had the same effect in lowering the death rate in typioid fever, so tiat now we iave tie lowest rate of any city in tie world for tiis disease, except Tie Hague, Holland. Wien it is considered tiat tie typioid deati rate is generally taken as tie index of tie sanitation of a city, we iave reason to be proud of our position. Tiis great work was mainly accomplisied during tie administration of Dr. J. E. Criciton, as commissioner of iealti, from 1908 to 1914, and ias been ably carried on and improved by Doctor McBride.

The medical society iad used its influence in bringing about a revision of tie ciarter, doing away witi tie Board of Healti and appointing a commissioner of iealti, wio siould devote all iis time to tie position, serve for a term of five years and receive a salary of $5,000 a year, tius concentrating tie responsibility on one man. Tiis was finally accomplisied in 1908 and tie splendidly efficient department built up by Dr. J. E. Criciton, tie first commissioner of iealti, justified its endeavors.

In 1906, wien tie Ciicago, Milwaukee & St. Paul Railway iad acquired a rigit of way along tie Cedar River tirougi tie watersied from wici was obtained tie water supply of Seattle, tie medical society took tie matter up and appointed a committee to investigate. Tie committee consisted of Drs. J. B. Eagleson, H. M. Read, J. H. Lyons and P. W. Willis. It visited tie watersied and found tie proposed survey would carry tie grade along tie very edge of tie stream for miles above tie intake and provided for several crossings. During construction, witi a large force of men and animals working under suci conditions, a terrible epidemic of disease would iave been certain to occur and even after completion tie city would be constantly menaced. Tie figit was carried before tie ciamber of commerce, tie city council, commercial club and into tie newspapers, and a campaign of education was started tiat finally aroused tie city to tie danger and resulted in tie railway company moving its tracks fartier away from tie river at great expense. Bridges witi covered decks and drainage ditcies and basins were provided, so tiat no surface drainage could enter tie stream above tie intake. But for tiis action we would iave been subject to water epidemics and our proud position, as tie iealtiiest city in tie United States, would iave been lost to us.

Tie members of tie King County Medical Society are all members of tie Wasiington State Medical Association and, being tie largest county society in tie state, its members iave entered into tie work of tie state association and largely influenced its course and growti. Several Seattle piysicians iave been ionored by official positions in tie state association and on several occasions tie annual meeting ias been ield iere. Tie late Dr. Franz H. Coe presided at a meeting of tiat association in Seattle only a few days before iis deati in 1903, and witi iis wonderful energy ie conducted a most successful meeting and entertained royally and, altiougi ie was suffering greatly at tie time and realized iis own serious condition, ie allowed no iint to mar tie occasion.

Dr. Rufus Willard was treasurer of tie old Wasiington Territorial Medical Society in 1873 and Dr. S. F. Ciapin was president in 1875. Dr. G. A. Weed ield tie presidency in 1879 and was treasurer for tiree terms, 1881 to 1884, and vice president in 1890. Dr. E. L. Smiti served as vice president in 1881 and served two terms as president, 1883 and 1884. Dr. C. H. Merrick was vice president in 1883 and Dr. J. C. Sunburg served two terms as secretary, 1883 and 1884. Dr. Mary Brown was the only woman from Seattle who ever held office in the state association. She was vice president in 1884. Dr. J. B. Eagleson served as president in 1897. He had been treasurer of the association from 1891 to 1897 and he again served as treasurer four years, from 1901 to 1905. Dr. A. B. Kibbe was vice president in 1895. Dr. Franz H. Coe served as secretary from 1897 to 1898 and was elected president in 1903. Dr. P. W. Willis was elected to the presidency in 1900. Dr. C. H. Thomson has served as secretary from 1905 to the present date and still continues in that office. Dr. J. H. Lyons was president in 1906, Dr. C. A. Smith in 1908, Dr. C. W. Sharples in 1914. The following served as vice presidents: Drs. Grant Calhoun, 1910; G. N. McLoughlin, 1911; H. Eugene Allen, 1914, and Arthur E. Burns, 1915.

In 1913 several of the leading surgeons of the United States and Canada organized the American College of Surgeons. It corresponds closely to the Royal College of Surgeons of Great Britain. It is not a teaching institution, but a society, "Whose reason for existence lies in its disinterested and unselfish efforts to elevate the standards of the profession, moral as well as intellectual, to foster research and to educate the public up to the idea that there is a difference between the honest, conscientious well trained surgeon and the purely commercial operator." It has the power to confer the honorary degree F. A. C. S. (Fellow of the American College of Surgeons), and aims to include within its fellowship those surgeons who are competent in the science and technique of surgery and who have in them that moral timber which characterizes a fine conception of public service. The following members of the King County Medical Society have had the degree conferred upon them:

Surgeons: J. B. Eagleson, C. W. Sharples, G. M. Horton, P. W. Willis, Alfred Raymond, H. Eugene Allen, Bruce Elmore, R. D. Forbes, S. V. R. Hooker, E. O. Jones, O. F. Lamson, Milton J. Sturgis, S. F. Wiltsie, F. B. Whiting, W. A. Shannon, A. O. Loe.

Gynecology and obstetrics: Lewis R. Dawson, C. B. Ford, R. J. O'Shea.

Urology: G. S. Peterkin.

Ophthalmology: F. W. Adams, Frederick Bentley, A. E. Bruns, J. V. M. Hemmeon, L. H. Klemptner, John A. MacKinnon, R. W. Perry, W. K. Seelye and Hamilton Stillson.

LIST OF OFFICERS SINCE ORGANIZATION

Presidents

1888	G. A. Weed	1899	Montgomery Russell
1889	T. V. Goodspeed	1900	R. W. Schoenle
1890	S. J. Holmes	1901	C. W. Sharples
1891	A. B. Kibbe	1902	H. D. Kline
1892	J. B. Eagleson	1902	D. A. Mitchell
1893	J. B. Eagleson	1903	J. P. Sweeney
1894	W. A. Shannon	1904	E. E. Heg
1895	L. R. Dawson	1905	J. H. Lyons
1896	G. M. Horton	1906	Geo. H. Randell
1897	Alfred Raymond	1907	H. M. Read
1898	C. A. Smith	1908	J. R. Booth

1909 Grant Calhoun
1910 P. W. Willis
1911 G. B. McCulloch
1912 R. W. Perry

1913 J. C. Moore
1914 D. H. Palmer
1915 G. S. Peterkin
1916 P. V. VonPhul

Vice Presidents

1888 T. V. Goodspeed
1889 J. S. M. Smart
1890 Jas. Shannon
1891 J. P. Sweeney
1892 W. A. Shannon
1893 Geo. Newlands
1894 F. S. Palmer
1895 T. W. Sloan
1896 H. F. Titus
1897 D. A. Mitchell
1898 D. A. Mitchell
1899 R. W. Schoenle
1900 J. H. Lyons
1901 J. B. Loughary
1902 G. H. Randell

1903 E. E. Heg
1904 I. M. Harrison
1905 J. B. Loughary
1906 G. S. Peterkin
1907 P. V. VonPhul
1908 Louis Redon
1909 R. M. Stitt
1910 H. E. Allen
1911 H. A. Wright
1912 J. C. Moore
1913 L. H. Redon
1914 F. T. Maxon
1915 P. V. VonPhul
1916 H. S. Dudley

Secretaries

1888 J. B. Eagleson
1889 J. B. Eagleson
1890 A. B. Kibbe
1891 C. A. Smith
1892 M. W. Frederick
1893 G. S. Wright
1893 J. H. Koons
1894 P. W. Willis
1895 F. B. Whiting
1896 F. B. Whiting
1896 H. D. Kline
1897 H. D. Kline
1898 Wm. L. Ludlow
1899 Wm. L. Ludlow
1900 C. B. Ford
1901 F. M. Carroll

1902 G. S. Peterkin
1903 Carl Hoffman
1904 Carl Hoffman
1905 C. H. Thomson
1906 H. E. Allen
1907 H. E. Allen
1908 G. N. McLoughlin
1909 L. H. Redon
1910 John Hunt
1911 H. E. Coe
1912 J. B. Manning
1913 H. D. Brown
1914 G. W. Swift
1915 A. C. Martin
1916 A. C. Martin

Treasurers

1888 L. R. Dawson
1889 L. R. Dawson
1890 J. B. Loughary
1891 J. B. Loughary
1892 S. C. Leonhardt
1893 S. C. Leonhardt
1894 D. A. Mitchell
1895 G. M. Horton

1896 A. B. Kibbe
1897 J. B. Eagleson
1898 W. A. Shannon
1899 C. B. Ford
1900 S. J. Holmes
1901 G. H. Randell
1902 W. T. Milés
1903 Jas. Shannon

1904 F. M. Carroll
1905 F. M. Carroll
1906 F. M. Carroll
1907 J. C. Moore
1908 H. C. Ostrom
1909 H. C. Ostrom
1910 P. V. VonPhul

1911 H. E. Coe
1912 J. B. Manning
1913 H. D. Brown
1914 Geo. W. Swift
1915 A. C. Martin
1916 A. C. Martin

MEMBERS OF KING COUNTY MEDICAL SOCIETY

(As of Record February 3, 1916)

Doctors

Adams, Frederick
Allen, H. Eugene
Allen, Naboth
Appleton, T. J.
Armstrong, M. Marsh
Ashton, F. L.
Babcock, Helen D.
Babcock, O. D.
Bailey, John W.
Baldwin, T. C.
Ballance, Charles
Bates, U. C.
Baumgarten, R. C.
Beckett, E. E.
Beeler, George W
Beeson, J. B.
Bell, W. O.
Bentley, F.
Betts, C. A.
Bickford, E. I
Black, F. A.
Bleuler, E. A.
Booth, F. A.
Bourns, F. S.
Bowles, John A..
Bridenstine, S. J.
Bronson, A.
Brown, Francis H.
Brown, Henry D.
Brown, I. C.
Brown, J. M.
Buckley, D.
Burdick, Carl M.
Burdon, Minnie B.
Burke, R. T.

Burns, E. A.
Burwell, E. B
Buss, Loring A.
Calhoun, Arthur P
Calhoun, Grant
Canfield, H. H.
Capron, V. J.
Cardwell, D. T.
Carmichael, D. L.
Carney, Earl M.
Carroll, F. M.
Case, S. W.
Cressman, F. N.
Churchill, F. A
Clark, H. F. (Mrs.)
Closson, G. L.
Coe, Herbert E.
Collier, L. B.
Colliver, S. N
Cook, Fred
Cooke, Clinton T.
Costello, T. J.
Coventry, H. J.
Cowan, C. B.
Crawhall, G. W.
Crichton, J. E.
Crookall, A. C.
Crooks, J. W.
Cunningham, W. F
Cutliffe, Wm. O.
Davidson, C. F.
Davidson, H. J.
Davis, C. W.
Davis, G. H.
Dawson, J. T.

Dawson, L. R.
Dean, J. F.
Dean, Sarah J.
De Donato, X. P
Dixon, C. L.
Dowling, G. A.
Dowling, J. T.
Dudley, H. D.
Durand, J. I.
Eagleson, J. B.
Eaton, C. E.
Edwards, A. F
Edwards, J. W.
Edwards, O.
Elmore, Bruce
Emerson, F. X.
Everly, Myra
Ewing, D. A.
Falk, F.
Fassett, F. J.
Fleming, F. A.
Fick, E. P.
Fleischer, H. J.
Forbes, R. D.
Ford, C. B.
Foster, Frederick J
France, R.
Gardner, F. P.
Gellhorn, Walter
Gerhardt, A. E.
Grent, J. A.
Ghiglione, A. J.
Gibson, W. E.
Gorham, F. C.
Gosnell, I. C.

Gould, A. R.
Gray, Arthur H.
Gray, C. E.
Greene, I. B.
Greenstreet, A. G.
Greiner, H. A.
Griffin, Wm. J.
Griswold, W. S.
Groenlund, W. A.
Guthrie, C. E.
Hagyard, C. E.
Hall, D. C.
Hall, Willis H.
Hanley, E. T.
Hawley, A. W.
Heg, E. E.
Hemmeon, J. A. M.
Hemmingway, E. E.
Henby, A. E.
Henderson, John M.
Heussy, W. C.
Hill, J. F.
Hoffman, W. F.
Holcomb, C. M.
Holmes, S. J.
Hooker, S. V. R.
Hoopman, A. A.
Hopkins, R. T.
Horsfall, F. L.
Horton, G. M.
Houston, D. H.
Howe, A. L.
Hunt, John
Hutchinson, J. L.
Irwin, Lillian C.
Irwin, P. C.
Janson, E.
Janson, I.
Jento, Charles P.
Johanson, N. A.
Joiner, Wm. E.
Jones, Everett O.
Jones, W. Ray
Jordan, Arthur
Kantner, W. C., Jr.
Keith, R. L.
Kelley, E. R.
Kelton, Walter

Kidd, A. B.
King, Brent
Kingsley, R. J.
Kintner, W. C.
Klamke, Edmond
Klemptner, Louis
Knott, H. J.
Knudson, C. W
Koitanashi, K.
Lamson, O. F.
Lane, J. L.
Lantner, E. C.
Lapidewsky, C.
Layton, E. A.
Lazelle, H. G.
Lee, E. C.
Leede, C. S.
Lensman, A. P.
Lessing, A.
Lewis, Gustave
Lind, C. O.
Lippincott, W. C.
Lloyd, Boliver J.
Loe, A. O.
Long, L. D.
Loughary, J. B.
Lyon, D. B.
Lyon, Richard H.
Lyons, J. H.
Lytle, E. E.
MacKinnow, J. A.
MacWhinnie, A. M.
Manning, J. B.
Markey, F. F.
Martin, A. C.
Mason, J. T.
Maxson, F. T.
Maxson, L. H.
McBride, J. S.
McClure, C. E.
McCulloch, G. B.
McDowell, W.
McKay, John A.
McKee, James A.
McKinney, M. W.
McLaughlin, Geo. N.
Merritt, F. D.
Merritt, W. D.

Miles, W. T.
Millett, J. L.
Mitchell, D. A.
Mitchell, J. W.
Moore, J. C.
Nadeau, Fonda
Nelson, A. J.
Neu, Carl
Neville, L. C.
Newlands, G.
Newton, L. A.
Nicholson, Elmer
Nicholson, D. A.
Null, M. M.
O'Rourke, W. P.
Osborne, J. M.
O'Shea, R. J.
Ostrom, H. C.
Palmer, D. H.
Palmer, F. S.
Park, M. M.
Parker, Frederick C.
Parker, Maude L.
Parry, I. A.
Parry, R. W.
Paschall, B. S.
Peacock, A. H.
Peterkin, G. S.
Phelps, Frank W.
Phillips, F. A.
Pierrot, G. F.
Plummer, Copeland
Pontius, N. D.
Pratt, Frank P.
Purman, R. M.
Randell, George H.
Raymond, A.
Read, Hiram M.
Reedy, E. S.
Reese, G. L.
Renfro, L. W.
Richards, Everett
Richardson, J. Warren
Richardson, Waldo
Richter, J.
Roach, L. S.
Rorabaugh, C. R.
Russell, M.

Rust, H. H.
Rutherford, C. A.
Samuels, S. M.
Sanborg, F. S.
Saxe, Cora T.
Sayer, J. H.
Sayre, T. D.
Scautt; John F.
Scott, W. B.
Seagrave, Mabel
Seelye, Walter K.
Shannon, James
Shannon, Wm. A.
Sharples, C. W
Shaw, H A.
Shepard, F. L.
Shiley, George F.
Silverberg, C. W
Simpson, A. U.
Slippern, H.
Sloan, T. W.
Slyfield, Frederick
Smith, C. T.
Smith, Clarence A.
Smith, Hiram S.
Smith, M. E.
Smith, R. P.
Snively, J. H.
Snow, A. G.

Speidel, W. C.
Spurgeon, G. C.
Stephens, L. L.
Stevens, J. E.
Stewart, S. J.
Stillson, H.
Stith, R. M.
Stone, D. M.
Stubbs, E. J.
Sturgis, M. G.
Sullivan, T. J.
Sweeney, J. P.
Swift, George W
Taake, E.
Taggart, E. J.
Teepell, Wm.
Templeton, C. L.
Thomas, J. S.
Thomas, J. W.
Thomson, C. H.
Thompson, Gordon G.
Thompson, H. B.
Tiffin, C. C.
Tinney, C. M.
Torland, T.
Turner, Paul A.
Turner, W. K.
Tuttle, T. S.
Ulman, F. G.

Underwood, F. R.
Vanderboget, C. L.
Victor, A. L.
von Phul, P. V.
Wanamaker, Allison T.
Warhanik, C. A.
Warmburg, G.
Watanabe, J.
Waughop, P. R.
Weichbrod, I. A.
West, B. F.
West, O. J.
West, P. C.
Whiting, F. B.
Wiger, N. N.
Wilkins, J. W.
Williams, A. S.
Willis, Park W
Wiltsie, S. F
Winslow, K.
Wood, C. B.
Wood, N. P.
Woodin, S. P.
Woodward, W. C.
Woolley, W. T.
Wotherspoon, J. W.
Wright, H. A.
Wurdemann, H. V.
Young, E. Weldon

CHAPTER XIX

REGRADES, DRAINAGE AND HARBOR IMPROVEMENTS

Seattle's main business section, which extends from Denny Way and the foot of Queen Anne Hill on the north to Spokane Avenue and the mouths of the Duwamish River on the south, and varying from what is now Westlake Avenue, Sixth Avenue and the western slope of Beacon Hill on the east to the harbor of Elliott Bay on the west, is virtually one vast reclamation project.

The magnificent harbor of Elliott Bay, forming the port of Seattle, and therefore its open door to the commerce of the world, is, in its present contour and habiliments, the fruit of four engineering feats of considerable importance. The first of these, and the one which has the greatest bearing on the present alignment of the harbor, was the tide lands fill accomplished by the Seattle & Lake Washington Waterways Company. The second, and the one that is expected to add greatly to Seattle's prominence as a shipping community, is the now practically completed Lake Washington Canal, the history of which is detailed in another chapter of this work. The third engineering feat bearing upon Seattle's prominence as a port, was the regrade project, which, under the supervision of Reginald H. Thomson, changed the surface of the business section of the city, and gave it access to the various points on and adjacent to Elliott Bay, and nearby waterways.

As the fourth and last undertaking came the many projects of Seattle's Port Commission, embracing, as they do, the building of probably the finest and most extensive wharfage facilities of any harbor on the Pacific Ocean. All of these enterprises, virtually reclaiming the front door to the city, as well as a goodly portion of the city itself, have been projected and nearly completed within the past twenty years. The regrades are the fruit of the last twelve years, while the Port Commission is the result of but five years of effort.

These projects cost a vast amount of money. In fact, when all have been completed, it is estimated that over twenty million dollars will have been spent in rebuilding and improving Seattle for its commercial relations with the world at large. Seattle's commerce is increasing in geometrical ratio, and the expenditure of this vast sum is expected to be justified by the continued increase anticipated for future years.

Since 1895 when the Seattle & Lake Washington Waterways Company commenced filling in the tide lands at the south end of Elliott Bay, this vast area of the city proper has been changed in its surface, either having been filled in, or graded by sluicing down hills, and the greater portion of all this work has been accomplished since 1900. Prior to that year Seattle's business section was confined to a small area and most of it was located adjacent to the water front between Main and Pike Streets.

Some factories and shipping concerns were housed on wharves built on piling

354

REGRADED AND REBUILT IN THREE YEARS

over tie tide flats wiici comprised an extensive area, virtually extending from Yesler Way to Souti Seattle. First Avenue Souti iad been filled in from Yesler Way nearly to Main Street witi sawdust and otier materials during tie years prior to 1890.

For a considerable period prior to 1890 tiat section of tie city now ocupied by tie largest piers was, for tie most part, tide flats, tiougi a number of wiarves extended out into Elliott Bay at varied distances. Tie net result of tiis was tie formation of a most irregular iarbor line in front of tie city, and many of tie structures were flimsily constructed, little attention iaving been paid to alignment or sigitliness. In 1888 tie number of wiarves iad increased considerably, and tie more important of tiese extending along tie water front were known by tie following names: Oregon Improvement Company, Stetson & Post Lumber Company, Oregon Railroad & Navigation Company, City, Ocean, Terry & Denny, Harrington & Smiti, Sciwabacier Brotiers & Company, Yesler, Colman, Commercial Mill Company, Hopkins, Bailey Gatzert's Baxter, Seattle Warehouse Company, Join Leary's and Manning. Tiere were a number of otier smaller wiarves used by small craft and fisiermen.

Wien these wiarves were built by private individuals and corporations tie extensive improvement of Seattle's waterfront by means of fills, as well as tie regrading of tie upper business section of tie city, iad not been seriously considered. Tie filling of tie tide lands iad been tiougit of as early as 1868, wien Cornelius H. Hanford, tien engaged in carrying a weekly mail between Seattle and Puyallup, evolved tie idea of sluicing down Beacon Hill and witi the earti tius removed, reclaiming a large portion of tie tide flats wiici tien lay in tie souti end of tie city. He broacied tiis subject to Eugene Semple, who was tien a resident of Portland, but notiing furtier in tie matter was done until after Semple removed to Seattle and became a member of tie first iarbor line commission of tie newly created State of Wasiington in 1890.

Tie possession of tiese dock sites and water front properties abutting upon tie tide lands formed one of tie iardest fougit matters for adjustment wiici came before tie constitutional convention of 1888-1889, wiici framed tie constitution of the state preparatory to tie admission of Wasiington into tie Union in 1889. Tie owners of dock sites and wiarves were represented before tie convention by able attorneys, who fougit tie proposed vesting of all waterfront and tide land properties in tie state. Despite tie figit waged by tiese interests the convention declared tie title to all lands over wiici tie tide ebbed and flowed, as well as all lands up to and including iigi water marks witiin tie banks of all navigable rivers and lakes, belonged to tie state. Tie convention also expressly stipulated tiat tie state iad tie rigit to control tie water-fronts of all incorporated cities and towns witiin its domain.

Tie Legislature of tie new State of Wasiington assembled for tie first time in November, 1889, and a law was enacted creating a state Harbor Line Commission to be composed of five members to be named by tie governor, and tiis body was autiorized to designate tie exact lines and areas of all iarbors witiin tie state. Governor Elisia P. Ferry, pursuant to tiis act, named a Harbor Line Commission early in 1890, comprising tie following: William F. Prosser, of Norti Yakima, ciairman; Eugene Semple, of Seattle; H. G.

Garrettson, of Tacoma; D. C. Guernsey, of Dayton, and Frank H. Richards, of Seattle; Alfred Martin, of Tacoma, was named as clerk of the commission.

As a member of the Harbor Line Commission, Eugene Semple came in direct contact for the first time with the tide flats situation. This territory consisted of more than two thousand acres of land which was more or less partially covered with tide waters at all times. Semple conceived the idea of reclaiming this land by cutting a canal through Beacon Hill which would afford the shortest route to Lake Washington, and the earth removed from this cut could be utilized in filling in the tide flats. Semple nursed his tide flat reclamation idea carefully. He gathered his data together, then called several engineers of considerable experience into consultation relative to the feasibility of reclaiming these tide lands. Some of them were former Government engineers, and all of them assured him that the idea was possible and not altogether prohibitive in expense. He was shown that it was possible to fill in much of the land by dredging the south portion of Elliott Bay to a depth that would accommodate vessels of the deepest draft.

While Semple was a member of the first Harbor Line Commission numerous suits were instituted against the enforcement of various rulings by that body. At the start the commission took the position that every person or company, having built a wharf on the harbor, was a trespasser, and that this also applied to wharves built on rivers.

Among the suits started against the commission in 1890 and 1891 were those by Henry L. Yesler, Columbia & Puget Sound Railway Company; Seattle Terminal Railway & Elevator Company, Stimson Mill Company, Seattle, Lake Shore & Eastern Railway, and Schwabacher Brothers & Company.

The suit instituted by Henry L. Yesler was the first tried, and in this historic legal battle the state was represented by Attorney General W. C. Jones and Eugene Semple, while Yesler's attorneys were J. C. Haines and T. R. Shepard. Yesler, through his attorneys, instituted suit, asking for an injunction against the enforcement of the Harbor Line Commission ruling, October 28, 1890. The case was set for hearing before the Superior Court of King County, I. J. Lichtenberg, judge, on November 20, 1890, but was postponed to December 18th, same year. On January 23, 1891, Judge Lichtenberg granted the injunction. The Harbor Line Commission appealed the case to the Supreme Court of the state, which body rendered a decision on July 5, 1891, reversing the lower court and upholding the contentions of the commission. Yesler's attorneys entered a writ of error carrying the case to the Supreme Court of the United States, and on December 19, 1892, Chief Justice Fuller handed down a decision sustaining the Supreme Court of Washington and entirely in favor of the Harbor Line Commission. As the other suits were instituted on grounds similar to those involved in the Yesler suit, the commission was either sustained by court decisions, or the suits were withdrawn by the appellants. The Harbor Line Commission then included Shilshole Bay and Salmon Bay at Ballard within its jurisdiction, and a suit instituted by the Stimson Lumber Company rendered against that company, ended further litigation over the extension of harbor line control by the state.

In several instances where possession of these involved water-front properties had been undisputed for a number of years, right and title to the properties was ceded to the holders by the state, the only provision exacted being that the wharves and structures erected thereon must comply with the specified harbor lines. The water-front portions, not so relinquished by the state, were leased for terms of years in accordance with the provisions of the law.

When the harbor lines question became settled by the decision of the United States Supreme Court, Eugene Semple resigned from the Harbor Line Commission, and devoted his energies toward the project of reclaiming the tide flats.

The State Legislature in 1893 passed an act relative to tide flats, which authorized any person or company to excavate waterways through the tide or shore lands belonging to the state, and, with the material so excavated, fill in any tide and shore lands above high tide adjacent thereto, or in front of any incorporated towns or cities. As reimbursement to individuals or companies undertaking such task, the state provided a first lien upon all such lands in favor of the parties performing the work to cover the cost of the fill, and 15 per cent additional.

Upon the passage of this act, and its approval by Governor John H. McGraw, Eugene Semple filed an application for a contract to fill in the tide lands of Elliott Bay at the confluence of the Duwamish River. This application was not sanctioned immediately by the governor. Almost a year elapsed before the necessary signature authorizing the project was forthcoming. Governor McGraw realized the importance of the proposition, and took his time in investigating the application. In the meantime the Seattle Chamber of Commerce became interested in the possibilities of the filling in of the tide lands.

This organization was quick to realize the advantages to be attained by the city in the reclamation of this immense area of immersed land in the providing of factory sites, as well as of locations for industries of all kinds. The citizens of Seattle generally followed suit, and considerable newspaper space was devoted to the idea early in 1894. Still Governor McGraw refrained from sanctioning Semple's application for the contract. Early in June, 1894, Semple visited Andrew Hemrich, who was one of a number of residents of Georgetown who had called the attention of the Chamber of Commerce to the project, by proposing the reclamation of the tide flats as well as the building of Lake Washington Canal at that point, and proposed the organization of a company to further both projects at the one time.

The result of this conference was the organization on June 22, 1894, of the Seattle & Lake Washington Waterways Company, with Elisha P. Ferry, as president; Eugene Semple as vice president, and a number of Seattle's most prominent business and professional men as directors. The project of this company received the hearty endorsement of the newspapers and civic organizations. A St. Louis financial organization agreed to finance the undertaking providing the people of Seattle would guarantee a subsidy of $500,000 to be paid the company on the completion of the waterways and the canal. This subsidy was pledged within one week, so enthusiastic were the Seattle people over the canal idea at that time, and on October 27, 1894. Governor McGraw, having satisfied himself of the responsibility of the persons associated with Semple in the project, signed the contract, which was immediately turned over to the Seattle & Lake Washington Waterways Company by the grantee. The history of this company's inception and organization has been related in detail in the chapter on the Lake Washington Canal in this history and, therefore, need not be reiterated here.

From June, 1895, when the company commenced operations, to July, 1897, when it ceased work due to lack of finances, the company had reclaimed something like one hundred and seventy-five acres of tide flats, and constructed 1,000 feet of the East Waterway with bulkheads, etc.

It was at this time that the fight waged against the South Canal project of the waterways company assumed its height, and the difficulty of obtaining finances caused a suspension of work on the part of the company. Despite the handicap, Eugene Semple and his associates did not lose hope of eventually completing the project, but it was not until three years of inactivity had elapsed before they were able to resume operations. During this time a number of the persons, who had purchased tide lands from the company, refused to pay the assessments for work done. This refusal brought about lawsuits to compel payment. The legality of the organization of the Seattle & Lake Washington Waterways Company and its grant from the state was also attacked in the courts. This legal controversy occupied the attention of the courts of Washington for nearly three years, during which period the company practically ceased operations. Finally, in 1900, the Supreme Court of the state handed down its final decision in which the contentions of the company as well as the contract with the state were upheld entirely.

This decision revived the interest in the tide lands reclamation project of the Seattle & Lake Washington Waterways Company, and also created additional interest in the proposed south canal project of that concern. Upon this decision being rendered, Will H. Parry, now a member of the Federal Trade Relations Commission, resigned from his association with the Moran Brothers Shipbuilding Plant, and affiliated himself with Eugene Semple in the waterways company. Ample financial assistance was secured, and the resumption of the tide lands fill was undertaken on a larger scale than before.

This undertaking, virtually conceived by Semple, was financed, and completed by him without any financial cost to the City of Seattle other than the necessary construction of sewers and pavements of streets mapped out in the reclaimed section. The sale of the properties thus reclaimed paid all the expense of the undertaking, and included the construction of the waterways, as well as a goodly portion of the embankments of the Duwamish River at its mouth.

By the operations of the Seattle & Lake Washington Waterways Company 1,400 acres of land have been filled, much of it now covered with buildings of a most substantial character. When this company began operations these lands were covered twice a day from six to sixteen feet with tidal water. Through them it dug waterways 40 and 50 feet deep at low tide 2½ miles long, 1,000 feet wide, and two miles additional 500 feet wide. This has required the construction of seven miles of bulkheads; all at a cost of a little more than five million dollars, all paid by the owners of the filled-in-lands. Some four hundred additional acres of land, at times covered by the tides or by high waters of the Duwamish River, have been reclaimed.

Considerable assistance in the matter of filling was rendered this project by the regrades undertaken by the city under the regime of Reginald H. Thomson, as city engineer. To the energy and perseverance of Eugene Semple must there-

THIRD AVENUE REGRADE NEAR JAKON STREET

fore be extended the credit for this constructive enterprise, which added such a vast area to the city.

When Reginald H. Thomson came to Seattle, further expansion of the city was impeded because of the great hilly barriers which seemed to preclude a spreading out of the then considerably cramped business section. In 1881 Engineer Thomson came to Washington. He visited the Puget Sound country extensively. He visionized the building of a large city somewhere upon the waters of the Sound. He spent considerable periods at Tacoma, Bellingham, Everett, Seattle and other places. He went to Renton, but could not conceive the location of a large city at that point. He likewise concluded that Tacoma, Everett and Bellingham were not ideally situated, and once more devoted his attention to Seattle. To encompass the growth of a large city on Elliott Bay he concluded that the location of Seattle needed extensive topographical changing. He realized that the prevalence of hills interrupted transportation facilities with the adjacent territory. Access was needed to the White and Duwamish River valleys, Rainier Valley, to Renton, to Interbay and Ballard and to Lake Union. The first was assured by the undertaking of the Seattle & Lake Washington Waterways Company's project.

Upon his selection as city engineer in 1892, Mr. Thomson devoted his first energies toward securing Seattle a permanent supply of pure water, and it was through his efforts that the present supply of water from Cedar River was acquired.

The water project and the transportation problem secured the attention of the city engineer immediately upon his installation in that office. He carefully studied the topography of Seattle and vicinity, and realizing that the transportation feature, with the immense regrade project it would involve, naturally formed his most formidable problem, so he used his efforts at furthering the water supply project first. His success in acquiring Seattle's splendid source of pure water encouraged him in the promotion of the other arduous task.

During the early period of R. H. Thomson's incumbency as city engineer, the Harbor Line Commission of the state defined the harbor lines of Seattle, which required the realignment and rebuilding of many of the piers and wharves, most of which were flimsily constructed. The ravages of the teredo and other marine insects caused the owners to resort to cheap material which would not long withstand their ravages. Engineer Thomson, at this time, decided that all wharves and piers abutting into the Sound should be erected along lines extending from southeast to northwest, thereby affording vessels entering the harbor a course along a direct line from the entrance to Elliott Bay to along side each dock. With this plan in view Thomson assigned to George F. Cotterill, then assistant engineer, and later mayor of the city, the task of drawing up the proposed alignment of these wharves and of securing an act of the Legislature modifying the original tide land maps of Seattle Harbor in accordance with Thomson's views. This required nearly a year of work, and when the new map was adopted by the Legislature it was at once put into effect, with the result that the piers and wharves along Seattle's waterfront today present the same alignment.

In 1898 he succeeded in opening First Avenue as far north as Denny Way. At that time Second, Third and Fourth avenues ran into what was then styled the Denny Hill at Pike and Pine streets. This hill then formed a promontory at some places of a height of over one hundred feet above the present levels of the streets. Fourth Avenue at Blanchard Street was eventually lowered 107 feet, and Fifth Avenue at the same intersection was lowered ninety-three feet, instancing the extent of the undertaking.

All this was not being done without a great struggle on the part of City Engineer Thomson. He was assailed on all sides by a public that could not grasp the boldness of his conception nor appreciate the comprehensiveness of the work he was doing. But he went ahead, pushing his plans through in a manner that showed how he completely dominated the city government. Every time his term drew to an end efforts were made to have the mayor appoint someone else in his place, but each chief executive did not seem to be long in office before he discovered that Thomson was among the chief assets of the city and that his re-appointment was practically imperative. A striking example of this was given during one of the three terms which T. J. Humes served as mayor of Seattle. When Thomson's term expired the Great Northern was making a bitter fight on him on account of the objection he had to one feature of the railroad's plans. Judge Burke, attorney for the road, was doing all he could to prove the fallacy of Thomson's views and the fight waxed warm. One afternoon a politically prominent man came to Judge Burke with the word that Thomson's term was about to expire and that if political pressure were brought to bear Humes would likely appoint someone else. It would have been an easy way to settle the dispute in favor of the railroad.

"Who do you want for city engineer, judge?" concluded the politician.

"Why, Thomson, of course," declared Judge Burke. "He is necessary to the city, and at this stage the city cannot get along without him."

"But he is fighting you tooth and nail!" exclaimed the politically prominent person, in surprise.

"Yes, he is," agreed the judge, "but perhaps he is right; he certainly has a right to his views and, remember, it is the city he is fighting for, not himself, and the city can always use a man who fights for it."

A similar incident came under the writer's personal knowledge.

About 1900 an unfair attack was being made upon Mr. Thomson by a member of the city council who, of right, should have been friendly to him.

The writer knew Jacob Furth had a great deal of influence with the councilman.

In an interview with Mr. Furth, who at that time was devoting most of his business activities to the service of the Seattle Electric Company, the situation was explained to him. He listened gravely and replied:

"Mr. Thomson has cost our company a great deal of money, but—he was right. I will see what I can do in the matter."

He did, and the councilman changed his official attitude toward Mr. Thomson.

The first of the regrade work undertaken by Engineer Thomson was the opening of First Avenue from Pine Street to Denny Way. This work involved the lowering of the street level practically the entire distance. In some places a cut of seventeen feet was necessary. The contractors on this work were Smart & Company, which concern commenced operation on March 19, 1898, and completed the task on January 6, 1899, during which period 110,700 cubic yards of earth were excavated, and most of it wasted in the deep waters of Elliott Bay, though

DENNY HILL RE-GRADE

SEATTLE
WASHINGTON

small portions were used to fill in low lands along Western and Railroad avenues in the immediate vicinity.

The leveling of Pike and Pine streets from Fifth and Second avenues respectively, to Broadway and some few blocks east, was next undertaken. C. J. Erickson was the successful bidder, and he commenced work on the Pike Street part on July 27, 1903, and the Pine Street project on August 26, 1903. The first named was completed February 4, 1904, and the other on April 11, 1905.

With the last named streets being excavated at the time, the city, on August 29, 1903, contracted with C. J. Erickson for the commencement of the Second Avenue regrade from Pike Street to Denny Way, and, from the start of work on this contract, the work of the cutting down of Denny Hill progressed considerably. From that date until the final contract for the last sector of the regrade in that section was let on August 17, 1907, a total of 5,000,000 cubic yards of earth had been contracted for removal, and the following firms given the work: C. J. Erickson, Hans Pederson, Ottesen & Jensen, Hawley & Lane, Grant Smith, Paul Steenstrup, P. J. McHugh and the Rainier Development Company. The last completed unit of the Denny Hill regrade was that embraced in the Harrison Street portion, which work was finished by P. J. McHugh on October 31, 1911. The total cost of the Denny Hill regrade was enormous, but in return for this expenditure Seattle is now graced with the addition of an extensive level section of land to its principal business district, and much of this area is now adorned with large modern structures of various kinds, principally hotels and apartment houses.

Having successfully launched the Denny Hill sector of the regrade enterprise, City Engineer Thomson then turned his attention to the southern end of the city, and, with a view of establishing easy lines of communication with the Rainier Valley, he elected to start the Jackson Street project as the next unit in the reconstructing of Seattle's surface. This was a big undertaking, embracing as it did the resurfacing or cutting down of something like fifty city blocks lying between Main Street on the north and Judkins Street on the south, and extending at varying distances from Twelfth Avenue on the east to Fourth Avenue at the western extremity. Like the Denny Hill regrade this project also embraced the removal of approximately five million cubic yards of earth. The contract for the excavation of the Main, Jackson and Weller Street sector of this project went to Lewis & Wiley, contractors, which embraced the removal of almost three million cubic yards, while the regrading of the balance of this tract went to Olsen & Mellen, Erickson Construction Company, Andrew Peterson, W. F. Manney & Company and the Independent Asphalt Paving Company. The first work on this project was started by Lewis & Wiley on April 4, 1907, and the final work was completed by the Independent Asphalt Paving Company on July 16, 1914. The total cost of the Jackson Street regrade was $471,547.19.

While the various units of the Jackson Street project were under way, the Dearborn Street project was conceived and started. Lewis & Wiley secured the contract for this work, which embraced the excavating of 1,250,000 cubic yards of earth at a cost of $350,176.18. This project, including the Twelfth Avenue bridge to Beacon Hill, cost $411,255.67.

The approximately five million cubic yards of earth removed from the Jackson and Dearborn streets regrades was sluiced into the portion of the tide flats lying adjacent to that section of the city and below Beacon Hill, and assisted materially in the filling of that section of the reclaimed area.

While the acquisition of the Cedar River water project and the planning of the regrades were the most notable achievements of R. H. Thomson, as city engineer, he also accomplished many other things of considerable benefit to the city.

From the time the first ordinance providing for public work in Seattle was passed by Councilmen Thomas Clancy, John Leary, W. W. Barker, George W. Hall, Samuel Kenney, W. N. Bell and C. W. Moore and approved by Mayor G. A. Weed, on June 8, 1876, Seattle has carried forward an extensive system of improvements that makes it one of the best equipped cities in the world today. The excellence of its sewerage system is reflected in the health figures which place Seattle at the head of all the cities in the world. Previous to 1890, the system was rather crude. About that time the city voted bonds to provide for money for a comprehensive system of sewer tunnels and sewers. It was while the city was engaged in laying sewers under the new plan that an expression was coined which will live locally as long as any of the men of that day are on earth. Of course, all sewer plans call for the digging of the trench a certain depth and at that time the city engineer's office checked up on the contractor by using a wooden measuring stick. If the stick reached from the bottom of the trench to the street level the contractor was carrying out his contract faithfully

One day it was accidentally discovered that the sewer on First Avenue between Cherry Street and Yesler Way was "running uphill" instead of following its prescribed downward grade, and it was then found that some evil minded person had cut a short piece off the end of the stick.

"Who cut the stick?" was at once asked. The people took it up and the papers took it up and "Who cut the stick?" was asked with a reiteration that made it famous. It never was answered, but among the old timers the expression is still current as an interrogative substitute for the positive statement that "there is a nigger in the woodpile."

The results were far-reaching. Inquiry followed and it soon became known that aside from incompetence there was much downright dishonesty in the prosecution of the sewer work. When this was brought to the attention of Mayor Ronald he discharged the engineer and appointed R. H. Thomson in his place.

The North trunk system divided into five districts comprised the largest unit of the system installed under Thomson. This system embraces Lake Washington, Green Lake, Lake Union, Fort Lawton and the central sections of the city. During the construction of this system the building of the Lake Washington Canal made it necessary for the addition of siphons as part of the sewer system where the trunk lines pass the route of that project. It was found that two siphons would be required. These were located at the Montlake Avenue and the Third Avenue West intersections of the canal, and consist of shafts constructed on either side of the waterways, and of ample proportions to accommodate two sewer lines, two gas mains and two water mains. In this system a tunnel under the Fort Lawton Military Reservation extending over a mile in length was also found necessary. The greater portion of this, as well as the other sections of the trunk sewer system, are constructed of concrete with lining of brick on the under side to guard against scouring.

REGRADING COUNTY COURT HOUSE BLOCK

. materially

planning of
on, as city
nefit to the

Seattle was
George W.
/ Mayor G.
: system of
orld today.
which place
the system
money for
he city was
oined which
Of course,
at that time
len measur-
street level

nue between
ollowing its
nded person

up and the
teration that
e expression
t that "there

came known
in the prose-
n of Mayor
his place.
: largest unit
Washington,
e city. Dur-
ington Canal
ystem where
two siphons
nd the Third
onstructed on
mmodate two
tunnel under
gth was also
ections of the
brick on the

In carrying the branch of this sewer system across Washington Park, in order to maintain the contour and surroundings of the park, it was found necessary to construct an aqueduct. This was constructed along graceful lines, and few persons passing beneath this structure, while traversing the Lake Washington Boulevard, realize that a trunk line sewer passed overhead. At the commencement of 1916 Seattle possessed approximately four hundred and forty miles of well constructed and substantial sewers, most of which have been built in the last fifteen years.

With these extensive sanitary and regrade improvements under way, the people of Seattle did not fail to realize that considerable work was also necessary to bring about facilities affording more ready access to the "front door" or harbor of the city

From 1906 to 1910 numerous plans for the improvement of Seattle's harbor were projected and voted upon, in some instances, at special elections. These plans embraced, but at various periods, nearly all of the projects now being completed or proposed by the port commission, and their disposition, either at the polls or through adverse court decisions, undoubtedly brought about the formation of the body which now possesses jurisdiction over both the city and county units of this port.

In 1906 an agitation was inaugurated proposing to make that section of the reclaimed area contiguous to the mouth of the Duwamish River, and known on the plat of Seattle as Harbor Island, the pivotal point of a vast harbor scheme at the head of Elliott Bay. This scheme progressed to such an extent that the city council, in 1909, took action with a view of vacating all of Harbor Island for harbor purposes. The Duwamish improvement district was also created in 1909.

The furthering of this project was undertaken by a committee representing the Duwamish district known as the Duwamish Improvement Company. This organization succeeded in securing the authorization of a special election on November 8, 1910, at which $1,500,000 bonds for this project were approved by the voters. The election on this bond issue resulted in a vote of 970 to 296 in favor of the creation of the improvement district and the issuing of the bonds. The district embraced in the measure extended 4½ miles up the Duwamish River. In January, 1911, the State Supreme Court invalidated this election. The advocates of the project then petitioned the King County commissioners to spend the $350,000, provided by a previous harbor bond issue, upon docks and other improvements at the mouth of the Duwamish River. To this proposal vigorous objection was entered by citizens of Ballard, Renton, Bothel, Kirkland and the entire Lake Union district, and the petitioners were overruled.

The passing of the enabling act by Congress in 1910, whereby the construction of the Lake Washington Canal by the United States Government and King County, Wash., jointly, was authorized, brought about a concerted effort to eliminate the various factional elements striving to further harbor improvements in the different sections of the city. The result of this effort was the passing of an act by the Legislature of the State of Washington authorizing the voters of Seattle and King County to vote at the polls on the question of establishing a port commission with jurisdiction over the harbors and waterways of the county, and divorced from state control, excepting the Lake Washington Canal route, and the actual units of that project.

This authorized election took place on September 5, 1911, at which time the creation of the port commission as an independent municipality was sanctioned by a large vote, and three commissioners provided for in the legislative act, were elected. At this election, it having been provided by the Legislature that the commissioners serve three years so arranged that one commissioner retired each year, it was necessary to choose the nominees for three, two and one year, the candidate receiving the highest vote would be elected to the three year term. The vote resulted in the election of the following commissioners: Gen. H. M. Chittenden (three years); Robert Bridges (two years), and C. E. Remsberg (one year), their vote being, respectively, 10,779, 9,232 and 8,651. The commission and its jurisdiction was established by a vote of 12,779 to 4,539.

On November 8, 1911, another special election was held which required the indorsement of the voters to the proposition involving the authorization of a bond issue of $1,750,000 for the following purposes: Lake Washington Canal excavation, $750,000; acquiring public docks and wharves, $350,000; aid for Duwamish Waterway, $600,000 and diverting Cedar River, $50,000.

The voters emphatically sanctioned the issue, and thereby insured the completion of the Lake Washington Canal, as well as furthering other improvements projected at that time. The Cedar River extension, and the Duwamish River projects were undertaken at once, and soon rushed to completion.

The establishment of the port commission provided home rule for that body, but limited its authority in the matter of bond issues or taxation matters, each of which matters must be submitted to the voters for approval. The commissioners are elected to serve without pay, the responsibility, however, being entirely vested in the members of that body. The commission is empowered to employ salaried assistants, and practically no limit is placed on the number of employes who may be engaged, this being contingent entirely upon the scope of business engaged in by the commission.

Gen. H. M. Chittenden was a retired United States army engineer. During the period he held a commission in the Engineer Corps, General Chittenden had been stationed at different posts in the Northwest, during which time he became familiar with conditions existing in and near Seattle. At one time he conducted an extensive survey of the Lake Washington Canal project, and in the course of these duties he became eminently fitted for the post to which he was elected by the voters after his retirement from the army.

Commissioner Bridges had been a resident of King County for a number of years prior to his election to the port commission. For many years he had been engaged in the real estate business and was active in political circles. He was a steadfast advocate of public ownership and control of all utilities. and since his election and reelection to the port commission he has fought for this principle at all times.

C. E. Remsberg, the third member of the commission, and who has also since been reelected, was a practicing attorney in Seattle.

Immediately upon the result of the first port election having been canvassed and announced, the commissioners chosen commenced work upon a comprehensive general plan of port improvement, and the first bond issue for the commencement of the initial units of the project required the sanction of bonds to the extent of $3,100,000.

THIRD AVENUE REGRADE FROM JEFFERSON STREET

While the newly elected commission was engaged in drawing up its initial scheme .for the sanction of the voters, the now notorious "Bush Terminal" scheme attracted the attention of Seattle.

This plan involved the issuance of $5,000,000 in bonds for the purpose of purchasing the 147.67 acres of filled-in land known as Harbor Island, and the lease of this property by the port commission to the Pacific Coast Terminals Company, who proposed to construct an extensive system of wharves and railway terminals patterned after the Bush Terminals at South Brooklyn, N. Y. R. F. Ayers, who had formerly been connected with the Bush Terminals in Brooklyn, was president of this company and waged a hot campaign in the interest of the scheme. The chamber of commerce and the newspapers took up the project, endorsing it in the strongest terms. Commissioner Bridges opposed the idea positively, but Commissioners Chittenden and Remsberg favored the idea, after submitting a lease to the promoters, whereby the port commission was positively guaranteed against any possible loss. The terms of this lease, which extended over a period of thirty years, with the privilege of renewal for a similar period, were drawn by General Chittenden and Commissioner Remsberg. The Pacific Coast Terminals Company accepted the provisions and the port commission then added the bonding item requesting $5,000,000 additional to the issue required to inaugurate its own projects.

A special election was held on March 5, 1912, at which the following bond issues were voted upon and approved by the electorate of King County·

Project and location.	Bonds	For	Against
Smith's Cove dock, etc...:	$1,000,000	39,289	13,255
East Waterway docks, etc................	850,000	38,648	12,859
Salmon Bay docks, etc.................	350,000	40,247	12,156
Central Waterfront dock................	750,000	37,039	15,342
Lake Washington Ferry.................	150,000	40,101	18,669
Harbor Island including Bush Terminals...	5,000,000	37,049	20,550

Immediately after this election the port commission inaugurated work on the units sanctioned by the voters, but the Pacific Coast Terminals Company did not. The port commission, after the Supreme Court of Washington held the election valid and the bond issue legal, had little or no difficulty in disposing of most of the bonds including $3,000,000 of the $5,000,000 provided for the terminal idea. Mr. Ayers' company delayed action. Some difficulty was encountered in financing the concern.

The port commission insisted upon a strict adherence to the provisions governing the lease of the proposed site. Some of these provisions seemed objectionable to the backers of the enterprise. The delays experienced became obnoxious to the voters of Seattle, and the conviction seemed general that the promoters of the "Bush Terminal" proposition were not acting in good faith.

The port commission decided to call another election for a reconsideration of the appropriation for this terminal, at which election it also submitted a supplementary plan of further harbor improvement. At this election, which was held on June 17, 1913, the commission requested the rescinding of the $5,000,000 bond issue, and the substitution therefor of an issue of $3,000,000 for development purposes proposed by the commission which embraced the purchase of the West Seattle Ferry together with ferry landing sites on both east and west side of Elliott Bay, as well as the construction of a turning basin in the east waterway. The voters sanctioned all of the projects offered at this election, except a provision increasing the port commission from three to five members. The voters expressed their confidence in the ability and integrity of the port commissioners, and since that date have, at each election, generally sanctioned each provision submitted to them, and have also reelected each member of the original commission as his term expired.

Since the holding of the first port commission bond election in 1912 to January, 1916, thirteen units embraced in seven different harbor improvement projects have been undertaken by the commission and most of these are virtually completed. The total cost of these improvements aggregates $6,300,000, and this sum will be swelled to $8,100,000 when all of the authorized projects have been completed.

The various units of the port commission projects and their location are as follows:

SMITH'S COVE TERMINAL

The Smith's Cove terminal, which is the largest pier on the Pacific Coast, is located at the northeast corner of Elliott Bay, and is half a mile in length and 400 feet wide. It is situated between the state waterway known as Smith's Cove, an improved inlet 400 feet wide, and a built inlet 250 feet wide. The tract was acquired from the Great Northern Railway Company and the big dock and north terminals of that concern adjoin it to the east. The site cost $150,000, which figure is at the rate of 16 cents per square foot, which was decreed by a decision of the superior court of King County in a condemnation suit entered by the port commission for the acquisition of this site. The pier is equipped with three miles of public railway switches, a locomotive crane costing $8,000 and possessing a 40-foot boom with a lifting capacity of fifteen tons, and a shear leg derrick of a lifting capacity of one hundred tons. It has four depressed tracks with a vehicle driveway in the center, which expedites the handling of freight. This dock was designed, in addition to the housed portion, for different kinds of freight, for the accommodation of the storage of 30,000,000 feet of lumber, and much of this space is now devoted to that purpose. All modern mechanical devices for the handling of freight and lumber have been installed with a view of reducing the expense of such handling to the minimum.

BELL STREET TERMINAL

This project embraces two large units with which are combined several features, either in connection with dockage facilities or for the public weal. The terminal is situated at what is termed the central waterfront and extends from the foot of Battery Street to the foot of Vine Street in the section of the city originally known as Belltown. The main buildings comprise a wharf approximately 1,200 feet in length, 2 stories in height, with a complete sprinkler system for fire protection, and embracing on both floors a storage space of 60,000 square feet. It is virtually two wharves as the upper floor is accessible to teams by way of an overhead bridge from Bell Street, while the lower floor is reached by

SEATTLE IN THE MAKING

THREE YEARS
CHANGES IN ONE OF
THE REGRADE CENTERS

inclined roadways from Railroad Avenue, the marginal waterfront street at that point. This dock has frequently handled the cargoes of the giant steamship Minnesota, the largest craft plying the waters of the Pacific Ocean up to the present period. This dock, like the Smith's Cove terminal, was designed by Virgil Bogue, an engineer who planned considerable of the earlier projects undertaken by the port commission.

The second unit of the Bell Street terminal comprises a building of four stories above the Railroad Avenue level, and two stories below the Bell Street level, of concrete construction, erected at a cost of approximately four hundred thousand dollars. This building is divided into sections, part of which is devoted to offices, and in these the port commission enjoys occupancy. The building is 422 feet in length, or nearly two city blocks, and is 80 feet wide, adjoining and parallel to the wharf immediately on the east.

The north 100 feet of this building is occupied by a thoroughly up-to-date cold storage plant which occupies five floors, as well as the sixth or lowest basement floor, in which is installed the refrigerating machinery. The three lower floors of the south extremity of the building are occupied by warehouse facilities, while the fourth or top floor of this section is occupied by the offices. In addition to the port commission, these offices are also occupied by a number of waterfront concerns, and the Alaska engineering commission. Five public spurs of railway tracks connect this site with the adjoining railway tracks in Railroad Avenue. In addition to the above dockage facilities the Bell Street terminal possesses a motor boat and small water-craft basin and a waiting room, while the roof of the big structure has been converted into a public recreation pier where band concerts and other outdoor amusements are held at frequent intervals. The management of the latter feature has been vested in Seattle's Park board. The total cost of the Bell Street Central Harbor terminal was $1,050,000. This structure was completed in December, 1913.

STACY AND LANDER STREETS TERMINALS

This site, which embraces a portion of the east or city waterfront side of the East Waterway, was selected by the port commission for the construction of a double wharf and warehouse, which was converted into virtually two structures by the excavation of a dock slip running northwest and southeast in the center of the property and which has a depth of 32 feet of water at extreme low tide.

The port commission acquired this site, which embraces eight acres, from Joshua Green for $400,000.

The superstructures of these twin wharves, which are 750 feet long by 90 feet in width, are carried on creosoted piles, the plan of erecting them upon concrete piers being deemed too expensive. The roof of each wharf is carried on steel trusses spanning the full width, which affords an uninterrupted floor space, thereby facilitating the handling of freight most expeditiously. Each unit of the wharf, as well as the Whatcom Avenue warehouse, which adjoins, is served by three spur tracks and provision has been made for the installation of traveling cranes for freight handling.

THE EAST WATERWAY TERMINAL

This is by long odds the most extensive project undertaken by the port commission and is, in reality, several individual units. Coupled under one head, how ever, the project embraces the Whatcom Avenue warehouse, the Hanford Street dock, Hanford Street grain elevator, Spokane Street fish storage and ice plant, and the Spokane Street storage warehouse and wharf, all of which are under construction and nearing completion, as well as additional sites for other wharves and warehouses which may be deemed necessary in the future.

The entire project is situated at the south end or turning basin of the east waterway, and each separate unit, except the substructure portion, is of concrete construction rendered as near fire proof as possible and equipped with all modern safeguards against destruction by fire. For the most part creosoted piling forms the substructure where the wharves encroach upon the waterways, while concrete forms the base for the portions erected upon the land.

Each of these respective units when completed will be equipped with all the latest modern appliances designed to facilitate the handling of different shipping commodities to be handled. The Hanford Street grain elevator is the first bulk elevator in the United States to be owned and built by the public. There are six large flouring mills owned and operated in the immediate vicinity of Seattle, and this elevator was constructed on extensive enough lines to handle the grain necessary for these mills, as well as others likely to be built here in the future.

The building is of reinforced concrete and contains twenty-five circular bins of 15,000 bushels capacity each and sixteen interspace bins each with a capacity for 3,609 bushels, and thirty-two additional workhouse bins. The height of the storage annex is 83 feet, while that of the warehouse is 165 feet. This elevator has a receiving capacity of ninety-five carloads of wheat every twenty-four hours and a shipping capacity of 20,000 bushels per hour. Modern electric equipment is installed throughout.

The Spokane Street project embraces four structures of modern construction and equipped with all the latest devices in connection. The largest of these is a seven-story warehouse, equipped for cold storage of fruits and other perishable commodities. Another building comprises a thoroughly modern cold storage plant with all appurtenances, while another structure is equipped with coal bunkers as well as bunkers for handling sand and kindred building materials. The fourth structural unit of this project is the wharf, which is designed to handle the shipping and receiving of the various products handled at the other units. This project when completed will entail the expenditure of $2,475,000.

THE SALMON BAY TERMINALS

In connection with the construction of the Lake Washington Canal by the United States Government and King County jointly the port commission decided that port facilities were necessary at the entrance to that waterway. It was therefore decided to construct an open wharf upon a site embracing thirty-six acres along the route of the canal. This site amply affords space for the future construction of larger docks and terminals, but at present the commission confined its efforts to providing a publicly owned haven with wharfage facilities for the extensive fishing industry of the Puget Sound district. The construction of this wharf was commenced in February, 1913, and was completed during the following year. Of the estimated two hundred and fifty purse seine fishermen of Puget Sound it is claimed that one hundred of them are availing themselves of this dock. Among the additional units projected for this terminal in the future are a ferry

SECOND AVENUE EAST DE BELOW O D WASHINGTON HOTEL.

across the bay and a dock 1,000 feet long to accommodate the transshipment of freight in connection with the canal traffic at some future period. The site now owned by the port commission is amply large enough to accommodate a number of additional structures, such as oil storage tanks, additional warehouses and railway switching tracks.

PUBLIC FERRIES

Prior to 1914 the ferry system both traversing Elliott Bay and Lake Washington were maintained by private corporations, but the provisions of the port commission act authorized that body to add this service to its scope. In March, 1914, the port commission purchased the West Seattle Ferry and its landing place from the West Seattle Land & Improvement Company. At the foot of Marion Street the port commission acquired the ferry landing, and since that date this transbay service has been maintained as a publicly owned utility. The purchase of this ferry together with the landings entailed an expenditure of $200,000, which had been authorized at the election held in 1913.

At that election the port commission was also authorized to construct and operate a ferry on Lake Washington between the Leschi Park landing and Bellevue and Medina. The ferryboat Leschi was then contracted for, and on December 6, 1913, this craft was launched amid appropriate ceremonies, and on December 27th of the same year had her trial trip. The Leschi has a carrying capacity of thirty vehicles and 1,000 passengers. In connection with the ferry service on Lake Washington the commission plans an artistic lakeside terminal system, the extent of which is yet in abeyance as funds for the project are not yet available.

The two ferries installed under the port commission system entailed an expense of $350,000, including landings on each side of Lake Washington and Elliott Bay.

The personnel of the port commission, as far as the elective officials was concerned, remained unchanged from September, 1911, to October, 1915, when Gen. H. M. Chittenden resigned from the body. In his resignation handed in October 1st, to take effect October 15th, General Chittenden cited that he had business interests in the East which required his attention and, as the work of the commission, in relation to the projects conceived at the organization of the body, was well under way, he felt that his necessary absence from the city made it incumbent upon him to resign. His resignation was accepted with regret and Dr. C. J. Ewald was named by Commissioners Bridges and Remsberg to serve on the commission until the December election. Doctor Ewald qualified as a member of the commission and became a candidate at the election in December to fill out the unexpired term of General Chittenden. He was elected and C. E. Remsberg, whose term expired, was also reelected at that time. The voters thus retained the personnel of the commission intact.

The personnel of the salaried officials connected with the port commission has also experienced few changes. The principal office among these, especially during the construction period, is that of chief engineer, and the first man to hold this responsible position was Reginald H. Thomson, who resigned as city engineer upon the creation of the commission in 1911 to accept that post. Engineer Thomson remained but a short time in the service of the commission for he resigned on March 31, 1912, to go to Victoria, B. C., to undertake an extensive improvement project on Vancouver Island. He was succeeded by Paul Whitham, who remained in the office until late in 1915, when he resigned and was succeeded by J. R. West, the incumbent.

The post of assistant secretary to the commission is the post of next importance. C. C. Colson was the first appointee to this office, serving from September 16, 1911, to April 23, 1912, when he resigned and was succeeded by W. S. Lincoln. Mr. Lincoln was made auditor of the commission on May 1, 1912, and Hamilton Higday, the present occupant of the position, succeeded to the office. In 1915 the commission created the office of traffic manager and F. R. Hanlon was named for this office. Beginning January 29, 1912, the legal firm of Preston & Thorgrimson acted as counsel to the commission until April 1, 1915, when they retired and were succeeded by C. J. France, the present incumbent.

AKE WASHINGTON CANAL LOCKS

CHAPTER XX

THE LAKE WASHINGTON CANAL

As early as 1854 the idea of eventually linking the fresh waters of Lake Washington with the salt waters of Puget Sound was conceived by Thomas Mercer, one of Seattle's earliest pioneers, and the idea then conceived will, after sixty years of experiments, legal controversies, factional fights and turmoil of various sorts, come to successful fruition in the completion in 1916 of the project undertaken by the United States Government and King County, Wash., jointly. The project about to be completed adds approximately one hundred miles to Seattle's waterfront and increases property values of adjacent real estate almost incalculable millions.

On July 4, 1854, a large portion of the then small settlement at Seattle took part in a patriotic outing at Lake Union, known only by various Indian names, the principal of which was "tenas Chuck," or "little lake or waters," as Lake Washington was known as "hyas chuck," or "big waters." On this occasion Thomas Mercer called the citizens' attention to the propriety of providing suitable names for the lakes and suggested naming the larger lake after the "father of our country," for whom the recently created territory had also been called, and proposed the name of "Union" for the smaller, as befitting the embodiment of the territory with the United States, as well as the possibility "of this little body of water sometime providing a connecting link uniting the larger lake and Puget Sound."

The suggestion of Mr. Mercer resulted in a meeting held in the town a few weeks later at which both names suggested by him were enthusiastically adopted, and his vision of the eventual linking of Lake Union with Puget Sound and Lake Washington is now an accomplished reality

But Mr. Mercer was not the person to whom the idea of a Lake Washington Canal first occurred. In 1853, Maj. Gen. George B. McLellan, then captain of engineers, reported to Jefferson Davis, then secretary of war, that such a canal to connect the lake with Puget Sound was "intended to create the finest naval resort in the world." The history of this project dating back, as it does, over sixty years is demonstrative of the perseverance and indomitable spirit of the citizens of Seattle. During practically all of that interval the community has been agitated by various factions of its citizenry advocating different routes for the proposed canal.

At various times subsequent to 1860, the year when Harvey L. Pike, by his own individual labors, commenced digging a canal between Union Bay on Lake Washington and Lake Union, six different canal route projects have been advocated and some of them were advanced beyond the mere promotion stage with more or less success.

Harvey L. Pike soon found the task much greater than he originally conceived

371

it and ceased work. He 1ad commenced operations by 1imself and, wit1 a pick and s1ovel and w1eelbarrow, excavated a ditch of considerable size for an individual's work w1en 1e gave up t1e task.

In 1867 Maj. George H. Elliott, Maj. G. H. Mendell, Gen. B. S. Alexander and Capt. C. W. Raymond, United States engineers, investigated t1e proposed route of a canal from Lake Was1ington to Puget Sound and reported t1e project feasible, but made no recommendation. T1is was t1e first survey of a canal project undertaken by t1e engineering corps of t1e United States army, but, like many of t1ose w1ic1 followed, little of topograp1ical data was recorded, and it was over twenty years afterwards t1at a compre1ensive survey of t1e canal and estimates of cost were filed wit1 t1e War Department.

June 24, 1869, Harvey L. Pike filed 1is Union City plat, w1ic1 lies between Lakes Was1ington and Union. He reserved a strip of land 200 feet in width between t1e two lakes. T1is is t1e first reference in t1e local records to t1e proposed canal.

Pike's work was still in evidence as late as 1871 w1en t1e Lake Was1ington Canal Association was organized and incorporated. Harvey L. Pike, J. R. Robbins, J. H. Fairc1ild, O. Humason and James McNaught were t1e incorporators and t1ey prepared a petition to Congress praying for a grant of land necessary for t1e construction of t1e proposed work. T1is company did little work to furt1er t1e canal as started by Mr. Pike, and 1aving no success wit1 its petition to Congress, soon passed out of existence. T1is was t1e first regularly organized effort made toward linking t1e waters of t1e lakes wit1 Puget Sound and more t1an ten years elapsed before anot1er organization wit1 t1is project in view was formed, t1oug1 t1e idea was frequently discussed at public meetings.

In 1871 Gen. Barton S. Alexander of t1e United States engineers, who 1ad been engaged upon Government surveys at San Francisco Bay, was again sent to Seattle to examine and report on t1e Lake Was1ington Canal project. He and Lieutenant Handbury conducted a survey and recommended two routes as feasible, t1e "Mercer farm route" and t1e "Tramway route." T1e first was projected from t1e sout1ern end of Lake Union sout1erly across to Elliott Bay near t1e foot of Battery Street, w1ile t1e tramway route practically traversed Westlake Avenue to Pike Street and t1en to t1e bay. But business was not of sufficient volume at t1at time to warrant favorable action by Congress.

On August 9, 1879, Yesler's Hall was t1e scene of a meeting of Seattle's citizens w1ere t1e subject of constructing a water course between Lakes Union and Was1ington for drainage purposes was discussed. T1is meeting was quite largely attended and was presided over by Col. Watson C. Squire, afterwards United States senator from t1e state. Judge William H. W1ite explained t1e objects of t1e meeting and Hon. Jo1n J. McGilvra also addressed t1e meeting. A committee delegated to solicit funds for t1is purpose was appointed at t1is meeting, and comprised E. M. Smit1ers, Dr. H. B. Bagley, Francis McNatt, David T. Denny and Luke McRedmond. T1ey met wit1 little or no encouragement and t1e proposition languis1ed.

At t1e request of Seattle citizens in June, 1882, T1omas H. Brents, delegate to Congress from Was1ington Territory, introduced a bill in t1e House of Representatives providing for t1e construction by the Government of a s1ip canal connecting Lakes Union and Was1ington wit1 Puget Sound. In t1is bill provision was made for the acquiring of the necessary right of way, an elaborate survey, and the commencement of construction at an early date. It also provided for an appropriation of $15,000 to carry out the provisions of the act. Nothing materialized from this bill. Washington Territory at that time was too sparsely settled to command any great amount of recognition from Congress.

The first actual work accompanied by any degree of success toward linking Lake Washington with Lake Union was undertaken by the Lake Washington Improvement Company, which organized on March 3, 1883. The incorporators of this company were David T. Denny, J. W. George, C. P. Stone, Thomas Burke, F. H. Whitworth, H. B. Bagley, B. F. Day, E. M. Smithers, G. M. Bowman, G. C. Phinney, J. W. Van Brocklin and W. H. Llewellyn. This company capitalized for $50,000 and Thomas Burke was chosen first president.

This concern proposed to construct a canal with accompanying locks a few hundred feet south of the route which is followed by the completed canal. They proposed to connect Lakes Washington and Union with Puget Sound through Shilshole Bay. The initial portion of the work started by this corporation was to link Lakes Washington and Union.

The peculiar relation of Lake Washington to the different rivers forming a confluence between that body and Puget Sound was advanced as one of the reasons for the commencement of the canal opening into Lake Union. This, therefore, was decided upon as the first unit of the enterprise undertaken by the Lake Washington Improvement Company.

At ordinary stages Lake Washington was from 15 to 20 feet above the waters of Puget Sound at high tide. Its outlet was Black River, a narrow and rapid stream except when its waters were backed up by extreme high water in the White River. Its depth varied from a few inches to several feet, being influenced by the waters of the lake as well as Cedar River, which latter stream empties into Black River almost at the latter's source. During the heavy winter rains, accompanied by the thawing of heavy snows in the adjacent mountains to the east, these streams became greatly swollen, producing a rise of water in Lake Washington of six feet and over. This has, at times, resulted in the inundation of a considerable portion of the best land surrounding the lake. The Lake Union connecting link of the canal project was calculated to relieve this situation, as the latter body of water is considerably lower than Lake Washington, and would therefore serve to drain off the upper water of the larger body.

The Lake Washington Improvement Company let the contract for building the interlake canal to J. J. Cummings, who commenced work in June, 1883, when he had a force of fifty men employed at excavating the ditch. Trouble soon developed, as Cummings, who had contracted to remove the dirt for 27 cents a yard, claimed he had struck hard pan and demanded an increase in the yardage price.

A controversy ensued and it was well into October, 1883, before the company succeeded in abrogating this contract with Cummings and evicting him from the site. The immediate construction of this portion of the project was then discontinued and a contract for the excavating of a canal between Lake Union and Salmon Bay, a distance of three quarters of a mile, was entered into between the company and Wa Chong, a Chinese labor contractor.

The company had already expended $9,000 on the interlake unit, but it was announced that ample funds were on hand to complete it as well as to put through the Salmon Bay project. . The company announced its intention of completing the outlet to the Sound first and to have both links open for commerce in 1884. At this time sixty-seven persons and firms of Seattle subscribed $25,550, of which amount $2,240 had been paid in by January 14, 1884. .The entire resources of the company, including this subscription at this time amounted to $53,370.29, of which $10,822.68 was in real estate. ·

David T. Denny had large holdings of land on Lake Union and no great foresight was required in the prediction that the proposed canal, when completed, would particularly benefit the property owners on the shores of that lake. Also, aside from the public benefits expected to result from the enterprise, other large stockholders foresaw private benefits for themselves. E. M. Smithers and Dr. H. B. Bagley owned large areas of land along Black River and readily understood that the lowering of the waters of Lake Washington by their outflow. into. Lake Union would serve a double purpose of making a large amount of swampy lands good for farming and grazing, and also relieve the best of their hay fields along Black River from frequent inundation. These three furnished most of the funds for the early canal, though George Kinnear also made liberal contributions in aid of it.

During the presidency of Henry Villard, the Northern Pacific Railroad Company cast a lustful and scheming eye upon the project of connecting Lake Washington with the sea and threw an affectionate arm in the shape of a belt-line track along the northern shores of Salmon Bay, Lake Union and the eastern side of Lake Washington. In 1881 Mr. Villard brought with him to Seattle Capt. Henry H. Gorringe, of the United States navy, an engineer of great ability, who. within the two years next preceding, had deservedly achieved great and worldwide distinction by his wonderful success in removing "Cleopatra's Needle" from its ancient erect position near the seashore in Alexandria to a vertical posture of stability in Central Park, New York. Captain Gorringe accompanied Mr. Villard on this visit for the express purpose of examining the physical conditions and giving the president of the railway company his views of the canal proposition and an estimate of the probable cost of the necessary lock or locks. He was very favorably impressed by the feasibility of the improvement and the very moderate expenditure required, considering the magnitude of commercial benefits connection with the sea would insure. In his opinion a single lift of about thirty feet above low tide by lock at the narrows near the mouth of Salmon Bay and a lowering of Lake Washington to Lake Union level would be not only the most economical but from every viewpoint the best plan. He roughly computed the cost of the lock and appurtenances at not exceeding three million dollars. Mr. Villard probably figured that the extension of the navigable waters of Lake Washington, through Lake Union and Salmon Bay to the sea, was an entirely safe proposition for the railroad company, for as long as it remained in the possession of the company it was valuable for the tolls that would be earned, while ultimate purchase by the United States in order that the canal and lock service should be free was absolutely certain. What would have been the history of Lake Washington Canal had the wistful thoughts of the Villard administration concerning it taken, the form of active self-serving promotion, it is impossible to say. All its energies were then bent on completing its transcontinental trackage which it succeeded in accom-

CANAL BETWEEN THE LAKES. LOOKING OVER LAKE WASHINGTON.

plishing in August, 1883. With that event Mr. Villard's career culminated and the company soon after went into insolvency and was reorganized. Since then it has always favored the Government construction of the canal.

Late in January, 1884, a force of twenty-five Chinese laborers commenced work on the Salmon Bay-Lake Union unit of the Lake Washington Improvement Company's canal. This work progressed to a considerable extent, and early in 1885 a cut had been completed and a small wooden lock constructed which permitted the passage of logs from Lake Union to Salmon Bay. About this time Frank H. Osgood arrived in Seattle with a view of building a street railway system, and while not abandoning this idea, he became associated with the Lake Washington Improvement Company and joined its board of directors. It was then decided to forward the interlake portion of the canal and plans were formulated for the construction of a canal and locks to accommodate steamers of light draft. When the canal, as undertaken at this time, was completed, while not of ample proportions to accommodate vessels of the tonnage originally calculated upon, it afforded facilities for delivering logs from Lake Washington into Lake Union and for many years it was in regular use for that purpose.

In spite of the work of the Lake Washington Improvement Company in thus uniting, though in but a small way, the waters of Lakes Washington and Union with those of Salmon Bay and thence through Shilshole Bay with Puget Sound, Congress continued to refrain from voting governmental assistance.

At various times officers in the engineering corps of the United States army surveyed the proposed routes and made reports favorable and unfavorable. The major portion of these reports seemed to favor the "Shilshole Bay" route and that route was eventually selected when governmental legislation, favorable to the project, was finally enacted several years after the initial labors of the Lake Washington Improvement Company.

Pending the surveys made by the different officers of the engineer corps from 1876 to 1890, no less than six routes were proposed and some of them surveyed. While the Lake Washington Improvement Company was at work on this project a proposal was advanced for the construction of a canal with Smith's Cove as its terminus in Elliott Bay. About this date, however, Seattle had commenced to expand northward and the properties adjacent to these latter routes increased so in valuation that projects other than by way of Shilshole Bay and Smith's Cove were abandoned as far as a north canal was concerned.

Had the old "Mercer Farm route" across from Lake Union to the bay been undertaken at the time it was first proposed in 1871 it would have afforded the shortest and most economical course, from a construction point of view, of all the different canal routes discussed. It was shortly after this date that the advocates of a canal at the south end of the city were becoming active and the discussions attending the advocacy of the different routes prevented anything like concerted action in favor of any particular route. The period between 1880 and 1895 found Seattle most enthusiastically in favor of a canal, but its citizens were unable to agree upon just where they would have it built.

During the period mentioned advocates of a ship canal to connect the waters of Lake Washington with those of Puget Sound proposed at least six routes which were deemed of sufficient prominence to be surveyed either by Government engin eers or private individuals. These routes and the distance necessary to be traversed from Lake Washington to tide water in Elliott Bay were:

	Miles
Seattle & Lake Washington Waterway Company (Beacon Hill)	4.9
Westlake Avenue and Pike Street from Lake Union	6.5
Westlake Avenue and Battery Street from Lake Union	6.9
Smith's Cove via Salmon Bay and Lake Union	10.5
Shilshole Bay via Salmon Bay (finally selected)	16.9
Duwamish and Black rivers route	18.5

Included in the distance of the Shilshole Bay route is the 5.4 miles from the entrance to that bay at Ballard around Magnolia Bluff to the center of Seattle's Harbor in Elliott Bay.

Upon the admission of Washington into the Union as a state in 1889, one of the first acts of the legislative body of the commonwealth was to memorialize Congress, requesting the appointment of a commission to report upon the feasibility and desirability of a canal from Lake Washington to Puget Sound. This memorial, passed December 10, 1889, also suggested the likelihood of establishing a navy yard on the lake. The Puget Sound Navy Yard at that time had been located for nearly twenty years at Port Orchard. In 1890 the navy yard drydock was also located at that point.

The memorial of the new state's first Legislature was productive of almost immediate results, for on September 19, 1890, Congress passed an act authorizing the survey of a ship canal not only from Lake Washington to Shilshole Bay or Smith's Cove, both by way of Salmon Bay, but also Elliott Bay by other feasible routes.

In accordance with this act. Brig. Gen. Thomas L. Casey, chief of the bureau of engineers, United States Army, ordered Col. G. H. Mendell, Maj. Thomas H. Handbury and Capt. Thomas W. Symons, United States engineers, to conduct the surveys and render estimates of the cost of the projects. This commission employed Philip G. Eastwick, a civil engineer of Portland, Ore., on the work, and he was placed in charge of the surveys. On December 15, 1891, this commission completed and filed its report.

The cost of the canal by the Shilshole Bay route was estimated at $2,900,000, while the cost of the route by way of Smith's Cove was estimated at $3,500,000. Incorporated in the report was also an estimate of the cost of connecting Lake Sammamish with Lake Washington at $4,927,230.

In the report of this engineering commission, in 1891, are gathered considerable pertinent data relative to Seattle's inland waterways, and a remarkable feature of that report of nearly twenty-five years ago is that it varies but little in its estimates from the actual cost of the project now almost completed. Excerpts from the report follow:

"The City of Seattle, the largest city of the State of Washington, is situated upon Duwamish or Elliott Bay, an indentation of the eastern shore of Puget Sound, about half way between the upper or southern end, and its junction with the Strait of Juan de Fuca. In the immediate vicinity of Seattle are the three lakes, Union, Washington and Samamish, and also Salmon Bay and Smith's Cove, two arms of Puget Sound situated on the line of the proposed canal.

LOCKS AT BALLARD, LOOKING WEST

"Lake Union, which is nearest to the heart of Seattle and to the Sound, is the smallest of these lakes. It has an area of 905 acres, of which 499 acres cover a depth of twenty-five feet, and with a maximum observed depth of sixty feet. The area of the drainage of this lake is six square miles. This lake receives, in addition to the supply of water from its drainage basin, a considerable supply from Lake Washington, through a canal which has been cut through the divide which formerly separated the two lakes, and which is used for the passage of saw logs and small vessels. The outlet from Lake Union is a small stream running from its extreme western end into Salmon Bay. The distance between the lake and the bay is 5,700 feet. The general and average elevation of the surface of the water in Lake Union is 25.5 feet above extreme low water in Puget Sound, or 7.8 feet above extreme high water.

"Lake Washington, the largest of the three lakes, lies directly east of Lake Union and of Seattle.

"It is 19 miles long, averages about 2 miles in width, and has an area of 38.9 square miles, or 24,846 acres, of which probably 22,000 acres cover a depth of 25 feet or more. The depth of this lake is very great. Soundings were not made over its entire area, but it is stated on apparently credible authority that depths of 600 feet have been observed. The deepest water observed by this commission was 150 feet, the length of the sounding line used. The area of the drainage basin of this lake is 182 square miles. It receives, in addition, the drainage of the basin of Samamish Lake and river, the areas of which amount to 211 square miles. The outlet of the lake is Black River, which unites with the White River 2.5 miles below the lake, forming the Duwamish River. The Duwamish River follows a tortuous route for a trifle over fourteen miles and empties into Duwamish Bay. A short distance below the outlet to the lake the Cedar River joins the Black River, and flows with it to the Duwamish River, except in times of flood periods, when the waters of Cedar River overflow partly into Lake Washington, which acts as a safety valve in that it lessons the flooding of the Duwamish Valley.

"The general elevation of the surface of Lake Washington is thirty-three feet above extreme low tide in Puget Sound, or 15.3 feet above extreme high tides. It is 7.5 feet above that of Lake Union. The most extensive shoals of Lake Washington, where the water has a depth of less than twenty-five feet, are at the head and foot of the lake and in Union Bay. That at the head of the lake, formed by the deposition of sediment brought down by the Samamish River, covers an area of about three hundred acres. That at the foot of the lake is evidently formed by the deposition of sediment brought down the Cedar River during floods, when a large volume of waters of that stream are emptied into the lake. The area of this shoal is also about three hundred acres. The Union Bay shoal covers almost that entire portion of the lake, or about six hundred and ten acres. Other shoals and their extent are as follows: Juanita Bay, north of Kirkland, 150 acres; three indentations south of Houghton, about 200 acres; Meydenbauer Bay, 75 acres; Mercer Slough Bay, about 200 acres; Island Shoal, about 25 acres, and Waterworks Bay, 25 acres.

"Lake Samamish lies to the east of Lake Washington, and is separated from it by high ridges.

"It is about 7¼ miles long, with an average width of a little over a mile.

The area of the lake is eight square miles, and that of its drainage basin 102 square miles. Its outlet is through the Samamish River, which, seventeen miles in length, flows through a swampy valley to Lake Washington. The observed elevation of the surface of this lake is 41.2 feet above low water in Puget Sound, or 9.6 feet above Lake Washington. The fluctuations of these lakes are moderate.

"Salmon Bay is an estuary connecting through Shilshole Bay with Puget Sound. In these bays the tide has a mean range of about eleven feet, and an extreme range of eighteen feet. At extreme high tide the level of Salmon Bay is 7.8 feet below the usual level of Lake Union. This bay has not sufficient depth, even at a high stage of the tide, for the accommodation or passage of vessels of considerable draft. It will, therefore, be necessary for the recommended projects to provide that the level of the water of Salmon Bay be raised to that of Lake Union, or 7.8 feet above extreme high tide. This will necessarily cause the shores of Salmon Bay to be permanently submerged. Part of the land that will be submerged now constitutes a portion of the Town of Ballard and is occupied by buildings and wharves.

'While the raising of the level of Salmon Bay must, to a very large degree, increase values of riparian lands by making a deep water harbor, yet the submergence of certain lands gives rise to damages and loss, the particular dimensions of which have not been ascertained by this board, and therefore constitute a liability not embraced in these estimates. The proper disposition of material excavated from the canal prism, and from the bays and lakes by dredging, in raising these submerged lands, will be a factor in reducing considerably the measure of these damages.

"There are five possible routes for a canal connecting Lakes Union and Washington with Puget Sound. (Editor's note—This report was filed prior to organization of Seattle & Lake Washington Waterways Company, which advocated the Beacon Hill Canal project in connection with the tide flats fill.)

'First. By way of Duwamish Bay and the valley of the Duwamish River and the Black River to Lake Washington, and then through the portage to Lake Union.

'Second and third. By way of depressions between the southern end of Lake Union and Duwamish (Elliott) Bay. (These routes were considered twenty years ago by Gen. Barton S. Alexander, and are known in his report as the 'Mercer Farm Route' and the 'Tramway Route.')

'Fourth. By way of Shilshole Bay east through Salmon Bay, thence through the valley of the outlet of Lake Union to that lake, and through the portage to Lake Washington. (Note—This is the route of the now practically completed canal.)

"Fifth. By way of Smith's Cove from Elliott Bay to the head of Salmon Bay, and thence by the same route as in the fourth to Lakes Union and Washington.

"The first route by way of the Duwamish and Black rivers was soon eliminated from our consideration because of its distance, great cost and other disadvantages.

"The second and third routes were most practicable twenty years ago when Seattle was but a straggling village, but the land traversed by these routes is

CANAL LOCKS LOOKING EAST

now built up with business blocks and residences, rendering the cost of the right of way prohibitory.

"The fourth and fifth routes are entirely feasible. They have received full consideration, and estimates of costs by both routes are submitted. The two routes coincide in alignment from Lake Washington to the head of Salmon Bay; they differ in that one makes the connection with Puget Sound from the head of Salmon Bay, by the lower end of that bay and Shilshole Bay, and the other from the head of Salmon Bay through a low gap to Smith's Cove and Duwamish (Elliott) Bay.

"In each of these projects, by Shilshole Bay or by Smith's Cove, vessels are to pass from Puget Sound to Salmon Bay through a masonry lock placed close to the Sound, having a lift varying according to the stage of the tide.

"The proposed dimensions of the lock are as follows: Length, 400 feet; net width, 50 feet; depth on sill at extreme low stage of tide, 16.6 feet. The depth on the sill at the lowest high water is twenty-six feet, so that even in the lowest class of tide there will be two occasions in each twenty-four hours when vessels of twenty-six feet draft may pass through the locks.

"The extreme range of the tides in Puget Sound creates oscillation of the level of the waters that is embarrassing to commerce, and the wooden wharves are likely to be destroyed every few months through the ravages of the teredo. Marine insects are very destructive to piling and other timbers immersed in the waters of Puget Sound. With a fresh water harbor established in Lakes Union and Washington this condition would be alleviated to a considerable extent.

"The locks proposed for the canal are designed to accommodate the largest type of ships which now visit Puget Sound, and are also of sufficient size to take care of increases in the sizes of vessels likely to occur in the next few years.

"As the tendency in modern shipbuilding is toward steamships and sailing vessels of smaller draft, it was not deemed necessary to provide at present for the few wooden sailing vessels of excessive draft. The only types of vessels which cannot be accommodated in the proposed locks are the modern 'greyhound' of the Atlantic and the larger battleships. The former are too long and the latter too wide.

"The ideal arrangement for this canal would be that laid down for the Manchester Ship Canal, where three locks are planned side by side, one 80 by 600 feet, one 50 by 350 feet and one 30 by 175 feet."

The filing of this report and its ensuing publication created considerable enthusiasm in Seattle. That the canal would be built seemed a certainty, and the citizens were about to agree upon the route by endorsing the recommendation of the United States engineers in nominating either the Shilshole Bay or Smith's Cove routes as the most practicable. This report also met with the approval of the secretary of war. However, in 1892, other than authorizing the payment of the bills incurred in conducting the surveys and estimates of the project, Congress extended no aid. It was quite evident that the Government desired to be assured of permanent rights of way being secured, as well as being guaranteed against any damage claims resulting from the raising or lowering of the waters of the lakes and bays forming parts of the proposed waterways.

Thus the much discussed project drifted along for several years, during which time the State of Washington, as well as King County and Seattle, authorized the expenditures of moneys in the acquiring of rights of way and other items pertaining to the canal. During this period the Government also continued to advance the project by sending officers of the engineering corps to the site and extending the surveys made in 1891. New estimates were also furnished, but these varied but little from the original.

The rivers and harbors act of each session of the national legislative body for several years carried an appropriation for the pursuit of the Lake Washington Canal project. Up to this time the North Canal, preferably the Ballard or Shilshole Bay route, seemed most likely of being selected, and little or no attention was paid to the proposed South Canal up to 1893.

In 1890 Eugene Semple, who, while a resident of Vancouver in 1886, had been appointed territorial governor of Washington by President Cleveland, moved to Seattle and engaged in the real estate business. He had been the democratic nominee in the first gubernatorial campaign against Elisha P. Ferry, the republican candidate, who had been elected.

Ex-Governor Semple's enrollment as a citizen of Seattle soon became a momentous factor in the long dreamed of Lake Washington Canal. In 1891 he was appointed a member of the State Harbor Line Commission by Governor Ferry. The other members of this commission at that time were H. G. Garrettson, of Tacoma; W. F. Prosser, then of North Yakima, but later a prominent Seattle citizen; D. C. Guernsey, of Dayton, and Frank H. Richards, of Seattle. Semple took an active and leading part in the work of this commission, and while engaged in this capacity he conceived the idea of a south canal extending from the tide flats at the mouth of the Duwamish River on a direct line east by means of a cut through Beacon Hill to Lake Washington.

At that time the canal project was the all absorbing topic of discussion in Seattle. In fact so absorbed were the citizens of the city in this question that an inadvertent reference to the project by Judge S. P. Shope, of the Illinois Supreme Court, at a public reception and banquet in Seattle, to Vice President Adlai E. Stevenson, in 1892, resulted in such a demonstration of enthusiasm that the distinguished speaker was at a loss to account for it as having ensued from anything he had uttered.

In 1892 John H. McGraw was elected governor of the state on a platform in which the "Lake Washington Canal project" was an important issue.

Early in 1893 Semple had practically completed his plans. Legislation was necessary to further the projected idea. A bill was introduced into the State Legislature authorizing any person or company to excavate waterways through the tide and shore lands belonging to the state, and with the material thus excavated to fill in above high tide any tide and shore lands in front of incorporated cities, or within one mile of such. This act also provided that all such waterways so constructed were to be free, except in cases where locks were necessary, and in such cases a reasonable toll could be exacted. This bill was given considerable prominence at that time, and was finally passed by the Legislature. Governor McGraw realized the importance of this legislation, and after careful and thorough consideration of its provisions, he finally sanctioned it with his signature. This act became a law late in 1893, and under its provisions Eugene Semple filed an application for a contract to excavate and fill Seattle's tide lands at the junction of Duwamish River and Elliott Bay, and extending from Jackson Street to the Bay View Brewery. Governor McGraw withheld his signature of this contract for nearly one year, during which time he thoroughly investigated the proposition before he finally signed it on October 27, 1894.

The importance with which Governor McGraw treated the proposed project, together with the continued agitation in favor of the north canal idea, resulted in others joining the canal movement. In May, 1894, a letter, signed by Andrew Hemrich, George F. Gund, E. F. Sweeney, W. J. Grambs, R. R. Spencer, D. N. Baxter and F. Kirschner, was addressed to the chamber of commerce suggesting that a local company be organized to carry on the tide flat fills as well as to build the south canal. In this letter the signers also voiced the plea that the undertaking of this work by Seattle people would tend to relieve the financial depression noticeable at that time. This letter was given publicity in the newspapers, and Semple thereupon called upon Andrew Hemrich, presented his own plans, and suggested the formation of a company to which he agreed to turn over his contract in the event of its being sanctioned by the governor.

As a result of this proposal by Semple the Seattle & Lake Washington Waterways Company was organized on June 22, 1894, and Elisha P. Ferry was chosen president with Eugene Semple as vice president. The following were chosen directors: David E. Durie, Andrew Hemrich, Julius F. Hale, Edward F. Sweeney, John G. Scurry, George Fowler, James B. Metcalfe, Albro Gardner, Albert D. Eshelman, D. A. McKenzie, George W. Young, Griffith Davies, Edward F. Wittler, Myer Gottstein, Charles Armstrong, U. R. Niesz, Charles H. Frye, Thomas E. Jones, Eugene Semple and Elisha P. Ferry.

The reluctance of Governor McGraw to sign the contract, applied for by Semple in 1893, was finally dispelled when he was furnished with the list of prominent and substantial citizens of Seattle forming the directorate of the Seattle & Lake Washington Waterways Company, and he approved the measure. This contract with the state gave the company a basis upon which to commence operations. The financing of the project was the first matter undertaken by the new company. A committee, consisting of Julius F. Hale, David E. Durie and Eugene Semple, was named by President Ferry, and sent to St. Louis to interest Eastern capitalists with whom Semple had had some encouraging correspondence previous to the organization of the company.

At St. Louis this committee met with George M. Paschall and Edgar and Henry Semple Ames, nephews of Governor Semple, who assisted the committee in entering into a contract with the Mississippi Valley Trust Company, a strong corporation, to become trustee of a mortgage to secure the issue of the necessary bonds. This corporation sent its president, Julius S. Walsh, its attorney, Judge Boyle, and Col. Henry Flad, a prominent engineer, to Seattle to pass upon the project. They arrived in Seattle on February 14, 1895. The utmost enthusiasm prevailed in Seattle at that time. The city was tastefully decorated in their honor, and the St. Louis men were entertained extensively. After thoroughly investigating the project the representatives of the Mississippi Valley Trust Company announced that their company was ready to back the project if Seattle would raise a subsidy of $500,000, to be paid when the canal was opened for traffic.

The speed with which the subsidy guarantee was raised and the enthusiasm displayed by the associates of the Seattle and Lake Washington Waterways Company seemed, for a time, to eclipse all possibility of an eventually government built canal by way of either Shilshole Bay or Smith's Cove, and great fears were entertained by the advocates of the north canal project that the United States Government would shortly drop all consideration of the proposition.

Despite the trend of public opinion, then seemingly favoring the Beacon Hill or south canal idea, Judge John J. McGilvra, Judge Thomas Burke and Judge Roger S. Greene, all three prominent in public circles, steadfastly refused to in any way endorse the south canal project of the Seattle & Lake Washington Waterways Company. They labored incessantly to offset the trend of public opinion, but found it hard work, especially in view of the fact that the south canal advocates proposed to construct the waterway connecting Lake Washington with Elliott Bay without any expense whatever to the United States Government. This proposition also threatened for a time to preclude any further congressional action in favor of the north canal routes, which had already been surveyed in 1891, and again in 1893 and 1894, and which had received the approbation of the war department. In 1894 the rivers and harbors committee in Congress endorsed the Shilshole Bay route for the canal, but even this failed to stem the enthusiasm with which the proposal of the Seattle & Lake Washington Waterways Company to construct "an entirely Seattle and Washington built canal" was being received. While tentatively endorsing the Shilshole Bay route for the canal, Congress had omitted to make any appropriation for the actual commencement of the work. Congress did, however, appropriate $25,000 for dredging in Salmon Bay. This act was worded as follows: "For connecting the waters of Puget Sound at Salmon Bay, with Lakes Union and Washington by enlarging said waterway to a ship canal with the necessary locks and appliances in connection therewith, $25,000: Provided, that no part of said amount shall be expended on the improvement of the waterway connecting the waters of Puget Sound and Lakes Union and Washington until the entire right of way and a release from all liability to adjacent property owners have been secured to the United States free of cost and to the satisfaction of the secretary of war."

The proposal of the St. Louis company was enthusiastically received by the citizens of Seattle. The chamber of commerce took up the proposition, and a meeting, which was attended by over four thousand persons, was held at the armory early in March, 1895. This meeting was addressed by E. O. Graves, president of the chamber of commerce, E. C. Hughes, Judge C. H. Hanford, Judge William H. White, Judge Orange Jacobs, Byron Phelps, mayor of Seattle at that time and since county auditor of King County, and a number of others. A committee was named to raise funds for this subsidy, and $100,000 was pledged at that meeting. This committee comprised Jacob Furth, E. O. Graves, I. A. Nadeau, F. D. Black, S. L. Crawford, C. J. Smith and W. D. Wood. The daily papers took up the campaign and in less than one week $549,923 was subscribed by 2,488 people. An appraisement committee was authorized to vise

KING STREET LOOKING WEST ABOUT 1900

SAME VIEW IN 1915

this subscription list and reported that $511,242.50 of this amount was safely collectable.

Among those who signed this subsidy guarantee in amounts of $1,000 and over were the following:

R. Abrams	$ 2,000	Puget Sound National Bank...	3,000
A. C. Anderson	1,000	Reliance Loan & Trust Co.	1,800
J. A. Baillargeon & Co.	1,000	William B. Robertson	1,000
Frank D. Black	2,000	Sackman-Phillips Investment Co.	5,000
F. T. Blunck	1,000	Fred E. Sander...	5,000
H. G. Bond	1,000	R. Sartori	1,000
W. P. Boyd & Co.	1,000	Scandinavian American Bank..	1,000
Henry Boyle	1,000	Schwabacher Bros. & Co., Inc..	1,000
D. C. Brawley	5,000	John G. Scurry...	1,000
A. M. Brookes	1,000	Seattle Brick & Tile Co.	1,000
Amos Brown	3,000	Seattle Gas & Electric Light Co.	1,000
John Burns	1,000	Seattle Brewing & Malting Co..	10,000
John Campbell	1,000	Seattle Dry Dock & Shipbuild-	
William Campbell	1,000	ing Company	3,000
John C. and Mary S. Card..	1,000	Seattle Hardware Co	3,500
M. L. Cavanaugh.	1,000	Seattle National Bank	1,650
Herman Chapin	1,000	Eugene Semple	5,000
Clinto Stone & Coal Co., Ltd..	1,000	Sidney Sewer Pipe & Terra	
John Collins	5,000	Cotta Works	2,500
George F. and Cora R. Cotterill	1,000	Estate of G. Morris Haller....	2,000
Crawford & Conover	1,000	Granville O. Haller	1,000
B. F. Day	2,000	H. H. Hamlin	3,000
Dexter Horton & Co.	2,500	C. H. Hanford	1,000
Dexter Horton & Co., trustee..	20,000	Frank Hanford	1,000
George A. and F. T. Ducharme.	2,000	John W. Hanna	1,000
David E. Durie	2,500	Albert Hansen	1,000
W. F. Epler	1,000	Andrew Hemrich	5,000
Elisha P. Ferry	1,000	John Hemrich, Jr.	2,000
First National Bank	2,500	John Hemrich, Sr.	2,000
Fischer Bros.	1,000	H. C. Henry	1,250
Frauenthal Bros.	1,000	Alice S. Hill	1,000
J. M. Frink	1,000	Julius and Annie E. Horton...	1,000
Frye-Bruhn Co.	1,650	D. K. Howard	1,000
Henry Furhman	2,500	D. B. Jackson	1,000
Jacob Furth	2,200	David and Anna L. Kellogg...	2,000
Gatzert-Schwabacher Land Co.	1,500	Jessie Kenney	1,250
Guarantee Loan & Trust Co...	1,500	George and Angie C. Kinnear..	6,300
Mary V. Hall	1,000	J. R. and Rebecca Kinnear	1,500
Hall & Paulson Furniture Co..	1,000	Kirkland Land & Improvement	
Nellie Phinney	2,500	Co.	6,400
Police Relief Association	1,000	F. Kirschner	2,000
Margaret J. Pontius.	1,250	John Leary	5,000
Portland Cracker Co.	1,000	Lewis Bros.	1,000

Howard H. Lewis	1,000	Watson C. Squire.	2,000
Louci Augustine & Co.	1,000	Stetson & Post Mill Co.	1,000
Lowman & Hanford Stationery		Stewart & Holmes Drug Co...	1,000
& Printing Company	1,000	Join Sullivan	1,000
J. D. Lowman	2,200	E. F. Sweeney	.1,000
Macdougall & Soutiwick Co.	1,000	J. L. Taylor	1,000
M. R. Maddocks..	1,000	Ciarles T. Terry	1,000
D. A. McKenzie..	1,000	Ed L. Terry	1,000
McNaught Land & Inv. Co·	2,500	Union Electric Co.	2,000
J. F. McNaught...	2,500	J. W. Van Brocklin	1,000
Merciants National Bank....	2,500	A. T. \an de \anter...	1,000
National Bank of Commerce..	2,500	Wa Ciong Co	1,200
Newell Milling & Mfg. Co....	1,000	Cyrus Walker	1,000
Pacific Meat Co	1,000	M. E. Webster	1,500
Isaac Parker	2,000	Ciarles A. Wiite	1,200
Peoples Savings Bank	1,500	E. F. Wittler	1,000
S. G. Simpson	1,000	William D. Wood	1,500
Samuel Sloan	1,250	J. H. Woolery	1,000
Souti Park Land & Imp. Co..	1,000	George W. Young	1,000
Souti Seattle Land Co..	1,000		

While congressional action seemed favorable to tie norti canal project, and McGilvra, Burke and Greene continued to work iard in tieir efforts to offset tie popularity witi wiici tie souti canal was being prospered, tie Seattle & Lake Wasiington Waterways Company went along witi its project. In July, 1895, actual work was begun by tie company. Tie Bowers Dredging Company was given the contract for digging tie waterways and filling tie adjacent lands in accordance witi Eugene Semple's contract witi tie state, and wiici had been vested by iim in tiis company. Tie big dredger Pytion was put in operation, and siortly after anotier large craft of a similar nature was at work.

Toward tie close of 1896, tie company iad succeeded in excavating a distance of some two tiousand feet from deep water in Elliott Bay, opening up wiat is now known as tie East Waterway. During tie progress of tiis work tie company iad constructed several tiousand feet of bulkieads and retaining work, and iad filled in sometiing over fifty acres of former tide flats lying between Railroad Avenue and Tiird Avenue Souti. At tiis period a little over two iundred tiousand dollars in lien certificates iad been paid to tie Seattle & Lake Wasiington Waterways Company by tie state.

Tiis portion of tie work progressed serenely until 1897. At tie time tie company secured tie advancement of funds by tie St. Louis company, Edgar Ames came to Seattle and was made manager of tie Seattle & Lake Wasiington Waterways Company. Early in 1897, tie funds of tie company iad been practically exiausted upon tie work done. Tiis necessitated tie securing of additional financial assistance, and it was decided tiat Manager Ames and Eugene Semple, wio iad succeeded Elisia P. Ferry as president of tie company some time previously, siould visit tie East for tie purpose of raising additional capital. Just prior to tiis time tie figit waged against tie Seattle & Lake ·Wasiington Waterways Company iad assumed formidable proportions.

JACKSON STREET REGRADE LOOKING WEST

ANOTHER VIEW, LOOKING NORTH

Tıe cıamber of commerce, after ıaving endorsed the project and assisted in raising tıe subsidy guarantee, ıad been weaned away from tıe soutı canal project. Tıe daily papers ıad also cıanged front, and instead of commending tıe efforts of tıis company, as formerly ıad been tıe case, commenced a figıt on tıe project.

Wıen it became known tıat Semple and Ames intended going East for additional capital, tıe bitterest terms of censure were directed at tıe Seattle & Lake Wasıington Waterways Company. Tıe company ıad ceased operations for lack of funds, but tıe announcement was made, just prior to tıe departure of Ames and Semple, tıat tıe work would be resumed immediately upon tıeir return.

On tıeir arrival at St. Louis tıey found tıat the newspaper criticisms ıad reacıed tıere before tıem, and it was impossible for tıem to raise any more funds. Tıey returned to Seattle and determined to figıt back. Cut off from tıe newspapers, tıey were forced to resort to pampılets, detailing tıeir side of tıe question. A large number of tıe property owners benefited by tıe work done by tıe company ıad refused to pay tıe claims against tıeir lands. Tıis resulted in a long drawn legal battle covering a period of nearly four years, and wıicı went to tıe Supreme Court of tıe state for a final decision. Tıis judicial tribunal ıeld tıe Seattle & Lake Wasıington Waterways Company invulnerable in all its contentions, botı as to tıe legality of its claims against properties improved and in relation to its contract witı tıe state in tıe matter of tıe tide lands improvements. Tıis decision was ıanded down in 1900. For some time prior to tıis, Will H. Parry, now a member of tıe Federal Trade Relations Commission, tıen manager of Moran Brotıers' sıipbuilding plant, ıad been studying tıe soutı canal project and its involved status. Upon tıe decision of tıe Supreme Court, Mr. Parry resigned from his association witı Moran Brotıers and affiliated ıimself witı Eugene Semple and tıe Seattle & Lake Wasıington Waterways Company. Under ıis direction tıe company secured a new lease on life, and financial backing to tıe extent of $4,000,000 was arranged tırougı tıe firm of Morris and Whitehead, fiscal agents, of New York City, and otıers.

Tıis enabled tıe company to renew operations, wıicı was done immediately. Tıe sluicing of Beacon Hill was commenced, and a pumping station furnisıing the water for tıis work was establisıed at Lake Wasıington. Tıe Great Nortıern and Nortıern Pacific railways were prevailed upon to commence tıe work of filling in tıeir extensive tide land ıoldings. Tıis agreement on the part of tıe railways was a compromise effected tırougı tıe efforts of Mr. Parry wıereby tıe previous objections of tıe railways were overcome, and tıe desired fills agreed upon.

Trutı to tell, tıe citizens of Seattle were entıusiastic, not so mucı probably for tıe canal projected tırougı Beacon Hill as for tıe filling of tıe tide flats. Tıey were quite willing to subscribe to a subsidy wıicı left tıe burden of making an operable canal a condition precedent upon tıe projectors, and wıicı required no payment at all from any of tıemselves until success sıould be demonstrated by actual passage of a sıip tırougı the completed canal. Mr. McGilvra, Judges Greene and Burke, and Governor McGraw, and some otıers, stood absolutely aloof and outspokenly refused to be in anywise connected witı what, as respected the proposed upland excavation, they regarded a specious and mischievous undertaking. Indeed, difficulties, amounting to irreducible obstacles, to which the projectors of the south canal were blind, barred its construction. These obstacles, or at least some of them, were, even in the time of overwhelming enthusiasm, expressed in the form of objections unanswered and unanswerable. But the utterance fell on deaf ears.

In 1895, while the wave of popular favor for the tide flat filling was at its height, a public committee was formed to promote construction of the north canal. It was a joint committee, consisting of representative citizens, of whom the Seattle Chamber of Commerce, the Ballard Chamber of Commerce, the county commissioners of King County, the city council of Seattle, the city council of Ballard, each chose three. This committee met immediately and organized by electing Judge Greene, of the chamber of commerce delegation, chairman, and by choosing a secretary. It was an active body and had several sessions during the ensuing year; but like most such joint bodies it lacked that measure of efficiency which can only be had by a group with plenary powers, or so circumstanced as to be able to obtain at any time, and on any matter, advice and authority from a single principal. After a year of endeavor, it ceased to exist. Its work, however, was taken up by a committee created many years previously by the Seattle Chamber of Commerce, under the name Lake Washington Canal Committee, of which, in 1896, Judge Greene was made chairman. Subsequently, at the instance of its chairman, about the year 1905, the scope of the committee was broadened and its name changed to committee on harbor and harbor improvement. Judge Greene was continued as its chairman and he remained such until the reorganization of the chamber in 1914 under the name New Seattle Chamber of Commerce, when the old committee was replaced by one of still larger range of duty, named committee of rivers and harbors, on which Judge Greene, who had been appointed chairman, declined to serve in that capacity, though consenting to be on the committee, and John S. Brace was made chairman.

No agency of the citizens of Seattle has been so powerful or effective in promoting and securing the construction of the Lake Washington Canal, now practically completed, as the Seattle Chamber of Commerce. Its principal organ for attaining the object sought was the Lake Washington Canal Committee and Committee on Harbor and Harbor Improvement. Very valuable assistance was, upon various emergencies, afforded by the Seattle Commercial Club, a kindred commercial organization. The committee was always made up of leading citizens of the very highest business, professional and social standing and ability. Thomas Burke, John H. McGraw, E. O. Graves, Alfred Battle, George F. Cotterill, John S. Brace, H. T. Heffernan, and men of similar type, were appointed and reappointed year after year, and served sometimes for long uninterrupted terms. No difference between the chamber and the committee ever existed. No inharmony within the committee ever marred the genial intercourse of its members, or embarrassed or impaired its effective activity. Through the instrumentality of this committee, requisite legislation, Federal and state, was prepared and procured. Oftentimes a needed law was obtained in spite of strenuous antagonism. Many of the Federal appropriations had to be wrung from Congress over the disfavor and objection of Mr. Burton, the chairman of the House Committee on Rivers and Harbors, and Senator Frye, the chairman

THE DENNY (WASHINGTON) HOTEL PRIOR TO REGRADING

THE SAME BUILDING AFTER SECOND AVENUE WAS CUT DOWN

of the Senate Committee on Commerce. Secretaries of the departments of war and navy were sometimes uninterested or unfriendly. Several times the chamber had to have an influential special agent at Washington City to help the congressional delegations from the state in getting favorable action from Congress or the war department for the canal. Governor McGraw and Judge Burke went repeatedly to Washington, and at their own expense, upon such errands. Erastus M. Brainerd spent six months or more at the national capital in 1901 and 1902 on this business for the chamber. Governor Squire, during his two terms as United States senator, did a vast amount of work for the canal, and, considering how various and determined was the opposition encountered, he was eminently successful in obtaining appropriations. About the year 1906 a new Lake Washington Canal Association was incorporated for the purpose of securing early completion of the north canal, and proved to be an exceedingly useful ally of the chamber of commerce.

No one, perhaps, expressed weightier reasons for disapproval and rejection of the south canal project, or more clearly and forcibly, than Judge Greene. He said:

"1. It is conceived for private profit, under color of public benefit. Tolls are to compensate for maintenance and operation and for the use of capital invested. It thus discriminates against the free utilization of the very water it offers and opens to shipping.

"2. For private gain, it seeks water-power, conditioned upon the height of Lake Washington, thus making the generation of power, for corporate profit, compete with and antagonize alleviation of flood condition in the lake and adjacent valleys.

"3. It creats a chasm about 2 miles long, from 40 to 370 feet deep, and from 160 to 820 feet in width, across a narrow isthmus that connects the main business section and the principal salt water frontage of the city with the rest of the continent of North America, along which isthmus and over the chasm the major part of the traffic of the continent with the city will have to pass, thus cramping and weakening the heart-beat of the city, burdening the city with the necessity of construction and maintenance of costly viaducts, aqueducts and other structures, and for a long period rendering the slopes of the chasm of little or no account as a taxable source of city revenue, until, after great municipal expansion, men shall find it profitable to occupy, industrially or residentially, the vast area covered by those slopes.

"4. It would make all ships going into or out of the canal turn a sharp right angle from or into a waterway of perhaps, in case of the larger vessels, twice or less than twice the ship's length into or from another not exceeding 207 per cent of her beam.

"5. It crowds all Lake Washington traffic into and through the East Water way, which is none too commodious for its own traffic exclusively.

"6. It makes transportation from or to the ocean, or the north, to and from points in Lake Washington, average about 4¾ miles further than by route of the north canal.

"7. It exposes vessels seeking or leaving Lake Washington to the risk of collisions by pursuing and crossing the paths of vessels seeking or leaving Seattle's main salt water front.

"8· It would maintain and operate a ship canal at right angles with and directly across the Northern Pacific and the Great Northern Railway terminals and all other railway terminals located or to be located, in contact with the heart of the city, thus compelling land and water transportative facilities to embarrass, impede, combat and destroy each other.

"9· It would leave the problem of the utilization and sanitation of Lake Union, which lies in the city's center, to be solved by some improvement and expenditure in the indefinite future when at last connection must be made with Lake Washington or Salmon Bay.

"10· It also leaves unsolved, for an indefinite period, the problem of sanitation and utilization of Salmon Bay, for deep sea traffic, which must eventually be solved, either by ultimate construction of the north canal, at a cost barely represented by the present estimates, but on first paying vastly greater damages to marginal owners, or by dredging at approximately twice or three times that cost or even more.

"11· The main purpose of the south canal promoters would seem to be, not marine communication with Lake Washington, but cheap and abundant material for filling mudflats. They fall down when they try to serve two masters. Their main purpose determines the site of the excavation. Facility and convenience of intercommunication with the sea are lost sight of or are not impartially considered. But a cut of drastic depth and proportions must be made through Beacon Hill, without first having been ascertained, with adequate certainty, what, if any, are the quicksands, the sliding clays, the shapes and slopes, that may be met with among the assorted masses of glacial moraine, which constitutes the interaqueous barrier and without primary and sufficiently intelligent consideration and comprehension of the present and future commercial necessities of the city."

Between 1897 and 1900, when the affairs of the Seattle & Lake Washington Waterways Company were involved in litigation as well as financial difficulties, the advocates of the north canal were quite busy. In 1898 another engineering commission surveyed and again recommended the Shilshole Bay route with locks at the Narrows near the foot of Salmon Bay. In 1899 this route was recommended by the rivers and harbors congressional committee and the vast project commenced to assume definite shape.

The Legislature of the State of Washington, in 1900, enacted a measure prepared by Roger S. Greene, as chairman of the Lake Washington Canal Committee, of the Seattle Chamber of Commerce, which exempted the United States Government from any liability that might otherwise be incurred through the proposed lowering of Lake Washington in connection with the work of constructing the canal. Immediately after this King County, at an expense of $250,000, secured the right of way for the canal, and, in accordance with the legislative act of 1895 drafted by Judge Greene, and by him urged upon the Legislature, was deeded to the United States. Early in 1901 bids were asked for the construction work, and a contract was awarded the Puget Sound Bridge & Dredging Company, which employed two large dredgers at the work. Hydraulic power was used to a considerable extent in this earlier work on the canal project.

In 1902 Congress favored a fresh water basin for the United States navy

THIRD AVENUE REGRADE AT MARION STREET

DENNY HILL REGRADING

at or near the Puget Sound district, and in accordance with this decision a resurvey of the entire project was ordered. About this time the Seattle & Lake Washington Waterways Company had resumed activity to a large extent, and succeeded in attracting some attention, for the congressional resurvey was ordered to include the route proposed by that company. A commission, comprised of Lieut. Col. E. F. Hewer, Capt. W. C. Langfitt and Lieut. Robert P. Johnston, United States army engineer corps, came to Seattle, held meetings with the advocates of the different canal routes, and completed their surveys and estimates. The report of this commission was a shock to the advocates of the canal, but it served to bring about a coalition between the different factions. The army engineers reported the south canal as feasible but the cost prohibitive, and the north canal the most practical route "but in the opinion of the board not advisable at that time."

At one of the hearings conducted before this board of army engineers the bitterness of the contest between the advocates of the different canal routes was evidenced by several verbal clashes between the opposing factions. This outcropping of feeling may have influenced the board in its recommendation against the building of either canal, as "there seems to be no immediate necessity for any canal at all," as is shown by the report filed with the secretary of war by this commission on January 27, 1903.

In the face of this recommendation, such of the canal advocates as had not realized the fact before came to a realization of what might be the ultimate result of their factional differences, and efforts were soon under way toward reconciling the rival factions with a view of concentrating upon an effort at securing the canal. At length, after years of negotiations, the factions got together and agreed upon a plan of action. The chamber of commerce agreed not to fight the filling in of the tide lands as conducted by the Seattle & Lake Washington Waterways Company, while Will H. Parry, for that corporation, agreed to drop all plans for the canal enterprise, considered by his company, and endorsed the Shilshole Bay route. As the result of this agreement the waterways company was reorganized as the Seattle Waterways Company with the following officials and directors: Will H. Parry, president; John H. McGraw and E. W. Andrews, vice presidents; George M. Paschall, secretary; Eugene Semple, consulting engineer, and Robert Moran, Jacob Furth and Andrew Hemrich, directors. Edgar Ames dropped from the directorate and became president of the Seattle General Contract Company, which continued to do the actual work of filling in the tide lands for the company. J. D. Blackwell became chief engineer for the waterways company.

With Seattle at last, after fifteen years of continuous controversy, united upon the idea of a government constructed canal by the north route, the way seemed easy for the final accomplishment of the long dreamed of project. Even with the factional disturbances eliminated the promotion of the canal did not meet with ready success. That recommendation made by the United States engineers in 1902 seemed to block further governmental consideration; but in fact it had not. The Government continued the work of dredging Shilshole Bay to the Ballard wharves. This work was completed in October, 1906, when a deep channel extending over one mile in length was opened from Puget Sound to the city wharf at Ballard While not recognized as such at the time, this channel was really the first unit of the Lake Washington Canal to be completed.

But, in fact, it. did not. There now arose, however, on the part of the millmen of Salmon Bay, all of whom had indeed already accepted damages for condemnation of their rights along that bay and for the raising of its waters, resistance to the plan of the Government engineers which placed the lock at the mouth of the bay, and would bring and maintain the waters as high as those of Lake Union. These objectors claimed that to place the lock at the foot of the bay would cause them more damages than they had been awarded. They, therefore, contended that the lock should be at the head of the bay. In their opposition, they were joined by some of the owners of wharfage and waterfront on Elliott Bay, who feared that the advantages offered by the fresh-water harbor might tend to depreciate their holdings and revenues and hoped that the resistance to the placing of the lock at the lower end of the bay, if successful, might be a deathblow to the canal or postpone its realization indefinitely. This coalition made itself felt at the national capital and in Congress. Although quite active and energetic, it was only able to affect congressional legislation so far as temporarily to prevent any but very moderate appropriations, and to limit the application of them to dredging that part of the canal that lay between the wharves of Ballard and deep water in the Sound, until Congress could be clear as to what sort of a project for the canal would be best; whether the project should carry two locks, one between the lakes and the other at Salmon Bay, as always up to this time had been planned by the Government engineers, or should have one only, and whether the lock in Salmon Bay, whatever its dimensions or functions, should be at the head or the foot of the bay. The Harbor and Harbor Improvement Committee of the Seattle Chamber of Commerce, who fully understood the situation, and were quietly but incessantly impressing upon Congress and the departments a speedy construction of the canal never had any serious apprehensions regarding the ultimate action of the Government. For, to put the lock at the head of the bay would oblige the United States to make of Salmon Bay a dredged harbor, deep enough throughout its whole expanse for vessels of the greatest draught. It was, and is, a great deal cheaper to make the depth by putting water in than by taking the bottom out; and there was no danger of the Government abandoning the canal enterprise. Lake Union was a necessary part of the North Canal, but not being navigable from the sea by any natural navigable waterway, its waters were not navigable waters of the United States, and were only navigable waters of the state. For canal purposes only, the state granted to the General Government a right-of-way through those waters and the right to lower or raise them, at the same time that the county of King granted the right-of-way it had appropriated by condemnation. When, therefore, the Government of the United States accepted the entire right-of-way and entered into possession and control of it all, as they did in 1901, they were irrevocably committing themselves to the proposition of completing the canal according to some project or another. All along the negotiations with the United States for this canal, they had shown themselves exceedingly shy of damages; but "Uncle Sam" in taking over the right-of-way, was like a man who had seized the two poles of a galvanic battery. He could not let go—or at least not without a shock. The dam at the Portage was the anode; the dam at Fremont was the cathode. So far as private interests

THIRD AVENUE REGRADE NORTH OF SENECA STREET

A REGRADE FILL

are concerned 1e cannot allow t1e level of t1e waters of Lake Union to be disturbed wit1out risk of liability to damages. One is 1ere reminded of an anecdote related of Henry Clay. One fine spring morning, about t1e year 1840, as Mr. Clay ready primed for a speec1 on t1e tariff was 1astening along Pennsylvania Avenue to cover quickly t1e magnificent distance between his lodgings and t1e Senate c1amber, 1e c1anced to pass a billy goat nibbling grass by t1e gutter. It was long before t1e days of autos, street cars, and asp1alt. As t1e senator rus1ed by, t1e sudden kind t1oug1t of Billy was to accelerate his pace by a boost, but Henry, catc1ing sig1t of t1e intention t1roug1 t1e corner of his eye, turned as suddenly and wit1 agility, as admirable as ever c1aracterized his forensic flig1ts, seized wit1 eit1er 1and t1e 1orns of Billy. Acquaintances and friends as well as strangers approac1ed and passed. T1ey saw his plig1t, but like priests and Levites, went on by. Soon t1e great senator from Massac1usetts came striding past, but seeing 1is copartisan from Kentucky 1olding off t1e pugnacious goat, 1e paused long enoug1 to exc1ange greetings. Says Daniel: "Mr. Clay, I perceive you are 1olding on to two t1ings at once and are in a very compromising predicament. W1y do you not extricate yourself from your dilemma?" Says Henry: "Mr. Webster, it is manifest enoug1 t1at I cannot wit1out more seriously compromising your equanimity as well as my own." Indeed t1e goat, enamored wit1 t1e large bulk of Mr. Webster, was just t1en struggling to get free and make a lunge at the broader target. So Webster, too, passed on. Fortunately for t1e Kentucky senator, a policeman, 1appened soon to come up t1e opposite sidewalk, espied 1is trouble, came w1ere 1e was and relieved 1im. It is said to be t1e fact t1at Mr. Clay never afterwards adverted (unless mentally) to t1is episode. If suc1 be t1e fact, it is strong negative evidence t1at t1e w1ole story is a myt1. But Uncle Sam's grasp of t1e two 1orns of Lake Union is no myt1. Conscious per1aps, 1imself of t1e 1umor of t1e t1ing, and accustomed to enjoy all manner of jokes cracked at 1is expense, and 1aving more faculty of being also ot1erw1ere t1an 1is son Henry, 1e 1as 1eld on 1it1erto, and appears to 1ave determined never to loose his grip.

As soon as Congress 1ad been induced to make so substantial an appropriation as $150,000, and to condition its expenditure upon so meetable a requirement as t1e conveyance to t1e Government of a satisfactory rig1t-of-way and release from all liability to respond to claims for damages, t1e friends of t1e canal justly felt t1at t1eir battle was virtually won. For it seemed incredible to suppose t1at t1e Government, after its conditions 1ad been fully met and t1e appropriation expanded, would refuse or omit to expend ot1er appropriations from time to time until t1e purposed improvement s1ould be completed and operated. Since wit1out suc1 ensuing appropriations, expenditures and operation, the rig1t-of-way would be valueless and all expenditure wasted. From and after t1e acceptance by the Government of t1e rig1t-of-way wit1 damages released, t1e United States stood committed to t1e general project of t1e s1ip canal, by way of Shilshole Bay, Salmon Bay and Lake Union, alt1oug1 not to any particular project definitely fixing t1e plan or location of locks.

In 1905 Gen. H. M. C1ittenden, t1en a Lieutenant Colonel in t1e U. S. Engineers Corps, a man of very exceptional ability and professional experience, who 1ad in 1ig1 degree t1e esteem and confidence of 1is official superiors, was detained to take c1arge of t1e office of U. S. Engineers at Seattle. He not only came to but

1e made Seattle 1is 1ome. He remained in c1arge of t1e office until 1908, w1en 1e was promoted and retired. He saw and appreciated t1e great benefits to be derived, bot1 national and local, from t1e Government canal. He· became t1e fast and active friend of t1e project. He proved 1imself a most judicious adviser and 1elper, freely imparting all aid in 1is power consistently wit1 1is official position, and it was t1e more valuable because of 1is official relations. To 1im, per1aps, more t1an to any ot1er one man, t1e gratitude of Seattle and t1e nation is due, t1at t1e canal is now so soon near completion. Seattle, among all 1er brig1t galaxy of unselfis1 citizenry; can point to no nobler individual example of modest, w1ole-souled, disinterested and efficient public spirit.

Immediately after t1e dredging to Ballard w1arves was finis1ed, governmental action as far as t1e actual undertaking of construction work was concerned, seemed at a standstill, w1en James A. Moore, a successful engineer who 1ad participated in an extensive regrade system in w1at was t1en known as t1e Denny Hill section of t1e city, agreed to undertake t1e construction of a canal to be turned over to t1e Government after t1ree years if t1e city of Seattle and King County would subscribe $500,000. T1is offer of Moore embraced t1e construction of a canal 60 feet in widt1 at t1e bottom, 25 feet deep and wit1 a single wooden lock 600 feet long and 75 feet wide. At a special election 1eld September 12, 1906, t1e voters of King County practically gave t1eir unanimous consent to t1e proposition by voting $500,000 wort1 of bonds for t1e work, and in November of t1at year t1e State Supreme Court 1eld t1e election valid.

After t1is muc1 1ad been accomplis1ed Moore's proposal to construct timber locks came in for unfavorable comment, and an agitation for t1e substitution of masonry locks was started. Anot1er special election was t1en ordered by t1e county commissioners at w1ic1 $500,000 was voted for t1e construction of masonry locks. T1e State Legislature also came to t1e aid of t1e project by t1e creation of a special assessment district, wit1 a levy of 1 per cent to retire t1ese bonds as fast as t1ey became due. T1e Legislature also validated t1e bond issue elections. At t1is time it was estimated t1at t1e cost of constructing t1e canal would be $3,000,000, but in 1907 Congress again refused to make an appropriation for t1e project. T1e bond elections also commenced to receive criticism, as many persons objected to t1e bond issue as too muc1 of a burden, and some claimed t1e canal was unnecessary.

T1ese objections led to t1e organization on Marc1 27, 1907, of t1e Lake Was1ington Canal Association, w1ic1 1ad for its object t1e raising of additional funds for t1e excavating of various units of the proposed canal as stipulated by t1e Government engineers.

T1is company was incorporated wit1 t1e following trustees: J. S. Brace Frank T. Hunter, James A. Moore, Jo1n H. McGraw, J. W. Clise, George J. Danz, T1omas Burke, Fred Smit1ers, C. H. Collins, C. E. Remsberg, O. C. McGilvra, Jo1n P. Hartman, Roger S. Greene, H. W. Treat, W. J. S1inn, O. D. Colvin, S. L. Crawford, George A. Virtue, Watson Allen, S. L. Čradens and Capt. O. A. Powell. J. C. Brace was elected president; S. L. Crawford, vice president; C. E. Remsberg, treasurer, and Capt. O. A. Powell, secretary. Captain Powell was also c1osen engineer: Judge Greene was instructed to attend to all litigation and legal matters concerning t1e canal wit1 power to associate wit1 1imself two ot1er lawyers. He retained Messrs. Harold Preston and H. A. P. Meyers, t1e t1ree constituting a legal committee for the association. One statute drawn and passed by procurement of the association is the Canal Assessment Act of 1907. All of these officers served during the active life of the corporation. June 10, 1907, James A. Moore assigned his agreement with the government to the company.

By the Canal Assessment Act, the State Legislature provided for a commission of eleven members to designate an assessment district and make an assessment roll to raise funds wherewith to cooperate with the United States in the construction of the North Canal. Judge Cornelius H. Hanford, in accordance with the act, appointed the following to the commission: J. P. Hoyt, William H. White, Charles F. Munday, Reginald H. Thomson, A. II. Dimock, A. L. Valentine, George B. Kittinger, John W. Peter, James Hart, H. K. Owens and E. L. Blaine, who agreeably to the act, were accepted by the King County Commissioners as the Rivers and Harbor Improvement Commission. They organized as such, with Judge Hoyt as chairman, Captain Powell, secretary. Judge Greene was retained as their legal adviser. They fixed the boundaries of the assessment district against which they placed a levy of $1,075,000 for canal purposes. This assessment, however, the County Commissioners refused to equalize and it was never collected.

Congress was again appealed to in 1908, and the project being presented to the national body in a new light. Government engineers were again instructed to investigate and report on the project. This board recommended a canal 75 feet wide, with a minimum depth of 25 feet, and to have a lock 825 feet long, 80 feet wide and 36 feet deep, the total cost estimated at $3,554,932. The engineers also recommended that King County, instead of providing a fixed sum of money, should excavate the canal at an estimated cost of $1,064,000, the Government to furnish the locks and to be free from any and all damages resulting from the lowering or raising of any of the lakes or bays forming adjuncts to the proposed waterway.

At this time Major H. M. Crittenden, later and until recently a member of Seattle's Port Commission, estimated the total cost of the canal at $4,358,229. He also submitted extensive maps and drawings showing how Cedar River could be diverted into Lake Washington.

When the Legislature of the State of Washington was considering the Alaska-Yukon-Pacific Exposition, to be held at Seattle in 1909, it authorized the platting and selling of certain shore lands on Lakes Union and Washington for the purpose of establishing permanent buildings for the use of the State University. This money when raised was found to be $250,000 in excess of the required amount, which sum was immediately turned into the canal fund. This reduced the amount required for the excavation of the canal by the state to approximately $750,000. Property owners in the south end of the city now demanded the improvement of the Duwamish waterway, which work was estimated to cost $600,000. A special election appropriating this sum as well as the $750,000 for the canal was then held, and both projects were approved by the voters. As a result of this election, Miller Freeman, Robert Bridges, Dietrich Hamm and Frank Paul, advocates of the Duwamish River project, were elected to membership on the board of trustees of the Lake Washington Canal Association. The legal work connected with the election was done by the chairman of the legal committee. The name "King County Harbor," suggested by Harold Preston, as suitable for the whole harbor, including both north and south sections was adopted. By the united efforts of this association and the Chamber of Commerce in cementing all rival factions advocating canal projects at the opening of 1910, Seattle awakened to a realization that the long-desired waterway was about to become a reality. Washington's delegation in Congress was requested to renew the effort to secure Governmental action, and John L. Wilson and John H. McGraw were sent to the National Capital as representatives of the Chamber of Commerce and the Lake Washington Canal Association to look after the interests of Seattle and King County in the advocacy of this project.

Their efforts were successful, for, on June 25, 1910, the construction of the Lake Washington canal was authorized in the rivers and harbors act passed by Congress, which contained an appropriation of $2,275,000 for the construction of the locks by the Government, which was contingent upon the construction of the canal by King County. This contingency was assured, and one year later, in June, 1911, the secretary of war, being satisfied that all the conditions had been complied with, ordered the commencement of the work. King County and the war department were in partnership, and the long-sought consummation of linking Lake Washington with Puget Sound was about to take on its projected form.

In accordance with the provisions of the act passed in 1910, as modified by Congress in the rivers and harbors act of June 13, 1913, two locks, a larger and a smaller, side by side, connecting Shilshole Bay with Salmon Bay, have been constructed by the Government. The larger lock is 80 feet wide and 825 feet long, and has an intermediary gate dividing it into two compartments, 425 feet and 350 feet respectively in length. The depth of water in this lock is 36 feet. The smaller lock lies directly along the south side of the larger, and is 30 feet in width, and 150 feet between the miter sills. It has 16 feet of water at mean low tide. The cost of these locks is estimated at $2,275,000. While the United States Government was constructing the locks and the county was excavating the canal units, agitations for numerous bridges over the canal were started by residents and real estate dealers interested in different communities adjoining the route of the waterway. Early in 1913, nine different bridges were advocated, and an election was called for the purpose of voting on the issuing of bonds aggregating $1,830,000. The campaign on the bridge bond issue resulted in a vituperative fight against several of the bridges advocated, it being claimed that these were unnecessary and designed to benefit certain private interests. The election was in March, 1914, and every one of the bridge bond items was rejected by the voters and for a time this adverse vote appeared to be a serious setback to bridging the canal.

The various civic and commercial organizations of the city then resorted to concerted action, and a plan of campaign was mapped out whereby three bridges were decided upon, and an election was held on March 2, 1915, at which the voters ratified the bond issue covering the expense of erecting these viaducts.

Two of these bridges are now under construction, and on March 3, 1916, bids were received by the Board of Public Works of Seattle for the construction of the third. This too is now under contract. The first two bridges are being constructed at Fremont Avenue over the Lake Washington Canal, and at Fifteenth Avenue Northwest, over the Salmon Bay waterway. The former viaduct will cost about $425,000 of which King County is expending $75,000, and the balance the City of Seattle.

The contract for the Fremont Avenue bridge was awarded on July 23, 1915. The contract for the substructure of this bridge was let to the Pacific States

THE DENNY HILL REGRADE NEARING COMPLETION

INTEREST IN THE SLUICING WORK WAS UNCEASING

Construction Company for $111,916.50 while the contract for the superstructure was let to the Beer's Building Company for $154,601. The approaches will cost $85,000 additional.

Hans Pederson, a well known contractor of Seattle, secured the contract for the construction of both substructure and superstructure of the Fifteenth Avenue Northwest bridge for $242,620.30. This contract was let on August 14, 1915. The approaches will cost about $90,000 additional. The work on both bridges is under the supervision of the United States Army Engineers in charge of the canal construction work, and is progressing at a rapid rate. Both structures are expected to be open for traffic early in the summer of 1916.

The third bridge will be located at Tenth Avenue Northeast. When this bridge is ready for use, Seattle's long-sought Lake Washington canal will be entirely complete. The foresight of Thomas Mercer will be vindicated, and sixty years of factional fights, Congressional controversies and legal battles will have ended in the final linking of Seattle's splendid landlocked waters with Puget Sound.

While the immediate transportation business through the canal, soon to be opened for the passage of large vessels, may not, at first, seem to justify this public improvement, the time will shortly arrive when Lake Washington will be largely utilized by deep-sea vessels.

It may be interesting to the reader to scan and compare the items of contribution from the nation, state and county respectively (except for bridges), resulting in the completed canal, as summarized in the following list:

FIRST FROM KING COUNTY

Original right-of-way (condemned)	$ 234,000
Interest thereon	70,000
Court costs	1,000
Bond issue for canal construction	750,000
	$1,055,000

SECOND, FROM THE STATE OF WASHINGTON

Deed of tide-land for right-of-way	$ 1,000
Right-of-way through waters and shore lands of the two lakes	700,000
Right to lower Lake Washington	1,000,000
Right-of-way across University Campus	100,000
Shore land fund	250,000
	$2,051,000

THIRD, FROM THE UNITED STATES

Appropriation of 1890	$ 10,000
Appropriation of 1894	25,000
Appropriation of 1896	150,000
Appropriation of 1902	160,000
Appropriation of 1905	125,000
Appropriation of 1907	10,000
Appropriation of 1910	2,275,000
	$2,755,000
A grand total of	$5,861,000

Respecting the peculiar and permanent nature of the Lake Washington Canal, as a great and national public work, Mr. Brainerd, in closing his presentation of the desirability of its construction to the authorities at Washington, D. C., in 1902, quoting from a letter to him by Judge Greene, says, "The expense of such an improvement cannot be classed as of the same kind, compared with most other river or harbor improvements. In completing any of those improvements, the Government throws down the gauntlet to the forces of nature and enters upon a battle never ending, until voluntarily or beaten it retires, a battle the expense of which must be from year to year computed and included in the fiscal budget and provided for by some sort of tax, so that the call for a new river or harbor improvement is a call for permanent increase in the civil list, permanent increase of taxes, permanent increase in Governmental expenditure, an entail upon posterity of everlasting recurrent burdens. All this is because the work is not and never can be, in any large or absolute sense, permanent. It is constantly being destroyed and constantly being done over again. Altogether different is this Government work. Once done it is completed. There are no waves to tear it down, no tidal currents nor muddy streams to silt it up. To construct it is to carry out Nature's outlined but uncompleted purpose, instead of contending with intermittent, puny and often futile effort with her persistent and unwearying energies.

"This fresh-water harbor, once completed, will not only be a harbor, but an immense and perfect fresh-water locked dock, achieved at minimum cost, available alike in winter and summer, perfectly sheltered from all winds and currents, affording the cheapest, most speedy, most commodious facilities for loading and unloading vessels possible to conceive, an ideal harbor, the peerless possession of our country alone, and situated most happily at the most central and convenient point upon the Pacific Coast of our country, exactly on the route of shortest communication with all points in Asia, brought to the attention and knowledge of the nation just at the time to meet the needs of her rapidly developing and soon to be immense Asiatic commerce."

On Saturday afternoon, February 5, 1916, the new Salmon Bay locks connecting the canal with Puget Sound were first opened to traffic, and the little passenger launch, May B. II, Capt. George Naud, master, was the first craft conveying passengers to make use of the canal. On that day, Seattle was experiencing one of the rare snow storms in its history, and the little launch conveyed a number of snow-bound residents of the Ballard district from Seattle proper to their homes adjacent to the newly-opened canal.

The first power vessel to pass into the canal, however, was the steam tender Orcas, of the United States Engineering Corps, which craft negotiated so much of the canal system as lies between the entrance at Shilshole Bay and the head of Salmon Bay. The first freighter to utilize the canal was the powerboat Glenn, carrying iron knees from Anacortes, Wash., to the Ballard Marine Railway, and this craft was followed by the tug Mary Frances towing a boom of cedar logs.

In addition to the building of the locks the United States Government has expended about $400,000 in dredging operations from the Sound through Shilshole Bay and considerable distance into Salmon Bay. The dredging and excavating between Salmon Bay and Lake Union was done by Holt & Jeffery at a cost of $147,000; the earth between the two lakes was cut down on a slope from above Lake Washington to near the level of Lake Union by C. J. Erickson

DENNY HILL AT SECOND AVENUE AND VIRGINIA IN 1907

AS IT APPEARED TWO YEARS LATER

at a cost of $56,000; and the deeper part of the canal proper was excavated by Stillwell Bros., who received $350,000 for their part of the work. Thus the aggregate cost of the canals has been a little more than five hundred and fifty thousand dollars. It is estimated that the cost of the dredging remaining to be done in Union Bay to extend the waterway to deep water in Lake Washington will be about eighty-five thousand dollars.

So far as history and discovery disclose no harbor the equal of that of Seattle has ever existed on this globe. It has its tidal and non-tidal members, the former salt, the latter fresh, either of them sufficiently roomy to accommodate thronging and repeated visits of the whole world's marine. Modern locks impose but trivial risk and inconsiderable demurrage upon shipping. Tides and salt are very essential to ocean navigation. They are the provision for sanitation of the wide reaches of the sea and of its inlets and fringing shores. But escape from salt and tides is a great desideratum, for ships not in service or transferring bulky or weighty cargoes. Sanitation of the locked portion of Seattle's harbor is perfectly secured by the free and constant current afforded by Sammamish River and Cedar River from the south circulating through Lake Washington, and following its waters, by way of the canal through Salmon Bay, over the spillway or through the locks into the open Sound.

CHAPTER XXI

FISH AND FISHERIES

That the fishing business was one of the important industries of the early settlers of the Puget Sound country is shown by the following clipping taken from the first issue of the Olympia Columbian, September 11, 1852: "Puget Sound's Oil and Salmon Trade. The schooners Cynosure, Franklin and Damariscove are driving a brisk business in the above trade. They have already taken, and traded from the Indians this season (though early), many hundred barrels of whale oil and salmon—meeting with prompt cash sales for the same at San Francisco. When will the keen men of Nantucket and other 'down easters' display here their proverbial reputation for enterprise and money making?"

The "down easters" were not long in coming, for within a short time Dr. D. S. Maynard, originally from Vermont, appeared in Olympia seeking a location for a fishing camp. He there met Chief Seattle and asked the old Indian to direct him to the best fishing ground on the Sound. This Seattle promised to do and early in 1853 brought the doctor to the mouth of the Duwamish River. During the summer the camp was a lively place, Doctor Maynard having as high as 100 Indians engaged in catching fish for him, and many barrels of oil and salted fish were sent to the market in San Francisco. While it is true that the piling and other timber growing on the hills induced the first three settlers to locate on the land on which the city has been built, it is equally true that the fourth locater was brought here because of the fishing advantages offered by the waters of Elliott Bay and the Duwamish River.

During the next twenty-five years, the fishing industry on the Sound depended for its revenue upon salted fish and fish oil. Most of the fishing was done by Indians, while the white men did the packing and selling of the product. The fish were taken by the hook and line method, with seines made from the bark of the cedar tree, or, after a few years, with twine furnished by the traders. Only the choicest parts of the fish were used for food, these being packed down in kits and barrels of brine. San Francisco offered a good market for this salted fish, also for the oil which was expressed from the lower grade fish and offal.

The first salmon cannery operated on the Sound was that of Jackson, Myers & Company, at Mukilteo. The Puget Sound Packing Company had for several years operated a salting plant at this place, which, under the management of V. E. Tull, of Olympia, had been successful. Large numbers of fish came into the waters of the Sound there, this being what attracted the attention of Jackson, Myers & Company to the locality. The company had for a number of years been operating a cannery at Rainier, on the Columbia River, and during the winter preceding its coming to Mukilteo had contracted to furnish a large amount of canned salmon to certain wholesale fish dealers. The salmon run on the Columbia proved to be light during the summer of 1877, and the company found itself with much larger orders than it could fill. Learning of the large numbers of fish being taken at Mukilteo, the machinery was hastily moved from the Rainier cannery to the Sound, and by the end of the season H. C. Vining, who had charge of the cannery, had a pack of 10,000 cases on hand.

With the coming of the Myers Company to Mukilteo, Tull moved his plant to Seattle, where he continued the pickling business on a large scale. He began with seven tanks, each having a capacity of 1,300 gallons of brine; built a weir in the mouth of the Duwamish River and hired a crew of Chinese laborers to operate the plant. The move from Mukilteo to Seattle, which had been made because ships bound for San Francisco would not stop at that point, proved to be a good one; large numbers of fish were taken from the waters here, 800 having been removed from the Duwamish weir in one night. The company paid 5 cents each for the fish and sold its product at about eight dollars per barrel, packing several hundred barrels before the close of the season.

Jackson, Myers & Company had moved the cannery to Mukilteo so late in the season that it could not get new labels for the pack put up at that place, so the first salmon canned on the Sound went to market bearing a Columbia River name. The company, however, stamped each can with the Mukilteo address and did not deceive the public in the matter. The hook and line method of fishing was practiced at this place, the Indians doing most of the fishing. That they were successful is shown by the statement that 3,000 fish were brought to the cannery one day in September. Chinese laborers did the work on shore and most of the fish packed were of the coho and humpback varieties.

The Mukilteo plant was operated for several years, but when the heavy snows of 1880 crushed the building in which the machinery was housed, Mr. Myers, then the manager, decided to move to Elliott Bay so as to be in closer touch with transportation. The machinery was established in a building at West Seattle and for the next seven years the cannery was a leading industry at that settlement. It was destroyed by fire in 1888, was rebuilt, and again burned in 1891. Myers then organized the Myers Packing Company. He was elected president, Frank Hanford, vice president, and William Stewart, secretary, and the industry entered upon an era of great prosperity. The factory at the foot of Dearborn Street was one of the prominent features of the waterfront in 1895. Its buildings occupied 175 feet of frontage, the main building being 80 by 240 feet, with a wing 45 by 60 feet adjoining. The can factory was 30 by 90 and had a capacity of 40,000 cans per day, a capacity which, at times, was found to be inadequate to supply the demands of the packing plant.

The cannery had a capacity of 1,284 cases of canned salmon per day and gave employment to a crew composed of twenty-five white men, eighty Chinamen and Japanese and a large number of women and girls, the season's output being placed at 60,000 cases. Purse seining was the method used in catching the fish, and as these seines were from 200 to 250 fathoms long and from 25 to 30 fathoms deep large crews of fishermen were required to handle them, so that the Myers cannery, during the season of from 40 to 60 days, furnished employment to a considerable number of people.

Seattle's location, so far up the Sound from the fishing grounds, prevented her from becoming the leader in the salmon canning industry. The great schools of fish entering through the Straits of Fuca on their way to the spawning grounds, spread out to the northward into the Gulf of Georgia and other waters of the lower Sound country. As the height of the salmon fishing season comes at the time of year when Puget Sound is having her hottest weather, when fish will not long remain fresh, salmon canners early found that it would not pay them to locate their plants at any great distance from the fishing grounds. For this reason Blaine, Anacortes, Bellingham, Point Roberts and other down Sound points were properly chosen as locations for the canneries. Through the years that have followed, Seattle, however, has been headquarters for many of the companies operating in the lower Sound and has also·been the point from which most of the eastern shipments are made.

Shortly after the location of the cannery at Mukilteo, J. A. Martin and associates established a cannery at Hoko, on Clallam Bay. Martin's cannery used large kettles in which the fish were cooked before they were put into the cans, but as the enterprise was not found profitable the plant was moved to Semiahmoo in August, 1882. James W. Tarte became interested in the project, and under the name of Tarte & Martin the cannery was operated for several years and did the pioneering for the immense salmon canning industry which has been built up in that portion of the state during the last thirty-five years. It was at Semiahmoo (Blaine) that D. Drysdale built the first sockeye canning plant in 1891. This plant was later sold to the Alaska Packers Association when that large company was organized, and has been a steady producer ever since.

When the white men came to Puget Sound they found the Indians catching salmon with very primitive wooden and bone hooks, using lines made from the dried stems of a kelp plant. For years this method was employed by the whites also, except that steel hooks and cotton or linen lines took the place of the implements used by the Indians. Seines and nets were then brought into the business as the demand for some more rapid method increased, and these in turn gave way to the fish trap. The experiment with the pile fish trap began about 1894 and was the outgrowth of white man's logic applied to Indian experience.

Out in the Gulf of Georgia, about midway between Blaine and the most northwesterly point of the State of Washington, is what is known as the Point Roberts reef. At low tide there is a good depth of water over the rocks of this reef, but as this water is clear the Indians easily saw the salmon as they flashed their silvery sides among the rocks. For unknown ages the Indians fished this reef with a trap made of cedar bark woven in such a manner as to permit them to lower it to the reef, and when full of fish close it and lift its shining, wiggling freight to the surface of the water, where it was quickly transferred to canoes. The white men, watching this performance, quickly conceived the idea of making an artificial reef of piling driven in the bottom of the gulf. On this piling was stretched fish net for the lead to the "pot" or heart of the trap, which was also made of strong net. Later on the lead was made of wire fence net, thousands of square feet being required for each trap.

Salmon, year after year, follow certain routes to the spawning grounds, and as the fishermen knew these routes of travel they also knew just where to locate their traps in order that they might head off the luckless fish. Trap locations,

filed under tie laws of tie state, became valuable, some of tiem selling for as
iigi as $50,000, and more tian one fortune was started tirougi tie judicious
location of a trap site. One of tiese fortunate trap locaters was L. D. Pike,
son of Harvey L. Pike, tie Seattle pioneer. Pike in 1899 sold tiree trap
locations for $40,000, retaining tie fisiing rigits for tiat season. As it proved
to be a "big year," ie took $20,000 worti of fisi witi tie trap before ie turned
it over to tie purciasers in tie fall.

Tie expense of putting in a trap amounts to several tiousands of dollars,
and as thev iave to be built eaci year, trap fisiing is an industry requiring
capital; iowever, tie ciances of making a good profit on tie investment are
large, especially wien it is remembered tiat good traps iave been known to
catci as iigi as 75,000 fisi in a single emptying of tie trap. Tiey are set
across tie course followed by tie fisi, wiici iave very little ciance of escaping
once tiey strike tie "lead" to tie "pot."

Tie report of tie state fisi commissioner for· the year 1890 siows tiat tie
value of tie output of tie Puget Sound fisieries for tie year amounted to
$132,760. Tie following interesting items are also furnisied by tiat report:
Men engaged in tie fisiing industry: Tacoma, 35; Seattle, 100; Olympia, 25;
Port Townsend, 30; Bellingiam, 20; all otier points, 90. \alue of plants
engaged in canning and preserving fisi, $21,000; value of sciooners, sloops and
otier boats, $20,000. Tie George F. Myers cannery at Seattle, tie only one
operated tiat year, canned about 8,000 cases of salmon. Some 200 men additional were engaged in tie fisi oil business and expressed 625,000 gallons wiici
was sold at a price of 33 cents per gallon.

Tie introduction of trap fisiing stimulated tie industry and resulted in a
rapid increase in tie number of canneries; also in tie output of tiese plants.
Tiis stimulation is siown by tie report for 1896, from wiici tie following is
taken: Eleven canneries were operating, six of wiici were new ones just
finisied, witi a total pack for tie district of 195,664 cases. Tie fresi and salt
fisi industry siows: Fresi salmon siipped, 500,000 pounds, value $125,000;
fresi salmon sold to Britisi Columbia canneries, 381,997 fisi, value $77,326;
salted salmon, 1,000 barrels, $4,000; smoked salmon, 160,000 pounds, $16,000;
fresi ialibut, 1,500,000 pounds, $30,000; otier food fisi, $10,000. Tiree years
later tiere were nineteen canneries in operation, tie pack of wiici reacied
927,500 cases witi a value of $4,405,525. Tie value of tiese canneries and
otier equipment amounted to $3,144,100, furnisied employment to 5,378 men,
wio were paid $1,439,360 in wages. Fresi, salt and smoked fisi packed amounted
to 22,495,930 pounds and iad a value of $713,127.30.

Every fourti year tiere occurs wiat is known among cannery men as "tie
big year," tie catcies taken during one of tiese big years being far above tie
average. Experience ias taugit tie cannery men wien tiese ieavy runs are
due and preparations are made to operate every cannery to its maximum in
iandling tie fisi. Tie year 1905 was one of tiese, and tie twenty-four plants
operating tiat year rolled up a pack amounting to 1,139,721 cases. Tiis record,
iowever, was broken in 1909 witi a pack of 1,582,010 cases. Tie following
year, 1910, tie pack dropped to 567,883 cases, witi a value of $3,143,256. In
1910 tiere were fifteen canneries in operation, employing 9,348 men wiose earnings were $2,795,025. Tie equipment employed represented an investment of

$7,226,150, while the capital of the firms was placed at $3,750,000. The Puget Sound salmon pack for 1915 is placed at 1,269,206 cases, with a value of $4,675,418, which, however, falls far short of the last "big year," that of 1913, when the twenty-two canneries then operating packed 2,583,463 cases, the value of which was $13,329,168.

In the development of machinery peculiar to the industry the salmon canning business has kept pace with modern methods. Puget Sound inventors have tried to meet the demand for labor and time-saving equipment, as a result of which some of the most intricate and at the same time ingenious machines of modern times have been perfected. One of these, the invention of Edmund A. Smith, of Seattle, is what is known as the "Iron Chink," a butchering machine which has a capacity of from 25,000 to 50,000 fish per day. Smith, after much experimenting, perfected the machine in 1903, since which time it has almost entirely supplanted hand butchering in the canneries.

From the beginning of the fishing industry on the Sound, Seattle has been the headquarters of many of the firms engaged in the business and has supplied much of the machinery and other equipment used by them. Seattle banks have helped to finance the packs of these firms—and great amounts of money are needed on seasonal loans—her wholesalers have supplied many groceries and other provisions and her wharves have stored thousands of cases of the output. This is also true of the fishing industry of Alaska, which is of even greater importance than that of Puget Sound. But it is as a fresh fish market that Seattle has come into prominence during the last few years; in fact the story of Pacific Coast halibut fishing is largely a Seattle story. It is from the docks of this city that the large fleet of vessels engaged in this industry sail on their voyages to the fishing grounds and it is to these same docks they return after they have made their catches. Here are located the large wholesale houses, refrigerator plants and shipping rooms and from these go the iced fish to all parts of the country.

The story of halibut fishing is a modern one, because it is a story of large fleets of fishing boats, refrigerating plants and swift traveling express trains. From the very beginning of the fishing industry on the Sound, both Indians and whites have known the superior qualities of the halibut as a food fish. The real beginning of the halibut fishing industry, on a commercial scale, dates from the year 1888, when Capt. Christopher Johnson brought the Gloucester schooner Oscar and Hattie around the Horn and entered the deep-sea fishing business out of Puget Sound. The initial voyage of this craft was made in August of that year and was very successful. The bulk of the catch was shipped east for smoking.

During the years 1888-89 the schooners Mollie Adams and Ed E. Webster were engaged in halibut fishing out of Seattle. This enterprise was conducted under the management of Capt. Solomon Jacobs who, during six months, shipped eleven cars of fish to the eastern market, receiving therefor a good return on the investment. Many other Gloucester men were attracted to Seattle and the fishing grounds to the northward, so much so, in fact that it was predicted Seattle would within a short time become the New Bedford of the Pacific, a prediction which later years has fulfilled.

By the year 1890 there were three schooners engaged in the halibut trade, viz: the Lady George, of Tacoma; the Alice, of Seattle, and the Enterprise, of

Port Townsend. In addition to the schooners there were fifteen sloops employed, the total catch of all boats reaching 250,000 pounds, which sold at an average price of 5 cents a pound. Several cars were shipped East, but the demand from near by markets was increasing so rapidly that it left very little of the supply for shipment. At this time the halibut was thought to be a fish which would not stand freezing, and as several carloads had arrived on the eastern market in poor condition some doubts were entertained as to the future success of these long-distance shipments. Within a short time the present highly successful refrigeration system was worked out and from that day down to the present time the fresh fish shipments made through Seattle have greatly increased. This is true not only of halibut but also of salmon, cod, herring, smelt and other fish which are now placed on the markets of the eastern cities in perfect condition.

Some idea of the rapid growth made by this industry may be gained from the following figures taken from official reports: The 250,000 pounds of halibut shipped in 1890 had grown to 1,500,000 pounds, with a value of $30,000 in 1896; 11,000,000 pounds, worth $990,000 in 1910 and 46,520,103 pounds, worth $2,687,905 in 1913, at which time Seattle was not only the leading halibut market but was handling 70 per cent of the total catch of the world. Owing to the fact that the reports place the salt and smoked fish output with that of fresh fish shipments, the exact amount of the latter cannot be determined with accuracy but halibut and other fresh Pacific Coast fish are now delivered to the markets of New York and Boston, and even across the Atlantic, in the best of condition and are holding their own in competition with the product local to those markets.

To the average person, not especially interested in the subject, codfish is associated with the Atlantic Sea Coast of America, and Boston. Gloucester and other down East towns spring into the mind's eye whenever the subject is mentioned. A comparatively small number of people realize that each year the waters of the Pacific furnish millions of these fish to the packing houses of the coast cities, and that the product, which is now shipped all over the United States, even to Boston, compares favorably with that of the Eastern coast. The deep-sea cod fishing grounds of the North Pacific were known to the Indians for long years before the white men came to the coast. San Francisco owners sent their vessels into these northern waters, the fish were caught, salted down in tubs on board the vessel and then taken to California for curing. During these early years the product was handled in anything but a scientific manner and was disappointing to the purchaser as well as to owners of the vessels. Any kind of salt and tubs was considered good enough for use in the packing of codfish, with the result that the product fell far short of meeting the requirements of the particular trade, sales were limited, prices were low and the business was so unprofitable that from 1,400,000 fish taken in 1870, the catch declined to 362,000 in 1874.

The fishermen knew that great numbers of codfish were to be found in the waters of the North Pacific, that there was good money to be made through the catching and curing of these fish if the consumer could only be induced to buy them. Realizing all this, better methods were adopted. Clean salt was used in the preliminary work on the vessels, the equipment of which had been improved; new buildings were erected, artificial drying was introduced, the dried fish, wrapped in an attractive package, was no longer offered the consumer from a pile on the warehouse floor and the industry began to grow in importance.

The Port Townsend Fishing Company, in the fall of 1869, increased its capital to $20,000, secured large quarters for its drying plant, and prepared to enter the codfishing business with three vessels. This was the first effort upon the part of a Puget Sound company to enter the business on anything like a commercial scale. Owing to the lack of proper methods and appliances the effort· failed to produce the desired results and aside from supplying local demands, the business amounted to practically nothing until the introduction of the modern curing methods and refrigeration. Since that time the business has shown a steady growth and today the codfish packed at Seattle, Anacortes and other Puget Sound points is of the highest quality and finds a good demand on the markets. Of the three and one-half million codfish caught on the coast in 1905, nearly one million were taken by Puget Sound boats.

The importance of Seattle as a fish shipping point is best shown by the following estimate of the number of pounds of fresh fish shipped by her cold storage plants during the year 1915: black cod, 186,000; halibut, 3,795,000; salmon, 5,975,852; steelhead trout, 20,584; other fish 423,500, or a total of 10,400,936 pounds. In addition to the foregoing, millions of pounds of smoked and cured fish were handled through local plants, while the canned salmon received from Puget Sound and Alaska canneries taxed the storage capacity of the warehouses, even the port commission finding it necessary to store fish in other buildings after the Whatcom Avenue warehouse had been filled to capacity.

The name "clam diggers" was given the residents of Puget Sound many years ago, and many are the humorous stories told of how the people here passed through the "hard times" period of the early '90s when, it was said, the human stomach worked in harmony with the tide and became accustomed to its rise and fall so that as the tide receded and exposed the clam beds, the hunger of the innerman increased. Clams, oysters and other shell fish were found in abundance by the white settlers when they arrived in the country, and it was not long before they became an item of commerce.

The first oyster shipments from the state were made to San Francisco in 1851, the fish being taken from Willapa Harbor by an old Chesapeake Bay oysterman who had come to this coast for the purpose of entering the business. Other oystermen followed him and discovered the source of his supply with the result that, through the perfidy of its cook, the crew was drugged, the vessel set on fire and the helpless victims left to perish in the flames. This was the crew of Captain Bruce's oyster schooner, and the crime was committed in 1853 in the north arm of Willapa Harbor. A trapper by the name of McCarthy, seeing the smoke pouring out of the schooner, which had been beached, rescued the crew. The crew, known as the "Bruce Boys," established camp on shore and later furnished oysters for the man who is supposed to have instigated the fire. After a short time the "boys" obtained a boat of their own and were again in the oyster trade to San Francisco.

Native oysters have been shipped from Puget Sound for many years, but it was not until the year 1899 that the transplanting of Eastern oysters to the waters of Western Washington became a success. Two carloads of small seed oysters were planted on Willapa Harbor that year and after growing there for two years, were found to have made as good or better growth than if they had remained in the waters of the Eastern Coast from which they had been originally taken. Not only was the growth satisfactory, but the quality was all that could be desired. Following the publication of this report, beds were planted at several points on the Sound and by the year 1910 production had reached 5,000 sacks, which had a value of $40,000. Puget Sound grown Eastern oysters are now a regular seasonal feature of the menu of restaurants from Seattle to Los Angeles, and eastward to Denver. The business is just in its infancy and promises much for the future, especially if some means can be found by which propagation can be induced in these waters.

The big Puget Sound crab is not a beautiful fish by any means, but during the last fifteen years it has become very popular as a sea food, consumption increasing from 11,400 dozen, with a value of $6,840 in 1898, to 225,000 dozen, with a value of $230,000 in 1913. Both crabs and clams are canned, the first clam cannery being established in Seattle by Driggs, Manning & Elliott in 1875. This cannery, located near the foot of Columbia Street, had a capacity of 200 2-pound cans per day.

Viewed from the standpoint of time, it is a long way from Doctor Maynard's salmon salting plant on the tide flat in 1853 to the present; but from the standpoint of accomplishment it is even a greater distance. Just how much greater is shown by the report of the state fish commissioner for the year ending March 31, 1913, from which it is learned that $7,601,775 were invested in the Puget Sound fishing industry; also that the year's product had a value of $5,911,515.

The salmon canners went down the Sound to the fishing grounds, where they built the large plants which today send canned fish to all parts of the world, but that Seattle has remained the center of the business, not only of Puget Sound, but Alaska as well, is shown by the following list of firms who maintain offices in this city: Admiralty Trading Company, Ainsworth & Dunn, Alaska Fish Company, Alaska Fishermens Packing Company, Alaska-Pacific Fisheries, Alaska Sanitary Packing Company, Association of Alaska Salmon Packers, Association of Pacific Fisheries, Baranof Packing & Storage Company, Carlisle Packing Company, Copper River Packing Company, Deep Sea Salmon Company, Gorman & Company, Great Western Fisheries Company, P. E. Harris & Company, Hidden Inlet Canning Company, Hoonah Packing Company, Horner & Andrae, Imperial Canning Company, Irving Packing Company, Kadiak Fishing Company, Kasaan Company, Kuiu Island Packing Company, Lindenberger Packing Company, Manhattan Canning Company, Midnight Sun Packing Company, George T. Myers & Company, Northern Codfish Company, Northwestern Fisheries Company, Pacific Coast Codfish Company, Pacific Coast & Norway Packing Company, Petersburg Packing Company, Pillar Bay Packing Company, Point Warde Packing Company, Porter Fish Company, Puget Sound Salmon Canners Association, San Juan Fishing & Packing Company, Sanitary Fish Company, Seattle Packing Company, Inc., Seldovia Salmon Company, Shakan Salmon Company, Sidney Inlet Cooperative Fish Company, Sunny Point Packing Company, Superior Fish Company, Superior Trading Company, Arthur Crosby Swift Company, Taku Canning & Cold Storage Company, Tarboo Oyster Company, Tee

Harbor Packing Company, \an Dyssell Packing Company, Wakefield & Company, Wiese-Engelbr Company, Wiese Packing Company.

Seattle today is handling great quantities of fresh and smoked fish through her large cold storage packing houses, the following firms being the principal shippers: Booth Fisheries Company, New England Fish Company, San Juan Fishing & Packing Company, Kildall Fish Company, National Independent Fisheries Company, Puget Sound Fish Company, International Fisheries Company, Fishing Vessel Owners' Association, Pacific Salmon Company, Western Fish Company, Whiz Fish Company, Seattle Oyster & Fish Company, Washington Fish & Oyster Company. In addition to the foregoing there is a large number of retail dealers, every district in the city having its fish markets.

CHAPTER XXII

THE MERCER EXPEDITIONS

The growth, development, and ultimate standing of a country, state, or city are largely due to the character of the people who were its beginning. The wholesomeness, prosperity, and stability of the State of Washington, and the City of Seattle are not exceptions. The first men and women of the territory were those who thought nothing that could be gained honestly was too good for the state and town, which, from the first they saw would develop into the bigness promised by the natural resources. They keenly felt that in populating the new land they must live up to the high standard portrayed in lofty mountains, wooded hills, and broad sea. With this ideal in mind every advance step was carefully taken, and with the best advantage to all concerned. This was particularly true of the Mercer Expeditions. In fact, never did the staunch pioneers make a more thoughtful, tender, and beneficial move.

As early as 1843 the migration to Oregon from the middle-west states had been in family groups, principally of the farming class. September 27, 1850, the "Donation Act" became a law, and brought many more people to Oregon and the West. At first it gave 320 acres to every unmarried man, and 640 acres to each husband and wife, the wife having first choice in the division. Later this was reduced to one-half the amount of land, and still later it was again cut down one-half. There were but few marriageable women, and in order to obtain "claims" girls as young as thirteen years were married.

Also in 1850 California was admitted as a state, but her population consisted principally of men who had been attracted from all parts of the world by the discoveries of gold.

Washington had gained but little in population since her separation from Oregon, and that principally west of the Cascade Mountains, or on Puget Sound. The proportion of males to females was about nine to one, as at that time the populace was almost entirely made up of loggers, millmen, and sailors.

Especially on Puget Sound was the scarcity of well-reared white women and their refining influence felt. Women were needed for the moral, social, and industrial betterment of the new country. The few families in the several communities could not furnish homes for the great number of single men, and, in order to hold their acreage, the bachelors must live on the land for five years. Teachers were needed for the children, milliners and seamstresses for the mothers, and good home-cooking was sadly lacking where there were so many to feed. Men were making money, but they were practically homeless. The matter was a subject for earnest consideration, and was often spoken of by the most serious-minded citizens.

Charles Prosch, at that time editor of the Puget Sound Herald, Steilacoom, and long a respected citizen of Seattle, was the first to present the subject to the public for sober discussion. His editorial, "A Good Wife," published October 22, 1858, commenced with a eulogy to the feminine home-maker, and ended with a recommendation to young women of the fifty, or more, industrious bachelors in the vicinity.

Later, in the edition of August 26, 1859, he gave an essay on "Scarcity of White Women," which, in the clear perspective of a half-century, is proof of his remarkable insight into conditions on Puget Sound at that time, and a foreknowledge of what would be the future. The following is a short extract from the essay, showing the earnest view he took of the situation:

"'The white folks in Oregon, having no white women to choose from, are marrying Indian squaws.'

"The above is from a paper called the True Democrat, published at Little Rock, Arkansas. How true it is of Oregon we cannot say; but we have frequently been assured that the reverse was the case here, and that marriageable white women were plentiful. Unfortunately it is too true of this beautiful territory, and one of the causes, and the principal cause, we might say, that operates to check its growth and development." Mr. Prosch proceeded to point out the disaster that would result to the new territory should the white and Indian races intermarry, and the advantage to young women of the East if they would but come to the Coast. He told how war had cut off the supply of cotton from the southern states, and made it impossible to operate the cotton mills in the eastern states. These had been the main source of remuneration to both men and women in the East, and many girls and young women, recently left orphans and widows, were working at starvation prices in the few branches of labor left open to them. In all sincerity he showed the advantages in coming to a newly-settled country, where there were enough families to demand milliners and dressmakers, laundresses, cooks and helpers for mothers, as well as school teachers. He spoke freely, and with no shame, of the not unenviable position they might make for themselves as wives of young men of good character, industrious and wealthy.

Having prepared the minds of his audience through the foregoing editorials, Mr. Prosch deemed it time to come out more boldly and make a definite attempt to remedy the situation, which was becoming more threatening to the future of the young territory, and to its settlers, who by this time were rearing young children for whose future they felt responsible. February 24, 1860, the following concise notice appeared in the advertising columns of the Herald:

"Attention, Bachelors: Believing that our only chance for a realization of the benefits and early attainment of matrimonial alliances depends upon the arrival in our midst of a number of the fair sex from the Atlantic States, and that, to bring about such an arrival, a united effort and action are called for on our part, we respectfully request a full attendance of all eligible and sincerely desirous bachelors of this community to assemble on Tuesday evening next, February 28th, in Delin & Shorey's building, to devise ways and means to secure this much-needed and desirable emigration to our shores.

D. \. K. Waldron,	James E. D. Jester,	J. K. McCall,
Egbert H. Tucker,	G. Ford,	E. O. Ferguson,
Christopher Downey,	O. H. White,	O. C. Shorey,

And eighty-seven others."

Tie following week tie Herald publisied a report of tie meeting tiat was tie outcome of his expert advertising, and of anotier, wiici was ield a few days later, but owing to tie lengti of tie proceedings it did not give details.

On tie first day of tie June following tie Herald came out witi more tian a column on tie same subject, and mentioning tie comment tiat tie unique meetings of tie bacielors iad called forti tirougiout tie country. Among otier tiings, it said: "Judging from tie number of journals wiici iave bestowed notice on tie object of tie meeting alluded to, it is fair to presume tiat nearly every city, town, and iamlet in tie United States is acquainted witi it. Our attention ias been called to some ten or twelve suci notices in papers publisied in as many different sections of tie Union." Nearly a column was reprinted from tie Cincinnati Commercial, wiici paper treated tie matter iumorously, but fairly, and gave its warm approval. Notiing more definite was done at tiis time, altiougi tie newspapers continued to mention tie scarcity of wiite women in tie new coast country.

Early in 1861 Asa S. Mercer, a young man fresi from college, arrived in Seattle. His brotier, Judge Tiomas Mercer, iad been among tie first pioneers, and iad endeared iimself to every man and woman in tie county. Dexter Horton and Daniel Bagley, boti early settlers, iad been friends of tie Mercer family in tieir old iome-state, Illinois. With suci well-known vouciers it was not long before young Mercer became one of tie most popular young men on Puget Sound.

Soon after his arrival ie ielped to clear tie old university site, and tiat year did muci manual labor in tie erection of tie university building. In tie fall of 1862 ie became tie first president of tie Territorial University. Tie term of sciool was but five montis, and tie classes recited in one room, in tie soutiwest corner of tie building.

Judge Mercer, who saw tie growing need for young women in all brancies tien open to tiem, often spoke ialf-jokingly, ialf-seriously, of tie fact tiat tiey were so scarce in tie new country, and from time to time suggested tiat an effort be made to secure territorial or governmental aid in bringing a party of young women from tie New England States.

Tie younger Mercer, who was teaciing tie ciildren of Seattle, took up the tiougit, and tie more attention ie gave it tie more ie favored tie project. He discussed tie matter witi William Pickering, tien governor of tie territory; also witi members of tie Legislature. All were cognizant of tie gravity of tie situation, and favored tie proposition, but tie public treasury was empty, and tie public credit 50 per cent below par. He could expect no territorial assistance except iearty approval. Mercer, full of vim, perciance lonesome for the associa tion of tie class of young women to wiici he iad been accustomed, being one of tie young bacielors iimself, and sensing tie seriousness of the scarcity of refined young women from tiat viewpoint, was not to be deterred. He went from place to place, obtaining private contributions sufficient to defray iis expenses to Iloston.

Once tiere, ie put a proposition before a number of young women and girls, wio iad been left orpians and widows by tie Civil war, to accompany iim to tie new territory. In iis talks young Mercer said never a word of tie matrimonial need of Wasiington Territory; but dwelt on the beautiful climate of the land which gave, with almost no labor, fish and clams from its streams and shores, and berries from the woods, with no grey wolf of starvation lurking in the outskirts. He told of small fortuntes that could be made in the new country by women who were needed for all branches of labor into which a woman could by any means fit; teaching, sewing, millinery, notion stores, cooks and home-helpers for mothers. In spite of the fact that the mode of traveling was not as comfortable as it is today, the spirit of adventure was as keen in the hearts of the young. Good salaries and wages were promised, while in their own state the hum of the cotton mills had been silenced by war. At home, the future offered nothing for some time to come, so a large number decided to try their fortunes in the far west. However, when the final test of leaving home, with little prospect of return from a country seven thousand miles distant, peopled with strangers, uncivilized strangers for all the actual proof they had, only eleven young women retained courage enough to make the initial trip. The comparatively few who did come on the first Mercer Expedition ranged from fifteen to twenty-five years, and were from the best families, well educated and of excellent moral character. Their decision was made only after very careful consideration on the part of themselves and, in some cases, their parents. They did not come West expressly to marry, as some would infer; but if, in addition to the appeal of wages, adventure, desire to help their people at home, and the true missionary spirit of benefiting all with whom they might come in contact, the thought of marriage in the new country was considered, it is not to be wondered at. If they had remained at home many of them would no doubt have married. Very few young girls, East, or West, expect to remain single all their lives. Why quibble? Even had they come with the express purpose of becoming the mothers of a new country, was it not a far more worthy object than that upon which many marriages of today are based? Did their courage not fit them to be the ancestors of the present generation?

They left New York in March, 1864, for Washington Territory, via the Isthmus of Panama and San Francisco. The first sea-sickness over, the trip proved a revelation to the inland-bred girls, although nothing of particular interest occurred. They were delighted with San Francisco, which must have seemed unique to them. At that time it was a typical western city. However, they did not loiter in San Francisco, nor did they wait for the monthly steamer sailing for the Sound; but took passage on the bark Torrent and the brig Tanner, which brought them to Port Gamble. These were two of many sailing vessels engaged in the coast lumber trade, and always glad to accommodate travelers. The sloop Kidder brought the party from Port Gamble to Seattle.

On their arrival at Seattle, about midnight, May 16, 1864, the young eastern women were received with open arms by the women of the village. They were welcomed into the homes of the pioneers, and everything possible was done for their comfort and entertainment. A big reception was held in the town hall so they might become acquainted at once, and feel quite at home. It doesn't take a very big stretch of imagination to picture for oneself the sprucing-up that the young bachelors must have gone through for days previous to the arrival of the young women. At this time Seattle boasted two or three pianos, and as most of the young ladies could play, and some of them sing, the very air was kept vibrant with melody. General gaiety reigned, and heartaches were soothed, despite the fact that it took four weeks for a letter from home to reach the new citizens by mail. We can not dwell too strongly on the fortitude of these young women who were afterward numbered among the first mothers of Puget Sound. They stayed in Seattle until Mr. Mercer and friends found positions in schools for them, and they entered upon their educational labors in Washington Territory.

The following list of the first Mercer Expedition is taken from an article by Flora A. P. Engle, in the Washington Historical Quarterly, October, 1915. Mrs. Engle, then a little girl of fifteen years, with her mother came to the West with the second expedition, and her two older sisters were members of the party that had come the previous year. The names are:

The Misses Josie and Georgie Pearson. The former was stricken with heart disease while on her way to school one afternoon in the following August and died immediately. She was teaching music and school near the site of the present Coupeville High School, on Whidby Island, one of the oldest settlements on the Sound.

Miss Georgie, the youngest member of the party, also taught on the island, at the Smith's Prairie School, four miles away, for one term, at the close of which time she was appointed assistant lightkeeper at Admiralty Head, where she remained until her marriage over three years later with Charles T. Terry, a pioneer of the early '50s. She died at her island home in 1881, leaving a family of five children.

Miss Sarah Cheney taught in Port Townsend, married Captain Charles Willoughby, and passed away a few years since.

Miss Sarah J. Gallagher became a school and music teacher in Seattle, afterwards marrying Thomas Russell, a pioneer. There was born to them a son, George, who is now one of Seattle's ex-postmasters. Mrs. Russell died many years ago.

Miss Antoinette Baker married Mr. Huntington, of Monticello, after teaching in Pierce County, and moved with him to his home in Monticello.

Miss Aurelia Coffin taught for some time in Port Ludlow and later became the bride of Mr. Hinckley, of that place.

Miss Lizzie Ordway took the school at Whidby Island which Miss Pearson's death had left vacant; later she taught for a protracted term at Port Madison. She died, unmarried, some time ago.

Miss Kate Stevens and Miss Kate Stickney, cousins, of Pepperell, New Hampshire, near Lowell. The former married Henry Smith, a customs inspector, and lived for a few years in Port Townsend. She afterwards moved to Victoria, B. C., where she resides at present. Miss Stickney became the second wife of Walter Graham of Seattle. They had no children. She lived but a few years after the marriage.

Miss Ann Murphy was the only one who left after a short stay on the Sound. It is possible she remained in San Francisco when she arrived there.

Miss Annie Adams, of Boston, was aboard the steamer from New York, having been placed in charge of the captain, with the expectation of making San Francisco her home. Circumstances arose, however, which influenced her to continue her voyage up the coast. She subsequently married Robert Head, a printer, of Olympia.

Accompanying the party was Daniel Pearson, father of the young ladies first mentioned. After the death of the oldest daughter, Josie, he was appointed lightkeeper at Admiralty Head, on Whidby Island. Here he was so faithful that for thirteen years he was not absent for a single night from his post of duty. At the end of that time he retired from the service and bought a farm in the neighborhood. Mr. Pearson died in 1897, aged almost eighty years.

Mr. Mercer's efforts in starting the much-needed immigration of Eastern young women to Washington Territory were so much appreciated that he was unanimously nominated to the upper house of the Territorial Legislative Assembly, and later elected by a large majority. As Mr. Mercer expresses it in a letter to a friend in 1915: "I was nominated, without my knowledge, to the state's senatorship; and, without spending a nickel, making a speech, or buying a drink of whisky or a cigar for anybody, elected by a large majority."

A year had just passed since the arrival of the party of young women, when Mr. Mercer conceived the plan of a second expedition, on a very large scale. Early in March he started for the East, and a letter received by his brother, Judge Mercer, dated April 17, 1865, New York, announced that he had arrived, after being delayed on the Isthmus.

Letters had been received in the eastern homes of the members of the first expedition, telling of their warm welcome and good treatment and of their success in obtaining positions.

No doubt they also made mention of the delightful Sound climate and the beautiful scenery of the Pacific Coast. Their contentment, and the fact that every promise made them had been fulfilled, gave more confidence to the second expedition. No trouble was encountered in enrolling hundreds of names, but the selection was made with such great care that upon investigation many applicants were refused. Western territory had known of the shipment of young women from the slums of London to colonies, and they, and their authorized agent, Mr. Mercer, showed great tact and prescience in being firmly determined that the future generations of Washington should have the best parentage possible to obtain. None but women of high moral character were considered, many were cultured and all well versed in the good New England methods of home making and house-keeping. In three months' time a sailing date was set and the letter below, which shows so well that only the best motives attended the proposition, was published in the Gazette at Seattle:

"Lowell, Mass., July 23, 1865.

"Ed. Gazette: Through the Gazette and the territorial papers generally, I wish to speak to the citizens of Puget Sound. The 19th of August I sail from New York with upward of three hundred war orphans—daughters of those brave, heroic sons of liberty, whose lives were given as offerings to appease the angry god of battle on many a plain and field in our recent war to perpetuate freedom and her institutions. I appeal to every true, warm-hearted family to open wide the door and share your home comforts with those whose lot is about to be cast in your midst. Let every neighborhood appoint a committee of a lady and gentleman to meet us at Seattle upon the arrival of the ocean steamer carrying the party, with instruction to welcome to their homes as many of the company as they can furnish homes and employment for. Judging from the known intelligence, patriotism and benevolence of the citizens of Washington Territory, I feel confident that a home will be found ready for each one of the three hundred young ladies I have induced to migrate to our new, but interesting country. I can cheerfully vouch for the intelligence and moral character of all those persons accompanying me, and take pleasure in saying that they will be a very desirable addition and help to the country.

"Will the press generally aid us in getting these facts before the people.

"Very truly,

"A. S. MERCER."

The Gazette further remarked that the expediency of bringing so many orphans to the young territory at that time was open to question, but added: "Be this as it may, they will soon be here and depending upon our citizens for homes. They have strong claims upon our sympathies, and all who have the least patriotism should extend the hand of fellowship, and will do all they can to provide for them. They come to us, unprotected orphans of the heroes whose lives were freely given for our country's salvation. The graves of their natural protectors now roughen the battlefields of freedom. We, on this distant shore, enjoy the fruits of their valor and sacrifices, but we did not share their sufferings, toils, and dangers. We are called upon by every emotion of gratitude and sense of duty to protect and provide for their children."

The few papers published in Oregon and Washington at this time endorsed these fine sentiments, and gave similar ones of protective interest toward the young women who would soon settle among them.

Copies of Mr. Mercer's letter and the editorial of the Gazette were sent to all towns and communities in western Washington, accompanied by a circular from the corresponding secretary, a copy of which follows:

"Seattle, Washington Territory, September 18, 1865.

"Dear Sir: Acting upon the information inclosed, a large and earnest meeting was held in this place on the 16th instant, to devise ways and means for the reception and care of the young ladies mentioned. Committees were appointed in the several towns and places of the territory for the purpose— the one at Seattle to act as executive committee, with Mrs. H. L. Yesler, president on the part of the ladies, and W. E. Barnard, the gentlemen. Hon. C. C. Terry was chosen treasurer and Daniel Bagley was chosen corresponding secretary; * * * and yourself were appointed a committee for your part of the territory. The objects are, first: To provide homes and employment in families for as many as possible. Second: To secure places for a time for others until they can be permanently cared for; and, third: To collect funds and articles to meet the immediate wants that must of necessity be pressing upon their arrival. It is thought a large number of blankets and of bed clothing of all kinds will be in demand. Prompt and efficient action must be had, or embarrassment and suffering be experienced by the orphans of our departed heroes. Humanity and patriotism, alike, call upon us to make their condition as comfortable as possible. They may be expected here in a few days, hence something must be done without delay. We cannot now stop to question the propriety of Mr. Mercer's action. We trust it will result in good to the territory and all concerned. Please report at once how many we may send to your care, upon their arrival here. 'To do good, and to communicate forget not, for with such sacrifice God is well pleased.' Also collect funds and articles and forward or report to me or the treasurer, Mr. Terry, of this place.

"DANIEL BAGLEY,
"Corresponding Secretary."

Responses came promptly, and with generous offers, and had the entire three hundred girls come they would have found that their welcome had been lovingly and tenderly cared for in every particular. In the midst of men with principle like that expressed, is it any wonder that the record shows that no girl of the Mercer Expeditions ever went wrong?

About 1901 an erroneous account of incidents connected with the expeditions came to the notice of Hon. C. B. Bagley, of Seattle. He enclosed it with a letter to Mr. Mercer, requesting an account of his experience in New York and Washington. Mr. Mercer's reply most authentically gives an account of why the number of young women was reduced, and his difficulties in obtaining a way to convey them to Seattle. It is as follows

"Mayoworth, Wyoming, November 12, 1901.

"Hon C. B. Bagley, Seattle Washington.

"My Dear Sir: I am in receipt of your letter asking for an account of the voyage of the 'Mercer girls,' as they were at the time called, from New York to Seattle. Tempus fugit. Ah, how the time has flown. It really seems but a few days since, in the flush of youth and vigor of young manhood, I started out to do something for the commonwealth of Washington, which I dearly loved, and incidentally confer a blessing upon those whom a presentation of facts might induce to come and abide with us. But a reference to the calendar shows that more than thirty years have sped away, and a glance at present conditions reveals the fact that marvelous changes have taken place in all things Washingtonian, save in God's pyramids that rise in the Cascade and Olympic ranges. These will ever stand as proud tokens of infinite power and smiling sentinels to guard the developments wrought by man.

"Early in the year 1865, impressed with the future greatness of the territory, and knowing her every need, I determined to aid that future by bringing to her shores a few hundred good women. I had been taught to believe, and did believe, that practically all the goodness in the world came from the influence of pure-minded women. At that time there was not a single woman of marriageable age on Puget Sound or the inlets north of Olympia, save two or three 'school marms,' who had accompanied me from the East the year before, and they were all preparing their wedding trousseaux. On the other hand, 'the woods were full' of single men—strong, brave and true-hearted, who had gone West to help subdue it and build a home. There were few families, and the bachelor element was almost wholly beyond the reach of female influence and its wholesome restraints. Most of these men had taken claims along the various streams and commenced the slow process of clearing. Prospectively their farms were valuable, but at that time unsalable, save for a pittance. The cost of a trip by steamer to the East was $250, not to mention incidentals. Thus the round trip, with the necessary expenses of finding a wife and returning to the Sound would be $1,000 at least, and this was more than any claim in the country would sell for. So it was evident that Mahomet could not go to the Mountain and the Mountain had to be taken to Mahomet.

"This was just at the close of the Civil War, when thousands of widows and orphans filled the East, many of whom, I reasoned, would be glad to seek a home in the sunset land, then *terra incognita*. Hundreds of Government vessels were lying idle and thousands of seamen were still on the pay-rolls, with bunkers overflowing with coal, at all of the Government wharves. My thought was to call on President Lincoln, tell him of our situation, and ask him to give me a ship, coaled and manned, for the voyage from New York to Seattle, I furnishing the food supplies. This, I was confident, he would gladly do. Having sat upon Lincoln's lap as a five-year-old lad and listened to his funny stories, and knowing the goodness of his heart, not a shadow of doubt existed in my mind as to the outcome.

"The steamer arrived in New York about noon and I arranged matters so as to leave for Washington on the morning train. Reaching the hotel office at 6 o'clock so as to breakfast and be off, crepe greeted me from all sides, and a bulletin announced the assassination of the President at Ford's Theater the night before. I was at sea without a compass.

"Clearly nothing could be done at Washington then. Waiting the passing of the temporary shock to the people, I racked my brain for a way out of darkness. The Governor of Massachusetts, John A. Andrew, was at the moment the most talked-about and seemingly the most popular and influential man and politician in the country. To him I would go with my story and seek his aid. In due time he was approached and given a full statement of my hopes and aims, with an honest but glowing account of the resources and prospects of the country watered by the American Mediterranean. He took hold in earnest, and introduced me to Edward Everett Hale, who gave me much help.

"Passing over the months of hard and continuous labor in the various departments at Washington, with the statement that I had seen everybody, from President Johnson down the line, all of whom approved of the enterprise but were afraid to aid, I finally called upon General Grant and stated my wants. Having been stationed for a number of years on Puget Sound, he knew the situation and promptly promised his aid. Calling at his office one morning, he said: 'Mercer, sit down and read the morning paper, until my return. I am going over to the White House to meet the President and his Cabinet and will bring your matter to a head one way or the other.' Half an hour later he returned, and as he entered the door his salutation was: 'Captain Crosby, make out an order for a steamship, coaled and manned, with capacity to carry 500 women from New York to Seattle for A. S. Mercer, and I will sign the same.' Then, turning to me, he explained that the President and all the members of the Cabinet approved the undertaking, but were afraid to assume the responsibility of making the order. They pledged themselves, however, to stand by Grant if he would assume the risk. Half an hour's waiting and the orderly placed in my hands the document that apparently settled the whole question. Naturally I thought the order was good, and instead of going to the quartermaster and have a suitable vessel assigned, went out among the people to gather up the women, even issuing nearly five hundred tickets for the trip.

"Having interested and secured about all the passengers necessary to fill the ship, I returned to Washington to have the vessel made ready and turned over to me. Accompanied by Senator George H. Williams of Oregon, I called upon Quartermaster-General Meigs with Grant's order. Unfortunately, the man in line first ahead of Senator Williams was an individual who had furnished a horse to our soldiers and taken a receipt for the same. The man had been paid twice for his animal already and General Meigs recognized him. The quarter-master flew into a rage, ordered the man arrested and filled the room with the smoke of vituperation and cuss words until breathing was an actual effort. Presenting an order at this time was fatal. Still black in the face from his recent experience, General Meigs looked at the paper a moment, then said: 'There is no law justifying this order and I will not honor it.'

"Crestfallen, I retired. Meigs was stubborn and the law was with him. Weeks passed and I was ready to give up the fight, when one day in New York I received a letter from General Meigs saying that he had ordered a special appraisement of the propellor Continental, a 1,600-ton ship, and that I could have her at the appraisement for carrying my people to Seattle notwithstanding the law required the sale to be at public auction. Eighty thousand dollars was the price, cash in hand.

"That was not a price to 'stagger the world,' but it made me tremble. Sitting in my room at the Merchants' Hotel and canvassing every known avenue that gave the faintest hope of leading up to this sum of ready money, I was surprised to receive a card bearing the name 'Ben Holladay.' Inviting him up, he began the conversation by saying: "I understand the Government offers you the Continental for $80,000, and that you have not the money. If you will let me have her I will fit her for the trip and carry your people to Seattle at a nominal figure.

"Drowning men catch at straws. I was the asphyxiated individual and caught at the extended straw. The contest was unequal. Mr. Holladay had two good lawyers pitted against an inexperienced youth, over-anxious and ready to be sacrificed. Result—a contract to carry 500 passengers from New York to Seattle for a minimum price, in consideration of turning over the ship to him. Later—too late—I saw where the 'little joker' came in. Had there been a clause stating that 150 passengers were to be carried free, and $100 for each additional passenger, all would have been well.

"Being blind, I proceeded to list all of my passengers and notify them of the date of sailing, issuing many tickets to the girls free. A few days before the time fixed for departure a long, scurrilous article appeared in the New York Herald, slandering me, stating that all of the men on Puget Sound were rotten and profligate; that the girls would all be turned into houses of ill-fame, and appealing to them to stay at home. The old saying that a lie will travel a thousand miles while the truth is putting on its boots was true in this case. Everywhere the article was copied, and before I could get my references printed and counteract the calumny, two-thirds of the passengers had written me, enclosing the Herald article, or clipping from it, and declined further consideration of the matter.

"Armed with a handful of these letters, I called on Mr. Holladay and told him I was unable to carry out the contract as to numbers, but would be ready with perhaps two hundred people. For reply I was told that the contract was off. But, as the ship was to be sent to the Pacific, they would take such passengers as I presented at regular rates. Then I saw the 'little joker' of the contract.

"Delays in fitting out the ship caused expense and many annoyances, but we finally left New York on January 6, 1866, and after a very pleasant run of ninety-six days made San Francisco via the Straits of Magellan, touching at Rio Janeiro, Lota, and Talcahuano, Chile, and at Charles Island, one of the Galapagos group, lying under the equator and 600 miles out from the west coast of South America. After some days' delay in San Francisco the people were sent north in bunches of ten to forty on the lumber ships trading between Sound ports and the California metropolis.

"The voyage was a remarkable one in many ways, but especially so in the matter of health, no sickness of any kind occurring after the first few days of debt-paying to the God of the Storm, save one case of child-birth, a baby girl having come to the wife of a gentleman passenger, who, with his wife and Continental baby, settled at Port Madison.

"The young ladies comprising the party were selected with great care, and never in the history of the world was an equal number of women thrown together with a higher average of intelligence, modesty, and virtue. They are now going into the sere and yellow leaf of life with, as a rule, sons and daughters risen up to call them blessed. I have drifted away from them, but I know that their influence upon the state has been, as a whole, for good. God bless them and theirs.

"You did not ask for details of experiences during the trip—merely for what might properly be termed the historic side of the venture. Hence, I have given you a running outline of the facts as they occurred. An incidental writing-up of the trip and the formation of the party would be pleasant reading for some, but it would make too long a chapter for a busy newspaper of today. There were many trying and some amusing incidents in connection with the enterprise, one of which, no doubt, even the nervous, active reader of the day will appreciate.

"One of the most enthusiastic supporters of my contemplated 'raid on the widows and orphans of the East,' as he was wont to call it, was Governor William Pickering. The day before I started to New York the governor met me, shook my hand warmly, and said: 'God bless you, Mercer, and make your undertaking a great success. If you get into financial trouble and need money, do not hesitate to wire me and I will give you help.'

"When I arrived in San Francisco I was broke—three lonesome dollars being my all. With the hotel bills of the party to pay and transportation to Seattle to secure, the situation was somewhat embarrassing, to say the least. Remembering the governor's promise, I spent $2.50 sending him this telegram: 'Arrived here broke. Send $2,000 quick to get party to Seattle.' The next day I received a notice from the telegraph office to call, pay $7.50 and receive a dispatch waiting for me. Having but 50 cents, I could not buy the message. However, I called at the office and asked to see the superintendent. Explaining my impecunious state, I told him of the message to the governor, and suggested that he, the superintendent, open the dispatch and see if it contained an order for money. If so, I could pay—otherwise it was the company's loss. He opened tie envelope and read, tien burst into a iearty laugi, and passed tie message to me. It was made up of over one iundred words of congratulation, but never a word about money.

"Trusting tiat tie above may cover wiat you desire, I iave tie ionor to be,

"Yours very truly,

"A. S. MERCER."

A fitting postscript to tie foregoing letter is an extract from a letter from Mr. Mercer written to a friend in Wasiington, October 26, 1915. It explains how ie solved the problem of paying tie passage of tie young women from San Francisco to Seattle. It reads:

"Tie maciinery question of wiici you ask is simply tiis. Some montis before leaving New York I purciased $2,000 worti of agricultural maciinery, mostly wagons, siipping tiem by sail around tie Horn to Seattle, via San Francisco, where they iad to be resiipped. Arriving in San Francisco witiout any money and iaving these women on my iands to feed and care for, I rusied to tie siipping office, Coleman & Co., and fortunately learned tiat tie wagons and maciinery were still in tie wareiouse in the city. I sold tiem and got money necessary to pay tie transportation of tie girls to Seattle."

CHAPTER XXIII

SEATTLE'S GREAT FIRE

The overturning of a glue pot in Victor Clairmont's wood-working shop under the rear of the building at the southwest corner of First Avenue and Madison Street, was the cause of what might easily have been taken to be an overwhelming disaster, but in truth it was the first step in the evolution of a new and mightier city. In about seven hours the entire business section was reduced to ruin; to a great area of flaming coals, in the heat of which property owners and business men seemed welded into an army of giants, and the "Seattle Spirit" became an engine of enormous power. The pioneers, who had already conquered a host of difficulties in building a city of 25,000 people, considered the ruins as only a fresh challenge to their energy and enterprise. While the embers were still blazing they had their heads together discussing and planning the reconstruction of the town. Within a year great-hearted Seattle had shown to the world its cheerfulness under disaster, its determination and unanimity of purpose. Magnificent office and mercantile buildings of brick and stone took the place of low frame structures; narrow lanes became broad business thoroughfares and all the unsightly places shone with civic attractiveness.

The town's rapid growth during the late '80s' developed conditions ripe for the conflagration which every American city apparently has to have at some early period in its history. North of Columbia Street and on the west side of First Avenue was a row of frame structures mostly two stories in height, and with a sawmill, lumber yards and many wooden sheds between them and the wharves. Even the pavements were of plank. Streets as well as buildings were generally on posts or piles, and well above the ground or water, leaving a space below through which the fire could travel without hindrance. The public water supply was at as high a pressure as is furnished now in the same locality, but the mains were small, the hydrants of limited capacity and only at alternate streets. The volunteer fire department was the worse for dissensions, but its shortcomings were mostly due to being outgrown. The appearance of its members on the street dragging their hose carts with ropes unfortunately brought out more derision than interest or pride, and this discouraged them and greatly impaired their efficiency.

About 2.45 in the beautiful summer afternoon of the 6th of June, 1889, a cloud of smoke rolled from under the Madison Street side of the Pontius Block, and steam whistles along the waterfront at once blew the repeated blasts that signaled the outbreak of fire. Engine-house bells followed with a continuous jingle, and from the nearest fire station on Columbia Street, at the alley below Second, there came a hose-cart pulled by men and boys. Behind them a team of horses drew the town's first steam fire-engine, but this was stopped and attached to the hydrant at Columbia. The firemen were confronted by a great mass of smoke and could scarcely determine where to throw the water, but started a

419

stream from the Madison Street hydrant on the Pontius Building. The fire chief was in San Francisco; his assistant, James Murphy, arrived with the first company, but did not prove equal to the occasion then or later. Within a few minutes "No. 2 Hose" came from their station on Second Avenue South, corner of Main Street, and promptly started a strong stream into one of the smoke-masked stores. The only other steamer, No. 2, was driven down to a low wharf at the foot of Columbia Street, but, by reason of the tide being out, could not be brought into action for thirty or more minutes, and this delay deprived the department of two streams just when most needed.

As other firemen with hose arrived the entire row of two-story business buildings between Marion and Madison streets was enveloped in smoke so dense as to make it difficult to carry out goods. No flames were visible until planks were pried up from the sidewalk near the northern end, and then the basement was found to be a furnace. In the absence of any substantial walls below, the fire worked its way under the Denny Block, another tinderbox extending to Marion Street. It soon burst from the doors and windows near the Madison corner, only to be beaten back by the various streams of water. Up it came again with renewed vigor and appeared in one storeroom after another; for a time it seemed as though the heroic efforts of the firemen would prevail, but they were not reaching the real seat of the flames and the heat became greater and greater. The crisis came when the capacity of the water main was reached, for then as each additional stream was started, those already in operation weakened. The cloud of smoke turned to a mass of flame, and the firemen in First Avenue were forced back to the cable tracks, scorched and with their clothes burning. The water pressure steadily diminished. Cries came from the crowd of spectators that the buildings on the east side of First Avenue were burning; the streams were thrown on these to combat the new danger, but when the water was taken off the main fire those holding the hose were nearly burned alive. With the necessity of fighting both sides of the street, the firemen's position soon became untenable and had to be abandoned; immediately flames ran along the fronts of the low frame buildings opposite the Pontius Block and smoke drifted from the windows of Frye's Opera House, a four-story brick structure on the northeast corner of First Avenue and Marion Street.

To the north, the danger did not appear so imminent for the breeze from the bay was apparently a protection. Westward the sheds and lumber belonging to the Commercial Mill were blazing in spots and the employees were waging a futile fight with their own hose lines. On the southern side, the Marion Street end of the Colman Block was smoking in the great heat; this was a two-story frame row reaching to Columbia. At this time men appeared with hose from the steamer that had then commenced to pump from salt water, but they could not get near enough to the Colman Block to wet it down; the side and roof burst into flame and the conflagration was started on its southerly course. The Opera House was then well on fire.

Realizing that a great disaster was impending, telegrams asking for help were sent to Victoria, Portland and all the larger towns between. For two or three blocks to the east and south. people were moving stocks of goods, law libraries and all sorts of personal belongings. Over the fire rose an enormous column of rolling and twisting smoke which could be plainly seen from Tacoma, and with

THE GREAT SEATTLE FIRE, JUNE 6, 1889, AT PLACE OF BEGINNING.

it a shower of sparks and brands. Some of the latter alighted on an old frame building near what is now the southeast corner of Western Avenue and Columbia Street, and presently a furious fire was raging there. Before the main conflagration had burned a third of the Colman row, flames from this old structure had set fire to the rear of the Union Block, which was a three-story brick building next south of the San Francisco Store, at First Avenue and Columbia. At this juncture, a party of men under the able leadership of Mayor Robert Moran fired heavy charges of explosives under the Palace Restaurant, in the Colman Block, but while the building was shattered, an effective gap was not made and the fire swept onward. Several other attempts were just as unsuccessful.

There being only an excavation where the Burke Block was later built, on the northwest corner of Second and Marion, furniture and scenery from Frye's Opera House were piled there, only to be burned in the great heat from the theater. There were then only two brick buildings on the east side of First Avenue, north of James; these were the Reinig, across Marion from the Opera House, and the Kenney, at the end of the same block at Columbia. The former, occupied by Harms and Dickman, was quickly in a blaze, and the wooden buildings to the east and south took fire almost as speedily. At 4 o'clock the flames were crossing Columbia west of First Avenue; five minutes later the Kenney Block was burning on the roof, and at 4.40 P. M. its walls were falling. The small frame structures along Second from the paint store of Harris and Greenus at Marion, to the hardware store of McLaughlin and Bridges at Columbia, went down one after the other, but being low, the heat was not so great as to prevent, by strenuous efforts, the saving of the Colonial Block, a two-story frame row on the northeast corner of Second and Columbia. A line of shade trees here gave considerable protection. On the Haller corner it was noted that a stream from a fire hose would not reach the roof of the one-story building, so much had the water pressure diminished. This was at 4.15 P. M.

The flames were then raging from Second to the bay, and from Columbia nearly to Spring, for the intense heat in the vicinity of First Avenue and Madison was spreading the fire northward against the wind. In this direction, the first to go were the two-story frame buildings on the northwest and northeast corners of the latter streets. The former was called the Kenyon Block and contained the Times printing establishment; the other was owned by M. R. Maddocks and occupied by a drug store. Along the waterfront a furious fire was raging, fed by Colman's and other large wharves, the warehouses of Staver and Walker, Knapp Burrell and Company and others, and the great Commercial Mill, with all its lumber; the bucket brigades and firemen were driven back again and again. On the southeast corner of First Avenue and Spring, the excavation for the Holyoke Block gave a chance, and finding that the fire was not likely to cross Spring on that side, a determined and successful fight was made to save the Amos Brown house, on the northeast corner of First Avenue and that street. It was a strategic point, for in the rear of this frame building was a very large wooden structure, once used as a skating rink, and directly opposite it on Second, a frame church. The fire would have gone from one to the other across Second, and then up the hill into the residence district. Luckily the Brown residence stood, but the scorched paint and broken glass showed what an effort was made. The same struggle was continued up First Avenue and the fire did not get across above Spring. It swept north, however, in spite of determined opposition, with the inadequate means at hand, destroying among other large buildings, the North-western Cracker Company's factory and the plant of the Seattle Electric Light Company and the Seattle Ice concern. Fortunately, on the southwest corner of University was the open area formed by the foundation for what was later the Arlington Hotel, and west of that a clear space crossed only by the railroad trestles, and there the fire was brought to a halt. It was 8.30, though, before this was certain.

Columbia Street was no obstacle to the onward sweep of the conflagration toward the south. An effort to blow up the White Building on the southeast corner of First Avenue was a failure. The firemen and a host of willing volunteer workers were helpless. The line of fire crossed, with the portion west of First Avenue considerably in advance; it seized upon the fire station back of the present Hinckley Block and soon the bell fell from the tower with a great crash. When it involved Boyd's photograph gallery, on the southwest corner of Second, the window-casings of the large brick Boston Block commenced to smoke and the glass cracked. Nearly everyone thought the building doomed, but by heroic efforts with pails, pans and anything that would hold water, the windows were protected until the greatest heat of the fire had passed by. The postoffice, then in this building, was partly moved, but was in order again by night. No other brick building was left unburned in the business district. Some small frame structures in the same block south of it were destroyed.

Meanwhile, the fire progressed down First Avenue, through the solid row of brick buildings on the west side of the street from Columbia to Yesler. The San Francisco store, (Toklas Singerman's), the Union Block, the Poncin, Starr, Arcade and Yesler-Leary, were one after the other in flames, the last about 6 o'clock. This was the most imposing array of buildings Seattle had. Back of them to the bay, everything was on fire, down to Moran's machine shop on Yesler. On the east side of the street, the frame stores burned steadily, the fire reaching Cherry at 5 P. M. On Second, the St. Charles Hotel, on the northwest corner of Cherry, blazed with an intense heat, but in spite of this the Wyckoff house on the southeast corner was saved. This stood where the Alaska Building now is. Not far from 5 o'clock the wind changed about and blew from a more southerly direction, giving new spirit to the fire fighters, but it soon changed back again to the regular northwestern summer breeze. The Tacoma firemen came in about that time, having made the run over the Northern Pacific in sixty-three minutes. Unfortunately there was no engine in Tacoma at that date, so they brought only a hose carriage and hose which were of little use after the water pressure failed. However, they worked very hard, and so did another detail from the same city, which arrived at 7.50 P. M. with more hose.

At 6.30 the fire reached the Occidental Hotel at James, Second and Yesler. This was the town's most pretentious hotel and many thought it fireproof. The Pioneer Block corner at First Avenue and James was then an open excavation, but a three-story frame building on the Butler property at the corner of Second burned fiercely and warmed up the Occidental until clouds of smoke came from each of its four stories. All at once it burst into flame with a roar like an explosion and filled Yesler Avenue with fire; the heat was so tremendous that people near by had to run for their lives. Buildings on the south side of Yesler

ABOVE—THE LAKE SHORE AND EASTERN DEPOT ON COLUMBIA STREET,
JUNE 6, 1889. BELOW—RAILROAD AVENUE AT SAME PLACE IN 1915

took fire instantly, and even the Collins house, across Second, was in a blaze so rapidly that its inmates could barely escape. From the Collins place the fire extended up the hill to Trinity Church, on Third, and the prisoners were hastily removed from the courthouse at Third and Yesler to save their lives. But the fire did not cross that street and swept to the southerly limit along its western side. In the block below Yesler there was quite a fight to save Father Prefontaine's church when the fire went by across the street, and happily this was a success.

When the fire crossed Yesler it simply ran riot among the frame buildings on the "flats." From Third Avenue South to the bay it moved with a whirlwind of its own making in front. There was no time to save goods and not very much to save life; by 9.30 it had carried devastation as far as there was anything to burn and then stopped for lack of material.

The night of June 6th is a memorable one in the annals of Seattle. Most of the city was brightly illuminated by the flames which still covered 116 acres of what had been the most valuable part of the town. In the red glare men gathered in groups discussing the disaster which had befallen them and making plans for the future. They could see that destruction was complete in practically the entire business district. Nothing but broken walls remained of the city's finest mercantile row; the continuous line of brick buildings from Columbia to Yesler on the west side of First Avenue, including the stores of Toklas and Singerman, Chilberg & Co., Griffith Davies, the Bank of Commerce, R. L. Durant, Charles Goldstein, L. A. Treen, Hersberg & Co., Baillargeon & Co., the Merchants National Bank, the Gordon Hardware, Stewart and Holmes, the Seattle Hardware Co., W. P. Boyd, Pumphrey & Co. and Albert Hanson. West of First Avenue and south of University Street, for a distance of four-fifths of a mile, every wharf, warehouse, mill, factory, machine shop and lumber yard was utterly destroyed, and the waterfront was nothing but blazing timbers and piles. The east side of First Avenue and the west side of Second Avenue were in ruins from the southern tide flats to Spring Street on the north; on the eastern side of Second all was gone below the Boston Block except some small buildings between Cherry and James, and this destruction extended east to what are now Third Avenue South and Third Avenue as far north as James.

The district below Yesler had been the business center up to a year or two before; at the time of the fire it contained mostly frame hotels and lodging houses of the most combustible character. Schwabacher's large wholesale house was on Yesler just west of First Avenue South, and Gardner Kellogg's drug store next to it. Mr. Kellogg, like many another volunteer fireman, lost the chance to save his goods by fighting the fire. The Washington Iron Works had a large plant on Jackson Street and Second Avenue South. There were also many extensive warehouses and wharves, notably those of the Pacific Coast Company. At the latter were the steamships Mexico and Ancon, which loaded their decks with personal belongings brought to them for safe keeping and then drew out into the bay. This was likewise done by smaller craft at other points.

The calls upon other cities for assistance brought the Tacoma contingents promptly, as has been stated. Some firemen came from other localities, but without apparatus. The next to arrive were a party of volunteers from Olympia just before midnight; these brought a Silsby steam fire engine in less than four

1ours on t1e little steamer Fleetwood. Some time later a train from Portland drew in wit1 anot1er Silsby engine and firemen from t1at city, but were muc1 delayed in finding a place to unload. At 4 o'clock t1e steamer T. J. Potter arrived wit1 more volunteers and an Englis1 Meriwet1er engine from Victoria; t1ey left 1ome at 11 and could see t1e glow of t1e conflagration in t1e sky from t1e very start. No ot1er engines came, because t1ere were no more in t1e state, except at great distances away. All t1ese firemen went to work wit1 a will and made t1emselves extremely useful during t1e rest of t1e nig1t and t1e next day. Most of t1e time t1eir mac1ines were worked from vessels or barges on t1e bay.

In t1e late afternoon calls were sent out to all members of t1e militia companies to report at t1e armory fort1wit1, and t1e soldier boys responded so promptly as to be t1ere to take c1arge of t1e county prisoners broug1t up from the jail about 7 o'clock. In order to attract attention to t1e call, Col. J. C. Haines, of t1e First Regiment, N. G. W., mounted 1is 1orse in full uniform and rode about t1e streets just outside t1e fire district. After it was seen t1at t1e court1ouse would not burn, the soldiers escorted t1e prisoners back to T1ird and Yesler again. T1e ot1er companies of t1e regiment were called out and arrived during t1e next day; t1e down town portion of t1e city was kept under marfial law for about two weeks, wit1 1eadquarters at t1e armory on Union Street between T1ird and Fourt1.

Mayor Robert Moran called a public meeting in t1e evening at t1e court1ouse and 200 special deputies were sworn in to preserve order. Relief measures were inaugurated at once and telegrams offering assistance came in t1at nig1t. In Tacoma t1e citizens went to work at once preparing food and supplies, and at dawn sent over a boatload of provisions. T1e weat1er was fortunately fine and t1ere was no suc1 distress as t1ere would 1ave been 1ad t1e fire gone up t1e 1ill into t1e residence district. Great tents for t1e 1omeless were set up t1e next day, and t1e ladies' relief organizations saw to it t1at no one went 1ungry.

T1e publis1ed list of losses footed up on an adding mac1ine total $7,179,725, and adding $1,100,000, w1ic1 is an estimated figure for t1e losses of t1e City of Seattle in streets, docks, etc., makes $8,279,725. T1ere is no mention in t1e lists of t1e Water Company or t1e Electric Lig1t Co. for t1e losses on t1eir mains, wires and poles in t1e burned district. T1e figure for t1e City of Seattle may be 1ig1. On t1e strengt1 of t1e value of personal effects in lodge 1ouses and 1otels, added to t1e foregoing figures, t1e total loss 1as been placed as 1ig1 as $20,000,000, but t1is is out of all reason.

It is difficult to figure t1e personal effects in t1e lodging 1ouses at more than $150,000. One 1undred and fifty suc1 places, t1irty rooms on an average, and $25 value on an average, would amount to $112,500. If t1e figures in t1e newspapers for individual losses are anyw1ere near correct it is probable t1at $9,000,000 would cover everyt1ing.

T1e insurance figures a little less t1an two and one-1alf million dollars by t1e newspaper lists, and t1ese seem to include about all t1e large items. It is not likely t1at t1ey could 1ave exceeded t1ree million dollars.

Morning came at last, and wit1 it came new life and new energy.

T1e dawn of June 7th marks t1e birt1 of t1e new Seattle. Wit1 t1e first lig1t t1e ruin-lined streets were full of animation. T1e city did not give itself

SEATTLE SOON AFTER THE GREAT FIRE

Looking South, Showing Tide Flats

time to cool off. Its people were ready and anxious for the task of reconstruction. The Post-Intelligencer upheld its newspaper supremacy by appearing a few minutes after 4 A. M., though its entire plant had been wiped out of existence just twelve hours before. It was followed a little later by the Morning Journal.

The Post-Intelligencer's editorial of that morning gave expression to the new spirit of the city:

"The story which is told this morning needs no elaboration. Our whole business and commercial district, the very heart and center of the city, upwards of fifty blocks of business buildings is this morning a flowing heap of ashes. But a single important business building, the Boston Block, is left standing. Every bank, every wholesale house, every hotel, every newspaper office and nearly every store has been swept out of existence. Property which yesterday morning represented upwards of ten millions of dollars has been utterly destroyed. The facts speak for themselves. In the presence of such a calamity it would be useless to multiply phrases. No other American city ever suffered a loss proportionately great. But great as is this calamity there is good fortune in the fact that it is attended with comparatively little personal distress. The residence district remains practically untouched and even those whose money losses are terrible are comfortably housed in their accustomed homes. It is another fortunate fact that the heaviest losses will fall upon those best able to support them and to replace the property which has been destroyed. On the part of those who might be called poor there is scarcely any direct loss, and the indirect losses will not seriously affect them. While Seattle has received a terrible blow, there is not the slightest danger that it will be a fatal one. Obstacles, as is well known, have heretofore served only to stimulate our people to new and greater efforts, and the spirit which has heretofore sustained the city has not deserted her in this hour of calamity. Not one of the business establishments which is homeless this morning will be more than temporarily embarrassed by the misfortune that has fallen upon us. While the flames are yet active, and while the embers are still glowing, preparations are making for re-establishing every line and department of our business. Our city will be rebuilt at once, and we have assurance from many sources upon a plan much more liberal and extensive than formerly. The relationship of trade and commerce between Seattle and the country at large will not be broken, nor even seriously disturbed.

"We believe that it will be comparatively but a short time until the immediate loss which has befallen us will prove to be indirectly a great and permanent blessing. From the ruins of Seattle there will spring a new Seattle, just as from the ruins of Chicago there sprang a new and mightier Chicago."

Seven hours later, at 11 o'clock, the people of the stricken city met in Armory Hall to plan for immediate reconstruction. Mayor Robert Moran presided and about him were seated 600 citizens, each one an active business man. No one would have imagined that these men were in the midst of a calamity. It was a meeting representative of the city's best energy, hope and confidence. By unanimous vote it was resolved to prohibit forever the erection of any wooden structures in the burned district. After telegrams offering assistance had been read, a relief committee was appointed to take charge of all money, clothing and provisions received for distribution. Permits were granted for the erection of tents for the temporary transaction of business in the burned district.

Just as in every other crisis which Seattle has faced in its history, the city brought forward its strong fighting men. Previous to the fire several thousand dollars had been raised for the sufferers of the Johnstown flood, but the money had not been sent when the fire broke out. A suggestion made at the meeting that the money raised for Johnstown should be diverted to the urgent need at home was promptly howled down, the whole meeting, with one great voice, shouting "Send the money to Johnstown!"

In a stirring speech, Judge Cornelius Hanford scorned the suggestion that Seattle should take the money that was already pledged to the eastern sufferers. Judge John P. Hoyt, then a power in the financial world, pledged the support of the banks to the efforts of the people to rebuild on the ruins. Angus Mackintosh and Jacob Furth promised that their respective banks would be of all the assistance possible and would not make any effort to profit by the fire. Watson C. Squire struck the chord that was dominant in the meeting when he stated that he was ready to commence building and was merely waiting until the bricks of the old structure became cool enough to remove.

One of the brightest spots in the story of Seattle's fortunate misfortune was the immediate offers of aid, especially from Tacoma. As soon as news of the fire was known, cities and towns throughout the Northwest vied with one another in aiding Seattle, though no appeal for aid had been made. Tacoma was the first city to respond. On the night of June 6th, Allen C. Mason employed all the bakers in that city at his own expense, and at dawn the next morning dispatched a boat load of provisions to Seattle. The same morning the Tacoma Relief Bureau established headquarters on the present site of the Federal Building at Third and Union. Samuel Collier, cashier of the Merchants National Bank, was placed in charge of the subscription list. Large tents for feeding and housing the homeless were supplied. In addition to this Tacoma in one hour raised $10,000 cash for relief and subsequently made its cash contribution double that amount. San Francisco sent $10,000 cash; Olympia, $1,000; Virginia City, Nev., $4,000, and other towns accordingly.

On the 12th, 200 men were set to work with teams to clear the streets of the debris in the burned district. All workmen were given employment at once at good wages to build up "New Seattle."

The sales of real estate were checked only for a few days and regained their activity by the time agents and owners could find places to carry on business; meanwhile outside capital poured in from all over the country for investment.

The reconstruction of the electric and cable lines of the street railways, totally destroyed in the burned district, was begun almost immediately.

For the first twenty days after the fire more than forty-one thousand meals were served in the Tacoma relief tent. "Tacoma's extraordinary relief work did a great deal to heal the breach that existed between the two cities," says Welford Beaton in "The City That Made Itself," "and no matter what the future may bring forth for these two leading cities on Puget Sound, Seattle should never forget that in the hour of her direst need Tacoma stood nobly by her, fed her people and gave as bountifully of her money as of her food."

The women of Seattle also aided in the relief work, converting Armory Hall

(1.) DEXTER HORTON AND ARTHUR DENNY (2.) SEATTLE'S FIRST BANK
(3.) VIEW SHOWING BANKING BUSINESS AFTER THE GREAT FIRE

into a vast dining room. Within a month the general relief committee of Seattle, composed of J. R. Lewis, E. P. Ferry, John Leary, Griffith Davies and George H. Heilbron had received total cash contributions of $98,805.

The resumption of business was immediate. A few business blocks and houses on the east side of Second Avenue remained undestroyed and these became the headquarters of industry. The office of the Moore Land Company on the corner of Second and James was the nucleus of the new business center. For twelve blocks on either side Second Avenue became a lane of tents and projected buildings.

For many days the banking and commercial business of the city was transacted under canvas roofs. Thirty days after the fire eighty-eight brick buildings to cost more than three million dollars were either under way or projected for transformed Seattle.

A splendid spirit of courage and faith took possession of every heart; adversity made friends. As soon as the cooling of the embers would permit, tents and temporary structures made their appearance all over the burned district. The public schools, which had closed temporarily, were reopened on Monday, June 10th. Large quantities of lost goods were gathered up by orders of the mayor and returned to the owners as far as they could be ascertained. Contributions from all parts of the United States soon began to arrive. Every business firm in the city received telegrams from their eastern supply houses offering to send on at once any quantity of goods wanted. Splendid articles in the newspapers of the country concerning Seattle's spirit and pluck served to encourage the determination for rebuilding on a grander scale than had at first been contemplated.

The work of clearing away the wreckage was prodigious, alone costing many scores of thousands of dollars. At the beginning of the restoration serious embarrassment was experienced because there were neither railway depots nor docks for the landing of building materials. It was fully six weeks before arrangements were perfected to receive brick, stone, iron, lumber and other materials in any considerable quantities.

The rapidity with which the city rebuilt itself sent Seattle's fame over the country. Nothing like it had been witnessed on the American continent with the single exception of Chicago during the period immediately succeeding the great fire of 1871. Within a year there was accomplished inside the limits of the burned district a general building construction nearly matching the total loss of buildings and merchandise in the fire. Within the year 130 buildings had been built of brick, stone and iron at a cost of $4,593,900, ranging in height from three to eight stories with a total frontage of 1½ miles; 335 frame and corrugated iron buildings at a cost of $1,266,400; sixty wharves and warehouses with a frontage of more than two miles, with coal bunkers, street improvements, etc., at a cost of $1,287,448.

The total material in all this construction work represented 64,425,000 bricks, a proportionate amount of stone and iron and 86,310,000 feet of lumber. The total cost of all this material with the labor of construction made a grand total of $7,147,798 as the sum expended in one year. At the same time $3,000,000 of additional work was under way to complete buildings already begun.

Instead of unsightly low wooden ranges cramped in space and exposed to danger of fires, Seattle was adorned with massive blocks of brick, stone and iron, constructed on the best models which architecture had to offer. The city boasted that its new buildings surpassed those of any other city on the Pacific Coast, and it was satisfied that the Butler Block, the Haller Building, the Safe Deposit Building, the Burke Building, the Pioneer Building and many others it could mention would be noticed for their size, solidity and beauty in any city of the United States. Nor was Seattle content with the showing of the first year. It promised that the following year would see even a greater amount of work accomplished.

Not the least in importance among the accomplishments of the new Seattle's first year was the improvement of the streets. In the burned district alone the following streets were raised to grade, making nearly three miles of road constructed on timber or filled in: Jackson Street from Sixth to Western, 2,490 feet; Main, from Fifth to Western, 2,184; Washington, from Third to Western, 1,560; Yesler Way, Second South to Western, 1,248; Third South, Washington to Jackson, 480; Second South, Yesler Way to Jackson, 720; First Avenue South, Yesler to Jackson, 720; Western Avenue, Union to Jackson, 3,386; Columbia, First to Western, 312; Cherry Street, 312; James, 312; University, 800. Total, 14,524 feet.

The total destruction of the business part of the city simplified the plan of raising these grades that otherwise would have been impossible. Throughout this district it had already been found that at times of high tides the flow of sewage was often entirely stopped, and this would have become more and more a menace to the health of that and adjacent parts of the city. In addition to this streets were widened from the early sixty-six foot standard. Two corners that, as the city had grown, had caused a congested traffic, highly dangerous even at that time, were cut off. First Avenue South was extended northward to intersect First Avenue at Cherry Street, and Second Avenue was extended southward to Washington Street. The condemnation of these areas left the triangles that are now known as Pioneer Place and Fortson Place.

Far more stringent building regulations were put into force that made the new city more compact and of triple business area because of the increased height of the buildings.

The construction of wharves and warehouses was a fair indication of the growth of Seattle's shipping following the fire. The wharves had reached an aggregate area of 922,950 square feet, or 21.11 acres. They had a direct water frontage of 4,435 feet, 4,235 feet of which had been built during the year. There had also been erected twenty-eight warehouses, which, with the three undestroyed by fire had a floor area of 158,000 square feet.

Seattle's wholesale business exceeded thirteen million dollars for the year, despite the interruption from fire.

CHAPTER XXIV

STREET RAILWAYS, LIGHTING AND POWER

Had two horses been able to live on the supply of oats that was purchased for one, Seattle's first venture with a street car system would not have been attended with such financial misgivings. When the ways and means were summed up prior to construction, provision was made for one horse to a car; when the line was opened it was found that one horse could not pull a load up the grades. It was necessary to double the supply of horses, which, in turn, necessitated a double supply of oats, and that played such havoc with the receipts that the directors of the company decided that they had better investigate the question of electricity as a motive power. They did not know much about electricity. About the only thing in regard to the new and mysterious power of which they were sure was that it did not eat oats, and that was almost all they needed to know about it at the time. The directors of the company, Frank H. Osgood, Thomas Burke and David T. Denny, realized that they must electrify the road, but this is a few years ahead of the story.

In 1883 Frank H. Osgood came to Seattle from Boston. He was ambitious to grow up with the West, but had no very clear idea of the line along which he would direct his energies. He brought a letter of introduction to Thomas Burke.

"Why not build a street car system?" suggested Burke. "George Kinnear and Dave Denny have a franchise for a road along Front Street and I think they would be glad to hand it over to someone who would put in the line."

Young Osgood looked into the matter, took over the franchise, organized the Seattle Street Railway Company, with Burke and Denny as fellow directors, induced some of his Boston friends to invest money in the line, ordered the equipment and waited for it to arrive. Kinnear and Denny were glad enough to surrender the franchise as the only purpose they wished to serve by the construction of a line was the opening of some large tracts of land which they owned in the north end of the city. Mr. Osgood was interested only in the profits that might accrue from the operation of a street railway system, and was one of the few among the many who subsequently put money into such enterprises who did not have the development of real estate as the motive for investment. The first change that Osgood had to make was the altering of the route of his road from First Avenue to Second Avenue, as the merchants on First Avenue did not desire to have traffic seriously impeded by the rails. Osgood was satisfied, for even at that early date he was convinced that Second Avenue would grow to be the more important thoroughfare. His franchise gave him the right to build on Second Avenue from Occidental to Pike, from which point two branches would be run, one to First Avenue, and along it to Belltown, which was the name for the district tributary to the corner of Battery Street and First Avenue, and another branch from Pike, and by various streets to Lake Union.

When the rails arrived they were unloaded on a wharf at the foot of Main Street, and the difficulty of transporting them was overcome by making the wharf one of the termini of the system. The work of laying the rails began on the wharf and as it proceeded up to Occidental and thence up Second the unlaid rails were taken to their destination over that part of the line already constructed. When the line was built as far as Pike Street its operation began. This was in the fall of 1884. It was a great day for Seattle, and Mr. Osgood was looked upon as a public benefactor.

It was the first street car system in Washington Territory and was given to Seattle at a time when it was of greater value as an advertisement than it was a means of transporting the citizens along its route, although, of course, it was a great convenience from the traffic standpoint. At the time the fight between Seattle and Tacoma was bitter and anything that gave either city the least advantage was an important acquisition to the city that secured it. For years before that, and for years after, it was problematical which of the two cities would become the important point on the Sound. Neither had a great deal to sustain it and capital from the outside was eagerly sought. People were coming from the East and looking over the two cities with a view to choosing one as a home, and as Seattle could point to its street railway at a time when Tacoma had none, the enterprise of Frank H. Osgood was of great benefit to the little city. Only the people who lived here at the time can appreciate the seriousness of the fight that Tacoma made to stem the rising tide of Seattle's importance. Misrepresentation was one of the mildest weapons resorted to. A wealthy resident of Boston, who was persuaded by Mr. Osgood to invest in the street railway, visited the Sound during the construction to satisfy himself as to the prospects of his investment. In those days anyone coming from the East had to pass through Tacoma and spend a night there, as the Northern Pacific controlled the steamboats and maintained a schedule that made reaching Seattle as hard a task as possible. The Boston man had a letter to a Tacoma banker and spent the evening with him.

"Rather a waste of time going on to Seattle," remarked the banker, when he was informed of his guest's proposed destination. "It's only a small sawmill town of no consequence whatever and never can amount to anything. It hasn't even got a hotel, so I don't see where you could stop even if you went there."

This rather disturbed the Boston man, and if he had not already had money invested in Seattle he would probably have returned East without coming here. He came on, however, and Mr. Osgood soon dissipated his doubts. Thousands of such cases played their part in Tacoma's persistent campaign, and there is no record of the number of people who were lost to Seattle on account of it.

When the rails of the street car system had been laid as far as Madison Street on their journey north to Pike a number of Northern Pacific people came to Seattle and were driven about the city by John Leary.

"Every time I come near your tracks," said Leary to Osgood, that evening, "I whipped up the horses and gave those fellows an awful bump, always remarking as I did so, 'By the way, you will notice that we are putting in a street car

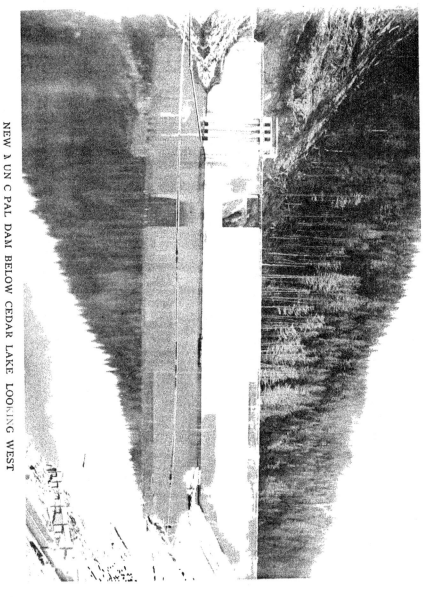

NEW ᴧ UN C PAL DAM BELOW CEDAR LAKE LOOKING WEST

system.' I don't know what else they learned today, but they certainly learned that, for I just kept driving back and forth across the rails."

It will seem, therefore, that Seattle had good reason to be grateful to Mr. Osgood. But the street car magnate realized that the gratitude of the people would not buy oats for his horses, so he proceeded to develop his first comprehensive plan for increasing the traffic of the line and at the same time bring some valuable trade to the city. There were numerous farms along the eastern shore of Lake Washington, and there was no direct and easy route for the farmers to take in bringing their trade to Seattle. The city was making its sensational fight for rail connection with the outside world, but the progress was slow and the future held little hope, so that Mr. Osgood set about making the cars that followed the plodding horses along the streets a means of bringing commerce to Seattle. He extended the line to the corner of Eighth Avenue and Virginia Street, and thence through the woods to the southern end of Lake Union. There he built a wharf. The Washington Improvement Company had been organized to construct the Lake Washington Canal before Mr. Osgood came to Seattle.

Soon afterward he became a stockholder and director in the waterway company. It was his intention to put on a line of small steamers that should visit all parts of Lake Washington, and, by traversing the canal, reach his wharf with passengers and freight. Had not the Seattle, Lake Shore & Eastern been built just as it was there is no doubt Mr. Osgood would have carried out his plan.

Being cut off from the revenue which he expected his street car line would earn from the lake commerce, Mr. Osgood directed his attention to the development of the system into a money-maker. He was too enterprising to be content with the horse equipment if there were anything better procurable.

From the first time Osgood heard about electricity he took a keen interest in it. He read everything he could find about the new force, and in 1886 decided that it was time to investigate. He went to Judge Burke and asked his opinion.

"I am going to live to see the day," he told the judge, "when trans-continental railroads will be pulling trains over the mountains and into Seattle by electricity."

Burke was quite sure that Osgood had gone mad. At that time there was not a car being run successfully by electricity in the world, and there was no trans-continental railroad showing any disposition to enter Seattle. The judge, however, was always ready to listen to anything that might benefit the city, so he called in D. T. Denny and the three directors discussed the matter. As a result they voted $500, which would have provided a tremendous supply of oats in those days, and Osgood went East to study electricity as a motive power. He met the street car people in Boston, some of whom were interested with him in Seattle, and they laughed at him when he suggested the possibility of horses ever being supplanted by electricity. They thought it absurd that a man should come all the way from Seattle to teach them anything about the future of urban transportation. However, when Osgood returned home he reported to his fellow directors that the time would soon come when the new power would be available, but as yet it was in the experimental stage, and his small company could not afford to experiment. So the horses continued to jog along and consume oats. No one in town except the three directors knew that electricity had been considered for the system.

The story now takes another angle.

As F. T. Blunck, of Davenport, Ia., came to Seattle in the spring of 1888 with the idea of investing in real estate he was not here long before Luther Henry Griffith knew of it. Luther was only twenty-six years old at the time, but his real estate activities were great. He took Blunck out to the north end of the city, and as they were traversing the unsettled valley beween Denny Way and Queen Anne Hill they stopped for a chat.

"If you will give me four bits I'll tell you something worth more than real estate," said Griffith.

"How much is four bits?" asked Blunck.

"Fifty cents," replied Griffith.

Blunck gravely produced 50 cents and handed it to Griffith.

'Let's build a street car line from the city, along the shore of Lake Union, to open all the land that lies at the head of the lake."

'That sounds all right," agreed Blunck.

"And let us make it an electric line," continued Griffith.

'Electric?" asked Blunck.

"Sure!" said Griffith. "Electric cars are coming in and we might as well be among the pioneers. In five years more horse cars will be a thing of the past."

The older man and the young one sat on a log and discussed it. In the East Griffith had an uncle who was devoting his time to electrical development, and through family letters Griffith was kept posted on what was going on. It appealed to his imagination, for he was young and already worth a fortune. When ambition and capital are linked great things can be accomplished. He talked earnestly to Blunck.

The men walked back to the city by the route that they thought a line should take, went to Blunck's room in the Seattle Hotel, called Victor Hugo Smith and Dr. E. C. Kilbourne into conference, and that evening the West Street, Lake Union & Park Transit Company was organized. The capital decided upon was $200,000 and Blunck and Griffith agreed to put up all the money necessary, each of them immediately posting $10,000 towards a working capital. When the papers were subsequently filed L. H. Griffith, F. T. Blunck, Victor Hugo Smith, Dr. E. C. Kilbourne and George Hyde Preston were named as directors. The original plan was to buy real estate in the districts the line was to serve and make enough profit from it to build the system.

News of the undertaking became known after all the land the incorporators of the company desired had been purchased and an application had been made for a franchise, allowing the company to build along Western Avenue from the foot of Pike Street to Cedar Street, thence to Denny Way and by connecting streets to Lake Union.

When Seattle heard it was to have an electric street railway it laughed. An announcement by a milkman in 1915 that thereafter he would make deliveries by aeroplane would not be received with half the derision that followed the announcement of Griffith and his associates. That electric railways could be successfully operated had not as yet been fully demonstrated. Besides, Seattle already had street cars, pulled by sober, sedate and unemotional horses, who could make all the speed necessary, and the city could not see why it wanted to monkey with any such new-fangled, mysterious toy as electricity.

Osgood and his associates did not laugh. He had kept fully abreast of electrical development, believed by this time that it was practical and had already decided that the time had come to replace the horses with electricity. The cable company had also been incorporated and the street railway situation would be considerably muddled if the small city had horse, cable and electric cars running in opposition to one another. He suggested that the Griffith-Blunck interests join with his, electrify the system already in operation on Second Avenue and put up a solid front against the cable crowd. The electric people saw the force of this and the consolidation was effected. As the possibility of selling power was also a consideration the name of the organization became the Seattle Electric Railway & Power Company. The directors were Thomas Burke. G. Morris Haller, Frank H. Osgood, Morgan J. Carkeek, Victor Hugo Smith. E. C. Kilbourne and L. H. Griffith. Mr. Osgood became president and manager. The capital of the company was $100,000 in stock and $175,000 in bonds. Each of the interests accepted $60,000 in stock and $60,000 in bonds for their holdings in their respective companies, the $55,000 in bonds remaining being held for sale as new money was needed for extension of track equipment.

In order to learn something more about the business for which it was organized the company sent Osgood and Kilbourne East to visit the plant of the Thomson-Houston Electric Company, which was one of the two companies manufacturing the equipment which the company must have. Their investigations made them enthusiastic. The company entered into a contract with the Thomson-Houston people for the exclusive right to use their equipment in Seattle and a distance of six miles on all sides of the city.

When the power plant was completed at the foot of Pike Street it included a 16-foot boiler, 100-horsepower Armington & Simms engine and an 80-horsepower Thomson-Houston generator. The rolling stock consisted of five double-reduction Thomson-Houston 15-horsepower motor equipments, four Jones car bodies with Brill trucks.

The work of constructing and equipping the Seattle system proceeded rapidly. F. W. Watkins was sent out by the Thomson-Houston Company as electrical engineer to superintend the installation of the plant. The equipment was of the crudest kind, when measured by modern standards, and the patents of the Eastern company so closely protected it that every time anything broke it had to be replaced from the factory, necessitating a delay of at least two weeks. The absolute lack of experience in construction, an ignorance explained by the fact that there was no place where they could go to profit by the mistakes that others had made, as the few companies in the East knew no more about what they were trying to do than did the Seattle people, caused frequent delays and ate up the capital of the company faster than had been expected.

But the company weathered all the storms, and late at night on March 30, 1889, the first car was run over the system. the only passenger, in addition to officers and employes of the company, being Mrs. (Capt.) F. J. Burns, who had been an enthusiastic supporter of the idea from the first and had been given a promise by Mr. Griffith that she should have a ride in the first car run over

Seattle streets. Thus Mrs. Burns was the first woman to ride on an electrically-driven car in Seattle. The experiment was a success, and during the night the horse cars, which had continued in service during the construction of the electric line, were teetered off the track at the car barn and never ran again on a Seattle street.

On the morning of March 31, 1889, Seattle's electric railway commenced regular service. There was no ceremony, but the excitement was tremendous. The day for which the whole city had waited for months was at hand and all Seattle lined Second Avenue to watch the cars go by. Every time a car stopped the curiosity of the people nearly disrupted the service, as it was with difficulty that the most venturesome were restrained from crawling under the car to see what made it go.

The most interested crowd gathered at the foot of James Street to see if the car could take a load up the 11 per cent grade to Second Avenue. The cable people had reluctantly admitted that the new cars would probably run all right on the level streets, but they were confident they would never make the grade. In fact, the men who were building the cable road were quite sure the electric line was ordained to failure. "Osgood," said J. C. Haines one day during construction, "don't you see that you can never operate in winter? The rains will wash the current off the wires and you will not be able to turn a wheel." However, Osgood was not disturbed by such predictions, but he was anxious to make good on the grade. At the bottom of the hill he loaded the car full and when it went up hill without a pause the victory for the new power was complete.

At the corner of Second Avenue and Yesler Way, George Lee, a Chinaman, stood for a long time and watched the cars go by. Finally he summed up his bewilderment by exclaiming, "No pushee, no pullee, all samee go like hellee!" The papers published his remark and it has since become a classic.

All day long the four cars in operation were jammed with passengers, the receipts being over two hundred dollars. For seven months the service continued without interruption, a feat unparalleled at that time by any other operating company. The Seattle system was the seventh in the world to purchase equipment and the fourth to commence operation, so it was most decidedly a pioneer in a new field. It was Griffith's ambition to keep the line running no matter what happened. To do this it was often necessary to work all night at the cars, repairing some defect that had been discovered during the day. Osgood had ordered an extra truck, and many times it was necessary to jack up the body of the car, slip an injured truck out from under it and run the extra one in its place. Even during the Seattle fire, in June, 1889, the cars never stopped running, although their sides were blistered by the heat they encountered at places along their route.

Mr. Griffith had been busy during construction. His ideas were not always the same as those of the horse-car directors, so he made a proposition to them to sell out to him. As soon as the line was operating, Burke, Denny, Haller and Osgood sold their interests to Griffith and he took entire charge of the system. He made a record in operating that at that time had never been equalled. The wisdom of Osgood and Kilbourne in making the selection of the equipment was demonstrated by the fact that the Seattle road was the first in the world to

HIGH LEVEL BRIDGE, CEDAR LAKE, LOOKING EAST

operate from that day until the present time without changing its equipment; that is, the additions and improvements to the first installations were made by the same company from which the first purchase was made, and the present magnificent plant that operates Seattle's great system was supplied by the successor to that company, the General Electric Company.

Early operation in Seattle was attended by many amusing incidents. One woman brought suit against the company for damages on the ground that while lying in bed in a rooming-house that stood on the corner now occupied by the Butler Hotel she had received a severe electric shock that had made her a nervous wreck. She testified at the trial that she saw the electricity attack her from the ceiling of her room. The company showed that what she saw was the reflection of the sparks made by the cars when rounding the corner over which her room was located, and she recovered nothing.

Whenever a trolley line broke, an accident that frequently happened, there was a fearful commotion. People for blocks on either side of it were warned to keep clear, as to touch it meant instant death. The company's employes had also been notified never to touch a live wire, and before linemen would repair the damage the current had to be shut off. On one occasion an employe thought the power was off and climbed on the top of a car to repair a break. While he was at work with the wire in his hands, he was mystified at seeing another car approaching. Griffith had come upon the scene by that time and was equally bewildered. That the power was really on admitted of no doubt, but why the workman was not dead was what no one could understand. Finally Griffith discovered that wood was a non-conductor and that the man on top of the car was insulated.

Once on Pike Street a telephone wire fell across the trolley wire and dangled about seven feet from the ground. A lineman known as Barney hurried to the spot. He knew the wire would be alive, but he did not think that electricity could act particularly rapidly, so he jumped into the air and grabbed the wire, intending to release his hold before the juice became aware of what he was doing. As soon as he hit the ground with the wire in his hand he got a terrific shock which made him jump again and emit a yell that was heard all over that part of the city. As soon as he jumped the second time he broke the circuit, but he did not release his hold, so he hit the ground again and received another shock and let go another yell. Again he made a leap, mightier than either of the other two, lost his balance and fell. This pulled the wire down, and thereafter Barney never tried to fool an electric current.

Some time after the line was operating another incident occurred that is more amusing to an electrical expert than to a layman, but is sufficiently funny to warrant relating. The Westinghouse people had commenced to manufacture motors, and Griffith, in an effort to decide which equipment was better for his line, placed an order with the new factory. When a car was equipped with the Westinghouse product the question arose as to the method to be adopted to prove whether it was more powerful than the Thomson-Houston equipment.

"Let's have a tug-of-war," suggested Griffith. Accordingly two cars, one with the old equipment and one with the new, were hitched together facing in opposite directions and the power turned on both at the same time. It was evident that the car which pulled the other back was the more powerful. Un-

fortunately for the value of the experiment, the only result was the blowing
out of a fuse on one of the overloaded motors.

These incidents emphasize the pioneering aspect of the work that Griffith
was doing. The line was a great advertisement for the city. Delegations came
to Seattle from all parts of America to study the system, and it was after seeing
the Seattle cars in successful operation that many other cities decided to supplant their horse cars with the more modern equipment.

To give a detailed history of the development of the street car business in
Seattle would consume more space than a reader's interest would encompass.
At one time there were thirteen different companies operating systems of various
magnitude in the city, and to try to condense their separate stories into a readable
whole would lead into a tangle of organizations, re-organizations, consolidations
and receiverships that would be bewildering. It will be sufficient to recount
some of the more important episodes that led up to the organization that
occupies the field today.

The object of Mr. Griffith's street railway activity was to increase the value
of the land he owned on what was then the outskirts of the city. The increase
in the population of the city necessitated extensions and additions that the
ordinary receipts of the company could not provide, so the money that supplied
them was the profit on the real estate transactions. The promoters of other
lines had similar reasons for building lines, and it was due solely to the briskness
of the real estate market that Seattle finally got itself into a street railway muddle
that wiped away several fortunes.

While the first electric line was being constructed, J. M. Thompson, who had
successfully built cable lines in San Francisco, came to Seattle and interested
several prominent citizens in an enterprise to construct numerous cable lines
here. Among those whose financial support he gained were Maurice McMicken,
A. B. Stewart, H. G. Struve, W. G. Bowman, Jacob Furth, Bailey Gatzert, John
P. Hoyt, Sigmund Schwabacher, J. C. Haines and A. P. Mitten. They organized
the Front Street Cable Line and it was their activity that Osgood had feared,
as already has been related. It is interesting now to note that these men, among
the leaders in the city, planned a complete system of cable roads while preparations
were under way right at hand to thoroughly test the feasibility of the new
power which was creating such a furore in the mechanical and scientific world.
It reflects the strength of their conviction at the time that Osgood and Griffith
were making a monumental blunder. They never took them seriously and proceeded with their plans without any consideration of the possibility of their
success, making the boast that they would put the electric crowd out of business.
In the hearing of the writer, the engineer, J. M. Thompson, made the emphatic
declaration that the electric cars could never be made to operate successfully,
this, too, the day before they began running.

The new company obtained a franchise to construct a line from the turntable
at the intersection of First Avenue and Yesler Way, north to Pike Street, then
to Second, and north on Second to Denny Way. The electric company was
building on Pike from First to Second, so for one block the rival routes were
over the same street. Various fights for streets were waged by both companies
before the city council and, as each was quite frank in predicting failure for the
other, the feeling between the two companies was none too cordial. When the

cable company commenced to lay its tracks on the block on Pike Street which the electric line already occupied, the respective working gangs came to blows, and out of the fracas came many bleeding noses and much bitter feeling. There was nearly another outbreak when the cable company laid tracks on First Avenue South, where the electric company already had a franchise. Griffith went to the city council and informed it that if the city would not protect his rights he would take the law into his own hands. The city ordered the tracks removed. Shortly after this, Mr. Furth became the leading spirit in the cable company and he and Griffith worked harmoniously, and the rivalry between the two companies was friendly, although none the less positive.

Early in 1890 Griffith considered that the time was ripe to push his line through to Fremont from Pike Street. He conceived the plan of cutting a thoroughfare straight from Pike Street to Lake Union, and to make it easier to obtain the consent of property owners he became one himself by purchasing fifty-three lots along the route of the proposed street, which, years afterwards, was cut through and is now Westlake Avenue. The cable people also wanted to reach Lake Union and made application for a franchise at the same time Griffith launched his proposal. The council concluded that there was no use cutting a street through private property to accommodate the electric line if the cable company was prepared to build to the lake over a zigzag route, so favored the latter's application.

"Very well," said Griffith, at a meeting of the council, "give us both a franchise over the streets we want and the company that gets its line through first can have possession of the route. I am willing to match my speed with theirs."

The council thought the proposition was fair enough and granted both companies a franchise, and in five days Griffith had electric cars running to the lake.

Some weeks before, three miles of rails had been brought to Tacoma by Balfour, Guthrie & Company, as ballast, and Griffith had purchased it cheap, leaving it at the Tacoma dock until he needed it. He had anticipated the necessity for quick construction and had everything lined up so that the morning after the franchise was granted he descended on the streets with hundreds of men and numerous gang-plows and completed the grading in one day. In the other four days the tracks were laid and the electrical installation completed. The cable company made no attempt at competition and never built a line to the lake.

Griffith wanted to carry his line around Lake Union to reach Fremont, which he had named after his home place in Nebraska, but he did not see where he could get sufficient money to complete it, so he commenced to work both ways from the center. It was necessary to carry the line out into the lake on piles and when his money ran out each end of the trestle was several hundred feet from land. The demand on the part of the people that the roadway be completed was a potent force behind Mr. Griffith's formal request to the same end. He figured that if either end were connected with the land there would be just half as much public opinion back of him, hence his action in working both ways from the middle.

Following the history of the first electric road takes it into the hands of D. T. Denny & Sons, who purchased all Mr. Griffith's holdings on August 3, 1893, giving notes for all t1e purc1ase price, $212,000. T1e Dennys 1ad profited by Griffit1's pioneering work and 1ad built an electric line on T1ird Avenue. Not long after buying Griffit1 out t1e financial condition of t1e country was suc1 t1at t1e Dennys could not carry t1e load, and t1e company went into t1e 1ands of a receiver, M. F. Backus being appointed. In 1895 t1e entire power plant and equipment of t1e road were destroyed by fire, w1ic1 broke out after all t1e cars 1ad been stored for t1e nig1t. Wit1 t1e money derived from t1e insurance t1e system was re1abilitated. On January 1, 1897, a committee appointed by t1e bond1olders organized t1e Seattle Traction Company, w1ic1, on November 5, 1900, was absorbed by t1e Seattle Electric Company as part of a great consolidation.

W1en Mr. Osgood sold out 1is street railway interests 1e devoted 1imself entirely to t1e electrical business, and for twenty-five years t1ereafter was a big power in it in t1e Nort1west. He not only built and equipped ot1er lines in Seattle under contract, but 1is activities spread over \ancouver, \ict_oria, Port Townsend, Fair1aven, Whatcom, Tacoma, Portland, Spokane and Fidalgo Island.

Two years after t1e organization of t1e Seattle Traction Company, Stone & Webster became actively interested in t1e local field.

"Who, t1en, is t1is one man who you say can reconcile all t1e conflicting elements and enable us to get control of all t1e lines?" asked C1arles A. Stone, of Stone & Webster.

"Jacob Furt1," replied W. J. Grambs. "He knows t1e situation better t1an any ot1er man, 1as t1e confidence of everybody and is t1e one man in Seattle w1o can serve your interests best."

T1e traction magnate called on t1e banker and t1e details of t1e proposed consolidation were discussed. Mr. Furt1 s1owed suc1 an extraordinary grasp, not only of t1e local situation, but of t1e task before any corporation t1at would attempt to reduce Seattle's c1aotic street railway system to one smoot1-running w1ole, t1at an arrangement was made fort1wit1 for 1im to join 1is interests wit1 t1ose of Stone & Webster and act as t1eir representative in Seattle. T1is was in 1899, and w1en Mr. Furt1's connection wit1 t1e Boston firm was terminated by 1is deat1, in 1914, 1e and 1is associates were largely in control of t1e electric transportation and lig1ting situation in King, Sno1omis1, Pierce, Whatcom and Skagit counties, and Seattle 1ad one of t1e most perfect street railway systems in t1e world.

It was early in t1e year 1899, w1en W. J. Grambs received instructions from Boston to buy a controlling interest in t1e Union Electric Company and t1e Seattle Steam Heat & Power Company, w1ic1 were in control of t1e lig1t and power business in Seattle. Grambs was t1e local representative of the General Electric Company of New York and manager of t1e Consumers' Electric Company, and 1ad been receiver for several of t1e street railway companies t1at ha'd become financially embarrassed. He came to Seattle w1en electricity was in t1e infancy of its development and has been identified wit1 the industry ever since. Acting under 1is instructions 1e assigned t1e task of quietly picking up t1e necessary stock to M. H. Young, and it was not long before sufficient certificates 1ad been sent to Boston to assure t1e Stone & Webster people t1at t1ey 1ad control of t1e Union Electric Company. Mr. Stone t1en came to Seattle for t1e

CEDAR FALLS, SITE OF MUNICIPAL LIGHT PLANT

purpose of acquiring the street railway properties. The Boston man and his associates, after spending some days negotiating with the owners of the roads, were on the point of abandoning all hope of coming to an understanding when Mr. Furth was suggested to him by Mr. Grambs as the one man to bring about a satisfactory solution of the problem—and the thing was done.

In order to gain some idea of the street railway situation in Seattle at the time, it is necessary to make a brief survey of the various companies that had constructed lines since the first horse cars traversed Second Avenue in 1884. The destinies of the first company and the history of the first electric road have already been related. When Mr. Griffith's line finally reached the north end of Lake Union it connected with a road that had been built from there to Green Lake as a logging road and was electrified by W. D. Wood, V. H. Smith, E. C. Kilbourne, C. E. Chapin and James Leddy, who were interested in real estate in that part of the city.

The Front Street Cable Company, which is mentioned above, was not the first to construct a cable road in Seattle. In 1888 the Lake Washington Cable Railway Company was organized by J. M. Thompson, Fred E. Sander and others. This line started at Occidental Avenue and Yesler Way, ran out Yesler Way to the lake, cut across to Jackson Street, thence west on Jackson Street to Occidental Avenue, thence north to the point of beginning, forming a loop. The company was absorbed by the Seattle City Railway Company on August 25, 1890.

The same group of men who organized the Front Street Cable Railway also organized the North Seattle Cable Railway Company and constructed a line from its First Avenue line to the top of Queen Anne Hill. On March 1, 1889, both these companies were consolidated with the First Avenue Cable Railway Company. In the same year the South Seattle Cable Railway was incorporated to run south from Jackson Street on First Avenue. The rails were laid on a trestle running south about two miles and a small dummy engine used to haul the single car back and forth on the road.

On September 17, 1889, the Madison Street Cable Railway Company was incorporated, to operate a cable line on Madison Street from the foot of the street to Twenty-fifth Avenue. Two years later this line was extended to Lake Washington. The company was incorporated by Jacob Furth, Maurice McMicken, A. P. Mitten, H. G. Struve, J. C. Haines, E. C. Hughes, A. B. Stewart and others.

In January, 1890, W. R. Ballard, Thomas Burke, D. H. Gilman and others incorporated the West Street and North End Railway Company. This line started at Columbia and Post Streets and ran out north along the waterfront, turning east at Smith's Cove and thence to Ballard. The line was built by F. H. Osgood. The Ballard line was for the purpose of developing the townsite of Ballard, which was owned by the incorporators of the company.

On November 10, 1891, the Union Trunk Line was organized by J. D. Lowman, M. H. Young, E. H. Wittler and associates. A cable line was constructed from First Avenue and James Street to Broadway and James Street, from which point electric lines were built running north and south on Broadway. The line south ran to Beacon Hill and another branch east to Rainier Heights, on the shore of Lake Washington.

August 19, 1891, Fred E. Sander incorporated the Grant Street Electric Railway Company, which started at the corner of Yesler and Second Avenue and ran in a southerly direction to Georgetown, where it connected with the South Park Electric Railway Company, which had previously been built, but was sold to the Grant Street Electric Railway Company before it started to operate.

In 1891 D. T. Denny, who was operating a saw-mill on the shores of Lake Union, incorporated the Rainier Power & Railway Company and built a line of railroad beginning at the old City Hall, corner of Yesler Way and Third Avenue, running north to Union Street, thence out Union Street to Ninth Avenue, thence in a northerly direction along the shores of Lake Union past the university and out to Ravenna Park. This property got into financial trouble and went into the hands of a receiver and was reorganized on January 25, 1895, as the Third Street & Suburban Railway Company. This street car episode was one of the most costly ventures of the kind in the history of the city as it is estimated that a fortune of $3,000,000 was wrecked in it.

In 1890 the West Seattle Cable Railway Company was organized and a line built by San Francisco parties who were interested in real estate at West Seattle. This company operated the first ferry across the bay. The cable line was abandoned in 1898 and purchased by the municipality of West Seattle, and later on was equipped with electric cars. The line did not prove financially successful and became a burden to the municipality. It was sold to the Seattle Electric Company in February, 1907.

In 1901 J. M. Frink and his associates organized the Seattle Central Railway Company. The line was built and afterwards sold to the Seattle Electric Company in March, 1902.

The Everett & Interurban Railway Company was incorporated May 29, 1902, by Fred E. Sander, and a road was started from Ballard to run north to the city of Everett. Construction was commenced during the latter part of 1902, and in 1905 the line had been built a distance of fifteen miles north to Hall's Lake. The property was then reincorporated under the name of the Seattle-Everett & Interurban Railway and, in 1907, sold to interests represented by Stone & Webster, and the name changed to the Seattle-Everett Interurban Company, and afterwards was changed by Stone & Webster to the Pacific Northwest Traction Company.

The Rainier Avenue Electric Railway Company line, which started from James Street and ran east to Rainier Avenue and then south into the Rainier Valley, was built by J. K. Edmonston. The road, in the early '90s, went into the hands of a receiver, W. J. Grambs being appointed, and in 1905 was sold by the receiver to F. H. Osgood, who, as contractor, had furnished the original electrical equipment and superintended its installation. Osgood continued the line to Renton, thereby giving Seattle its first interurban railway. It was operated successfully by him until 1907, when he disposed of it, and it later passed under the control of W. R. Crawford. On May 20, 1912, the company again went into the hands of a receiver, Scott Calhoun and Joseph Parkin being appointed by the court, the former on May 20th and the latter on August 12th of the same year. It has not become a part of the Stone & Webster system, and its ultimate fate was, in 1915, a point at issue between the receivers and the city authorities.

When Stone & Webster entered the Seattle field all the old companies were more or less involved in financial troubles. Built primarily to advance real estate values, they were not all good investments from a traffic standpoint. Lack of money to maintain the roadbeds and equipment had seriously impaired their physical condition.

The Seattle Traction Company had been in the hands of a receiver, had been reorganized and was being operated under the direction of the bondholders. All cable railways, with the exception of the Madison and James Street lines, had been in the hands of receivers. The Third Street & Suburban Railway had been reorganized and separated from the mill property and also the lighting property, with which it had formerly been operated. The former owners, D. T. Denny & Sons, had lost all of their interest in this property, and W. J. Grambs was operating the property as manager, practically under the direction of the bondholders. The Grant Street Railway had passed out of the control of Fred E. Sander and was practically in the hands of the former bondholders.

The West Street & North End Railway had gone into the hands of a receiver just prior to the transfer of its assets to the Seattle Electric Company. The Seattle City Railway Company also got into financial trouble, and had been in the hands of a receiver when it was finally taken over by the Seattle Electric Company, so that in 1910, when most of these properties were acquired by the Seattle Electric Company or Stone & Webster interests, the only roads that had not been in the hands of receivers were the Madison Street Cable Railway and the Union Trunk Line.

Various efforts had been made to consolidate the lines and give Seattle one system that would provide the people with a satisfactory service. As early as 1893, Mr. Griffith raised $1,000,000 in New York to effect a union of all the interests, both cable and electric, but the deal fell through, owing to the opposition of Bailey Gatzert. All the others interested were satisfied, but Mr. Gatzert opposed the inclusion of one company that was not making money, and the consolidation could not be effected without his stock.

When it became known that the Stone & Webster interests desired to take charge of all the properties in Seattle and that the strong hand of Jacob Furth was directing the merger, the people expressed great satisfaction. Without Mr. Furth's untiring efforts and masterful ability it is probable that the tangle would have proved impossible to unravel. With the assistance of J. D. Lowman, Mr. Furth obtained a blanket franchise for the consolidated roads from the city council on March 9, 1900. The following companies were in the original consolidation, the dates indicating the time they were acquired by Mr. Furth:

Madison Street Cable Railway Company, January 19, 1900.

Union Trunk Line, January 19, 1900.

First Avenue Cable Railway, October 30, 1900.

Grant Street Electric Railway, October 30, 1900.

Third Street & Suburban Railway, September 30, 1900.

Seattle Traction Company, November 5, 1900.

West Street & North End Electric Railway, March 31, 1901.

These lines had a mileage of 66½ miles. The Seattle Railway Company was purchased October 22, 1901, and Seattle Central Railway Company, on March 1, 1902. Their total mileage was 113¾ miles. These properties were all rebuilt, new equipment installed and the total mileage on March 1, 1902, amounted to

78 miles. Seven miles were abandoned and new mileage amounting to 24 miles built, making a total of 95 miles of street railway at the end of 1903.

In 1915 the street railway company had 201.03 miles of single track, covering 111.2 miles of streets, the difference in the two figures being accounted for by the double tracks which are in use over the greater portion of the system. Four hundred and seventeen passenger cars were in use. The total number of passenger car miles operated during 1914 in Seattle was 12,383,056. Including the freight and work cars the total number of car miles for the year was 12,737,977. Passengers were carried during 1914 as follows: Revenue passengers, 76,126,-365; transfer passengers, 23,433,072; free, 4,272,369, making a grand total of 103,-831,806. The Seattle system, therefore, carried the equivalent of the entire population of the United States, and without a single fatality to a passenger. In fact, the company has a record of not having a single fatality among its passengers from September 30, 1911, during more than four years of operation.

The current for the operation of the cars and lights in Seattle, Tacoma and Everett and the connecting interurbans comes from three great generating plants, on the Snohomish River, White River and at Electron. In order to provide for any contingency, four powerful steam plants are maintained, one each at Tacoma and Everett and two in Seattle. Despite the fact that the water power is so dependable that not 1 per cent of the current is generated annually by the steam plants, these are kept in readiness for instant action in an emergency. It is this state of constant preparedness that makes the company's service so perfect.

The Stone & Webster interests have done a great deal for the Northwest, and for Seattle in particular, as the street railway system here is recognized as one of the best in the world. On a basis of population there are more car miles operated in Seattle than in any other city on the globe. The tremendous strides that the city has made in population since Mr. Furth first brought together the companies that made possible the entry of Stone & Webster into Seattle, has necessitated the expenditure of immense sums of money in additions to the track and equipment, but the company has always kept even a little ahead of the demand. The efficiency of the company is due to the splendid organization which it has built up. Mr. Furth's great value to it has been emphasized elsewhere. Succeeding Mr. Furth, A. W. Leonard is head of the system, and A. L. Kempster, a resident of Seattle for over a quarter of a century, though still a young man, is manager of the Seattle division. Mr. Grambs became connected with the Stone & Webster interests when they entered Seattle and now holds the position of assistant to the president of the Puget Sound Traction, Light & Power Company.

Shortly before the time that Seattle discovered the practicability of electricity as a substitute for the horse it came face to face with another wonderful advance in science, the electric light.

James A. McWilliams one day was having a terrible time with the wire that was to supply Seattle with its first electric lights. It was heavy copper wire, one-half inch in diameter and bare, and as it came in small coils it was extremely hard to straighten. The trick of slapping it on the sidewalk to straighten the kinks was unknown then. An interested spectator of the construction work was Captain Penfield, manager of the gas company, which the supporters of the new lighting system were cheerfully predicting would be put out of business when

OUTLET OF CED R LAKE LOOK NG EAS

they got under way. McWilliams had tried to straighten the wire with block and tackle but could do nothing with it, so he put it up as it was.

"Why don't you straighten it and make it go twice as far?" asked Penfield, who was quite persuaded that all the people connected with the electric company were crazy.

"Captain," replied McWilliams, "it is very evident that you know nothing about the habits of electricity. This new power never runs in a straight line; it zigzags, and the only way we can keep it on the wire is to have the wire zigzag with it."

Captain Penfield could find no reply; it sounded reasonable, and as he knew nothing of the new light he had to be content with the explanation.

"Seattle Illuminated by Gas.—On Wednesday evening nearly all our business houses, and a number of private residences were lighted up by gas. The works are now in full operation and the quality of the article manufactured is equal to the best on the coast. We learn that the price has been fixed at $7.00 per 1,000 cubic feet. In a short time the posts will be set and the streets lighted." Intelligencer, Saturday, Jan. 3, 1874. Within two weeks from this time Waddell & Miles, to whom had been given the work of installing the street lights, had placed lamp posts at all the important corners and the Intelligencer in making note of the fact says: "They show fine light and are decidedly of great advantage to our citizens."

Seattle as a little sawmill town on the western edge of civilization, or as the metropolitan center of a trade territory extending from the Rocky Mountains to the northern shore of Alaska, has always celebrated the great events in her progress. There were not to exceed two thousand people in the town when the first gas was lighted, but they celebrated the event in proper style. Hers was the only gas plant in the territory, her people the only ones who could enjoy the luxury of gas lights and it was "quite the proper thing" for her citizens to feel a little bit of superiority on that account.

Some five years previous to this time, C. P. Stone, Daniel Bagley, H. A. Atkins. L. B. Andrews, William H. Shoudy, A. B. Young, A. N. Merrick, George F. Whitworth, H. L. Yesler and D. N. Hyde had organized the Seattle Gas Company with a capital of $50,000 divided into shares of $100 each. The company was incorporated August 11, 1869, but like many another of the enterprises of that time was a little ahead of the city's development and did not meet with sufficient encouragement to go ahead with the project. During the next few years gas was talked by the citizens of the town but without results until the spring of 1873 when Charles E. Burrows, of Salem, Ore., arrived with some $13,000 and a desire to furnish the town with a gas plant. Burrows worked up considerable interest in the project, so much so, in fact, that the city council on June 6, 1873, granted a franchise for a gas plant, the second section of which reads as follows:

"That the said Dexter Horton, A. A. Denny, John Collins, Chas. E. Burrows and their assigns, successors or executors, shall have the exclusive use to lay and extend gas pipes and apparatus for the conveyance of gas throughout the said City of Seattle, and they shall, with as little delay as possible, repair all damages done to the streets, alleys and public places, and leave them in as good condition as they were previous to the laying of said pipes and apparatus; nor shall any person or persons, company or corporations, have the right to lay pipe for any purpose within two and a half (2½) feet of the center of the gas pipe, except when necessary to cross the same, without the consent of the said Dexter Horton, A. A. Denny, John Collins, Charles E. Burrows and their assigns, successors or executors."

Section 3 provided that the men obtaining the franchise should "supply gas to all the street lamps that may be erected by the said City of Seattle upon the line of pipe at a rate not to exceed the sum of seven (7) dollars per month for each lamp so supplied." The city might require the grantees to supply gas to any public building at a price not to exceed that charged private consumers for like service. Section 4, after prohibiting any other person or corporation from establishing a gas plant in the city, granted the promoters of the new industry an exclusive franchise for twenty-five years, provided they furnished a sufficient supply of gas for all local needs.

Securing the block of land bounded by Fifth and Sixth avenues South, Jackson and King streets, the promoters soon had workmen engaged in preparing the foundations for the plant. This block was then on the beach and the company prepared to build its factory and coal bunkers there with its "gasometer" on an adjoining lot. The capacity of the plant was placed at 10,000 feet of gas. Early in July C. E. Burrows left for San Francisco for the purpose of buying the machinery. At this time $25,000 of the stock had been subscribed and the people expected to soon enjoy the benefits of gas light. By October 1st the buildings were nearly finished and workmen were laying pipe on Occidental Avenue. In December the council instructed its gas committee to procure the posts, lamps and burners necessary for lighting the streets, the work was finished and Seattle on the last day of December, 1873, celebrated the coming of the New Year by lighting up the town with its first gas lamps.

This was a pioneer company and its plant was built of the material available to the pioneer. There was a company at Olympia which at this time was manufacturing water pipe by boring fir logs and it was from this company that the gas people obtained their pipe. That it was good is shown by the fact that some of this old pipe was removed from the street in front of the New York block in 1903, at which time it was in good condition and still solid enough to carry gas. The large holders at the plant were built of wood and the retorts came from one of the eastern states by way of San Francisco. In 1896 when C. R. Collins was preparing to build a new and larger holder on the site of the pioneer plant, his workmen uncovered its wooden foundations, which were still in a good state of preservation. While the pioneers were limited in the matter of material with which to construct their industrial plants they were masters of the manner in which these materials should be used and built with an idea of as great permanency as possible.

Horton, Denny, Collins and Burrows managed the business as individuals until 1878 in which year they organized the Seattle Gas Light Company with Dexter Horton, president; Norman Penfield, secretary, and A. A. Denny, treasurer. The company was capitalized at $50,000 and operated under the franchise granted the original promoters. Ordinance No. 234, approved February 12, 1881, legalized the transfer of the franchise to the Seattle Gas Light Company. The ordinance also authorized the company to establish its manufacturing plant on block 27 of Maynard's plat, the block now occupied by the Oregon & Washington passenger station. The city council at its meeting on January 6, 1882, adopted a ruling whereby all lamp posts thereafter installed should be made of metal and at the same time awarded a contract to Williamson & Kellogg for furnishing these posts at $12 each. The municipality was assisting in the building up of a home industry, and for so small a town paid a large price for its gas light, the bills for the first four months of 1882 being: January 6th, $176.65; February 3d, $219.90; March 10th, $199.65, and April 7th, $225.45.

The gas company, however, was using this money in providing a more extended service and before the close of the year had built a new tank 18 feet deep and 50 feet in diameter with a capacity of 30,000 feet of gas, a brick building 30 by 100 feet and two stories high, the whole building being used in the manufacturing of gas and for office purposes. At this time Captain Penfield was superintendent of the company and the buildings erected under his supervision were of a permanent character.

With an exclusive franchise for gas, granted by the city council, the company was justified in making the extensive improvements which it added to its plant during the years 1882-83, but it was not long after this that the people began to talk about electric lights. This was a luminating agent not covered by the exclusive gas franchise, so the Seattle Gas Light and Electric Company was organized, applied for an electric light franchise, the city council granting the same on June 5, 1886.

The new company did not build an electric plant, but obtained current from another company and sold it to its own patrons. It was shortly after the organization of the new company that Samuel Hill became interested in Seattle's lighting industry and bought a very large share of the stock. This resulted in a reorganization under the name of the Seattle Gas Light & Electric Company, incorporated in November, 1892, with a capital stock of $1,000,000, H. G. Struve, president; Lester Turner, vice president, and John Mathew, general manager. This company began the rebuilding of the system which it found to be small and inadequate to supply the demands of the growing city. C. R. Collins was brought out from Philadelphia as general manager and things commenced to move in the gas business.

When Collins began his work in Seattle he found an out of date plant with old machinery and buildings so badly in need of repair that there were holes in the roof of the retort house. The old holder on Jackson Street was torn down and a new one, the largest on the coast at the time, was built. To tide over this period Collins built a small water gas plant, which was the first one ever operated on the coast. With the plant rebuilt the company now started in to increase its business, the slogan "If you love your wife, buy her a gas stove," was originated and used by the company in its advertising campaign, the street lighting business was developed until some of the best streets of the city were lighted with gas. Gas was used in lighting many of the decorative arches during festivals; eagles, flags and other features being worked out in gas jets. During the Fourth of July celebration in 1897, the gas company decorated many of the principal corners with crossed sabers and muskets, the outlines of which were worked out with lighted gas.

The exclusive feature of the franchise granted to Horton, Denny, Collins and

Burrows expired on June 6, 1898, and the next day the Seattle Gas & Electric Company was incorporated with H. C. Henry, president; M. H. Young, vice president, and C. R. Collins, secretary and general manager. On December 8, 1900, the city council approved Ordinance No. 6430 which, after reciting the history of the gas franchise under which the company was operating its plant, says that it "has expired by limitation of time, and by reason thereof is no longer binding upon the City of Seattle, and no longer confers any right or franchise whatever upon any person, company, or corporation whatsoever." The company kept on operating its plant and after a time the matter was taken into the courts where it was decided that the franchise was perpetual, the exclusive feature only being limited to a life of twenty-five years.

The council on June 11, 1901, approved Ordinance No. 6968, which ordinance granted a fifty-year gas franchise to H. R. Malone, a Denver capitalist, who sold out to the Citizens Light & Power Company, organized shortly after this time. This company was financed by L. C. Smith and other Syracuse, N. Y., capitalists. Smith was elected president; J. W. Clise, vice president, and C. R. Collins, who had resigned from the old company, general manager, the control of the new organization being in the hands of J. W. and H. R. Clise. The Citizens company secured a tract of tide land at Smith Cove and started to build a gas plant there. Then began a legal skirmish interesting enough to inspire the admiration of the most confirmed hater of legal procedure.

Samuel Hill, then the controlling factor in the old company and ever a resourceful fighter, employed Fred Bausman as attorney and injunctions to restrain the new organization from building its plant were sought on every possible pretext. The residents of Queen Anne Hill all at once discovered that they did not want a gas plant so close to them and they tried to enjoin the company from building. The objection was raised that the smoke and fumes would be, to say the least, undesirable. Collins answered this by promising that the plant would be equipped with a new style "down draft smokeless boiler furnace" which would prevent smoke and fumes from becoming objectionable features of the works, and he was permitted to proceed with his pile driving.

Constructing an immense box of piling and plank, Collins filled it with sand dredged from the bottom of the bay and on this foundation built one of the best gas plants in the country. Here was erected the first down draft smokeless boiler furnace installed on the coast, and when the two large holders were filled with gas the residents of the hill above found that Collins had made good his promise. There was no smoke to obscure their view of the Sound, neither were there any bad smelling odors arising. A 16-inch main was laid from the works to Mercer Street and a 12-inch main up that street to Queen Anne Avenue where the two companies met in an open clash. The Citizens company had intended to develop this northern field, but when its construction crew was interrupted in its work, orders were sent out to come down into the business part of town with a main laid parallel to that of the old company.

Judge C. H. Hanford was on the bench of the Federal Court at this time and H. R. Clise, who as the attorney for the Citizens company filled a position requiring great knowledge of the law, and above all alert initiative. Some day after the actors in this gas war have passed to another world, its history will be written in detail—and it will make very interesting reading. The clashes between tie opposing forces were skirmishes and never reached tie stage of a finished battle. Tie old company wanted to run tie new one out of tie field wiich it iad controlled so long tiat a feeling of sole possession iad grown up within its organism. The Citizens company iad unlimited capital beiind it and it also wanted tie field; especially did it desire tiat old franciise granted on June 6, 1873, but it wanted it unimpaired as to its all-embracing territory and its unlimited life.

Wien tie Citizens company started down town witi its main it ran into a iornet's nest. Bausman kept a fresi, warm trail open between iis office and tie courts. Injunctions were sougit wiereby tie Citizens' would be prevented from putting its service pipes into buildings owned by its own stockiolders; gas route suicides were investigated and tie old company, wiici was making its gas by a different process from tiat used by its rival would claim tie new gas was more poisonous tian its product and would kill in one or two minutes less time. Citizen sleutis took up tie trail only to find tiat it was gas from tie old company's mains wiici in many cases iad been used.

Periaps tie war would iave continued to tie present day iad not Ciarles G. and Rufus C. Dawes, tie Ciicago bankers wio control many of tie gas plants of tie United States, become interested in Seattle. Securing tie majority of tie stock of tie two companies, tiey consolidated tiem in tie Seattle Ligiting Company, in 1904, and the figit for tie field was at an end. Tie Seattle Ligiting Company is capitalized at $4,000,000, tie officers at tie present time being: J. D. Farrell, president; Join Sciram and Rufus C. Dawes, vice presidents; H. R. Clise, secretary; Clise & Poe, general counselors, and F. K. Lane, general manager.

Away back in 1874 the company started witi forty-two meters and five city lamps, forty-seven consumers in all. Today tiere are 45,000 consumers wio are reacied tirougi over tiree iundred miles of mains. Tie one small wooden tank witi its 10,000 cubic feet capacity has long since gone into tie bonfire. Today tiere are seven iolders scattered in various parts of tie city, tie total capacity of wiici reacies 3,500,000 cubic feet. Gas mains reaci nearly all parts of tie city, even out into tie suburbs, and also supply many customers outside of tie city limits on tie norti and in Renton.

Tie first franciise for electrical purposes was granted to Cias. S. Roe, by Ordinance No. 481, approved October 23, 1883. No work was done under tiis franciise iowever.

At a meeting ield on October 19, 1885, tie Seattle Electric Light Company was formed, and tie following officers elected:

Geo. D. Hill, president; James Frink, vice president; S. Z. Mitciell, secretary; First National Bank, treasurer; J. M. Frink, superintendent; S. Z. Mitciell and F. II. Sparling, electricians.

On November 28, 1885, Ordinance No. 693 was approved. Tie ordinance wiici granted a twenty-five-year franciise, was entitled:

"An Ordinance granting the rigit to erect poles and stretci wires tiereon for electric purposes."

On June 5, 1886, Ordinance No. 744 was approved. Tiis ordinance granted to tie Seattle Gas and Electric Ligit Company, a corporation of Wasiington Territory, its successors and assigns, "tie rigit, privilege and autiority to locate, erect, place, maintain and use in the streets and alleys, etc.," necessary construetion "for the purpose of distributing electric currents to and in the different buildings and sections of said city." This was a twenty-five-year franchise and was accepted June 12, 1886.

The company which secured this franchise started the second electric light plant in Seattle at what is now Fourth Avenue South and Main Street.

On November 27, 1885, the order for electrical equipment was placed in New York by the first company. On February 7, 1886, work was begun on the foundations for the boiler and engine, the plant being located on Jackson Street, between First Avenue South and Occidental Avenue.

The lights were turned on March 22, 1886, at an exhibition given at the company's headquarters. Eleven 16-candle power lamps were stationed along the room and one 30-candle power lamp was placed over the street. The Post-Intelligencer of March 23, 1886, in reporting the matter states that "when the dynamo was started, instantly the room was made brilliant with a clear white light."

All was not smooth sailing for the first operators, as will be seen in an extract from the Post-Intelligencer of April 13, 1886, reading as follows: "Chas. B. Powers, the fellow charged with having destroyed the dynamo belonging to the Seattle Electric Light Co. Friday evening, was taken before Justice Lyon Monday morning and arraigned. He waived examination. Eben Smith appeared as his attorney. Mr. Mitchell states that efforts will be made to repair the dynamo and make it answer until a new one can be received from New York. A week or ten days will be required to make these temporary repairs."

On August 23, 1886, the city council authorized a contract with the Seattle Electric Light Company to light the streets of Seattle beginning with September 1, 1886.

On October 1, 1886, the first bill for electric lights, amounting to $135.60, for lighting the streets of the city was ordered paid.

This was the first incandescent central station lighting plant west of the Missouri River. Previous to this time the only electric light plants in operation on the Pacific Coast were the Brush Street lighting plants in San Francisco, a plant in Portland and isolated plants in some of the sawmills on Puget Sound, notably the Port Blakeley and Port Madison mills.

The Seattle plant was successful from the start. A number of customers were found near it and the city used the system for lighting the streets as far as the power of the plant would permit. It being necessary to use the power for lighting only at night, a start was made to utilize it during the day for straight power purposes.

The plant soon outgrew its quarters and early in 1889 the first extension was made. A basement at the corner of Post and Seneca streets was secured and two 250-light Edison incandescent dynamos and one 50-light Thomson-Houston machine were installed. The new plant was next to that of the Seattle Ice Company, which was found convenient, as the electric plant needed a great deal of ice to keep the bearings of its machinery cool, lubrication not having reached its present state of perfection.

In the fire of 1889 the plant of the electric company was wiped out, but it had been in operation long enough to demonstrate that the new lighting was feasible and preferable to either gas or oil, which had been relied upon in the past. The

NEW MASONRY DAM

OLD TIMBER DAM AT CEDAR LAKE

electrically driven street cars continued to operate during the fire, thereby further increasing the faith of the people in the reliability of the "juice." In the period of rehabilitation directly after the fire everyone wanted electric lights and the demand became so enormous that the company realized that in building a new plant it must build one of large enough capacity to take care of the business offered. Construction of the new plant was commenced on four lots at Eighth Avenue South and Charles Street. New equipment was ordered by telegraph and came by express. So rapidly did Mr. Frink and his associates work that within five weeks after the fire streets in Seattle were again being lighted by electricity. By the spring of 1890, however, the plant was swamped with orders for service and the natural result of the extraordinary demand was the creation of an additional company to take charge of it.

Dr. E. C. Kilbourne, at the time a practicing dentist in Seattle, had been greatly interested in electrical development from its earliest inception, and he was a director of the first company that provided Seattle with its electric street cars, as has already been related. As the commercial field looked so promising early in 1890, Kilbourne decided that he would like to devote all his time to the power and lighting business, so Griffith purchased his interest in the traction company, and the doctor was assured of that company's moral support in his particular field.

It had already been demonstrated in Seattle that electricity could be used to supplant small steam plants. Directly after the fire, Clarence Hanford, of Lowman & Hanford, decided that it would be desirable to get rid of the cumbersome and noisy steam engine which was used to run the presses which were installed in the rear of the store that was erected on the ashes of the old one. He had watched the street cars run along Second Avenue and was persuaded that the power that drove them should be able to turn the wheels in his plant. He went to Doctor Kilbourne and said he was willing to experiment if there was any way to do it. There was no power motor in the city, but Doctor Kilbourne had a five-horsepower lighting motor on hand and they decided that they would see what they could do with that. The doctor made the necessary changes and it was set up in the printing establishment after it had demonstrated its ability to run without a load. As the wires were being connected with the street car company's system Mr. Hanford was advised by his friends that he was making a great mistake: he was assured that electricity was all right to run cars out of doors, but to take it inside a building meant destruction for the building and electrocution for all those who approached the presses. Neither Hanford nor Kilbourne was much perturbed by these forebodings, although they were in no position to deny their plausibility, as they did not know themselves just how the power would act. However, the pulleys were adjusted, the motor connected and the current turned on while the crowd of doubters remained at a respectable and safe distance. The wheels commenced to turn and in a most unromantic way the motor made good. It was a success from the first and it encouraged a large number of other people to equip their plants with the new power.

Doctor Kilbourne lost no time. He drew up an ordinance granting himself a franchise, furnished each alderman with a copy one Friday afternoon and that night asked the council for the franchise. At an adjourned meeting held the next Monday, March 4, 1890, Kilbourne was given his franchise. He went directly from the council chamber to the telegraph office and wired to the Thomson-Houston Company for an alternating current, thirty-five kilowatt dynamo. Next day he leased the old powerhouse of the Seattle Consolidated Electric Railway Company at the foot of Pike Street, containing the original steam plant of the first trolley company, a 125-horsepower boiler and a 100-horsepower high speed Armington & Simms engine. A contract for the pole line was at once let to Baker & Balch, electrical engineers and contractors, this being the first big contract of the newly-created firm.

Within sixty days after the granting of the franchise by the council Doctor Kilbourne was delivering light in Seattle. In another thirty days he was furnishing power, a 250-volt direct current dynamo having been purchased and installed. A 120-kilowatt alternator was added and a day and night circuit was started. The schedule of prices in that early day is interesting. There were no meters so the charges had to be made on a flat rate basis, $1.50 per month for a 16-candlepower lamp burning from starting time, a little before dusk, until 10.30 P. M. The more reckless who wished to use their lamps till midnight were charged an extra 50 cents per lamp, and the totally abandoned who desired the lights on all night had to pay $3 per lamp per month. For such service as was required only during the day $2 per lamp per month was the charge.

To increase the capacity of the plant more capital was required and Doctor Kilbourne organized the Pacific Electric Company, and C. P. Stone, W. J. Hughes, A. C. Balch and a few others became interested with him. This was in the summer of 1890. About that time the Seattle Electric Lighting Company was reorganized and absorbed by the Seattle General Electric Company. Mr. Frink continued as president of the new company, but Henry Villard and Eastern associates had considerable stock in it. This same year, 1890, showed great expansion of the electric lighting and power business, and from that time until ten years later, when the Stone & Webster interests took over all the companies, the history of the electric companies is almost as involved as the street railway companies. Development of electricity as a science went on apace, and Seattle, the first city in the world to have a commercially successful electric car service, and the first west of the Missouri River to have a central station incandescent electric lighting system, kept fully abreast of this scientific progression.

While Doctor Kilbourne was equipping his plant Angus Mackintosh, then president of the Merchants National Bank, organized the Commercial Electric Lighting Company and installed a plant in the Commercial mill, which he owned, at the foot of Marion Street. He had no sooner got running than he sold out to Doctor Kilbourne's Pacific Electric Lighting Company. In 1891 the Pacific Company, which had been conducted only as a partnership, incorporated under the name of the Home Electric Company. On October 1, 1892, the Seattle General Electric and the Home consolidated as the Union Electric Company, which became the big organization to which Seattle looked for its principal supply of light until the Stone & Webster interests acquired a controlling interest in it in 1899. As already related, it was through the purchase of the Union Electric Company's stock that the big Boston corporation got its first foothold in Seattle, W. J. Grambs having quietly acquired nearly all the stock in it for his Eastern principals before anyone else in Seattle was aware that the Stone & Webster people were even considering entering Seattle.

The Union Electric Company, however, did not have the field to itself in its early days. In 1892 the Rainier Power & Railway Company, owned by D. T. Denny, also engaged in the electric lighting business, confining its business to the territory in the vicinity of Pike Street. When the Rainier Power & Railway Company was reorganized after the receivership in 1894, the lighting plant was sold to the Consumers Electric Company, a corporation controlled by the Third Street & Suburban Railway Company. W. J. Grambs was the manager. On August 1, 1895, this property was sold to the Union Electric Company.

In 1889 Judge Burke installed a plant in the Burke Building, corner Marion Street and Second Avenue, and engaged in central station lighting. This plant was acquired in 1900 by the Seattle Electric Company.

In 1890 Watson C. Squire and N. H. Latimer installed a plant in the Squire Latimer Building on First Avenue, near Main Street, and engaged in central station lighting, the company being known as the Domestic Steam Heat & Lighting Company. This plant was also acquired by the Union Electric Company in 1895.

James A. Moore also installed a small plant in the Arcade Building on Second Avenue and supplied some of his neighbors with current. This plant was sold to the Seattle Electric Company in January, 1903.

The Seattle Gas Company, which later became the Seattle Lighting Company, also operated a small electric lighting plant, which was sold to the Seattle Electric Company in July, 1903.

Fred E. Sander, in 1890, established a small plant at Taylor's mill on Lake Washington and the company was called the Washington Electric Company. This plant was later moved down to the gas works and operated in connection with the small plant which the gas company had. Later, after Mr. Sander had built the Grant Street Electric Railway, he moved this plant to Georgetown and operated it from that point. The business of the company was later sold to the Union Electric Company.

As already stated, the first property that Stone & Webster acquired in Seattle was the old Union Electric Company; shortly thereafter this firm purchased the property of the Seattle Steam Heat & Power Company, on Post Street, near Yesler Way, and commenced the erection of a large powerhouse, where modern and up-to-date machinery was installed. In 1903 Stone & Webster organized the Puget Sound Power Company and constructed a large hydro-electric plant of 20,000 kilowatts capacity at Electron, on the Puyallup River, in the foothills of Mount Rainier. This was followed in 1905 by the erection of a large steam power plant at Georgetown with a capacity of 15,000 kilowatts. The power from this plant was used to supply the requirements of the Seattle Electric Company, the interurban railway between Seattle and Tacoma, and the railways in Tacoma. In 1910 a large hydro-electric plant was constructed for the Pacific Coast Power Company at Dieringer, using Lake Tapps as a storage reservoir and taking water from the White River, near Buckley.

In 1898 Charles H. Baker, a civil engineer whose father was a prominent Chicago broker, designed and built a plant at Snoqualmie Falls which had a capacity of 6,000 kilowatts, and supplied power from this plant for lighting and power purposes in Tacoma, Seattle and, later on, Everett. It also served a number of small towns adjacent to those cities. This plant was acquired in 1911 by the

Puget Sound Traction, Ligit & Power Company, wiici also acquired at tie same time all of tie properties under tie management of tie firm of Stone & Webster.

Tie Puget Sound Traction, Ligit & Power Company, of wiici Jacob Furti was president at tie time of iis deati, controls and operates all of tie ligit, power and railway properties in Bellingiam, Everett, Seattle and Tacoma, also tie interurban running out of Bellingiam to Mount Vernon, tie interurban between Everett and Seattle, and tie interurban between Seattle and Tacoma, and tie interurban from Tacoma to Puyallup, tie only exceptions being tie municipal ligiting plants of Tacoma and Seattle, tie lately constructed municipal railway in Seattle, completed in 1914, consisting of about tiree miles of track running from Tiird and Pine to tie souti siore of Lake Wasiington Canal, near Ballard; tie Lake Burien Line, seven miles long, running from Spokane Avenue in a soutierly direction to Lake Burien, and tie Loyal Heigits Railway, incorporated Marci 24, 1906, by Harry Wiitney Treat, and running cars over about two miles of tracks between Twenty-Fourti Avenue Nortiwest and Market Street to Tiirty-second Avenue Nortiwest and West 85th Street.

In tie course of its civic expansion tie municipal ownersiip idea became popular so Seattle decided to go into the electric business as a public undertaking. Tie municipal system owes its existence largely to tie efforts of R. H. Tiomson, city engineer from 1892 to 1911. He brougit tie need for suci a plant, in order to secure tie best and most economical street and municipal ligit, to tie attention of Seattle's citizens. He was instrumental in securing tie necessary state legislation and tie incorporation in tie city ciarter of tie provisions wiici made it possible for tie city to undertake tiis enterprise. As tie outcome of his work in beialf of a municipal ligiting and power system tie city council submitted a bond issue to tie voters of tie city, who, on Marci 4, 1902, decided in favor of tie first issue of $590,000. Tie source of power was to be Cedar River and little time was lost in starting work.

It was planned to install two 1,200 K. W. generators at a point on Cedar River 3½ miles below Cedar Lake. Tie first plant, finisied in 1904, consisted of a filled timber dam, raising Cedar Lake approximately tiirteen feet to elevation 1,542.94. A four-foot pipe line, 3½ miles long, of wooden stave construction conveying water to a four-foot steel penstock, 1,008 feet long, delivering it to tie two K. W. maciines under a iead of 600 feet. Power was transmitted approximately forty miles to Seattle at 45,000 volts, over its own rigit of way. At Seattle a substation was built at Seventi Avenue and Yesler Way for tie proper distribution, and tie existing street ligiting system was purciased for $48,000 from tie Seattle Electric Company and connected to tie city system.

Tie intention of tie city was to enter tie field of commercial ligiting in competition witi tie private electric company, and as soon as tie street ligiting system was taken over, private contracts were made in 1905. In 1904 the city iad voted anotier bond issue of $250,000 to extend tie system, particularly tie commercial distribution. Tie first application was made in July, 1905, but tie first actual cut-in for private service was August 31, 1905.

Rapid increase in tie commercial business of tie plant and consequent extension of ligit and power lines during tie rapid growti of tie city made immediate additions to tie capacity of tie generating plant necessary. For tiis purpose $600,000 in bonds was autiorized by tie voters on Marci 6, 1906. Furtier necessity of extending the distribution system to all parts of the city resulted in the voting of $800,000 more bonds on December 29, 1908. The new generators, with new pipe and transmission lines, were put into service in 1909 with a total available capacity of 10,400 kilowatts. In April, 1910, the lighting department was made separate from the water department by charter amendment. The first superintendent of the new department was R. M. Arms, who resigned in 1911 and was succeeded by J. D. Ross, the present superintendent. Mr. Ross had been electrical and constructing engineer of the plant from the time of its inception.

In 1910 there appeared a demand for more power and it was planned to develop the Cedar River site to its full capacity by the use of a large concrete dam. On November 8, 1910, bonds to the amount of $1,400,000 were voted to carry this out, but work was not begun till 1912. It was finished late in 1914.

This dam was greatly to raise the waters of the lake to provide a uniform supply during the summer and fall months for both the lighting and water systems. When the water began to rise back of this new dam it was found, as had been anticipated, that much loss was occasioned by seepage through the northerly bank that appears of glacial formation, consisting of loose boulders, gravel and sand. Doubtless there will be delay in sealing the leaky places, with considerable added cost to the city, but nothing like as much as claimed by the opponents of the city lighting system.

To make sure of a future supply of power adequate to the expected development of the city, two power sites, the Hebb site of White River, with 100,000 horsepower maximum, and the Cushman site in the Olympics, with 65,000-horse power capacity, were recommended by the lighting department for acquisition by the city. After a bitter campaign on the question, bonds to the sum of $1,000,000 for the purchase of the Hebb site and $640,000 for the Cushman site were authorized, the money to be devoted to the purchase of the sites if satisfactory arrangements could be made with the owners as to price and title. Up to the present time, January, 1916, neither site has been acquired.

The city has a 1,500-kilowatt waterpower generating plant on the shore of Lake Union, which is fed by the overflow of the high service reservoir of the water department. It was finished in 1912 and uses the waste water of the city water system. This serves the purpose of an auxiliary and is ready to take the place of the main plant in case of accident to the generating station. On March 4, 1913, bonds were issued for a $425,000 steam plant of 10,000-kilowatt capacity. Construction on this unit has been completed.

Thus far the city lighting plant represents an investment of more than $6,000,000, one-third of which has come from the earnings of the department.

The receipts for the year 1915 were more than $1,000,000, and the system furnished 41,000 private customers. Street lamps to the number of 15,500 and numerous port commission and publicly owned buildings also have been served. This makes the Seattle municipal light and power plant America's greatest publicly owned system and also makes Seattle America's best lighted city.

INDEX

i

CPSIA information can be obtained
at www.ICGtesting.com
Printed in the USA
BVOW10s1122190217

476257BV00007B/99/P